CHILD ABUSE:
An Annotated Bibliography

compiled by

DOROTHY P. WELLS

in consultation with

Charles R. Carroll

The Scarecrow Press, Inc.
Metuchen, N.J., & London
1980

Library of Congress Cataloging in Publication Data

Wells, Dorothy Pearl, 1910-
    Child abuse, an annotated bibliography.

    Includes index.
    1. Child abuse--United States--Bibliography.
2.   Child abuse--Treatment--United States--Bibliography.
3.   Child abuse--Law and legislation--United States--
Bibliography. 4. Child abuse--Services--United States.
I.   Title.
Z7164.C5W37   [HV741]   016.3627'3   79-21641
ISBN 0-8108-1264-9

CONTENTS

ACKNOWLEDGMENTS

The compilation of this bibliography would not have been possible without the privilege of occupying one of the several research offices in the Alexander M. Bracken Library of Ball State University. To the Director of Libraries, Dr. Ray R. Suput, I am indebted for assignment to one of these offices.

The encouragement and support of Donald Siefker, Head of Reference Service and the Division of Information Sources, provided me with the impetus to persevere in my efforts.

For their utmost patience and helpfulness in procuring from other academic institutions voluminous materials for perusal and annotation, I am deeply appreciative to Veva McCoskey, Head of Inter-Library Loan Service, and her staff, Treva DuBois and Bessie Miller.

Contributing significantly by annotating many materials and through consultation has been Dr. Charles R. Carroll, professor of Physiology and Health Sciences and Administrative Assistant in the Department of Physiology and Health Science.

Barbara C. Stewart, now librarian at the John F. Kennedy School in West Berlin, Germany, translated and annotated many articles in the German language on child abuse. Marjorie K. McConnell, Ball State emerita, performed this same service for articles in the French language. The assistance of these two gifted individuals has added to the completeness of this publication.

Several annotated U. S. Government bibliographies were drawn upon in the compilation of this bibliography. I am grateful for the privilege of being able to freely make use of this material. Most of these materials are listed in the "Bibliographies" section.

Acknowledgment and thanks are extended to the personnel of

the following abstracting services who granted me permission to
draw upon for my annotations their abstracts which pertained to the
subject of child abuse and neglect:

Abstracts for Social Workers. National Association of Social
Workers, Inc., Publications Dept., 2 Park Ave., New
York, N.Y. 10016.

Abstracts on Criminology and Penology (formerly Excerpta Crim-
inologica) and Abstracts on Police Science. Hugo de Groot-
straat 27, Leiden, The Netherlands.

Criminal Justice Abstracts (formerly Crime and Delinquency
Literature). National Council on Crime and Delinquency,
Continental Plaza, 411 Hackensack Ave., Hackensack,
N.J. 07601.

Dissertation Abstracts International. The dissertation titles
and abstracts contained here are published with permission of
University Microfilms International, publishers of Dissertation
Abstracts International (copyright by University Microfilms International, 300 N. Zeeb Rd., Ann Arbor, Mich. 48106), and
may not be reproduced without their prior permission.

Excerpta Medica Publications: Psychiatry Excerpta Medica,
Public Health, Social Medicine and Hygiene Excerpta Medica,
Radiology Excerpta Medica, and Rehabilitation and Physical
Medicine Excerpta Medica. Excerpta Medica, 305 Keizers-
gracht, P.O. Box 1126, Amsterdam, The Netherlands.

Journal of Studies on Alcohol. Abstracts reprinted by per-
mission from Journal of Studies on Alcohol (copyright by
Journal of Studies on Alcohol, Inc.), Rutgers Center of
Alcohol Studies, Smithers Hall, Allison Rd., Rutgers, The
State University of New Jersey, Piscataway, N.J. 08854.

Mental Retardation and Developmental Disabilities Abstracts.
American Association on Mental Deficiency, 5101 Wisconsin Ave., N.W., Washington, D.C. 20016.

Psychological Abstracts. American Psychological Association,
1200 Seventeenth St., N.W., Washington, D.C. 20036.
Copyright by the American Psychological Association. Abstracts reprinted by permission and identified in the bib-
liographic annotations by the symbol (P.A.).

Women's Studies Abstracts. Rush Publishing Co., Inc.,
Box 1, Rush, N.Y. 14543.

PREFACE

Gross physical abuse and neglect of children is not a new
sociological phenomenon. In 18th-century England where child abuse,
neglect, and infanticide occurred frequently, the first real changes
came through the infant welfare movement. A few sensitive men
who occupy important positions in pediatric history perceived the
barbarous waste of human potential and attempted to correct this
social wrong. Today, we have come a long way in our general perception of the value of the lives of children. However, contemporary noxious societal forces of a more sophisticated nature which
are now infringing on families are causing maltreatment of offspring
in alarming proportion.

The child protective movement in the United States had its beginnings in the 1870's when the American Society for the Prevention of
Cruelty to Animals (ASPCA) intervened in a situation of extreme abuse
in the landmark case of a nine year old named Mary Ellen. On the recommendation of a New York social worker, Henry Bergh founded the
(New York) Society for the Prevention of Cruelty to Children. It was the
world's first such organization. Other societies, modeled after the New
York organization, were soon established in several cities.

In 1946 Dr. John Caffey in his diagnostic findings in children
noted traumatic battering. Literature on the problem, however, remained minimal until 1962 when Dr. C. Henry Kempe's article on
the subject appeared in the <u>Journal of the American Medical Associa-
tion</u> and skyrocketed in the news. Since that time the proliferation
of writings particularly in the United States and England has been
inconceivably extensive and comprehensive.

When compiling this bibliography on child abuse and neglect
I could only feel my way into the vast maze of available materials.

vi

Writings of a historical nature seemed essential to the understanding of the total problem of child abuse. Consequently, several such writings have been included. Although some sources earlier than 1962 are listed, the bulk of the works stem from that date when the news media first introduced in a major way the extent of the problem to today's public. A cut-off date was essential if publication was to be timely, so the date of December 1976 was selected. Since that time many publications on the subject have appeared and a supplement to this bibliography might be indicated.

Not discounting the value of the works dealing solely with neglect, such as that found in the poor areas of Appalachia, and those concerned solely with sexual molestation of children, this bibliography has omitted much of that material and concentrated chiefly on physical and psychological abuse and intentional neglect of children.

Works of varied format include non-book materials, such as video-cassettes and films; directories, handbooks, manuals, and newsletters; books and chapters of books; journal articles; pamphlets, dissertations; and government publications. Foreign language references are included. Because of the volume of materials cited, a subject approach was deemed necessary for efficiency of use. Cross-referencing has been employed extensively for entries which fit in multiple categories.

Dorothy P. Wells
June 1979

KEY TO ABBREVIATIONS

EDRS	ERIC Document Reproduction Service
HC	hard copy
il.	illustrated
ℓ.	leaves
MF	microfiche
p.	page(s)
P. A.	Psychological Abstracts
por(s).	portrait(s)

BIBLIOGRAPHIES

1. Colorado. State Department of Social Services. Library. "What Are We Doing to Defend Them? Abused and Neglected Children." Library Counselor, v. 27, no. 4. The Library, 1972. 42 p. Annotated.

    The title of this annotated bibliography is in the nature of a challenge, not only to the helping professions, but to all concerned and compassionate adults. It includes 173 citations subdivided under the following subject headings: General Reading; Legislative and Medical Aspects; Treating the Parents; Protective Services; and Sexual Abuse.

2. Council for Exceptional Children. Information Services and Publications. Child Abuse. A Selective Bibliography. Exceptional Child Bibliography Series No. 601. 1976. 24 p. Available from: CEC Information Services and Publications, The Council for Exceptional Children, 1920 Association Drive, Reston, Virginia 22091. $4; also from EDRS: MF-$0.83; HC-$1.67, Plus Postage.

    This bibliography contains approximately 80 abstracts and associated indexing information for documents or journal articles published from 1968 to 1975 and selected from computer files of CEC and ERIC. Titles were chosen in response to user requests and analysis of current trends in the field.

3. Court, Joan; Thomson, Lynda. Battered Child Syndrome: Bibliography. National Society for Prevention of Cruelty to Children, 1 Ridinghouse Street, London, England W.1, 1968.

4. Davis, Gwendolyn; Higgins, Judith. "Child Abuse. A Bibliography." il. pors. School Library Journal, 23:29-33, November 1976.

    The authors have compiled an annotated bibliography of 38 books, pamphlets, periodical articles, films, and filmstrips dealing with child abuse. The entries are more appropriate for high school readers, as technical material oriented primarily to professionals has been omitted.

5. DeLay, D. R. An Annotated Bibliography of Early Warning Signals of Child Abuse and Neglect. Athens, Georgia: Regional Institute of Social Welfare Research, November 27, 1973. 39 p.

    One hundred and five publications and their descriptions are

1

listed under the major categories of child abuse and neglect. Each category is divided into sections concerned with a parent or parent substitute profile, child profile, parent and child profile, or a family profile. Each category is further subdivided into psychological, sociological, sociopsychological, sociocultural, medical, and legal orientations.

6. International Reference Organization in Forensic Medicine and Sciences. Bibliography of References on Battered Child and Infanticide. The Organization, Wichita, Kan. , 1972. 32 p.

7. Kline, Donald F.; Hopper, Mark A. Child Abuse: An Integration of the Research Related to Education of Children Handicapped as a Result of Child Abuse. Final Report. Logan: Utah State University, Department of Special Education, 1975. 136 p. Available from EDRS: MF-$0. 76; HC-$6. 97, Plus Postage.
The literature on child abuse is reviewed in terms of a concept analysis. Also presented is an annotated bibliography of approximately 550 journal articles, 18 books, 6 dissertations, and 40 pamphlets on child abuse. The bibliography is alphabetical by author within format categories and includes bibliographical data and a brief nonevaluative description.

8. Kretschman, Karen L. Selected Bibliography on Child Abuse and Neglect. Austin, Tarlton Law Library, University of Texas School of Law, 1976. 26 ℓ. (Tarlton Law Library Legal Bibliography Series: No. 12)
Kretschman was not able to find any bibliographies solely of government documents on the subject of child abuse and neglect. Since the government is excellent in providing information on this topic, this bibliography is designed to fill the gap. Included are documents of the following nature: House, Senate, Presidential, Departmental, Federal, Texas State and other state documents, and Government periodical sources.

9. National Committee for Prevention of Child Abuse. Medical Bibliography. Chicago, 1976. 6 p.
Over 200 entries are listed. While the bibliography is intended to aid medical professionals, it will also serve others concerned about the prevention and treatment of child abuse.

10. Naughton, M. James; Steepe, Stephanie K. ; Mart-Nibbrig, Marilyn. Child Protective Services: A Bibliography with Partial Annotation and Cross-Indexing--1976. Seattle: Washington University, Health Sciences Learning Resources Center, 1976. 621 p. Available from: Health Sciences Learning Resources Center, University of Washington, Seattle, Washington 98195. $15; Also from EDRS: MF-$1. 16, Plus Postage.
Contained in the bibliography are citations for 1500 publications concerned with child abuse and neglect of which 700 include abstracts. Titles are listed alphabetically by author under broad subjects or

child protective service case types.   A final listing is strictly alphabetical by author with abstracted articles asterisked.

11.   U.S. Children's Bureau.   Bibliography on the Battered Child.
      Rev. ed.   Washington, D.C.:   Social and Rehabilitation Ser-
      vice, 1969.   22 p.
      Presented is a reference list intended to provide to research
investigators, clinicians, and the lay public bibliographical information on the battered and abused child in order to advance understanding of this critical psychological and social problem.   It includes
only those references beginning with 1968.   The references are ar-
ranged alphabetically by year.

12.   _____.   Bibliography on the Battered Child.   DHEW Publi-
      cation No. (OHD) 74-5.   Washington, D.C.:   Social and Re-
      habilitation Service, February 1974.   15 p.
      This is a reissue of portions of the Bibliography on the Bat-
tered Child, revised July 1969.   The selected portions include references of early and classic works about child abuse published in
the sixties which are not duplicated in other bibliographies.

13.   _____.   Children Who Need Protection: An Annotated Bib-
      liography, compiled by Dorothy M. Jones.   U.S. Department
      of Health, Education, and Welfare, Washington, D.C. , 1966.
      75 p.
      This bibliography, with one exception, covers all aspects of
child neglect including child abuse, child welfare, maternal deprivation, protective services, social casework, the courts, and state
legislation.   The one exception is in the area of cultural deprivation.
Material covering child neglect in foreign countries has been limited
to publications and articles published in the English language.

14.   U.S.   ERIC Clearinghouse on Early Childhood Education.   Re-
      search Relating to Children, March 1976-August 1976, by
      Dorothy O'Connell, et al.   191 p.
      Issued twice a year.   Includes abstracts of research in pro-
gress and recently completed research; also includes, "Child Abuse
and Neglect: A Bibliography, " which updates previous ERIC Clearinghouse on Early Childhood Education bibliographies.

15.   U.S.   National Center on Child Abuse and Neglect.   Child
      Abuse and Neglect Research: Projects and Publications.
      (DHEW).   paper $25 a year; single number $15.   Published by
      the National Technical Information Service (NTIS).
      Issued twice a year--in May and November.   This publication
and its companion volume, Child Abuse and Neglect Programs, are
designed to make the information in the National Center's computer
system available for direct public and professional reference.   Most
of the publications included were selected from journals, books, and
other sources that are readily accessible to scholars and practitioners.   The research project descriptions, on the other hand, came
exclusively from a survey conducted.

16. U.S. National Institute of Mental Health. Selected References on the Abused and Battered Child. October 1972. 11 p. (DHEW Pubn. No. HSM 73-9034). $0.20-Supt. of Documents.
    This bibliography was derived from references and materials available in the library of the National Institute of Mental Health, the Children's Bureau, and the National Library of Medicine. Since several bibliographies on the battered child have been published prior to 1969, this bibliography includes only those references beginning with 1968. The references are arranged alphabetically by year.

17. _____ . Violence at Home: An Annotated Bibliography, compiled and edited by Mary Lystad, Division of Special Mental Health Programs. Washington, D.C.: Superintendent of Documents, 1974. 95 p.
    Intended by the National Institute of Mental Health for use by social scientists and mental health professionals, the annotated bibliography contains summaries of 190 studies on violent behavior among family members published from 1945 to 1974. Citations are grouped under 10 major topics; 55 citations pertain to violence of parent to child.

18. U.S. National Library of Medicine. Child Abuse. January 1970 Through July 1973. 303 Citations. Literature Search No. 73-28. 15 p.; Also: Child Abuse, August 1973 Through December 1975. 353 Citations. Literature Search No. 75-29, 22 p. (DHEW)
    NLM Literature Searches are computer-generated bibliographies produced by the Library's Medical Literature Analysis and Retrieval Systems (MEDLARS). Selection of topics is made on the basis of significant current interest in the subject matter. Each Literature Search has been given a descriptive title and may include a brief explanation of the specific point of view of the search.

CASE STUDIES

19. Adelson, Lester. "The Battering Child." Journal of the
    American Medical Association, 222:159-161, October 9,
    1972; Criminologist, 8(27):26-33, 1973.
    Presented are case studies of five infants, all less than one
    year of age, who were killed by children eight years old or younger.
    All died from craniocerebral trauma, resulting from either assaults
    with a blunt instrument or being dropped to the floor or both. Two
    had been bitten. It is concluded that the preschool child is capable
    of homicidal rage when he is provoked by what he considers to be
    a threat to his sense of security.

20. _____. "Homicide by Pepper." Journal of Forensic Sci-
    ences, 9:391-395, July 1964.
    This case study details how a 42-month-old girl died of as-
    phyxia following the pouring of a large amount of pepper into her
    mouth and throat by her mother. Death was due to the occlusion
    of air passages by pepper.

21. _____. "Homicide by Starvation; the Nutritional Variant of
    the 'Battered Child.'" Journal of the American Medical
    Association, 186:458-460, November 2, 1963.
    The deaths of five infants from starvation arising from neglect
    were investigated by the Cuyahoga County Coroner's Office. Autop-
    sies disclosed no congenital or acquired disease which could explain
    the marasmus which characterized all the children. Death was at-
    tributed to wanton disregard of the children's nutritional needs and
    successful criminal prosecution was carried out in four cases.

22. _____. "Slaughter of the Innocents: A Study of Forty-Six
    Homicides in Which the Victims Were Children." New
    England Journal of Medicine, 264:1345-1349, June 29, 1961.
    Forty-six homicides in which the victims were infants and pre-
    adolescent children were studied. Serious mental illness, loss of a
    parent's temper and sexual assault were the most common precipi-
    tating factors. An unusually large proportion were killed by methods
    rarely or never utilized to murder adults. (Journal Summary Modi-
    fied.)

23. Allison, Patricia K. Exploration of a Program of Preventive
    Intervention in the Early Parent-Infant Interaction. D. S. W.
    Northampton, Mass., Smith College, School for Social

Work, 1974. 295 p. (Available from University Microfilms, Ann Arbor, Mich. (75-1649).)
An extensive case study examines new ways to identify infants
potentially at risk due to parental pathology and the usefulness of
establishing a program of preventive intervention during the immediate postpartum period in potential child abuse cases.

24. Ameli, N. O.; Alimohammadi, A. "Attempted Infanticide by
    Insertion of Sewing Needles Through Fontanels. Report of
    Two Cases." Journal of Neurosurgery, 33:721-723, De-
    cember 1970.
The insertion of sewing needles through the fontanels of an unwanted baby is apparently an ancient practice of which there are
still instances in Iran and other Moslem countries, Hungary, and
Poland. This peculiar method of attempted infanticide is described
in two case studies. (Journal Abstract Modified.)

25. Anchorage Child Abuse Board, Inc. Statistical Description of
    Cases Followed by the Anchorage Child Abuse Board, Inc.,
    October 1972-March 1975, by M. Andreini and S. Green.
    Alaska, 1975. 10 p.
In the statistical description are seven different considerations,
such as proportion of abusing families in which drug abuse or alcoholism is a problem. The types of abuse most frequently found
were detailed. Other considerations were the age of mothers, size
of families, percent of alcohol and drug abusers, percent of multi-
problem families. Recommendations for intervention and treatment
are given.

26. Bachara, Gary H.; Lamb, William R. "Psycho-social Dwarf-
    ism: A Case Study of Neglect and Reversibility." Journal
    of Pediatric Psychology, 1(2):23-24, Spring 1976.
Presented is a case study of an abused, neglected infant who
made significant gains as a result of careful foster home placement.
It is concluded that placement in a warm, stimulating foster home
is essential for maximum therapy, in conjunction with other psychiatric and remediation intervention, chemotherapy, family counseling,
perceptual motor training, and/or language therapy.

27. Banagale, Raul C.; McIntire, Matilda. "Child Abuse and Neg-
    lect: A Study of Cases Reported to Douglas County Child
    Protective Service from 1967-1973." Part I. Nebraska
    Medical Journal, 60(9):353-360, September 1975.
The 2,570 child abuse and neglect cases reported to Douglas
County (Nebraska) Child Protective Service are reviewed from 1967
to 1973. This is the first review to ascertain the incidence rates,
types, extent and distribution pattern of child abuse and neglect
cases in Omaha. Also discussed are the success of agency intervention and the essential changes to improve the present program
concerning child abuse and neglect. (Journal Abstract Modified.)

28. _____; _____. "Child Abuse and Neglect: A Study of
    Cases Reported to Douglas County Child Protective Service

from 1967-1973." Part 2. <u>Nebraska Medical Journal,</u>
60(11):439-440, November 1975.
The co-authors report the reasons which cause physicians to
hesitate in making a report of child abuse and/or neglect. They
also offer suggested changes for improving the present program
concerning child abuse and neglect in Douglas County (Nebraska):
legislation, education, program management, and establishment of
a family crisis forum.

29. Barbre, Constance. "So Short a Life, So Small a Flame."
<u>The Journal of Practical Nursing,</u> 20:36-37, October 1970.
The author presents a case history of a battered ten-week-old
female infant who eventually died following a second attack by the
father. Detailed medical aspects of the infant are included.

30. "Battered Babies Never Fully Mend." <u>Medical World News,</u>
7(45):47, 1966.
The hospital records of 20 abused children were compared at
the time of injury and one-and-a-half to 11 years later. Results of
findings.

31. "The Battered-Child Syndrome." <u>Journal of the Tennessee
Medical Association,</u> 64(4):346-347, 1971.
In a study of 662 cases of physical abuses of children, the
father was responsible in about 38 percent of the cases, the mother
in about 29 percent, and both in 5 percent. One apparent reason
for such abuse is the parental opinion that beating will teach the
child obedience or knowledge. Among the hidden reasons may be
a competition for the love of the spouse or some abnormality in the
child which offends and disappoints the parent, and in some cases
the conviction that the child does not belong to them.

32. Bender, Barbara. "Self-Chosen Victims: Scapegoating Behavior Sequential to Battering." <u>Child Welfare,</u> 55:417-422,
June 1976.
The cases of two boys, 8 and 10 years of age, are described.
Victims of severe physical abuse, they developed a pattern of behavior that perpetuated their scapegoat role with peers and adults
outside the family. Long treatment gradually reduced the scapegoating behavior without removing either boy from his home. (P.A.)

33. Berg, Pamela Ione. <u>Parental Expectations and Attitudes in
Child-Abusing Families.</u> Ph.D. University of Southern
California, 1976. Available from University Microfilms,
P.O. Box 1346, Ann Arbor, MI 48106 ($20-Hard Copy,
$10-Microfiche). Order number not given.
This study was designed as an exploratory effort to systemati-
cally investigate differences in parental expectations and childbearing
attitudes between parents whose children had been physically abused
and a control group of nonabusing parents.

34. Billingsley, Andrew. "Family Functioning in the Low Income
Black Community." <u>Social Casework,</u> 50(10):563-572,

December 1967.

Cites two unpublished studies and results about two groups (of 40 each) of randomly selected low income families headed by women. Percentages for black and white families who abused their families are given.

35. Birrell, R. G.; Birrell, John H. "The Maltreatment Syndrome in Children: A Hospital Survey." Medical Journal of Australia, 2:1023-1029, 1968.

A series of 42 maltreated children over 31 months is reported from the Royal Children's Hospital, Melbourne. Statistics are presented as to nature of abuse, type of injury, and number of admissions and average stay in hospital. Reasons why parents abuse their children are given. The need for a notification law with freedom from suit appears essential. Medical and diagnostic aspects are discussed as well as the importance of a team approach to the problem.

36. Boisvert, M. J. "The Battered-Child Syndrome." Social Casework, 53(8):475-480, October 1972.

Child abuse in 20 families was studied in order to develop a typology for classification and treatment and to provide the rudiments of a guide for planning intervention strategy. Each case was divided into a typology of either uncontrollable or controllable abuse and then delimited into classes according to the pathology of the abusing parent or parent substitute as given by the data.

37. Braun, Ida G.; Braun, Edgar J.; Simonds, Charlotte. "The Mistreated Child." California Medicine, 99(2):98-103, August 1963.

The co-authors present seven different case studies of abused and neglected children. In each instance, a description of what actually was done is followed by an outline of a management approach which might result in better follow-up of cases which might occur in the future.

38. Brown, Marsena; Pappas, Margaret M. Eight Children with Suspected Inflicted Injury: A Follow-Up Pilot Study. Master's Thesis, University of Southern California School of Social Work, Los Angeles, June 1965.

39. Browne, William J.; Palmer, Anthony J. "A Preliminary Study of Schizophrenic Women Who Murdered Their Children." Hospital and Community Psychiatry, 26:71+, February 1975.

This is a report of a preliminary study of nine schizophrenic women who murdered one or more of their children.

40. Buglass, Robert. "Parents with Emotional Problems." Nursing Times, 67:1000-1001, August 12, 1971.

Thirty case histories involving young mothers with emotional disturbances who battered their offspring are discussed. All of the subjects were reported to have benefited from psychiatric treatment.

The author feels that there is a definite need for mothering skills training based on his personal observations.

41. Bührdel, P. "Das Vernachlässigungssyndrom beim Kind" [Neglect Syndrome in the Child]. Deutsche Gesundheitswesen, 25:1352-1354, July 16, 1970.
  Quoting 15 cases treated in the University Children's Clinic of Leipzig, the author describes the typical symptoms of gross children's neglect. The author attempts to characterize the committers. If there is justified suspicion of children's neglect, each physician is liable to notification of the competent authorities. (Journal Abstract.)

42. Bull, Olwyn; Bull (Mrs.). "A Family Affair." Nursing Mirror and Midwives Journal, 133:26-29, November 19, 1971.
  A daughter-mother team presents the case of Peter, an unwanted and wilfully neglected child from age three until his present age of twelve. Afflicted with the coeliac syndrome, Peter makes a slow but remarkable recovery under the care of a foster family.

43. Burland, J. Alexis; Andrews, Roberta G.; Headsten, Sally J. "Child Abuse: One Tree in the Forest." Child Welfare, 52(9):585-592, November 1973.
  A review of the records of 28 children who experienced parental abuse or severe neglect indicates the complexity of the parent-child relationship, and the necessity of meeting the child's and the parents' dependency needs, rather than focusing exclusively on the abuse itself as the major concern. (Journal Abstract.)

44. Button, Alan. "Some Antecedents of Felonious and Delinquent Behavior." Journal of Clinical Child Psychology, 2(3):35-37, Fall 1973.
  A series of case studies by the author indicated that child abuse was quite common in the group of juvenile delinquent boys studied. A quote from one of the subjects indicated that despite the fact he had experienced abuse as a child he would treat his own children the same way. Characterization of the family environments are given.

45. Bwibo, N. O. "Battered Child Syndrome." Eastern African Medical Journal, 49:934-938, November 1972.
  The battered child syndrome causes many permanent injuries or death in children in North America. Eight cases with two deaths seen among East African children are presented. The etiology, clinical features and management are discussed. Doctors are urged to have their eyes open in order to recognize cases in East Africa. (Journal Abstract Modified.)

46. Cadol, Roger V., et al. Prospective Study in Child Abuse: The Child Study Program. Final Report. Denver, Colo.: Department of Health and Hospitals. 1976. 100 p. Available from EDRS: MF-$0.83; HC-$4.67, Plus Postage.
  Presented is the final report of the Child Study Program, in which the following objectives were investigated with 140 abused

children (from birth to 72 months old): whether abused children are
developmentally different from non-abused children, whether there
are differences between children who sustained non-accidental trauma
(NAT) and children who failed to thrive (FTT), and the effectiveness
of an intervention program. Reported are results of comparisons of
the experimental groups with one another and non-abused controls.
Tables presenting descriptive data on the subjects, biological parents, environmental factors, the abusive incident, and the abusers
are included.

47. "Children: The Hard Case." Newsweek, 82:32, July 16, 1973.
     por.
     Dr. Joseph Farrar is under indictment for the murder of a
17-year-old student. According to witnesses, the student consumed
roach poison, but because Farrar thought she was faking illness, he
kept her from receiving medical attention. Farrar operates Artesia
Hall, a school designed to shape up even the wildest youth. It is
located in a swamp north of Houston, Texas. The terror that Farrar created at the academy is only now being revealed.

48. Chodkiewicz, J. P.; Redondo, A.; Clouin-Moral, M. "Les
     Enfants battus hospitalisés en neurochirurgie. (Problèmes
     cliniques et médicolégaux)" [Battered Children Hospitalized
     in Neuro-Surgery. (Clinical and Medico-Legal Problems)].
     Medecine Legale et Dommage Corporel, 7:21-26, January-
     March 1974.
     In the light of verifications obtained from a series of 21 cases
of battered children hospitalized in neurosurgery in three Parisian
medical departments these last six years, the authors underline the
following points: the frequency of probable unsuspected maltreatment, the severity of symptoms, the extreme severity of the prognosis, the emergency and difficulty of a rapid diagnosis, and the
necessity of more efficient collaboration between different medico-
social, judiciary and police services. (English Abstract Modified.)

49. Clarke, A. D. B. "Commentary on Koluchova's 'Severe De-
     privation in Twins: A Case Study.'" Journal of Child
     Psychology and Psychiatry and Allied Disciplines, 13(2):
     103-106, 1972.
     Koluchova's on-going study of twin boys who suffered extreme
deprivation between 18 months and seven years, and who thereafter
received remedial treatment, is discussed in the context of relevant
literature.

50. Cohen, Michael I.; Raphling, D. L.; Green, P. E. "Psycho-
     logic Aspects of the Maltreatment Syndrome of Childhood."
     Journal of Pediatrics, 69:279-284, August 1966.
     Case histories of 12 families in a military environment treated
at a psychiatric outpatient clinic for behavior involving child abuse
are reviewed.

51. Colarossi, G.; Bonanni, E. "Traumi domiciliari ed ingestione
     di corpi estranei. Statistica degli anni 1957-1967 della

Clinica Pediatric di Roma" [Home Injuries and Ingestion of
Foreign Bodies. Statistics of the Years 1957-1967 of the
Clinica Pediatrica of Rome]. Minerva Pediatrica, 22:1696-
1702, August 25, 1970.
The authors examined 1320 children from 0 to 12 years of age
admitted to the Pediatric Clinic of Rome during 11 years (1957-1967)
for traumas or various accidents having happened in domestic sur-
roundings. These accidents occur more often to male children, and
generally during the second year of their life. The greatest percentage comes from workmen's and small tradesmen's families.
Five-tenths percent of the children were beaten by their parents.
(English Summary Modified.)

52. Corey, Eleanor J.; Miller, Carol L.; Widlak, Frederic W.
    "Factors Contributing to Child Abuse." Nursing Research,
    24(4):293-295, July-August 1975.
    Compared are the background demographic characteristics and
medical data of 48 hospitalized battered children with those of 50
hospitalized nonbattered children of the same age group (up to six
years of age). Factors investigated included sibling presence,
mothers' marital status, and perpetrator's sex. (P.A.)

53. Creighton University. Department of Pediatrics. Child Abuse
    and Neglect. A Study of Cases Reported to Douglas County
    Child Protective Service from 1967-1973. Omaha, Neb.,
    1973. 39 p.
    Between August 1967 and December 1973, 2,570 cases of child
abuse and neglect were reported to the Douglas County (Nebraska)
Child Protective Service. Age of abused child, sex of perpetrator,
socioeconomic status of families, type of injuries, percent of neglect
cases, percent accounted for by private physicians, percent of termination of parental rights by court action, etc., were reported.
Recommendations were for improved legislative definition, better
initial investigative methods, more accurate screening of cases,
more widespread education, and earlier identification of abuse potential.

54. Croll, Ramah. "Poor Tina: The Story of a Beaten Child."
    Liquorian, 61:38-40, October 1973.
    This is the tragic story of Tina, a battered three-year-old.
Foster parents gave her much love and attention, under which she
seemingly thrived physically, but eventually the fact had to be accepted that she was microcephalic as a result of a skull fracture
she had suffered. She now lives her very limited life in an institution.

55. D'Ambrosio, Richard. No Language but a Cry. Garden City,
    N.Y.: Doubleday, 1970. 252p.
    As a young psychologist, the author tells of his first experi-
ence with a maltreated child who could not speak for the first 12
years of her life. It is a story of human suffering beyond belief.
The doctor gives an account of his extended treatment and her as-
tonishing recovery.

56. _____ . "No Language but a Cry." Good Housekeeping,
171:64-67+, August 1970.
This is an abbreviated account of the story presented in the
book by the same title.

57. Davies, J. F.; Jorgensen, J. D. "Battered, but Not Defeated;
The Story of an Abused Child and Positive Casework."
Child Welfare, 49:101-104, February 1970.
It is essential that the battered child receive not only medical
care for physical damage but other support to strengthen and maintain his vital balance. In this case report, Martin represents a
host of children. Where the abused child lived did not determine
the outcome of his life but rather how he lived, the quality of services offered and the quality of the people who entered his life. In
Martin's case, the vital balance turned toward emotional health and
a push for growth and health, instead of illness, as the child welfare agency emphasized.

58. DeCourcy, Peter; DeCourcy, Judith. A Silent Tragedy: Child
Abuse in the Community. Port Washington, N.Y.: Alfred
Pub. Co., 1973. 231 p.
Presents 12 case histories of child abuse which occurred in
two U.S. communities. Police reports, psychological findings,
children's agency actions, and court disposition in the cases are
presented and discussed. (P.A.)

59. Degos, R., et al. [Silverman's Syndrome, So-Called Battered-
Child Syndrome (a case)]. Bulletin de la Société Française
de Dermatologie et de Syphiligraphie, 78:288-289, 1971.

60. Dorman, S. "Child Abuse: A Review of 69 Cases." Clinical
Proceedings, 31(11):256-262, December 1975.
The family dynamics of child abuse are reviewed, and statistics
from 69 randomly selected cases of 135 reported at Children's
Hospital National Medical Center in 1973 are presented and com-
pared to previously published statistics.

61. Draft Report of Phase I of the Family Development Study.
Boston, Mass.: Children's Hospital Center, 1974. 153 p.
Phase I of the Family Development Study was designed as
descriptive epidemiologic case-control study of Children's Hospital
patients. "Cases" included a variety of presenting conditions in
which it was believed that specific factors affecting the capacity of
a family to nurture and protect a child under four years of age
might form a common and significant part of their etiology. "Controls" were comparable acute medical conditions matched on age,
race, and very roughly on socioeconomic status. The study included
303 children on the inpatient division of the Hospital and 257 out-
patients visiting its Emergency Clinic.

62. Duncan, Glen M.; Frazier, Sherrert H.; Litin, Edward M.,
et al. "Etiological Factors in First-Degree Murder."
Journal of the American Medical Association, 168:1755-1758,

November 29, 1958.
Case studies of six prisoners convicted of first-degree murder
revealed that remorseless physical brutality at the hands of the parents had been a constant experience for four of them. In interviews
transparent evasions and calculated lying were manifested by most
of the parents. Intervention by physicians in known sadistic family
patterns may well avert a later violent crime.

63. Duncan, Jane W.; Duncan, Glen M. "Murder in the Family:
     A Study of Some Homicidal Adolescents." American Journal
     of Psychiatry, 127:1498-1502, May 1971.
     Five cases are presented in which a homicidal adolescent's
abrupt loss of control was associated with a change in his interpersonal relationship with the victim, together with a sequence of
events progressively more unbearable and less amenable to his control. The authors suggest criteria for assessing the adolescent's
potential for homicidal behavior within the family. A history of
parental brutality is a significant consideration. (Journal Abstract.)

64. Ebbin, Allan J.; Gollub, M. H.; Stein, A. M., et al. "Bat-
     tered Child Syndrome at the Los Angeles County General
     Hospital." American Journal of Diseases of Children, 118:
     660-667, October 1969.
     The social histories and significant medical findings of 50
parentally battered children were studied. The 50 children represented one percent of admissions to the Children's Division of the
Los Angeles County-University of Southern California Medical Center
over one year and about half of those suspected of being assaulted
by an adult.

65. Edgar, W. M. "Battered Baby Syndrome." (Letter). British
     Medical Journal, 1 (5439):924, April 3, 1965.
     A 21-year-old British man pleaded guilty to manslaughter and
was sentenced to five years imprisonment in the death of the 18-
month-old son of the woman with whom he had been living. Re-
portedly, the man had discovered that the child's father was Black.
The child suffered multiple injuries.

66. Elmer, Elizabeth. "Child Abuse: A Symptom of Family
     Crisis." In: Pavenstedt, E., ed. Crisis of Family Dis-
     organization. New York: Behavioral Publications, 1971.
     103 p.
     A follow-up study of child abuse at the Children's Hospital of
Pittsburgh is discussed. In almost all of the 22 cases the mother
was responsible for the maltreatment. The findings of the study
reveal the stresses that caused mothers, sometimes repeatedly, to
lose control and resort to violence directed at the child. The need
for preventive measures is stressed, and social conditions are seen
to be the major causative agents. Remedial measures, under present
conditions, are difficult.

67. _____. Children in Jeopardy: A Study of Abused Minors
     and Their Families. Pittsburgh: University of Pittsburgh

Press, 1967. xi, 125 p. illus. (Contemporary Community Health Series). Pitt Paperback.

This is a comparison follow-up study of 50 children who were admitted to Children's Hospital, Pittsburgh, Pennsylvania, over a period of 13 years with multiple bone injuries.

68. _____. Fifty Families Study: A Study of Abused and Neglected Children and Their Families. Pittsburgh: University of Pittsburgh School of Medicine, June 1965.

69. _____; Gregg, Grace; Wright, B., et al. "Studies of Child Abuse and Infant Accidents." Mental Health Program Reports, (5):58-59, December 1971. Also in: U.S. National Institute of Mental Health. The Mental Health of the Child. Program Reports of the National Institute of Mental Health, 343-370, June 1971.

Factors determining whether a child will be abused were investigated in two studies. In the first study, characteristics of 50 families where abuse of the children was strongly suspected were analyzed and current interviews were attempted. The second study analyzed factors involved in childhood accidents and how to distinguish a true accident from an abusive one. The studies are described in detail.

70. Evans, Sue L., et al. "Failure to Thrive: A Study of 45 Children and Their Families." American Academy of Child Psychiatry Journal, 2:440-457, 1972.

Forty families of children failing to thrive fell into three groups. A case exemplifying each of the groups is presented. Some of the families in the third group actually burned or beat their children.

71. "Events of Puberty." British Medical Journal, 4(5626):317-318, November 2, 1968.

A syndrome of deviation from normal growth due to intrafamilial deprivation has been observed in 16 children. Characteristic features are listed which disappeared on hospitalization. Emotional status of mothers is given.

72. Evseeff, G. S. "A Potential Young Murderer." Journal of Forensic Sciences, 21(2):441-450, 1976.

Longitudinal study of six people who committed homicides or exhibited a potential for homicidal behavior was undertaken over a period of ten years. The data were obtained through psychiatric interviews, psychological testing, and examination of all available records. It was concluded that homicidal proneness can be anticipated in people who as children suffered from physical and emotional abuse, witnessed violence, and were sexually traumatized through incestuous experiences or their equivalents. (Journal Summary Modified.)

73. Fehaiel, A. E., et al. [Silverman's Syndrome: Apropos of a Case]. Tunisie Medicale, 52(5):223-229, September-October 1974.

74. Feinstein, Howard M.; Paul, Norman; Esmiol, Pattison. "Group Therapy for Mothers with Infanticidal Impulses." American Journal of Psychiatry, 120:882-886, March 1964.
    This article details a report of a study of mothers with infanticidal impulses. These mothers shared several biographical characteristics and ranged clinically from obsessional neurotics to borderline psychotics with some common symptomology. Group psychotherapy was found to offer a number of therapeutic advantages.

75. Fessard, C.; Maroteaux, P.; Lamy, M. "Le Syndrome de Silverman: fractures multiples du nourrisson (etude de seize observations)" [Silverman's Syndrome: Multiple Fractures in Infants (Study of 16 Cases)]. Archives Françaises de Pediatrie, 24:651-666, June-July 1967.
    In 1953 Silverman drew attention of doctors and radiologists to the possibility of unrecognized injuries in the etiology of certain fractures in the baby which until then had not been recognized. For several years, many English-language publications have insisted on the neuropsychic disorders revealed by a thorough examination of the environment of these children. The study of these 16 observations shows that this syndrome is still a source of many diagnostic errors whose social and medical importance must not be misunderstood.

76. Fisher, Samuel H. "Skeletal Manifestations of Parent Induced Trauma in Infants and Children." Southern Medical Journal, 51:956-960, August 1958.
    Six cases of parental induced trauma in infants and children are presented. Two of these were in children accidentally injured in stable home environments, and four were in children whose parents were emotionally ill. Two cases resulted in the death of the child and the imprisonment of the parent or parents.

77. "Follow-Up Clinic: 18: The Tragedy of Mary, Clive and Penny--A Lesson We Are Not Yet Ready to Learn." Midwife and Health Visitor, 8:62-65, February 1972.
    A case history is presented in which three children of an abusing family all die mysterious deaths, after a series of major and minor injuries. Eventually, the parents are charged with criminal neglect, convicted, and sentenced to four years imprisonment.

78. Fomufod, Antoine K.; Sinkford, Stanley M.; Louy, Vicki E. "Mother-Child Separation at Birth: A Contributing Factor in Child Abuse." (Letter). Lancet, 2(7934):549-550, September 20, 1975.
    The association of birth weight, gestational age, neonatal problems, and duration of stay in the hospital immediately after birth with future child abuse was studied retrospectively in cases of child abuse seen at the District of Columbia General Hospital over a one-year period. The hypothesis that early and prolonged neonatal hospitalization interferes with the development of natural maternal-infant bonding and sets the scene for even greater distortions at a later date is supported.

79. Freedman, David A.; Brown, Stuart L. "On the Role of Co-
    enesthetic Stimulation in the Development of Psychic Struc-
    ture." Psychoanalytic Quarterly, 37:418-438, July 1968.
    Case histories of two children confined in almost total isola-
tion in infancy are compared to those of two children in India reared
during infancy by wolves, to differentiate the effects of an absence
of coenesthetic experience and a distorted experience.

80. Friedman, Stanford B.; Morse, Carol W. "Child Abuse: A
    Five-Year Follow-Up of Early Case Finding in the Emer-
    gency Department." Pediatrics, 54(4):404-410, October
    1974.
    In a five-year follow-up study on child abuse, out of an origi-
nal 156 children under age six studied, all cases of suspected abuse
and neglect, and a random sample of accidents, were included in an
investigation involving interview of parents and a survey of medical
facilities for subsequent contact with these children.

81. Galdston, Richard. "The Burning and the Healing of Children."
    Psychiatry, 35:57-66, February 1972.
    Five percent of 100 children admitted to the surgical wards of
the Children's Hospital Medical Center between 1964 and 1970 for
burn injuries were thought to be the victims of child abuse. Galdston discusses the burning and healing of the 100 children, including
trauma incurred, regression, etc.

82. _____. "Observations on Children Who Have Been Physi-
    cally Abused and Their Parents." American Journal of
    Psychiatry, 122:440-443, October 1965.
    This report summarizes observations of young children who
were admitted to Boston's Children's Hospital Medical Center for
physical disorders due to parental abuse. Responses of the children
to management, the psychodynamics of abusing parents and differences in forms of abuse are discussed.

83. Gautier, E. "Démonstrations cliniques. Embryopathie de
    l'aminoptérine, Kwashiorkor, Enfant maltraité, Listéroise
    congénitale et saturnisme, Maladie de Weil" [Clinical Dem-
    onstrations. Aminopterin Embryopathy, Kwashiorkor, Child
    Abuse, Congenital Listeriosis and Lead Poisoning, Weil's
    Disease]. Schweizerische Medizinische Wochenschrift, 99:
    33-42, January 11, 1969.
    Five children are described in whom the pathologic condition
was directly ascribable to abnormal behavior or incompetence of
their parents. (Journal Abstract.)

84. Gibbens, T. C. N. "Violence to Children." Howard Journal
    of Penology and Crime Prevention, 13(3):212-220, 1972.
    Discussed are the recurring themes in the history and per-
sonality of the offenders in cases involving violent cruelty to children, with special reference to the 32 men and 7 women offenders
examined for this study. Aggressiveness could be traced to many
influences in their childhood: disorganization of home life and the

marriage, illegitimacy, the lack of psychophysical mechanisms responsible for the development of maternal feelings and responses, mental illness, depressive illness, and loss of control. Both parents practicing cruelty arises from quality of marriage itself.

85. _____, et al. "Violent Cruelty to Children." British Journal of Delinquency, 6:260-277, April 1956.
Study on characteristics of men and women (total of 39) imprisoned for cruelty to children (mostly abuse; two cases of neglect) in Great Britain.

86. Girodet, Dominique. "Les Jeunes Enfants maltraites; étude medico-sociale de 110 observations hospitalières" [Maltreated Infants: A Medico-Social Study of 110 Hospital Cases]. Paris: Universite Rene-Descartes, 1973. Pages not given.
A sample of 110 maltreated children were examined in light of their socio-economic and medical family backgrounds. The first section deals largely with characteristic forms of maltreatment. The contributing factors to poor mother-child relationships among premature children (of which there were 18 percent) are given. Environmental studies did not identify common familial characteristics. After hospital treatment, about half the children returned home; the other half went to institutions.

87. Goldson, Edward; Cadol, Roger V.; Fitch, Michael J., et al. "Nonaccidental Trauma and Failure to Thrive." American Journal of Diseases of Children, 130(5):490-492, May 1976.
Charts were reviewed of 140 children who were discharged from Denver General Hospital with diagnoses of nonaccidental trauma or failure to thrive. The findings are reported.

88. Gormsen, Harald; Vesterdal, Jørgen. "Barnemishandling. 20 tilfaelde, heraf 11 med død til følge" [Child Abuse. The Battered Child Syndrome. 20 Cases, 11 of Which Were Fatal]. Ugeskrift for Laeger, 130:1203-1209, July 18, 1968.
An account is presented of 20 cases of ill-treatment of children from the period 1939-1967, 11 of which proved fatal. Nine of the 20 cases occurred in 1967. Fifteen of the 20 culprits were mentally abnormal and nine of these were mentally retarded. According to Danish law, notification of such cases to the authorities for the protection of children and young persons is compulsory. (Journal Abstract Modified.)

89. Gornall, P.; Ahmed, S.; Jolleys, A., et al. "Intra-Abdominal Injuries in the Battered Baby Syndrome." Archives of Disease in Childhood, 47:211-214, April 1972.
Six case studies of battered children suffering from intra-abdominal visceral injuries are presented. In addition to visceral lesions, all the children were found to have histories and physical signs clearly pointing to the diagnosis of the battered baby syndrome. Epigastric and small intestinal injuries predominated in these

children, and in this respect the pattern of trauma differs from that
seen in children injured in road traffic and other accidents. (Journal Abstract Modified.)

90. Green, Arthur H. "A Psychodynamic Approach to the Study
and Treatment of Child Abusing Parents." Journal of the
American Academy of Child Psychiatry, 15(3):414-429, Summer 1976.
The author presents the psychodynamics of the distorted patterns of family interaction encountered in a study of 60 cases of
child abuse. Child abuse is regarded as a dysfunction of parenting
in which the parent misperceives the child due to his own frustrating
childhood experiences. The beating represents the parent's attempt
to master trauma passively experienced as a child. The child abuse
syndrome is conceptualized as the project of three factors: the
parent's abuse-prone personality, the child's abuse-provoking characteristics, and environmental stress. (Journal Summary Modified.)

91. _____. "Self-Destructive Behavior in Physically Abused
Schizophrenic Children. Report of Cases." Archives of
General Psychiatry, 19:171-179, August 1968.
An investigation concerning self-destructive behavior in schizophrenic children found that the periodic physical abuse which the
child demonstrated, such as head-banging, was due to overall rejection and stimulus deprivation. Although painful to the child, this
physically abusive contact may compensate for the deficiency of
tactile and kinesthetic stimulation.

92. _____; Gaines, Richard W.; Sandgrund, Alice. "Child
Abuse: Pathological Syndrome of Family Interaction."
American Journal of Psychiatry, 131:882-886, August 1974.
Patterns of family interaction frequently encountered in 60
cases of child abuse are described. The maltreatment syndrome
is described as the end result of three potentiating factors: the
abuse-prone personality of the parent, characteristics of the child
that make him vulnerable to scapegoating, and current environmental stress. Role reversal was a prominent feature in the psychodynamic makeup of these families. (Journal Abstract Modified.)

93. _____; _____; _____. Psychological Sequelae of Child
Abuse and Neglect. See entry 2107.

94. Green, Orville C. "Sizing Up the Small Child." Post-Gradu-
ate Medicine, 50:103-109, October 1971.
Several case studies of undersized children who otherwise appear normal and do not show evidence of congenital anomalies are
presented. Factors identified in delayed or stunted growth include
constitutional delay, pituitary insufficiency, emotional deprivation,
pituitary insufficiency induced by child battering, willful starvation,
and hypothyroidism.

95. Greengard, Joseph. "The Battered Child Syndrome." Medical
Science, 15:82-91, March 1964.

Greengard presents case studies of Cook County (Chicago) Hospital infant patients as illustrative of the total problem of child abuse, and then discusses the clinical and sociological aspects of the battered child syndrome.

96. Gregg, Grace S.; Elmer, Elizabeth. "Infant Injuries: Accident or Abuse?" Pediatrics, 44:434-439, September 1969.
Observations were made of 146 children who were accidentally injured or abused, and 113 children were studied in detail. The injuries of the abused group tended to be more severe and to be followed by serious sequelae more often than those of the accidentally injured, but the two groups were difficult to differentiate on the basis of history alone. Other findings such as developmental retardation, patient's ordinal position, family density, and ability to cope with stress were more useful. (Journal Abstract Modified.)

97. Griswold, B. B.; Billingsley, Andrew. Personality and Social Characteristics of Low-Income Mothers Who Neglect or Abuse Their Children. Berkeley: California University, School of Social Welfare, undated. 16 p.
The welfare records of 40 white women with illegitimate children and 14 without illegitimate children were reviewed to identify deviant psychosocial factors among mothers who abused or neglected their children. The results of the review are detailed. Fragmentary evidence suggests that data for black families would be significantly different from the present study.

98. Harder, Thoger. "The Psychopathology of Infanticide." Acta Psychiatrica Scandinavica, 43(2):196-245, 1967.
Children are the victims of almost half the total number of murders in Denmark. The killers are predominantly the parents, who frequently commit suicide immediately afterwards; therefore there are not many who can be put to mental observation. The killing by parents of their own children has not hitherto been made the subject of a collective survey in this country. The material presented consists of 19 persons who had been mentally observed on account of their having killed, or attempted to kill, their children.

99. Hart Hansen, Jens P. "Barnesmishandlingogsa i Gronland" [The Battered Child Syndrome--Also in Greenland]. Ugeskrift for Laeger, 136:1213-1215, May 27, 1974.
Three typical cases of the battered child syndrome in Greenland are presented to stress the fact that it is necessary to be aware of this phenomenon also in Greenland. (Journal Summary.)

100. Heins, Marilyn. "Child Abuse--Analysis of a Current Epidemic." Michigan Medicine, 68:887-891, September 1969.
After a brief description of the nature, historical development, clinical picture, and diagnostic procedures of child abuse, Heins presents the results of a study of child abuse cases admitted to Detroit General Hospital over a 16-month period, beginning in September 1969.

101. Hick, John F. "Sudden Infant Death Syndrome and Child Abuse." Pediatrics, 52:147-148, July 1973.
   The author suggests that a foster home setting might have provided a more controlled situation for the Steinschneider Study. Because of the potential for child abuse in the family history and the danger of hospital-acquired infection, a foster home would have established control over these two variables and perhaps led to a different outcome.

102. "High Risk Abuse Children Should Be Identified in Clinical Setting." U.S. Medicine, 6-7, December 15, 1973.
   In this study of 60 abused children, it was found that child abuse was the end result of interaction of three variables: parental personality attributes which contribute to their "abuse proneness" and are incompatible with adequate child-rearing; characteristics of the child which increase the likelihood of his being abused; and immediate environmental stresses which maximize the burden of child-rearing.

103. Holczabek, W.; Lachmann, D.; Zweymüller, E. "Sturz im Säuglingsalter" [Falls in Infancy]. Deutsche Medizinische Wochenschrift, 97:1640-1646, October 27, 1972.
   Three hundred and eighty out-patient and in-patient case notes of infants (under one year of age) who had been brought to the hospital because of an accident were analyzed. Almost half of those having severe injuries (17) had skull fractures, in thirteen there were fractures of the upper and lower limbs and in six of the clavicle. In the first of the two fatal cases there had been other injuries as well as battered baby syndrome. (English Summary Modified.)

104. Holland, Cathleen Grant. An Examination of Social Isolation and Availability to Treatment in the Phenomenon of Child Abuse. Master's of Social Work Thesis. Smith College Studies in Social Work, 44(1):74-75, 1973.
   Social isolation and availability to treatment were examined in 52 cases of abused or neglected children reported in the records of a child and family service agency. Major findings were that the families were, on the whole, socially isolated. In spite of the isolation, however, over half had made contacts with community services around issues of familial and parenting stress prior to referral for abuse. A significant number of them were helped in terms of the diminution of social isolation and strengthening of family functioning, as well as diminished abuse. (Journal Abstract Modified.)

105. Holman, R. R.; Kanwar, S. "Early Life of the 'Battered Child.'" Archives of Disease in Childhood, 50(1):78-80, January 1975.
   The obstetric histories and early lives of 28 subsequently abused children are reviewed. Causes for abuse are explored. These and other difficulties may be regarded as "environmental pressures" leading to child abuse by susceptible individuals.

106. Holter, Joan C.; Friedman, Stanford B. "Child Abuse: Early
Case Finding in the Emergency Department." Pediatrics,
42:128-138, July 1968.
In two surveys of children seen in the emergency department
at the University of Rochester Medical Center, 7 of 69 cases and
7 of 87 cases were suspected of having injuries due to maltreatment.
Empirically, certain types of injuries were found to be most commonly associated with childhood abuse. Findings of the surveys are
discussed in terms of the preventive function and role of an emergency department. (Journal Abstract Modified.)

107. _____; _____. "Etiology and Management of Severely
Burned Children. Psychosocial Considerations." American Journal of Diseases of Children, 118:680-686, November 1969.
In assessing the emotional makeup of the families of severely
burned children, it was found that 10 of the 13 families involved in
this study had major psychological and social problems within the
family units prior to the burn incidents. In these 10 cases, the
gross emotional disturbances within the families appeared to have
propelled the children into tragic situations resulting in severe burns.
(Journal Summary Modified.)

108. _____; _____. "Principles of Management in Child
Abuse Cases." American Journal of Orthopsychiatry, 38:
127-136, January 1968.
Procedures for a team-diagnosis approach to child abuse are
suggested. Seven girls and 12 boys, aged one month to five years,
who were hospitalized at a university medical center were studied
from different vantage points. Findings indicated: Families were
often social isolates; marked psychopathology or mental retardation
in 14 of 18 families studied; characteristic personality patterns.

109. Horn, P. "Child-Battering Parent: Sick but Slick." Psychology Today, 8(7):32, 35, December 1974.
A study undertaken to illustrate the abusive parents' ability
to appear normal is described. Thirteen non-battering parents and
13 convicted child-battering parents were matched by age, sex, income, education, number of children, and marital status. The two
groups were given a series of personality tests and an I.Q. test.
Results of the study are presented. Indications are that abusive
parents tend to overcompensate in preventing awareness of their
violent impulses.

110. Hwang, Woon Tai, et al. "Battered Child Syndrome in a
Malaysian Hospital." Medical Journal of Malaysia, 28(4):
239-243, June 1974.
Seven battered child syndromes were treated in the University
Hospital Kuala Lumpur. Three of the children were under three
years of age. The clinical features include bruises, scalp hematoma, radiological evidence of fractures of skull and abdominal
visceral injuries. The importance of team work between the doctors and social workers, and hospitalization of the suspected child

at the initial stage, were stressed. An appeal to medical practitioners and others for cooperation in detection of cases was made.

111. Hyman, C. A. "I. Q. of Parents of Battered Babies." (Letter). British Medical Journal, 4:739, December 22, 1973.
A criticism of the results showing that nearly half of the mothers of a series of child batterers were of borderline normal intelligence or below based on the averaged scores of four Wechsler Adult Scale subtests. The validity of this use of subtest scores is questioned. Another study using a short form of the W.A.I.S. revealed no differences in spatial perceptual abilities between battering mothers and controls.

112. "Iowa Child Abuse Study." Children Today, 5(1):30-31, January-February 1976.
The present social situations of abused children who had been treated at the University of Iowa Hospitals for their injuries from July 1965 to December 1973 were investigated. The results of the findings are reported.

113. Ironside, Wallace. "The Infant Development Distress (IDD) Syndrome: A Predictor of Impaired Development?" Australian & New Zealand Journal of Psychiatry, 9(3): 153-158, September 1975.
A follow-up study was conducted of eight infants displaying the IDD syndrome and eight matched healthy infants for 6.75 years. A checklist was used to conduct interviews, and children were visited in their homes. The findings are presented. Enhancement of the mother-infant relationship and family dynamics appear to be the critical factors in treatment. (P. A.)

114. Isaacs, Susanna. "Physical Ill-Treatment of Children." Lancet, 1:37-39, January 6, 1968.
Presents results of a survey done in a child psychiatry department over a three-year period in which 22 of 699 families presented with evidence of child abuse. Also cites a survey by Gibbens and Walker published in pamphlet form in 1956.

115. Jenkins, Richard L.; Gants, Robert; Shoji, Takeshi, et al. "Interrupting the Family Cycle of Violence." Journal of the Iowa Medical Society, 60:85-89, February 1970.
Presented is a case history of a nine-year-old boy who battered two sibling infants in an outburst of violent resentment toward a brutal stepfather. The child tended to model the violent behavior of the stepfather in the home environment, yet appeared to be able to function in outside social relationships and in school.

116. Johnson, Betty; Morse, Harold A. "Injured Children and Their Parents." Children, 15:147-152, July 1968.
The need for a comprehensive, coordinated community protective service was clearly demonstrated in a study of 101 children in 85 families, known to have been abused during an 18-month

period in 1963-64. At the end of the study, child care had improved in 33 families, and 80 percent of the children were no longer in danger of subsequent injury. (Author Abstract Modified.)

117. Johnson, Clara L. Child Abuse in the Southeast: Analysis of 1172 Reported Cases. Athens, Ga.: Regional Institute of Social Welfare Research, University of Georgia, 1974. 153 p.
Presented is an analysis of 1172 reported cases of child abuse in the eight southeastern states in Region IV (Georgia, Alabama, Florida, North Carolina, South Carolina, Tennessee, Kentucky, and Mississippi). The methodology of the study including aims, sampling procedure, and data collection and processing is given in Chapter 1. A summary, reflection, and conclusion are included in Chapter 7. Also provided is a summary of the significant findings.

118. _____. Child Abuse: Some Findings from the Analysis of 1172 Reported Cases. Athens, Georgia: Regional Institute of Social Welfare Research, 1975. 12 p. (Paper presented at the Annual Meeting of the Southern Association of Agricultural Scientists, New Orleans, La., February 2-5, 1975). Available from EDRS: MF-$0.76, Plus Postage. HC not available.
A sample of 1172 cases of both confirmed and unconfirmed child abuse was analyzed in an attempt to identify major demographic variables which might be associated with differential case handling. The data was collected by transferring previously recorded information on child injury cases from state central registries to a standardized form.

119. Justice, Blair; Duncan, David F. "Life Crisis as a Precursor to Child Abuse." Public Health Reports, 91:110-115, March-April 1976.
Many of the theories as to the causation of child abuse assign some role to stress--life change events. If an excessive number or magnitude of such life change events occur, the person affected may be said to be in a state of life crises. A questionnaire was administered to 35 abusing parents and 35 matched controls who had experienced problems with their children but had not been abusive. The two groups were compared for their life change scores on the Social Readjustment Rating Scale for the year before their abuse or problems began with their children. Results are given.

120. Kaleita, Thomas; Wise, James H. "An MMPI Comparison of Child Abusers with Two Groups of Criminal Offenders." Clinical Proceedings, 32(8):180-184, September 1976.
Twenty-five child battering parents were compared with forty violent and forty non-violent criminal offenders on the Minnesota Multiphasic Personality Inventory (MMPI). Except for sex sampling bias, none of the groups proved to be significantly different from one another when each of the 12 scales were separately compared. Profiles for the child battering groups indicated highest scores on Psychopathic Deviate (Pd) and Schizophrenic (Sc) scales. These

findings support the "sick but slick" personality cluster suggested by Wright. (Journal Summary.)

121. Kaplun, David; Reich, Robert. "Murdered Child and His Killers." American Journal of Psychiatry, 133:809-813, July 1976.
The authors studied 112 cases of child homicide in New York City in 1968-1969 to identify contributing social and psychiatric factors and to determine the fate of the surviving siblings and the degree of involvement of the city's social agencies with the families. Results of the findings are given. The authors present case illustrations and offer guidelines for improved prevention by psychiatrists and social workers. (Journal Summary Modified.)

122. Keen, J. H.; Lendrum, J.; Wolman, B. "Inflicted Burns and Scalds in Children." British Medical Journal, 4(5991): 268-269, November 1, 1975.
Ten children who had been burnt and six who had been scalded by parents or those caring for them were seen over three years. Staff caring for burnt children should be aware of this type of inflicted injury. X-ray skeletal surveys should be carried out in doubtful cases and a case conference initiated. (Journal Abstract Modified.)

123. Kenel, Mary Elizabeth. A Study of the Cognitive Dimension of Impulsivity-Reflectivity and Aggression in Female Child Abusers. Ph.D. The Catholic University of America, 1976. 81 p. Available from: University Microfilms. Order No. 76-20,229.
The purpose of this study was to investigate the dimensions of impulsivity and aggression in child abusers in order to facilitate diagnosis, treatment, and prediction of high-risk caretakers.

124. Kennell, J. H.; Wolfe, Jerauld, R., et al. "Maternal Behavior One Year After Early and Extended Post Partum Contact." Developmental Medicine and Child Neurology, 16(2):172-179, 1974.
This study reports observations of maternal behavior in 28 human mothers of full term infants. Apparent were measurable differences for as long as one year between mothers with early and extended contact with the infant and those who were separated shortly after birth. A disproportionately high percentage of mother disturbances force an examination of present prenatal practices.

125. Kent, James T. "A Follow-Up Study of Abused Children." Journal of Pediatric Psychology, 1(2):25-31, Spring 1976.
Presented are some of the findings of a retrospective follow-up study of abused children in Los Angeles, undertaken to investigate the effects of abusive environments on the psychosocial development of children. Kent concludes that abusive environments do have specific effects independent of low socio-economic status and general family dysfunction, and that these effects are in part reversible with intervention through foster home placement.

126. Klein, Michael; Stern, Leo. "Low Birth Weight and the Battered Child Syndrome." American Journal of Diseases of Children, 122:15-18, July 1971.
Fifty-one cases of battered child syndrome seen over a period of nine years at the Montreal Children's Hospital were reviewed to explore the possibility that low birth weight predisposes to this condition (23.5 percent were low birth weight infants). A high degree of isolation and separation of infant from parents in newborn period were other common factors. (Journal Summary Modified.)

127. Koel, Bertram S. "Failure to Thrive and Fatal Injury as a Continuum." American Journal of Diseases of Children, 118:565-567, October 1969.
Three cases of failure to thrive in infancy were investigated but no pathologic diagnosis was made. Within months after discharge, each was readmitted, critically ill from trauma. Two infants died. Fattening a puny infant is satisfying to the staff, but the child remains at risk of subsequent violence if he is sent back to untreated parents. (Journal Summary.)

128. Kogutt, Marvin S.; Swischuk, Leonard E.; Fagen, Charles J. "Patterns of Injury and Significance of Uncommon Fractures in the Battered Child Syndrome." American Journal of Roentgenology, Radium Therapy and Nuclear Medicine, 121:143-149, May 1974.
The case histories and X-rays of 95 physically abused children (49 boys, 46 girls, 6 weeks to 8 years old) were reviewed to document patterns of injury. There were positive radiographic findings in 66 percent, which were fractures in 55 percent. These fractures are described.

129. Koluchová, Jarmila. "Further Development of Twins After Severe and Prolonged Deprivation: A Second Report." Journal of Child Psychology and Psychiatry and Allied Disciplines, 17:181-188, July 1976.
A previous (1972) report on the good development of twins after severe and prolonged deprivation is followed up, and progress over three further years is described. See entry below.

130. _____. "Severe Deprivation in Twins: A Case Study." Journal of Child Psychology and Psychiatry and Allied Disciplines, 13(2):107-114, June 1972.
This is an interesting case study of a set of identical twins reared in isolation from the age of 18 months to seven years. When discovered by child welfare personnel and examined, their mental age was three years. After placement in a foster home for a period of approximately two years, they seemed to approach normal in terms of I.Q. and physical size. See entry above.

131. "Koluchová's Twins." (Editorial). British Medical Journal, 2(6041):897-898, October 16, 1976.
This editorial reviews the case of the Koluchová twins of

Czechoslovakia who had been isolated and cruelly treated from the age of 18 months to seven years by their stepmother. Because of their remarkable recovery when placed with a foster mother, it is tempting to write-off the importance of the early years. But other research with a different theoretical basis should maintain the balance.

132. Kreisler, L.; Straus, P. "Les Auteurs de sévices sur les jeunes enfants" [The Perpetrator of Cruelty Upon Young Children. A Psychological Approach]. Archives Françaises de Pediatrie, 28: 249-265, 1971.
   A sample of 110 cases of child abuse were observed in a Paris hospital. Four of these cases were studied with emphasis on the psychological characteristics of those who inflict physical abuse upon young children. Conclusions are given concerning practical pediatrics and prevention.

133. Krieger, Ingeborg. "Food Restriction as a Form of Child Abuse in Ten Cases of Psychosocial Deprivation Dwarfism." Clinical Pediatrics, 13:127-133, February 1974.
   Ten children (7 boys, 3 girls, 27-120 months old) with psychosocial deprivation dwarfism presented with complicating symptoms of malabsorption. Their physical and mental conditions are described. Direct and indirect evidence indicated that food had been persistently restricted by the mothers, who had the personality traits commonly seen in abusing mothers.

134. Kunstadter, Ralph H.; Singer, Myron H.; Steinberg, Rose. "The 'Battered Child' and the Celiac Syndrome." Illinois Medical Journal, 132:267-272, September 1967.
   The case history of a boy, hospitalized five times between the ages of three years nine months and six years one month, shows an association between celiac syndrome and child abuse. The characteristics of celiac or malabsorption syndrome are provided, as well as other symptoms the child manifested. Surveillance of the child's home revealed an unstable environment in which the father drank and physically abused the mother. In a residential psychiatric treatment center, the child showed both physical and emotional recovery. At age seven, he appeared ready for the third grade and had made up much of the deficiency in growth.

135. Kushnick, T.; Pietrucha, D. M.; Kushnick, J. R. "Syndrome of the Abandoned Small Child." Clinical Pediatrics, 9(6): 356-361, June 1970.
   Records of 39 abandoned children seen during a 12-month period in the Newark City Hospital were reviewed. The children, how and when abandoned, their ages and physical condition, and something of the family background are described. Social service and child welfare agencies, the police, and the courts were involved in the disposition of several of the cases. The data also indicate that insufficient care was taken to obtain adequate family histories and complete medical examinations.

136. Lampard, F. Gillian; Reid, Dorothy A. "Nanook of Eskimo Point." Nursing Times, 65:1472-1473, November 13, 1969.
Nanook, a 20-month-old Eskimo boy, was brought to the Eskimo Point Canada nursing station in a moribund state suffering from severe exposure. Remarkably, he showed apparently complete recovery, although he did not initially respond to affection when he had improved physically. Placement by the Children's Welfare Department was being effectuated.

137. Lauer, Brian; Ten Broeck, Elsa; Grossman, Moses. "Battered Child Syndrome: Review of 130 Patients with Controls." Pediatrics, 54:67-70, July 1974.
The medical and social service records of the 130 battered children under 10 years of age admitted to San Francisco General Hospital during a six-year period were reviewed. Only children with physical injuries were included. A control group was selected from concurrent admissions. The results of the findings are given.

138. Lukianowicz, Narcyz. "Attempted Infanticide." Psychiatria Clinica, 5:1-16, 1972.
A study is presented of 20 women who attempted infanticide. Clinical syndromes of the patients were reviewed and their personality, their marriage, their attitude toward pregnancy, their own childhood, the psychodynamics of their behavior, the precipitating factors and the methods employed in the attempted child slaying were discussed. The religion of the patients, their social class and housing conditions were reviewed. Ways of preventing infanticide were discussed. (Author Abstract Modified.)

139. _____. "Battered Children." Psychiatria Clinica, 4:257-280, May 6, 1971.
Reports of 18 children diagnosed as abused in three clinics in Northern Ireland. The mean age of the mothers was 22 years and 24 years for the fathers. In 14 cases the batterer was the mother, in two cases the father, and in two cases both parents participated in the battering. In this study, 14 of the 18 children were the only child, and the mothers expressed rejection of the infant in all cases.

140. _____. "Infanticide." Psychiatria Clinica, 4:145-158, 1971.
An analysis of infanticide covers definition, typology, three extensive case reports, and psychiatric evaluation. The cases illustrate late overt infanticide where the mothers killed all their children.

141. McRae, Kenneth N.; Ferguson, C. A.; Lederman, R. S. "The Battered Child Syndrome." Canadian Medical Association Journal, 108:859-860, 863-868, April 7, 1973.
The experience of the Children's Hospital of Winnipeg from 1957 to 1971 with abused infants and children is presented with

statistical data on 132 children. Details as to incidence, source and types of abuse, are presented along with a discussion of the management of the problem.

142. Mainard, R.; Berranger, P. De; Cadudal, J. L. "Une conséquence fréquente et grave de l'alcoolisme parental: les sévices commis sur les enfants" [A Frequent and Serious Consequence of Parental Alcoholism: Child Abuse]. La Revue de l'Alcoolisme, 17:21-31, 1971.
Alcoholism was found in 65 percent of the parents of 32 French children hospitalized following parental brutality; both parents were alcoholics in 20 percent; the fathers alone in 39 percent; mothers alone in 6 percent. Alcoholism was found in 82 percent of the 200 social welfare cases involving children abused by their parents.

143. Malee, T. J. "Drug Abuse in a Small Community." Rocky Mountain Medical Journal, 69(5):66-67, May 1972.
A 5-year-old girl was hospitalized after ingesting an overdose of the tranquilizer Placidyl which had been prescribed for her mother, a known drug user. Four days after she had been hospitalized and while she was visited by her mother, the girl once again ingested Placidyl. The child was placed in the care of the county welfare department, and the mother referred for psychiatric evaluation and care.

144. Manciaux, M.; Deschamps, J. P. "L'Enfant victime de mauvais traitements" [The Battered Child]. Vie Medicale au Canada Français, 4(3):244-247, 1975.
The syndrome of the battered child is reviewed, based on 27 case studies. Suggested prophylactic measures are included.

145. Maroteaux, P., et al. "Les Séquelae du Syndrome de Silverman (Fractures multiples du nourrisson, syndrome dit des 'enfants battus'). Etude de seize observations." [Sequelae of Silverman's Syndrome. (Multiple Fractures in the Infant, So-Called 'Battered Child' Syndrome). Study of 16 cases]. Presse Medicale, 75:711-716, March 22, 1967.
In a follow-up study of 16 observations of Silverman's syndrome, the authors show that, in many of these, non-conspicuous sequels may be present. Some are easily predicted, such as articular limitations of elbow and the hip. Others, as described, are singular enough. The non-exceptional occurrence of anomalies in the peripherical retineal field remains unexplained in its nature and pathogenesis. The expression "battered child syndrome" is perhaps debatable since some of the involved children are probably the object of excessive manipulations, but not voluntary ill-treatment. (English Summary Modified.)

146. Martin, Harold P. Follow-Up Studies on the Development of Abused Children. JFK Child Development Center, National Center for Prevention and Treatment of Child Abuse and Neglect. (Unpublished Manuscript, 1973.)

This paper reports two follow-up studies of abused children. In the first study of 42 children, 33 percent were mentally retarded, and 43 percent were neurologically impaired. The second study focused on 38 abused children who had suffered less severe trauma but 36 percent of the group were undernourished at the initial examination and 18 of the 21 still exhibited growth retardation. Learning and behavior problems were common findings.

147. Martin, Helen L. "Antecedents of Burns and Scalds in Children." British Journal of Medical Psychology, 43:39-47, March, 1970.
A study of the circumstances surrounding the burns and scalds in 50 children is analyzed. The injuries usually stemmed from a breakdown in protection by the parents or by failure of the child to heed known hazards. The article notes the vast difference between injuries such as these and parental abuse.

148. Meinick, Barry; Hurley, John R. "Distinctive Personality Attributes of Child-Abusing Mothers." Journal of Consulting and Clinical Psychology, 33(6):746-749, December 1969.
Distinctive personality attributes of child-abusing mothers are studied. To explore hypotheses derived from contemporary child-abuse writings, groups of 10 abusive (A) and 10 control (C) mothers, matched for age, social class, and education, were compared on 18 personality variables. Characteristics of abusive mothers are an inability to empathize with their children, severely frustrated dependency needs, and a probable history of emotional deprivation.

149. Meyers, Stephen A. "The Child Slayer: A 25-Year Survey of Homicides Involving Preadolescent Victims." Archives of General Psychiatry, 17:211-213, 1967.
Eighty-three cases of felonious homicide involving preadolescent victims in Detroit from 1940 to 1965 were studied. Psychosis was the most common precipitating factor, and the one most prevalent among the accused mothers.

150. Michael, Marianne K. "The Battered Child." Iowa Journal of Social Work, 3(3):78-83, 1970.
The author presents the results of a case study of 28 abused children reported in the period from October 1, 1965, to December 31, 1969. All of these children were reported from University Hospitals to local county departments of social services and to county attorneys as suspected abused children.

151. _____. "Follow-Up Study of Abused Children Reported from University Hospitals." Journal of the Iowa Medical Society, 62:235-237, May 1972.
Discusses a study of the reporting policy formulated by University Hospitals which only sees patients referred by a physician. The records of 28 cases were reviewed and findings indicate that 85 percent of the victims were under three years old, in 16 of the 28 families both parents were present, and 84 percent had three or less children.

152. Money, John; Annecillo, Charles. "IQ Change Following Change of Domicile in the Syndrome of Reversible Hyposomatotropinism (Psychosocial Dwarfism): Pilot Investigation." Psychoneuroendocrinology, 1(4):427-429, September 1976.
The authors instituted a program of IQ testing before and after domicile change to investigate whether catch-up intellectual growth might accompany catch-up somatic growth in cases of reversible dwarfism with suspected or proven child abuse. Follow-up studies were conducted on sixteen patients. Results draw attention to the living environment as a powerful determinant of IQ and its changes, especially in the context of reversible pituitary (growth hormone) failure, occurring along with child abuse or neglect. (P.A.)

153. _____; Wolff, Georg. "Late Puberty, Retarded Growth and Reversible Hyposomatotropinism (psychosocial dwarfism)." Adolescence, 9(33):121-134, Spring 1974.
A case report of a 16-year-old boy who was diagnosed as suffering from battered child syndrome, reversible hyposomatotropic dwarfism, and delayed puberty is presented. Evidence from 11 other cases of reversible hyposomatotropic dwarfism is also presented.

154. _____; _____; Annecillo, C. "Pain Agnosia and Self-Injury in the Syndrome of Reversible Somatotropin Deficiency (Psychosocial Dwarfism)." Journal of Autism and Childhood Schizophrenia, 2(2):127-139, April-June 1972.
Hospital and social service records of 32 patients, 23 boys and 9 girls, with reversible behavioral symptoms in a syndrome of dwarfism characterized by reversible inhibition of growth in stature are surveyed and discussed. In 22 of these cases severe physical punishment had occurred in the original home environment. Management and treatment of the cases, as well as the results of same, are given. Self-injury, pain agnosia, and related syndromes are briefly discussed.

155. Moore, Jean G. "Yo-Yo Children." Nursing Times, 70(49): 1888-1889, December 5, 1974.
Emotional child battering was investigated in 23 children who had witnessed violence between their parents. Characteristics of the children were frequent introversion, unexplained temper tantrums, fatigue, and underachievement in school. Health visitors with contacts within the community are urged to help discover these problem families and ensure protection for the children.

156. Morse, Carol W.; Sahler, Olle Jane Z.; Friedman, Stanford B. "A Three-Year Follow-Up Study of Abused and Neglected Children." American Journal of Diseases of Children, 120:439-446, November 1970.
Twenty-five children from 23 families were studied approximately three years after hospitalization for injuries judged to be sequelae of abuse and gross neglect. About one-third were suspected of again being victims. Seventy percent were judged to be outside the normal range of intellectual, emotional, social, and

motor development. Often mental retardation or motor hyperactivity
may have preceded the abuse. More attention to rehabilitation to
these families is needed. (Journal Summary Modified.)

157. "Mother Confines Three to House for Ten Years." Life, 49:
     29-30+, August 29, 1960. il.
     This is an account of a Tecumseh, Ontario, mother who kept
her three dwarfed youngsters, now 18, 15, and 13 years of age,
confined to a small playroom-bedroom for $10\frac{1}{2}$ years. Taken to the
hospital, they were found to have the physiques and emotions of 9-,
7-, and 5-year-olds. Mother claimed she hid them to shield them
from other children's ridicule and to get past landlords who frowned
on big families.

158. Muir, Martha F. "Psychological and Behavioral Characteris-
     tics of Abused Children." Journal of Pediatric Psychology,
     1(2):16-19, Spring 1976.
     Two case studies reveal important clues concerning views of
the world, typical defensive mechanisms, intactness of ego, and
capacity to form meaningful relationships which can be gained from
interpersonal interactions and projective data with abused children.
Reviewed are current research findings concerning these children's
psychological and behavioral characteristics and presented are relevant case history data as a step toward developing effective therapeutic interventions for children of abuse.

159. Muller, S. "Als Frau K. die Nerven durchgingen--Dokumen-
     tation zur Kindermisshandlung" [When Mrs. K. Lost Her
     Cool. A Documented Case of Child Abuse]. Neue Praxis,
     3(1):44-56, 1973.
     Between 30,000 and 80,000 cases of child abuse are recorded
in the German Federal Republic annually. Muller presents a case
study selected from files of a child welfare office.

160. Myers, Steven A. "The Child Slayer: A 25-Year Survey of
     Homicides Involving Preadolescent Victims." Archives of
     General Psychiatry, 17:211-213, 1967.
     This is a study of preadolescent felonious homicides in Detroit
over a 25-year period. Myers cites actual incidents and presents
statistics regarding the deaths. He covers details, such as who was
the murderer and how it was accomplished.

161. _____ . "Maternal Filicide." American Journal of Diseases
     of Children, 120:534-536, December 1970.
     Of 83 preadolescent victims of felonious homicide in the city
of Detroit from 1940 to 1965, 35 were slain by their mothers. The
majority of the mothers were judged to be overtly psychotic, a considerable number schizophrenic. (Modified Journal Summary.)

162. Neimann, N., et al. "Les Enfants victimes de sévices"
     [Children Victims of Maltreatment]. Pediatrie, 23:861-875,
     December 1968.
     Public opinion has tended to blame doctors and social services

because diagnosis in child abuse cases have come too late to save
the child. The problem has a triple aspect: medical, social and
judicial. These various aspects were studied in 79 observations
made between 1959 and 1965 in Nancy.

163. Newberger, Eli H.; Reed, R. B.; Daniel, J. H., et al.
     Toward an Etiologic Classification of Pediatric Social Ill-
     ness: A Descriptive Epidemiology of Child Abuse and
     Neglect, Failure to Thrive, Accidents and Poisonings in
     Children Under Four Years of Age. (Paper presented at
     the Biennial Meeting of the Society for Research in Child
     Development, Denver, Colo., April 10-13, 1975). 17 p.
     Available from EDRS: MF-$0.76; HC-$1.58, Plus Post-
     age.
     The underlying common origins of pediatric social illnesses
in children under age four are examined. Subjects were 560 children
admitted to the Children's Hospital Medical Center in Boston. Children admitted with pediatric social diagnoses were matched on the
basis of age, race, and socioeconomic status with control children
who were without pediatric social diagnoses.

164. Nichtern, S. "The Children of Drug Users." Annual Progress
     in Child Psychiatry and Child Development, (Part X):545-
     551, 1974.
     Case records of children of heroin addicts revealed that nearly
all of these children are neglected, and some show evidence of
physical abuse. Some suffered from malnutrition, and many were
withdrawn, lacking in animation, and generally inhibited in their responses. This rapidly growing population demands increasing attention.

165. Nurse, Shirley M. "Familial Patterns of Parents Who Abuse
     Their Children." Smith College Studies in Social Work,
     35:11-25, October 1964.
     A study of cases selected from the files of the New York
County Family Court, Juvenile Term, confirms previous studies that
common factors in cases of physically abused children are: the selection of a single victim--usually an unwanted, devalued child; parental protection of each other rather than the child; and repetitious
assaults by the abusing parent. Studies of causes are also noted.

166. O'Hearn, Thomas P., Jr. A Comparison of Fathers in Abu-
     sive Situations with Fathers in Non-Abusive Situations.
     Ph.D. Denver University, Colorado. Graduate School of
     Arts and Sciences. 1974. 149 p. Available from Uni-
     versity Microfilms, 75-01872.
     Twenty-three abusive fathers were matched with 23 non-abusive
fathers on the basis of age, income, age of children, and number of
children under five years of age. The matched pairs were compared
on the following variables: internal vs. external control; social isolation; acceptability to others; powerlessness; empathy; dogmatism;
self-esteem; assertiveness; and ego strength.

167. Oliver, J. E. "Microcephaly Following Baby Battering and
      Shaking." British Medical Journal, 2(5965):262-264, May
      3, 1975.
      This article focuses on cases of microcephaly following the
rough handling of babies. It discusses how this rough handling often
leads to mental retardation. Other forms of abuse which were
found with siblings are also considered. The case studies involved
operations performed, the kind of care given, and follow-up studies
regarding progress of the children.

168. _____; Cox, Jane. "A Family Kindred with Ill-Used Chil-
      dren: The Burden on the Community." British Journal
      of Psychiatry, 123:81-90, July 1973.
      A family pedigree is described in which representatives from
at least three generations were subjected to severe ill-usage as
children. This family pedigree is representative of a number of
others in the locality which are also under study. Many members
of this kindred, and their husbands, wives and children, had received extensive social and medical help from numerous professional workers in many areas over long periods of time. To date,
this help has not prevented the tendency to the perpetuation of child
abuse and neglect in successive generations. (Journal Summary.)

169. _____; _____; Taylor, Audrey, et al. Severely Ill-
      Treated Young Children in North-East Wiltshire. Research
      Report 4. Oxford University (England). Department of
      Clinical Epidemiology, August 1974. 88 p.
      A clinical study of 38 severely abused children under four
years of age seen during a seven-year period ending in 1971 is presented. The discussion deals with the extent of the problem, difficulties in ascertainment, methods of ascertainment, and prevention.
Case vignettes of 34 children are presented.

170. _____; Dewhurst, K. E. "Six Generations of Ill-Used Chil-
      dren in a Huntington's Pedigree." Postgraduate Medical
      Journal, 45:757-760, December 1969.
      A Huntington's chorea pedigree of six generations illustrates
the interaction of environmental and genetic factors, which causes
prolonged suffering to children reared in such families. The majority of children from at least four of the six generations were subjected to both active cruelty and passive neglect. Family planning
and therapeutic abortion remain the only means of preventing Hunt-
ington's chorea.

171. _____; Taylor, Audrey. "Five Generations of Ill-Treated
      Children in One Family Pedigree." British Journal of
      Psychiatry, 119:473-480, November 1971.
      Five generations of ill-treated children are described with
some detail. The families contain numerous members who suffer
from mental illness, profound disturbances of personality, and
degrees of subnormal intelligence. Implications for preventive
medicine, particularly for family planning, are discussed.

172. O'Neill, James A., Jr. "Deliberate Childhood Trauma:
     Surgical Perspectives." Journal of Trauma, 13:399-400,
     April 1973.
     A series of 110 battered children demonstrates the serious-
ness of the child abuse problem. Of the patients, seven percent
died and 10 percent suffered permanent disability. Eighty percent
showed signs of repeated injury and about two-thirds had more than
one fresh injury when first seen. Psychological scars, neglect,
and malnutrition have all been associated with abuse. It is recommended that the physician employ a non-accusative approach toward
the problem. He should also overcome his reluctance to report
suspected abuse.

173. _____; Meacham, W. F.; Griffin, P. P., et al. "Pat-
     terns of Injury in the Battered Child Syndrome." Journal
     of Trauma, 13:332-339, April 1973.
     The authors describe their experience with 110 children who
were the victims of physical abuse seen over the last five years.
Most patients were less than two years of age and were injured by
a member of the family. Causes for abuse and types of injuries
encountered were given.

174. Palmer, C. H.; Weston, J. T. "Several Unusual Cases of
     Child Abuse." Journal of Forensic Sciences, 21(4):851-
     855, 1976. Tables 1.
     All childhood deaths which occurred in New Mexico during
1974 and 1975 were reviewed. Nine fatal instances of abuse were
identified representing the entire spectrum of physical abuse: neglect, abuse in a single episode of injury, repetitive abuse, or
sexual abuse. Several cases are summarized. These are unusual
either in the distribution of pathologic findings or in the problems
encountered in court presentation.

175. Pashayan, H.; Cochrane, W. A. "Maltreatment Syndrome of
     Children." Nova Scotia Medical Bulletin, 44:139-142,
     June 1965.
     Seven case histories describing clinical findings of the bat-
tered child syndrome are presented. Characteristic lesions, classical radiological findings, laboratory tests, and patterns of slow
development are explained. Observation of the family reveals socioeconomic stress and parental inadequacy.

176. Patscheider, H. [Two Unusual Cases of Fatal Child Abuse].
     Archiv für Kriminologie, 155(1-2):19-27, January-February
     1975.

177. Paulson, Morris J.; Afifi, Abdelmonen A.; Chaleff, Anne,
     et al. "A Discriminant Function Procedure for Identifying
     Abusing Parents." Life Threatening Behavior, 5(2):104-
     114, 1975.
     Discriminant function analysis was used to derive a more re-
fined scale of a linear combination of selected items for identifying
potential or actual abusive parents. A sample of 15 males and 18

females was selected from 60 abusive parents, each identified as the primary abusive parent in the home. The Minnesota Multiphasic Personality Inventory of each parent was subjected to a series of discriminant function analyses.

178. _____; _____; Thomason, Mary L., et al. "The MMPI: A Descriptive Measure of Psychopathology in Abusive Parents." Journal of Clinical Psychology, 30:387-390, July 1974.

Studied a total of 60 child-abusing parents and 100 nonabusing parents (controls) to determine (a) whether the MMPI could differentiate between the two groups and (b) given the varying degrees of responsibility and participation in the abuse and/or maltreatment of a child, the degrees to which the nonabusing spouse manifested psychological conflicts that may have directly or indirectly contributed to the abusive parent's act of violence. (Journal Summary Modified.)

179. _____; Schwemer, Gregory T.; Bendel, Robert B. "Clinical Application of the Pd, Ma and (OH) Experimental MMPI Scales to Further Understanding of Abusive Parents." Journal of Clinical Psychology, 32(3):558-564, July 1976.

The MMPI scales Pd(4) and Ma(9), corrected for K, are two clinically significant scales that in earlier published research differentiated between abusive parents and a like sample of nonabusive psychiatric outpatient parents. Standard ANOVA procedures were applied to data from 166 subjects, and nine experimental subscales of Pd, eight experimental subscales of Ma, and the Megargee Overcontrolled Hostility Scale (OH) were scored to compare a sample of abusive and non-abusive parents. (Journal Summary Modified.)

180. Pawlikowski, Andrzej. "Losy dzieci z rodzin alkoholikow" [Fates of Children from Families of Alcoholics]. Problemy Alkoholizmu, 7(7):4-6, 1972.

The situation, problems, and prospects of children from 100 families of alcoholics were studied. The data were obtained from the Cracow district court of law and from professional mental health workers. The most drastic 23 case histories are presented. The children were starved, maltreated, beaten, forced to lead a promiscuous life, could not learn, or became alcoholic.

181. Pelikán, L., et al. [Severe Deprivation Syndrome in Twins Following Prolonged Social Isolation]. Ceskoslovenska Pediatrie, 24:980-983, November 1969.

182. Pollitt, Ernesto; Eichler, Aviva Weisel; Chan, Chee-Khoon. "Psychosocial Development and Behavior of Mothers of Failure-to-Thrive Children." American Journal of Orthopsychiatry, 45:525-537, July 1975.

The social development, emotional adaptation, and functioning of mothers of failure-to-thrive children, and of a group of matched controls were studied. Results show that maternal behavior of the mothers of the failure-to-thrive group, while showing no overt psychopathology, did differ substantially from that of the control group. (Journal Abstract.)

183.   Rees, Alan; Symons, John; Joseph, Michael, et al. "Ven-
           tricular Septal Defect in a Battered Child." British Medi-
           cal Journal, 1(5948):20-21, January 4, 1975.
       The case of a five-year-old girl is discussed along with the
events surrounding her ventricular septal defect (VSD).   Her defect
was caused by a kick in the chest from her stepfather.   She also
had various other injuries.   The authors discuss the procedure for
caring for the injury along with some statistics regarding other VSD
cases involving child abuse.

184.   Reidy, Thomas J., Jr.   The Social, Emotional and Cognitive
           Functioning of Physically Abused and Neglected Children.
           Ph. D.   DePaul University.   1976.   124 p.   Available
           from University Microfilms, 76-14, 743.
       Three groups of children, twenty physically abused, sixteen
neglected, and twenty-two normal children were used in this study.
It is the first study to provide empirical evidence that child abuse
and neglect has serious consequences for the children involved.
Physical harm is only a portion of the damage caused by deprivation and abuse.   Severe behavioral, emotional and cognitive excesses and deficits were demonstrated.

185.   Resnick, Phillip J.   "Child Murder by Parents: A Psychiatric
           Review of Filicide."   American Journal of Psychiatry, 126:
           325-334, September 1969.
       The author reviews 131 cases of child murder and proposes
a new classification of filicide by apparent motive: altruistic,
acutely psychotic, unwanted child, accidental, and spouse revenge.
The high frequency of altruistic motives distinguishes filicide from
other homicides.   The psychodynamics of the filicidal impulse are
explored.   (Journal Abstract Modified.)

186.   Riley, R. L.; Landwirth, J.; Collipp, P.J., et al.   "Failure
           to Thrive: An Analysis of 83 Cases."   California Medi-
           cine, 108(1):32-38, January 1968.
       Among a series of 83 children hospitalized for failure to
thrive, 26 cases showed evidence of maternal deprivation.   History
revealed child beating in several of these cases.   The importance
of hospitalization, obtaining a complete social history, and evaluation of siblings in cases of failure to thrive are emphasized.

187.   Robertson, B. A.; Hayward, M. A.   "Transcultural Factors
           in Child Abuse."   South African Medical Journal, 50:1765-
           1767, October 9, 1976.
       Of 54 battered children referred to a children's hospital in
Cape Town, South Africa, the "Cape Coloured" children were abused
most frequently by the father and the white children by the mother.
The high incidence of Coloured fathers in the sample did not seem
to be related to alcohol misuse; 16 percent of the Coloured and 11
percent of the White families in the sample misused alcohol, compared with the national rates of 4 and 2 percent, respectively.

188.   Robertson, Isobel.   "Follow-Up of Five Severely Deprived and

Malnourished Siblings, After Their Placement in Foster Care." South African Medical Journal, 50(21):799-800, May 15, 1976.

Five siblings, neglected and malnourished to the extent that they had become nutritional dwarfs, were placed in foster care. Their weights and heights were recorded at the time of placement, and at intervals for the following six years. (Journal Summary Modified.)

189. Rolston, Richard Hummel. The Effect of Prior Physical Abuse on the Expression of Overt and Fantasy Aggressive Behavior in Children. Ph.D. The Louisiana State University and Agricultural and Mechanical College, 1971. 130 p. Available from University Microfilms, 71-29,389.

Behavioral and personality characteristics of children who had previously suffered severe physical abuse or punishment at the hands of their parents or parent surrogates, and who had subsequently been removed from parental custody and placed in foster homes were investigated. The major implications of the study are the long-term duration of the effects of child abuse and the incongruity between the lack of aggressive behavior in this sample of abused children and the aggressive behavior manifested by such children in previous studies.

190. Russell, Patricia A. "Subdural Haematoma in Infancy." British Medical Journal, 2:446-448, 1965.

The author reviews 25 case studies, involving subdural hematoma in infancy. All of the cases were of children under two and a half years of age who had a history of trauma. Russell also gives the common signs and symptoms and discusses plans of treatment. He suggests thorough follow-up be implemented in such cases.

191. Sandgrund, Alice; Gaines, Richard W.; Green, Arthur H. "Child Abuse and Mental Retardation: A Problem of Cause and Effect." American Journal of Mental Deficiency, 79: 327-330, November 1974.

The impact of child abuse on cognitive development was investigated by comparing physically abused, neglected, and nonabused (control) children who were matched for age, sex, and socioeconomic status (SES).

192. Sanford, D. A.; Tustin, R. D. "Behavioural Treatment of Parental Assault on a Child." New Zealand Psychologist, 2(2):76-82, 1973.

A novel approach to a young father's inability to tolerate his 13-month-old daughter's crying is described. Prior to treatment the man, who found the child tolerable at best, beat her when she cried. A treatment program was instituted to increase the father's tolerance for loud noise.

193. Santhanakrishnan, B. R.; Vasanthakumar Shetty, M.; Balagopala Raju, V. "PITS Syndrome." Indian Pediatrics, 10(2):97-100, February 1973.

38 / Child Abuse

Three cases of parent-infant traumatic syndrome (PITS) were
observed in India. One child died of sustained injuries and recidivism was noted in all cases. The families were drawn from the
middle and lower socioeconomic classes. Stresses due to pregnancy
and child rearing contributed to the abuse in all cases. Because
India lacks the social welfare facilities, therapeutic measures must
concentrate on counseling.

194. Scherrer, P. "Contribution a l'etude psychopathologique des
      parents bourreaux de leurs enfants" [Contribution to the
      Study of the Psychopathology of Parents Tormenting Their
      Children]. Annales Medico-Psychologiques, 2(5):813-846,
      December 1975.
      Reviews world literature on personality characteristics re-
ported among child-abusing parents and adds eight case histories
from personal experience. Basic to all is a demand for behavior
by the child which would serve as a reassurance, but which the
child is unable to give, hence a permanent state of parental frustration leading to aggression and punishment. (P.A.)

195. Schreiber, Flora R. Sybil. Chicago: Henry Regnery, 1973.
      359 p.
      Sybil is the case history of 11 years of psychoanalysis of a
woman with sixteen personalities, two of which were male. This
book is based on psychiatrist's notes, diaries, tape recordings, and
many interviews with the principal selves involved. The subject, a
schizophrenic who was severely abused as a child, suffered from
lengthy blackouts and first sought analysis in 1954. The story of
the efforts of her analyst, Dr. Cornelia B. Wilbur, is also included.

196. Schreiber, L. H. "Ätiologie der Kindesmisshandlung" [Etiology
      of Maltreatment of Children]. Recht der Jugend und des
      Bildungswesen, 18(7):201-211, 1970.
      A study was made of all maltreatment cases tried between
1960 and 1968 (333 cases). An abundance of exact data were obtained. The data are compared with the findings reported by other
German investigators.

197. _____. "Misshandlung von Kindern und alten Menschen"
      [Maltreatment of Children and the Elderly People].
      Kriminalistik Verlag (Hamburg) 1971 Kriminologische
      Schriftenreihe Band 48. 167 p.
      This study of criminal records concerns all cases tried in
the German Federal Republic between 1960 and 1968 involving maltreatment of children or elderly people by members of the family:
333 cases of child abuse (out of 835 cases reported to the police)
and 46 cases involving elderly people (out of 69 reported cases).
The sociological and psychological aspects of these two types of offense are compared.

198. Schwokowski, C. F. "Schwere traumatische Zerstörung
      beider Kniegelenke und multiple Gesichtshämatome bei
      cinem 8 Monate alten Säugling" [Severe Traumatic

Destruction of Both Knee Joints and Multiple Face Hematomas in an 8-Month-Old Infant. A Contribution on the 'Battered Child Syndrome']. Zentralblatt für Chirurgie, 92:2484-2487, September 2, 1967.
This case involved not only subdural hematomas and multiple fractures, but also a less frequently described loosening of the epiphysis of the upper right shin bone with dislocation. The relatively young parents gave no evidence for the cause of the injuries, but there was little doubt it was of criminal nature. It was recommended that the child be removed from the home. Cooperation between the welfare and police is stressed to find the best alternative for the child.

199. Scott, P. D. "Fatal Battered Baby Cases." Medicine, Sciences and the Law, 13:197-206, July 1973.
Family, social, and psychiatric facts relating to 29 fatally battered children (less than five years old) in which the fathers had been remanded to London's Brixton prison on charges of killing their children were presented. The data were compared with those provided by Skinner and Castle (1969), who dealt with 78 battered children treated in a social agency.

200. _____. "Tragedy of Maria Colwell." British Journal of Criminology, 15:88-90, January 1975.
Death-by-abuse of Maria Colwell is discussed in terms of her background as a child and her home life. The procedures involved in her case are revealed and why it came to the attention of the public. Communication between the various services was lacking which led to Maria's return to home and eventual death by her step-father. Many services were at fault and through this case maybe solutions to communication can be found.

201. Segal, Rose S. A Comparison of Some Characteristics of Abusing and Neglecting, Non-Abusing Parents. D.S.W. New York, Columbia University, School of Social Work, 1971. 291 p. University Microfilms, 72-01386.
A study compared 32 couples who neglect their children with 31 couples who abuse their children in order to determine classifying characteristics between abusing and non-abusing parents. Interviews were used to obtain data, and research methods are explained. Evaluation included economic, social, and cultural criteria. Family interaction was a major determinant of differences between the groups of parents and revealed varying attitudes to child rearing and family life.

202. Silver, Larry B.; Dublin, Christina C.; Lourie, Reginald S. "Does Violence Breed Violence? Contributions from a Study of the Child Abuse Syndrome." American Journal of Psychiatry, 126:404-407, September 1969.
A study covering three generations of families of abused children supports the themes that violence breeds violence and that a child who experiences violence has the potential of becoming a violent member of society in the future. The authors believe that the

physician has a critical role and responsibility in interrupting this cycle of violence. (Journal Abstract.)

203. Simpson, Keith. "Battered Babies: Conviction for Murder." British Medical Journal, 1(5431):393, February 6, 1965.
On January 19, 1965, a 19-year-old father became the first Englishman to be convicted of murder in a case involving child abuse. The man was implicated in the death of two children 10 months apart, an illegitimate daughter and a son born in wedlock. Prosecution was initiated only after the second death.

204. Skinner, Angela E.; Castle, Raymond L. 78 Battered Children: A Retrospective Study. London, England: National Society for Prevention of Cruelty to Children, September 1969. 24 p. (Available from: NSPCC Information Department, 1 Riding House Street, London WIP BAA, 5 shillings, $0.65.)
A retrospective study of 78 cases of the battered child syndrome analyzes the victims, the families, the battering adults, and the legal and social work intervention which followed.

205. Smith, Selwyn M. The Battered Child Syndrome. See entry 1553.

206. _____. "Child Abuse Syndrome." British Medical Journal, 3:113-114, July 8, 1972.
Smith reports on the results of examinations of 103 cases of "unexplained injuries" in children under five years of age in the course of a broadly based research project. Presents statistics concerning the children and also makes some inferences as to the cause of the abuse.

207. _____. "134 Battered Children. A Medical and Psychological Study." British Medical Journal, 3(5932):666-670, September 14, 1974.
The results of a controlled investigation of 134 battered children are given. Difficulties with the child were attributable to interaction with neurotic mothers. Prevention may lie in educating mothers in the basic physical and psychological requirements of children and overcoming their reluctance to avail themselves of medical care.

208. _____; Hanson, Ruth. "Failure to Thrive and Anorexia Nervosa." Postgraduate Medical Journal, 48:382-384, June 1972.
A case study of an anorexia nervosa mother who battered her elder male child from early babyhood and, in collusion with her psychopathic husband, starved to death her 10-week-old daughter, is reported. With regard to the possible underlying psychopathology, the mother exemplified the pattern of the battering parent. The possibility of failure to thrive and battering of children existing on a continuum is explored.

209. _____ ; _____ . "Interpersonal Relationships and Child-
    Rearing Practices in 214 Parents of Battered Children."
    British Journal of Psychiatry, 127:513-525, December
    1975.
    The self-reported child-rearing practices of 214 parents of
battered babies were characterized in a few but not all respects by
demanding behaviour which exceeded that to be expected in relation
to their social class and age. Inconsistency in child management
was noted in the comparison between lack of demonstrativeness and
emotional over-involvement, and between physical punishment and a
tendency to be lax in the supervision of the child, and was remi-
niscent of parents of delinquents. (Journal Summary Modified.)

210. _____ ; _____ ; Noble, S. "Parents of Battered Babies:
    A Controlled Study." British Medical Journal, 4:388-391,
    November 17, 1973.
    A controlled investigation of parents of battered babies was
made to determine the nature of these parents. The results indicate that they are young, predominantly lower class, and prema-
turely parents. Among the mothers 76 percent have an abnormal
personality and 48 percent are neurotic. Borderline or subnormal
intelligence and a record of crime are frequent for both parents.
Among fathers 64 percent have abnormal personality, more than
half being psychopaths. (Author Abstract Modified.)

211. _____ ; Honigsberger, L.; Smith, C. A. "E. E. G. and
    Personality Factors in Baby Batterers." British Medical
    Journal, 3(5870):20-22, July 7, 1973.
    Electroencephalograms (EEG) and personality factors were
studied in parents who battered their children. Out of 35 parents,
eight had an abnormal EEG. All of these were found to be psychopathic, of low intelligence, and to be persistent batterers. The
presence of an abnormal EEG strongly suggests that some baby batterers are more closely related to those who commit acts of violence and that taken as a whole, they are not a homogenous group
about whom it is safe to generalize. (Author Abstract Modified.)

212. Solli, R. "Child Abuse (Norwegian)." Nordisk Kriminaltek-
    nisk Tidsskrift, 42(3):41-44, 1973.
    Solli reports on a two-year-old girl who was fatally battered
by her mother who attempted to lay the blame on the girl's sister.
The child presented with lesions, including fresh and old bite-marks
all over her body, as well as lesions on the lips and bleeding from
the mouth.

213. Spieker, Gisela; Mouzakitis, Chris M. Alcohol Abuse and
    Child Abuse and Neglect: An Inquiry into Alcohol Abusers'
    Behavior Toward Children. Alcohol and Drug Problems
    Association of North America. 27th Annual Meeting, New
    Orleans, La: 12-16 Oct. 1976. 17 p.
    The Association, between the variables of alcohol abuse and
child abuse and neglect, investigated the cases of 42 alcohol abusers

who had responsibility for the care of children. Data indicated that the children of these alcohol abusers were more often neglected than physically abused. Helping services for alcohol abusers and for their children are seen as necessary for the protection of the children and the diminution of emotional problems within families.

214. Staak, M.; Wagnes, Th.; Wille, R. "Zur Diagnostik und
       Sozialtherapie des vernachlässigten Kindes" [On the Diag-
       nosis and Social Therapy of the Neglected Child].
       Monatsschrift für Kinderheilkunde, 115:199-201, April
       1967.
The information in this article is based on investigations of clinical material from 1956-1965 with most cases (28 out of 32) being studied at the Institute for Legal Medicine at Kiel. Two types of child abusers, the indolent type and the ambivalent type are defined. The ambivalent abuser (overt) showed greater ability to respond to therapy and change.

215. Steinfels, Peter. "Laura's Bastille of Silence." Common-
       weal, 93:270, December 11, 1970.
In this case study of personal tragedy, the author describes each incident of abuse to Laura initiated by her mentally ill parents. Steinfels also discusses her removal from her parents, her courageous battle for life each day, and the doctor who was continually by her side during her institutionalization.

216. Stender, W. "Folgezustände nach Kindesmisshandlung" [Con-
       sequences of Child Abuse]. Monatsschrift für Kinderheil-
       kunde, 118:342-343, June 1970.
A table presents the increase in the reported number of cases of abuse and neglect in Berlin from 1960-1968. The cases studied include 42 from the Children's Clinic in Berlin 1967-1968. Discussed are the character of the abuser, social consequences, and problems, such as the doctor's oath of silence. More cooperation and centralization of effort is needed by doctors, police, etc. There are also legal problems. Because there has been no satisfactory solution to these problems a case is often settled to the disadvantage of the abused child.

217. Stephenson, P. Susan; Lo, Nerissa. "When Shall We Tell
       Kevin? A Battered Child Revisited." Child Welfare,
       53(9):576-581, November 1974.
This case study concerns a battered child who was removed from his family and placed under foster care. Presented are the many problems faced by professionals in dealing with Kevin. Timing and circumstances were two critical factors in deciding when and whether to tell the abused child why he was taken from his parents.

218. Sturdock, P. W., Jr. Report on Child Abuse and Neglect in
       Montana from January 1, 1974 Through June 30, 1974.
       Helena, Montana State Dept. of Social and Rehabilitation
       Services, November 1974. 22 p.
       Extensive statistical analyses of the characteristics of the

children and the parents, and specific referral sources involved in abuse cases are presented for a 6-month period in 1974.

219. Sussman, S. J. "The Battered Child Syndrome." California Medicine, 108:437-439, June 1968.
Socio-medical aspects of 23 episodes of physical abuse among 21 children are reported. Discussed are incidence and severity of abuse in California and participation in therapy.

220. Sweden. Socialstyrelsen. Barn som far illa: en undersökning om barnmisshandel och skadlig uppväxtmiljö/utg. av Socialstyrelsen i samarbete med Allmänna barnhuset: illustr., Angélica Serrano-Punell. Karlshamn: Nya Lagerblads tr. -AB [distr.], 1975. 86 p.

221. Taipale, V.; Moren, R.; Piha, T., et al. "Experiences of an Abused Child." Acta Paedopsychiatrica, 39(3):53-58, 1972.
A child abuse follow-up report illustrates the psychological development of a battered child. The case involves a 7-year-old boy who was less than three years old when he suffered multiple fractures and contusions inflicted by his stepfather. The extensive case history shows that the boy was placed in eight different institutions, homes, and hospitals. These traumatic moves had a greater psychologically damaging effect than the original abuse. This case emphasizes the need for careful placement of abused children in order to achieve successful follow-up care.

222. Terr, Lenore C. "A Family Study of Child Abuse." American Journal of Psychiatry, 127:665-671, November 1970.
Ten battered children and their families were evaluated over a six-year period. The family dynamics leading to child abuse are classified under four different categories. Several suggestions for using a family approach in treating battered children are offered.

223. _____; Watson, A. S. "The Battered Child Rebrutalized: Ten Cases of Medical-Legal Confusion." American Journal of Psychiatry, 124:1432-1439, April 1968.
Followed over a two-year period were ten battered children and their families. The handling of each case from a medical, legal, and social work standpoint was evaluated. It was felt that children were further traumatized because of confusion, poorly coordinated efforts, delays, and failure by agencies and individuals to assume responsibility for appropriate action. Suggestions are offered for better management.

224. Trude-Becker, Elisabeth. "Bissspuren bei kindesmisshandlung" [Traces of Human Bites in Child Abuse]. Beitraege zur Gerichtlichen Medizin, 31:115-123, 1973.
Vestiges of human bites are noted frequently, along with other signs of outrage, in the assault and battery of infants. Eight out of 38 cases of abuse showed cicatrices of a human bite in addition to alternative hematoma. Invariably, the cause of death was subdural

hematoma. The idea is conveyed that a third party was involved,
possibly an over-strained female delinquent where there was a dis-
integration of emotional stasis.

225. "Tug of Opinion." Economist, 252(6837):30, September 7,
      1974.
      The concern is with the abuse-death case of Maria Colwell.
Discussed is why her death has become the center of a tug of
opinion between the members of the committee of inquiry appointed
after her death. There is a crucial difference of attitudes between
the members regarding why Maria was not taken from home when
abuse was evident.

226. Unverbesserlich, vom Heim ins Zuchthaus: eine Dokumenta-
      tion. Edited by Matthias Borgmann and Egmont Elschner.
      2., verb. Aufl. Berlin: Verlagskollektin Roter. Oktober
      [1970]. 55 p., illus. (At head of title: UVB)

227. Vesin, C.; Girodet, D.; Straus, P. "Les Sévices exercés
      contre les jeunes enfants. Etude clinique de 110 observa-
      tions" [Brutality Towards Young Children. Clinical Study
      of 110 Cases]. Medecine Legale et Dommage Corporel,
      4:95-107, April-June 1971.
      This is a clinical study of 110 cases observed at Bretonneau
Hospital, 1958-1969. There were more cases reported in 1969 than
1958, doubtless because of greater alertness to the problem. Gradual re-introduction of child into family after attempts to educate
parents under the supervision of social workers is recommended.
It is seldom necessary to permanently remove the child from the
family.

228. "Violence at Home." (Editorial). Public Health, 84:53-56,
      January 1970.
      A brief review covers the major points of a study of battered
children undertaken by the National Society for the Prevention of
Cruelty to Children. The average circumstances of the battered
child and his parents are described. Prevention and treatment require a wider distribution of present knowledge and a more understanding approach to problems of stress and crisis in people with
character disorders, as well as a multidisciplinary approach to
therapy and to research.

229. Wathey, R.; Densen-Gerber, J. Preliminary Report on the
      Sociological Autopsy in Child Abuse Deaths. Chicago,
      American Academy of Forensic Sciences, 27th Meeting,
      February 20, 1975. 26 p.
      A case of child abuse and neglect covering two generations is
presented in detail and subjected to a sociological autopsy.

230. White, G. de L.; Househam, K. C.; Ngomane, D. "Child
      Abuse Among Rural Blacks." (Letter). South African
      Medical Journal, 50(30):1499, September 11, 1976.
      Presented are two case histories--a male and a female--both

three years old. The abuse took place in rural areas and in each
case, the mother worked in Durban and the child was cared for by
an aunt.

231. Wight, Byron W. "The Control of Child-Environment Inter-
      action: A Conceptual Approach to Accident Occurrence."
      Pediatrics, 44:799-805, November 1969.
A one-year longitudinal survey was made of 77 children under
the age of one who had been referred to Children's Hospital in
Pittsburgh for X-ray examination. The survey was designed to uncover relationships between the child's home environment and the
cause of the injury. The injuries, including 16 cases of suspected
child abuse, were divided into five categories. All groups of injuries were associated with lack of adequate parental control.

232. Wright, Logan. The "Sick but Slick" Syndrome as a Per-
      sonality Component for Parents of Battered Children.
      New Orleans, La., American Psychological Association
      Annual Meeting, September 1974. 9 p. Also in: Journal
      of Clinical Psychology, 32(1):41-45, January 1976.
A battery of personality tests were administered to 13 parents
who had been convicted in court of battering their children and 13
matched controls. Battering parents appeared to be psychopathically
disturbed. They presented, whenever possible, a distorted picture
of themselves as healthy and not likely to abuse their children.
This tendency, therefore, is referred to as the "sick but slick syndrome."

233. Young, Leontine. Wednesday's Children: A Study of Child
      Neglect and Abuse. New York: McGraw-Hill Book Co.,
      1964. 195 p. (First McGraw-Hill Paperback Edition,
      1971).
This book is an account of a detailed study of parents indifferent to their children, who neglect, beat, torture, and sometimes
murder them. The author looked for broad outlines of family behavior and used these observations to fill in more of the details of
the outline. Information was taken entirely from case records
which follow families over a period of from one to as long as 15
and 20 years. Chapters are devoted to causes, the protectors, the
family dilemma, the preventive approach, and the need for public
awareness and assistance.

234. Zlotnik, Gideon. "Børnemishandling--et materiale fra
      retspsykiatrisk praksis" [Child Abuse. A Material from
      Court-Psychiatric Practice]. Ugeskrift for Laeger, 133:
      567-572, March 26, 1971.
A [Danish] account is presented of 23 cases of child abuse
from a court-psychiatric practice. The individuals concerned had
been submitted to mental observation. On the basis of review of
these cases, the impression was gained that these actions had been
undertaken by very young parents with personalities showing character defects which had affected their emotional and social adaptation.
(Journal Summary.)

235. Zuckerman, Kenneth; Ambuel, J. Phillip; Bandman, Roselyn. "Child Neglect and Abuse. A Study of Cases Evaluated at Columbus Children's Hospital in 1968-1969." Ohio State Medical Journal, 68:629-632, July 1972.

Sixty reported cases of child neglect and abuse are reviewed and analyzed to determine the major physical and socioeconomic factors. All of the cases were reported to appropriate police or other law enforcement agencies but follow-up was not always possible.

DETECTION AND DIAGNOSIS

236. Adams, P. C.; Strand, R. D.; Bresnan, M. F., et al.
    "Kinky Hair Syndrome: Serial Study of Radiological
    Findings with Emphasis on the Similarity to the Battered
    Child Syndrome." Radiology, 112:401-407, August 1974.
    Two cases of Menkes' Syndrome (kinky hair disease) were
studied by serial radiologic examination of the extremities and by
selected studies of the central nervous system. The findings of
flared and fragmented metaphysis as signs of trauma and evidence
of brain damage are similar to those in cases of child abuse.

237. Altman, Donald H.; Smith, Richard L. "Unrecognized Trauma
    in Infants and Children." Journal of Bone and Joint Sur-
    gery, 42-A; 407-413, April 1960.
    Five case studies of traumatically induced bone lesions are
presented. In none of these young patients was there any history of
trauma obtainable at the time of admission. Diagnosis of injury to
bones can be made with a relative degree of certainty on initial
X-ray examination, but recognition of trauma induced by adults or
older siblings will save considerable time and effort in an attempt
to arrive at a diagnosis calling for removal of the child from its
environment. (Journal Summary Modified.)

238. "...And Don't Overlook Whiplash Hematoma." Emergency
    Medicine, 4:184-185, January 1972.
    Shaking a child, although generally considered to be an ac-
ceptably humane form of punishment, may be nearly as dangerous
to an infant as a series of violent blows. The commonest signs
and symptoms of hematoma are described. The physician should
look closely for other signs of battering for here is a chance to uncover the incipient battered child and the incipient battering parent.

239. Anderson, William R.; Hudson, R. Page. "Self-Inflicted Bite
    Marks in Battered Child Syndrome." Forensic Science,
    7(1):71-74, January-February 1976.
    Examination of a child abuse victim revealed bite marks on
both arms. These lesions are usually pursued as a clue to the
identity of the specific perpetrator. We demonstrated that the bite
was from the victim. Importance of this phenomenon in evaluation
of bite injuries is discussed. (Journal Summary.)

240. Andrews, John P. "The Battered Baby Syndrome." Illinois
    Medical Journal, 122:494, November 1962.

47

The diagnosis of unrecognized trauma to infants, along with the more common signs of the battered baby syndrome, is the focus of this brief article.

241. Antoni, P. "A megkínzott-gyermek syndroma" [The Battered Child Syndrome]. Orvosi Hetilap, 106:1934-1937, October 10, 1965.
Based on three personal cases, clinical features and differential diagnostics of a well defined clinical entity, the "tormented child syndrome" with bone and skin injuries, poor physical condition and untidy appearance are presented. Prevention measures are suggested.

242. Arcadio, F., et al. "Forme exceptionelle de sévices a enfant. Introduction de treize aiguilles a coudre dans le corps" [Unusual Form of Child Abuse: Introduction of 13 Sewing Needles into the Body]. Medecine Legale et Dommage Corporel, 2:274-275, July-September 1969.
Thirteen sewing needles were found in the body of a young boy, son of a North African father. Was this child abuse or some sort of initiation ritual? The police were unable to determine this point or to apprehend the guilty family.

243. Aron, J. J.; Marx, P.; Blanck, M. F., et al. "Signes oculaires observes dans le Syndrome de Silverman" [Ocular Symptoms Observed in Silverman's Syndrome]. Annales d'Oculistique, 203:533-546, June 1970.
The Silverman syndrome is a bone syndrome in which X-ray examination reveals the after-effects of numerous often misunderstood fractures of the young child. It is often accompanied by skin signs, effects on the mucous membranes of the mouth and nose, and ocular symptoms. The 18 cases reported here all show ocular symptoms: chorio-retinal spots, essentially peripheral and temporal, or retinal detachments. (English Summary Modified.)

244. Auvert, B.; Degos, R.; Theron, H.-P. "Syndrome des enfants battus (Syndrome de Silverman): Un cas avec atteinte cornéene" [Syndrome of Battered Children (Silverman Syndrome): A Case with Corneal Lesion]. Bulletin des Societes d'Ophtalmologie de France, 71:1093-1098, December 1971.
This is a case of corneal lesion. These lesions may be a symptom of Silverman's syndrome. Other symptoms are: radiological indications, clinical indications, mouth and nose lesions, lesions of the eye, and a particular etiology.

245. Baher, Edwina; Hyman, Clare; Jones, Carolyn, et al. At Risk: An Account of the Work of the Battered Child Research Department, NSPCC. See entry 2204.

246. Bai, K. Indira; Rao, K. W. Subba; Subramanyam, M. V. G. "The Battered-Child Syndrome." Clinician, 37(5):199-203, 1973.

The battered child syndrome, clinically encountered in young children under two years of age who have been subjected to trauma or physical abuse either by parents or guardians, can be detected by the information offered by parents/guardians, clinical findings, the repetitive nature of the traumatic episodes, or localization of bony lesions.

247. Bakwin, Harry. "How to Recognize the Abused Child."
     Consultant, 3:36-38, May 1963.
     By presenting a case history, the author describes the techniques in diagnosing instances of child abuse. Bakwin offers several clues to determine if violence was a cause of injury in children: evidence of repeated injury; subdural hematoma, bruises, broken noses, bony irregularities; and the appearance of being chronically ill or underweight.

248. _____. "Multiple Skeletal Lesions in Young Children Due
     to Trauma." Journal of Pediatrics, 49:7-15, July 1956.
     Trauma is probably the most common cause of skeletal changes in infants and adults. The clinical manifestations are generally mild and easily overlooked. The radiographic bone lesions are subperiosteal ossification, metaphyseal fractures, avulsions, gross fractures, impacted fractures, and epiphyseal displacements. The outcome is good unless the growing cartilage has been injured. (Journal Summary Modified.)

249. Ballantine, Thomas V. N. "Kids in Crisis: A Surgical Grab
     Bag." Emergency Medicine, 8(5):181-199, May 1976.
     In this comprehensive article on surgical problems related to young people, Ballantine discusses Trauma X--the battered child syndrome. Clues to child abuse lie in the discrepancy between the history and the physical examination, a prolonged interval between the time of injury and presentation for its treatment, the peculiar nature of the injury, a history of having had medical care in many different places, and abandonment of the child after treatment.

250. Barmeyer, George H.; Anderson, Lee R.; Cox, Walter B.
     "Traumatic Periostitis in Young Children." Journal of
     Pediatrics, 38(2):184-190, February 1951.
     The acute limping leg of early childhood, traumatic in origin, is frequently the result of periosteal separation. Roentgenograms delayed beyond the point of clinical recovery will demonstrate an ossifying periosteal reaction in many cases. Ultimate radiologic resolution is complete. (Journal Summary.)

251. Barness, Lewis A. "What's Wrong with the Hip?" Clinical
     Pediatrics, 9:467, August 1970.
     In this "mystery story," Barness presents a short case study of a ten-week-old infant brought to a hospital emergency ward because of swelling of the left leg. X-ray of the hips and thighs revealed a spiral fracture of the left femur, later diagnosed as a battered child case. A better initial history would have suggested the correct diagnosis at the outset, according to the author.

252. Baron, Michael A.; Bejar, Rafael L.; Sheaff, Peter S.
"Neurologic Manifestations of the Battered Child Syndrome." Pediatrics, 45:1003-1007, June 1970.
An infant with symptoms mimicking organic brain disease was treated months for neurologic disease until she finally showed external bruises. All neurologic findings disappeared within one week after hospital admission. This experience showed that battered child syndrome must be included in the differential diagnosis of developmental failure with diffuse or nonfocal neurologic signs, and that all infants showing these symptoms should be hospitalized. (Journal Abstract Modified.)

253. "The Battered Baby." British Medical Journal, 5487:601-603, March 5, 1966.
The "battered baby syndrome" describes a collection of symptoms and signs occurring in children who have suffered repeated injuries at the hands of their parents or others. This article explains the cases which may be missed, the recognition of the syndrome, the action which must be taken if a diagnosis is under suspect, and recommendations on how to involve community agencies and law officers, as well as prevention measures.

254. Bennett, A. N. "Children Under Stress." Journal of the Royal Naval Medical Service, 60(1-2):83-87, Spring-Summer 1974.
Bennett presents the origin of the term "battered baby" and describes various diagnostic criteria. A classification of child abuse is suggested as follows: true infanticide, the wasted and neglected child, deliberate cruelty, and the mildly battered child. Various treatment programs are also discussed.

255. Berant, Moshe; Jacobs, J. "A 'Pseudo' Battered Child." Clinical Pediatrics, 5:230-237, April 1966.
A boy of two years eight months was admitted to Hadassah University Hospital in Jerusalem with a clinical picture of scurvy, in which the differential diagnoses of sepsis, leukemia, syphilis, Still's disease, and the "battered child" syndrome were considered and excluded.

256. Berlow, Leonard. "Recognition and Rescue of the 'Battered Child.'" Hospitals, 41:58-61, January 16, 1967.
Definitive action often is not taken by those who come in contact with abused children, not only because of a resistance to personal involvement but also because clear directives are lacking. Current legal requirements for reporting child abuse are outlined and lists of telltale signals for distinguishing between accidental and intentional injuries are provided. (Journal Abstract Modified.)

257. Bhattacharya, A. K. "Multiple Fractures." Bulletin of the Calcutta School of Tropical Medicine, 14:111-112, July 1966.
Two siblings were hospitalized for recurrent painful swellings of the limbs which they contracted on the same day. Radiological

examination revealed old fractures of both humeri in each child; characteristic epiphyseal and subperiosteal reactions were present. A landlord to whom the mother had entrusted the children was apparently responsible.

258. _____; Mandal, J. N. "Battered Child Syndrome: A Review with a Report of Two Siblings." Indian Pediatrics, 4:186-194, April 1967.

Two young siblings, presenting simultaneously with recurrent painful swellings of limbs, apparently represent the first Indian report of the battered child syndrome. Multiple fractures, epiphyseal separation, and periosteal reaction were noted in both children.

259. Birrell, R. G. "The 'Maltreatment Syndrome' in Children." Medical Journal of Australia, 2:1134-1138, December 10, 1966.

A series of maltreated children suffering injury and neglect involving two deaths is described. Neglect, fractures, soft-tissue injuries of varying ages and an unsatisfactory history should give rise to suspicion of the syndrome, together with no new lesions appearing in the hospital. Any attempt at rehabilitating the family should not be undertaken at the risk of the child. It is suggested that there should be legislation along American lines.

260. Blanck, Marie-France. "A propos de deux cas de syndrome de Silverman avec décollement de rétine" [Two Cases of Silverman's Syndrome with Retinal Detachment]. Bulletin des Societes d'Ophtalmologie de France, 73(9-10):881-885, September-October 1973.

This is a study of two cases of detached retinas in young children. Detachment of retina may be a sign of Silverman's syndrome.

261. Bleiberg, Nina. "The Neglected Child and the Child Health Conference." New York State Journal of Medicine, 65: 1880-1885, July 15, 1965.

Bleiberg describes a study which explored the possibility of finding cases of child abuse and neglect in New York City's preventive health program in which children are brought in for routine medical check-ups. Physicians working in child health stations were asked to report on such cases, which numbered 18 during a one-year period.

262. Blount, J. G. "Radiologic Seminar 138: The Battered Child." Journal of the Mississippi State Medical Association, 15: 136-138, April 1974.

Multiple fractures in different stages of healing, exaggerated periosteal reactions, frequent metaphyseal fragmentation with epiphyseal separation, soft tissue injuries, head injuries, and evidence of prior injury unexplained by history are indicative of a battered child.

263. Bolz, W. Scott. "The Battered Child Syndrome." Delaware

Medical Journal, 39:176-180, July 1967.
Bolz presents a case history of a battered child whose condition was only recognized after death together with diagnostic criteria
and differential diagnoses.   Especially noteworthy is the fact that
this case occurred in an Air Force family in central Delaware in
socioeconomic and medical circumstances which apparently did not
seem conducive to the genesis of this syndrome.   (Journal Summary
Modified.)

264.   Borland, Marie, ed.   Violence in the Family.   See entry
       2360.

265.   Bowen, D. A.   "The Role of Radiology and the Identification
       of Foreign Bodies at Post Mortem Examination." Journal
       of the Forensic Science Society, 6:28-32, January 1966.
In the case of battered children, radiology is of great value
in the diagnosis of unsuspected fractures of the chest and limbs and
of healing fractures.   Unexplained fractures of the long bones, particularly if repeated, and subdural hemorrhages offer fairly conclu-
sive evidence of abuse.

266.   Boysen, Bette E.   "Chylous Ascites.   Manifestation of the
       Battered Child Syndrome." American Journal of Diseases
       of Children, 129(11):1338-1339, November 1975.
A child had chylous ascites and other findings suggestive of
child abuse.   He had a spontaneous remission, with conservative
therapy.   A lymphangiogram showed the area of leakage into the
peritoneal cavity.   The discussion includes a brief review of literature on chylous ascites.   (Journal Abstract.)

267.   Bratu, Marcel; Siegel, Bernard; Dower, John C., et al.
       "Jejunal Hematoma, Child Abuse, and Felson's Sign."
       Connecticut Medicine, 34(4):261-264, April 1970.
A 22-month-old patient with intramural jejunal hematoma related to traumatic abuse has been reported and previous reports of
similar patients reviewed.   Physicians should be aware of this unusual complication of blunt abdominal injury, especially associated
with the battered child syndrome.   (Journal Summary Modified.)

268.   Brings, E. G.   "Sudden and Unexpected Death." (Letter).
       Pediatrics, 39(5):792-793, May 1967.
The use of alcohol or nasal decongestants may be operative,
in rare instances, in sudden unexpected death in infants.   Two cases
are cited: a 4-month-old boy, who since the age of 4 days, had
been underfed and repeatedly given a mixture of whiskey and water
to pacify him, was hospitalized with several maladies.   A 2-year-
old girl who drank beer since infancy was admitted to the same
hospital in a moribund condition.   Diagnosis would be difficult without a history of use.

269.   Brody, Howard; Gaiss, Betty.   "Ethical Issues in Screening
       for Unusual Child-Rearing Practices." Pediatric Annals,
       5(3):106-112, March 1976.

This is an ethical critique of Helfer's article, "Early Identification and Prevention of Unusual Child-Rearing Practices" appearing in Pediatric Annals, 5(3):91-105, March 1976. Issues raised include: balance between the rights of all parties concerned; distinctions between after-the-fact and before-the-fact intervention; mandatory vs. voluntary programs of screening; and the emotional effects of labeling parents as "high risk" through false-positive test results.

270. Bwibo, N. O. "Battered Child Syndrome." East African
       Medical Journal, 48:56-61, February 1971.
    The case of battered child syndrome in an eight-year-old boy presenting with multiple superficial injuries is described. The clinical features and principles of management of the syndrome are described. (Journal Summary.)

271. Caffey, John. "Infantile Cortical Hyperostosis." Journal of
       Pediatrics, 29:541-559, November 1946.
    Description and discussion of six cases of infantile cortical hyperostosis. Findings indicate patients suffering from new diseases, causes unknown--scurvy, rickets, syphilis, bacterial osteitis, neoplastic disease, traumatic injury--all cited as causative aspects. Characteristics common to all patients: 1) tender swelling deep in soft tissues, 2) cortical thickenings in skeleton, 3) onset during first three months of life.

272. _____. "Multiple Fractures in the Long Bones of Infants
       Suffering from Chronic Subdural Hematoma." American
       Journal of Roentgenology, Radium Therapy and Nuclear
       Medicine, 56:163-173, 1946.
    Describes six infants with subdural hematoma and associated multiple fractures in the long bones. Explains that although it was agreed that the injuries were of traumatic origin, parents were not identified as perpetrators of abuse.

273. _____. "The Parent-Infant Traumatic Stress Syndrome:
       (Caffey-Kempe Syndrome), (Battered Babe Syndrome)."
       American Journal of Roentgenology, Radium Therapy and
       Nuclear Medicine, 114:218-219, February 1972.
    Caffey presents a brief history of the radiographic discovery and early development of the parent-infant traumatic stress syndrome (PITS) and current status of radiographic findings in it. Unlike the term "battered child" which may be unjust when used before parental guilt has been legally established, PITS is a fairer term. It accuses no one, yet does indicate the causal, emotional, social, and economic stresses which plague the parent.

274. _____. "Significance of the History in the Diagnosis of
       Traumatic Injury to Children." Journal of Pediatrics,
       67(5):1008-1014, November 1965.
    A discussion covers four sources of evidence of trauma in diagnosing child abuse: history, physical examinations, laboratory tests, and radiologic examinations. Better diagnostic techniques are needed to identify children's injuries. A new field of pediatric

traumatology could study medical, social and epidemiologic aspects
of the problem.

275. _____. "Some Traumatic Lesions in Growing Bones Other
        Than Fractures and Dislocations: Clinical and Radiological
        Features." British Journal of Radiology, 30:225-238, May
        1957.
        Clinical and radiological features of repeated trauma. Morbid
anatomy and causal mechanisms are pictured.

276. Cameron, J. M.; Rae, L. J. Atlas of the Battered Child
        Syndrome. Edinburgh, Scotland: Churchill Livingstone,
        1975. 90 p.
        A medical atlas of the diagnostic and radiological signs of the
battered child syndrome includes extensive photographs and radio-
graphs of selected cases. The way in which various types of injuries
are caused is examined to prepare the physician for questions that
will arise in legal proceedings. Consideration is also given to eye
injuries characteristic of the battered infant. Prevention and treatment are briefly discussed, and the critical role of the physician in
identifying and reporting such cases is stressed.

277. _____, et al. "The Battered Child Syndrome." Medical
        Social Law, 6:2-21, January 1966.
        Discussion is of clues to battered baby syndrome, related to
nature of injuries, time taken to seek medical advice and recurrent
injuries, which should assist the physician in diagnosis; and parame-
ters of the problem: aspects of making differential diagnosis, social
aspects, and psychiatric aspects.

278. Camps, F. E. "When Infant Death Occurs." Nursing Mirror
        and Midwives Journal, 133:14-15, November 12, 1971.
        General comments on undue punishment or neglect as a cause
of mortality are discussed within the context of infant death. Camps
stresses the importance and enormous responsibility of early recognition of child abuse by those in the medical and welfare services.
Sudden and unexpected infant deaths are also examined.

279. Camps, Francis. "Sudden Deaths in Infants." Midwife and
        Health Visitor, 9:113-116, April 1973.
        In this article, written shortly before his death, the author
discusses two important pediatric and social problems--child cruelty
and the battered baby syndrome and unexpected infant deaths. (Journal Abstract.)

280. Carter, Jan, ed. The Maltreated Child. See entry 750.

281. "Child Abuse and Neglect." Special Children, 1(2):71-72, Fall
        1974.
        It is most important to be able to recognize situations in
which abuse or neglect may exist. An Index of Suspicion is provided from the standpoint of history, physical examination, and
radiologic manifestations.

282. Ching, T. T.; Singleton, E. B.; Daeschner, C. W., Jr. "Skeletal Injuries of the Battered Child." American Journal of Orthopsychiatry, 6(10):202-207, 1964.
When the typical roentgenographic features of traumatic lesions are demonstrated in a battered child, no other etiologic factor needs to be considered. Many authors have commented on the futility of extensive laboratory studies. A good history is emphasized.

283. Clark, J. M. "Roentgen Diagnosis of Skeletal Trauma." Applied Radiology and Nuclear Medicine, 4(1):27-31, 1975.
In diagnosis and treatment of skeletal trauma, the role of radiology is discussed. A brief overview of bone development is presented as a basis for discussion of diagnosis, as well as the battered child syndrome.

284. Claus, H. G. "Knochenveränderungen nach Kindesmisshandlung" [Bone Changes Following Battered Child Syndrome]. Radiologe, 10:241-248, June 1970.
Roentgenologists and surgeons should devote more attention to the battered child syndrome. Unusual hemorrhages and injuries to the trunk of the body should be cause for suspicion of child abuse. Especially broken bones in various places and in varying stages of healing would seem to indicate this possibility. One must be suspicious when a child has a subdural hematoma along with a fracture, or when the degree and type of injury doesn't coincide with the described accident.

285. Cochrane, W. A. "The Battered Child Syndrome." Canadian Journal of Public Health, 56:193-196, May 1965.
When an injured child presents with a picture of certain physical characteristics, a rather classical family history, and evidence that no new lesions occur once the child is hospitalized, the physician, or health personnel, should manifest a high index of suspicion. The radiologist should be alerted to suggest a diagnosis when classical radiological findings are found.

286. Connell, John R. "The Devil's Battered Children. The Increasing Incidence of Wilful Injuries to Children." Journal of the Kansas Medical Society, 64:385-391, September 1963.
Connell presents three case studies to illustrate the difficulties in establishing guilt associated with child abuse. However, detecting the child under abuse is highly successful. A diagnostic acrostic abstract, urging the physician to be curious about all childhood injuries, is also offered.

287. Constable, H.; Gans, G. (Letter). "Unnecessary X-Rays?" British Medical Journal, 1:564, 1970.
This is a letter concerning the practice of delaying radiologic diagnosis defended in an earlier letter. Pointed out is the fact that the law makes mandatory a complete skeletal survey in cases of skeletal injury of any child under two years.

288. Corcelle, L.; Théodorides, M. "Syndrome de Silvermann
     [sic]. A propos d'une observation familiale" [Silverman
     Syndrome. Apropos of a Family Case]. Bulletin des
     Societes d'Ophtalmologie de France, 67:644-647, July-
     August 1967.
     In this study of a brother and sister, the diagnosis is not
clear. It may be a case of Silverman's syndrome, or it may be
a case of the mistreatment of children with low resistance to certain physical afflictions of the bones and eyes. Of the five children
in the family, four had bone deformations. The two children observed had cataracts and other ocular defects, but the father also
had cataracts.

289. Crawford, C. S. "The Battered Child." New Physician,
     576-579, September 1971.
     Diagnostic signs characteristic of child abuse are discussed
and appropriate diagnostic procedures are described. Three important operation principles regarding child abuse are proposed.
With these three principles in mind, the physician can direct most
of his intellectual energy to the detection of battered children.
Guidelines are provided for interpreting the findings.

290. Cremin, B. J. "Battered Baby Syndrome." South African
     Medical Journal, 44:1044, September 12, 1970.
     In a letter to the editor, Cremin emphasizes the role which
radiologists play in the diagnosis of the battered baby syndrome.

291. Crown, Barry; Redlener, Irwin; Benson, Irene. "Attitudes to
     Children's Accidents." (Letter). Lancet, 1(7959):590,
     March 13, 1976.
     This letter refers to one by R. F. N. Duke in which he asks
that the benefit of the doubt be given parents where there is only
suspicion of abuse. The authors argue that in almost all cases of
abuse the family presents an abnormal picture which may be manifest in numerous ways. They urge those involved in treating suspect cases to ask questions until they are thoroughly satisfied.

292. "Cruelty to Children." British Medical Journal, 5372:1544-
     1545, December 21, 1963.
     The main part of this article deals with the "battered baby
syndrome" and why diagnosis is so important. If a diagnosis is
missed the child will be returned after recovery, or be left to recover, in the presence of its parents who may do more injury to it.
Clinical and radiological investigations can produce irrefutable proof
that the affected child was cruelly beaten.

293. Cullen, J. C. "Spinal Lesions in Battered Babies." Journal
     of Bone & Joint Surgery, 57(3):364-366, August 1975.
     To demonstrate the radiological appearances of trauma to the
spine, the case histories of five young children are presented.
These injuries were thought to be inflicted by either parent or
guardian.

294. Dargan, E. L. "Pancreatic Pseudocysts in Childhood."
    Journal of the National Medical Association, 58(3):179-181,
    May 1966.
    Although rare, pancreatic pseudocysts should be considered
in the differential diagnosis of abdominal masses in children with a
history of trauma and may be of significance in battered children.

295. Davies, J. M. "Battered Child Syndrome: Detection and
    Prevention." Nursing Mirror & Midwives Journal, 140:
    56-57, June 12, 1975.
    Davies discusses the incidence of baby-battering in the United
Kingdom and then describes the role of the health visitor in detecting
and preventing the battered child syndrome. Emphasis is placed on
detection of signs of stress, formation of "parentcraft" classes, and
obtaining cooperation of the parents.

296. Department of Health and Social Security. The Battered Baby.
    London, England, February 1970. 11 p.
    The clinical manifestations of the battered baby syndrome and
methods that medical professionals may utilize to deal with it are
discussed. The importance of early recognition is emphasized.

297. Diethelm, L.; Kostner, P. "Zur Röntgeniagnostikder Wirbel-
    säule" [Concerning the X-Ray Diagnoses of the Spinal
    Cord]. Radiologe, 12:281-287, September 1972.
    This is a discussion of the problems of X-raying spinal cords
after trauma, i.e., both technical and diagnostic criteria. Some
cases described were handled by the authors, while others have been
discussed previously in the literature. It is imperative to further
reduce the unsatisfactory X-ray examinations.

298. Dine, Mark S. "Tranquilizer Poisoning: An Example of Child
    Abuse." Pediatrics, 36:782-785, November 1965.
    A case study of deliberate perphenazine (tranquilizer) poisoning
by a parent is presented as an example of child abuse. Symptoms
included prolonged sleep, convulsions, and hyperpyrexia. Suggestions
for making the diagnosis include a high index of suspicion on the part
of the physician and routine testing for phenothiazines and other psy-
chotropic drugs in patients with convulsions of undetermined etiology.
(Journal Summary Modified.)

299. Duke, R. F. N. "Attitudes to Children's Accidents." (Letter).
    Lancet, 1(7953):257, January 31, 1976.
    A mother with an injured child is possibly quizzed too thor-
oughly by the casualty department staff for fear of missing a maltreated child. Such intensity may produce more social harm than
missing a few cases. Those investigating should give the benefit of
the doubt where they are merely suspicious, for accidents do happen.

300. Durigon, M.; Caroff, J.; Derobert, L. "Histologie pulmonaire
    de 123 morts subites ou suspectes d'enfants de moins d'un
    an" [Pulmonary Histology of 123 Sudden or Suspicious

Deaths of Children of Less Than a Year Old]. Medecine
Legale et Dommage Corporel, 4:287-293, July-September
1971.
A pulmonary histological examination is an indispensable part
of every autopsy of a child less than one year old. In the case of
the newborn, it gives a diagnosis of respiration, a fact of great importance in questions of infanticide. In the case of the young baby,
a natural death can be verified when there is evidence of broncho-
pneumonia, alimentary inhalation, or a hemorrhaging lung.

301. Ebeling, Nancy B. Child Abuse: Intervention and Treatment.
See entry 1268.

302. Eckert, William G. "Slaughter of the Innocents." Journal of
the Florida Medical Association, 54:256, March 1967.
Eckert details the detection of unsuspected violence in a 13-
month-old child who had been severely beaten by its father.

303. Elmer, Elizabeth. "Hazards in Determining Child Abuse."
Child Welfare, 45(1):28-33, January 1966.
The purpose of this study was to determine some of the difficulties in identifying who is abused. The necessity for careful social
evaluation of families suspected of abuse is becoming apparent.
Among the areas for inquiry are: the ordinary patterns of child
care, variations in care that may occur and reasons for them, the
history of the caretakers, family events occurring at the time of
the child's injuries and the typical reactions of family members to
stress.

304. _____. "Identification of Abused Children." Children, 10:
180-184, September 1963.
This article explains why it is difficult to identify abused
children from normally injured children, and how hospital staffs
may learn to identify abused children with multiple-bone injuries
by X-ray. Specific facts regarding findings of 50 children with
multiple bone injuries are also provided.

305. "Failure to Thrive, Threat to Survival." Emergency Medicine, 2:41, October 1970.
Three short case studies illustrate the need of physicians to
suspect that a child is being emotionally, physically, or nutritionally
deprived by his parents if he is emaciated and apathetic and then
thrives after admission to a hospital.

306. Fairburn, A. C.; Hunt, A. C. "Caffey's 'Third Syndrome'--
a Critical Evaluation. ('The Battered Baby')." Medicine,
Science and the Law, 4:123-126, April 1964.
This paper describes seven cases where multiple fractures
were found in infants which on investigation proved to be the result
of parental violence and not of any abnormality.

307. Fatteh, Abdullah V.; Mann, Geoffrey T. "The Role of Radiology in Forensic Pathology." Medicine, Science and the

Law, 9:27-30, January 1969.
This paper illustrates and stresses the importance of radiology in the investigation of various types of deaths, including cases
of battered child syndrome, seen in the practice of forensic pathology.

308. Faure, J.; Gau, G.; Couderc, P., et al. "Le Syndrome de
Silvermann [sic] ou syndrome des enfants battus a propos
d'un cas" [Silverman's Syndrome or Battered Child Syndrome: A Case]. Medecine Legale et Dommage Corporel,
1:139-141, April 1968.
Cases of multiple bone fracture with intracranial hematomas
have given rise in recent years to many controversies as to their
etiology. The actuality of an injury cannot always be determined by
medical examination alone; police and social research must also be
done. Numerous diseases may cause fractures and hematomas.
Observation of family environment and of parents is essential before
a definite diagnosis can be made.

309. Finberg, Laurence. "A Pediatrician's View of the Abused
Child." Child Welfare, 44:41-43, January 1965.
This pediatrician believes that the availability of X-ray evidence is a genuine advance in the diagnosis of physical child abuse.
He has found the following six types of neglect to produce serious
consequences: direct physical abuse, undernutrition, malnutrition,
refusal to accept necessary medical advice, neglect of child care
leading to accidental poison ingestion, and self-induced abortion or
general health abuse on the part of the pregnant woman. In conclusion, he states that work toward resolution should be comprehensive, involving medical, judicial, and social work disciplines.

310. Fischer, L.; Imbert, J.-C.; David, M., et al. "Luxation
traumatique atteignant successivement les deux hanches
chez une enfant. Discussion de facteurs prédisposants"
[Traumatic Luxation Successively Affecting Both Hips in
a Child: Predisposing Factors]. Lyon Medical, 222:
263-266 passim, September 7, 1969.
Observations of a child who had suffered displacement of both
hips. Was this a case of Silverman's disease, a syndrome of battered children?

311. Fiser, Robert H.; Kaplan, Joseph; Holder, John. "Congenital
Syphilis Mimicking the Battered Child Syndrome. How
Does One Tell Them Apart?" Clinical Pediatrics, 11:305-
307, May 1972.
Congenital syphilis is on the increase in the U.S., yet un-
familiarity with its expressions may lead to errors in diagnosis.
This paper describes a case which mimicked the battered child syndrome, and which developed after a maternal non-reactive serologic
test for syphilis early in gestation.

312. Fontana, Vincent J. "The Battered Child--1973. When to
Suspect Child Abuse." Medical Times, 101:116-120

passim, October 1973.
Fontana details a physician's index of suspicion for detection
of child abuse which he claims is getting worse, not better.   While
it is difficult and distasteful to accept that parents' maiming of
children is becoming commonplace, nevertheless, family physicians
must learn to be suspicious, because it is what's happening.   Two
doctors recently lost a large lawsuit for failure to diagnose assaultive parents. (Journal Abstract Modified.)

313. _____. "Battered Child Syndrome and Brain Dysfunction."
Journal of the American Medical Association, 223(12):
1390-1391, March 19, 1973.
Fontana presents a number of the warning signals indicative
of possible future battering, such as a combination of minor physical
symptoms, evidence of emotional disturbance, and possibly nutritional neglect and abuse.

314. _____. "The Diagnosis of the Maltreatment Syndrome in
Children." Pediatrics, 51(4):780-782, April 1973.
In the Symposium on Child Abuse held in 1971, important
aspects of diagnosing the maltreated child by the physician were
discussed.   Diagnosis must encompass the physical examination,
questionable history as to the cause of physical condition, and diagnostic X-ray findings.   A precise differential diagnosis to rule out
other organic causes must be undertaken, and a social service investigation can confirm the diagnosis of mistreatment in a specific
patient.

315. _____. The Maltreated Child: The Maltreatment Syndrome
in Children. See entry 1281.

316. _____. "The Maltreatment Syndrome in Children." Hospital Medicine, 7-25, 1971.
The child is the victim of emotionally crippled parents. Maltreatment Syndrome is preferable to "Battered Child Syndrome" because the term encompasses multiple minor physical evidence of
emotional and physical neglect and abuse, including nutritional deprivation.   Brief case descriptions with illustrations.   Gives signs
of physical abuse and neglect.

317. _____. "When to Suspect Parental Assault." Resident and
Staff Physician, 48-52, August 1973.
Guidelines for recognizing possible child abuse are presented.
The necessity of diagnostic X-rays to speak for the child is stressed.
A differential diagnosis is recommended to eliminate scurvy and
rickets, infantile cortical hyperostosis, syphilis of infancy, and ac-
cidental trauma.

318. _____; Donovan, D.; Wong, R. J. "The 'Maltreatment
Syndrome' in Children." New England Journal of Medicine, 269:1389-1394, December 29, 1963.
The circumstances and signs of the maltreatment syndrome
are typified in three case histories.   In two infant siblings, the

eldest sister expired at two years of age; an autopsy revealed multiple injuries. Investigation failed to uncover malicious intent in the injuries sustained by the remaining sibling. As a result of being thrown on the floor, multiple injuries were observed in a 6-week-old child. Presumably, multiple intercranial damage and subdural hematomas have resulted in blindness and mental retardation, which were noted at follow-up.

319. Friedman, Morris S. "Traumatic Periositis in Infants and Children." Journal of the American Medical Association, 166:1840-1845, April 12, 1958.
    The characteristic etiology and course of traumatic periostitis is illustrated by the case histories of seven children up to 10 years of age. Frequently, the traumatic event itself was forgotten until frank disability led to thorough investigation. The symptoms sometimes suggested the paralysis of poliomyelitis, but roentgenograms showed characteristic periosteal lesions, explained the unwillingness of the child to use the affected extremity, and led to the recollection of the injury, sometimes related to parental maltreatment.

320. Furness, J. "Bite Marks in Non-Accidental Injuries of Children." Police Surgeon, 6:75-87, 1974.
    This article pertains to using the dental casts of bite marks for comparison with possibly suspected persons or animals. For illustration, five cases are described.

321. Gans, Bruno. "Battered Babies--How Many Do We Miss?" Lancet, 1:1286-1287, June 13, 1970.
    The case of a 5-month-old infant observed in a London hospital in 1969 illustrated the fact that physicians and others are reluctant to diagnose battered child syndrome even when presented with abundant evidence. Part of the reluctance of the authorities to make the diagnosis resulted because the parents were nice people.

322. _____. "Unnecessary X-Rays?" British Medical Journal, 1:564, February 28, 1970.
    Gans states that any injury in a child under the age of two makes a complete skeletal survey mandatory. Such an infant must be considered to be an instance of "battered-baby syndrome" until proven otherwise. Only radiological examinations of the whole child will reveal old and healing injuries, which are virtually pathognomonic. It is worth remembering that any subsequent battering carries a 10 percent mortality.

323. Gee, R. J. "Radiology in Forensic Pathology." Radiography, 41(485):109-114, May 1975.

324. Gianotti, F. [Proceedings: Infantile Familial Bullous Recurrent Dermatitis with Eyelid, Lip, and Genital Localizations and Otorrhagia, and Fatal Course: Hetero-Provoked Pathomimial]. Annales de Dermatologie et de Syphiligraphie, 102(4):403-405, 1975.

325. Giedion, A. [The Repeated Skeletal Trauma in the Infant and Small Child in X-Ray Films]. Praxis, 57:191-196, February 13, 1968.

326. Giertsen, J. C., et al. "Barnemishandling. Meddelelse om et Dodelig Tilfelle" [Child Abuse. A Case Report with Fatal End]. Tidsskrift for den Norske Laegeforening, 92: 2251-2253, November 30, 1972.
    This Norwegian case concerns a two-year, five-month-old boy, the son of a psychopathic father and a mother with consid--ably reduced mental faculties. After a thorough medical examination and on repeated questioning, the father admitted that the boy was not found dead. He became angry with the boy when trying to wash him, caught his feet and held him upside down, shaking him. This must possibly be considered as a cause of the subdural hematoma.

327. Gostomzyk, J. G.; Rochel, M. "Befinden der Misshandlung und Vernachlässignung von Kindern" [Findings in Child Abuse and Child Neglect]. Beitraege zur Gerichtlichen Medizin, 31:102-109, 1973.
    At the University of Mainz, Department of Pediatrics and Forensic Medicine, 54 cases of battered children and 19 cases of neglected children were registered between the years 1960 and 1970. In nearly 50 percent of the children, skeletal injury through radiological signs could be proved. These radiographic manifestations are described.

328. Grantmyre, Edward B. "Trauma X--Wednesday's Child." Nova Scotia Medical Bulletin, 52:29-31, February 1973.
    The physician must be suspicious of the possibility of the diagnosis of Trauma X (battered child syndrome) in any infant or child where the extent of injuries is considerably greater than expected by the history. Parental factors common to most of these cases of child abuse are discussed. The moral, legal, and ethical responsibility of the physician to report these cases has been emphasized.

329. Green, Karl. "Diagnosing the Battered Child Syndrome." Maryland State Medical Journal, 14:83-84, September 1965.
    Physicians are urged to become aware of the wide range of possible indicators of the battered child, to apply this knowledge of this syndrome to all cases they care for, and to report all cases where there is legitimate suspicion of a battered child.

330. Greengard, Joseph. "The Battered-Child Syndrome." American Journal of Nursing, 64:98+, June 1964.
    Physicians and nurses must be familiar with the commonly found symptoms-complex if cases of non-accidental injury to infants and toddlers do not go undetected. The pathology and signs to arouse the suspicions are described by a Chicago pediatrician.

331. Greinacher, I. "Rontgenbefunde beim sogenannten battered child syndrom" [Roentgenological Findings in the Battered

Child Syndrome]. Fortschritte auf dem Gebiete der Roentgenstrahlen und der Nuklearmedizin, 113(6):704-710, 1970. In the battered child syndrome, radiological examination often provides only limited information. In any suspected case, it is advisable to repeat examination after two weeks; more definite changes may then be present. Reviewed is a relatively large clinical series to analyze the radiological findings.

332. Gross, C. A.; Biber, Michael P. "Re: Child Abuse." (Letter). Journal of the American Medical Association, 235:2475-2476, June 7, 1976.
Gross congratulates Biber on his article, "Iatrogenic Skull Fracture Depression by Use of a Head Clamp," but criticizes him for not suspecting child abuse. Biber replies that the purpose of the article was to alert medical personnel to a potential hazard of mechanical head restraint. Battering was irrelevant to the main point of the article.

333. Guandolo, Vincent; Silver, Larry; Barton, William, et al. "Grand Rounds: The Battered Child Syndrome." Clinical Proceedings, 23:139-160, May 1967.
The authors present a case study of a child admitted to a children's hospital on three different occasions because of traumatic injuries. The battered child syndrome was suggested not only by the repetitive nature of these admissions but also by the type of injuries involved. To support this suspicion were the physical findings of an unclean, poorly cared for, malnourished, anemic, and withdrawn child. Important was the fact that the child thrived on hospital care. Responses of lawyers, social workers, and physicians are included. (Journal Summary Modified.)

334. Guarnaschelli, John; Lee, John; Pitts, Frederick W. "'Fallen Fontanelle' (caida de Mollera). A Variant of the Battered Child Syndrome." Journal of the American Medical Association, 222:1545-1546, December 18, 1972.
A case of subdural hematoma occurred secondary to manipulation by a folk practitioner for fallen fontanelle (caida de mollera). This variation of the battered child syndrome should be a consideration when dealing with patients of Latin-American background because folk concepts of disease and their related "remedies" are sometimes important factors in case histories. (Journal Abstract.)

335. Gwinn, John L.; Barnes, George R., Jr. "Radiological Case of the Month." American Journal of Diseases of Children, 109:457-458, May 1965.
The history obtained from the parents of a 5-week-old girl admitted to the hospital for the first time was very misleading. The final radiological diagnosis: battered child syndrome with multiple rib fractures and metaphyseal fractures of the left femur. The final clinical diagnosis: subarachnoid hemorrhage with cerebral contusion and battered child syndrome. (Journal Summary.)

336. _____; Lewin, Kenneth; Peterson, Herbert, Jr. "Roent-
    genographic Manifestations of Unsuspected Trauma in In-
    fancy." Journal of the American Medical Association, 176:
    926-929, June 17, 1961.
    Twenty-five cases of unsuspected trauma in young children
have been recognized in a two-year period in Los Angeles. They
presented characteristic roentgenographic manifestations and multiple
sites of bony involvement. The history and clinical aspects were
frequently misleading, and the fact of willful, repeated injury to the
child was generally either unrecognized or concealed by the informant. Recognition of these findings becomes important in safeguarding
the infant from further injury.

337. Gyepes, Michael, et al. "Metaphyseal and Physeal Injuries in
    Children with Spina Bifida and Meningomyeloceles." Ameri-
    can Journal of Roentgenology, 95:168-177, 1965.
    Children with spina bifida and meningomyelocele who are not
fully paralyzed are more prone to suffer injuries resulting in metaphyseal and physeal injuries to the lower extremities. Trauma is
the main cause.

338. Haas, L. "Injured Baby." British Medical Journal, 5462:
    645, September 11, 1965.
    Haas expresses concern that birth trauma is no longer the
only reason for subdural haematoma during infancy. He suggests
that subdural haematoma may be the first real sign of some types
of child abuse, and that professionals should become aware of this
indication. One case study is given as an example.

339. Hall, M. H. "The Diagnosis and Early Management of Non-
    Accidental Injuries in Children." Police Surgeon, No. 6:
    17-74, 1974.
    This article gives instructions on interviewing and examination
in cases of non-accidental injury to children. The physical manifestations of non-accidental injuries are described elaborately. Fifty-
five photographs are of paramount instructive value.

340. Hamlin, Hannibal. "Subgaleal Hematoma Caused by Hair-
    Pulling." Journal of the American Medical Association,
    204:339, April 22, 1968.
    Hamlin suggests that the most likely cause of childhood sub-
galeal hematoma is a vigorous hair-pull by the grip of an enraged
adult. This condition should be another clue to the "battered-child
syndrome."

341. Hamory, J. "Exploring Complaints of Child Abuse--The
    Problem of Inquiry." The Australasian Nurses Journal,
    4:15+, October 1975.

342. Harcourt, Brian; Hopkins, David. "Ophthalmic Manifestations
    of the Battered-Baby Syndrome." British Medical Journal,
    3:398-401, August 14, 1971.
    Eleven battered babies with ocular manifestations of their

abuse were studied. Eight suffered a permanent impairment, ten had extensive intraocular hemorrhage, indicating that hemorrhage is an important diagnostic feature in the battered baby syndrome.

343. _____ : _____ . "Permanent Chorio-Retinal Lesions in Childhood of Suspected Traumatic Origin." Transactions of the Ophthalmological Societies of the United Kingdom, 93:199-205, 1973.

The authors report the well-known association of retinal and pre-retinal hemorrhages with subdural hematoma or effusion in young children. In many such cases, there is a suspected or proven traumatic etiology, and a number of affected children fulfill some or all of the diagnostic criteria of the battered child syndrome. They recommend that the possibility of physical maltreatment be considered by the examiner of an infant with subdural hematoma.

344. Hawkes, C. D. "Craniocerebral Trauma in Infancy and Childhood." Clinical Neurosurgery, 11:66-75, 1964.

In this technical article, Hawkes describes several types of head injuries. When infants present with skull fracture or subdural hematomas, neurosurgeons are advised to be alert to the possibility of child abuse and search for multiple injuries to other parts of the skeleton. This is particularly true when the reason for the injury is unclear or when the family situation is such that one might suspect abuse.

345. Heiskanen, O.; Kaste, M. "Late Prognosis of Severe Brain Injury in Children." Developmental Medicine and Child Neurology, 16(1):11-14, February 1974.

346. Helfer, Ray E. "The Battered Child--in 1973. What to Do When the Evidence Hardens." Medical Times, 101(10): 127-128, October 1973.

A noted authority details his own approach to the definitive diagnosis of child abuse. He advises family physicians to approach the problem as they do any other serious, life-threatening situation. (Journal Summary Modified.)

347. _____ . The Diagnostic Process and Treatment Programs. Washington, D.C., National Center for Child Abuse and Neglect. Report No. DHEW (OHD) 75-69, 1975. 44 p. Available from Govt. Prtg. Office; also from EDRS: MF-$0.76; HC-$1.95, Plus Postage.

Provided for physicians and nurses is information on the diagnostic process and treatment programs for abused and neglected children and their families.

348. _____ . "Early Identification and Prevention of Unusual Child-Rearing Practices." Pediatric Annals, 5(3):91-105, March 1976.

Helfer proposes the adoption of early identification programs which seek to screen for those parents who are more likely to have problems with parent-child interaction than the general population.

A prevention counterpart of the screening program attempts to intervene with educational and training experiences, thereby changing or eliminating the basic causes of unusual rearing practices that produce children with a variety of difficulties. The school system must be convinced to start parenting courses for students in the elementary, junior high, and senior high school levels.

349. _____. "Seven Guidelines in Child Abuse Cases." Resident and Staff Physician, 19(8):57-58, August 1973.
Recommended in child abuse cases is a diagnosis which includes a complete physical examination of the child, a precise history, and diagnostic X-ray findings. Knowledge in the area of child abuse is such that diagnosis should be made in over 75 percent of the cases. The problem is seen as bringing successful therapeutic programs to abusive families.

350. _____; Kempe, C. Henry. Child Abuse and Neglect: The Family and the Community. See entry 617.

351. Henderson, J. G. "Subdural Haematoma and 'Battered Baby.'" (Letter). British Medical Journal, 3(5619):678, September 14, 1968.
Further research is necessary to elucidate the significance of subdural hematoma as an indication of child abuse. Subdural hematoma has been described in physically abused children as has retinal hemorrhage with and without subdural hematoma. On the other hand, at least one child has been observed with extensive fractures and meningitis but without subdural hematoma; while a recent study of subdural hematoma in infants presented no data on the number who sustained injury as a result of physical abuse.

352. Herbich, J., et al. ["Differential Diagnosis in Child Abuse."] Beitraege zur Gerichtlichen Medizin, 31:97-101, 1973.

353. Hiller, H. G. "Battered or Not--A Reappraisal of Metaphyseal Fragility." American Journal of Roentgenology, Radium Therapy and Nuclear Medicine, 114(2):241-246, February 1972.
Results of a retrospective study of 145 non-battered children and 25 battered children showed that multiple epiphyseal plate fractures, up to the present considered to be almost certain evidence of battering, may in fact be due to an underlying bone defect. The evidence for this theory is presented. The advisability of accepting multiple epiphyseal plate fractures as definite roentgenologic evidence of battering is thus doubtful.

354. Hogan, M. "The Eye of the 'Battered Child.'" Archives of Opthalmology, 72:231-233, 1972.
This is a case of traumatic retinal detachment which was probably bilateral in a seven-month-old infant who had been battered. Hogan states that this condition should be considered a possibility in the differential diagnosis of retinoblastoma.

355. Hudson, Phoebe. "The Doctor's Handy Guide to Chronic Child Abuse." Journal of the Medical Society of New Jersey, 70:851-852, November 1973.
Guidelines are presented to help the doctor detect chronic abuse of very young children. Clues to maltreatment are given. The importance of the whole picture in making an evaluation is stressed.

356. Hussey, Hugh H. "The Battered Child Syndrome: Unusual Manifestations." (Editorial). Journal of the American Medical Association, 234(8):856, November 24, 1975.
Hussey lists eleven uncommon manifestations of child abuse in addition to the "whiplash-shaken infant syndrome" caused by manual shaking. Originally noted by Kempe, the unusual manifestations range from retinal hemorrhage to uncommonly jittery babies.

357. Ilona, B., et al. "The 'Battered Child Syndrome' and the 'Shaken Infant Syndrome.'" Orvosi Hetilap, 117(42):2544-2547, October 17, 1976.

358. Ingraham, Franc D., et al. "Subdural Hematoma in Infancy and Childhood." Journal of the American Medical Association, 112(3):198-204, 1939.
Case reports depict intracranial hemorrhage with formation of subdural hematomas. Conditions occur more frequently in the undernourished, and in the majority of instances there is trauma. A wide variety of neurological treatments are offered.

359. Jackson, Graham. "Child Abuse Syndrome: The Cases We Miss." British Medical Journal, 2:756-757, June 24, 1972.
One hundred cases of injury to children 12 years old or less were randomly chosen from the files of two British hospitals. When cases with clear causation and those with inadequate histories were discarded, 18 cases strongly suggestive of child abuse remained. Despite these obvious signs, it appears that the possibility of child abuse was not considered in the original diagnoses, indicating that hospitals should review their files to help identify children at risk of abuse.

360. James, H. E.; Schut, L. "The Neurosurgeon and the Battered Child." Surgical Neurology, 2(6):415-418, November 1974.
Without a clear history in a child, the neurosurgeon should suspect neglect or trauma. Lack of recognition of this situation can lead to brain damage or death. Of a series of 45 children suspected of abuse at the Children's Hospital of Philadelphia, the neurosurgeon was consulted in 20. Conditions of these patients are given.

361. Jennett, Bryan. "Head Injuries in Children." Developmental Medicine and Child Neurology, 14:137-147, April 1972.
This is a general article concerning head injuries of various kinds in children, including those of the battered baby. Whenever a battered baby is suspected, the likelihood of head injury should be

considered even though there is no direct evidence: the fundi should
be examined and the skull X-rayed.

362. Jones, Henry H.; Davis, Joseph H. "Multiple Traumatic
    Lesions of the Infant Skeleton." Stanford Medical Bulle-
    tin, 15:259-273, August 1957.
    The co-authors describe multiple skeletal lesions in infants
insofar as they may be related to undiagnosed traumatic experiences.
Several case studies emphasize the need for medical practitioners
to recognize such lesions so that infants may be spared extensive
diagnostic procedures and, if indicated, removed from offending environments. (Journal Introduction Modified.)

363. Keeney, Ronald E. "Enlarging on the Child Abuse Injury
    Spectrum." (Letter). American Journal of Diseases of
    Children, 130(8):902, August 1976.
    Reference is made to an unusual manifestation of injury re-
lated to child abuse. The case illustrates vividly the potential for
severe multisystem involvement in physical child abuse. The blatant
discrepancies between the explanation for the child's injuries and
the actual findings re-emphasize the need to remain alert to such
discrepancies when dealing with pediatric trauma.

364. Kempe, C. Henry; Silverman, Frederic N.; Steele, Brandt F.,
    et al. "The Battered-Child Syndrome." Journal of the
    American Medical Association, 181:17-24, July 7, 1962.
    Described is the incidence, clinical manifestations, psychiatric
aspects, and differential diagnosis of the battered child syndrome,
as well as management procedures. Such a syndrome should be
considered with evidence of bone fracture, subdural hematoma,
failure to thrive, soft tissue swellings, or skin bruising, and in
any child who dies suddenly, or where the degree and type of injury is at variance with the history given regarding the occurrence
of the trauma.

365. Kiffney, G. T., Jr. "The Eye of the 'Battered Child.'"
    Archives of Ophthalmology, 72:231-233, August 1964.
    A case of a traumatic retinal detachment is presented which
was probably bilateral, occurring in a 6-month-old infant who was
a victim of the "battered child syndrome." This condition should
be considered as a possibility in the differential diagnosis of retinoblastoma. (Journal Summary.)

366. Kim, Taek; Jenkins, Melvin C. "Pseudocyst of the Pancreas
    as a Manifestation of the Battered-Child Syndrome. Re-
    port of a Case." Medical Annals of the District of Colum-
    bia, 36:664-666, November 1967.
    An extensive case history describes diagnosis and treatment
of pseudocyst of the pancreas following inflicted trauma. Physicians
should be aware that abdominal trauma can produce this formation.

367. Kirchner, Sandra G.; Lee, Ying T. "X-Ray of the Month.
    Child Abuse." Journal of the Tennessee Medical Association,

66:1053-1054 passim, November 1973.
Radiographic findings pointed to the diagnosis of child abuse in
a 22-month-old male infant weighing 13 pounds, 15 ounces, who was
admitted to the hospital at the request of his local health department
because of failure-to-thrive. The findings are fully described. The
differential diagnosis is discussed. The patient responded well to
treatment, and he was brought into the protective custody of the
court and transferred to a foster home.

368. Köttgen, U. "Kindesmisshandlung" [Child Abuse]. Monatsschrift für Kinderheilkunde, 115:186-192, April 1967.
Reviewed is the research on the problems of identifying, discovering, and reporting child abuse. The psychology of the abuser
is also discussed. Whether or not the doctor is by law forced to
report cases as in the USA, he is still responsible for the fate of
the child. Case studies, as well as illustrations of bone structure
damage, are presented.

369. _____; Greinacher, I.; Hofmann, S. "Zur röntgendiagnostik
der kindesmisshandlung (Battered Child Syndrome)" [X-ray
Diagnosis of the Battered Child Syndrome]. Zeitschrift für
Kinderchirurgie und Grenzgebiete, 6(3):384-392, 1968.
Even if details of the injury are not known in the case of a
battered child, a description of the classical and typical X-ray appearance which are visible in the first years of life can lead to a
diagnosis with considerable certainty. Although these X-ray signs
are not widely recognized, they are important.

370. Krauland, Von W. "Morphologische Aspekte der traumatischen
Hirnschädigung" [Morphological Aspects of Traumatic Brain
Damage]. Wierner Medizinische Wochenscrift, 118:742-
746, September 21, 1968.
The connection between primary and secondary traumatic brain
damage is discussed. Krauland concludes that the problem of differentiating the primary brain damage from the secondary has not
yet been solved. He advocates a close morphological analysis of
the case along with its clinical history over that of a statistical comparison of cases which cannot be compared.

371. Krige, H. N. "The Abused Child Complex and Its Characteristic X-Ray Findings." South African Medical Journal,
40:490-493, June 11, 1966.
The interpretation of traumatic lesions in young children will
always remain a difficult problem. With the increasing knowledge
of the etiology of diseases, the incidence of the more frequently encountered simple direct trauma is often sadly ignored. A missed
diagnosis is the commonest cause of failure in the treatment of a
child with the battered syndrome. The predominant findings are
radiologic and the doctor is often astounded by the severity and extent of the pathology revealed.

372. Krivine, F., et al. "Le syndrome de Silverman en stomatologie" [Silverman's Syndrome in Stomatology]. Revue de

Stomatologie et de Chirurgie Maxillo-Faciale, 74:343-352,
June 1973.
In connection with four cases in stomatological practice of
the battered baby syndrome, the authors endeavor: to define the
type of lesions which should alert practitioners; to determine the
family background responsible; to define the type of child most often
found with this syndrome. The authors conclude by recalling the
disorders with which Silverman's syndrome should not be confused.
(Eng. Abstr.)

373. Kuss, J. J., et al. "Le Syndrome de l'enfant battu: a propos d'une observation" [Battered Child Syndrome: Apropos
of a Case]. Tunisie Medicale, 52(4):187-190, July-August
1974.
Through reporting a case of a battered child, the authors
draw attention to the existence of child abuse and its detection.
Their purpose is to alert all those who are concerned with the
care of children.

374. Laing, S. A.; Buchan, A. R. "Bilateral Injuries in Childhood: An Alerting Sign." (Letter). British Medical
Journal, 2(6041):940-941, October 16, 1976.
The child health service in Leicestershire has nominated a
small number of senior clinical medical officers, who have developed
an expertise in the diagnosis of non-accidental injury to children, to
see most of the cases and then give advice and, where necessary,
attend court to give evidence. As more information about the normal
range of minor injuries was needed, a project was undertaken in
which children attending 10-day nurseries were inspected every day
and all injuries were recorded. None of the 1543 injuries were bilateral, e.g.,--affecting both sides of the head or both arms. Doctors should be particularly vigilant when seeing children with bilateral
trauma.

375. Lansky, Lester L. "An Unusual Case of Childhood Chloral
Hydrate Poisoning." American Journal of Diseases of
Children, 127:275-276, February 1974.
While hospitalized, a 3-year-old girl went into coma on four
separate occasions. Toxic quantities of chloral hydrate were isolated from the child's blood, urine, and gastric contents. Mother
had tried to poison the child with the drug, it was discovered.
Demonstrated is the value of perseverance in clarification of an ill-
defined clinical problem. (Journal Summary Modified.)

376. Leaverton, David R. "The Pediatrician's Role in Maternal
Deprivation." Clinical Pediatrics, 7(6):340-343, June
1968.
Maternal deprivation must be viewed biomedically and psycho-
socially, and covers an extensive range of symptoms, many of
which are difficult to distinguish. There is a wide variance of conditions due to maternal deprivation and a checklist of several factors
common to each is presented. All physicians and pediatricians must

begin to recognize the problem as early detection is essential to successful resolution of the problem.

377. Leavitt, Jerome E., comp. The Battered Child: Selected Readings. See entry 521.

378. Leikin, Sanford L.; Guin, Grace H. "Clinical Pathological Conference: The Battered Child Syndrome." Clinical Proceedings, 19:301-306, November 1963.
        In great detail, the co-authors present the case of a $4\frac{1}{2}$-year-old girl who was apparently healthy until three days before admission to a hospital for periorbital edema and ecchymoses. After autopsy and lengthy investigation, it was learned that the victim had been battered by the 12-year-old son of a baby-sitter.

379. Lentle, B. C. "Pycnodysostosis: A Case Report." Journal of the Canadian Association of Radiologists, 22:210-214, September 1971.
        Pycnodysostosis, an uncommon bone disease, has features in common with a number of diseases and syndromes including battered child syndrome. A case history is presented of a child with multiple bone fractures, increased bone density, and other distinctive features of the disease. Data for differential diagnoses are given.

380. Levine, Lowell J. "The Solution of a Battered-Child Homicide by Dental Evidence: Report of Case." Journal of the American Dental Association, 87:1234-1236, November 1973.
        Human bite marks left on the body of a 6-week-old homicide victim were used to help solve the crime. A limited number of persons had had the exclusive opportunity to cause the skull fractures that resulted in the death of the infant. Examination of the bite marks contributed to suspicion of a $4\frac{1}{2}$-year-old child. (Journal Summary.)

381. Levine, Milton I. "Traumatic Injuries in Children: Modern Concepts. A Pediatrician's View." Pediatric Annals, 5(10):4-7, October 1976.
        Levine discusses presentations given at a symposium where a group of surgeons experienced in the modern approach to the diagnosis of the damage incurred in traumatic incidents during childhood and the most effective methods of treatment were brought together.

382. Lis, Edward F.; Frauenberger, George S. "Multiple Fractures Associated with Subdural Hematoma in Infancy." Pediatrics, 6(6):890-892, December 1950.
        An infant with subdural hematoma associated with multiple fractures was presented. The etiology was not established. (Journal Summary.)

383. Lloyd-Roberts, G. "The Diagnosis of Injury of Bones and

Joints in Young Babies." Proceedings of the Royal Society of Medicine, 61:1299-1300, December 12, 1968.
Injuries to the limb bones of babies under one year old have appearances strikingly different from those of older children and adults. Characteristic radiographic signs are given. Where the injuries have resulted in assault, lesions are likely to be widespread and of varying age. They are readily distinguishable from those of scurvy and osteomyelitis and are less easily distinguishable from those of infantile cortical hyperostosis.

384. McAnarney, Elizabeth. "The Older Abused Child." (Letter).
Pediatrics, 55(2):298-299, February 1975.
The author encourages diagnosis of abuse and neglect not only on young children, but also on adolescents. Older children and teenagers may be reluctant to give accurate histories of abuse, fearing retaliation from parents. However, access to school authorities is easily available for those who might seek help there. A further definition of the magnitude of teenager abuse is necessary, utilizing health care facilities, schools, and youth activity centers.

385. McCauley, Mary Ann. "Burns, Bruises May Lead to Total Family Counseling." American Nurse, 7:6,15, October 1975.
Provided for the nurse are nine signals alerting her to possible maltreatment of children, seven questions she should ask herself when making a physical assessment of the child, and a Statement on Child Abuse adopted by the Executive Committee, Division on Maternal and Child Health Nursing Practice.

386. McCort, J.; Vaudagna, J. "Visceral Injuries in Battered Children." Radiology, 82:424-428, March 1964.
Presents case histories of ten children with unexplained visceral trauma where abuse was suspected. States that four of the ten died, emphasizing the seriousness of visceral trauma in the battered child syndrome. Explains that evidence of abuse and neglect was found in six of the ten patients as manifested by poor nutrition, contusions, brain damage, and/or multiple skeletal fractures.

387. McHenry, Thomas; Girdany, Bertram R.; Elmer, Elizabeth. "Unsuspected Trauma with Multiple Skeletal Injuries During Infancy and Childhood." Pediatrics, 31:903-908, June 1963.
This report concerns the experience at the Children's Hospital of Pittsburgh with 50 children who had skeletal lesions considered to be the result of trauma. The initial impressions of house officers ranged through the gamut of possible skeletal disorders and blood dyscrasias. The seriousness of this disease is indicated by the deaths of five of the infants and the continued injury of others after their return home from the hospital. (Journal Summary Modified.)

388. Mackler, Stuart F.; Brooks, Arthur L. "Diagnosis and Treatment of Skeletal Injuries in the Battered Child Syndrome." Southern Medical Journal, 58(3):27-32, 1970.

Discusses the battered child syndrome along with a brief overview of its history, diagnosis, and classic X-ray manifestations. Other diagnostically similar conditions are also called to the attention of the reader.

389. McLay, W. D. "The Battered Baby Syndrome." Police Surgeon, No. 5:95-106, 1974.
Besides describing autopsied cases of the battered baby syndrome, McLay reviews diagnostic aspects and stresses the importance of X-rays. Also discussed are measures of prevention.

390. Manson, Gordon. "Neglected Children and the Celiac Syndrome." Journal of the Iowa Medical Society, 54:228-234, May 1964.
Three cases of starved children are reported on whom the diagnosis of celiac syndrome was made following the demonstration of malabsorption. The clinical histories had been convincing, and the physical findings had been consistent. Yet, subsequent information revealed unequivocal evidence of starvation. It is emphasized that the clinical history should be questioned, and that starvation, for whatever reason, should be considered in the differential diagnosis of any child who presents with severe nutritional depletion. (Journal Summary Modified.)

391. Manzke, H.; Rohwedder, H. J. "Röntgenologie traumatischer skelettveranderungen beim saugling und kleinkind. (Battered Child Syndrome)" [Roentgenology of Traumatic Skeletal Lesions in Infants and Small Children. Battered Child Syndrome]. Chirurgische Praxis, 15(4):631-640, 1971.
Diagnosis, in cases of metaphyseal fragmentation, periostium findings, cortical hyperstosis, greenstick fractures, and fissures, can be effectively established only through X-rays. Case histories are too lacking in knowledge. There may be various causes for these injuries, such as birth trauma, the battered child syndrome, etc. Personal cases are presented.

392. ________; ________. "Traumatische Knochenvëranderungen beim Säugling, insbesondere nach Misshandlungen" [Traumatic Bone Changes in Infants, Especially Following Abuse]. Monatsschrift für Kinderheilkunde, 115:197-199, April 1967.
This is a technical description of the X-ray diagnosis of traumatic bone changes and includes X-ray illustrations. While these changes may be due to a physical condition or accident, most often the cause is child abuse.

393. Mintz, A. A. "Battered Child Syndrome." Texas State Journal of Medicine, 60:107-108, February 1964.
Described are some of the problems of diagnosis in child abuse cases. Psychological aspects relating to the parent and child are discussed, and the importance of reporting is stressed.

394. Morris, T. M. D.; Reay, H. A. J. "A Battered Baby with

Pharyngeal Atresia." <u>Journal of Laryngology and Otology,</u> 85:729-731, July 1971.

A case report of a seven-month-old girl with difficulty in breathing, a history of feeding difficulties, and two broken ribs is presented. In following months numerous procedures (reported in detail) were performed to remove pharyngeal obstruction. Three months later the child was readmitted with a broken femur. A review is presented of possible cause-and-effect relationships between battering and pharyngeal defects. It is sometimes difficult to tell if the defect is congenital or of traumatic origin.

395. Mushin, Alan S.; Morgan, Gwyn. "Ocular Injury in the Battered Baby Syndrome. Report of Two Cases." British <u>Journal of Ophthalmology,</u> 55:343-347, May 1971; <u>British</u> <u>Medical Journal,</u> 3:402-404, August 14, 1971.

Childhood ocular injuries resulting from physical abuse are easily confused with pseudoglioma, Coat's Disease, lens dislocation, and any form of intraocular hemorrhage. Ocular pathologists may be the first to recognize that these lesions are of a traumatic origin. Two detailed case histories of child battering illustrate commonly seen eye injuries.

396. <u>National Conference on Child Abuse: A Summary Report.</u> See entry 1371.

397. Naumann, Peter. "Kindesmisshandlungen" [Child Abuse]. <u>Munchener Medizinische Wochenscrift,</u> 109:1703-1704, August 18, 1967.

Naumann writes of his own experience after reading about the work on child abuse at the Kiel Clinic. A girl nearly two years old was brought to him by the parents who earnestly explained her injuries as the result of falling. Completely taken in by the parents' pose, Naumann misdiagnosed the case. The next day he learned from the police that it was child abuse. The child had died of internal injuries. Naumann praises the research done at Kiel which opens the eyes of doctors.

398. Nomura, F. M. "The Battered Child 'Syndrome.' A Review." <u>Hawaii Medical Journal,</u> 25:387-394, May-June 1966.

Child abuse should be suspected when a child presents with unexplained trauma, evidence of multiple or repeated injuries, and where there is a marked discrepancy between the physical findings and the report of the parents. On the basis of characteristic findings, the diagnosis can often be established. Methods of treatment and prevention are suggested.

399. Nong, The Anh. "'Pseudo-Battered Child' Syndrome." (Letter). <u>Journal of the American Medical Association,</u> 236(20):2288, November 15, 1976.

The purpose of this letter is to help American doctors avoid a misdiagnosis of Cao Gio, a Vietnamese medical practice. Because of ecchymoses on a child's chest and back, a father was suspected of child abuse. After being jailed, he committed suicide.

400. Nwako, Festus. "Child Abuse Syndrome in Nigeria." International Surgery, 59(11-12):613-615, November-December
1974.
The child abuse syndrome is not uncommon in Nigeria. Every
hospital handling accident cases should be aware of this fact. Diagnosis is based on a high degree of suspicion and pathognomonic
radiologic and other features. We recommend setting up detection
organizations in each state to handle suspicious or proven cases of
child abuse. (Journal Summary.)

401. O'Doherty, N. J. "Subdural Haematoma in Battered Babies."
Developmental Medicine and Child Neurology, 6:192-193,
April 1964.
When infants suffer physical assault, careful clinical examina-
tion goes a long way towards the diagnosis or exclusion of subdural
hematoma. Provided are symptoms to alert the examining physician.

402. Oettinger, Katherine B. "The Abused Child." Childhood Education, 41:235-237, January 1965.
Identifying the abused child is a major problem in child abuse.
Guiding principles for the reporting of the physically abused child
are offered along with a discussion of the various backgrounds of
abused children, what type of parent abuses and why. The community should become more aware of this major problem.

403. Ott, John F. "Neglected or Physically Abused Children."
Journal of the South Carolina Medical Association, 60:309-
315, October 1964.
Discusses the clinical and social manifestations, as well as
the psychiatric, legal, and medical implications of child abuse from
a diagnostic point of view. Recommends that every effort be made
to identify cases and, wherever necessary, remove these children
from the custody of their inhumane parents.

404. Ounsted, Christopher; Lynch, Margaret; Roberts, Jacqueline.
"No Not Non-Accidental Injury." (Letter). Lancet, 2(7991):
913, October 23, 1976.
The authors believe there is danger in using the euphemism
"non-accidental," for it blinkers everyone so they see only the in-
juries. Serious forms of child abuse may produce no visible trauma.
The cause of injury is another symptom of underlying bonding failure.
Intensive treatment can reverse the situation.

405. Palomeque, F. E.; Hairston, M. A., Jr. "'Battered Child'
Syndrome: Unusual Dermatological Manifestation." Archives of Dermatology, 90:326-327, September 1964.
This is the report of a case of a $2\frac{1}{2}$-year-old boy admitted to
the Louisiana State University pediatric service of Charity Hospital
of Louisiana in New Orleans who presented with dermatitis of the
scalp and numerous pigmented lesions in bizarre pattern on his back,
chest, and arms as well as other symptoms. With the help of social workers, the story of abuse became clear.

406. Pickel, Stuart, et al. "Thirsting and Hypernatremic Dehydration--A Form of Child Abuse." Pediatrics, 45:54-59, January 1970.
    Three cases of hypernatremic dehydration following periodic water deprivation by psychotic mothers are presented as examples of child abuse. This represents a previously unreported form of child abuse and a previously unrecognized cause of hypernatremia in children in the range from 2-8 years of age. From acute changes in body weight and sodium concentration in serum in the period of hydration, it was deduced that the dehydration sustained by these children was not associated with salt deficits. (Journal Summary.)

407. Pickering, Douglas. "Neonatal Hypoglycaemia Due to Salicylate Poisoning." Proceedings of the Royal Society of Medicine, 61:1256, December 1968.
    A 19-day-old girl was hospitalized in a near moribund state and suffering from convulsions. Because the child's parents told conflicting stories, it was not possible to determine whether aspirin had been administered deliberately to poison the child, or whether the parents had merely attempted to quiet the child and accidentally administered an overdose.

408. _____. "Salicylate Poisoning as a Manifestation of the Battered Child Syndrome." (Letter). American Journal of Diseases of Children, 130(6):675-676, June 1976.
    The mother gave her infant aspirin; the borderline between deliberate and accidental poisoning is not always easy to define. Later the child was readmitted to another hospital after being assaulted by her mother. It would seem reasonable to examine samples of the blood and urine of battered babies on admission for evidence of poisoning until the incidence of this manifestation is determined.

409. _____; Moncrief, Martin; Etches, P. C. "Non-Accidental Poisoning and Child Abuse." (Letter). British Medical Journal, 1(6019):1210-1211, May 15, 1976.
    Two cases of non-accidental poisoning are reported to alert social workers, lay magistrates, and doctors. In the first case, the mother used aspirin. The child was returned home against pediatric and psychiatric advice. Eight years later the same child was admitted for severe battering. In the second case, amitriptyline was found in the baby's urine and the mother was later caught in the hospital giving the child more.

410. Platou, Ralph V.; Lennox, Robert; Beasley, Joseph D. "Battering." Bulletin of the Tulane Medical Faculty, 23: 157-165, May 1964.
    Twenty-five pediatric physicians report information about frequency and types of child abuse in their contacts with 5,039 infants and children in offices, hospitals, clinics or homes during a two-week period. Stressed is the clear duty that physicians have in the major role of detection and then in assisting allied disciplines in a concerted effort toward prevention.

411. Potts, William E.; Forbis, Orie L. "Willful Injury in Childhood." Journal of the Arkansas Medical Society, 59:266-
270, December 1962.
This is a summary of the information obtained from 71 Arkansas physicians who answered a questionnaire concerned with the
abused child. It presents radiologic evidence and psychiatric aspects of child abuse.

412. Pringle, Mia K. "Identifying Deprived Children." Proceedings of the Royal Society of Medicine, 67(10):1061-1062,
October 1974.
Provided are three basic assumptions in identifying deprived
children--those deprived of continuous, consistent, and loving care
and those who are deprived of the intellectual stimulation needed to
promote full development of their innate natures. Pringle advocates an "at risk" register for children psychologically vulnerable
in order to prevent harmful effects. She outlines a course of action in ensuring early professional involvement.

413. Renvoize, Jean. Children in Danger. The Causes and Prevention of Baby Battering. See entry 645.

414. "Report from the Identification Work Group." C. Henry
Kempe, Chairman. Clinical Proceedings, 30(2):37-38,
1974.
In the report of the Identification Work Group of the National
Conference on Child Abuse, the question of whether the definition
of child abuse should be expanded and standardized, is discussed.
Two definitions were adopted, one for the identification of children
whose problems must be reported, and the second for identification
of children in need of services. A recommendation for the provision of health to all children as a means of access was also
adopted.

415. Rose, Cassie B. "Unusual Periostitis in Children." Radiology, 27:131-137, 1936.
Five cases of hospitalized children are reported because of
the close similarity of the X-ray and wide divergence of the clinical
findings; to emphasize the value of co-ordinating history and clinical
findings in the interpretation of X-ray evidence; and because of comparative rarity of some feature of each of these cases.

416. Rosenblatt, E.; Greenland, C. "Early Identification of Child
Abuse." Dimensions in Health Service, 52:10-12, May
1975.
The fact that health professionals in Ontario were found with
the lowest rate of reporting child abuse led to the home accident
and injuries study (HAIS). Its principal objective was to work with
pediatricians and hospital emergency staff to encourage the early
identification and reporting of abused and neglected children. The
work of HAIS is described.

417. Roth, Frederick. "A Practice Regimen for Diagnosis and

Treatment of Child Abuse." Child Welfare, 54(4):268-273, April 1975.
   A description of a step-by-step system for identifying child abuse cases and delivering the services and treatment required by the families and their children is presented. Developed by the Quincy District Office of the Illinois Department of Children and Family Service, this simplified system of abuse identification allows two things: quickly and accurately deciding how serious the situation is, and determining the kind of treatment needed to help the family.

418. Rupprecht, E., et al. [Clinical and Roentgenologic Symptoms of Child Neglect and Child Abuse]. Kinderaerztliche Praxis, 44(3):113-123, March 1976.

419. _____, et al. [On the Differential Diagnosis of Multiple Skeletal Trauma in Childhood]. Radiologia Diagnostica, 17(5):615-625, October 1976.

420. Salmon, James H. "Subdural Hematoma in Infancy. Suggestions for Diagnosis and Management." Clinical Pediatrics, 10:597-599, October 1971.
   The symptoms of subdural hematoma in infants is given. In conjunction with other fractures and bruises, hematoma suggests battered child syndrome. Detailed instructions are presented on performing subdural taps. When recognized early and treated properly subdural hematoma in infants carries an excellent prognosis.

421. Sauer, H., et al. [Differential Diagnosis-Accident in Childhood--Child Abuse]. Zeitschrift für Allgemeinmedizin: der Landarzt, 50(27):1171-1172, September 30, 1974.

422. _____; Kurz, R.; Fink, M. "Thoracoabdominale und Knochenverletzungen bei kindesmisshandlungen (Battered Child Syndrome)" [Thoracoabdominal and Bone Lesions in Child Abuse (Battered Child Syndrome)]. Monatsschrift für Unfallheilkunde, 78(11):533-543, 1975.
   The problems of diagnosis are described through the examples of five cases of abused children with fractures or thoracoabdominal injuries. First measures are suggested.

423. Shaw, Anthony. "The Surgeon and the Battered Child." Surgery, Gynecology and Obstetrics, 119:355, August 1964.
   This is a discussion of the clinical manifestations of abuse. The physician's responsibility in such cases is described.

424. _____. "Would You Have Missed This Battered Baby?" Hospital Physician, 9(3):59,62-63, 1973.
   A case report of a baby recuperating from an accidental head injury and examined for possible abuse is presented. He was kept at the hospital until a social worker could contact the parents about rehabilitation therapy. A list of clues in diagnosing child abuse is included.

425. Sheriff, Hilla. "The Abused Child." Journal of the South
     Carolina Medical Association, 60:191-193, June 1964.
   The radiologic manifestations of trauma are specific, and the
metaphyseal lesions in particular occur in no other diseases of
which doctors are aware. The findings permit a radiologic diagnosis even when the clinical history seems to refute the possibility of
trauma. Under such circumstances, the history must be reviewed,
and the child's environment carefully investigated. (Journal Summary Modified.)

426. Silverman, Frederic N. "The Battered Child." Manitoba
     Medical Review, 45:473-477, October 1965.
   The damage done to children under two years of age by adult
abuse is demonstrated through a series of striking X-rays. The
strictly medical handling of such cases is compared with the psychiatric aspect and the legal responsibility.

427. _____. "The Roentgen Manifestations of Unrecognized
     Skeletal Trauma in Infants." American Journal of Roent-
     genology, Radium Therapy and Nuclear Medicine, 69(3):
     413-427, March 1953.
   Examined are types of injuries associated with trauma and
abuse. In terms of specificity of injuries, an early landmark study
of types of abuse gives some indications of the reactions of parents
when interviewed about the trauma detected in their children.

428. _____. "Unrecognized Trauma in Infants, the Battered
     Child Syndrome, and the Syndrome of Ambroise Tardieu."
     Rigler Lecture. Radiology, 104:337-353, August 1972.
   Silverman points out the various aspects of diagnosing the battered child syndrome and adds an additional note which indicates
that Ambroise Tardieu (1818-1879) published a book on abuse and
maltreatment that lists symptoms and conditions very similar to
those presented by Kempe, and others, in their book on child abuse.

429. Sims, B. G.; Cameron, J. M.. "Bite-Marks in the 'Battered
     Baby Syndrome.'" Medicine, Science and the Law, 13:
     207-210, July 1973.
   Since 1969, bite marks have figured significantly as a feature
of the battered child syndrome. The clinical details of three cases
and the use of dental evidence based on photographs of the bite
marks and wax impressions of the mother's teeth to pinpoint responsibility are discussed, and other injuries commonly found in the battered child syndrome are reviewed.

430. Slovis, Thomas L.; Berdon, Walter E.; Haller, Jack, et al.
     "Pancreatitis and the Battered Child Syndrome. Report
     of 2 Cases with Skeletal Involvement." American Journal
     of Roentgenology, Radium Therapy and Nuclear Medicine,
     125(2):456-461, October 1975.
   The clinical problems described in these two patients emphasize the need not only to relate pancreatitis to the battered child
syndrome but also to distinguish between the bone changes due to
direct trauma and those related to pancreatitis.

431. Smith, E. Ide. "Trauma in Children." Journal of the Oklahoma State Medical Association, 62:511-517, November 1969.
    A discussion covers etiology, diagnosis, and treatment of trauma, the leading cause of death in children. Careful emergency room examination and patient history enable proper diagnosis and treatment. Abused children usually suffer multiple trauma, and symptoms are often difficult to identify. Five tables present causes of various trauma-related deaths, etiology of burns, and the age and sex of burn victims.

432. Smith, Marcus J. "Subdural Hematoma with Multiple Fractures." American Journal of Roentgenology, Radium Therapy and Nuclear Medicine, 63:342-344, 1950.
    A case is reported in which the presence of multiple fractures of the long bones aided in establishing the diagnosis of subdural hematoma in an infant. (Journal Summary.)

433. Starbuck, George W. "The Recognition and Early Management of Child Abuse." Pediatric Annals, 5(3):27-41, March 1976.
    Through a series of photographs, Starbuck sensitizes the physician to the recognition and management of non-accidental injury (NAI) in children. Recognition and immediate treatment of NAI are inseparable from prevention, long-term treatment, and long-term follow-up and evaluation of cases through an entire generation. The author concludes that if treatment is effective, NAI and neglect will be prevented in children still unborn.

434. Stefani, F. H.; Ehalt, Heidi. "Non-Oxygen Induced Retinitis Proliferans and Retinal Detachment in Full-Term Infants." British Journal of Ophthalmology, 58(5):490-513, May 1974.
    A clinical and histological review is presented of ten bilateral and five unilateral cases (collected over the last 19 years) of retinal detachment with retinitis proliferans in the eyes of full-term infants who had not been given supplemental oxygen. Discussed are the diseases and conditions to be considered in the differential diagnosis, among which is the battered baby syndrome.

435. Stevenson, W. "Battered Baby Syndrome." Medical Journal of Australia, 2:1073, 1973.
    Letter and answer concerning possible missed cases of child maltreatment in the Royal Children's Hospital-Brisbane. Cases surveyed. Includes information on reporting law.

436. Stone, N. H.; Rinaldo, L.; Humphrey, C., et al. "Child Abuse by Burning." Surgical Clinics of North America, 50:1419-1424, December 1970.
    This article explains that burns are the primary injury in 10 percent of abuse cases. The physician must recognize intentional burns and act to prevent subsequent injury.

437. Stone, Richard K.; Harawitz, Alan; San Filippo, Anthony, et al.

"Needle Perforation of the Liver in an Abused Infant."
Clinical Pediatrics, 15:958-959, October 1976.
The purpose of this report is to present a hitherto unreported
and unique cause of abdominal trauma in an abused child.   Chest
and abdominal X-rays confirmed the presence of a radio-opaque
needle-shaped foreign body just below the right diaphragm.   A
needle was found and removed from the left lobe of the liver.

438.   Storey, Bruce.   "The Battered Child."   Medical Journal of
       Australia, 2:789-791, November 14, 1964.
Reviewed are six case studies from Australian literature, all
of which involved unexplained fractures and child abuse diagnosis.

439.   Straus, P.; Compere, R.; Livchitz, J., et al.   "L'Apport de
       la radiopediatrie au dépistage des enfants maltraites.   Ses
       limites" [Contribution of Radiopediatrics to the Detection
       of Child Abuse.   Its Limitations].   Annales de Radiologie,
       11:159-169, 1968.
Four children subjected to ill-treatment are described.   Radiology plays an important role in confirming that a child has been
ill-treated and allows a distinction to be made from other conditions
which may be confused with these injuries.   The clinician, as Nie-
mann points out, should complete the assessment by the detection
of other signs of ill-treatment and throw light on underlying causes
in order to rectify it.   (Journal Summary Modified.)

440.   Straus, P.; Dirodet, D.; Vesin, C.   "Del'accident méconnu
       au sévice.   Contribution au diagnostic du: 'Syndrome de
       Silverman'" [From Unrecognized Accidents to Deliberate
       Injuries: Diagnosing Silverman's Syndrome].   Annales de
       Pediatrie, 19(10):651-659, October 2, 1972.
Included are the symptoms indicative of child battering.
Faulty diagnosis may occur in cases of generalized ecchymoses or
in subdural hematomas (postnatal), diagnosed as vitamin C deficiencies, or in fractures which may be diagnosed as bone disease.   Difficulties encountered in the diagnosis are primarily due to the extreme youth of the victim, the confusing clinical picture, and the
abuser's denial of the act.

441.   Sussman, Sidney J.   "Skin Manifestations of the Battered-
       Child Syndrome."   Journal of Pediatrics, 72:99-101,
       January 1968.
This report is concerned with skin lesions of the battered
child, noting characteristics which distinguish such lesions.   Illustrated.

442.   Swischuk, Leonard E.   "The Battered Child Syndrome:
       Radiologic Aspects."   Southern Medical Bulletin, 58(3):
       24-26, June 1970.
Skeletal injuries in infants and children indicative of the battered child syndrome, and their radiologic manifestations are described to increase the roentgenologist's awareness of the syndrome.

443. _____. "The Beaked, Notched, or Hooked Vertebra: Its Significance in Infants and Young Children." Radiology, 95:661-664, June 1970.
Conditions producing hooked or notched vertebrae in infants are reviewed. This abnormality is sometimes seen in battered children due to acute trauma or hyperflexion of the spine. It is often associated with neuromuscular problems, and in battered children is commonly noted in those with subdural hematoma, permanent brain damage, and chronic hypotonia. Despite the variety of seemingly unrelated conditions in which notched vertebrae exist, all cases involve hypotonia, exaggerated thoracolumbar kyphosis, and anterior herniation of the nucleus pulposus.

444. _____. "Spine and Spinal Cord Trauma in the Battered Child Syndrome." Radiology, 92:733-738, March 1969.
Six cases of battered child syndrome with spinal injury and one case with both spine and spinal cord injury are presented. The significance of the various vertebral injuries is discussed, and mechanisms of injury are postulated.

445. "TMA X-ray of the Month." Journal of the Tennessee Medical Association, 66:1053-1056, 1973.
This is a case study that arrives at a final diagnosis of battered child syndrome.

446. Talbert, James L.; Felman, Alvin H. "Identification and Treatment of Thoracoabdominal Injuries in 'Battered Children.'" Southern Medical Bulletin, 58(3):37-43, 1970.
The range of diagnostic devices and their capabilities in evaluating abdominal and genitourinary trauma are reviewed. Characteristic radiographic features of skeletal or soft tissue injuries may confirm the diagnosis of battered child syndrome. In general, the guidelines of management are analogous to those for adult care; however, significant emphasis should be placed on follow-up to prevent fatal recurrences.

447. Tate, R. J. "Facial Injuries Associated with the Battered Child Syndrome." British Journal of Oral Surgery, 9:41-45, July 1971.
A report on six cases of abused children whose injuries included facial trauma emphasizes the importance of correctly diagnosing battered children.

448. Taylor, David; Bentovim, Arnon. "Recurrent Nonaccidentally Inflicted Chemical Eye Injuries to Siblings." Journal of Pediatric Ophthalmology, 13(4):238-242, July-August 1976.
Two siblings are described with non-accidentally inflicted chemical eye injuries; the etiology, the nature of the chemical agent, the family background, and the problem of diagnosis and management are discussed. (Journal Summary.)

449. Teng, Ching Tseng; Singleton, Edward B.; Daeschner, C. W., Jr. "Inflicted Skeletal Injuries in Young Children."

Pediatrics Digest, 53-66, September 1964.
This article is an attempt to familiarize pediatricians, orthopedists, and radiologists with the diagnosis and other aspects of the
battered child syndrome. Metaphyseal infractions, subperiosteal
hemorrhage, epiphyseal-metaphyseal separations, multiplicity of
trauma, and evidence of repeated injuries are common characteristics of the syndrome as detailed in several case studies.

450. _____, et al. "Skeletal Injuries of the Battered Child."
     American Journal of Orthopedics, 6:202-207, October
     1964.

451. Thomas, G. Initial Views on Research on Early Warning
     Signals of Child Neglect and Abuse. Atlanta, Ga., Social
     and Rehabilitation Service Conference on Early Warning
     Signals of Child Abuse, November 27-29, 1973. 7 p.
A state of the art presentation on early warning signals of
child abuse and neglect includes brief definitions of terms, current
knowledge of early warning signals, and suggestions for future research. Resources of the Regional Institute of Social Welfare Research at the University of Georgia are briefly outlined.

452. Touloukian, Robert J. "Abdominal Visceral Injuries in Bat-
     tered Children." Pediatrics, 42:642-646, October 1968.
The injuries noted in the title tend to be caused by a punch
or blow delivered to the mid-abdomen. It is pointed out that the
fractures usually associated with Battered Baby Syndrome may not
be present in this form of abuse. The author presents a plea to
suspect visceral injury in any abused child who has abdominal complaints.

453. _____. "Battered Children with Abdominal Trauma." GP,
     40:106-109, December 1969.
Battered children with abdominal visceral injuries usually
suffer pancreatic, duodenal, mesenteric, and proximal jejunal injuries, whereas accidental trauma is more often associated with
lateral abdominal injuries, such as renal, splenic, and hepatic disorders. Early diagnosis of distinctive abdominal visceral injuries
is important in recognizing child abuse cases to prevent further
battering. Abdominal injuries are the second major cause of death
in child abuse cases.

454. Trube-Becker, Elisabeth. "Obduktion beim Plötzlich Gestor-
     benen Kind" [Autopsy After Sudden Death in Infancy Abso-
     lutely Indicated]. Medizinische Klinik, 66:58-59, January
     8, 1971.
In cases of sudden death in infants, an autopsy is especially
important. Doctors and the police should help in clearing up the
cause of death--to either remove or verify the suspicion of violence.
The experience of the author is that more than 50 percent of the
children on which autopsy was performed did not die a natural death.

455. Tseng, S. S., et al. [Battered Child Syndrome Simulating

Congenital Glaucoma]. Archives d'Ophthalmologie, 94(5): 839-840, May 1976.

456. "...Two by Abuse." Emergency Medicine, 8(7):140-142, July 1976.
Physicians are warned that when they diagnose pancreatitis in a child under five years of age, they should also order a full radiologic skeletal survey. Such a procedure could reveal the phenomenon of pancreatitis secondary to child abuse. A follow-up radiologic survey six weeks to two months later is also recommended.

457. Weidenthal, Daniel T.; Levin, Daniel B. "Retinal Detachment in a Battered Infant." American Journal of Ophthalmology, 81(6):725-727, June 1976.
A 12-week-old battered infant boy had bilateral retinal detachments. The retina in the left eye was considered inoperable, but retinal detachment surgery was performed in the right eye. This retina was reattached and limited vision was restored. The history, the location of the retinal pathology, and the absence of a lens colomboma helped differentiate this result of physical abuse from a congenital retinal detachment. (Journal Summary.)

458. Weston, W. J. "Metaphyseal Fractures in Infancy." Journal of Bone and Joint Surgery, 39(b):694-700, 1957.
Three cases of metaphyseal fractures in infants are described. Obstetrical trauma was probably responsible in two cases, and in the third case direct injury was admitted by the parents. These fractures are associated with bone destruction and periosteal new bone formation in the metaphyses. They are important because they can be confused with syphilis, tuberculosis, scurvy, osteomyelitis and neoplasm. The fractures respond to conservative treatment and usually heal rapidly in a matter of weeks. (Journal Summary.)

459. Wheelock, Seymour E. "The Abused-Child Syndrome." Hospital Topics, 44:95+, April 1966.
Wheelock recommends vigilance on the part of physicians in an attempt to reduce the growing number of child abuse cases. He presents a seven-point index of suspicion to be used by a physician in determining whether or not a child has been mistreated. Differential diagnoses are also included.

460. "When They're Angry." Newsweek, 59:74, April 16, 1962. il.
An index for diagnosing child battering is being developed by radiologist, Dr. John Gwinn. An increase in the number of battered child syndrome cases has created a need for accurate diagnostic methods. Most commonly, abused children suffer fractures of the arms and legs. Without tangible evidence, says Newsweek, that the child was deliberately injured by the parents, no doctor cares to become involved in legal action.

461. "Whiplash Injury in Infancy." Medical Journal of Australia, 2:456, August 28, 1971.

In any case of infantile subdural hematoma, and no marks of injury at all, there is a possibility of assault, and the physician should keep this fact in mind. He should attempt to find out as tactfully as possible whether or not the baby's head had been shaken.

462. Wickes, Ian G.; Zaid, Zafar H. "Battered or Pigmented?" British Medical Journal, 2:404, May 13, 1972.
This article concerns Mongolian spots and how they resemble battered areas on a child. Mongolian spots consist of grey-blue areas of pigmentation over the sacral area, buttocks, back and shoulders. They are usually seen in brown or black babies but rarely in white babies. Observations should be made with care.

463. "Willful Injuries to Children." (Editorial). What's New (Abbott Laboratories), 228, Summer 1962.
This is a review of many cases of child abuse and infanticide, many of which were difficult to prove, such as excessive cooling of the infant. Advocated is complete autopsies of children who die under unknown circumstances or where the cause of death cannot be reasonably substantiated by natural disease syndromes.

464. Woolley, P.; Evans, W. "Significance of Skeletal Lesions in Infants Resembling Those of Traumatic Origin." Journal of the American Medical Association, 155:539-543, 1955.
Discussed are the various patterns of skeletal trauma in relation to family patterns. Explained is that chronic skeletal lesions in infants showed a correlation to what are described as unstable families.

465. Wurfel, Lois J.; McCoy, W. T. "Radiographic Features of the Battered Child Syndrome." Journal of the College of Radiologists of Australia, 9:220-223, October 1965.
The radiographic features of 26 children known to be suffering from battered-child syndrome included gross fractures, metaphyseal fractures, epiphyseal displacements, and periosteal reactions. Recognition of the radiologic findings, which are often the sole evidence for the syndrome, is important so that appropriate action can be taken to prevent an expected recurrence of the violence. Informational aids for differential diagnoses are given.

466. "X-Rays in Focus. Bone Diseases in Children." Pictorial. Part 7. Nursing Times, 72:25-28, (center pages), July 8, 1976.
This article is devoted to two diseases of bone which occur in children: rickets and the battered baby syndrome. Radiology forms an important part in the diagnosis of both of these disorders.

467. Yeatman, Gentry; Shaw, Constance; Barlow, Matthew J., et al. "Pseudobattering in Vietnamese Children." Pediatrics, 58(4):616-618, October 1976.
In America, linear bruising on children has been considered synonymous with child abuse. With the large influx of Vietnamese children, physicians need to be aware of the practice of coin-

rubbing--a lay practice for ailments including fever, chills, and headaches. Oil is applied to back and chest with cotton swabs, skin is massaged until warm, and firm downward strokes with the edge of a coin are used until petechiae or frank purpura appear.

DIRECTORIES, HANDBOOKS, MANUALS, AND
NEWSLETTERS

468. American Humane Association. Children's Division. American Humane Magazine. Denver, Colo. (Magazine Subscription, $5.50).
Official national voice of humane activity, published monthly. Each edition includes news of both child and animal protective services. Content includes news and general feature stories on people and issues pertinent to the protection of children, adults and animals.

469. _____ . _____ . The Fundamentals of Child Protection: A Statement of Basic Concepts and Principles in Child Protective Services. Denver, Colo., 1955. 71 p. $2.
A manual on basic concepts, principles and practices for social work practitioners in this specialized field.

470. _____ . _____ . The National Child Protective Services Newsletter. Denver, Colo. No charge for single copies.
A quarterly report of activities of AHA's Child Protection program and other topics of interest to the field.

471. Bundy, Mary Lee; Whaley, Rebecca Glenn. The National Children's Directory: An Organizational Directory and Reference Guide for Changing Conditions for Children and Youth. College Park, Md.: Urban Information Interpreters, 1976. 300 p.
The main portion of the directory contains organization profiles of 665 local and national professional and citizen groups working to change conditions for children and youth.

472/3 Caring, a journal published by the National Committee for Prevention of Child Abuse.
The aim of this journal is to call attention to the urgent child abuse problem and to provide useful information. Free copies only to members of the Committee. Non-members interested in obtaining a copy, or non-members and members interested in obtaining multiple copies are invited to request price information from Caring, Publishing Department, Suite 510, 111 E. Wacker Drive, Chicago, Illinois 60601.

474. Child Protection Report: A Biweekly National Letter on Programs to Prevent Child Abuse and Neglect. Published by:

Child Protection Report, 1301 20th Street, N. W. , Washington, D. C. 20036.
Keeps one fully informed about important new development in the child welfare field. These professionals share a common concern: what society is doing for--and to--children. It is the only newsletter devoted to providing information on what is happening in all the professional disciplines engaged in federal, state, and local programs to prevent and treat child abuse and neglect.

475. Future Homemakers of America. Resource Papers. Child Abuse and Neglect. Washington, D. C. , May 1975. 9 p.
Presented for use by adult leaders of the Future Homemakers of America is information on the problem of child abuse and neglect in the U. S. Concise discussions on various topics are included.

476. International Association of Chiefs of Police. Child Abuse. (Training Key: No. 07). Gaithersburg, Md. , 1974. 5 p.
A training manual.

477. Johnston, Carol A. The Art of the Crisis Line for Child Abuse Prevention: A Training Manual for Volunteers. Parental Stress Service, Inc. , Santa Clara Ave. , Oakland, Calif. 94610 ($5). 1976. 64 p.
The Parental Stress Service training program for volunteers to work on crisis lines in child abuse prevention is described in this manual.

478. Jones, Mary P. Dealing with Child Abuse and Neglect: A Self-Teaching Manual for the Social Worker. [s. l. :s. n.], 1975. 82 p.

479. McIntosh, Joseph W. ; McQueen, Carolyn, eds. A Guide for the Prevention of Child Abuse. Health Science Division, Columbus College, Columbus, Ga. 31907. n. d. 16 p.

480. National Committee for Prevention of Child Abuse. The National Directory of Child Abuse Services and Information. Chicago, 1974.
The Directory lists over 135 public and private child abuse treatment and prevention agencies from across the United States. It includes name, address, telephone number, and contact person for each agency; type of service provided, complete program descriptions, geographic and service indexes.

481. _____. Prevent Child Abuse. Chicago, 1976. 4 p.
This pamphlet is an immediate educational and reference guide through the maze of child abuse and neglect. It gives an overview of some of the causes, symptoms, legal implications, and procedures surrounding child abuse. It includes national direct service organizations; as well as government and private resources; it describes some volunteer opportunities, encourages persons experiencing problems where and how to seek help, and includes a bibliography.

482. New York Foundling Hospital. Center for Parent and Child
Development. Practical Approach to Management of Child
Maltreatment. A Working Manual for Identification, Reporting, Treatment, and Intervention. New York, 1975.
85 p.
A working manual for a training program sponsored by the
New York Foundling Hospital emphasizes early detection and prevention. Consideration is given to legislative mandate and guidelines, program descriptions, record-keeping materials, guidelines
for intake and determination of progress, and criteria for termination of service. The child protective system is outlined and investigation and notification forms are provided. A model multidisciplinary
program for treatment of maltreating parents is described.

483. Oberg, M., ed. "Child Health Conference--Nurses' Resource
Manual (#21-1502)." National League for Nursing Publications, League Exchange, 101:1-127, 1975.

484. Parents Anonymous, Inc. I Am a Parents Anonymous Parent.
Inglewood, Calif., 1974. 32 p.
A handbook providing information on Parents Anonymous, a
program to help abusing parents.

485. _____. Parents Anonymous Chairperson-Sponsor Manual.
1975. 47 p. Available from: Parents Anonymous, 2810
Artesia Boulevard, Redondo Beach, Calif. 90278. $4;
also from EDRS: MF-$0.83, Plus Postage.
Presented is a manual which focuses on the Chairperson-
Sponsor relationship of Parents Anonymous (PA), an organization
for helping parents with child abuse problems. Also provided is
an application form for becoming a PA volunteer.

486. _____. Parents Anonymous Chapter Development Manual.
Inglewood, Calif., 1974. 18 p.

487. _____. Parents Anonymous International Chapter Directory.
Redondo Beach, Calif., 1975. (Cover title: Parents
Anonymous National Directory).

488. Regional Institute of Social Welfare Research. Child Abuse
and Neglect: Handbook for Social Workers in Georgia.
Athens, Georgia University, 1976. 14 p. (Available
from the Institute, 468 N. Milledge Ave., Heritage Bldg.,
Athens, Ga. 30602. $0.50; also from EDRS: MF-$0.83;
HC-$1.67, Plus Postage).
Guidelines are provided for the social worker in reporting
cases of suspected child abuse and neglect as required by Georgia law.

489. U.S. National Center on Child Abuse and Neglect. Child
Abuse and Neglect Reports. DHEW Publ. No. (OHD) 76-
30086.
Child Abuse and Neglect Reports is the official newsletter of
the National Center on Child Abuse and Neglect. The intention is to

publish it four times a year. It attempts to keep readers up to date with factual, objective accounts of present and future activities of the NCCAN: provide summaries of research and other important findings resulting from their grants; and provide a medium for the exchange of ideas between child protective services agencies and concerned professionals and lay people throughout the country who believe they have something to contribute to the common cause. (From Preface.)

490.   Washington State Medical Association. Subcommittee on the Abused Child. The Abused Child Primer, by D. C. Phillips. Olympia, Wash., July 1974. 19 p.

Guidelines for early identification, reporting procedures, and methods of rehabilitation for abused children and their families in the state of Washington are presented. Some of the services available to abusive parents and their children are surveyed.

491.   Wolman, Irving J.; Freedman, Alan R., eds. "Clinical Pediatrics Handbook: The Abused or Sexually-Molested Child: Clinical Management." Clinical Pediatrics, 8(5): 16 B, May 1969.

A CP handbook issued monthly. It has been a widely-read and popular special feature of Clinical Pediatrics journal for $3\frac{1}{2}$ years. This particular issue covers the physically-abused child, family assessment, and a table providing "Clues to Possible Abuse in Physical Examination of Injured Child."

492.   Zurcher, J. C. Identifying the Battered or Molested Child. A Handbook for School Staff Members. See entry 2347.

EDUCATION

493. Acute Phase, Consulting Pediatrician. Mike Williams Asso-
      ciates, 329A 17th Street, Manhattan Beach, Calif. 90266.
      1/2 inch videocassette (sony) B&W 20 min., 1974.
      The role of pediatric consultant in a child abuse case is
demonstrated in data gathering necessary for support of the diagnosis, determining safety of home and the development of long-term
treatment programs. The demonstration follows a consultation by
Dr. C. Henry Kempe of the National Center for the Prevention and
Treatment of Child Abuse and Neglect with a patient. The material
is designed for individuals who are involved with helping the abused
child and his family.

494. Acute Phase Pediatric. Mike Williams Associates, 329A
      17th St., Manhattan Beach, Calif. 90266. 1/2 inch video-
      cassette (sony) B&W 20 min., 1974.
      An interview with a physician who admits a child abuse patient
to the hospital is presented dealing with necessary data collection,
hospitalization procedure and the maintenance of a nonconfrontation
approach to parents. The material is designed for individuals who
are involved with helping the abused child and his family. The
demonstration includes an introduction and summary by Dr. Barton
Schmitt of the National Center for the Prevention and Treatment of
Child Abuse and Neglect and a patient interview by Dr. David Manchester, Pediatric Resident of the Colorado General Hospital.

495. Acute Phase, Social Worker. Mike Williams Associates,
      329A 17th St., Manhattan Beach, Calif. 90266. 1/2 inch
      videocassette (sony) B&W 20 min., 1974.
      A social work interview in a child abuse case is presented
demonstrating data collection for diagnosis, and provision of answers
for parents, with emphasis on family dynamics and the establishment
of mutual trust with parent(s). The patient interview is conducted
by Joy Chandler, a social worker with the NCPTCAN. The material is designed for individuals who are involved with helping the
abused child and his family.

496. American Humane Association. Children's Division. Plain
      Talk About Child Abuse, by Herb Stoenner. Denver, Colo.
      24 p. $.40.
      Six articles from The Denver Post which expose the myths
and stereotypes popularly accepted about parents who neglect or

abuse their children. An interpretation for the general public of the
nature and dimensions of neglect and abuse, its causation, and treatment.

497. _____. _____. Selected Readings. Denver, Colo. 59 p.
     $.75.
     A compilation of eight selected excerpts and an annotated bib-
liography designed to furnish background material for training sessions on Child Protective Services.

498. The Battered Child. Motion Picture. National Education
     Television and Radio Center. Made by WTTW. 1969.
     2 reels, 29 min. each. Sound, B&W. 16 mm. Price:
     $265; Rental $15.25; Catalog No. C51977. Based on the
     book of the same title, edited by Ray E. Helfer and C.
     Henry Kempe. Contact: Indiana University, Audio-Visual
     Center, Bloomington, Ind. 47401. (812) 337-8087.
     A documentary study of child abuse. Shows a team of doctors
and social workers at the University of Colorado Medical Center
working with actual cases of child abuse in an effort to determine
the causes of physical child abuse as well as to treat children affected mentally.

499. "Challenge: Advocacy for the Abused Child." Keynote, 3(3):
     15, 18, 1975.
     The professionals, volunteers, and members of the Boys'
Clubs of America are encouraged to champion the cause of the
abused and neglected child on local and national levels. How they
can help is outlined.

500. Child Abuse. Motion Picture. 29 min. sound, color. 16 mm.
     Price: $395. Available from AIMS Instructional Media
     Services, Inc., 626 Justin Avenue, Glendale, Calif. 91201.
     Focuses on the legal aspects of child abuse with which law
enforcement personnel should be familiar. However, in the interest
of giving the topic perspective and context, some sociological and
tactical observations are in order. The viewer is cautioned that
there are different opinions concerning the causes of child abuse,
the number of cases per year, the role of law enforcement, custody
of the children, and the method of treatment or punishment of the
parent. There are, however, many areas of broad consensus.

501. Child Abuse and Neglect. Filmstrip. Parents' Magazine
     Films, 1975. 5 color filmstrips and 3 cassettes (or one
     record). 6 to 10 m. per s. (Children in Crisis). Audio
     script booklet by Dr. Vincent J. Fontana. Discussion
     Guide. Price: $58. Contact: Parents' Magazine Films,
     Inc., 52 Vanderbilt Avenue, New York, N.Y. 10017.
     (212) 685-4400.
     Distinguishes between discipline and abuse. Points out the
problems of the abusers and gives laymen an idea of how to spot
child abuse and when to intervene. Discusses treatment and prevention. Useful in family-living units of health education, home economics, psychology or sociology courses from 10th grade up.

502. Child Abuse and the Police. Motion Picture. color. 30 min.
$415; Rental $25. Produced by the Attorney General of
California, 1973. Contact: AIMS Instructional Media
Services, Inc., 626 Justin Ave., Glendale, Calif. 91201.
(213) 240-9300.
This film shows a family's involvement with the police and
the law in a child abuse case. A training film, it also shows how
doctors and police determine that a child's injuries are the result
of abuse.

503. Child Abuse: Cradle of Violence. Motion Picture. color.
20 min. $340; Rental $40. Produced by Mitchell-Geb-
hardt Film Co. for Bonanza Films, 1976. In Arkansas,
Kansas, Louisiana, Missouri, Oklahoma, and Texas, contact: Motorola Telegrams, Inc., 7919 Cliffbrook Dr.,
Suite 243, Dallas, Tex. 75240 or call collect (214) 661-
8464. In Alaska, Hawaii, and Illinois, contact: Motorola
Teleprograms, Inc., 4825 N. Scott St., Suite 23, Schiller
Park, Ill. 60176, or call collect (312) 671-0141. In all
other states, contact: the Illinois address, or call toll-
free (800) 323-1900.
This film takes a different look at child abuse and its prevention. Parents discuss direction provided by self-help groups of
former abusive parents and by community services such as parental
stress hot lines and classes teaching parental skills.

504. The Child Beater. Motion Picture. B&W. 12 min. Rental
$18. Contact: Jean Stiman, Division of Child Psychiatry,
Children's Memorial Hospital, 2300 Children's Plaza,
Chicago, Ill. 60614. (312) 649-4589.
This film shows a single parent whose inability to cope leads
to child abuse.

505. Children in Peril. Motion Picture. American Broadcasting
Co. 22 min. sound, color. 16 mm. Price $350;
Rental $30. Contact: Xerox Films, Xerox Educational
Publications, 245 Long Hill Road, Middletown, Conn.
06457. (203) 347-7251.
According to medical authorities, the leading cause of infant
death in the U.S. may well be murder at the hands of the infant's
own parents. According to the film, there were some 60,000 reported cases of child abuse in the U.S. in 1974, and an estimated
two children die of abuse each day in this country alone. The film
also reveals that child abusers are not strikingly different from non-
abusive adults.

506. Cipher in the Snow. Motion Picture. color. 24 min. $265;
Rental $14. Produced by Brigham Young University,
1973. Contact: Brigham Young University, Media Marketing W-STAD, Provo, Utah 84602. (801) 374-1211, x 4071.
An award-winning film, this dramatization of psychological
abuse is based on the true story of a boy no one thought was important until his sudden death one snowy morning.

507. Criteria for Diagnosis. Cassette. Department of Human Development, College of Human Medicine, Michigan State University, East Lansing, Mich. 48823. AT 1 7/8 IPS cassette. 30 min. 1974.

The form of a diagnosis to examine the history and present
behavior of a family to assess environmental aspects which may lead
to child abuse and neglect is examined. The material is designed
for individuals who are involved with helping the abused child and
his family. A manual is included which presents brief introductory
remarks, a self-assessment quiz, a brief discussion about the material covered with references, and a summary of related instructional materials available.

508. The Crying Need. Motion Picture. color. 30 min. Free
loan in Virginia only. Produced by WBRA-TV, Roanoke,
Virginia, 1974. Contact: Office of Communications, Virginia Department of Welfare, 8007 Discovery Drive, Richmond, Va. 23288. (804) 786-8771.

Available only to Virginia residents, this film focuses on child
abuse in Virginia and includes information on help available.

509. Developing Community Programs. Cassette. Department of
Human Development, College of Human Medicine. Michigan State University, E. Lansing, Mich. 48823. AT
1 7/8 IPS cassette. 30 min. 1974.

The major components, the individuals involved, the developmental sequence, and cost of a coordinated community child abuse
and neglect program are considered. The material is designed for
individuals who are involved with helping the abused child and his
family. A manual is included which presents brief introductory remarks, a self-assessment quiz, a brief discussion about the material covered with references, and a summary of related instructional materials available.

510. Diagnostic Child Abuse and Neglect Via Physical Findings.
Slide Series with Cassette Tapes. Available from: Mike
Williams Associates, Box 564, Manhattan Beach, Calif.
90266.

This slide series is a presentation of physical descriptions of
the results of various types of abuse, including burns, bruises, bone
injuries, and failure to thrive.

511. Dispositional Conference. Videocassette. 1/2 inch. (sony)
B&W. 20 min., 1974. Mike Williams Associates, 329A
17th Street, Manhattan Beach, Calif. 90266.

A weekly team conference for child abuse case disposition is
portrayed emphasizing the multidisciplinary approach. The conference's purpose is to consolidate all data collected, establish trust
and communication between disciplines, identify all problems of the
family and establish priorities for immediate and long-term follow-up.

512. Don't Give Up on Me. Motion Picture. color. 28 min.
$375; Rental $50. Produced by Cavalcade Productions,

1975. In Arkansas, Kansas, Louisiana, Missouri, Oklahoma, and Texas, contact: Motorola Telegrams, Inc., 7919 Cliffbrook Dr., Suite 243, Dallas, Tex. 75240, or call collect (214) 661-8464. In Alaska, Hawaii, and Illinois, contact: Motorola Teleprograms, Inc., 4825 N. Scott St., Suite 23, Schiller Park, Ill. 60176, or call collect (312) 671-0141. In all other states, contact: the Illinois address, or call toll-free (800) 323-1900.

Accompanied by an instructor's manual and useful for social workers, the film's emphasis is on understanding and helping parents so overwhelmed by problems that they lash out at their youngsters. Only one character in the cast, a social worker, is played by a professional actor. Therapists, counselors, and abusive parents and their children play themselves.

513. The Dynamics of Child Abuse. Videotape. (S-574-74). color. reel. 1/2" EIAJ 1, 37 min. October 1974. Contact: Fort Wayne Public Library, 900 Webster Street, Fort Wayne, Ind. 46802. Attention: Steven Fortriede.

Taped at Lutheran Hospital, Dr. James Hill and Mrs. Norma Pinney, R.N., answer questions about child abuse. The questions cover such subjects as: distinction between child abuse cases and other injuries; causes, both deep-seated and obvious, of child abuse; constructive attitudes for emergency room personnel toward the abused child and his parents; the S.C.A.N. (Suspected Child Abuse and Neglect) approach; the responsibilities of the nurse in a suspected child abuse case; and some of the methods being used to prevent actual violence in families prone to child abuse. The tape strictly avoids the emotional approach so often adopted by those who point out the excesses of child abuse.

514. Education Commission of the States. Education for Parenthood: A Primary Prevention Strategy for Child Abuse and Neglect. Report No. 93 from the ECS Child Abuse Project, by Oralie McAffee and Shari Nedler. Denver, Colo., December 1976. Available from the Commission: $3.50; also from EDRS: MF-$0.83; HC-$2.06, Plus Postage.

In this booklet the importance of parent education as a preventive strategy for child abuse is discussed. Many individual differences exist in the area of needs, strengths, and weaknesses related to effective child-rearing and parental competencies.

515. _____. Education Policies and Practices Regarding Child Abuse and Neglect and Recommendations for Policy Development. Report No. 85. Denver, Colo., April 1976. 72 p. Available from the Commission; also from EDRS: MF-$0.83; HC-$3.50, Plus Postage.

This report documents the findings and implications of a nationwide assessment of current education policies and practices regarding child abuse. The report offers guidelines to help education policy makers formulate child abuse policies.

516. Families Anonymous. Videocassette. 1/2 in. (sony). B&W.

20 min. 1974. Mike Williams Associates, 329A 17th
Street, Manhattan Beach, Calif. 90266.
A group meeting with Walt and Joan Hopkins and members of
a Families Anonymous Group from the NCPTCAN is demonstrated,
noting the kinds and use of interaction between abusive or potentially
abusive parents with professional supervision. The material is designed for individuals who are involved with helping the abused child
and his family.

517. Fragile--Handle with Care. Motion Picture. color. 26 min.
$125/free loan. Produced by KTAR-TV Productions in co-
operation with the Independent Order of the Foresters,
1975. Contact: Mr. James Martin, High Court of Southern
California, 100 Border Avenue, Solana Beach, Calif. 92075.
(714) 755-5158.
Narrated by Bill Cosby, the film shows that abuse of children
is an old but increasing problem and examines why parents abuse
their children and what happens to the children, both physically and
mentally. The film looks at ways of preventing child abuse and
deals with the legal considerations involved. The situations portrayed are reenactments of authentic case histories.

518. Frequently-Asked Questions on Child Abuse and Neglect. Cassette. AT 1 7/8 IPS. 30 min. 1974. Department of
Human Development, College of Human Medicine, Michigan
State University, East Lansing, Mich. 48823.
A collection of questions and answers from various lectures
and presentations which have been most often asked concerning child
abuse and neglect is presented. The material is designed for individuals who are involved with helping the abused child and his family.
A manual is included which presents brief introductory remarks, a
self-assessment quiz, a brief discussion about the material covered
with references, and a summary of related instructional materials
available.

519. Helfer, Ray E.; Caufield, Barbara A.; Lieber, Leonard, et al.
A Look at Child Abuse. Chicago: National Committee for
Prevention of Child Abuse, 1976. 33 p.
Written in laymen's terms, this booklet provides comprehensive,
fundamental information that will help teachers, volunteers, physicians, troubled parents, students, better understand and deal with
abuse.

520. Lay Therapy. Videocassette. 1/2 in. (sony). B&W. 20
min. 1974. Mike Williams Associates, 329A 17th
Street, Manhattan Beach, Calif. 90266.
A meeting of lay therapists with a social worker and a psychiatrist is excerpted to illustrate the origin of lay therapy, some
of the roles a lay therapist plays in helping the family, the importance of professional supervision and sharing of the lay therapist's
own personal reactions. The discussion includes Helen Alexander,
Dr. Ruth Kempe, and several lay therapists from the NCPTCAN.

521. Leavitt, Jerome E., comp. The Battered Child: Selected
        Readings. Morristown, N.J.: General Learning Corp.,
        1974. 268 p.
        An interdisciplinary textbook consisting of 46 articles on child
abuse includes chapters on: recognition and treatment of battered
children; psychological observations and approaches to child abuse;
the legal aspects of child abuse; sociological and social work perspectives; the medical aspects of child abuse; educators' responsibilities
with regard to child abuse; and preventative suggestions. Each
chapter has an introduction, summary, and study questions.

522. Low View from a Dark Shadow. Motion Picture. B&W
        30 min. $165; Rental $9.50. Catalog No. ES977. Pro-
        duced by WMUS-TV for Public Television Library, 1968.
        Contact: Indiana University, Audio-Visual Center, Bloom-
        ington, Ind. 47401. (812) 337-8087.
        This is a dramatization of the psychological abuse an eight-
year-old boy suffers at the hands of his alcoholic parents. The film
compares the wholesome atmosphere of a good foster home with his
inevitable psychological destruction if he is allowed to return to his
natural mother.

523. Management of the Battered Child Syndrome. Videocassette.
        3/4 inch. color. 18 min. 1972. $25. New York, Net-
        work for Continuing Medical Education.
        The reasons for child abuse are demonstrated in an unrehearsed
conversation with the mother of a patient. Three experts offer some
practical advice on coping with parents once child abuse has been
diagnosed and the underlying problems identified. For physician's
use only. Also available in other video formats.

524. Meckes, R. E. Training Curriculum for Lay Therapists.
        Philadelphia, Pa.: Saint Christopher's Hospital for Chil-
        dren, 1975. 26 p.
        The training curriculum presented for lay therapists at the
Demonstration Center is designed to delineate the roles and responsibilities of lay therapists as well as to develop skills in dealing with
abused children and their families.

525. Mohamoud, J. Training for Strengthening of Parenting Skills.
        Ottawa, Ill.: Illinois Valley Community College, 1975.
        51 p.
        The materials, procedures, and rationale for conducting a 10-
session parent training workshop for abusive or neglectful parents
are presented. Parent evaluations of program effectiveness were
enthusiastic and positive.

526. Mohr, W. H.; Steblein, Jr., J. E. "Mental Health Work-
        shops for Law Enforcement." FBI Law Enforcement Bul-
        letin, 45(1):3-8, 1976.
        This article deals with a three-day (later two-day) training
program at the Niagara County Law Enforcement Academy, Sanborn,

N. Y., for police officers of five different police forces. Among the nine selected topics were family problems and child abuse.

527. Mother-Infant Interaction. Videocassette. 1/2 inch. (sony). B&W. 30 min. 1974. Price: $80; Rental $20. Contact: Mike Williams Associates, P.O. Box 564, Manhattan Beach, Calif. 90266. (213) 545-3512.

A series of first delivery room interactions between mother and child are depicted. A technique is demonstrated for the early identification of not only normal behavior, but that which may indicate potential problems with mother-child interaction. The interactions were taped at the University of Colorado Medical Center. The material is designed for individuals who are involved with helping the abused child and his family.

528. National Center on Child Abuse and Neglect. Child Abuse and Neglect: What the Educator Sees. Color Filmstrip, Tape Cassette, Discussion Guide. Office of Child Development, (DHEW), and distributed by The Council for Exceptional Children. Available directly through CEC, 1920 Association Drive, Reston, Va. 22091. Price $14.50.

This filmstrip is designed for inservice training for teachers and administrators, as well as nurses, social workers, psychologists, counselors, and those involved in law enforcement and correctional programs. It illustrates three main categories of child maltreatment--physical abuse, sexual abuse, and neglect--and the indicators of these forms of abuse by which the observant, concerned educator may identify them.

529. National Conference on Child Abuse: A Summary Report. See entry 1371.

530. Practical Aspects of Treatment Programs--Is the Home Safe? Cassette. AT 1 7/8 IPS. 30 min. 1974. Department of Human Development, College of Human Medicine, Michigan State University, E. Lansing, Mich. 48823.

The various treatment modalities and where they fit into the abnormal rearing cycle abusive parents have experienced are reviewed. The material is designed for individuals who are involved with helping the abused child and his family. A manual is included which presents brief introductory remarks, a self-assessment quiz, a brief discussion about the material covered with references, and a summary of related instructional materials available.

531. The Process of Developing a Diagnosis. Cassette. AT 1 7/8 IPS. 30 min. 1974. Department of Human Development, College of Human Medicine, Michigan State University, E. Lansing, Mich. 48823. (517) 353-4583.

The actual sequence of events important in the diagnosis and management of abuse and neglect cases is considered. A manual is included which presents brief introductory remarks, a self-assessment quiz, a brief discussion about the material covered with references, and a summary of related instructional materials available.

532. Psychiatric Diagnosis. Videocassette. 1/2 inch. (sony). B&W. 20 min. 1974. Mike Williams Associates, 329A 17th Street, Manhattan Beach, Calif. 90266.

A psychiatric interview in a case of child abuse is demonstrated, showing data collection for diagnosis and provision of answers for parents, with particular emphasis on the determination of whether or not patient falls into either psychotic or sociopathic classification and recommendation of the treatment modality or modalities most likely to be effective.

533. "Question-and-Answer Review (Quiz: Child Abuse and Neglect)." Pediatric Annals, 5(3):130-131,135, March 1976.

A series of 12 questions considers various aspects of child abuse and neglect. Specific items deal with reporting procedures, legal penalties, parental rights, management, and therapy. Answers are provided to the multiple choice and yes/no items.

534. "Report from the Education Work Group." T. Webster, Chairman. Clinical Proceedings, 30(2):46-48, 1974.

In the report from the Education Work Group of the National Conference on Child Abuse, the identification of specific groups having a vital role in prevention and treatment of child abuse is discussed. The roles of the general public, special public contacts, legislators, police, judiciary personnel, educators, social service agents, and health professionals are outlined as they relate to the problems of educating the public and each other on steps dealing with child abuse. Emphasis is placed on identifying what information needs to be disseminated in order to address most effectively the multiple problems in identifying, treating, and preventing child abuse.

535. Reward and Punishment. Motion Picture. color. 14 min. $225/Rental $25. Produced by Peter Jordan, 1974. Contact: CRM McGraw-Hill Films, Del Mar, Calif. 92014. (714) 481-8184.

The principles of reward and punishment are outlined by Dr. James Gardner, child psychologist. He discusses the use and abuse of punishment, its positive applications as well as negative effects.

536. Role of the Juvenile Court Judge. Videocassette. 1/2 inch. (sony). B&W. 20 min. 1974. Mike Williams Associates, 329A 17th Street, Manhattan Beach, Calif. 90266.

Excerpts of an interview are presented, focusing on a judge's views concerning child abuse and neglect and on how the courts can positively intervene with the families.

537. Second Chance. Motion Picture. color. 12 min. Rental $18. Contact: Jean Stiman, Division of Child Psychiatry, Children's Memorial Hospital, 2300 Children's Plaza, Chicago, Ill. 60614. (312) 649-4589.

This film portrays the results of emotional abuse on a child admitted to the hospital and follows the child's progress as she responds to tender-loving care.

538. Slack, Patricia. "Planning Training for Coping with Non-Accidental Injury." Nursing Times, 72(40):1561-1563, October 7, 1976.

Area Review Committees, to monitor training taking place for all those professionals and staff who work with children, were set up throughout the country and they are tackling the problem of training in a variety of ways in coping with non-accidental injury to children. Their aims are to prevent, to identify, to take positive action, and to follow up. Training program needs fall into three groups: single disciplinary training, self-teaching aids, and inter-disciplinary training.

539. Summary of an Instructional Program on Child Abuse and Neglect for Workers in this Field. Cassette. AT 1 7/8 IPS. 30 min. 1974. Department of Human Development, College of Human Medicine, Michigan State University, E. Lansing, Mich. 48823.

A six-part instructional program on audio-cassettes for individuals who are involved with helping the abused child and his family is summarized. The series examines the environmental factors contributory to child abuse and neglect, sample diagnosis and diagnostic procedures for use with target families, practical aspects of treatment programs, and developing community programs. The summary is accompanied by a manual.

540. Ten Bensel, Robert W. The Battered Child Syndrome. 100 colored slides (film) 2" x 2" (in box). (Medcom famous teachings in modern medicine.) Includes "Pana-vue 3" hand viewer and descriptive text. New York, 1971.

541. This Child Is Rated X. Motion Picture. color. 52 min. $550; Rental $40. Produced by NBC-TV, 1971. Contact: Films, Inc., 1144 Wilmette Ave., Wilmette, Ill. 60091. (312) 256-6600.

This is a study of the abused child's rights and the inequities of juvenile justice in four states.

542. "Training Unit on Child Abuse Prevention Opens." Pediatric News, 7(3):17, March 1973.

The National Training Center for the Prevention and Treatment of Child Abuse established by the University of Colorado School of Medicine is described. Diagnostic and treatment facilities are available and courses are offered to teach lawyers, social workers, judges and health professionals how to deal with the problem of child abuse.

543. War of the Eggs. Motion Picture. color and B&W. 27 min. $325 and $160; Rental $18.95 and $12.95. 1971. Contact: Paulist Productions, P.O. Box 1057, Pacific Palisades, Calif. 90272. (213) 454-0688.

Written by Michael Crichton and starring Elizabeth Ashley and Bill Bixby, this film is a sensitive dramatization of the child battering syndrome, focusing on the husband-wife relationship.

544. Whiting, Leila. "Defining Emotional Neglect." Children To-
        day, 5(1):2-5, January 1976.
The definition of emotional neglect was considered in a one-day workshop conducted in Montgomery County, Maryland, to sensitize the community to the problems of child abuse and neglect. The two objectives of the workshop were to provide those working with emotionally neglected children an opportunity to learn some new skills and to help participants develop new insights into the meaning of emotional neglect.

545. Women of Valor: Family Aids to Battering Parents Training
        Package. Motion Picture. color. 31 min. $285; Rental
        $35. Produced by H. Lee Pratt, 1973. Contact: Trikon
        Productions, P. O. Box 21, La Jolla, Calif. 92038. (714)
        459-5233.
A dramatization, this film follows a child through the hospital, custody, and juvenile court system. With a manual and slides, the film shows how volunteer supervision of the home allows the child to return.

546. World of Abnormal Rearing. Cassette. 30 min. AT 1 7/8
        IPS. 30 min. 1974. Department of Human Development,
        College of Human Medicine, Michigan State University,
        East Lansing, Mich. 48823.
An overview of the various aspects of the environment and family history which often produce child abuse and neglect is presented. A manual is included.

ETIOLOGY (STUDIES OF CAUSES)

547.   Allen, Ann Frances.   "Maltreatment Syndrome in Children."
            The Canadian Nurse, 62:40-42, April 1966.
        Many aspects concerning the maltreatment syndrome in chil-
dren are discussed, including three distinct groups in child trauma:
those resulting from a specific cause and known to be accidental;
those that occur in an unprotected environment, where parents are
indirectly to blame; and those caused by direct abuse from parents,
guardians, or siblings.   Allen also discusses ways of determining if
the injury was the result of accident or abuse.

548.   Baden, M. M.   "Pathology of the Addictive States."   In:
            Richter, R. W. (Editor).   Medical Aspects of Drug Abuse.
            Hagerstown, Md.: Harper and Rcw, p. 189-211, 1975.
        There is a growing awareness of a significant incidence of
battered, neglected, and abused children born to addicted mothers.
Physicians are implored to consider carefully the possibility of child
abuse in cases evidencing frequent or multiple injuries.   An addict
mother may intentionally injure a child or may not know how to care
properly for a child.

549.   Baher, Edwina; Hyman, Clare; Jones, Carolyn, et al.   At
            Risk: An Account of the Work of the Battered Child Re-
            search Department, NSPCC.   See entry 2204.

550.   "Battered Babies."   British Medical Journal, 3:667-668, Sep-
            tember 20, 1969.
        Findings of this study indicate that parents of battered babies
generally appear to have long-standing emotional problems and are
commonly between 20 and 30 years old.   Many of the fathers had
criminal records and were unemployed at the time of the incident.
The battered children were all very young, and over half of them
were under a year old.   There was a high risk to subsequent children in families where the first born was battered.

551.   "The Battered Child."   Newsweek, 71:68, June 3, 1968.
        Growing concern over the battered child syndrome is detailed.
Suggestions are offered as to what kind of parents assault their children.   Parents of abused children were themselves abused as children.   Battered children, says Newsweek, should be separated from
their parents and provided with good medical care.

552. "Battering Parent: Battered Child Syndrome." Time, 94:77+,
November 7, 1969.
    One characteristic all battering parents appear to have is that
they themselves had been battered, either physically or emotionally.
All had experienced a sense of intense, pervasive, continuous demand
from their parents, and a sense of constant parental criticism.
Over-disciplined and deprived of parental love in their infancy, they
look to their own children for what they missed.   Legal action simply reinforces a parent's conviction that he or she is always being
disregarded, attacked, and commanded to do better.   Focusing on
parents and overcoming feelings of rejection has reduced cases.

553. Beck, Mildred B.   "The Destiny of the Unwanted Child: The
Issue of Compulsory Pregnancy." In: E. Reiterman, ed.,
Abortion and the Unwanted Child.   New York: Springer
Publishing Co., Inc., p. 59-71.
    The unwanted child is characterized as one who has biological
parents only, the parents do not care for him and on occasion fail
to take him home from the hospital; he is abandoned psychologically
and frequently physically; he is neglected or abused, sometimes by
malnutrition, as well as psychologically.   To lay to rest the adage
that unwanted pregancies become wanted children after birth, Beck
observes that more than 300,000 American children are daily in
foster care.

554. Bell, Gwyneth.   "Parents Who Abuse Their Children."
Canadian Psychiatric Association Journal, 18(3):223-228,
June 1973.
    The heart of the problem of child abuse appears to be a fail-
ure of the parents to develop a normal nurturing relationship with
their children, either because they lacked proper parental models
themselves, or because of a disruption in the neonatal relationship
between mother and child.   Suggestions for management, prevention
and treatment are given.

555. Belson, Abby A.   "Help Us Before We Hurt Our Child Again."
Family Health, 7:26-31, June 1975.
    Factors prominent in the etiology of child abuse and potential
treatment of this problem are reviewed.

556. Bendix, Selina.   "Drug Modification of Behavior: A Form of
Chemical Violence Against Children." Journal of Clinical
Child Psychology, 2(3):17-19, Fall 1973.
    The use of amphetamines for behavior modification in children
raises many questions and problems.   Side effects are numerous
and may be severe in children and include physiological drug dependence.   All too often the child's real problem goes unnoticed as the
symptoms are masked by the amphetamines.

557. Bishop, Frank I.   "Children at Risk." Medical Journal of
Australia, 1:623-628, March 20, 1971.
    Bishop believes that physical and emotional abuse of children
results from a disturbance of the parent-child relationship and

interaction, and that the real parental motivating factors are completely outside the parents' conscious awareness. Babies at risk can be found in the following categories: illegitimate children, premature babies, congenital malformed infants, twin pregnancies complicated by maternal illness, babies conceived during depressive illness of the mothers, frequent pregnancies with excessive workload, and infants born to mothers in psychotic states.

558. _____. "Perception, Memory and Pathological Identification as Precipitating Factors in Parental Attacks on Children." Medical Journal of Australia, 2(7):243-245, August 16, 1975.
Examined are the origins and the importance of pathological identification of the parents of the child who was maltreated. The understanding of these identifications suggests methods of effective preventive action without recourse to the undesirable practice of removing the child from the home, other than in exceptional circumstances.

559. Blaine, Graham B., Jr. "Child Abuse." In: Are Parents Bad for Children? New York: Coward, McCann & Geoghegan, 1973 (p. 90-95).
This short chapter examines some of the causes of child abuse.

560. Branigan, Eileen, et al. An Exploratory Study of the Neglected-Battered Child Syndrome. Dissertation, Boston College of Social Work, 1964.

561. Breig, Joe. "Radiography of a Battered Child: Physical Punishment of Children." Ave Maria, 99:24, February 8, 1964.
Breig interprets the Scriptural verse--"He who spares the rod hates his son." To him, the word "rod" stands for parental encouragement, gentle goading and guidance, remonstrance, exhortation, leadership--everything that love moves a parent to do for a beloved son or daughter.

562. Brosseau, B. E. "Battered Child and Unwanted Pregnancy." (Letter). Canadian Medical Association Journal, 112:1039, May 3, 1975.
In reply to an earlier exchange between investigators who concluded that unwanted pregnancy often resulted in child abuse, Brosseau offers the results of conflicting research which indicates that 90 percent of the abused children's parents stated that they had wanted the pregnancy.

563. Bryant, Harold D.; Billingsley, Andrew; Kerry, George A., et al. "Physical Abuse of Children--An Agency Study." Child Welfare, 42:125-130, March 1963.
This paper reports some of the findings of a study of physical abuse conducted by the Massachusetts Society for the Prevention of Cruelty to Children. Who does the referring, in what families does

abuse occur and why, what are the characteristics of the abusing
adults, and who are the children who are abused.

564. Bylinsky, G. "New Clues to the Causes of Violence."
     Fortune, 87:134-142,146, January 1973.
     A discussion of social and physical causes of violent behavior
includes a comparison between mother-deprived rhesus monkeys and
abusive parents. Monkeys who were reared with mother surrogates
failed to develop maternal affection and seemed indifferent to their
own children. Like abusive parents, these monkeys frequently attacked and sometimes killed their infants.

565. Caffey, John; Silverman, Frederic N.; Kempe, C. Henry;
     et al. "Child Battery: Seek and Save." Medical World
     News, 12(22):21-25, 28, 32-33, 1972.
     Child battering is discussed in terms of family dynamics, of
how a case can be recognized and what the attending physician can
do to forestall its repetition. Generally, child abuse centers on one
particular child in a family, and while unwanted children are more
likely to be battered, many battered children are desperately wanted.
There are three key elements involved in child battering: battering
parents likely had poor mothering; young child does not give them
the love they never had; and batterer is involved in a crisis which
precipitated abuse. Society has overstressed the fact that women
must have children for fulfillment.

566. Carloni, G.; Nobili, D. "Il Figlicidio" [Infanticide]. Rivista
     Sperimentale di Freniatria e Medicina Legale delle Aliena-
     zioni Mentali, 46(4):1095-1131, 1972.
     The occurrence of and reasons for infanticide are discussed.
Motives for infanticide include brutality, revenge on a spouse, jeal-
ousy, mental illness, and killing for social reasons to preserve
honor. The means are often the same: strangulation, beating to
death, defenestration or poisoning.

567. Carter, Jan, ed. The Maltreated Child. See entry 750.

568. Chase, Naomi Feigelson. A Child Is Being Beaten: Violence
     Against Children, An American Tragedy. New York: Holt,
     Rinehart and Winston, 1975. 225 p.
     The problem of child abuse and neglect is surveyed by utilizing
numerous case reports and personal interviews. The problem is reviewed historically, and cultural norms which have made children
second class citizens are critically examined. The inadequacies of
the helping services in the U.S. are explored from the family courts
to the various social service agencies and institutions. The higher
incidence of child abuse among poor and minority groups is only a
reflection of social inequality in the U.S. society and the wide acceptance of physical discipline of children. The family as a source
of nurturance for children is in peril due to the mobility of the population, the emphasis on individualism, and the value placed on success. Some suggestions to remedy these problems are included.

569. _____. A Child Is Being Beaten. "Review." New Republic, 173:28-30, November 22, 1975, by T. J. Cottle.
A Child Is Being Beaten is not just a book which studies child abuse, but an historical account of the effects of our society on family life and human growth. Chase explains that the real causes of child abuse are poverty, unemployment, lack of housing and health care, and torn families. She details a tragic reality perpetuated by our way of life.

570. Chesser, Eustace. Cruelty to Children. London: V. Gollancz, 1951; New York: Philosophical Library, 1952. 159 p.
The first two parts of this book deal mainly with the problem of cruelty from the standpoint of overburdened motherhood, broken homes, rejection of mother instinct, the lack of cultural pursuits in leisure and recreation, and the neuroses of civilization. The last part deals with individual responsibility which is rarely taught in schools and is limited by the shortcomings of society and the question of punishment, prevention and treatment.

571. "Child Abuse and Injury." Military Medicine, 130:747-762, August 1965.

572. "Child Abuse: Family Social Disease." (Editorial). Canada's Mental Health, 21(6):16-17, November-December 1973.
This is a discussion of the causes and treatment of the child abuse syndrome. The basic cause of the syndrome is a mothering deficiency in one or both parents. Abused children are used for parents' emotional gratification without regard to their needs; they grow up with the same emotional failures and tend to treat their children as they were treated.

573. Clark, Karen N. Knowledge of Child Development and Behavior Interaction Patterns of Mothers Who Abuse Their Children. Ph.D. 1975. Wayne State University, Detroit, Mich. 122 p. Available from University Microfilms, Order No. 76-10, 931.
The primary purpose of this research was to investigate variables that contributed to the problem of child abuse. Inadequate knowledge of modal age behavior was hypothesized as one variable. The nature and quality of the mother-child dyadic interaction delineated a cluster of other variables. Seven indices were used to analyze the interactive responses. A profile of self-identified child abusers was identified as distinguishable from non-abusers. Characteristics that would be amenable to modification through educational programs were discussed.

574. Cohen, M. I. Neglect and Abuse of Children in the Middle Class. Master's Project. Simmons College, Boston, Mass., May 1971. 120 p.
A survey of social workers in Child Protective Services of Massachusetts was performed to determine etiological factors of child abuse and neglect in middle class families. The survey

revealed that less than 13 percent of the middle class families carried by the respondents were involved in child abuse and neglect. Statistical data concerning nine variables are analyzed.

575. Coigney, Virginia. Children Are People Too: How We Fail Our Children and How We Can Love Them. New York: William Morrow, 1975. 228 p.

The way adults feel about children and the way they raise children are examined. Reasons for the growing hostility toward the young are surveyed, noting that children in industrialized societies are not longer considered as assets but rather as liabilities. The scope and impact of child abuse and neglect are explored in depth, citing efforts in identification and treatment. Discussions are also included on laws relating to children, labeling and misguided treatment in schools, sexual repression of youth, public services for children, the effect of advertising on children, family planning, innovative thoughts on children and their relations with adults. The United Nations Declaration of the Rights of the Child and the U.S. Bill of Rights are provided as appendices.

576. Cole, Larry. Our Children's Keepers: Inside America's Kid Prisons. New York: Grossman, 1972. 152 p.

Training schools, youth guidance centers, and juvenile centers are examined and found to be chaotic, overcrowded prisons. Common examples are cited of the maltreatment of children who often are merely dependent and not delinquent, many of whom were turned over to the state because their parents mistreated them. Situations in New York, Denver, Louisiana, and San Francisco are described, including instances of beating, improper medical care, solitary confinement, barbed wire, and babies in cages. Preliminary plan for alternative families are offered.

577. Coppolillo, H. P. "Drug Impediments to Mothering Behavior." Addictive Diseases, 2(1-2):201-208, 1975.

578. Court, Joan. "Battering Parents." Social Work, 26(1):20-24, 1969.

The threshold of aggression in predisposed parents may be lowered by such things as lack of sleep occasioned by a crying baby. There appears to be a lack of normal verbal and physical interchange in the relationship between mother and child. Since social workers are generally the persons involved in child abuse cases, they are encouraged to develop a working relationship with the abusive parent and to convey their concern for the suffering and deprivation of the parents.

579. Dalhousie University. School of Law. Child Abuse in Nova Scotia. See entry 2217.

580. Dalton, Katherine. "Children's Hospital Admissions and Mothers' Menstruation." British Medical Journal, 2:27-28, April 4, 1970.

The results of interviewing 100 mothers indicate positive

relationship between mothers' menstruation and children's admission
to hospitals for accident or illness because of mothers' paramenstrual stress.

581. _____. "Paramenstrual Baby Battering." (Letter). British
       Medical Journal, 2(5965):279, May 3, 1975.
   According to Dalton, child battering is mainly caused by premenstrual tension. Mothers who have strong maternal urges will,
in a sudden fit of premenstrual irritability, lose control and injure
their much loved offspring. Premenstrual tension and irritability
are valid causes of some child abuse battering.

582. Dine, Mark S. "Slaughter of the Innocents." (Letter).
       Journal of the American Medical Association, 223:81-82,
       January 1, 1973.
   Dine reports on two cases of child abuse. In each case, the
mother was out of the baby's room when a sibling did the abusing.
The parents' responsibility for the safety of their infant under any
circumstances remains paramount.

583. Draft Report of Phase I of the Family Development Study.
       See entry 61.

584. Drogendijk, A. C., Sr. [What Kind of Parents Are Those
       Who Abuse Their Children?] Nederlands Tijdschrift voor
       Geneeskunde, 115:224-226, February 6, 1971. (Dutch)

585. Earl, Howard G. "10,000 Children Battered and Starved.
       Hundreds Die: Some Parents Admit Guilt--Intensive Two-
       Year Study of Battered and Maltreated Children Reveals
       the True Story Behind Abused Youngsters." Today's
       Health, 43:24-31, September 1965.
   Detailed are the horrid results of child abuse. An interview
with supervising probation officer at the San Francisco juvenile court
discusses the kind of children that are battered, the kind of parent
that batters, and specific incidents. Earl then explains legal implications of abuse, citing California's special law on child abuse.

586. Elmer, Elizabeth. "Child Abuse: The Family's Cry for Help."
       Journal of Psychiatric Nursing and Mental Health Services,
       5:332+, July-August 1967.
   Child abuse is usually the result of accumulated stresses on
the family, often associated with the lower socioeconomic classes.
Among the factors involved in the family stress is the birth of
several children close together. Prematurity also seems to be a
significant factor. Abusing families usually lack emotional support.
The community, medical people, and the extended family must help
the family by making themselves available when needed.

587. _____. "Failure to Thrive, Role of the Mother." Pediat-
       rics, 717, April 1960.
   Described are the effects of a mother's lack of nurturing on
the growth and development rate of infants. The predominant lack

of the father in the home reduces support for the mother. Five
case histories.

588. Evans, Philip. "Infanticide." Proceedings of the Royal So-
         ciety of Medicine, 61:1296-1298, December 12, 1968.
      After presenting a brief history of the phenomenon of infan-
ticide, Evans discusses various causes of infant killing: namely,
religion, culling, family planning, shame, commerce, anger, and
mental illness, including puerperal psychoses.

589. Everts-Goddard, J. E. "Kindermishandeling" [Child Abuse].
         Proces, 52(2):39-43, 1973.
      Parents who abuse their children are characterized.

590. _____. "Kindermishandeling: Ouders en Situaties" [Mal-
         treatment of Children: Parents and Situations]. Sjow,
         3(16):358-360, 1975.

591. _____; Sint-Van Den Heuvel, M. K. "Kindermishandeling
         Kent Veel Oorzaken" [Child Abuse Has Many Causes].
         Sjow, 3(8):163-165, 1975.
      Generally, children who demand extra attention run a graver
risk of being maltreated than normal, healthy children who give
their parents satisfaction.

592. Fergusson, David M. The Correlates of Severe Child Abuse,
         in Collaboration with G. Dickinson. Wellington, N. Z.:
         Department of Social Welfare, Research Division, 1973.
         19 p. (Technical Research Report no. 1)

593. _____. Factors Associated with the Serious Ill-Treatment
         of Children, in collaboration with David P. O'Neill. Wel-
         lington, N. Z.: Department of Social Welfare, Research
         Division, 1973. 21 p. (General Research Report, no. 1)

594. _____; Fleming, Joan; O'Neill, David P. Child Abuse in
         New Zealand. Wellington, N. Z.: Department of Social
         Welfare, Research Division, 1972. 342 p.
      Some of the results of a New Zealand national survey designed
to provide information on the characteristics of incidents of child
abuse, the nature of the family situation in which abuse took place,
and the characteristics of the children and adults involved in these
incidents are reported. The study sample included all cases of
alleged or suspected child abuse that came to the attention of the
Child Welfare Division during the survey year, 1967. The survey
form, illustrative case histories, and raw data are appended.

595. Ferrier, P. E. "Das Kind als Opfer von Misshandlungen und
         Vernachlässigung" [The Child as Victim of Abuse and Ne-
         glect]. Pro Juventute, 57(7):205-207, 1976.
      The core of the problem lies in a poor parent-child relation-
ship. The author explains which factors increase a child's risk of
falling victim to abuse. He maintains that a medical practitioner

should act as coordinator in family counseling and in supervision of these children. (Journal Summary.)

596. Fisher, Gary; McGrath, Bob. The Abusers. Milford, Mich.:
Mott Media, 1975. Paperback. 213 p.
        This is an incredible account of the sordid life of Gary Fisher, a drug addict, who was emotionally deprived and abused as a child by alcoholic parents. Grasping many times for a straw to pull himself out of the mire, he eventually became fully rehabilitated. He is now raising, besides a son of his own, two adopted children who had been severely abused. The book offers a list of additional recommended reading, ways to avoid child abuse, and how to counsel in child abuse cases.

597. Fontana, Vincent J. "Child Abuse in Megalopolis." New York State Journal of Medicine, 76:1799-1802, October 1976.
        According to Fontana, the dramatic increase in child abuse and neglect is attributed in part to fiscal crisis, cutbacks in necessary preventive and treatment programs, and other family-oriented intervention services for those in need, unemployment, and the consequential added stresses in an already stressful environment.

598. _____. Child Abuse in the Name of Discipline. New York: New York Foundling Hospital Center for Parent and Child Development, 1976. 6 p. Available from EDRS: MF-$0.83; HC-$1.67, Plus Postage.
        Fontana discusses the connection between corporal punishment and child abuse; analyzes the difference between discipline and abuse; and asserts that there are sociological, psychological, and biological characteristics typical of promoters of corporal punishment.

599. _____. Somewhere a Child Is Crying: Maltreatment-- Causes and Prevention. New York: American Library, 1976. (A Mentor Book in paperback; an authorized reprint of a hardcover edition published by Macmillan Publishing Co., 1973.) 264 p.
        Some of the problems involved in reporting, diagnosing, punishing, and preventing child abuse are outlined. The battered child, sexual abuses, and psychological neglect are detailed. The extent of the battered child syndrome has been minimized in the eyes of the public. Some of the statistical and human interest findings of the Mayor of New York City's Task Force on Child Abuse and Neglect are itemized. The legal rights of children are discussed. Most states do not have a good social welfare system to protect children once a problem family is identified. The social costs of failing to provide care for abused children are emphasized.

600. _____. "Which Parents Abuse Children?" Medical Insight, 3:16+, October 1971.
        Linking the battered child syndrome with the spirit of violence in society, Fontana describes the traits and characteristics of

abusing parents. He also summarizes the signs and symptoms of the maltreatment syndrome.

601. _____. "Why Do People Beat Up Their Kids?" U.S. Catholic, 28-32, March 1974.
Fontana describes child abuse as a medical-social disease of epidemic proportions. He then describes the various causes of maltreatment, characteristics of abusing parents, signs of child abuse, and efforts to protect the abused child.

602. Friedrich, William N.; Boriskin, Jerry A. "Ill-Health and Child Abuse." (Letter). Lancet, 1(7960):649-650, March 20, 1976.
In analyzing 424 cases of physical child abuse reported to the Harris County child welfare office in Houston, Texas, during the 17-week period ended mid-April, 1975, the authors found some support for Pasamanick's suggestion that children with a number of childhood disorders can precipitate parental distress and result in abuse. The findings are presented.

603. Gallagher, Carol. "Was Cinderella an Abused Child: A Discussion of Six Fiction Books for Elementary and Junior High School Children Which Contain Child Abuse." Catholic Library World, 48:73-75, September 1976.
This is a discussion of six fiction books for elementary and junior high school children which contain child abuse. The books, written within the last ten years, are examined in view of their long-range effects on the young reader and the climate of fostering child abuse they may create. The author questions too steady a diet of books like these without adult-directed programs of discussion. Children should feel hopeful--that something can be done if things are really bad.

604. Gibbens, T. C. N. "Violence in the Family." Medico-Legal Journal, 43(3):76-88, 1975.
The problem of violence in the family is a complex problem involving overlap between many factors. It is difficult to distinguish between causal factors in those cases serious enough to reach the courts and those which are not. The characteristics of abusive parents and their children are explored at length.

605. Gibson, J. "Parental Abuse of Children. Part I: An Attempt to Identify Some Characteristics More Commonly Found. Part II: Jane, Mark and Baby Timothy." Social Work Today, 5(2):51-54 and 5(3):71-75, 1974.
Part I draws together current thought and writing on aspects of the problem: categories of maltreatment of children; background and personality of child battering parents; types of children at risk; warning signs. Part II describes a case which illustrates several factors in child maltreatment identified in Part I.

606. Gil, David G. "Legally Reported Child Abuse: A Nationwide

Survey." (p. 135-158). In: Social Work Practice, 1968.
New York: Columbia University Press, 1969.
Reported are characteristics of abused children and their
families, perpetrator types and injuries and how inflicted.

607. _____. "Unraveling Child Abuse." American Journal of
Orthopsychiatry, 45(3):346-356, April 1975.
This paper attempts to clarify the dynamics of child abuse,
and to suggest approaches to primary prevention. Child abuse is
redefined, within egalitarian value premises, as inflicted gaps in
children's circumstances that prevent actualization of inherent potential. Levels of manifestation and causal dimensions of child abuse
are identified, and their multiple interactions are traced. Primary
prevention is shown to be essentially a political, rather than a
purely technical or professional, issue. (Journal Abstract.)

608. Gillespie, R. W. "The Battered Child Syndrome: Thermal
and Caustic Manifestations." Journal of Trauma, 5:523-
534, July 1965.
The characteristic pattern of repeated injury has been observed in this study as well as the other manifestations of the battered child syndrome. Society's responsibility to the child extends
beyond the provision of care of these injuries. These children de-
serve protection from further abuse.

609. Goode, W. J. "Force and Violence in the Family." Journal
of Marriage and the Family, 33(4):637-648, November 1971.
Goode posits three conditions when violence in the family may
occur: when family structures and values are violated; during the
socialization of children; when illegitimate force is used vis-a-vis
the child in the sense that parental demands are such that the child
cannot fulfill them. In the last case child abuse is the result.

610. Gottlieb, David, ed. Children's Liberation. Englewood
Cliffs, N.J.: Prentice-Hall, 1973. (Paper). 181 p.
The articles in this book chronicle the debilitating social and
educational environments, the lack of legal and moral rights, the
institutional discrimination, and other means by which children are
victimized. The reasons for this discrimination are isolated and
recommendations are made which point the way towards a more
humane society.

611. Green, Arthur H. "The Child Abuse Syndrome and the Treatment of Abusing Parents." In: Pasternak, S. A., ed.
Violence and Victims. Holliswood, N.Y.: Spectrum Publications, Inc., p. 169-180, 1975.
The roles and motivations of the participants in child abuse
are explored within the context of the family and its immediate environment, and a logical treatment program is developed for abuse-
prone parents from a body of clinical observations and research
data gathered from a large number of abused children and their
mothers. Case reports illustrate the personality characteristics of
abuse-prone parents, the characteristics of the child which contribute

to his abuse and treatment as a scapegoat, and the role of current environmental stress. Some treatment goals for parents are provided. A multiservice approach is required to attain these goals.

612. Grislain, J. R.; Mainard, R.; DeBerranjer, P.; et al. "Sévice. Problèmes legales et sociales" [Child Abuse. Social and Legal Problems]. Annales de Pediatrie, 15: 440-448, June-July 1968.

Despite the unquestionable role of psychological factors and the circumstances in the home and neighborhood, alcoholism remains the principal cause of child abuse in the Western world. Because of interaction between alcoholism and poverty, poor housing, family circumstances, an occupation which exposes the person to alcoholic beverages, emotional problems, and (particularly among women) psychosis or mental deficiency, it is difficult to isolate any single factor, but the control of alcoholism would be a valuable first step in the prevention of child abuse.

613. Guttmacher, Alan F. "Unwanted Pregnancy: A Challenge to Mental Health." Mental Hygiene, 51:512-516, October 1967.

Guttmacher asks those attending the annual dinner of the New York Clinic for Mental Health to help reduce the incidence of unplanned conceptions and to support the efforts of Planned Parenthood. An unwanted pregnancy may result in only partial adjustment; legal or, far more commonly, illegal abortion; the child being rejected or resented after its birth; in extreme cases, being physically abused; or it being abandoned. Man's irresponsible sexuality and unchecked reproduction contribute to huge, crushing, overwhelming forces.

614. Hanson, Ruth; Smith, Selwyn M. "I.Q. of Parents of Battered Babies." (Letter). British Medical Journal, 1:455, March 9, 1974.

It is commonly assumed that parents who batter their children have a low intelligence quotient. While it has been argued that this is not so, the authors feel low I.Q. is one of many abnormal parental attributes. They discuss the type of tests they used in identifying this factor, the W.A.I.S., and why they came to their conclusion.

615. "Hard Times for Kids, Too: Child Abuse as a Consequence of Economic Strain." Time, 105:88, March 17, 1975.

Economic strain is an increasing important factor in the increase in child abuse cases. Better methods of reporting also cause figures to go up. Fontana, head of N.Y. Task Force on Child Abuse, attributes the increase to the stresses and strains that our society is suffering today--the frustrations, the poor quality of life, the increase in drug addiction and alcoholism, and unemployment. People who lose their jobs often suffer loss of self esteem and experience unfocused rage. No one knows why one person takes out his frustrations on children and another does not. To some extent violence runs in families.

616. Harris, Susan B., ed. Child Abuse: Present and Future. Chicago: National Committee for Prevention of Child Abuse, 1975. 273 p.
    A compilation of ideas and information presented during the 1974 National Symposium, Child Abuse: Present and Future, sponsored by the National Committee for Prevention of Child Abuse and the Illinois Department of Children and Family Services, including panel discussions on causes of child abuse; profiles of abusers; situations that encourage abuse; child abuse research; interdisciplinary coordination; nonprofessional support; an outreach supportive service project; and views of the future.

617. Helfer, Ray E. Child Abuse and Neglect: The Family and the Community, edited by Ray E. Helfer and C. Henry Kempe; preface by Walter F. Mondale. Cambridge, Mass.: Ballinger Pub. Co., 1976. 438 p.
    The major purpose of this volume is to help the thousands of individuals now working in the field of child abuse and neglect to implement effective, efficient, and coordinated programs of family assessment, treatment, and learning, both in this country and abroad. It is divided into six sections: Dysfunction in Family Interaction; Assessing Family Pathology; Family Oriented Therapy; The Community; The Family and the Law; Early Recognition and Prevention of Potential Problems with Family Interaction.

618. _____. "The Etiology of Child Abuse." Pediatrics, 51(4):777-779, April 1973.
    In the Symposium on Child Abuse held in 1971, the factors contributing to child abuse were discussed, stressing that three components usually occur in some type of sequence and are almost always seen in one or both parents: the potential for abuse; a very special kind of child; and a crisis or series of crises. A crisis may precipitate the abuse where the other components are present. Solving the crisis alone is not enough.

619. Hindman, Margaret. "Children of Alcoholic Parents." Alcohol Health and Research World, Winter:2-6, 1975-1976.
    Among the unseen casualties of alcoholism are the children of alcoholic parents. Such children are subject to a high risk of developing alcoholism in their adult years, to an alarmingly high incidence of emotional and behavioral disorders, and to child abuse and neglect. In some areas, studies of child abuse and neglect implicate alcoholism in as many as 90 percent of reported cases, reflecting the frequent violence within families of alcoholic persons.

620. Hyman, Clare A. "I.Q. of Parents of Battered Babies." (Letter). British Medical Journal, 4:739, December 22, 1973.
    In discussing the Smith study concerning I.Q. of parents of battered babies, Hyman takes an opposing viewpoint regarding the outcome of the study. She contends that it is not simple stupidity which explains a parent's behavior as the W.A.I.S. Test results indicated. She believes more causes should have been examined and a

more reliable test used to its fullest extent, not just half the findings of one test.

621. "In a Nation of Boredom." (Editorial). Medicine, Science and the Law, 16(1):1, January 1976.
This editorial examines an underlying cause of child abuse--the change in domestic life. Non-accidental violence to children is seldom seen in certain races and religions, e.g., in Jewish families the father is the head of the family and the mother is domestic head and there is a strict maintenance of the family unit, together with constant contact with grandparents.

622. Ireland, W. H. "The Intricacies of Violence Against Children in American Society." Clinical Pediatrics, 10:557-558, 1971.
A brief recap of some of the significant findings of a nation-wide survey. Discusses incidence, characteristics of abusers and the conditions under which abuse takes place.

623. James, Howard. The Little Victims: How America Treats Its Children. New York: David McKay Co., 1975. 374 p.
This book is an in-depth account of child abuse in all of its various aspects by a humanitarian, roundly knowledgeable, and well-experienced in the total world of children. It is a strong appeal to those who are willing to read and to learn. James presents a historical account of children used as chattel, the difficult lot of the deviant (physically handicapped), and those institutionalized. He lays bare the ills of the American mating system; the family system; and the educational, welfare, mental, and mercantile systems. The last section pertains to seeking solutions, and the author lists 67 ways in which the individual can help.

624. Jordan, Bill. Poor Parents: Social Policy & the Cycle of Deprivation. London: Routledge & Kegan, 1974. 200 p.

625. Juhasz, Anne McCreary. "To Have or Not to Have--Children? That Is the Question." Journal of School Health, 43:632-635, December 1973.
Juhasz contends that child abuse, among other problems, is one of the consequences of having unwanted children. Therefore, one of the most important decisions any female could make is to have only "wanted" children.

626. Justice, Blair; Justice, Rita. The Abusing Family. See entry 1334.

627. Kempe, C. Henry; Silverman, F. N.; Steele, Brandt F., et al. "The Battered-Child Syndrome." Journal of the American Medical Association, 181:17-24, July 7, 1962.
Beating of children occurs among people with good education and stable financial and social backgrounds, as well as among those with a psychopathic personality or of borderline socioeconomic status. From the little available data, it would appear there is a

defect in character structure which allows aggressive impulses to
be expressed too freely. Other aspects of the etiology of child
abuse are discussed.

628. Kline, Donald; Christiansen, James. Educational and Psycho-
      logical Problems of Abused Children. Final Report. See
      entry 2310.

629. Komisaruk, R. "Clinical Evaluation of Child Abuse-Scarred
      Families: A Preliminary Report." Juvenile Court Judges
      Journal, 17(2):66-70, Summer 1966.
A study of the child abuse problem consists of data gathered
from interviews of parents involved in 65 cases referred to the
Wayne County Juvenile Court in Detroit over a 4-year period.

630. Lascari, Andre D. "The Abused Child." Journal of the Iowa
      Medical Society, 62:229-232, May 1972.
In this study of abusive parents, it was found that most of the
parents had been abused as children. Prosecution of the parents,
it is argued, would be counterproductive and is not recommended.

631. Linklater, John. "Baby-Bashing." Spectator, 233:174-175,
      August 10, 1974.
Linklater questions some of the reasons given for baby-
bashing. He believes it can best be explained by considering the
nature of man as an evolutionary animal. It seems extraordinary,
he says, that it should now need careful research to establish what
has for so long been widely known by farmers, zoologists and by
most schoolboys who breed pet rats. Society in its collective adolescence is attempting to defy the archetype.

632. Lynch, Margaret A. "Ill-Health and Child Abuse." Lancet,
      2(7929):317-319, August 16, 1975.
Experience in working with families in which child abuse has
occurred suggests that bonding failure is related in part to the
pregnancy, perinatal experience, and early ill health of the abused
proband and parents. Treatment during these periods may help in
the prevention of child abuse.

633. Lystad, Mary Hanemann. "Violence at Home: A Review of
      the Literature." American Journal of Orthopsychiatry,
      45:328-345, April 1975.
Studies on family violence have analyzed the phenomenon from
psychological, social, and cultural perspectives. A review of the
literature shows that the available evidence is not contradictory,
leading to the conclusion that a comprehensive theory of violence at
home must take into account factors at these several levels, placing
individual functioning within the social group and within the culture
norms by which the group operates. A theory of violence at home,
and suggestions for further research, are offered. (Journal Summary.)

634. Macías, Raymundo; Chagoya, Leopoldo. "Formas de Agresion

al Niño en la Familia" [Forms of Child Abuse in the
Family]. Gaceta Medica de Mexico, 109(4):235-244, April
1975.

635. Maden, Marc F. Significant Factors in Child Abuse: Review
of the Literature: Prepared for the University of Oregon
Health Sciences Center, School of Medicine, Department
of Psychiatry. Boulder, Colo.: Resources Development
Internship Program, Western Interstate Commission for
Higher Education, 1974. 60 p.

636. Martin, Harold P., ed. The Abused Child: A Multidisciplinary Approach to Developmental Issues and Treatment.
See entry 1355.

637. Nagi, Saad Z. Child Maltreatment in the United States: A
Cry for Help and Organizational Response. See entry
2242.

638. Nau, Elisabeth, et al. "Kaspar-Hauser-Syndrom" [The Kaspar-
Hauser Syndrome]. Munchener Medizinische Wochenschrift,
108:929-931, April 29, 1966.
By the example of a "Kaspar-Hauser Syndrome," the authors
discuss its multiple interrelated pathogenesis, the joint action of
heredity-dispositional, cerebro-organic, and environmental factors.
The significance of a clarification of the polyetiological determination of these cases of neglect of children in an expert's opinion in
criminal procedures is emphasized. (English Abstract Modified).

639. Newberger, Carolyn M.; Newberger, Eli H. "Inadequate
Mothers." (Letter). Lancet, 1(7897):42-43, January 4,
1975.
To attribute to the mother alone the source of the many
causes and manifestations of child abuse is to blame one who is a
victim herself. The simple concept of "inadequacy" in a mother
and subsequent practices lead logically to punitive social policies,
which divide families rather than strengthen them.

640. Olson, Robert J. "Index of Suspicion: Screening for Child
Abusers." American Journal of Nursing, 76:108-110,
January 1976.
Olson presents a practical means of identifying problem
parents so that prevention and intervention can be undertaken. A
table, "Index of Suspicion: Identification of Parents Who Are Potential Child Abusers," is provided.

641. Opp, Thomas E. "The Vulnerable Baby." The Nursing
Journal of India, 66:63-65, March 1975.
Some babies are more vulnerable than others to abuse.
Feeding and sleeping behavior are crucial aspects, since nothing
is more exasperating than the slow feeder or poor sleeper. Babies
born with physical defects or mental handicaps are special problems.
Such babies are not only "at risk," but mothers must get over the

loss of a hoped-for normal child and become adjusted. Only when
vulnerable babies become victims do we learn about them.

642. Pakrasi, Kanti; Sasmal, Bibhas. "Effect of Infanticide on Sex-
Ratio in an Indian Population." Zeitschrift für Morphologie und Anthropologie, 62:214-230, May 1970.
The Jhareja Rajputs were once notoriously addicted to the
cruel practice of killing all new-born females in their society. Under governmental pressures the Jharejas had to preserve more newborn females, and the result was that the high sex-ratio among them
could not but decline simultaneously. This paper highlights the features associated with such phenomena of rising female population and
declining high sex-ratio in Jhareja population. (Journal Summary
Modified.)

643. Pasamanick, Benjamin. "Ill-Health and Child Abuse." (Letter). Lancet, 2(7934):550, September 30, 1975.
The association of maternal tension and signs of brain dysfunction in the baby at the first routine examination at age 40 weeks is
related to findings that abnormal pregnancy, prematurity, and illness
are associated with child abuse.

644. Rapp, D. J. "Allergic Children's Behavior May Push Parents
to Abuse." (Letter). American Medical News, 18(23):6,
June 9, 1975.
The contribution of the allergic-tension-fatigue syndrome in
children to abusive behavior by their parents is considered.

645. Renvoize, Jean. Children in Danger. The Causes and Prevention of Baby Battering. London: Routledge & Kegan
Paul, 1974. 193 p.
A woman, whose problems became unmanageable when her
husband went blind, physically and mentally abused one of her children. Examinations are then made of definitions, characteristics of
battering parents, and causes of child abuse. Various protective
agencies criticize one another Diagnosis, treatment, and preventive measures are considered.

646. _____. "Have You Stopped Beating Your Baby?" The
Times (London) Educational Supplement, 3081:22, June 14,
1974.
The author reviews some cases of child abuse and explores
the reasons behind it. Means of preventing and treating are suggested.

647. Resnick, Phillip J. "Murder of the Newborn: A Psychiatric
Review of Neonaticide." American Journal of Psychiatry,
126:1414-1420, 1970.
Mothers who commit neonaticide differ from other mothers
who kill older children in that they are younger, more often not
married, and less frequently, psychotic. The most common motive
stems from illegitimacy, although other reasons include extra-mari-
tal paternity, rape, and viewing the child as an obstacle to parental

ambition. The unmarried groups include two subgroups which are described.

648. "Retreating to Barbarism?" Ave Maria, 97:17, April 6, 1963.
The unknown author looks upon physical punishment as a step back into barbarism. The whipping post and the public humiliation of the stocks are now considered wrong for adults--why are similar brutalities for young people considered permissible and desirable? If we physically punish children, let's administer the same to parents who park overtime, are late to work, etc.

649. Roberts, Albert F. , ed. Childhood Deprivation. Springfield, Ill. : Charles C. Thomas, 1974. 209 p.
Ten papers address issues of childhood deprivation which is defined as an act or series of acts which results in a child being physically, morally, medically, emotionally, socially, or educationally neglected or abused. Among some of the topics considered are: Studies of Children Deprived of Human Contact, Interaction and Affection; Human Behavior and the Social Environment; The Effects of Social Deprivation on Personality; Affectional Deprivation and Child Adjustment; The Abused Child; etc.

650. Rogers, David; Tripp, John; Bentovim, Arnon, et al. "Non-Accidental Poisoning: An Extended Syndrome of Child Abuse. " British Medical Journal, 1(6013):793-796, 1976.
Six cases of persistent non-accidental poisoning of children by their parents are reported. The underlying disorder may include marital conflict, over-involvement between parent and child, or drug abuse in the parents. A suggested plan of action for managing this problem is outlined.

651. Ryan, James H. Suffer the Little Ones. Nashville, Tenn. : Aurora Publishers, 1972. 176 p.
This book is a fictional account of a classical case of child abuse (eventually ending in murder) from the standpoint of the abuser, the law and the criminal court, community reaction, and one pediatrician's attempt to educate the public and help treat and rehabilitate the abuser. Also included are the unethical maneuverings of a drug company that fought to keep a drug on the market, knowing full-well that it contained a poison lethal to children. The author's chief aim in writing this book was to help prevent child abuse through understanding. All crime should be approached from a therapeutic rather than a punitive approach, he theorizes.

652. Sattin, Dana B. ; Miller, LtC. John K. "The Ecology of Child Abuse Within a Military Community. " American Journal of Orthopsychiatry, 41:675-678, July 1971.
The residence patterns of child abuse cases occurring in the military community were compared to those of non-abusing military families. It was found that child abuse cases were more likely to occur in the "Dyer Street" section of El Paso and that they were more likely to live in this area than other military families. A possible explanation that prior personality variables and/or financial or

other environmental stresses were responsible was offered.   (Journal Summary.)

653. Sauer, Louis W.   "Pediatric Problems of Teen-Age Parents. "
        Journal of the International College of Surgeons, 43(5):556-
        559, May 1965.
        Five important pediatric problems concerning children of mar-
ried teenagers have been briefly presented: early feeding and nursing care; prevention of premature birth; preventable birth defects;
diagnosis of the battered-child syndrome, and detection of congenital
syphilis.   (Journal Summary.)

654. _____.   "Problems of Teen-Age Parents. "   PTA Magazine,
        59:27-28, October 1964.
        Sauer discusses answers to problems that face teenage mothers
and fathers.   Some of the concerns he finds most often involved feeding the baby, immunizations, child care, prematurity and birth defects.   Battered baby syndrome is one problem usually unforeseen
by parents.

655. Scott, P. D.   "Parents Who Kill Their Children. "   Medicine,
        Science and the Law, 13(2):120-126, 1973.
        The annual incidence of filicide by mothers and fathers in
England and Wales leads to discussion on classification of the killers,
with particular emphasis on the difficulties associated with the criteria of motive and depression.   A modified classification is suggested and applied to the cohort made available by Morris and Blom-
Cooper (1964).

656. Smith, Selwyn M.   "The Battered Child Syndrome--Some Re-
            search Findings. "   Nursing Mirror and Midwives Journal,
            140:48-53, June 12, 1975; Royal Society of Health Journal,
            95(3):148-153, 1975.
        The author reviews the causes of child abuse as found by
other researchers.   He then gives a report of his own research findings in a study of 134 battered children and their families.

657. Soeffing, Marylane.   "Abused Children Are Exceptional Chil-
            dren. "   Exceptional Children, 42:126-133, November 1975.
        Soeffing reports that no major comprehensive research has ex-
amined the existence of a handicap as a causative factor of abuse
and neglect.   However, several researchers have reported findings
which reveal a possible relationship.   Other studies have indicated
that abused children are seen as different or difficult to raise.   Responsibilities of educators and federal programs are outlined.   Research and services are recommended.

658. Steele, Brandt F.   "Violence in Our Society. "   The Pharos
            of Alpha Omega Alpha, 33(2):42-48, April 1972.
        The author indicates that abusive parents constantly refer to
three main themes which are named.

659. Stephenson, P. S.   Project Toddler: Interim Report.   See
            entry 1444.

660.   Stern, Leo.   "Prematurity as a Factor in Child Abuse."
        Hospital Practice, 8:117-123, May 1973.
        Stern raises the possibility that among the consequences of re-
cent advances in management and low weight and ill newborns is that
the early interpersonal relationship between infant and mother is altered in an undesirable way while infant is hospitalized for diagnosis
and treatment.   Stern's statements are based on a study of child
abuse cases at Montreal Children's Hospital over a nine-year period
of 51 abused children.

661.   Stover, William H., Jr.   "Assumptions on Battering Ques-
        tioned." (Letter).   Pediatrics, 55(5):748, May 1975.
        Stover questions findings made by Lauer and others, in a re-
view of the battered child syndrome.   He says that the conclusion
that "minority children were less likely to be abused than whites"
is based on an unlikely assumption that hospitalization rates of non-
whites and whites are equal for all causes except battering.   The
conclusion that "non-white families were less likely than white families to be involved in child battering" is based on that assumption
and on the assumption that family size of white and non-whites is
equal.

662.   Stultz, Sylvia L.   Childrearing Attitudes of Abusive Mothers:
        A Controlled Study.   Ph.D. Cornell University, 1976.
        116 p.   Available from University Microfilms, Order No.
        76-21, 124.
        Ten mothers of young children (under eight) in each of three
groups were included in this study.   The women were either mothers
of abused, handicapped, or "normal" children.   The hypotheses with
regard to high use of power and low levels of empathy by abusive
mothers received support from the data.

663.   Swanson, D.; Bratrude, A.; Brown, E.   "Alcohol Abuse in a
        Population of Indian Children."   Diseases in the Nervous
        System, 7:4-6, 1972.
        The most drastic case histories (23) are presented out of 100
families of alcoholics.   The children were starved, maltreated,
beaten, forced to lead a promiscuous life, could not learn, sometimes ran away from home, or became alcoholic.   The alcoholic
parents lose control over their actions, demoralize and destroy their
own children.

664.   "Their Prison Was Home."   Newsweek, 56:43, August 8, 1969.
        A family who kept three children imprisoned in the home did
so at first because no one would rent to a family with six children.
Later, the neglected victims became very different from others their
age so isolation continued.   Now teenagers, the three weigh from 29
to 55 pounds and stand from 3'2" to 4'2".   Why are the children un-
dersize when they were not undernourished?   Are they victims of
congenital defects?   Are they the ages they claim to be?

665.   Van Stolk, Mary.   "Who Owns the Child?"   Childhood Educa-
        tion, 50:258-265, March 1974.
        Van Stolk identifies the basic reason for child battering as the

parents' adult response to their own abusive childhood experience.
Pointing out that a child will model his behavior after his parents,
the author asks if violence perhaps breeds violence. She concludes
that Western society is still mirroring cultural beliefs of the past,
because of its reluctance to interfere with the ownership rights of
the parents.

666. "Violent Parents." (Editorial). Lancet, 2:1017-1018, Novem-
     ber 6, 1971.
     This editorial states that only 5 percent of batterers are ill
in the psychiatric sense; most are "inadequate" and emotionally unable to respond to the child's needs. Discussed is the difficulty of
getting the diagnosis and then dealing with it. Increased mother-
baby contact during the infant's stay in a nursery may be a way to
decrease subsequent chances of battering.

667. Walters, David R. Physical and Sexual Abuse of Children:
     Causes and Treatment. See entry 2422.

668. Witkowski, J. [Nazi Camp for the Children in Łódź].
     Przeglad Lekarski, 24:73-81, 1968.

669. Young, Leontine. Wednesday's Children: A Study of Child
     Neglect and Abuse. See entry 233.

670. Young, Marjorie. "Multiple Correlates of Abuse: A Systems
     Approach to the Etiology of Child Abuse." Journal of
     Pediatric Psychology, 1(2):57-61, Spring 1976.
     The author presents a model which considers the complexity
of factors entering an event of child abuse. Young identifies predisposing factors, mediating factors, situational stress, and the immediate precipitating situation as parts of a complex interactional
system which may or may not evoke the abuse response in a parent.

FEDERAL AND HEALTH-BASED PROGRAMS

671.   American Academy of Pediatrics.   Task Force of the Committee on Infant and Preschool Child.   A Descriptive Study of Nine Health-Based Programs in Child Abuse and Neglect. Evanston, Ill. , April 1974.   113 p.
Data and impressions gathered from a questionnaire and a one-day visit to nine health-based child abuse programs throughout the U. S. are reported.   Procedural guidelines for each program are outlined and discussed.   Completed questionnaires are included along with summary descriptions of each program.   A general discussion compares the programs in terms of community approaches and needs and treatment problems.

672.   Berkeley Planning Associates, Inc.   Cost Analysis Design and Pretest Results.   Evaluation, National Demonstration Program in Child Abuse and Neglect.   Berkeley, Calif. , April 1975.   116 p.   Prepared for Health Resources Administration (DHEW), Washington, D. C.
Cost analysis of the 11 demonstration projects within the National Demonstration in Child Abuse and Neglect is being performed to determine efficiency of and economics of scale in the projects; investigate the costs of generic activities in the field and related unit costs; develop information necessary for determining cost-effectiveness of alternative service strategies for abuse and neglect families; determine project resource increases; and provide cost management information.

673.   _____ .   First Site Report, Part Two: Community System. Evaluation Demonstration Program in Child Abuse and Neglect.   Berkeley, Calif. , October 1974.   80 p.   Prepared for Health Resources Administration (DHEW), Bethesda, Md.
A report presents tables of overview data on the community setting of each of 11 child abuse and neglect demonstration projects, including population characteristics; readily available data on incidence and reported cases of abuse and neglect; and characteristics of applicable reporting laws.   Brief discussion of agencies handling most cases and their approaches, interagency coordination and conflict, and treatment shortcomings in each community is also included.

674.   _____ .   Second Site Visit Report.   Evaluation, Demonstration Program in Child Abuse and Neglect.   Berkeley, Calif. , December 1974.   78 p.   Prepared for Health Resources Administration (DHEW), Washington, D. C.

A report based on data gathered from visits to 10 of 11 child
abuse and neglect demonstration projects reviews their progress
since an earlier visit. Summaries of each project's developments
discuss specific activities in the areas of community and professional
education, agency coordination, legislation, case management, community treatment and services, research and evaluation, and program
administration and implementation.

675. Cohn, Ann Harris; Ridge, Susan Shea; Collignon, Frederick G.
"Evaluating Innovative Treatment Programs in Child Abuse
and Neglect." Children Today, 4(3):10-12, May-June 1975.
The focus here is the 11 demonstration projects in the field
of child abuse and neglect. Located across the U.S. and Puerto
Rico, each of the projects involves treatment, education, protection
services and evaluation processes. Evaluations of the programs determined the effectiveness, efficiencies, and inefficiencies, what is
still needed, what worked, and how research could develop answers
to theoretical questions.

676. DeGraff, B. J.; Ridge, S. S. Preliminary Quality Assessment Design Evaluation, National Demonstration Program
in Child Abuse and Neglect. Berkeley, Calif., Berkeley
Planning Associates, Inc. June 1975. 51 p.
Development of quality assessment procedures for evaluation
of case management and performance of treatment services of the
11 projects of the National Demonstration Program in Child Abuse
and Neglect is described. Four project visits are planned to gather
data for refining the quality assessment design.

677. General Records of the Children and Youth Projects, U.S.
Department of HEW, Health Services and Mental Health
Administrations, reports on "Promoting the Health of Mothers and Children by 1972."
Presented are reports from the Children and Youth Projects
on child abuse projects in 13 states. Reports include number of
cases reported and specify the type and kind of project established.

678. "One Child Dies Daily from Abuse: Parent Probably Was
Abused." Pediatric News, 9(4):3, 59, April 1975.
The National Center for the Prevention and Treatment of Child
Abuse and Neglect at the University of Colorado currently operates
five pilot programs which are described. The basic goal of the
Center is the creation of effective programs of child abuse identi-
fication, prevention, and treatment in every county in the country.

679. U.S. Air Force. Medical Service, Air Force Child Advocacy
Program. Washington, D.C., AF Regulation 160-38,
April 25, 1975. 8 p.
The regulation establishing the Air Force Child Advocacy program is discussed. The regulation assigns responsibility and explains Air Force policy and procedures for identification, prevention,
treatment, evaluation, documentation, medical and nonmedical management, follow-up, and disposition of suspected and established

child abuse or neglect cases as defined in the regulation. It establishes an HQUSAF Child Advocacy Program Committee and institutes a system for submission of incident reports through the corresponding committee at installation level.

680. U. S. Intradepartmental Committee on Child Abuse and Neglect. Research, Demonstration and Evaluation Studies on Child Abuse and Neglect. Report No. DHEW-OHD-75-77, 1975. 32 p. Available from Supt. of Documents, $.80; also from EDRS: MF-$0.76; HC-$1.95, Plus Postage.
This booklet describes 38 projects funded during Fiscal Year 1974 by the Intradepartmental Committee on Child Abuse and Neglect. Projects include community prevention programs, child protection, family resource centers, mother-infant attachment, the demography of child abuse, and the effect of birth order on the mother-child relationship. Project descriptions are organized by funding agency. The principal investigator or project director is listed for each described project, and a brief synopsis of the purpose of the project is given.

681. U. S. National Center for Child Abuse and Neglect. Federally-Funded Child Abuse and Neglect Projects 1975. Report No. DHEW-OHD-76-30076. Washington, D. C., 1976. 62 p.
Listed are approximately 160 federally supported projects (completed or current) directly related to child abuse and neglect. Provided for each listing are grant number, name of the project, a brief description of the project, a contact name and address, project dates and the amount of funding. Grants are indexed by principal investigators and institutions, titles and numbers, and states.

682. U. S. Office of Child Development. (DHEW). Child Abuse and Neglect Activities. Publ. No. (OHD) 75-4. 1975. 16 p. Available from EDRS: MF-$0.76; HC-$1.58, Plus Postage.
This report gives in detail recent federal activities and funding related to child abuse and neglect.

683. Ariés, Philippe. Centuries of Childhood: A Social History
of Family Life. Translated from the French by Robert
Baldick. New York: Alfred A. Knopf, 1962. 447 p.
A French historian studies the development of ideas about
children and child care between the Middle Ages and the early nineteenth century.

684. Bakan, David. Slaughter of the Innocents: A Study of the
Battered Child Phenomenon. See entry 2354.

685. Bloch, Harry. "Dilemma of 'Battered Child' and 'Battered
Children.'" New York State Journal of Medicine, 73:799-
801, March 15, 1973.
The history of the battered child dilemma is traced from ancient times to the twentieth century.

686. Chase, Naomi Feigelson. A Child Is Being Beaten: Violence
Against Children, An American Tragedy. See entry 568.

687. Demause, Lloyd. "Our Forebears Made Childhood a Night-
mare." Psychology Today, 8(11):85-88, April 1975.
Demause reports on a five-year study that he and his col-
leagues did on the history of child care and child abuse. From antiquity's infanticide to 19th-century manipulation, the human track
record on child-raising is bloody, dirty and mean. Only lately, and
only now in small numbers, do parents feel that children need aid
and comfort, not brutality. Six evolutionary modes seeming to describe the major trends of parent-child relations in the more advanced parts of the West are given.

688. Doriadis, Spyros. "Mothering and Frederick II." Clinical
Pediatrics, 9(9):565-566, 1970.
Maternal deprivation child abuse has been recorded since
608 B. C. in Athens.

689. Fontana, Vincent J. The Maltreated Child: The Maltreatment Syndrome in Children. See entry 1281.

690. Goldstein, Harold. "Child Labor in America's History."
Children Today, 5:30-35, May-June 1976.
Today, despite more than a century of state laws and four
decades of federal control, many children are working illegally or

under substandard conditions. Covered are the origins of child labor,
early protective legislation, the establishment of the National Child
Labor Committee, the push for a Federal Child Labor Law, the current legal status, and child labor today.

691. Hartman, Mary S. "Child-Abuse and Self-Abuse: Two Vic-
         torian Cases." History of Childhood Quarterly, 2(2):221-
         248, 1974.
      Two cases of child abuse that occurred in nineteenth-century
England are reported. In both situations, the Marsden daughters
(1855) and Constance Kent (1860), the parents came to regard them
as expendable. These cases provide some views on three decades:
education, corporal punishment, and the moral responsibility of children.

692. Helfer, Ray E. , comp. The Battered Child. See entry 1512.

693. Housden, Leslie George. The Prevention of Cruelty to Chil-
         dren. New York: Philosophical Library, 1956. 406 p.
      This book is on child abuse and neglect in England. It is di-
vided into three sections: The Past, The Present, and The Future.
The Past treats on the history of children at work, i. e. , the cruelty
of child labor during the nineteenth century when England was in an
enviable condition. Also treated in this section are the deplorable
living conditions under which children existed or died. The Present
details some of the deplorable living conditions of today and the beginning of awareness of the situation among those in a position to
help. The Future deals with the personal, social, and material environment in the cradle of cruelty, the need for education in the
home--health visitors, residential training for mothers--formal education, and prevention.

694. Judge, C. ; Emmerson, R. "Some Children at Risk in Vic-
         toria in the 19th Century." Medical Journal of Australia,
         1(13):490-495, March 30, 1974.
      The lamentable conditions of the reform schools in Australia
set up during the second half of the 19th century to care for the
large number of delinquents and orphans generated by the gold rush
are described. It is suggested that a review of these heinous conditions may help avert similar fates for the estimated 100, 000 at-
risk children in Australia today.

695. Kellum, Barbara A. "Infanticide in England in the Later
         Middle Ages." History of Childhood Quarterly, 1(3):367-
         389, 1974.
      Literary sources have revealed that massive infanticide during
the Middle Ages was an extensive phenomenon. Economic and social
pressures played a large role and the very commonality of infanticide may well have allowed it to be condoned even in court. The
light punishments and pardons due to "insanity" were probably directly related to the idea that infants and small children were
troublesome, as well as to general societal callousness.

696. Kline, Donald; Christiansen, James. Educational and Psychological Problems of Abused Children. Final Report. See entry 2310.

697. Langer, William L. "Infanticide: A Historical Survey. "
History of Childhood Quarterly, 1(3):353-367, 1974.
Infanticide (willful destruction of newborn babies through exposure, starvation, strangulation, smothering, poisoning, or through the use of some lethal weapon) has been viewed with abhorrence by Christians almost from the beginning of their era. Yet in these days of world population crisis there can hardly be a more important historical question than that of the chronically superfluous population growth and the methods by which humanity has dealt with it. The author gives an historical review of the subject.

698. Mindlin, Rowland L. "Background to the Current Interest in Child Abuse and Neglect. " Pediatric Annals, 5(3):10-14, March 1976.
Mindlin presents this article so that the current wave of sympathy for abused children does not curiously subside. He names three basic themes stemming from much of the violence to children. He then details various historical events in the U. S. regarding child abuse and neglect, including establishment of orphanages and foundling hospitals, etc.

699. Peiper, Von A. "Umgekehrte Kinderheilkunde" [Reversed Pediatrics]. Wiener Medizinische Wochenschrift, 117:895-899, October 1967.
Documented is the history of the crippling and emasculating of children for the purposes of using them in begging, or as keepers of harems, or as papal singers. Peiper cites proof that this custom has been with us since before Christ. He quotes many authorities on the subject from countries such as France, Germany, and Italy. Through these quotes, he provides a detailed description of how the crippling took place and for what purpose.

700. Roberts, Albert F. , ed. Childhood Deprivation. See entry 649.

701. Ryan, William Burke. Infanticide: Its Law, Prevalence, Prevention and History. See entry 1115.

702. Smith, Selwyn M. The Battered Child Syndrome. See entry 1553.

703. Van Stolk, Mary. The Battered Child in Canada. See entry 806.

704. Walters, David R. Physical and Sexual Abuse of Children: Causes and Treatment. See entry 2422.

HOSPITAL'S ROLE

705.   "An Antidote for Child Abuse. (Special Child Abuse Treat-
            ment Team at Baltimore's Sinai Hospital)." Human Be-
            havior, 4:61+, September 1975.
    This article is introduced by a case report of a young black
woman who maltreated her child.   Trying to support an illegitimate
child before having graduated from high school, and turned out by
her mother, she was unable to cope.   Through the efforts of the
Sinai Hospital treatment team, this young lady is in her junior year
of college and living with her baby who is thriving.   Over a two-
year period the team has served 30 families, including over 150
people.   Plans are being made to set up satellite child abuse treatment centers at several locations throughout the city.

706.   Barnes, Geoffrey B.; Chabon, Robert S.; Hertsberg, Leonard
            J.   "Team Treatment for Abusive Families." Social Case-
            work, 55(10):600-611, December 1974.
    The Sinai Hospital in Baltimore, Maryland, instituted in 1971
a child abuse project using a multidisciplinary team approach to aid
families in which a child had been physically abused.   The composition of the team is given.   What is unique in the program described
is the specific way in which team members behave toward and offer
services to these families.

707.   Bliss, Ann.   "The Emergency Department: Gateway to Help
            for Child Abuse."   (Editorial).   Journal of Emergency
            Nursing, 2(1):10, January-February 1976.
    The emergency department has emerged as the first line of
defense against child abuse.   Primary responsibility for detecting
and managing the disease has fallen on the emergency department
nurse and the physician.   To proceed from suspicion of child abuse
to reporting it, medical personnel must feel legally and profession-
ally secure.   The team approach is perhaps one of the most workable solutions.

708.   Boardman, Helen E.   "A Project to Rescue Children from In-
            flicted Injuries."   Social Work, 7:43-51, January 1962.
    Boardman describes the results of a staff project of Children's
Hospital of Los Angeles undertaken in September of 1959 to deal with
non-accidental injury to children.

709.   Callaghan, K. A.; Fotheringham, B. J.   "Practical Manage-
            ment of the Battered Baby Syndrome."   Medical Journal
            of Australia, 1:1282-1284, June 27, 1970.

A practical programme of management of the battered baby syndrome is set out in some detail. This is the programme presently carried out in the Department of Child Health at the Adelaide Children's Hospital, Inc. It is hoped that a similar system of investigation and management may be applicable to other paediatric centres in Australia and elsewhere. (Journal Summary.)

710.   Chabon, R. S.; Barnes, G. B.; Hertzberg, L. J. "The Problem of Child Abuse: A Community Hospital Approach." Maryland State Medical Journal, 22:50-55, October 1973.
A multidisciplinary team formed at Sinai Hospital in Baltimore to deal with the problems of abused children and their families is discussed. The organization and function of the team and plans for expansion of the program are described. Preliminary results are discussed and future directions for evaluation indicated.

711.   Cleveland Metropolitan General Hospital. The Parenting Program for the Prevention of Child Abuse, by Lalle Gabinet. Cleveland, Ohio. 10 p. Available from EDRS: MF-$0.83; HC-$1.67, Plus Postage.
Described is the Parenting Program for the Prevention of Child Abuse which employs home visits to upgrade home environments and to prevent physical abuse of children up to six years of age. The program focuses on four major areas: psychological support of the parent; obtaining social services that are needed; resolution of inner conflicts which contribute to the danger of child abuse; and parent education in the area of parenting skills.

712.   Cosgrove, John G. "Management and Follow-Up of Child Abuse." Journal of the Medical Society of New Jersey, 69:27-30, January 1972.
Cosgrove offers a brief overview of the management and follow-up of child abuse cases at the Martland Hospital Unit in Newark, New Jersey, over the period of a year. Also included is the specific input employed and the philosophy that undergirded it.

713.   Daniel, Jessica H.; Hyde, James N., Jr. "Working with High-Risk Families: Family Advocacy and the Parent Education Program." Children Today, 4(6):23-25, 36, November-December 1975.
The authors describe the Family Development Study which has been conducted over the past two years at Children's Hospital Medical Center, Boston, and which is supported by a grant from the Office of Child Development. A long-range objective is to begin exploring certain non-traditional modes of intervention in working with families whose children have been identified as being at risk. Two modes of intervention--Family Advocacy and Parent Education Program (PEP)--have been tentatively employed for working with high-risk families.

714.   Donnan, S. P. B.; Duckworth, P. M. "Suspected Child Abuse: Experience in Guy's Hospital Accident & Emergency Department." Guy's Hospital Reports, 121:295-298, 1972.

In common with other hospitals, cases of child abuse coming
to Guy's Hospital Accident Department appear to have been missed.
A proportion of these missed cases were fortunately detected subsequently, especially on the ward. Statistics are presented concerning
experience at Guy's over the past few years and a policy is outlined
for attempting to cope more adequately with the problem by cooperation between the Accident, Paediatric and Medical Social Work Departments. (Journal Abstract.)

715. Gray, Jane. "Hospital-Based Battered Child Team." Hospitals, 47:50-52, February 16, 1973; Nursing Digest, 1:28-
31, August 1973.
A well-designed team approach to handling cases of child abuse
or neglect may be a timely solution to this spreading "disease."
Centers of specialists in case-finding documentation and follow-up
care of the abused, neglected, and deprived child are being developed
by hospitals and city and county governments. Physicians, medical
social workers, and public health nurses are all available for consultation regarding the most beneficial manner to help a battered
child and his family. The hospital's first role is to recognize the
abused or neglected child.

716. Irwin, C. S. "The Establishment of a Child Abuse Unit in a
Children's Hospital." South African Medical Journal, 49
(28):1142-1146, July 5, 1975.
The aims of setting up a Child Abuse Unit in a children's hospital are detailed; the procedure for the education of staff, details
of training and establishment of a program are outlined; and the outcome is considered. The cooperation of the medical profession is
sought in setting up programs for the prevention of child abuse.

717. Joyner, Edmund N., III. "The Battered Child." New York
Medicine, 26(9):383-385, September 1970.
Problems still arise from a lack of good communication between the medical profession, the social workers, and the judiciary;
the reluctance of some physicians to report cases; and the lack of
adequately trained medical and social service personnel. It is suggested that each hospital form a committee on child abuse consisting
of a pediatrician, a psychiatrist, an administrator, and a social
worker. This committee would be responsible for educating the
medical staff to recognize cases of child abuse and for carrying out
the hospital's mandated reporting responsibilities.

718. _____. "Child Abuse: The Role of the Physician and the
Hospital." Pediatrics, 51:799-803, April 1973.
In the Symposium on Child Abuse held in 1971, the role of the
physician and the hospital in dealing with cases of child abuse was
examined in New York State, stressing that this can be divided into
five separate but interrelated roles. One method of performing these
functions thoroughly is through organization of a child abuse and neglect committee or team of professionals.

719. Kalisch, Beatrice J. "What Are Hospitals Doing About Child

Abuse? Report of a Nationwide Survey." <u>Hospital Topics,</u>
52(6):21-24, June 1974.
A nationwide survey of 120 hospitals to determine hospital response to child abuse and to decipher the programs and procedures
in operation is discussed. Details are given of the survey procedure
and its results.

720. Kempe, C. Henry. "The Battered Child and the Hospital."
<u>Hospital Practice,</u> 4:44-57, October 1969.
Beyond caring for the paramount needs of a battered child,
the hospital should turn to treating the parent. Failure in mothering
behavior usually reflects deep isolation or having been abused herself
in childhood. A therapeutic, not punitive, approach can result in the
safe return of children to their homes.

721. _____. <u>Helping the Battered Child and His Family.</u> See
entry 1339.

722. Leivesley, S. "The Maltreated Child--a Cause for Concern."
<u>Medical Journal of Australia,</u> 1:935-936, April 29, 1972.
When child abuse is suspected, admitting the child to the hospital not only affords a safe environment for the child, but it provides an opportunity to investigate the case, refer the parent to a
psychiatrist or social worker, and use a team approach in deciding
what is best for the child's future.

723. Lloyd-Still, John D.; Martin, Barbara. "Child Abuse in a
Rural Setting." <u>Pennsylvania Medicine,</u> 79(3):56-60, March
1976.
This article summarizes the experience of The Milton S. Her-
shey Medical Center located in a semi-rural area of central Pennsylvania which has provided a unique opportunity to observe the ecology
of child abuse and neglect, with special reference to three high risk
groups: "fundamentalist" religious groups whose members believe
that God expects them to vigorously punish their children, personnel
on military bases, and the poor because of their more frequent crises.

724. Ludwig, S.; Heiser, A.; Cullen, T., et al. "You Are Sub-
poenaed." <u>Clinical Proceedings,</u> 30(6):133-147, June 1974.
An account of a Grand Rounds devoted to child abuse as it is
dealt with at the Children's Hospital National Medical Center is presented. The importance of strict adherence to established hospital
policy is stressed. An Assistant Chief of the Juvenile Division of
the Corporation Counsel outlines the role of the doctor in court, and
the importance of being fully aware of the case in all its details is
emphasized.

725. Lynch, Margaret A.; Roberts, Jacqueline; Gordon, Margaret.
"Child Abuse: Early Warning in the Maternity Hospital."
<u>Developmental Medicine and Child Neurology,</u> 18:759-766,
December 1976.
Early detection of families with a high potential for abuse can

lead to effective prevention. In the Oxford area, over half the mothers referred to our service for bonding failure had had contact with
a maternity hospital social worker around the time of delivery. In
this paper we present the results of an investigation of how such
women can be distinguished from the general body of maternity hospital social work referrals, so permitting preventive action to be
taken. (Journal Introduction.)

726.   ; Steinberg, Derek; Ounsted, Christopher. "Family
        Unit in a Children's Psychiatric Hospital." British Medi-
        cal Journal, 5963:127-129, 1975.
    Treatment facilities at a children's psychiatric hospital, where
mothers are admitted with their children and the treatment concen-
trates on the psychotherapy of the family problems that underly baby
battering and the distress generated in the families of children with
developmental disorders, are described.

727. Meyers, Alan; Cooper, Carol; Dolins, David. "Child Abuse:
        Hospital Combats Neglected Health Crisis." Hospitals,
        48:46-49, September 1, 1974.
    The Yale-New Haven Hospital developed a hospital-based and
community-wide program to identify, report, and provide follow-up
care for abused children and rehabilitation for their parents. The
program has been nicknamed DART which stands for Detected, Admitted, Reported, and Taken (from the home). With the program,
the DART committee hopes to encourage more reporting of child
abuse and discourage repeated child abuse.

728. Newberger, Eli H. "The Myth of the Battered Child Syndrome:
        Focus on Parents' Inability to Nurture Child." Current
        Medical Dialog, 40:327-330, April 1973.
    Children's Hospital in Boston focuses on Trauma X (house eu-
phemism for child abuse) as an illness stemming from situations in
the child's home setting which threatens its survival. Its basic idea
is to come to grips with specific problems of parents' lives--poor
health, inadequate housing, no child care, and legal and monetary
difficulties. It means cooperating constructively with public and
voluntary agencies to enhance a family's capacity to care for its
children.

729.   ; Hagenbuch, J. J.; Ebeling, N. B.; et al. "Reduc-
        ing Literal and Human Cost of Child Abuse: Impact of a
        New Hospital Management System." Pediatrics, 51:840-
        848, May 1973.
    This study was designed to demonstrate the effectiveness of a
community effort to provide more adequate preventive and therapeutic
service to the victims of child abuse and their families. Social service personnel were integrated into a consultation group in an academic pediatric hospital, leading to a reduction in medical cost and
in the risk of reinjury subsequent to the diagnosis of child abuse.

730. "Outreach Program Helps Eliminate Child Abuse." Hospitals,
        50(15):37-38, August 1, 1976.

The Outreach Supportive Services program at Presbyterian-University of Pennsylvania Medical Center in Philadelphia was initiated in 1971. It is based on the belief that child abuse and neglect can be attributed to parental lack of self-confidence in raising children or to deficient child-rearing skills. By replacing these feelings with positive attitudes and skills, the team personnel have found, the probability of recurring abuse can be almost eliminated.

731. Paneth, Janice. "Deflation in an Inflationary Period: Some Current Social Health Need Provisions. " American Journal of Public Health, 62:60-63, January 1972.
This paper is an attempt to bring to the attention of health personnel, concerned with the physical, emotional and mental well-being of the patients we serve, an overview of some of the Mount Sinai Hospital Social Service Department's experiences with current societal provisions for specific health and maintenance needs. (Journal Summary.)

732. Paull, Dorothy; Lawrence, Robert J. ; Schimel, Beverly. "A New Approach to Reporting Child Abuse. " Hospitals, 41: 62-64, January 16, 1967.
A standing hospital committee for the abused child can do much not only to protect the defenseless child but also to relieve individuals of the moral and legal burden of reporting such abuse, the authors contend. They describe the composition, responsibilities, and achievements of such a committee at one hospital. (Journal Summary.)

733. Pfeifer, Donald R. ; Ayoub, Catherine. "An Approach to the Prophylaxis of Child Abuse and Neglect. " Journal of the Oklahoma State Medical Association, 69(5):162-167, May 1976.
A community hospital SCAN Team at Hillcrest Medical Center, Tulsa, Oklahoma, detected an epidemic of child abuse. A comprehensive preventative program was developed to keep children from being sent home to die.

734. Rowe, Daniel S. ; Leonard, Martha F. ; Seashore, Margretta R. ; et al. "A Hospital Program for the Detection and Registration of Abused and Neglected Children. " New England Journal of Medicine, 282:950-952, April 23, 1970.
Described is a program for the early detection of abused children called DART which has been set up at the Yale University Medical Center.

735. Shaw, Anthony; Carr, Corinne H. "A Team Approach to Child Abuse. " Virginia Medical Monthly, 101:366-372, May 1974.
The goals, composition, and operation of the Committee for Child Protection at the University of Virginia Hospital are outlined. Three cases illustrative of the functioning of the committee are briefly presented. A greater role on the part of Virginia physicians in local, state, and national programs against child abuse is strongly urged.

736. Snedeker, Lendon. "Traumatization of Children." New England Journal of Medicine, 267:572, September 13, 1962.
Discusses hospital procedure in dealing with suspected cases of child abuse.

737. Taylor, M. R. H.; Kevany, J. P. "Battered Babies in Hospital. Pathways for Their Care." Irish Medical Journal, 69(4):79-83, 1976.
Management of battered children in Ireland by hospital staff and social workers is outlined through a flow chart based on practical experience. Such a chart is felt to be helpful to all those who play an active part in management of the problem.

738. "'Team' Held Best Hope in Child-Abuse Intervention." Pediatric News, 9(3):76, March 1975.
Hospital-based multidisciplinary teams represent the current best hope for intervention in cases of child abuse, since this approach benefits the child, the parents, and the community at large. The make-up of the team at DeWitt Army Hospital and the advantages of this approach are given.

739. Ten Bensel, Robert W. "Neuro-Pediatrics Conference. Battered Child Syndrome." Minnesota Medicine, 49:1429-1436, September 1966.
Pediatric conferences--an integral part of the Comprehensive Clinic Program--are held every Wednesday at the University of Minnesota Hospitals. As the case of a battered five-month-old white female unfolds through those reporting at a conference, the reader is given a clear picture of the diagnosis and management of the case. Final recommendations of the conference are presented.

740. Tracy, J. J.; Clark, E. H. "Treatment for Child Abusers." Social Work, 19(3):338-342, 1974.
The child abuse program at Presbyterian-University of Pennsylvania Medical Center attempted to treat the parents of abused children using a social learning model. The model involves identifying behavioral goals followed by specific techniques for achieving them, and stands in contradistinction to treatments based on primary psychological modification.

741. Weinbach, Robert W. "Case Management of Child Abuse." Social Work, 20(5):396-397, September 1975.
Child abuse presents issues that are distinct to hospital administrators and staff. Recent reports not only provide clear identification of management problems in child abuse cases but suggest as well the need for a comprehensive program of case management at all levels of service. This article examines the sources of difficulty and proposes a comprehensive approach for hospital personnel. There is a definable obstacle existing in the medical setting that prevents the effective handling of child abuse cases. (Journal Introduction Modified.)

742. Wolkenstein, Alan S. "Evolution of a Program for the Man-

agement of Child Abuse. " <u>Social Casework</u>, 57(5):309-316, 1976.

A hospital's program for the management of child abuse, which provides an organized structure for dealing with the problem, is described.

743. _____. "Hospital Acts on Child Abuse. " <u>Hospitals</u>, 49(6): 103-104, 106, March 16, 1975.

Discussed is a program to help abused children and their families in Milwaukee Children's Hospital. In order to facilitate programming, three categories of abuse were identified: abused child, suspected abuse, and undetermined. The program coordinates state and local government agencies and other community sources. Reasons for its success are enumerated.

INCIDENCE

744. American Humane Association. Children's Division. High-
     lights of 1975 National Data. Denver, Colo. No charge
     for single copies.
     A report of the national study on child neglect and abuse re-
porting which offers a breakdown of 294,796 official reports by status,
type, number of children, sources of report and who was the abuser-
neglecter.

745. Anderson, J. R. "Child Abuse." Virginia Health Bulletin,
     26(2). 20 p. 1973.
     In the past six years, 266 child abuse cases were reported.
Twenty-one resulted in death; 35 percent involved children under six
months of age. Child abuse, neglect, and the approaches to the
problem being taken at all levels of government are discussed.

746. Baldwin, J. A.; Oliver, J. E. "Epidemiology and Family
     Characteristics of Severely Abused Children." British
     Journal of Preventive and Social Medicine, 29(4):205-221,
     1975.
     A retrospective study (1965-1971) was made of severe child
abuse in northeast Wiltshire, as well as a prospective study for 18
months from January 1972. This was done after a consultative
period with persons involved in increasing the awareness of the
phenomenon. A rate of one per thousand children under four years
old was obtained with a death rate of 0.1 per thousand.

747. Breen, Ed. "Child Abuse--How-Who-Why." Today's Family
     Digest, 25:16-22, January 1970.
     After describing some tragic examples of child abuse, Breen
discusses the incidence and causative factors of maltreatment of
children. Although the statistics indicate the seriousness of physical abuse, the problems of neglect and mental abuse often go unde-
tected.

748. Brown, G. W. "Child Abuse in Alaska." p. 461-467. In:
     Shephard, R. J.; Itol, S., eds. Circumpolar Health,
     Toronto: Univ. of Toronto Press, 1976.

749. Bynum, Alvin S. "A Report on the Battered Child: Indiana,
     1966." Journal of the Indiana State Medical Association,
     60:469, April 1967.
     A consultant with the Indiana Department of Public Welfare

comments on the incidence of reported cases of child abuse in Indiana during 1966. Bynum concludes that a broader educational program is needed to inform the many groups of people who might be
affected by an incident of child abuse.

750. Carter, Jan, ed. The Maltreated Child. Westport, Conn.:
     Technomic Publishing, 1976. 156 p.
     Sixteen different contributors from a variety of professions,
such as a neurosurgeon and member of the Tunbridge Wells study
group, a social worker and medical sociologist, a profession of child
health, etc. write about various aspects of child abuse in Britain:
the dimensions of it, characteristics of parents and children, medical
diagnosis, social assessment and services, treatment, and the law.

751. "Child-Abuse Problem." Christianity Today, 17:32, July 6,
     1973.
     Discussed is the rising problem of child abuse. Statistics on
incidence are given--nearly 60,000 reported cases each year. Various projects are identified, such as the "parent-aide" project that
works toward prevention through the parents. Also discussed is how
and why everyone should become involved in the prevention of child
abuse.

752. Claus, H. G. "The Intricacies of Violence Against Children
     in American Society." Clinical Pediatrics, 10(10):557-558,
     October 1971.
     Statistics reveal information about child abuse.

753. Cohen, Stephan J.; Sussman, Alan. "Incidence of Child Abuse
     in the United States." Child Welfare, 54:432-443, June
     1975.
     This article is part of the authors' book tentatively entitled:
Child Abuse: Guidelines for Legislation. Their study of estimates
on fatalities, variations in laws, problems of analysis, and national
estimates suggests that "estimated" and even "official" rates of incidence, which often serve as "evidence" demonstrating the need for
legal or social programs, should be received with a degree of caution.

754. Colclough, I. R. "Victorian Government's Report on Child
     Abuse: A Reinvestigation." Medical Journal of Australia,
     2:1491-1497, December 30, 1972.
     Some of the findings of the Victorian Government's Depart-
mental Committee established to investigate cases of child maltreatment are summarized. The results of a similar survey conducted
by a fifth year medical student are also presented and compared
with the Committee's reports. The discrepancy between the results
of the two surveys is believed to be due to the inadequate methods
of investigation adopted by the Committee. (Journal Summary.)

755. Dalhousie University. School of Law. Child Abuse in Nova
     Scotia. See entry 2217.

756. Dörmann, U. "(FRG) Sonderstatistik: Vollendete Tötungsdelikte an Kindern 1968-1974 (BRD)" [Special Statistics:
Successful Homicidal Offenses Against Children During
1968-1974]. Kriminalistik, 29(10):465, 1975. Tables 3.

757. Eisenmenger, W. , et al. [Child Abuse in Munich in the
Years 1961-1971]. Beitraege zur Gerichtlichen Medizin,
31:92-96, 1973.

758. Farn, Kenneth T. "Deaths from Non-Accidental Injuries in
Childhood. " (Letter). British Medical Journal, 3(5979):
370-371, August 9, 1975.
Farn discusses the Registrar General's statistical reviews of
child abuse deaths and how the coroner's court acts upon death no-
tifications. The six verdicts a coroner can hand down are discussed
along with arguments pertaining to better ways of determining a child
abuse death. The author believes that the current statistics are
correct and that the means of reporting these cases are also good
and correct.

759. Fergusson, David M. ; Fleming, Joan; O'Neill, David P.
Child Abuse in New Zealand. See entry 594.

760. Fontana, Vincent J. The Maltreated Child: The Maltreatment
Syndrome in Children. See entry 1281.

761. _____. "Physical Abuse of Children. " Pediatrics, 45:509-
510, March 1970.
The author feels that David Gil's report of his survey of child
abuse deserves comment to avoid misconceptions that may arise from
it. He states that Gil's comments distort the true nature of child
abuse and do a disservice to those who are working toward its prevention. Gil's statement that the Battered Child Syndrome is a relatively infrequent occurrence would be altered by his presence in any
pediatric emergency room of a large hospital. He encourages such
studies but cautions generalizations and conclusions based on a limited, reported number of child abuse cases.

762. Franklin, Alfred White. "Statistics of Child Abuse. " (Letter).
British Medical Journal, 3(5975):98-99, July 12, 1975.
Admitting that child abuse certainly exists and is a reality,
the author contends that it is often exaggerated by society. He feels
that child abuse cases should be classified and categorized. He also
feels that something has caused the "strain" of child abuse, and until the cause or causes are definitely found, it is up to society to
protect the integrity of the family and defend the children.

763. Friedrich, William N. "Epidemiological Survey of Physical
Child Abuse. " Texas Medicine, 72(10):81-84, October 1976.
Harris County Child Welfare intake reports of physical child
abuse for a 17-week period during 1974-1975 were analyzed. An
analysis of reporters and reporting patterns was also performed.
Results are provided.

764. Gelles, Richard J. "Demythologizing Child Abuse." The
     Family Coordinator, 25(2):135-141, April 1976.
     The idea of a dramatic rise in child abuse is one of the main
myths which clouds the clear perception and understanding of the
problem of child abuse and neglect in America.   Inaccuracies concern facets of the problem, such as what is child abuse, how much
abuse is there, what is the cause of abuse, and what is the impact
of prevention and treatment programs which are being instituted.
This paper addresses these "myths" in order to demythologize the
issue of child abuse and facilitate a clearer and more accurate understanding of this phenomenon.   (Journal Summary.)

765. Gil, David G. "First Steps in a Nationwide Study of Child
     Abuse." p. 61-79.   In: Social Work Practice, 1966.
     New York: Columbia University Press, 1966.
     This research project deals with incidence of child abuse,
family characteristics, circumstances of abuse and nature of injury,
as well as intervention.

766. _____. "Physical Abuse of Children.   Findings and Impli-
     cations of a Nationwide Survey." Pediatrics, 44:Suppl:857-
     864, November 1969.
     Gil offers a critical analysis of a 1967 study undertaken to
obtain systematic information on the number of legally reported incidents of child abuse in the U.S., the distribution patterns of these
incidents, the characteristics of the children, families, and perpetrators involved, the circumstances surrounding the incidents, and
the measures taken by health, welfare, and law enforcement authorities in dealing with reported incidents.

767. _____. Violence Against Children--Physical Child Abuse
     in the United States.   Cambridge, Mass.: Harvard Uni-
     versity Press, 1970.   Paperback edition with new preface
     and appendix, 1973.
     Reported are findings of a nationwide survey of the incidence
of child abuse reported through legal channels throughout the U.S.
in 1967 and 1968.   Included are additional findings of sample surveys
of the public knowledge, attitudes and opinions about child abuse.

768. _____. "Violence Against Children." (Letter).   Pediatrics,
     49:641, April 1972.
     This article supports the author's book by the same title, in
response to a book review by E. H. Newberger (Pediatrics, 48:688,
1971).   Newberger claimed that Gil failed to explain the disparity
between his estimate of the incidence of child abuse and low reporting level, and that his data is insufficient to derive hypotheses.   Gil
defends his study and states that the book review misrepresents it.

769. Gray, James J.   Trends in Child Abuse Reporting in New
     York State, 1966-1972.   See entry 962.

770. Hartl, H. "Verletzungen im Neugeborenen-, Säuglings und
     Kleinkindesalter" [Injuries in Newborns, Infants and Small

Children]. Wiener Medizinische Wochenschrift, 120:702-704, October 10, 1970.
In 1967, 43 percent of all children who died in the Federal Republic died of accidents. Hartl discusses categories of injuries: birth, poisoning, and burn injuries and those resulting from child abuse. Often doctors can intercede and help through knowledge of the social and psychopathic relationships of individual families.

771. Hawaii State Department of Social Services and Housing. Division of Public Welfare. A Statistical Report on Child Abuse in Hawaii. Honolulu, 1967-1968. 17 p.
A statistical report on child abuse in Hawaii in 1967 and 1968 presents data on geographical distribution, age, religion, month of abuse incident, type of injury, and psychosocial factors; similar data are presented for child neglect.

772. _____. A Statistical Report on Child Abuse and Neglect in Hawaii. Honolulu, 1969. 23 p.
This 1969 statistical report suggests that the increased number of cases reported reflect an increased public awareness rather than an actual increase of incidents. Reports of abuse most frequently occurred through the schools, whereas reports of neglect came more often from a neighbor.

773. _____. A Statistical Report on Child Abuse and Neglect in Hawaii. Honolulu, 1970-1971. 17 p.
The 1970 and 1971 statistics indicate a rate of abuse reporting in 1970 that more than doubled the rate in 1969, coincident with the establishment of the Child Protective Service Center. The largest reporting source was school personnel, and next was medical personnel.

774. Helfer, Ray E.; Gil, David G. "Physical Abuse of Children." Pediatrics, 46:651-652 concl., October 1970.
In this letter to the editor, Helfer criticizes an article published earlier by D. G. Gil ("Physical Abuse of Children: Findings and Implications of a Nationwide Survey." Pediatrics (Suppl.), 44:857, 1969). Deep concern is expressed about Gil's definition of physical abuse; the use of reports from 1967 which was, for many states, the first or second year of their reporting law; and reaching conclusions that cannot be supported by data. Gil replies briefly to Helfer's criticism and defends the original analysis of a nationwide survey, including definitions used and conclusions drawn.

775. Howells, J. G. "Deaths from Non-Accidental Injuries in Childhood." (Letter). British Medical Journal, 3(5984):651-652, September 13, 1975.
Reference is made to Dr. K. T. Farn's notion that the statistical machinery which records those elements apposite to estimating the number of child battering deaths is not capable of error. Howells discusses how it might not be the machinery but the human factor that makes statistical assessment greatly erroneous. He discusses sources which may invalidate estimates of child abuse deaths and more or less sees investigation of cases as necessary.

776. Illinois State Department of Children and Family Services.
Office of Research and Development. Child Abuse Reporting. Fiscal Year 1974. Springfield, 1974. 5 p.
A report compares statistics of suspected child abuse and neglect cases, reported and registered in Illinois in fiscal year 1974
with statistics from fiscal year 1973. Data tables are included.

777. Kansas State Department of Health. Child Abuse. Topeka,
Kansas. 1971. 9 p.
During the years 1969-1971 Kansas took significant steps
against child abuse. The result of these steps is described as to
incidence during the two-year period. The children are identified
as to age, race, type of injury, etc. , as are perpetrators.

778. Karlsson, A. "The Battered Child Syndrome in Iceland. "
Nordisk Psykiatrisk Tidsskrift, 25:112-118, 1971.
In assessing the incidence of the battered child syndrome in
Iceland, it was concluded that it is less than in other culturally-
related societies. Special social factors, such as smallness of pop-
ulation, are believed to be the reason.

779. Kline, Donald; Christiansen, James. Educational and Psychological Problems of Abused Children. Final Report. See
entry 2310.

780. Leavitt, Jerome E. "Battered Child. " Instructor, 75:50+,
March 1966.
Leavitt refers to recent headlines in newspapers identifying
the battered child syndrome as epidemic in proportion. He discusses
our state of knowledge of and attempts to deal with the problem of
child abuse. As compared with our scientific advance, social advance in the world lags appreciably, he concludes.

781. "Legally Reported Child Abuse: A Nationwide Survey. " Social
Work Practice, 1968. National Conference on Social Welfare. New York: Columbia University Press, 1968.

782. Loria, S.; Harlap, S.; Drapkin, I. Child Injury in West Jerusalem. (Paper presented at the First International Symposium on Victimology, held from 2-6 September 1973,
Jerusalem.)
Records were studied of 290 Jerusalem children admitted to
the hospital for injuries during a $3\frac{1}{2}$-year period. There were a
number of suspected cases of the battered child syndrome identified
but numerically neglect appeared to be the greater problem. Those
neglected clearly represented only a fraction of child neglect and
deprivation in the community. Suspected child abuse showed a less
clear-cut social distribution and was not confined to any ethnic, educational or standard-of-living group.

783. Lyons, Michael M. "Pediatric Forensic Pathology. " New
York State Journal of Medicine, 72:816-819, April 1, 1972.
The New York Medical Examiner's Office provides data for a

statistical report on childhood deaths. Eight headings cover different causes of death and several groupings discuss child abuse. Trauma remains a chief cause of death in children under 14 years old, while blunt-force trauma accounts for over 80 percent of serious injuries in children.

784. Nagi, Saad Z. <u>Child Maltreatment in the United States: A Cry for Help and Organizational Response.</u> See entry 2242.

785. National Society for the Prevention of Cruelty to Children. "Two a Day?" <u>Economist</u>, 254:27-28, March 29, 1975.
Statistics regarding child battering and case referrals in Britain are detailed. Referrals made by the public was up, but the overall case referral was down. In Britain alone, two children die every day from savage assaults made on them by their parents. All other deaths of children under 16 years was about one-seventh of that total.

786. National Symposium on Child Abuse, Rochester, N.Y. 1971. <u>Collection of Papers Presented at a National Meeting in Rochester, N.Y., October 19, 1971, to Explore on an Interdisciplinary Basis the Problems of Child Abuse and Sexual Exploitation of Children.</u> (Symposium presented by the Children's Division of the American Human Association in conjunction with the association's 95th annual meeting.) 1972. 72 p. $1.
An interdisciplinary exploration of child abuse and sexual exploitation of children. Papers given examined the intensity of the problem and discussed the legal, medical, and protective aspects of the problems.

787. New York State. Department of Social Services. <u>Cases of Suspected Child Abuse and Maltreatment Reported to the NYS Central Child Abuse and Maltreatment Register--1973.</u> Program Brief No. 2. Albany, April 1974. 4 p.
Statistics on cases of suspected child abuse and maltreatment reported to the New York State Child Abuse and Maltreatment Register for the calendar year 1973 are reported. Data are presented by county and month, including New York City as a separate entity and including case fatalities as a separate category.

788. New York State. Legislative Assembly. Select Committee on Child Abuse. <u>Report.</u> New York, 1972. 168 p.
Deaths attributed to suspected parent maltreatment and reported by the New York Central Registry, the State Medical Examiner's Office, plus 150 other deaths of children attributed to someone other than a parent, brings the total number of child deaths in New York City alone to approximately 200 in 1971. The New York State Select Committee on Child Abuse presents its findings and recommendations.

789. Newberger, Eli H.; Daniel, Jessica. "Knowledge and Epidemiology of Child Abuse: A Critical Review of Concepts." <u>Pediatric Annals,</u> 5(3):15-21+, March 1976.

The coauthors discuss the paucity of essential family supports, the heavy reliance on foster-home care, and the contradictions between philosophy and practice in management and prevention of child abuse. The epidemiology of child abuse is reviewed in terms of incidence, prevalence, duration, sampling bias, and confounding (the mistaking of a spurious association for a causal relationship).

790. _____; Haas, Gerald; Mulford, Robert M. "Child Abuse in Massachusetts. Incidence, Current Mechanism for Intervention, and Recommendation for Effective Control." Massachusetts Physician, 32(1):31-38, January 1973.
Presented are the detailed findings and recommendations of the Governor's Committee on Child Abuse convened in Massachusetts in 1970. From the results of a questionnaire study, Newberger's conservative extrapolation estimates the total number of abuse and neglect cases in the state at 7,290.

791. North Carolina State Department of Human Resources. Division of Social Services. Neglect and Abuse of Children in North Carolina. Special Report No. 30. Raleigh, January 1975. 32 p.
Statistical information generated from the North Carolina Central Registry's Report of Alleged Child Abuse or Neglect, DSS-CW-301, for the year beginning January 1972 is provided. Selected statutory definitions of abuse and neglect are also included.

792. Peckham, Catherine S.; Jobling, Megan. "Deaths from Non-Accidental Injuries in Childhood." (Letter). British Medical Journal, 2(5972):686, June 21, 1975.
Viewing child abuse as a very important problem, the authors present statistics regarding deaths of children from the Registrar General. They point out that such violence can be dealt with if the nature and extent of the problem are fully understood, but child abuse is extremely hard to determine if death has occurred.

793. Pennsylvania State Department of Public Welfare. Bureau of Child Welfare. 1973 Child Abuse Report. Harrisburg, 1974. 31 p.
The statistics for reported cases of suspected child abuse in Pennsylvania in 1973 are presented along with brief discussions of the history, various forms, parental characteristics, etiology, and legal aspects of the problem. In the seven years of mandatory reporting, almost 6,000 cases have been recorded in the state.

794. Pugh, R. J. "Battered Babies." Lancet, 2:466-467, August 29, 1970.
During a 3-year period, 24 infants with parent-inflicted injuries were admitted to a British hospital serving a population of 400,000. These figures indicate that approximately one child in 1,000 will be hospitalized due to battering in infancy. The nature of the injuries of these 24 infants is described. Three of them died.

795. Ryan, William Burke. Infanticide: Its Law, Prevalence, Prevention and History. See entry 1115.

796. Schloesser, Patricia T. "The Abused Child." Bulletin of the
      Menninger Clinic, 28:260-268, September 1964.
      This article reports on 85 cases of child abuse which occurred
in Kansas during 1962 and 1963. Involved were a high proportion of
very young parents.

797. Schrag, Peter. "Fine Tuning: The Epidemic That Never Was."
      More, 6:22, 24, February 1976.
      Schrag questions incidence statistics presented by news media
on child abuse and claims that television loves new ailments. Schrag
considers this effort a mask for straight propaganda on behalf of individuals and organizations pushing programs and "remedies" which
are often untested and which represent extensive intrusions into the
lives of those they purport to help.

798. "Shelter: Children's Center Deluged with Child Abuse Cases."
      New Yorker, 45:21-22, July 5, 1969.
      New York City's Children's Center is unable to effectively
meet the needs of the children, because of the drastic increase in
numbers. The problem is described in dealing with the deluge of
child abuse cases.

799. Simons, Betty; Downs, Elinor F.; Hurster, Archer; et al.
      "Child Abuse: Epidemiologic Study of Medically Reported
      Cases." New York State Journal of Medicine, 66:2783-
      2788, November 1, 1966.
      An epidemiologic study of child abuse in New York City was
carried out to achieve a better understanding of the problem. The
New York City child abuse registry was the source for data collection. The survey revealed abuse patterns which are detailed in four
different categories. Identifying these epidemiologic factors helps
define child abuse etiology and provide needed social services for
children.

800. _____; _____; Hurster, Madeline M., et al. Child
      Abuse: A Perspective on Legislation in Five Middle-Atlan-
      tic States, and a Survey of Reported Cases in New York
      City. See entry 1125.

801. Smith, Selwyn M. The Battered Child Syndrome. See entry
      1553.

802. Solomon, Theodore. "History and Demography of Child
      Abuse." Pediatrics, 51(4):773-776, April 1973.
      In 1969 approximately 2,600 cases of child abuse were reported
in New York City. Since the inception of the city registry in New
York, the local rate of child abuse case reports has increased 549
percent. Extrapolation, by Solomon, from California and Colorado
data indicate that between 200,000 and 250,000 children are in need
of protective services.

803. Stainton, M. Colleen. "Non-Accidental Trauma in Children."
      The Canadian Nurse, 71(10):26-29, October 1975; Infirmiere
      Canadienne, 17(12):20-23, December 1975.

Stainton discusses non-accidental trauma in children in relation to degrees of abuse in child battery, child abuse, failure-to-thrive, and child neglect. Also presented are some guidelines for prevention and treatment.

804. Thompson, E. "Child Abuse Is No Myth." Instructor, 83: 84-85, 1974.
    Interview with social worker indicating general prevalence of child abuse. Differentiates abuse and neglect and physical and psychological abuse.

805. U. S. Congress. Senate. Labor and Public Welfare Committee. See entry 1168.

806. Van Stolk, Mary. The Battered Child in Canada. Toronto: McClelland and Stewart, 1972. 127 p.
    An overview of the plight of the battered child in Canada is presented. Topics discussed include dimensions and history of child abuse: the role of the parent in relation to the child, to society, and to class; the respective roles of physician, social worker, and the community; the legal ramifications of child battering and the need for a reporting law, emphasizing the law as a potential source of protection for the child. Child battering is also related to the broad spectrum of cultural violence. In conclusion, the rights and limits of parenthood are presented. It is asserted that mistreatment of children reflects a continuation of our ignorance and our political and legislative impotency in the face of old customs and traditions.

807. Walters, David R. Physical and Sexual Abuse of Children: Causes and Treatment. See entry 2422.

808. Washington (State); Department of Social and Health Services. Child Abuse, 1974. Olympia, State of Washington, 1975. 14 p.

809. Webb, K. W.; Burt, M. R.; Friedman, F. G. A.; et al. Report and Plan for Recommended Approaches and Methods for Determination of National Incidence of Child Abuse and Neglect. Vol. 1 and Vol. 2. See entries 2266 and 2267.

810. Wichlacz, Casimer R.; Randall, Dolores H.; Nelson, James H.; et al. "The Characteristics and Management of Child Abuse in the U. S. Army--Europe." Clinical Pediatrics, 14(6):545-548, June 1975.
    A 12-month epidemiologic study of child abuse and neglect within a population of 100, 000 U. S. military personnel and family members in a geographic area of 5, 400 square miles in Germany is reported. The data consist of cases which came before the Child Abuse and Neglect Board at a U. S. Army General Hospital in Germany during the fiscal year 1971-1972. Causes for this problem are outlined. Involved in the intervention were various military and German agencies and facilities. Lack of child welfare resources is a major obstacle to recognition and treatment.

811. Wisconsin State Department of Health and Social Services.
Division of Family Services. <u>Child Abuse in Wisconsin,</u>
by D. Roberts and M. Adler. <u>Madison, 1974. 13 p.</u>
Data generated from Wisconsin's child abuse reporting system
and central registry during 1974 are discussed. Findings reported
are incidence, type of injuries, fatalities, sex ratio of children
abused, characteristics of abusers, how cases were handled, etc.
The increase in number of cases reported during 1973 and 1974 is
attributed to increased awareness and revised reporting procedures.

812. Zalba, Serapio R. "Battered Children. " <u>Transaction,</u> 8:58-
61, July 1971; Reprint: <u>Science Digest,</u> 70:8-13+, December 1971.
A conservative estimate of between 200,000 and 250,000 physically abused children in the U. S. need protective services each
year, of whom 30,000 to 37,500 may have been badly hurt. Parents
come from complete range of socioeconomic classes; they can be
characterized as highly impulsive, socially isolated, in serious difficulties with their marriage or with money, etc. Only when individuals are convinced that involving themselves in these difficult situations is important will there be positive results.

LAWS: LEGAL, MEDICO-LEGAL, AND REPORTING ASPECTS

813. "The Abused Child Law. " Wisconsin Medical Journal, 68:31-32, January 1969.
    The 1967 Wisconsin Legislature strengthened the previous child abuse law, adding dentists and hospital administrators to those required to report child abuse. City police were added to the list of proper county authorities to be notified. Civil immunity was added to the criminal immunity provision.

814. "The Abused Child Law. " Wisconsin Medical Journal, 69:25-26, January 1970.
    The Wisconsin Abused Child Law states that the enactment of the law makes it mandatory in Wisconsin for physicians and surgeons, nurses, hospital administrators, dentists, social workers, and school administrators to report suspected cases of child abuse to law enforcement or welfare agencies. The text also describes the required follow-up reports, penalties for non-compliance, and notes that criminal immunity is granted where report is made in good faith.

815. "The Abused Child, Parents, and the Law. " Rhode Island Medical Journal, 47:89-90, February 1964.
    A meeting of the subcommittee of the Child Welfare Services Advisory Committee of the Rhode Island Department of Social Welfare was held in Providence in December 1963 to study the need for child abuse legislation. It was a unanimous opinion of those present that the State of Rhode Island should promptly develop legislation.

816. "Abused Child: Problems and Proposals. " Duquesne Law Review, 8:136-160, Winter 1969-1970.
    Examined are some of the problems encountered in making adequate laws for child abuse prevention which touch on such factors as patient-client relationships and civil vs. criminal laws and the adversary system employed in courts. Model legislative system is proposed as a solution for prevention and rehabilitation.

817. "Adoption Denied to Prospective Mother Who Abused the Adoptive Child: H. v. Children's Services Division, 522 P. 2d 225 (Oregon), Court of Appeals of Oregon. May 20, 1974. " Social Welfare Court Digest, 20(4):5, 1975.
    In H. v. Children's Services Division, the Court of Appeals of Oregon affirmed the denial of adoption, where a police investigation report and evidence indicated that the wife had consulted a therapist

after becoming alarmed at her conduct in administering several
spankings to the infant proposed for adoption.

818.   Allen, Hugh D.   "The Battered Child Syndrome.   3.   Legal
       Aspects. "   Minnesota Medicine, 52:345-347, February 1969.
       The Minnesota state law concerning reporting of child abuse
is discussed.   Health personnel must report such cases under penalty of law for not doing so.   Reporting constitutes no basis for liability.   Hennepin County experience reflects that reporting does get
action appropriate to the individual case.

819.   _____ ; Ten Bensel, Robert W.; Raile, Richard B.   "The
       Battered Child Syndrome.   IV.   Summary. "   Minnesota
       Medicine, 52:539-540, March 1969.
       More cases of abused children are being reported because of
increasing awareness; incidence of abuse may not be changing.   It
is suggested that the state law be amended to permit any person to
report a suspected battered child without fear of liability and also
that Minnesota establish a central reporting agency.

820.   Allen, M.   "Child Maltreatment in Military Communities. "
       Juvenile Justice, 26:11-20, May 1975.
       Deficiencies in handling problems of child abuse and neglect
in the military community include the absence of a welfare department and the presence of a system of justice which contains no family or juvenile courts and no civil provisions for domestic relations
law.   Currently, virtually all Army posts in the U. S. have established procedures for child protection.   The experience at Beaumont
Army Medical Center near Fort Bliss is recounted.   Using it as a
model, the Army is currently drawing up an Army-wide regulation
to establish guidelines and procedures.   Four general categories of
federal-state jurisdictions are described.

821.   American Humane Association.   Children's Division.   Mar-
       shalling Community Services on Behalf of the Abused Child,
       by Vincent De Francis, William H. Ireland, and Winford
       Oliphant.   Denver, Colo.   30 p. $. 35.
       Implications of and differences in 47 state laws for reporting
child abuse; suggested changes for maximizing child protection; implementation of reporting laws in a state-administered program and
in a county-administered setting.

822.   _____ .   _____ .   Termination of Parental Rights--Balanc-
       ing the Equities, by Vincent De Francis.   Denver, Colo. ,
       1971.   20 p. $. 50.
       Explores the problem of termination of parental rights and the
legal complications which surround the process.   Basic data with respect to the rights of parents and children, and variations on the
theme of how parental rights are affected, are presented and discussed.

823.   Anderson, Doris.   "Let's Follow Quebec's Lead on Child
       Abuse. "   (Editorial).   Chatelaine, 48:2, March 1975.

This is an overview of the child abuse problem in Canada. Anderson cites Quebec's legislation which makes the reporting of child abuse compulsory. She urges the rest of Canada to follow Quebec and pass tougher laws.

824. Andrews, C. "The Maria Colwell Inquiry." Social Work Today, 4(20):637-644, 1973.
A public inquiry was made into the care and supervision provided by local authorities and other agencies in relation to Maria Colwell, and the coordination between them. Maria was killed by her stepfather; she was subject to a supervision order at the time, and she had previously been subject to a care order. Andrews refers to some of the issues relevant to social work which were pinpointed in the summing-up speeches by counsel at the inquiry.

825. "An Appraisal of New York's Statutory Response to the Problem of Child Abuse." Columbia Journal of Law and Social Problems, 7(1):51-74, Winter 1971.
The problem of child abuse and New York's statutory response to it are discussed. The nature of child abuse is considered, including discussions of who are the abused, who are the abusers, and the role of the physician. The difficulty of proving that the injuries of the child results from the action or inaction of the parents is examined. Solutions to this problem developed by Family Court judges, notably the application of the doctrine of res ipsa loquitur, are reviewed. Special consideration is given to the pertinent provisions of the New Article 10 of the Family Court Act entitled Child Protective Proceedings.

826. Areen, J. "Intervention Between Parent and Child: A Reappraisal of the State's Role in Child Neglect and Abuse Cases." Georgetown Law Journal, 63:887-937, March 1975.
Part I gives an overview of the current neglect process and an analysis of the competing interests of child, family and state. Part II is devoted to an examination of the historic antecedents of the present neglect process and illuminates the way the law has defined and protected the competing interests in each of three eras. Three specific issues are considered in the intervention of these problems. Part III assesses the current patchwork of standards and dispositions of the fifty states and the District of Columbia. A final section presents specific recommendations for drafting future neglect statutes.

827. Arkansas. Legislative Council. Research Dept. Survey of Legislation to Protect the Battered Child. Little Rock, 1964. 2, 12 ℓ. (Its Research report, no. 123)

828. Arnold, George L.; Hurd, Jeanne L. "Child Protection: A Suggested Role for Members of the Wyoming State Bar." Land & Water Law Review, 9:187-208, 1974.
We are becoming increasingly aware of the serious problems of child abuse and neglect. Professors Arnold and Hurd believe that because of the complex nature of these problems, the solution lies

in a multidisciplinary approach. The legal profession is one of the necessary disciplines. Professor Arnold suggests that members of the legal profession in Wyoming are in a unique position to lead the way to a solution. (Journal Summary.)

829. Askwith, Gordon K. "Authority, Prevention, and a New Child Welfare Act. " Child Welfare, 46:407-409, July 1967.
Through the operation of a child aid society in Ontario, Canada, the 1965 Child Welfare Act provides guidance, counseling, and protection for abusive families and preventive counseling for non-abusive families. In implementing the preventive aspects of the law, the element of authority is essential. In being forced to accept guidance, the rights of parents raises some question but to meet the needs of children in marginal families there is a need.

830. Baher, Edwina; Hyman, Clare; Jones, Carolyn, et al. At Risk: An Account of the Work of the Battered Child Research Department, NSPCC. See entry 2204.

831. Bard, E. Ronald. "Adjournment in Contemplation of Dismissal: A Legal Mechanism for Accountability. " Juvenile Justice, 27(3):11-14, August 1976.
A general overview, and then examination of specific sections, of the new law (Section 1039, New York Family Court Act) is provided. The law attempts, through the mechanism of quasi-contractural arrangement, to bring about a negotiated agreement between the natural parents (and their attorney); the child (and its attorney); the social services agency (and its attorney); and the court. Upon the breach of the contract the agreement breaks down and the parties face the adjudicatory phase with its often unsuccessful outcome for any of the parties.

832. _____. "Connecticut's Child Abuse Law. " Connecticut Bar Journal, 48:260-278, September 1974.
The Connecticut Child Abuse Law, initially enacted in February 1965, is discussed. Recent revisions to improve reporting and investigation and to safeguard the child further are reviewed. Six areas for further improvement are given.

833. Bates, F. "Redefining the Parent/Child Relationship: A Blueprint. " University of Western Australia Law Review, 12:518-534, December 1976.

834. "Battered-Child Cases. " America, 110:559, April 25, 1964.
Public concern is reflected in the mounting pressure for legislation. Physicians should be able to report suspected maltreatment without fear of prosecution for defamation. There is a need for a coordinated system of reporting and cooperation between physicians and police.

835. "Battered Child Law. " (LSA RS 14:403). Journal of the Louisiana State Medical Society, 119:317, August 1967; 122(8): 247-250, August 1970.

This article presents the requirements of the Louisiana State Battered Child Law. It describes the proper formal procedures to follow and also states the consequence for failure to do so. This law does not allow the physician-patient or husband-wife relationships as grounds for withholding evidence.

836.   "Battered Child Law Costs Four Physicians." Pediatric News, 7(3): March 1973.
This is a report of insurance companies for four physicians who agreed to pay a $600,000 settlement in what is thought to be the first application of a state law requiring physicians to report suspected cases of child abuse.

837.   "Battered Child Law Reporting Procedure Places Moral Obligation on Physician." Texas Medicine, 63:120, May 1967.
Physicians have been granted immunity from civil and criminal liability for reporting cases of battered children under a 1965 Texas law. However, reporting is not mandatory, leaving the decision with its moral and ethical considerations up to the physician. Where protection of the child is involved, it is important that the report be made quickly and to the proper authority.

838.   "Battered Child Law Takes Effect July 1." Illinois Medical Journal, 127:570-571, May 1965.
Obligations of physicians and hospitals to report suspected cases of child abuse under the 1965 child abuse law in Illinois are detailed. Addresses and phone numbers of the 23 local and regional offices of the Department of Children and Family Services are included.

839.   "Battered Child: Logic in Search of Law." San Diego Law Review, 8:364, March 1971.
The purpose of this article is to try to achieve some perspective in the problem of child abuse by analyzing significant aspects and to clarify the legal issues so as to bring them closer to solution. In order to solve the problems and meet the issues, which the legal framework has avoided, legal reform is necessary.

840.   "Battered Child--Louisiana's Response to the Cry." Loyola Law Review, 17:372, 1970-1971.
The growing awareness of the problem of child battering has prompted state legislatures and social agencies to take action. Every state has defined offenses for which battering parents may be prosecuted. A thorough examination of the Louisiana law is presented

841.   "Battered Child Syndrome." America, 116:236, February 18, 1967.
Enactment of federal legislation is needed to seriously bind physicians to report every case of child abuse and to protect them against legal action.

842.   Beck, Rochelle. "The White House Conference on Children: An Historical Perspective." Harvard Educational Review, 43(4):653-668, November 1973.

Review of seven White House Conferences on Children and discussion of general trend: increases in Federal expenditures; role of
the states in using Federal funds; importance of the family.

843.   Becker, Thomas T. "Due Process and Child Protective Pro-
            ceedings: State Intervention in Family Relations on Behalf
            of Neglected Children. " The Cumberland-Samford Law Re-
            view, 2(2):Fall 1971.
    This article is intended to stimulate interest in legislation de-
signed to provide due process of law for respondents in proceedings
to determine child neglect, without sacrificing on the altar of due
process the rights of the neglected child. (Conclusion Summary.)

844.   Becker, Walter. "Züchtigungsrecht und Misshandlung von
            Kindern" [The Right to Discipline and Child Abuse]. Zen-
            tralblatt für Jugendrecht und Jugendwohlfahrt, 60(11):478-
            480, 1973; Therapie der Gegenwart, 113(8):1382, 85-86,
            August 8, 1974.
    The author defines parental maltreatment of children as abuse
of parental power, especially in the case of pre-school children.
Particularly in physical terms, the boundary between what the law
permits and what it forbids is often ill-defined. Becker holds that
what is needed is a change of attitude, of new moral views on the
parent-child relationship. Some recent examples from German Federal jurisprudence, which indicate that pertinent views are changing,
are presented.

845.   Belgrad, G. "The Problem of the Battered Child. " Univer-
            sity of Maryland Law Forum, 11(2):37-49, Winter 1972.
    Abuse is defined for purposes of legislation and for remedial
social action. The profile of the abusive parent is reviewed. The
extent of child abuse in the U. S. is explored, citing an incidence of
13. 3-21. 4 cases per 1, 000 persons annually. Model child abuse
statutes are examined, commenting on the two most salient features:
the selection of the social welfare or law enforcement agency as the
report-receiving resources in the community, and the grant of immunity from suit.

846.   Bell, D. O. ; Graham, W. N. ; White, F. W. "A Recommen-
            dation for Court-Appointed Counsel in Child-Abuse Pro-
            ceedings. " Mississippi Law Journal, 46(5):1072-1095, 1975.
    A survey of existing child abuse legislation is presented, and
recommendations for alteration of the existing Mississippi child abuse
law are made. It is recommended that counsel be provided for every
child brought before the court in its investigation of child abuse al-
legations.

847.   Belzer, R. "Child vs. Parent: Erosion of the Immunity
            Rule. " The Hastings Law Journal, 19:201-222, 1967.
    Lengthy review of torts involving child-parent litigation. Shows
bias of the court changing from total immunity from prosecution for
parents to creation of children's rights.

848. Bennett, Robert F. "Families in Stress." Compact, 10:13+,
Summer 1976.
Courts and legislatures are beginning to realize that a punitive
approach to child abuse and neglect is not effective. A double-page
chart provides State Action on Child Abuse and Neglect. Legislation
is moving into two directions: broadening the categories of those
who are mandated to report and providing statutory penalities for
failure to report.

849. Bergman, N. W. "Family Law. Termination of Parental
Rights. A New Standard for Balancing the Rights of Parents, Children, and Society." Emory Law Journal, 24(1):
183-194, Winter 1975.
The decision by the Georgia Court of Appeals in In re Levi,
181 Ga. App. 348, 206 S. E. 2d 82 (1974), that freed a 16-month-old
infant for adoption by its foster parents is discussed. The rationale
used by the court in this case reflects the gradual shift in the way
children are viewed by the law.

850. Bern, Joseph. "The Battered Child, the Family, and the
Community Agency." California State Bar Journal, 557-
567, July-August 1969.
This article represents an attempt to help practicing attorneys,
judges, and legislators to examine the California laws relating to the
battered child, and to pinpoint specific areas of vagueness, conflict,
and inconsistency in existing law.

851. _____. "California Law: The Battered Child, the Family
and the Community Agency." Journal of the State Bar of
California, 44(4):557-567, 1969.
This article reports on many areas in which California laws
pertaining to child abuse are not clearly defined: definition, accusa-
tion of abusers, reporting procedures, and subsequent legal action.
Urges that examination and clarification of these areas be done immediately.

852. Bernstein, Arthur H. "Hospital Liability for Battered Children." Hospitals, 50(5):95-97, March 1, 1976.
Hospitals are involved in most of the proceedings of prosecutions of child abuse because outpatient and emergency department
personnel are a likely source of reports of battered children. Bernstein reviews the circumstances leading up to battered child legislation in the states and interprets responsibility in light of it. The
material is not intended to be legal advice and should not be used
to resolve legal problems.

853. "Better Protection for the Defenseless--Tennessee's Revised
Mandatory Child Abuse Reporting Statute." Memphis State
University Law Review, 4:585-593, Spring 1974.
The 1973 revision of the 1965 Tennessee Child Abuse reporting
law offers many advantages over the previous statute: guarantees of
immunity and confidentiality, the waiver of testimonial privileges, the
abolition of accusatory reporting, and the establishment of central

registries. Legislation alone will not eradicate abuse and neglect. The law's ultimate effectiveness depends most importantly on public concern.

854. Bialestock, Dora. "Custody of Children." (Letter). Medical Journal of Australia, 2:1128, December 22, 1973.
Bialestock contends that at present in Australia the child's right to normal growth is not protected in any way as vigorously as the adult's right to privacy. She cites the nuclear family detached from a supporting and protective community as the source of large numbers of children who fail to thrive and are battered. Furthermore, she states that only when the law accepts that the care of children is synonymous with custody of children will there be a way to ensure all children the right to normal, predictable growth and development.

855. Birrell, John H. "'Where Death Delights to Help the Living.' Forensic Medicine--Cinderella?" Medical Journal of Australia, 1:253-261, February 7, 1970.
In dealing with the scope of forensic or legal medicine, Birrel addresses the problem of maltreated children. He discusses the incidence of child abuse in Australia and the public reaction in terms of existing and proposed legislation to counter this social problem. Other forensic topics examined are drug dependence, alcohol abuse, sex offenses, and murder.

856. Björck, S. [It Is Often Relatives Who Report Child Abuse]. Tidskrift for Sveriges Sjukskoterskor, 41(15):5-7, August 29, 1974.

857. Borland, Marie, ed. Violence in the Family. See entry 2360.

858. Bowerman, E. E. The Law of Child Protection. London: Sir Isaac Pitman & Sons, Ltd., 1933. 124 p.
This book is historically interesting from the standpoint of British laws governing parental rights and responsibilities; schools, institutions, and the treatment of juvenile offenders; employment of children and young persons; and the prevention of cruelty and kindred offenses. Various laws are described, such as the Infant Life Preservation Act of 1929, the Children's and Young Persons' Act, 1933, etc.

859. Brown, H. "Background and Promise: Juvenile Courts and the Gault Decision." Children, 15:87-89, 1968.
Describes the effect of the Gault decision on the Juvenile Court System.

860. Brown, Rowine Hayes. "Battered Child." Medical Trial Technique Quarterly, 20:272-281, Winter 1974.
Aspects of the battered child syndrome, drawn from the Cook County Hospital experience, are summarized for a legal audience: injuries, victims, death rate, offenders, diagnosis, treatment, etc. In abuse cases brought to criminal trial the evidence must be beyond

reasonable doubt, but in a civil suit a lesser degree of evidence will suffice.

861. _____. "Child Abuse: Attempts to Solve the Problem by Reporting Laws." Women Lawyers Journal, 60:73-78, Spring 1974.
Brown describes and analyzes the various state "Battered Child Reporting Laws" enacted between 1963 and 1967. She details the purposes of such laws, who is required to report, what injuries are to be reported, to whom reports are to be made, control registries, immunity from liability for reporting, and results of the legislation.

862. _____. "Controlling Child Abuse: Reporting Laws." Case and Comment, 80(1):10-16, January-February 1975.
A review covers provisions of the state reporting laws relating to cases of child abuse: number of states that require reporting, permissive reporting, who reports and to whom, the function of central registries, the physician-patient privilege, etc. Suggested future action is given.

863. _____; Fox, E. S.; Hubbard, E. L. "Medical and Legal Aspects of the Battered Child Syndrome." Chicago-Kent Law Review, 50:45-84, Summer 1973.
An extensive review covers the history of the medical aspects of child abuse as well as the legal aspects. The details of the Illinois Child Abuse Law are summarized. Types of evidence for the child abuse case are described, and the importance of preparing such witnesses as physicians and social workers is stressed.

864. Burke, K. M. "Evidentiary Problems of Proof in Child Abuse Cases: Why Family and Juvenile Courts Fail." Journal of Family Law, 13(4):819-852, 1973-1974.
The evidentiary problems of proof that confront the juvenile and family courts in child abuse cases are examined. The extralegal factors creating these problems are considered, and several proposals aimed at alleviating them are presented.

865. Burns, Alice; Feldman, Myra; Kaufman, Anita, et al. Child Abuse and Neglect in Suffolk County. See entry 2211.

866. Burt, Robert A. "Forcing Protection on Children and Their Parents: The Impact of Wyman vs. James (91 Sup. Ct. 381)." Michigan Law Review, 69:1259-1310, June 1971.
This article is a discussion of the legal principles vis-à-vis child abuse and focuses on one of the major concerns implicated in Wyman vs. James: the government's power with regard to: intrusion into the family and home, the right to privacy while receiving assistance, and the right to determine her own needs.

867. _____. "Protecting Children from Their Families and Themselves: State Laws and the Constitution." Journal of Youth & Adolescence, 1:91-111, March 1972.
In recent years, the Supreme Court has imposed stringent pro-

cedural requirements on juvenile delinquency laws. In the past year, however, the Court has refused to extend these procedural stringencies to analogous child protective state laws. This article explores generally the rationale for court application, by constitutional mandate, or procedural safeguards to a broad range of child protective legislation.

868. Butler, O. H. "The Value of Bite Mark Evidence." International Journal of Forensic Dentistry, 1(1):23-24, 1973.
An increased awareness of bite mark evidence has increased among investigators in cases of murder, rape, assault and battered children. The four bases of bite mark evidence are given and the practical preparation of bite mark evidence for presentation in court is described.

869. Buttenweiser, H. "Children Are Not Chattels." Trial Law Quarterly, 8:28-29, 36, 1972.
Explains that children's rights are now receiving more attention than in the past but that case law and statutes are falling behind reality.

870. Cameron, J. M. "Infanticide." Nursing Times, 67:1371-1372, November 4, 1971.
Although condemned in many cultures, infanticide has been widely practiced in others for superstitious or economic reasons. The laws of Great Britain concerning infanticide, the concealment of pregnancy and the birth of a child if the child is found dead or missing, and criminal abortion are reviewed. Prosecution under all of the laws is frequently complicated by the difficulty of proving whether the infant was capable of separate existence and whether it died before or after birth.

871. Carpenter, James W. "Parent-Child Dilemma in the Courts." Ohio State Law Journal, 30:292-309, Spring 1969.
The purpose of this article is to explore the legal framework which has been constructed to deal with the problems presented by those children who are not properly cared for by their parents or guardians. Problems confronting the courts in cases dealing with abused, abandoned, delinquent, dependent, and neglected children involve balancing the interests of the child against those of the parents and society.

872. Carter, Jan, ed. The Maltreated Child. See entry 750.

873. Chandler, C. B. "Children and the Law." Practitioner, 213(1275):335-344, September 1974.

874. Chase, Naomi Feigelson. A Child Is Being Beaten: Violence Against Children, An American Tragedy. See entry 568.

875. Cheney, Kimberly B. "Safeguarding Legal Rights in Providing Protective Services." Children, 13:86-92, May-June 1966.

Cheney explains the need for state legislation authorizing protective services to intervene where child neglect is apparent. There is also a discussion of due process of law regarding the parents' right of bringing up children, various types of neglect, and the primary goals of protective services regarding such neglect.

876. "Child Abuse." Virginia Health Bulletin, 26(2, series 2):1-20, October, November, December 1973.
A review of the problem of child abuse and neglect in Virginia and the approaches to the problem being taken at all levels of government includes a description of the different aspects of child abuse, as well as a history of the legal aspects. Recommendations of the Governor's Task Force are given.

877. "Child Abuse and the Law: A Mandate for Change." Howard Law Journal, 18:200-219, 1973.
This article compares the various child abuse laws in the U. S. and pleads for change where needed. Child abuse legislation and court decisions indicate that courts and legislators have begun to realize that the protection and care of the child is not at the absolute discretion of the parent, but is the responsibility of the larger society. The assumption that the child must remain with the parent at all costs is no longer pervasive.

878. "Child Abuse: Another Attempt at Solving the Problem." Catholic Lawyer, 13:231-242, Summer 1967.
Previews the problem, discusses the difficulty of diagnosing child abuse, and reports on what the law has done. The attitude of doctors, the course chosen by judges in making disposition of cases, the reporting by obstetricians of seemingly unwanted children can all help prevent wasted lives and help eliminate the torture many infants must endure.

879. Child Abuse Prevention and Treatment Act. Statutes at Large, vol. 88 (1974). U. S. Code, Suppl. IV, 1971-1974, Title 42, Sections 5101-5106. U. S. Code Congressional and Administrative News, vol. 1 (1974). Congressional Record, vol. 119 (1973).
Financial assistance is provided for a demonstration program and to establish the National Center on Child Abuse and Neglect.

880. "The Child-Abuse Problem in Iowa. The Extent of the Problem, and a Proposal for Remedying It." Journal of the Iowa Medical Society, 53:692-694, October 1963.
A survey into the problem of child abuse by the State Department of Social Welfare and the State Department of Health in Iowa indicated that prompt and effective action is essential. There is no requirement for reporting or legal protection for doctors or hospital personnel. About all they can do is whisper suggestions to a social worker or county nurse. The proposed Model Statute by the U. S. Children's Bureau is presented.

881. "Child Abuse Prompts Plan for State Legislative Action: Pro-

posal of the Education Commission of the States. " Intellect, 102:283-284, February 1974.
The Education Commission of the States called on all states
to expand and improve their legal statutes on child abuse to provide
more adequate protection for the victims, more substantive preventive efforts, and broader interstate cooperation. The suggested legislation was formally adopted in November of 1973 by the ECS Steer-
ing Committee.

882. "Child Abuse: Scourge of Society. " (Editorial). Journal of
the Medical Association of the State of Alabama, 46(5):17,
November 1976.
Discussed is the decision of the Alabama Court of Criminal
Appeals on October 31, 1976, declaring a section of the Alabama
Criminal Code relating to child abuse unconstitutional. The Alabama
Legislature in 1977 will now need to pass a new law redefining in
both the body and the title of the act the offense involved. The law
is not the complete answer to the depravity of this heinous scourge
of society. An aware and dedicated public to its eradication is
needed.

883. "Children's Liberation. " Trial, 10(3):11-16+, May-June 1974.
The use of First Amendment rights and the equal protection
clause of the Fourteenth Amendment for protection of children is discussed. The harm done to children by their caretakers, from gross
child abuse to mislabeling children as retarded, or tracking them in-
correctly into low ability groups, is seen as evidence for the need
for legislation to regulate such violations of children's rights.

884. Childs, Marjorie M. "The 1970 White House Conference on
Children--The Child Advocate. " Women Lawyers Journal,
58:7-11, 35, Winter 1972.
The delegates to the 1970 White House Conference on Children
concentrated on seven major topics. The broad topic of Laws, Rights
and Responsibilities included the Child Advocate. This particular
forum started with the proposition that an independent representative
for children--the Child Advocate--is urgently needed in every community. It was recommended that Congress create national, state,
local, and neighborhood councils of child advocacy. Implementation
and funding of the child advocacy programs are discussed.

885. Ciano, M. C. "Ohio's Mandatory Reporting Statute for Cases
of Child Abuse. " Western Reserve Law Review, 18:1405-
1413, 1967.
The amended Ohio reporting law of 1965 expands the number
of persons required to report child abuse cases. Two other significant provisions are the granting of civil and criminal immunity and
the suspension of the physician-patient privilege. Comparisons between the first law and the amended law, and with other state laws
are discussed.

886. Clymer, James N. "Torts: The Battered Child--a Doctor's
Civil Liability for Failure to Diagnose and Report. " Washburn Law Journal, 16:543-551, Winter 1977.

Clymer believes that the increasing recognition of the physician's unique position and ability to recognize and diagnose the battered child syndrome will likely result in a corresponding increase in successful attempts to hold the non-reporting physician liable to the victimized child whose injuries are compounded as a result. (Journal Summary Modified.)

887. Coburn, D. "Child-Parent Communications: Spare the Privilege and Spoil the Child. " Dickinson Law Review, 74:599-633, 1970.
Legal brief and proposed legislation granting children rights of privileged communication with parents and Bill of Rights protection.

888. Coigney, Virginia. Children Are People Too: How We Fail Our Children and How We Can Love Them. See entry 575.

889. Columbia Law School Project on Child Abuse Reporting Legislation. The Child Abuse Reporting Laws: A Tabular View. Washington, U. S. Children's Bureau; for sale by the Supt. of Doc. , U. S. Govt. Print. Off. , 1966 (revised 1968). 46 p. (Prepared under Child Welfare Research and Demonstration Grants Program, no. PR-800.)

890. "Confidentiality for Informants. " British Medical Journal, 1(6023): 1476-1477, June 12, 1976.
The House of Lords will soon be asked to decide whether the NCPCC can keep confidential the name of an informant in an unfounded charge of baby battering. The Court of Appeal ruled that the mother was entitled to know the informant's name. Unless the House of Lords is persuaded that the Child and Young Peoples Act of 1969 places the NSPCC on a par with government agencies, it seems doubtful that the Court of Appeal decision will be reversed. This could bring about tragic results if the publicity given to the decision led doctors, or the public, to exaggerate the legal perils when making a report.

891. "Constitutionality of the Illinois Child Abuse Statute. " Northwestern University Law Review, 67(5):765-772, November-December 1972.
The action of the Illinois Supreme Court in overturning a conviction of a child abusing stepfather (People v. Vandiver) is discussed.

892. "Conviction of Cruelty to Child Upheld--Struck Child with Plastic Bat. " Social Welfare Court Digest, 20(8):5, August 1975.
The decision by the Superior Court of New Jersey in State v. Rivera, which affirmed the conviction of cruelty to a child and the acquittal of a charge of atrocious assault and battery, is reported.

893. Coughlin, B. "The Rights of Children. " Child Welfare, 47: 138-142, 1968.
A discussion of the rights of children in a philosophically ori-

ented analysis which ties in the origin of "human" rights with the
Kent and Gault decisions. Makes a case for emphasizing the protection of children over infringement of parents rights.

894. Council of State Governments. Committee of State Officials
on Suggested State Legislation. "Physical Abuse of Children. " Suggested State Legislation, 24:66-68, 1965.
Suggested legislation in the form of mandatory reporting by
medical personnel and institutions of certain physical abuse of children is offered. Provisions of such a law include: the declaration
of policy, reports, immunity from liability, admissibility of evidence,
and penalty for violation.

895. "Courts: Seen and Not Heard: The Child's Need for His Own
Lawyer in Child Abuse and Neglect Cases. " Oklahoma Law
Review, 29:439-445, Spring 1976.

896. "Cry Rises from Beaten Babies. " Life, 54:38-39, June 14,
1963.
This is a double-page spread and a highly illustrated article
of two battered babies; one of them at two months of age suffered
30 broken bones. For reasons criminological, psychological or
sociological, there is an upsurge of brutal cases of child beating.
Doctors are unwilling to become involved. Two states, California
and Wyoming, require them to report. Other states are being urged
to pass the necessary laws.

897. Curran, William J. "The Revolution in American Criminal
Law: Its Significance for Psychiatric Diagnosis and Treatment. " American Journal of Public Health, 58:2209-2216,
December 1968.
Examined are recent changes in American criminal law which
have important health consequences. Among those discussed are the
development of the Battered-Child Reporting Laws, laws which provide legal immunity to medical professionals in reporting child battering, child abuse reporting forms, and provisions for the investigation of cases by law-enforcement agencies, welfare agencies, or
both.

898. _____ . Tracy's "The Doctor as a Witness. " 2nd ed.
Philadelphia: W. B. Saunders, 1965. 196 p.
This book is to inform the doctor about preparing for a trial
and giving testimony on medico-legal matters. One chapter is based
on what makes a good medical witness and another on privileges and
obligations of the doctor-witness, still another on testimonies in malpractice cases, etc.

899. Dalhousie University. School of Law. Child Abuse in Nova
Scotia. See entry 2217.

900. Daly, Barbara. "Willful Child Abuse and State Reporting
Statutes. " University of Miami Law Review, 23:283-346,
Winter-Spring 1969.

The major portion of this article deals with the legislative response to child abuse, including the purpose clause of mandatory reporting statutes, making the report, identity of the recipient, contents of the report, immunities granted to reporters, abrogation of evidentiary privileges, the central registry, the effect of failure to report, and the child's remedies. The Florida reporting statute is also examined and recommendations for improvement of such laws are offered.

901. Davidson, Arthur T., Sr. "Child Abuse from an Attorney's Standpoint." Journal of the National Association, 68(6): 534-536, November 1976.
Davidson interprets the New York child abuse law from the standpoint of the Family Court Act (the judicial arena in which legal ajudication may be sought) and the Child Protection Act of 1973 which created a section in the Department of Social Services to deal exclusively with the abused child and the neglected child.

902. De Francis, Vincent. "Child Abuse--the Legislative Response." Denver Law Journal, 44(1):3-41, 1967.
The reporting laws in cases of child abuse are tools for discovering and identifying abused children. A full complement of services to treat the problem, protect the child, and preserve the family must evolve if the problem is to be solved. In the 1962 amendments to the Social Security Act, Congress required that child protective services be a part of all public child welfare programs, but it failed to appropriate the necessary funds for implementation. Child protective services must be created and expanded with or without federal assistance.

903. _____. "Due Process in Child Protective Proceedings." The Cumberland-Samford Law Review, 2(2):1-24, Fall 1971.
This is an examination of the legal proceedings as a result of the Gault and Kent decisions. Hearing, notice, council, standard of proof, evidence, self-incrimination, are explained and evaluated.

904. _____. "Laws for Mandatory Reporting of Child Abuse Cases (need for and types of legislation enacted by states in the last three years)." State Government, 39:8-13, Winter 1966.
In this article Vincent De Francis, Director of the Children's Division of the American Humane Association, deals with the need for legislation requiring that evidence of physical abuse of children be reported, particularly by doctors and medical personnel, to appropriate public authorities. The central objective, he underlines, should be to protect children rather than to punish parents. With this end in view he suggests a number of approaches, legal and otherwise. And he points to a wide range of laws, most of them mandatory, enacted in forty-seven states in the last three years for reporting of child abuse. (Journal Introduction.)

905. _____; Lucht, Carroll. Child Abuse Legislation in the 1970's. Revised edition updated to 1974. Denver, Colo.:

American Humane Association, Children's Division.   208 p.
$2.50.
Report and analysis of current child abuse laws.   Reflects
changes; records status of laws in each state; calls attention to novel
approaches; discusses problem areas; and challenges some concepts.
Highlights selected language.   A guideline for legislation.

906. Deleury, E.   "La Loi concernant la protection des enfants
       soumis à des mauvais traitements" [The Law Concerning
       the Protection of Children Subjected to Bad Treatment].
       L. Q. 1974, c. 59.   Les Cahiers de Droit, 16:937-959,
       1975.

907. Dembitz, Nanette.   "Child Abuse and the Law--Fact and Fic-
       tion. "   Record of the Association of the Bar of the City of
       New York, 24:613-627, December 1969.
       Dembitz discusses various mistakes in passage of the New York
Child Abuse Act, difficulties of proving child abuse, medical testimony, eyewitnesses, incidence of child abuse, characteristics of
abusing parents, summoning of parents to court, and protective procedures for the abused child.

908. "Des mesures séverès pour protéger les enfants maltraités"
       [Some Severe Measures for the Protection of Abused Chil-
       dren].   Canadian Medical Association Journal, 111:193,
       July 20, 1974.
       In a recent memoir the public prosecutor of Quebec recom-
mends that every adult who had knowledge of an act of child abuse
be held responsible for reporting such an act to the authorities.
This person in return would have the protection of the law.   The
public prosecutor believes that this proposed new law would make
much easier the task of doctors, nurses and educators.

909. Devine, J. R.   "A Child's Right to Independent Counsel in
       Custody Proceedings: Providing Effective 'Best Interests'
       Determination Through the Use of a Legal Advocate. "
       Seton Hall Law Review, 6(2):303-335, Winter 1975.
       The child's right to independent counsel in custody hearings is
examined, particularly as it pertains to such proceedings in New
Jersey.   The power of courts to determine custody matters is traced
from the common law doctrine of parens patriae.   The concept of
the child's best interests employed by various state courts is reviewed.

910. Dewees, Phillip E.   "The Role of the Family Doctor in the
       Social Problem of Child Abuse: Comments on New Legis-
       lation Affecting the Legal Immunity of Physicians. "   North
       Carolina Medical Journal, 27:385-388, August 1966.
       This paper deals primarily with recent legislation designed to
protect the abused child and the physician who treats him.   Also discussed are the physician's reluctance to intervene in suspected cases
of child abuse, and the Abused Child Law enacted in North Carolina.

911.   Dobson, M. W.   "The Juvenile Court and Parental Rights."
       Family Law Quarterly, 4(4):393-408, December 1970.
       Attempts of the court to prevent cruelty and moral harm to
children may actually destroy what little home life the child has by
the stress of legal and agency intervention.   The removal of children from the home by the juvenile court system is often the final
unbearable stress that causes a family to disintegrate.   The state,
acting parens patriae, cannot supply the love even an extremely inadequate parent feels for his own child.

912.   "Doctors and Hospitals Must Report Child Abuse: Recent Su-
       preme Court Ruling Doesn't Invalidate State Law."   (Edi-
       torial).   Illinois Medical Journal, 140-141, July 1971.
       The director of the Illinois Department of Children and Family
Services believes that a ruling of the Illinois Supreme Court striking
down a nineteenth century child welfare law in no way affects the
validity of the 1965 Child Abuse Reporting Law.   The defects of the
older statute are apparently not present in the 1965 law, which requires physicians and hospitals to report all cases of suspected child
abuse to the Department of Child and Family Services within 24 hours
and provides immunity to the reporter.   The director hopes that the
Supreme Court Decision does not discourage reporting.

913.   Doll, P.-J.   "Secret professionnel médical et protection de
       l'enfance martyre" (Loi no. 71-446 du 15 juin 1971) [Med-
       ical Professional Secrecy and Protection of Martyred Child-
       hood].   Medecine Legale et Dommage Corporel, 4:217-221,
       July-September 1971.
       Recent law in France gives doctor protection from violation
of Hippocratic Oath in cases of child abuse.   He has protection of
law if he testifies and also if he invokes professional secrecy.

914.   "Domestic Relations--Appointment of Counsel for the Abused
       Child--Statutory Schemes and the New York Approach."
       Cornell Law Review, 58:177, November 1972.

915.   Donovan, Thomas J.   "Legal Response to Child Abuse."   Wil-
       liam & Mary Law Review, 11:960-987, Summer 1970.
       This article discusses several legal aspects of child abuse
laws, including: reporting statutes, common law attitudes, removal
of children from the family, and the effectiveness of legal interventions.   Accompanying the article is a state-by-state listing of the
various provisions occurring in child abuse laws of the 50 states.

916.   Downs, W.   "Juvenile Courts and the Gault Decision. II.   An
       Invitation to Innovation."   Children, 15:90-96, 1968.
       A review of the 1966 Gault decision, in light of a child's right
to due process when accused of a crime.

917.   Driscoll, P.; Hickey, J. P.   "Child Abuse: Legal Aspects of
       Physician's Duty."   Trial and Tort Trends, 394-419, 1967.
       The legal responsibilities of physicians in the identification and
reporting of cases of child abuse are considered.   The significance

of X-ray examination in providing diagnostic evidence is discussed. Legislation establishing the responsibility of physicians and possible civil liability for reporting are considered, including legal precedents for breaking doctor-patient confidentiality.

918. Eads, W. "Child Protection." Stanford Law Review, 21:1129-1155, 1968-1969.
A review covering the historical role of juvenile probation departments in caring for neglected and abused children; jurisdictions of juvenile-probation departments, law enforcement agencies and CPS units, effective implementation of CPS; and the establishment of a central depository for child welfare statistics.

919. Ebeling, Nancy B. Child Abuse; Intervention and Treatment. See entry 1268.

920. Edelman, Peter D. "The Massachusetts Task Force Reports: Advocate for Children." Harvard Educational Review, 43(4):639-652, November 1973.
The process of building a task force is seen as a useful way to be an advocate for children's activities. Task force involves identifying problems, setting the problem-solving process in motion, making the problem small enough to work with, specificity of goals, involvement of leading citizens, and reporting.

921. Education Commission of the States. Child Abuse and Neglect in the States: A Digest of Critical Elements of Reporting and Central Registries. Denver, Colo., March 1976. 26 p. Available from the Commission, 300 Lincoln Tower, 1860 Lincoln Street, Denver, Colo., 80203. Paper $1; also from EDRS: MF-$0.83; HC-$2.06, Plus Postage.
The first section of this document lists for each state: who must and who may make reports of suspected child abuse, what form the report should take, when and to whom it should be made, penalties for failure to report and legal immunities for those who file reports. The second section, which deals with state central registries, lists for each state: whether a central registry is present in the state statute, what parties have access to reports stored in the registry, and penalties for improper use or release of reports.

922. _____. Child Abuse and Neglect: Model Legislation for the States. Report No. 71. Denver, Colo., March 1976. 72 p. Available from the Commission, 300 Lincoln Tower, 1860 Lincoln Street, Denver, Colo., 80203. HC $3, prepayment required; also from EDRS: MF-$0.83; HC-$3.50, Plus Postage; also from National Committee for Prevention of Child Abuse, Chicago.
This report is a model for state legislation for child abuse and neglect. This model act was designed to meet the requirements outlined in Public Law 93-247 which was enacted by the federal government in 1974. The model is outlined with sections covering every aspect of child abuse and the law.

923. _____. A Comparison of the States' Child Abuse and Neg-
    lect Reporting Statutes. Report No. 84. Denver, Colo.,
    March 1976. 9 p. Available from the Commission, 300
    Lincoln Tower, 1860 Lincoln Street, Denver, Colo., 80203.
    $1; also from EDRS: MF-$0.83, Plus Postage.
Each of the 50 states has a child abuse and neglect reporting
law. An overview of these various statutes is provided in table
form, giving the following information: citation; year enacted; effective date; requirement for mandatory reporting; reportable age;
definitions of child abuse; requirement for education/school report;
immunity, civil and criminal; requirement for mandatory investigation; confidentiality of records; penalty; cooperation with law courts
and state agencies; appointment of guardian ad litem; administrative
proceedings and existence of trained personnel and facilities; and
provision for dissemination of information.

924. _____. Task Force on Early Childhood Education. Child
    Abuse and Neglect: Alternatives for State Legislation.
    Report No. 6. By Brian G. Fraser. Denver, Colo.,
    1973. 95 p.
Recommended state legislation offered on one page with commentary and explanation on the opposite page. This report with its
draft bill can serve as a model or checklist for new legislation action.

925. Eighmie, Dorland. "Legislation: Child Abuse." Journal of
    the International Association of Pupil Personnel Workers,
    16:98-99, March 1972.
Various provisions of the Florida Statutes pertaining to child
abuse are listed, including a 1971 amendment placing a mandatory
reporting requirement on teachers and any other employee of a public facility serving children who has reason to believe that a child
has been subject to abuse.

926. "Evidentiary Problems in Criminal Child Abuse Prosecutions."
    Georgetown Law Journal, 63:257-273, October 1974.

927. Felder, Samuel. "A Lawyer's View of Child Abuse (Emphasis
    on the Law in New York State)." Public Welfare, 29(2):
    181-188, Spring 1971.
The role of the lawyer in cases of child abuse involves the
protection of all parties concerned; the child, the community, and
the respondent. The 1969 New York child abuse law was inadequate
and corrections in this act were made one year later, providing
clearcut indications for protection of the child. The great need is
the appropriation of funds to effect the child protective services
specified by the law.

928. Ferguson, William M. "Battered Child Syndrome. Attorney
    General's Opinion Regarding the Reporting of Such Occur-
    rences." Journal of the Kansas Medical Society, 65:67-69,
    February 1964.
Because of the increasingly high incidence of the "battered

child syndrome" in Kansas, an official opinion regarding the reporting of such cases was requested from the Attorney General. The opinion is primarily directed to physicians of the State of Kansas, since, other than the parents, they are the ones who would most likely have knowledge of child abuse.

929. _____. "The Reporting of Child Abuse: Cases in Kansas." Bulletin of the Menninger Clinic, 28:269-270, September 1964.
This article details a 1963 judicial opinion of the Attorney General of the State of Kansas concerning the reporting of instances of child abuse by physicians.

930. Ferro, Frank, ed. "Combatting Child Abuse and Neglect: Symposium." Children Today, 4:Inside Cover, May 1975.
This article focuses on The Child Abuse Prevention and Treatment Act of 1974 and discusses how the law was brought into being and why it is needed. Seven elements which are essential to an effective child protective system are also identified.

931. Fetherstone, W. M. "Nobody's Baby?" Law Society Gazette, 69(35):873, 1972.
The conditions which must be satisfied under the Children and Young Persons Act of 1969 in regard to child abuse cases are outlined. If the parent freely acknowledges his fault but convinces the court it was a single lapse which will not recur, the court has no choice but to dismiss the case. Tragic results have occurred in a number of such cases. Casework visiting, rather than prosecution of the parents, was intended by the new Act's machinery. If criminal proceedings are not taken by the police and NSPCC authorities, there is a possibility that no order will be made. A subsequent juvenile court order is strengthened if criminal proceedings are taken.

932. Ficarra, Bernard J. "Pioneer Laws for Child Protection." International Journal of Law and Science, 7(2):68-71, April-June 1970.
Presents a brief history of laws for the protection of infants and children, from ancient practices to present day battered child laws.

933. "First Degree Murder Indictment of Parents. Child Neglected." Social Welfare Court Digest, 16(12):1, December 1971.
The Court of Appeals of Oregon upheld a lower court dismissal of an indictment, which alleged that a husband and wife had committed first degree murder by "willfully failing and refusing to secure and provide him with adequate sustenance, and medical and hygienic care." Causes for dismissing the indictment are given.

934. Fisher, Gordon David. "Interdisciplinary Management of Child Abuse and Neglect." Pediatric Annals, 5(3):114-128, March 1976.
Fisher discusses the legal rights and responsibilities with re-

gard to children as determined by the government's power of sover-
eign guardian of persons under a disability such as minority.   Three
types of laws are detailed: criminal laws; child abuse reporting
laws; and adoption laws.

935.   Fontana, Vincent J.   The Maltreated Child: The Maltreatment
        Syndrome in Children.   See entry 1281.

936.   _____.   Somewhere a Child Is Crying, Maltreatment--
        Causes and Prevention.   See entry 599.

937.   Ford, Donald.   "The Battered Child Syndrome--the Law. "
        Nursing Mirror and Midwives Journal, 140(22):58, June 12,
        1975.
        Defines the provisions of the law under Section I of the Chil-
dren and Young Persons Act of 1969.   There is no prosecution in the
juvenile court.   The grounds on which the child may be brought before the court are set out in the Act: "His proper development is
being avoidably prevented or neglected or his health is being avoidably impaired or neglected or he is being ill treated. "

938.   Ford, R. J.; Smistek, B. S.; Glass, J. T.   "Photography of
        Suspected Child Abuse and Maltreatment. "   Nursing Digest,
        4:35-36, September-October 1976; Biomedical Communica-
        tion, 12-17, June 1975.
        Guidelines for photographing child abuse and maltreatment in
the preparation of legal evidence are discussed.

939.   Forer, L.   "Rights of Children: The Legal Vacuum. "   Amer-
        ican Bar Association Journal, 55:1151-1156, 1969.
        Inclusive review of issues concerning the rights of children.
Concise summary.   Reference source on general topic of child rights.

940.   Foster, Henry H. , Jr.   "Violence Toward Children: Medico-
        legal Aspects. "   Bulletin of the American Academy of Psy-
        chiatry and the Law, 4(4):336-340, 1976.

941.   _____; Freed, Doris Jonas.   "Battered Child Legislation
        and Professional Immunity. "   American Bar Association
        Journal, 52:1071-1073, November 1966.
        The coauthors discuss the enactment of new child abuse legis-
lation and the statutory immunity granted to reporters of suspected
child abuse cases.

942.   _____; _____.   "Bill of Rights for Children. "   Family
        Law Quarterly, 6(4):343-375, Winter 1972.
        Emphasizes importance of legal recognition of children as
persons and their rights as individuals.   The authors list 10 principles or rights of children such as love, support, firm treatment,
regard as a person, attended to, earned money, medical care, etc.

943.   Fotheringham, B. J.   "Legislative Aspects of the Battered
        Baby Syndrome in the Various States of Australia. "   Med-
        ical Journal of Australia, 2(7):235-239, August 17, 1974.

The status of current legislation in Australia concerning the
battered baby syndrome is reviewed. Some legal mechanism exists
in each state and territory for dealing with battered infants and statutory provisions are listed. Although uniform legislation is not an
absolute necessity, a standard form of approach by means of multidisciplinary committees would be helpful.

944. Franklin, Alfred W., ed. Concerning Child Abuse. See entry
2224.

945. Franklin, Lee R. "An Exception to Use of the Physician-
Patient Privilege in Child Abuse Cases." University of
Detroit Law Journal, 42:88-94, October 1964.
This article is devoted to an analysis of the legislative denial
of the physician-patient privilege in child abuse cases. Describing
the new legislation as a social reaction to reports of abused children,
Franklin cites the prevailing philosophy of the courts as the strong
basis for new reporting laws.

946. Fraser, Brian G. "Independent Representation for the Abused
and Neglected Child: the Guardian Ad Litem." California
Western Law Review, 13:16-45, 1976-1977.
A guardian ad litem is a person, not necessarily a lawyer,
who is appointed by the juvenile court to protect the interests of a
child. The historical concept, duties, and functions of the guardian
ad litem are explored, and how a child abuse case works its way
through the court is explained.

947. _____. "Pragmatic Alternative to Current Legislative Approaches to Child Abuse." American Criminal Law Review, 12:103-124, Summer 1974.
Current legislative approaches to the problem of reporting
suspected cases of child abuse are examined, noting possible future
statutory trends and surveying several legislative innovations. The
inappropriateness of prosecuting child abuse cases is stressed, focusing on a pragmatic and therapeutic alternative already in use.

948. Friedman, Robert M.; Helfer, Ray E.; Katz, S. N.; et al.
Four Perspectives on the Status of Child Abuse and Neglect
Research. See entry 2225.

949. Friedrich, William N.; Boriskin, Jerry A. "Child Abuse and
Neglect in North Dakota." North Dakota Law Review,
53:197-224, 1976.
Views on the psychological aspects of child abuse and neglect,
the reporting system, the juvenile court, the criminal court system,
termination of parental rights, foster homes, and therapy for abusing parents are presented in an effort to help those in the legal system become aware of the current thinking in these vitally important
areas. (Journal Summary Modified.)

950. Friel, Leo F.; Saltonstall, Margaret B. "Legal Protection of
the Drug-Addicted Infant." Child Welfare, 53:493-497,
October 1974.

This article is an excerpt from a study of the Massachusetts Committee on Children and Youth. It was recommended that, to protect the rights of the child, the physician or hospital must have the authority to report the birth of a drug-addicted infant to the Inflicted-Injury Unit of the Family Department of Public Welfare and to the Division of Family Health Services of the State Department of Public Health. Recommendations also included responsibilities of the Inflicted-Injury Unit in drug-addiction cases.

951. Galliher, K. "Termination of the Parent-Child Relationship: Should Parental I. Q. Be an Important Factor?" Law and the Social Order, 855-879, 1973.
Refers to a recent Iowa Supreme Court decision, which placed primary stress upon parental I. Q. as a rationale for permanent deprivation. Examines the nature and reliability of I. Q. tests and concludes that I. Q. has no proper place in termination proceedings.

952. Ganley, P. M. "The Battered Child: Logic in Search of Law." San Diego Law Review, 8(2):364-403, March 1971.
Various aspects of the battered child syndrome are discussed to clarify legal issues involved.

953. Gesmonde, J. "Emotional Neglect in Connecticut." Connecticut Law Review, 5(1):100-116, Summer 1972.
The psychiatric, social, and legal aspects of the emotional neglect problem in Connecticut are examined to arrive at a workable standard for state intervention in such cases. Consideration is given to the juvenile court's broad discretionary powers of disposition once neglect has been found to exist. The procedure in Connecticut for reporting and prosecuting cases of child neglect is reviewed.

954. Gibson, A. G. "Non-Accidental Injury to Children." British Medical Journal, 4(5888):359, 1973.
Discusses the term "non-accidental injury to children" from the standpoint of a legal definition.

955. Gil, David G. Testimony of Dr. David G. Gil, Brandeis University, at Hearing of U. S. Senate Subcommittee on Children and Youth on the "Child Abuse Prevention Act." S. 1191. (93rd Congress, 1st Session). March 26, 1973. 10 p. Available from EDRS: MF-$0.65; HC-$3.29. Journal of Clinical Child Psychology, 2(3):7-10, Fall 1973.
This testimony concerning physical abuse of children proposes a definition of child abuse and neglect based on the inherent equal worth of all children and a belief in their equal social, economic, civil, and political rights. Child abuse or neglect is considered the responsibility of individuals, institutions, and society as a whole with the underlying cultural cause rooted in widespread acceptance of physical discipline. The witness argues for additions to the Child Abuse Prevention Act, including a clear definition of child abuse and neglect, a statement of children's rights, a rejection of all forms of physical force against children in the public domain, and specification of a minimal living standard for children.

956. Goldman, J. "Washington, Day Care. " (Editorial). Day
Care and Early Education, 2(1):21-23, September 1974.
The Department of Health, Education, and Welfare has begun to
implement the 4-year, $85 million Child Abuse Prevention and Treat-
ment Act passed in January 1974. The Act establishes the National
Center on Child Abuse and Neglect, which will be a part of the Office of Child Development in DHEW, to collect and disseminate information of child abuse and provide funds for a demonstration program and grants to the states. Abuse and neglect are defined according to the law.

957. Goldney, R. D. "Abusing Parents: Legal and Therapeutic
Aspects. " Medical Journal of Australia, 2(11):597-600,
1972.
Stresses the need for a moratorium period on obligatory reporting, which would allow battering parents to seek help without
fear of immediate prosecution. Also suggests the establishment of
family courts designed to work with abuse cases.

958. Goodpaster, G. S. ; Angel, K. "Child Abuse and the Law:
the California System. " Hastings Law Journal, 26:1081-
1125, March 1975.
The California law relating to the reporting, processing, and
handling of child abuse cases as it operates in Los Angeles County
is discussed and analyzed.

959. Gordon, Henrietta L. "Emotional Neglect. " Child Welfare,
24-27, February 1959.
A general appeal for court action on emotional neglect as well
as physical abuse/neglect.

960. Gottlieb, David, ed. Children's Liberation. See entry 610.

961. Governor's Task Force on Child Abuse. Child Abuse. Richmond, Va. , July 1973. 14 p.
A report of the Governor's Task Force on Child Abuse examines shortcomings of the 1966 Virginia child abuse law and makes
recommendations for a new law.

962. Gray, James J. Trends in Child Abuse Reporting in New
York State, 1966-1972; a Report Prepared by James J.
Gray, Sr. , Albany, New York State Department of Social
Services, Office of Research, 1973. 31 p. , illus. (Program Analysis Report, No. 51); (New York State Department of Social Services pub. no. 1157, 4-73.) Free:
1450 Western Avenue, Albany, N. Y. 12203: Attn: Supervisor, Philadelphia Unit.

963. Green, D. W. , III. "Parent and Child--Child Beating--Recent
Legislation Requiring Reporting of Physical Abuse. " Oregon Law Review, 45(2):114-123, February 1966.
A brief overview of the problem of physical abuse of children
emphasizes legislation up to 1966, specifically the law of mandatory

reporting in Oregon. Oregon passed a mandatory reporting law in
1963, but it contained no provisions of immunity for persons reporting or of centralization of reports filed, rendering it ineffective.
The 1965 Oregon Legislature added these needed provisions to the
law.

964. Grumet, Barbara R. "The Plaintive Plaintiffs: Victims of the
    Battered Child Syndrome." Family Law Quarterly, 4(3):
    296-317, 1970.
    After a brief presentation on the history, symptoms, and prob-
lems attending physician diagnosis of child abuse, Grumet describes
battering parents and their children. She then offers the following
solutions to child abuse: reporting laws, prosecution of parents,
removal of the child, and treatment of the parents. She concludes
that basic reforms in the judicial system are needed to insure that
each case is handled in the best possible manner.

965. Hall, Douglas A. "State of Maine Department of Health and
    Welfare: Protecting the Abused Child in Maine." Journal
    of the Maine Medical Association, 65(6):148-149, June 1974.
    Maine laws protecting the abused, or battered, child are
briefly reviewed, and the intent of the Department of Health and
Welfare to expand and broaden these laws is discussed. Reasons
that make doctors reluctant to file reports are examined; the range
of services offered to protect the child are listed, and a suggested
format for reporting child abuse, together with a list of regional offices, is given.

966. Hallinan, Patricia. "A Physician Examines Professional Neg-
    lect of Abused Children." Journal of Pediatric Psychology,
    1(2):38-40, Spring 1976.
    As an advocate for abused children, Hallinan rebukes both the
medical profession for failing to report cases of child abuse and the
present judicial system for its medieval treatment of abused children.
She recommends that hospitals, rather than physicians, be mandated
to report, and that a special judicial group be trained to deal with
battered children. Especially deplored is the tendency of the courts
to protect by clothing the brutality and its perpetrators in the utmost
secrecy.

967. Hannig, Jeffrey. "Physicians and Surgeons--Infants--Physi-
    cian's Liability for Noncompliance with Child Abuse Report-
    ing Statute." North Dakota Law Review, 52:736-744, Sum-
    mer 1976.
    In North Dakota, as in most other states, the physician can
be held liable if he had "reasonable cause to suspect" child abuse
and yet did not report it. Hopefully, civil liability for noncompli-
ance with reporting statutes will help governmental agencies in detecting and preventing child abuse.

968. Hansen, Richard H. "Child Abuse Legislation and the Inter-
    disciplinary Approach." American Bar Association Journal,
    52(1):734-736, August 1966.

A discussion of recent developments in child abuse statutes
shows that some statutes require only physicians to report cases of
child beatings, while others apply to teachers, nurses, social workers, or anyone in a position to know of such cases.   Twenty-seven
states currently provide legal immunity for those reporting.

969.   . "Doctors, Lawyers and the Battered Child Law. "
         Journal of Trauma, 5:826-830, November 1965.
         Hansen discusses the Nebraska battered child law, who should
report suspected cases of abuse, protection for those reporting, the
legal doctrine of "privilege, " penalties for failure to report, and to
whom the report should be made.

970.   . "Legal Implications of the Battered Child Syndrome. "
         Nebraska State Medical Journal, 50:595-597, December 1965.
         Hansen discusses a study of the Nebraska Committee for Chil-
dren and Youth for a group of physicians.   He then offers an analysis
of the resulting legislation pertaining to the reporting of suspected
child abuse cases and describes the waiving of the doctor-patient
privilege in judicial proceedings regarding children, incompetents,
or disabled persons.

971.   . "Suggested Guidelines for Child Abuse Laws. "
         Journal of Family Law, 7:61-65, Spring 1967.
         The child abuse laws and implementing procedures that exist
in 49 states do not solve the problem of protecting children from
their families.   New measures are necessary.   On first report or
judicial hearing, a judge should be empowered by law to direct studies, financed by the court if necessary, bringing to focus on the
family all community resources: pediatric, psychological, psychiatric
and social welfare.   Since abused children usually do not live to be
brought to court a third time, the second report of abuse should in-
voke a variety of existing legal measures for protection of the child.

972.   Harper, Fowler V. "The Physician, the Battered Child, and
         the Law. " Pediatrics, 31:899-902, June 1963.
         Harper discusses proposed legislation concerning the reporting
of child abuse cases by physicians.   He analyzes the problems of
mandatory reporting by physicians having cause to believe that abuse
has been inflicted and the physician-patient privilege.

973.   Harper, Robert G. ; Eyberg, Shelia M.   "Child Abuse: Psy-
         chological Evaluation and Court Testimony. " Journal of
         Pediatric Psychology, 1(2):80-82, Spring 1976.
         Outlined are the basic psychological procedures to be employed
and guidelines for the presentation of psychological findings in a child
abuse hearing.   The authors contend that the psychologist's familiarity with courtroom procedure is essential to smooth and confident
testimony, especially when under attack by cross-examination.

974.   Hart, Walter M. "The Law Concerning Abuse of Children. "
         Journal of the South Carolina Medical Association, 61:391,
         December 1965.

Dr. Hart discusses the various sections of the South Carolina Act Requiring Reports of Certain Physical Abuses of Children. Also described are the provisions for immunity from liability and the penalties for violations.

975. Hartley, Albert I.; Ginn, Robert. "Reporting Child Abuse." Texas Medicine, 71(2):84-86, February 1975.
The reporting of child abuse in Texas, which is mandatory under Texas law, is discussed. The handling procedure among 189 physically abused youngsters treated during a six-year period are discussed. Only in five was a physician called upon to appear in court and no reporting physicians were subject to civil or criminal suits arising out of their association with any of the children.

976. Healey, R. O. "Legislative Aspects of the Battered Baby Syndrome in the Various States of Australia." (Letter). Medical Journal of Australia, 2(14):540, October 5, 1974.
Australia's Minister for Youth and Community Services reports that he has appointed a project team to investigate what legislative provisions might be desirable for the protection of children, including the ill treatment of children.

977. "Health and Welfare Legislation Enacted by the Rhode Island General Assembly--January Session. 1971." Rhode Island Medical Journal, 54:437-438 passim, September 1971.
Among various pieces of legislation enacted by the 1971 Rhode Island General Assembly was one mandating the reporting of cases of child abuse by any individual who has reasonable cause to believe that a child has been battered or abused.

978. Helfer, Ray E., comp. The Battered Child. See entry 1512.

979. _____; Kempe, C. Henry; eds. Child Abuse and Neglect: The Family and the Community, edited by Ray E. Helfer and C. Henry Kempe. See entry 617.

980. "Helping Physicians Protect Children: Illinois Law to Exempt Physicians from Libel Suits by Parents." Christian Century, 82:516, April 28, 1965.
As of July 1, 1965, physicians will be required to report suspected cases of child abuse to the Illinois Department of Children and Family Services. This new law will exempt any physician from a libel suit which parents may file in response to such a report.

981. Hendriksen, D. G. "The Battered Child: Florida's Mandatory Reporting Statute." University of Florida Law Review, 18:503-511, 1965-1966.
In response to the needs of the battered child and his family, the Florida Mandatory Reporting Statute was enacted. While the law does provide for the identification of such cases, an evaluation of it shows that it should be amended for the specific reasons given.

982. Hicks, G. M. "State vs. McMaster: Due Process in Termin-

ation of Parental Rights. " Willamette Law Journal, 8(2):
284-293, June 1972.

The Oregon statute which covers termination of parental rights
of those who are "unfit by reason of conduct or condition seriously
detrimental to the child" is criticized as vague and imprecise. It
is hoped that a committee of the Oregon State Legislature preparing
a proposed revision of the Juvenile Code will adopt a provision for
the termination of parental rights which provides for the welfare of
children and at the same time is sufficiently clear and definite to
safeguard the constitutional due process rights of parents.

983. Hochhauser, L. "Child Abuse and the Law: A Mandate for
Change. " Howard Law Journal, 18(1):200-219, 1973.

A summary of the status of the law and child abuse covers
the reporting laws, protective services, criminal laws, and juvenile
court acts. The federal Child Abuse Prevention and Treatment Act
creates a needed National Center on Child Abuse and Neglect established under HEW to provide technical assistance, conduct research,
publish reports, and serve as an information clearinghouse.

984. Hoel, Hans W. "The Battered Child. " Minnesota Medicine,
46:1001, October 1963.

Discussed is the need for mandatory reporting laws. However,
the author deplores the emphasis placed on the punitive aspects of
the law's enforcement which he views as counterproductive for both
the abused child and the family.

985. Holder, Angela R.; Johnson, T. D. "Child Abuse and the
Physician. " Journal of the American Medical Association,
222(4):517-518, October 23, 1972.

The authors describe the typical case of child abuse and the
responsibilities and exemption from liability under the child protection statutes. They also pose the question of abuse when medical
aid is denied because of religious beliefs of the parents and state
that this reason is irrelevant to reporting the situation to the proper
authorities.

986. Hoshino, George; Yoder, George H. "Administrative Discretion in the Implementation of Child Abuse Legislation. "
Child Welfare, 52:414-424, July 1973.

Results are reported of a study conducted about 12 months
following the enactment of an amendment to the Pennsylvania Child
Abuse Reporting Law requiring county child welfare administrators
to notify police immediately of all reports of suspected child abuse.
The study was designed to determine how county administrators re-
acted to the legislation and translated the policy into operation. It
was concluded that the law made virtually no difference in the way
suspected abuse cases are handled.

987. Illinois. Department of Children and Family Services. Division of Planning, Research and Statistics. A Survey of
the First Year: Illinois Child Abuse Act. Springfield, Ill.,
1966. 32 p., illus.

988. Illinois State Department of Children and Family Services.
     The Abused Child Act. (As Amended Through September
     7, 1973). Springfield, Ill., September 1973. 3 p.
     The Illinois Abused Child Act (The Act) was passed in 1965
and amended. The provisions of the amended law are fully detailed.

989. "Illinois Supreme Court Review: Constitutionality of the Illi-
     nois Child Abuse Statute." Northwestern University Law
     Review, 67(5):765-772, 1972.
     The ruling of the Illinois Supreme Court in the case of a man
accused of beating his stepdaughter is examined. It is suggested
that the wording of the child abuse statute raises questions of ambiguity of meaning and interpretation.

990. "In the Child's Best Interests: Rights of the Natural Parents
     in Child Placement Proceedings." New York University
     Law Review, 51:446-477, June 1976.
     There is no simple set of recommendations which would solve
all of the complex problems which arise in various child placements.
It is believed, though, that the proposals provided can reduce the
number of children who are initially separated from their parents
by defining the rights of the natural parent in relation to the child's
need for a stable, secure, permanent family. For those children
who must be separated, the goal of these reforms should be to re-
unite them with their natural parents as soon as possible, or in the
alternative, to free them to establish themselves promptly in a new
and permanent home. (Journal Conclusion.)

991. "Indiana's Statutory Protection for the Abused Child." Val-
     paraiso University Law Review, 9(1):89-133, 1974.
     The four ways Indiana provides statutory protection for abused
children are examined. It is suggested that this framework needs
thoughtful additions, revisions, and consolidations, and that implementation should begin with the enactment of a broad child protection article as part of Indiana's family law.

992. "Infanticide Cases Before Magistrates." British Medical
     Journal, 2(5453):118, July 10, 1965.
     A bill has been introduced in Parliament to reform the British
infanticide law under which approximately 20 mothers per year are
tried before assize courts. The current law is described. The proposed bill would change the law by giving jurisdiction to the magistrate, eliminating imprisonment and formalizing the hospitalization
option, and restricting the publicity that may be given to an infanticide case. The bill's sponsor eventually hopes that infanticide would
be dealt with by a special non-criminal Family Court.

993. Insero, Peter P., Jr. "Legislation--Child Protection Proceed-
     ings Under Article 10 of the New York Family Court Act."
     Buffalo Law Review, 20(2):561-566, Winter 1971.
     Revised Article 10 of the Family Court Act of New York State,
"Child Protection Proceedings," is discussed, and important facets
of Article 10 are given. The relaxed evidentiary provisions will as-

sist in establishing proof of abuse, and the new definitions of abuse and neglect will increase the circumstances in which the Family Court may intervene to aid children.

994. Institute of Judicial Administration, Inc.   Juvenile Justice Standards Project.   Final Draft.   Model Child Abuse and Neglect Reporting Law, New York, American Bar Association, January 1975, 50 p.

A model child abuse and neglect reporting law aims to assure that appropriate protective services will be provided to abused and neglected children and that appropriate services will be offered to families of abused and neglected children in order to protect such children from further harm and to promote the well-being of the child in his home setting.   Recommendations for the establishment of a central register of child abuse are provided.

995. Isaacs, Jacob L.   "The Law and the Abused and Neglected Child. "   Pediatrics, 51(4):783-792, April 1973.

In the Symposium on Child Abuse held in 1971 two areas of New York State law as it relates to child abuse were examined on a question and answer basis including laws which mandate the reporting of suspected cases of child abuse and the child protective proceedings of the Family Court.

996. Isaacson, L. B.   "Child Abuse Reporting Statutes: The Case for Holding Physicians Civilly Liable for Failing to Report. "   San Diego Law Review, 12(4):743-777, July 1975.

The proposition that physicians who fail to report suspected cases of child abuse do so at the cost of incurring civil liability for injuries subsequently inflicted upon these battered children is examined with respect to the Allen-Cologne Act, a bill enacted by the California State Legislature in 1963.

997. Jackson, A.   "Court Procedures in Child Abuse. "   Midwife Health Visitor & Community Nurse, 11:329+, October 1975.

998. James, Joseph, Jr.   "Child Neglect and Abuse. "   Maryland State Medical Journal, 21:64-65, July 1972.

Physicians in Maryland may refer to a set of guidelines in order to deal with cases of child neglect and abuse.   In this state a report to the police is suggested.   The article highlights the reporting program in Maryland.

999. Janec, J. ; Haicl, Z.   "Two Case Histories of Children Maltreated by Their Parents. "   Prakticky Lekar, 49(23):902-903, 1969.

Review of case histories of two children hospitalized with injuries contracted through parental punishment stresses the importance of cooperation between courts and medical authorities in detection of maltreatment.

1000. Jaso, Hector.   "The Battered and Abused Children Act of the State of Rhode Island. "   Rhode Island Medical Journal, 58 (11):474-475, November 1975.

The Battered and Abused Children Act of the State of Rhode Island is spelled out for the benefit of physicians in light of their responsibilities. Physicians or others who want a copy of the Act should request it by writing or calling Protective Services, Child Welfare Services, 333 Grotto Avenue, Providence, Rhode Island 02906 (401-277-2791).

1001. Johnson, Clara L. Child Abuse: Public Welfare Agency-Juvenile Court Relationships. Paper presented at the Annual Meeting of the Southern Association of Agricultural Scientists, Rural Sociology Section (Memphis, Tennessee, February 1974). 6 p.
This paper explores the relationship between public welfare agencies and juvenile courts in cases involving child abuse.

1002. _____. Child Abuse: State Legislation and Programs in the Southeast. Athens: Regional Institute of Social Welfare Research, University of Georgia, 1973. 117 p.
Reported is a study of child abuse legislation and state programs relating to principles of reporting abuse in the eight southeastern states in Region IV.

1003. Johnston, G. David. "Evidence--Marital Privilege Exception Expanded to Include One Spouse's Testimony Against Other in Federal Child Abuse Prosecutions." Cumberland Law Review, 7:177-184, Spring 1976.
Johnston reports that the Federal Court of Appeals for the Eighth Circuit considered the anti-marital facts privilege's well-established "exception by necessity," which allows adverse testimony where the accused spouse has committed an offense against the witness spouse. In affirming the defendant's conviction, the court held that the "exception" should be expanded to include crimes committed against the child of either spouse.

1004. Kansas City Times. "A New Missouri Approach to the Agony of Child Abuse." Missouri Medicine, 67(1):56, 1970.
This editorial comments on a new Missouri law which requires mandatory reporting of suspected cases of child abuse.

1005. Kaplan, Eugene N. "Domestic Relations--Appointment of Counsel for the Child--Statutory Schemes and the New York Approach." Cornell Law Review, 58(1):177-190, 1972.
Various statutory schemes for the appointment of counsel in child abuse cases are discussed, and the report of the New York State Assembly Select Committee on Child Abuse (1972) is analyzed.

1006. Katz, Sanford N. When Parents Fail: The Law's Response to Family Breakdown. Boston: Beacon, 1971. 251 p.
Katz, a professor of law, analyses the process of state intervention into the parent-child relationship.

1007. Kelley, Florence M. "Role of the Courts." Pediatrics, 51 (4):796-798, April 1973.

In the Symposium on Child Abuse held in 1971, the role of
New York State courts in dealing with cases of child abuse was examined. The chief source of court action in such cases is the Family Court, which examines information supplied by medical and social
personnel regarding the alleged abuse or neglect, listens to parental
testimony, and arrives at a decision as to the final disposition of
the child. A particular burden is placed on the judge since he alone
must make the ultimate decision.

1008. Kempe, C. Henry. "Duty to Report Child Abuse. " (Edi-
         torial). Western Journal of Medicine, 121(3):229, Septem-
         ber 1974.
       Kempe comments on the problem of malpractice liability for
failing to report child abuse as detected by physicians.

1009. _____. Helping the Battered Child and His Family. See
         entry 1339.

1010. Kerde, C. "Gerichtsmedizinische Aspekte zu Problemen der
         Kindesmisshandlung" [Medico-Legal Features of Child Abuse
         Problems]. Kinderaerztliche Praxis, 42(11):513-518, 1974.
       In 1967 obligatory reporting of criminal action against life and
health was established. Kerde discusses the problems of criminal
action and avoidance as they apply to children. Social services and
agencies of detection should cooperate.

1011. Kerssemakers, I.; Van De Loo, K. J. M. "Infanticide. "
         Nederlands Tijdschrift voor Kriminologie, 17(1):28-44,
         1975. (Dutch)
       Since the motive is usually quite different in the killing of a
child, it is usually considered another kind of crime. Various countries, in their penal codes, recognize this fact through special infanticide articles as respects the mother who murders her newly
born child. Terminology of infanticide, filicide, neonaticide, and
lactenticide are distinguished.

1012. Kiel, F. W. "Forensic Science in China--Traditional and
         Contemporary Aspects. " Journal of Forensic Sciences,
         15(2):201-234, April 1970.
       An extensive review of historical and contemporary aspects
of forensic science in China includes the topic of infanticide. Fathers
in traditional China exercised the right of infanticide because of su-
perstition or economic necessity. In certain regions in the 19th
century, 40 percent of the female infants were killed. Laws in contemporary China prohibit infanticide.

1013. Knight, B. "Forensic Problems in Practice. IX. --Infant
         Deaths. " Practitioner, 217(1299):444-448, September 1976.

1014   _____. "Perinatal Deaths and the Law. " Nursing Mirror
         and Midwives Journal, 140(6):74-75, 1975.
       Most cases of true infanticide (death of a child caused by the
mother during the first 12 months of life) involve unmarried, young

girls. Prior to 1922 such a crime was labeled murder and was
punishable by death, but the Infanticide Acts reduced the penalty to
imprisonment. Legally, the burden of proof is on the physician to
determine that the child was in fact a live birth, the law assuming
that all babies are born dead unless proved otherwise. Proving this
is extremely difficult.

1015. Kohlhaas, Max, et al. "Kindesmisshandlung und ärztliches
         Berufsgeheimnis" [Child Abuse and Medical Ethics]. Zeit-
         schrift für Rechtsmedizin, 63:176-182, April 26, 1968.
         In light of the current legal procedure, the physician may de-
cide whether to file a complaint or not in cases of mistreatment of
children. Further discussed is whether a physician should be obliged
to report a crime according to the provisions of §138 StGB ("Non-
filing of complaints in planned or premeditated crimes") and §330c
("Non-assistance to victims") when there is a suspicion of a recurrence of the crime. It is felt that both possibilities should be rejected for legal, as well as medical-ethical reasons. (Journal Summary Modified.)

1016. _____. "Schweigepflicht ist nicht Vorbeungungspflicht"
         [Obligatory Discretion Does Not Represent Responsibility
         for Prevention]. Deutsche Medizinische Wochenschrift,
         93:1974-1975, October 11, 1968.
         The German legal system seems to be becoming more dehu-
manized, especially when one considers the topic of child abuse.
Doctors are no longer required to report to the police. Each doctor
must weigh in his own mind what is best for the child and parent.
There is a discussion of possible child-abuse situations confronting
the doctor in the light of his right to remain silent.

1017. Kohlman, Richard J. "Malpractice Liability for Failing to
         Report Child Abuse." California State Bar Journal, 49:
         118-123+, March-April 1974; Western Journal of Medicine,
         121(3):244-248, September 1974.
         The legal responsibility and culpability of physicians in cases
of child abuse are discussed. Malpractice liability for negligently
failing to diagnose a case of the battered child syndrome and theories
of civil liability are examined.

1018. Lamb, Robert L. "New Child Abuse Law Explained." Penn-
         sylvania Medicine, 79(2):30, February 1976.
         The new Child Protective Services Law, Act 124, 1975, of
the state of Pennsylvania is explained for the benefit of physicians.
It supersedes all previous child abuse statutes.

1019. Lazenby, Herbert C. "Do We Need Child Abuse Law?"
         Washington State Journal of Nursing, 37:6-8, March 1965.
         Lazenby discusses the need for a child abuse law in the state
of Washington, along with needed clarification of the state's child
welfare bill and the establishment of demonstration projects to help
families involved in child abuse and neglect.

1020. Leavitt, Jerome Edward, comp. The Battered Child: Selected Readings. See entry 521.

1021. LeBourdais, Eleanor. "Look Again. Is It Accident or
Abuse?" Canadian Hospital, 49:26-28, January 1972.
Legislation which requires reporting of suspected cases of
child abuse is relatively new in Canada; however, cases are often
not reported because social workers, clergy, educators, or physicians do not wish to become "involved." Studies of Skinner and
Castle and Morris, Gould, and Matthews are cited.

1022. Ledakowich, Ann. "Child Abuse Decision Reversed by Supreme Court of California." Medical Times, 104(12):47-48,
December 1976.
This article is a review of a child abuse case in which the
Supreme Court of California recently decided that a physician faces
potential malpractice liability for failing to diagnose and report the
battered child syndrome.

1023. _____. "Malpractice Decisions You Should Know About."
Medical Times, 104(8):91-92, August 1976.
This is a review of a medical malpractice lawsuit for failure
to detect and report the battered child syndrome in California. Although the Court of Appeal held that the complaint failed to state a
cause of action for malpractice, it added that the physician may be
held for damages to the infant for breach of statutory duty to report
injuries which appear to the doctor to have been inflicted upon a
minor by other than accidental means. The case was remanded for
trial against the doctor and hospital.

1024. "Legal Protections Against Child Abuse." Children, 13(2):43-
48, March-April 1966.

1025. "Legal Recognition of the Battered-Child Syndrome." Catholic
Lawyer, 10:240-251, Summer 1964.
These notes and comments deal with the evolving legal concerns of preventing and managing cases of child abuse. Recent legislation in New York and California is reviewed along with the psychology of child abuse and community response and solutions.

1026. "Legally Reported Child Abuse: A Nationwide Survey." Social
Work Practice, 1968. National Conference on Social Welfare. New York: Columbia University Press, 1968.

1027. Leger, Lucien. "Pour protéger les enfants martyrs les méd-
ecins sont-ils tenus a la délation. Une ambiguité à dis-
siper" [To Protect Abused Children, Are Physicians
Forced to Report the Cases? An Ambiguity to Clear Up].
Presse Medicale, 79:1261, May 29, 1971.
Amendments to articles 62 and 378 of the French penal code
produced some ambiguities in need of clarification. Are physicians
forced to report cases of child abuse?

1028. "Legislation and Litigation." (Editorial). Journal of the
        American Dental Association, 75(5):1081-1082, November
        1967.
        Legislation in 22 states and the District of Columbia requires
dentists to report cases of suspected child abuse, and 10 jurisdictions define failure to report a misdemeanor. The lack of central
registries in most states makes difficult an assessment of how well
health personnel are reporting. In 17 of the 23 jurisdictions the
doctor-patient privilege is waived.

1029. "Legislation as Protection for the Battered Child. I. The
        Problem and Its History." Villanova Law Review, 12(2):
        313-323, Winter 1967.
        Mandatory reporting laws by themselves are not a solution to
the problem of child abuse. Other components of a complete treatment of the situation include provisions which are named. It is the
responsibility of the legal profession to correct shortcomings in the
various states which do not provide such complete protection.

1030. "Legislation: Child Abuse." Journal of the International
        Association of Pupil Personnel Workers, 15:101-103,
        March 1971.
        Detailed in this article are the several provisions of the Child
Abuse Law of the State of Ohio, including reporting of suspected
cases and the management of abused children and their abusive parents.

1031. Legislation for the Protection of Animals and Children. New
        York: Columbia University, 1914. 96 p. (Bulletin of so-
        cial legislation on the Henry Bergh foundation for the pro-
        motion of humane education, no. 2)
        "The summary of legislation to 1913 was prepared by F. B.
Williams, esq. who also wrote the articles interpreting administration and recent legislation for animal protection. Dr. C. C. Carstens ... prepared the corresponding interpretation of child protective legislation. The added material, bringing the summary down
to 1914, was prepared and incorporated by Professor R. C. McCrea."
(Prefactory Note.)

1032. "Legislative Efforts to Control Child Abuse in Washington."
        Washington Law Review, 40:916, 1965.
        Discusses the Washington State statutes on child abuse and
presents some serious shortcomings which make effective prevention
difficult. Suggests some alternatives.

1033. Leibsker, D. "Privileged Communications--Abrogation of the
        Physician-Patient Privilege to Protect the Battered Child."
        DePaul Law Review, 15:453-461, 1966.
        The Children's Bureau model act for reporting cases of child
abuse is compared with the 1965 Illinois act. The Illinois act contains an immunity clause but no penalty clause. It is suggested that
the law be amended to include mandatory reporting by teachers, social workers, nurses, and marriage counselors, as well as various

doctors and Christian Science Practitioners, to the Department of
Children and Family Services.

1034. L'Epée, P.; Lazarini, H. J. "Mise en oeuvre des expertises"
      [Use of Expert Testimony]. Medecine Legale et Dommage
      Corporel, 6:85-93, January-March 1973. (Fre)
      Emphasized is the great importance of expert legal and med-
ical testimony when dealing with cases of physical, sexual, and drug
abuse of minors. More courses in forensic medicine are needed in
universities, and more doctors and lawyers should be required to
take them.

1035. Levi, Stuart; Schuh, Sara. "Issues on Child Abuse and Neg-
      lect in South Carolina." Journal of the South Carolina
      Medical Association, 72(4):119-123, April 1976.
      In the South Carolina child abuse laws professional and lay
opinion is sharply divided on the legislative issues. Some support
updating the present law and others believe the present law adequate.
Because of conflicting opinions, the purpose of this article is to discuss various issues which have surfaced. Among conflicts generated
by child abuse legislation is that between parental right groups and
child advocacy groups.

1036. Levine, Richard Steven. "Access to 'Confidential' Welfare
      Records in the Course of Child Protection Proceedings."
      Journal of Family Law, 14(4):535-546, 1975-1976.
      The attorney's right to child welfare records to effectively
represent the client is analyzed.

1037. _____. "Caveat parens: A Demystification of the Child
      Protection System." University of Pittsburgh Law Review,
      35(1):1-52, Fall 1973.
      Through an examination of the operation of child welfare agen-
cies and the interests of parents suspected of neglecting or abusing
their children, the lack of procedural safeguards for the parents in
intervention by the child protection system is described.

1038. Litsky, Herman. "Child Abuse--Some Perspectives." Ca-
      nadian Welfare, 44:13-14, July-August 1968.
      A family court judge discusses child abuse in terms of the
abused child's best interests, rights of the abusive parents, and society's clamor for punishment of the parents. Litsky concludes that
law will not prevent the tragedy of a single violent outburst of abusive behavior, but may intervene in behalf of the child and prevent
recurrence of cruel treatment.

1039. McCloskey, Kenneth D. "Torts: Parental Liability to a
      Minor Child for Injuries Caused by Excessive Punishment."
      Hastings Law Journal, 11:335-340, February 1960.
      Considers the doctrine of immunity, as evidenced in various
court cases--pro and con.

1040. McCoid, Allan H. "The Battered Child and Other Assaults

Upon the Family: Part I. " Minnesota Law Review, 50(1): 1-58, November 1965.

A legal discussion reviews literature on the development of the medico-social concept of the battered child syndrome and analyzes the steps taken to promote identification of abuse, specifically, mandatory reporting statutes. Numerous aspects that directly concern the physician, who is considered the person most responsible for identification and initial treatment of the syndrome, are discussed.

1041. McDaniel, Charles-Gene. "Legalized Child Abuse. " The Progressive, 12-13, January 1976.

This article pertains to corporal punishment in schools and child-care institutions. McDaniel, a Missouri psychologist, notes that this practice is legalized only in the U. S. , the United Kingdom, Germany, and parts of Switzerland.

1042. McGrath, Melba. "Early Sorrow: Some Children of Our Times. " Family Law Quarterly, 8:91-99, Spring 1974.

Many ills beset children because lawmakers have been exceedingly slow in responding to their needs. Touched upon is the right of the adopted child to know his origin and the many faces to this coin; the exploration of Vincent J. Fontana's book, Somewhere a Child Is Crying, and the need that becomes more obvious daily that there must be a Bill of Rights for Children.

1043. McKenna, J. James. "Case Study of Child Abuse: A Former Prosecutor's View. " American Criminal Law Review, 12: 165-178, Summer 1974.

The death by abuse of a nine-year-old Maryland girl in 1972 is discussed from the point of view of the prosecutor. The practical problems of prosecuting a child abuse case are outlined. There is a continual need for the presence of the law enforcement and prosecutorial disciplines in the overall treatment of child abusers and their offspring.

1044. "Mandatory Reporting of Injuries Inflicted by Other than Accidental Means upon Children Under the Age of Eighteen Years. Legislation Passed at the January, 1964, Session of the Rhode Island General Assembly. " Rhode Island Medical Journal, 47:398-399, August 1964.

This article details the Rhode Island law mandating the reporting of non-accidentally caused physical injuries, sustained by children, by physicians, and institutions to appropriate public authorities. The intent of the legislation is to prevent further abuses, safeguard and enhance the welfare of such children, and preserve family life wherever possible.

1045. Marer, Jack W. "Development of the Law of the 'Battered Child Syndrome. '" Nebraska Medical Journal, 51:368-372, September 1966.

The history of child abuse from Caffey's paper in 1946 to the passage of state laws in the 1960's is recounted, and the findings of a 1962 study of the American Humane Society are summarized. The

Nebraska law requires reporting to the County Attorney, and contains an immunity clause; failure to report is a misdemeanor, and conviction results in a fine. A companion law provides for waiver of the doctor-patient privilege.

1046. Marker, G.; Friedman, P. R. "Rethinking Children's Rights." Children Today, 2(6):8-11, November-December 1973.
A discussion urges the legal profession to recognize and insure children's rights as persons. Those rights which are basic to human development are named. Expansion of these rights to children in institutions, exceptional children, and mentally retarded children is attributed to three precedent-setting court cases which are briefly described. Rights yet to be articulated by the legal profession are also named.

1047. Martin, Harold P., ed. The Abused Child: A Multidisciplinary Approach to Developmental Issues and Treatment. See entry 1355.

1048. Martin, Helen. "Child Abuse in Kansas." Community Health, 2(5):4-6, 1968.
Reviews legislation enacted in Kansas in 1965 and 1967 pertaining to child abuse cases.

1049. "Maryland Laws on Child Abuse and Neglect: History, Analysis and Reform." University of Baltimore Law Review, 6:113-136, Fall 1976.
Although Maryland was among the first jurisdictions to enact protective legislation for abused and neglected children, the Maryland legislature must continue to respond to the plight of these victims. The author traces the development of the Maryland child abuse and neglect laws, analyzes the effectiveness of these laws today, and discusses those changes necessary to afford Maryland children the fullest protection possible. (Journal Introduction Modified.)

1050. Matysiak, Josef. "Pojecia 'znecania sie' oraz 'rozpijania maloletniego w swietle kodeksu karnego" [The Concepts of Maltreatment and Inducing a Minor to Drinking in the Light of the Polish Penal Code]. Problemy Alkoholizmu, 7(4): 5-6, 1972.
The Polish penal code is discussed with reference to the concepts of maltreatment and inducing minors to drink. The Polish law considers as maltreatment any action intended to harm a member of the household either physically or morally. The penal code punishes maltreatment with one to 10 years' imprisonment, the punishment being more severe in those cases when the maltreated person attempts suicide as a result of ill treatment. The offense of selling alcoholic drinks to minors is punishable with one to three years' confinement.

1051. Merrill, Edgar J. "Reporting of Abused or Battered Children." Journal of the Maine Medical Association, 56:119-120, May 1965.

The major purpose of a new law in Maine is to require mandatory reporting by physicians and institutions in cases where there is reasonable cause to believe that a child under 16 years of age has had physical injury inflicted upon him by other than accidental means. The goal of this law is to provide protection for the child, not punishment of the parents.

1052. Miles, A. E. W. "Forensic Aspects of Odontology: A Museum Exhibit." Proceedings of the Royal Society of Medicine, 64:112, February 1971.
At a meeting of the Royal College of Surgeons, Prof. Miles speaks of the latest permanent exhibit added at the Odontological Museum. On Forensic Aspects of Odontology, it includes advances in knowledge of bite marks which can be a feature of the battered baby syndrome. Dental expertise now seems largely resolved. The interest of the Home Office in compiling a register of experts in this field seems to have established a reasonable mechanism whereby police and forensic pathologists make use of this expertise.

1053. Mondale, Walter F. "Burdened Family." Trial Magazine, 10:12-13+, May 1974.
The activities of the Senate Subcommittee on Children and Youth, created in 1971 for focus on the special interests of children and youth, are described. The Child Abuse Prevention and Treatment Act, the main thrust of which is to support programs to prevent, identify, and treat child abuse, is discussed.

1054. _____. "Child Abuse: Issues and Answers." Public Welfare, 32(2):9-11, 1974.
Background information and legislation regarding child abuse are discussed. Various aspects of the Senate subcommittee's investigation into existing state laws and federal programs are reviewed. Funding is discussed and synopsis of the Child Abuse Prevention and Treatment Act is provided.

1055. Montana State Department of Social and Rehabilitative Services. Child Welfare Service Bureau. Montana Laws Relating to Abused, Neglected and Dependent Children or Youth. (Section 10.1300-1322). Helena, undated. 9 p.
The requirements of the Montana statute dealing with child abuse are given. If after a hearing the child is found to have been abused, dispositions of a wide variety are open to the court, ranging from return to the home to commitment to the Montana Children's Center. The law also provides some regulations regarding foster home operation and payment for foster care.

1056. Moore, John L., Jr. "Reporting of Child Abuse." Journal of the Medical Association of Georgia, 55:328-329, July 1966.
Details of the 1965 Georgia statute on child abuse are summarized. Reporting is required of health personnel in suspected abuse cases involving children under 12 who have been physically injured by a parent or caretaker. Immunity is provided for claims

made in good faith. Objections to the statute include an insufficient concern for siblings, and the possibility that mandatory reporting may deter the parents from seeking medical assistance.

1057. "More of the Same." Nation, 198:339, April 6, 1964.
Many more child abuse cases are being detected as such. This article questions the value of a law proposed to the New York legislature requiring authorities to report cases of brutality. It states that child abuse is a disease of society and will become less frequent only when the causes are removed. It is felt that the proposed law is only a verbal attack on the problem.

1058. "More on the Battered Child." New England Journal of Medicine, 269:1437, December 26, 1963.
An expression of concern for reporting of battered children, noting need for laws to protect and assist any physician and family in need of help.

1059. "Mother Guilty of 'Neglect'--Baby Injured in Charge of Babysitters." In Re M., 357 N.Y.S. 2d 354 (New York) Family Court of City of New York. New York County. May 20, 1974. Social Welfare Court Digest, 19(11):6, 1974.
In Re M., the Family Court of City of New York found a mother guilty of neglect on charges that she failed to provide proper medical treatment and to report injuries sustained by her two-year-old child, who had been injured while in the charge of babysitters, in that she delayed 12 hours before taking the injured child to a hospital. The Court ruled that failure to exercise a minimum degree of care resulting in improper supervision is irresponsible.

1060. Naeve, W.; Lohmann, E. "Methodik und Beweiswert Körperlicher Sofort-Untersuchungen lebender Personen nach Straftaten" [Methodology and Conclusiveness of Physical Examinations of Living Persons Immediately After Criminal Offenses]. Journal of Legal Medicine, 72(2):79-99, 1973.
The indications and conclusions of physical examinations performed immediately after the offense on 503 living victims and accused persons by the Hamburg Institute of Forensic Medicine are reported. The findings showed that an immediate physical examination of victims and accused persons, particularly in cases of suspicion of child sex offenses, and violent crimes may contribute greatly to an evaluation of testimony; to a reconstruction of the crime; to the nature of the criminal instrument used; and to a determination of the time of the crime.

1061. Nagi, Saad Z. Child Maltreatment in the United States: A Cry for Help and Organizational Response. See entry 2242.

1062. National Committee for Prevention of Child Abuse. Independent Representation for the Abused and Neglected Child: The Guardian Ad Litem by Brian G. Fraser. Chicago. 45 p. This booklet is a reprint from the California Western Law Review. Available from the Committee, Suite 510, 111 E. Wacker Drive, Chicago, Ill. 60601. $1.75 ea.

A guardian ad litem is a person, not necessarily a lawyer, who is appointed by the juvenile court to protect the interests of a child. The booklet explores the historical concept, duties, and functions of the guardian ad litem; and explains how a child abuse case works its way through the court.

1063. _____. Professional Papers: Child Abuse and Neglect. Chicago, 1973-1974. 230 p.
A group of 11 papers compiled by the National Committee for Prevention of Child Abuse explores a number of aspects of the child abuse problem. Dealt with are the legal aspects, the social and related factors in child abuse, and finally, local child abuse programs.

1064. National Conference on Child Abuse: A Summary Report. See entry 1371.

1065. National Organization on Legal Problems of Education. Child Abuse: A Teacher's Responsibility to Report, by Roberta Gottesman. Topeka, Kansas, 1975. 6 p.
Recent state legislation aimed at dealing with the problem of child abuse has been confined to statutes affecting the reporting of abuse. The statutes all have two fundamental elements: a designated class of persons--teachers, doctors, social workers--who do the reporting, and oral and written reports that are made to officials so that they take action. Four desirable items for reporting statutes are given.

1066. National Symposium on Child Abuse, Rochester, N.Y., 1971. See entry 786.

1067. National Symposium on Child Abuse, 2d, Denver, 1972. See entry 1981.

1068. National Symposium on Child Abuse, 4th, Charleston, S.C., 1973. Seen entry 1982.

1069. National Symposium on Child Abuse, 5th, Boston, Mass., 1974. See entry 1983.

1070. Nelsen, Lloyd H. "The Abused Child Law." Utah Public Welfare Review, 16-21, Winter 1966.

1071. New York State Department of Social Services. Trends in Child Abuse Reporting in New York State 1966-1972. Program Analysis Report No. 51, April 1973. Publ. No. 1157 (4-73). 31 p.
History and operation of the New York State Child Abuse Register is provided, along with cases of suspected child abuse reported from 1966-1972. By showing trends in reporting--e.g., who makes reports, disposition of cases, some characteristics of the abused children and alleged abusers--this analysis report can provide indications of the effectiveness of the program, where improvements have been made and where they are needed. Charts, tables, and appendices.

1072. Niedermeyer, K. "Kriminelle Kindesmisshandlung durch die
      Mutter." In Medizinischjuristische Grenfragen. Heft 11.
      [Criminal Maltreatment of Children by the Mother]. In:
      Medicolegal Borderline Questions. vol. 11. VEG Gustav
      Fischer Verlag, 37-49, 1971. Tables 1.
      This article compares the rules on penalization of maltreat-
ment of children in the Penal Code of the German Democratic Republic (1968) with previously valid rules. Personal observations show
that some 50 percent of the offenders are women. There is no prevalence of oligophrenic mothers among them, but mothers on the
border of mental deficiency are numerous. The often immature offenders usually show a superficial attitude to life.

1073. "Observations on the Establishment of a Child-Protective-
      Services System in California." Stanford Law Review,
      21:1129-1155, May 1969.
      The California Child Protective Services Act, the Veneman
Act, represents California's first major break with its practice of
dealing with neglect and abused children through juvenile courts and
probation departments. It provides for the creation "as rapidly as
possible" of the statewide system of welfare-administered social services designed to ensure adequate care and supervision for all children. Observations on the Act are provided.

1074. Oettinger, Katherine B. "The Facts Behind Battered-Child
      Laws." Medical Economics, 41(17):71-75, 1964.
      Examines whether it is realistic to expect the child abuse
laws to protect children from abusive parents.

1075. Okell, C.; Butcher, C. H. H. "Battered Child Syndrome."
      The Law Society's Gazette, 66:587, September 1969.

1076. Oregon State Legislature. Joint Interim Committee on the
      Judiciary. The Non-Delinquent Child in Juvenile Court:
      A Digest of Case Law. By E. W. Browne and L. Penny.
      Reno, Nev.; National Council of Juvenile Court Judges,
      1974. 100 p.
      Some of the problems facing the juvenile court judge in cases
of juvenile neglect and dependency and changes in case law are related in 151 cases and 11 authoritative sources. Definitions of such
situations as neglect, child abuse, etc. are first reviewed. Procedures covered and information relating to disposition and philosophy
of disposition are given. Matters of custody, termination of parental
rights, etc., are also considered.

1077. "Oregon's Child Abuse Legislation: Some Additional Pro-
      posals." Willamette Law Journal, 5:131-139, Spring 1968.
      In 1967 the reporting provisions of the Oregon law were ex-
panded to include other professionals (besides doctors and medical
personnel), such as teachers and social workers. The creation of
a central registry, the inclusion of a social service agency in reporting procedures, and the expansion of the immunity clause to
teachers and other professionals would provide a wider scope of
services and a broader attack on the problem.

1078. "Our Children's Keepers. " Journal of the Canadian Dental
        Association, 37:245, June-July 1971.
    The need for legislation on child abuse in Canada is examined
in this editorial.   Greater severity in the courts might produce a
deterrent effect.

1079. Pachman, D. J.   "The Illinois Child Abuse and Neglect Re-
        porting Acts Past and Present. "   Illinois Medical Journal,
        149(2):175-184, February 1976.
    Provisions of the Illinois Abused Child Bill of 1965 relevant
to physicians are reviewed, and potential changes that may arise
from a proposed Abused and Neglected Child Reporting Bill are considered.   Child abuse and neglect registry data for Illinois through
fiscal year 1975 are presented, and reasons why child abuse and
neglect continues to be a major problem are proposed.   The provisions of the 1965 Act and its subsequent amendments are reviewed.

1080. "Parent Accused of Child Beating May Not Claim the Doctor-
        Patient Privilege to Prevent Medical Testimony. "   Univer-
        sity of Kansas Law Review, 12:467-469, March 1964.
    The Attorney General of the state of Kansas has ruled that
the parents of a minor child, as his natural guardians, do not have
the right to claim the doctor-patient privilege in behalf of such minor
child in cases of suspected child abuse.   The duty of a physician to
reveal cases of child abuse is a duty owed to the child, who is unable to protect himself, to society, and to his profession.   This ruling is in accordance with the principles of medical ethics of the
American Medical Association.   A concurrent ruling holds that a
physician who carries out this duty cannot be sued for defamation
should he be in error.

1081. "Parent-Child Tort Immunity: A Rule in Need of Change. "
        University of Missouri Law Review, 27:191-207, 1972.
    Develops the concept that parental immunity from prosecution
by the child grows out of societal conditions in which, without the
family, a child would perish.   Explains that such a situation no
longer exists and the immunity laws have become similarly outdated.

1082. Parizeau, Alice.   "Sommes-nous tous des assassins?" [Are
        We All Assassins?]   Criminologie, 8(1-2):167-174, 1975.
    The concept of parental authority as supreme with respect to
children is discussed.   Cases known to doctors of maltreatment,
cruelty or incest, and the difficulty of proving them before the courts
are discussed.   The question of the extent to which society should
recognize the rights of children instead of continuously demanding
that they respect its norms is examined.   (Journal Summary Modified.)

1083. Parker, Graham E.   "The Battered Child Syndrome.   The
        Problem in the United States. "   Medicine, Science and the
        Law, 5:160-163, July 1965.
    A review of child abuse legislation examines reporting pro-
cedures, social agency responsibility, purpose of the laws, and im-

plications for the medical profession.   Specific laws from Colorado, Idaho, and Wyoming are presented.   State laws differ on mandatory reporting, age qualification for the child, and responsibility for case disposition.

1084.   Paulsen, Monrad.   "Child Abuse Reporting Laws; the Shape of the Legislation. "   Columbia Law Review, 67:1-49, January 1967.
Described and analyzed are the existing child abuse reporting statutes of 1967.   Specific topics treated include model statutes, requirement of reporting abuse, state legislation, mandatory or permissive reporting, injuries to be reported, statutory plans for handling reports, central registries, practical effects of reporting legislation, and recommendations for improving legislation in New York State and their implementation in New York City.

1085.   _____.   "The Legal Framework for Child Protection. "   Columbia Law Review, 66(4):679-717, April 1966.
Paulsen examines the general legal framework within which the problem of child abuse has been located and some of the legal and social issues involved.   Consideration is given to criminal law (cruelty to children statutes and the privilege to discipline one's children): juvenile court acts; authorization of child protective services; and reporting laws.   The author concludes, that from the battered child's standpoint, the usefulness of the entire legal framework ultimately depends upon the effectiveness of the interventions for which the law provides.

1086.   _____.   "Legal Protections Against Child Abuse. "   Children, 13:42-48, March-April 1966.
Four types of legal provisions directly related to child abuse are discussed: provisions of criminal law invoked to punish those inflicting harm upon children; juvenile court acts which initiate protective supervision of the abused child or order his removal from the home; legislation authorizing or establishing protective services for abused children as part of comprehensive programs; and child abuse reporting laws which encourage the reporting of child abuse.

1087.   _____; Parker, Graham; Adelman, Lynn.   "Child Abuse Reporting Laws--Some Legislative History (Based on a Survey of 47 States).   George Washington Law Review, 34:482-506, March 1966.
This is an historical analysis of the factors responsible for the enactment of numerous state laws to curb child abuse between 1962-1966.   The influential roles of the American Humane Society, the U. S. Children's Bureau, mass media, professionals who deal with children, and voluntary associations are examined.

1088.   "Physically Abused Child Held 'Deprived. '"   Social Welfare Court Digest, 17(4):2, April 1972.
The Supreme Court of North Dakota affirmed a judgment terminating parental rights over a child who has suffered numerous unexplained injuries while in the care of his father.   The court held

that the child was "deprived," that the mother failed to protect, nurture, and care for the child, and that the circumstances were likely to continue.

1089. "Physicians Required to Report Child Beatings." Minnesota Medicine, 46:876, September 1963.
An amendment to the Minnesota Statutes, passed by the 1963 session of the legislature, now requires that beatings, or similar treatment of minors, under the age of 16 years, be immediately reported to proper police authorities. In addition, no such report shall be made the subject matter or basis for any suit for slander or libel.

1090. Piersma, Paul. "Protection for Abused Children: Review of Recent Legal Developments." Journal of Pediatric Psychology, 1(2):77-79, Spring 1976.
Although all states now have abuse reporting statutes, Piersma identifies four areas of serious legal difficulties: standards for state intervention, the vagueness test; abuse reporting, problems with central registers; emergency protective orders, the need for an early hearing; and legal counsel for parents and children. The author concludes that efforts should be made to develop precise, realistic standards and carefully developed procedures for the protection of children.

1091. Plaine, Lloyd Leva. "Evidentiary Problems in Criminal Child Abuse Prosecutions." Georgetown Law Journal, 63:257-273, October 1974.
The nature of child abuse cases often yields a lack of admissible evidence. The use of res ipsa loquitur principles to support an inference of guilt in child abuse cases, prompted by the difficulty of directly proving abuse, is neither a widely used nor the best means of circumventing the evidentiary difficulties. Courts and prosecutors must devise alternative methods of securing admission of evidence of abuse. An examination of the types of evidence available in child abuse cases reveals potential theories of admissibility; the exceptions to the exclusion of character and hearsay evidence have a special significance in such cases. (Journal Summary.)

1092. Plonka, H. "Kinder als Zeuge im Strafverfahren gegen Angehörige" [Children as Witnesses in Criminal Proceedings Against Relatives]. Polizeiblatt, 37(6):93-95, 1974.
In cases of child abuse, the rights of the child and the parents and the physician's responsibility are outlined according to the law. Some guidelines are given for the police. The formalities of instructing the witness should be dealt with as soon as possible in order to ensure valid evidence. Injuries and traces of maltreatment should be photographed (in color); witnesses must be questioned and personal observations recorded.

1093. Pospišil-Završki, K. , et al. "Alkoholizan i čl. 196. KZ-- zlostavljanje i zapuštanje maloljetnika" [Alcoholism and Paragraph 196 of Criminal Law--Abuse and Neglect of Minors]. Neuropsihijatrija, 16:49-53, 1968. (Croatian)

Of the 62 persons (30 women) who were tried in Zabreg during 1960-1965 for violations of Article 196 of the criminal code (abuse and neglect of minors), alcoholism was recorded in the legal documents of 37 (25 women) and confirmed clinically in 23 (3 women). Of all the defendants, only 18 (2 women) were convicted of violating Article 61a of the criminal code, requiring compulsory treatment of criminals who have "devoted themselves to the consumption of alcohol."

1094.   Prince, Russell C.   "Evidence--Child Abuse--Expert Medical Testimony Concerning 'Battered Child Syndrome' Held Admissible."   Fordham Law Review, 42:935-942, May 1974.
This is a detailed and well-footnoted article which presents a history of the legal difficulties in proving actual child abuse in the court system.   Highlighted is the case of People v. Henson (33 N. Y. 2d 63, 304 N. E. 2d 358, 349 N. Y. St. 2d 657, 1973) which established the admissibility of the diagnosis of "battered child syndrome" in criminal prosecutions as circumstantial proof that the child's injuries were not accidental.

1095.   Raffalli, Henri C.   "The Battered Child: An Overview of a Medical, Legal, and Social Problem."   Crime & Delinquency, 16:139-150, April 1970.
One of the applicable principles of law is the natural right of the parent to the care and custody of his children--a right that imposes on him the corresponding legal duty to care for them.   Care includes the responsibility to train, educate, and discipline.   But at what point does discipline cross the border into child abuse?   A diagnosis of child abuse is difficult primarily because of the demands of the doctrine of substantiation.   Legally, the question of doctor-patient privilege (can the doctor ask the parent to pay for X-rays to be used in evidence against him?) raises the whole spectrum of problems relating to constitutional guarantees against self-incrimination.   (Journal Summary Modified.)

1096.   Ramsey, Jerry A.; Lawler, Byron J.   "Battered Child Syndrome."   Pepperdine Law Review, 1:372-381, 1974.
The case of California physicians who failed to report a case of child abuse in the face of highly convincing evidence is recounted. It is suggested that criminal sanctions are not of sufficient severity and the incidence of prosecution not sufficiently frequent to result in an effective implementation of the mandatory reporting laws.

1097.   Rayford, Linwood; McCall, Frances; Miller, Morris, et al. "The Social and Legal Aspects of the Battered Child in the District of Columbia: Panel Discussion."   Clinical Proceedings, 24:375-393, December 1968.
Four persons of the medical and legal professions relate some of their experiences with battered children.   A panel discussion covers questions concerning the difficulty of bringing cases of child abuse to court, what legislation is needed, the role of the public health nurse, the need for a search warrant to inspect suspected homes, etc.

1098. "Recognition and Protection of the Family's Interests in Child Abuse Proceedings." Journal of Family Law, 13:803-813, 1973-1974.

1099. "Recommendation for Court-Appointed Counsel in Child-Abuse Proceedings." Mississippi Law Journal, 46:1072-1095, Fall 1975.

1100. Reed, R.; Melli, M.; Wald, M.; et al. "A Conference on Child Abuse." Wisconsin Medical Journal, 71:226-229, 1972.
A discussion by a panel of four professionals representing the legal, medical, and social viewpoints concerned with child abuse, involving the problems of detection, and aiding and prosecuting the adult who abuses the child.

1101. Reinhart, John B.; Elmer, Elizabeth. "The Abused Child. Mandatory Reporting Legislation." Journal of the American Medical Association, 188:358-362, April 27, 1964.
Advantages and disadvantages of the Children's Bureau proposed law requiring physicians to report instances of suspected child abuse are presented. Value of the model legislation lies in ordering conflicting values held by physicians, extending rational management of abuse problems, and facilitating detection of dangerous situations.

1102. "Report from the Legislative Work Group." Clinical Proceedings, 30(2):39-41, 1974.
In the report from the Legislative Work Group of the National Conference on Child Abuse, the means by which federal and state legislation concerning child abuse and neglect can be enacted as well as guidelines for such legislation are discussed. Financial assistance for the prevention of abuse and neglect in addition to support for the protection, treatment, and rehabilitation of these children is suggested as a national priority.

1103. "Report Suspected Child Abuse." Illinois Medical Journal, 141:587, June 1973.

1104. Richette, Lisa Aversa. The Throwaway Children. New York: Dell Publishing Co., 1969. 341 p.
Until recently, children were regarded as the chattels of their parents, and even now courts remain hesitant in child custody matters. Americans are unaware and uncaring about what goes on in the juvenile court and the machinery established to deal with children in trouble or in need of protection. The problems of the juvenile court are explored, and areas where reform should be instituted are cited. The courts and social workers continually affix delinquent labels to troubled children, trapping them in a downward spiral of delinquency that leads to further branding by society and its courts. The Supreme Court decision in re Gault, which extended due process to juveniles, is discussed. The U.S. is at least 30 years behind in its social planning. To reform the delinquency field will require a massive volunteer citizen effort and much greater funding.

1105. Rieger, H. J. "Meldung von Kindesmisshandlungen durch den
        behandelnden Arzt" [Reporting of Child Abuse by the Attend-
        ing Physician]. (Letter). Deutsche Medizinische Wochen-
        schrift, 99:211, February 1, 1974.
    Is an attending physician required by law to report suspicion
of a case of child abuse to criminal or other social authorities?
And does he make himself liable for prosecution if his report proves
later to be incorrect? Lawyer H. J. Rieger answers both these
questions negatively. The doctor has no legal obligation to report
his suspicions. However, he can weigh the cricumstances and if
the child is liable to continue to be abused, he will normally report
it. It becomes a matter of conscience.

1106. The Rights of Children. Cambridge, Mass.: Harvard Edu-
        cational Review, 1974. 391 p.
    A collection of writings covers the development of the concep-
tions of children's rights; child advocacy; and social policy for children. Among the nine specific topics included is alternative policies
for helping abused and neglected children.

1107. Riley, Nancy M. "The Abused Child." Rocky Mountain Med-
        ical Journal, 68:33-36, September 1971.
    Most states have adopted the basic provisions of the U. S.
Children's Bureau's 1962 Model Act for the States for the Mandatory
Reporting by Physicians. Under that act, physicians and other medical personnel are required to report suspected child abuse to legal
authorities. Violation of the act is a misdemeanor. There is also
a provision for civil and criminal immunity for persons reporting.
Other aspects of the law are described.

1108. Robbins, Jerry H. The Legal Status of Child Abuse and Neg-
        lect in Mississippi, April 1974. 101 p. Available from
        EDRS: MF-$0.75; HC-$5.40, Plus Postage.
    This paper, one of a series sponsored by the governor's of-
fice of education and training, presents the text of Mississippi law
on child protection; discusses the statutory provisions in other selected states, examines significant case law in Mississippi and other
states; presents model acts that have been adopted by a number of
states; and makes specific recommendations for improving Mississippi
State Law.

1109. Rodham, H. "Children Under the Law." Harvard Educa-
        tional Review, 43:487-514, 1973.
    Discusses the changing status of children under the law. Cur-
rently law reform is shifting toward helping children in two ways:
by extending to children rights legally granted to adults; and by recognizing the unique needs and interests of children as legally enforce-
able rights. Conflict in establishing rights of children lies in our
value on the doctrine of parens patriae versus our value on the importance of the nuclear family.

1110. Root, Irving; Scott, Wayne. "The Clinician and Forensic
        Medicine." California Medicine, 119(3):68-76, September
        1973.

Largely, this article is prepared from lectures given at the Forensic Medicine Committee of the San Bernardino County Medical Society. Its purpose is to introduce some of the aspects of forensic medicine that may be encountered by any physician and will make him more comfortable and more useful to his patients in such matters. Forensic medicine should be a part of the training and basic medical armamentarium of every physician. The medical truth of every case provides that essential aspect that society requires.

1111. Rosenberg, Arthur Harris. "Law-Medicine Notes. Compulsory-Disclosure Statutes." New England Journal of Medicine, 280:1287-1288, June 5, 1969.
Compulsory disclosure laws for physicians include reporting of gun wounds, drug users, and child abuse. The mandatory reporting laws hinder the physician's use of discretion and latitude in treating their patients.

1112. Rush, Florence. "Is Children's Liberation a Part of Women's Liberation?" Woman's World, 1:6-7, July-September 1972.
Delving into the oppression of children, the author discovered that men are not only not interested in children, but are generally without concern for all those who are helpless and dependent. As to the question of whether women in the movement should struggle for the liberation of children, the answer is yes, as long as the children are females!

1113. Russell, Donald Hayes. "Law, Medicine and Minors-IV." New England Journal of Medicine, 279:31-32, July 4, 1968.
A brief history of child protection emphasizes the need for more effective child abuse laws. Mandatory laws should provide protection for children, prevent informers from litigation, define areas of responsibility, and present guidelines to implement social services.

1114. Russell, R. L.; Rodgers, E. J., Jr. "Child Abuse--the District Attorney's Role." Prosecutor, 10(2):129-132, 1974.

1115. Ryan, William Burke. Infanticide: Its Law, Prevalence, Prevention and History. London: J. Churchill, 1862.

1116. Saury, H. "Les expertises médicales en rapport avec les violences à enfants, les attentats aux moeurs, les toxico-manies (en dehors des expertises psychiatriques). Le point de vue du magistrat" [Medical Expert Testimony in Child Abuse, Indecent Behavior and Drug Addiction (Excluding Psychiatric Expert Testimony). Viewpoint of the Magistrate]. Medecine Legale et Dommage Corporel, 6:82-84, January-March 1973.
Saury, a juvenile judge of Montpellier, writes about expert medical testimony being of prime importance in cases of physical abuse, indecent conduct, and drug addiction involving minors.

1117. Schloegel, E.; Fordyce, K. "Schools--Corporal Punishment

Without Civil or Criminal Liability. " West Virginia Law
Review, 72:399-407, 1970.
Discusses what is and what is not permissable corporal punishment by teachers in schools in light of laws and case decisions.
Explains that various states use differing criteria for determining
both civil and criminal liability for torts committed upon students
under a broad authority which most states give teachers to corporally
discipline children.

1118. Schuchter, Arnold. Child Abuse Intervention: Prescriptive
         Package. Boston: Boston University, Mass Center for
         Community Resource Development, 1976, 171 p.
         Written from a criminal justice perspective, the report on
child abuse intervention provides a model system that emphasizes
prompt medical treatment for the child and due process for both
parents and children. It is recommended that court action take the
form of a civil proceeding whenever possible. Part I provides a
framework for the prescriptive package on child abuse intervention
and Part 2 describes the operation of the model system. The final
section is a framework and guide for child abuse decision-making
and includes a detailed comparison of existing and proposed model
systems for handling child abuse intervention, a model decision making guide, and questions and answers on handling child abuse for
justice system personnel.

1119. Scranton, William M. "State Legislation of 1963 of Interest
         to Physicians. " Pennsylvania Medical Journal, 66:23-26,
         October 1963.
         Discussion of "Battered Child" Bill requiring physicians to
report suspected cases and provisions of immunity from civil or
criminal liability which might result from such reports.

1120. "Secret Professionnel et Enfants Martyrs" [Professional
         Secrecy and Abused Children]. Semaine des Hopitaux de
         Paris, 47:Suppl. 14:263-267, November 26, 1971. (Fre)
         On May 7, 1971, the French National Assembly voted an
amendment to Article 373 of the penal code which tended to favor
the "protection of the abused child. " Before this time professional
secrecy had been almost absolute in France. The highlights of the
debate in the National Assembly and the text of the law of June 15,
1971, are given.

1121. Shepherd, Robert E. , Jr. "The Abused Child and the Law. "
         Virginia Medical Monthly, 93:3-6, January 1966; Washington
         and Lee Law Review, 22:182-195, 1965.
         A discussion covers legal aspects of child abuse. The usual
approach to abuse cases is stated in the verdict found in Carpenter
vs. Commonwealth (Virginia Supreme Court of Appeals, 1947). Despite these legal precedents, problems in reporting still exist. A
mandatory reporting law would establish a clear path for physician
reporting and, in conjunction with a protective services bill, would
deemphasize the punitive aspects of such legislation.

1122. Sherman, Gilbert. "The Abused Child--New York State. "
New York State Dental Journal, 36:109, February 1970.
Sherman reports on a conference on "The Abused Child" held
at the Nassau County Family Court. Salient and pertinent features
in the implementation of Article X of the Family Court Act are listed.
The author urges dentists to report actual or suspected cases of
child abuse to the local Department of Social Service or to the police.

1123. Silver, Larry B.; Barton, William; Dublin, Christina C.
"Mandatory Reporting of Physical Abuse of Children in the
District of Columbia: Community Procedures and New Legislation. " Medical Annals of the District of Columbia,
36:127-130, February 1967.
The District of Columbia law for reporting of child abuse
cases and community procedures for handling such cases are discussed in detail. The limitations of these statutes are included.

1124. Simons, Betty; Downs, Elinor F. "Medical Reporting of
Child Abuse Patterns, Problems and Accomplishments. "
New York Journal of Medicine, 68:2324-2330, 1968.
Presented is a description of child abuse reporting patterns
which became apparent after the Child Abuse Registry was instituted
in New York City in 1964. The results of an experiment were reported which gave a dramatic increase in the reporting rates of the
target group: department heads of city hospitals.

1125. _____; _____; Hurster, Madeline M. , et al. Child
Abuse: A Perspective on Legislation in Five Middle-Atlan-
tic States, and a Survey of Reported Cases in New York
City. New York: Columbia University School of Public
Health and Administrative Medicine, February 1966.

1126. Sint-Van Den Heuvel, M. K.; Everts-Goddard, J. E. , eds.
Kindermishandeling [Child Abuse]. See entry 2176.

1127. Smith, Eugene L. "Parent and Child--Title 2 of the Texas
Family Code. " Family Law Quarterly, 8(2):135-155, 1974.
Title 2 of the Texas Family Code, which regulates the major
legal aspects of the parent-child relationship, is described. The law
was passed in 1973 and was a revision of the laws in force in the
state since its beginning.

1128. Smith, Homer A. "The Legal Aspects of Child Abuse. "
Southern Medical Bulletin, 58(3):19-21, 1970.
Discusses legal protection of abused children and mandatory
reporting of suspected abuse as provided by the Oklahoma statutes
annotated in Title 21 of Oklahoma Laws. All possible attempts are
made to keep the child with his own parents and only when all methods fail is the child put up for adoption.

1129. Smith, Jack L. "New York's Child Abuse Laws: Inadequacies
in the Present Statutory Structure. " Cornell Law Review,
55:298-305, January 1970.

This article discusses the inadequacies in the present statutes of New York's child abuse laws. In particular, Article 3 and Article 10 are cited for their overlapping and duplicating aspects

1130. Smith, Selwyn M. The Battered Child Syndrome. See entry 1553.

1131. Snedeker, Lendon. "Notes on Childhood Trauma." New England Journal of Medicine, 275:1061-1062, November 10, 1966.
A statute enacted in Massachusetts on September 15, 1964, requires physicians to report suspected cases of child abuse to the Department of Public Welfare, and provides for immunity against defamation suits resulting from the report. One limitation of the law is that it deals only with active trauma and not neglect. The Massachusetts law differs somewhat from the laws of the surrounding New England states. Some opposition to the law has been observed among physicians. One group feels that it impairs the physician-patient relationship, while another feels that it provides an unnecessarily high regard for parental rights.

1132. "Social Work Student Influences Legislation." (Editorial). Child Welfare, 44(6):346, June 1965.
Mary Ann McElroy, a student at the University of North Dakota, Division of Social Work, was given credit for changing a state bill on the battered child and reversing the philosophy behind the bill. Illustrated here is the effectiveness of citizen participation, supported by knowledge and facts, in the legislative process.

1133. Solomon, Theo; Berger, Deborah; Pessirilo, Gloria. The Mayor's Task Force on Child Abuse and Neglect. New York: Center for Community Research, 1970.
A report on child abuse as a major health and social problem in New York City and the creation of the Mayor's Task Force to examine the social, medical, and legal services involved in programs of child protection. Specific purpose was to evaluate the effectiveness of the 1964 New York State Child Abuse Law and the administrative machinery set up to carry out its mandate.

1134. Somerhausen, C. "La protection des enfants martyrs" [Protection of Maltreated Children]. Revue de Droit Pénal et de Criminologie, 52(10):1084-1090, 1972.
The French law of 15th of June 1971 to protect children who are victims of maltreatment, must be regarded as supplemental to section 62 of the Penal Code (reporting crimes) and section 378 (professional discretion). The author would like to see a similar section introduced in the Belgian Penal Code. Physicians have the possibility (not the obligation) to report cases to social welfare and health services. It can be ignored.

1135. Stamm, M. J. "Battered Children: Doctor, Parents, and the Law." Journal of the Kentucky Medical Association, 74(2):89-93, February 1976.

While state law in Kentucky requires certain people, especially doctors, to report cases of child abuse, many are reluctant to do so. Further legislation enacted to make doctors liable for not reporting may encourage more physician involvement. A significant problem in litigating abuse cases is the absence of adequate legal counsel to represent the child. Litigation is further hampered by the requirement for irrefutable, direct evidence in abuse cases.

1136. Stark, Jean. "Battered Child--Does Britain Need a Reporting Law?" Public Law, 1969:48-63, Spring 1969.
A discussion analyzes factors behind child abuse reporting legislation in the U.S. and compares them with similar factors in Britain.

1137. Stern, U. "Straflosigkeit bei Verletzung des Berufsgeheimnisses Infolge Pflichtenkollision" [Immunity Against Violation of Professional Secrecy Due to Conflicting Obligations]. Munchener Medizinsiche Wochenschrift, 112:1967-1970, October 23, 1970.
A doctor is constantly required to make certain decisions. At times he can easily be confronted with a real problem of conflicting obligations arising from the fact that, whatever action he takes, he is compelled to violate one or the other of two legally protected rights. This conflict of conscience which a doctor experiences in making his decisions is fully recognized by our legislation if the decision which he makes is one that violates professional secrecy. Criminal law condones his action by granting him immunity and thereby approving his decision, whatever it may be. No legal liability, let alone a criminal offense, can be derived from a purely ethical obligation. (English Summary.)

1138. Stoetzer, J. B. "The Juvenile Court and Emotional Neglect of Children." University of Michigan Journal of Law Reform, 8(35):351-374, Winter 1975.
Juvenile emotional well-being is not well defined in legislative terms. Standards for state intervention in cases of emotional neglect should be established. The courts must find a causal relationship between parental conduct and its adverse impact on the child in order to intervene, and where emotional neglect is involved, the courts must be prepared to look for its nonphysical effects. A note of caution is sounded against premature intervention on the part of the courts.

1139. Strauss, P. "The Relationship Between Promise and Performance in State Intervention in Family Life." Columbia Journal of Law and Social Problems, 9:28-62, 1972.
Informal position paper with panel reactions. Describes, from various points of view, the shortcomings of state intervention. Relates abused and neglected children to a form of institutional abuse.

1140. Sullivan, Michael F. "Child Neglect: The Environmental Aspects." Ohio State Law Journal, 29(1):85-115, Winter 1968.

Neglect law, if haphazardly applied, represents a threat to some of our most closely held values. A temptation to use it loosely exists; this temptation can be curbed by both the legislature and the judiciary if strong positive actions are taken. The legislature can mold the approach taken by the judiciary by drafting statutes which define neglect in terms of the effect on the child and by emphasizing the seriousness of the effect. In the final analysis, however, the success or failure of neglect law lies with the court. (Journal Summary Modified.)

1141. Sussman, Alan. "Reporting Child Abuse: A Review of the Literature." Family Law Quarterly, 8(3):245-313, Fall 1974.
A literature review covers fifteen different aspects of the reporting of child abuse.

1142. _____; Cohen, Stephan J. Reporting Child Abuse & Neglect: Guidelines for Legislation. Text ed. Cambridge, Mass.: Ballinger Pub., 1975. 255 p.
The focus of this book is primarily addressed to issues of reporting child maltreatment. The Office of Child Development requested the Institute of Judicial Administration and the authors to prepare a revised version of the 1963 model act. Forty-two national experts on child abuse and neglect assisted. This book contains the resulting model legislation, commentary and supporting papers. The authors hope that the suggestions offered will serve to place child abuse and neglect reporting in its proper social and legal perspective and facilitate the delivery of the necessary care and treatment to those children most in need of protection.

1143. Teague, Russell E. "Kentucky Legislation Concerning Reporting of Abused Children." Journal of the Kentucky Medical Association, 64:584, July 1966.
Kentucky legislation enacted in 1964 requires all persons who suspect that a child under 18 has been willfully injured by a parent or guardian to report in writing to the local law enforcement officers with a copy to the Department of Child Welfare. The law also provides immunity for any liability that may stem from the reporting and waives the physician-patient and husband-wife privileges. Kentucky plans to establish a central registry of child abuse incidents and begin detailed follow-ups of these cases.

1144. Theisen, William Maurice. Implementing a Child Abuse Law: An Inquiry into the Formulation and Execution of Social Policy. Ph.D. Washington University, St. Louis, Missouri, 1972. 187 p. Available from University Microfilms, Order No. 73-13716.
A new Missouri child abuse law was used to study the processes of social policy formulation and execution, and the procedures used by health, education, and welfare, and judicial organizations to implement the statute are described. The ways these organizations affect the quality and quantity of services available to abuse victims are discussed.

1145. Thomas, Mason P., Jr. "Child Abuse and Neglect: Historical Overview, Legal Matrix, and Social Perspectives."
North Carolina Law Review, 50:293-349, February 1972;
54:743-746, June 1976.
Comprehensive discussion and analysis of abuse and neglect,
including review of the history of child abuse from Biblical times
to the present. Thorough recommendations for judicial reform and
improved legislation.

1146. _____. "North Carolina's Child Abuse Reporting Law."
Popular Government, 41:6-9, Spring 1976.
North Carolina's mandatory law of 1971 repealed the 1965
voluntary law. These laws have served to increase public awareness
and understanding of the problems of child abuse and neglect. Reporting has increased dramatically since the mandatory law was
adopted. A summary of the law is given. A table presents the
abuse cases in North Carolina 1971-1975.

1147. Tocchio, Octavio Joseph. Legislation and Law Enforcement
in California for the Protection of the Physically Battered
Child. Ph.D. American University, Washington, D.C.,
1967. 426 p. Available from University Microfilms,
Order No. 67-12, 045.
A comprehensive study of the effectiveness of California legislation and law enforcement in controlling and preventing child battering involved documentary research; analysis of case studies; and
a survey of opinion from practitioners of law, medicine, public
health, social work, and law enforcement.

1148. Trewartha, Robin. "Are We Responsible When a Child Is
'Battered'?" Probation Journal, 21(1):22-24, 1974.
The Probation Service opinion of and attitudes toward the battered child are discussed. The follow-up suggestions were made in
study group paper to help in the process of observation. The constructive rather than punitive role of Probation Service workers is
stressed.

1149. Tripp, N. "Acting 'in Loco Parentis' as a Defense to Assault
and Battery." Cleveland-Marshall Law Review, 16:39-49,
1967.
Article which quotes from various cases concerned with the
"in loco parentis" rule in the U.S. Points out that teachers stand
in "loco parentis" to pupils, and their criminal liability is determined on nearly the same basis as others who stand in "loco parentis."

1150. Trube-Becker, Elisabeth. "Kindesmisshandlung in gericht-
lichmedizinischer Sicht" [Maltreatment of Children from a
Legal Medical Viewpoint]. Deutsche Zeitschrift für die
Gesamte Gerichtliche Medizin, 55:173-183, September 1,
1964.
Dealt with is the legal-medical aspects of child abuse with
emphasis on cases where death results. Especially discussed are

eight cases of small children who died from parental child abuse.
A table presents the circumstances and the sentences delivered the
parents. There is little difficulty determining if child abuse has
been committed. There is great difficulty determining that it was
willful. Many problems exist because of the protective circle of the
family. The judge may deliver an unbelievably light sentence due
to the right of the parent to punish.

1151. _____ . "Zur Kindesmisshandlung" [On Child Abuse].
Medizinische Klinik, 59:1649-1653, October 16, 1964.
    This is a discussion of the legal and clinical aspects of child
abuse. The law 223bSt6B is interpreted and a table is presented to
describe 11 cases of child abuse at the Legal-Medicine Clinic in Dus-
seldorf that ended in death. The table includes sex, age, marital
status of mother, diagnosis, cause of death, abuser, kind of abuse,
reason given by abuser for injury and the judgment in five of the 11
cases.

1152. Underhill, E. "Pour-quoi les enseignants et les professionnels
médico-sociaux restent-ils silencieux devant les parents qui
maltraitent leurs enfants?" [Why Do Teachers and Medico-
social Professionals Keep Silent When Confronted with Parents Who Maltreat Their Children?]. Revue Internationale
de L'Enfant, 21:16-22, 1974.
    The author (a lawyer) makes suggestions for better legislation
to prevent cases of child maltreatment with fatal results. She sus-
pects, in actuality, the figures she presents on child abuse in various countries may be a hundred times higher. She focuses on the
fact that physicians, social workers, and teachers keep silent about
cases known to them and why they do so. She proposes legislation
pertaining to abortion facilities, rights of foster parents, and making
failure to notify the authorities punishable.

1153. "Unfit Parents--ORS 419. 523 (2) (a). " Willamette Law Journal, 5:177, 1968.
    Article which focuses specifically on Oregon's statute which
permits termination of parent-child relationship. Explains that, put
into practice, it is virtually impossible to terminate the relationship
because of the Court's increasingly sympathetic attitude toward the
parent. Points out that there is some question that this was the intent of the legislature when the law was enacted, however, the conditions of "unfit" were not specified.

1154. U. S. Children's Bureau. The Abused Child: Principles and
Suggested Language for Legislation on Reporting of the
Physically Abused Child. Washington, U. S. Government
Printing Office, 1963. 13 p.

1155. _____ . Legislative Guides for Termination of Parental
Rights and Responsibilities and Adoption of Children, by
Harriet L. Goldberg, 1961. Publ. No. 394. (FS3. 209)
    This publication has to do with court methods available in
child abuse and neglect cases.

1156. U. S. Congress. Child Abuse Prevention and Treatment Act. Report Together with Dissenting Views from Committee on Education and Labor to Accompany S. 1191. H. R. 685, 93 Cong., 1st sess., November 30, 1973. 11 p.
A national center on child abuse and neglect is recommended.

1157. _____. Public Law 93-247, 93rd Congress, S. 1191, January 31, 1974: An Act to Provide Financial Assistance for a Demonstration Program for the Prevention, Identification, and Treatment of Child Abuse and Neglect, to Establish a National Center on Child Abuse and Neglect and for Other Purposes. Congress of the U. S., Washington, D. C. (Report No. PL-93-247). 1975. 5 p. Available from EDRS: MF-$0.83; HC-$1.67, Plus Postage.
Presented is the Child Abuse Prevention and Treatment Act (Public Law 93-247) which was enacted on January 31, 1974, and amended on January 3, 1975. Described are the activities of the national center. A definition of the term "child abuse and neglect" is provided. Demonstration programs and projects are covered in regard to authorization for making grants to, and entering into contracts with, public agencies or nonprofit private organizations, and states. Authorizations for expenditures are listed, and an advisory board is described in terms of membership, functions, and reporting procedures.

1158. _____. House of Representatives. Child Abuse Prevention: Hearing Before the Subcommittee on Labor, Social Services, and the International Community of the Committee on the District of Columbia, House of Representatives, 93rd Congress, Second Session on H. R. 15779 and H. R. 15918 to Establish an Agency for the Prevention of Child Abuse in the District of Columbia. Washington, D. C., Congress of the U. S., House Committee on the District of Columbia, 1974. 161 p.
Presented is the text of the hearing held in August on two house bills (H. R. 15779 and H. R. 15918) to establish an agency for the prevention of child abuse in the District of Columbia. Included are the full texts of the two bills and statements by persons representing such groups as the Children's Hospital National Medical Center, the Community Task Force on Child Welfare reform, the Juvenile Justice Clinic of the Georgetown University Law Center, the government of the District of Columbia, and the National Center for the Prevention and Treatment of Child Abuse and Neglect.

1159. _____. _____. Committee on Education and Labor. Selected Subcommittee on Education. To Establish a National Center on Child Abuse and Neglect: Hearings, October 1--November 12, 1973, on H. R. 6379, H. R. 10552, and H. R. 10968, bills to Provide for the Establishment Within the Department of Health, Education, and Welfare of the National Center on Child Development and Abuse Prevention, to Provide Financial Assistance for a Demonstration Program and for Other Purposes. 1974, v+ 292 p. bibl. table (93d Congress, 1st Session). Paper.

1160.   _____. _____. District of Columbia Committee.
Hearing Before Subcommittee No. 3 of the Committee on
the District of Columbia, House of Representatives, 89th
Congress, First Session, on H. R. 3394, H. R. 3411, and
H. R. 3814 "To Provide for the Mandatory Reporting by
Physicians and Institutions in the District of Columbia of
Certain Physical Abuse of Children, " June 10, 1965.
Washington, D. C. 20402: Govt. Prtg. Office, 1965.

1161.   _____. Senate. Adoption and Foster Care, 1975. Hearings Before the Subcommittee on Children and Youth.
94th Congress, 1st Session, 1975.
Proposed federal policies affecting the adoption of children
and their placement in the foster care system are examined. Physically and emotionally handicapped children due to child abuse or
neglect are included.

1162.   _____. _____. Child Abuse Prevention and Treatment
Act. Report from Committee on Labor and Public Welfare
to Accompany S. 1191. July 10, 1973. 12 p.

1163.   _____. _____. To Designate the Period of February
9 Through February 15, 1975, as National Child Abuse
Awareness Week, by Mr. Mondale and Mr. Stafford. 94th
Congress, 1st Session, 1975.

1164.   _____. _____. Labor and Public Welfare Committee.
Subcommittee on Children and Youth. Child Abuse Prevention Act, 1973: Hearings, March 26--April 24, 1973,
on S. 1191, to Establish a National Center on Child Abuse
and Neglect, to Provide Financial Assistance for the Prevention, Identification, and Treatment of Child Abuse and
Neglect, and for Other Purposes. 1973.. vi+ 695 p. bibl.
il. tables. charts (93rd Congress, 1st Session) Paper.
A record of the Senate hearings on The Child Abuse Prevention Act of 1973 is presented. A copy of Senator Mondale's bill to
establish a national center on child abuse is included. The objectives of the hearings were to investigate the magnitude of the problem in the U. S. and to clarify a definition of the problem. A complete transcript of the hearings and related materials are followed
by three appendixes which deal with medical and legal literature,
child abuse programs, and press reports.

1165.   _____. _____. _____. Child Abuse Prevention and
Treatment Act, 1974, Public Law 93-247 (S. 1191), Ques-
tions and Answers, Analysis, and Text of Act, Prepared
for Subcommittee on Children and Youth; April 1974. 1974.
10 p. (Committee Print, 93d Congress, 2d Session). Y4,
L11/2:C43/9
This booklet contains questions and answers concerning the
Child Abuse Prevention and Treatment Act, an analysis of the Act
by the Congressional Research Service, and a copy of the actual text.
The question and answer section provides information about the ra-

tionale for the Act, the amount of money available for its implementation, as well as its demonstration programs and state technical assistance program. The actual text of the Federal legislation is the final section of the booklet.

1166. _____ . _____ . _____ . Child Abuse Prevention and
Treatment Act, 1974. 93d Congress, 2d Session, Public
Law 93-247 (S. 1191), January 31, 1974. 10 p.
A copy of the 1974 Child Abuse Prevention and Treatment Act includes questions and answers pertaining to the law and an analysis by the Library of Congress.

1167. _____ . _____ . _____ . Comprehensive Headstart,
Child Development and Family Services Act of 1972: Bill
Text and Section Analysis Prepared by the Subcommittee
on Employment, Manpower and Poverty. Committee Print.
92nd Congress, 2d Session, 1972.
Child abuse and family services are included.

1168. _____ . _____ . _____ . Rights of Childrens, 1972:
Hearing Before the Subcommittee on Children and Youth of
the Committee on Labor and Public Welfare. U. S. Senate
92nd Congress. Part 2: Appendix--Selected Readings on
Child Abuse and Day Care. 1972. 823 p. Available
from: Subcommittee on Children and Youth, Room 506,
Senate Annex, U. S. Senate, Washington, D. C. 20510 (no
charge).
Some of the basic documents that shed light on the incidence and legal aspects of child abuse are provided in this appendix. In addition, a report--"Windows on Day Care" issued by the National Council of Jewish Women is provided. Part 1 of this document is on the Examination of the Sudden Infant Death Syndrome.

1169. _____ . _____ . Select Committee on Equal Educational
Opportunity. Justice for Children. Committee Print, 92nd
Congress, Second Session, 1972.
The address of Walter F. Mondale, December 9, 1970.

1170. U. S. Department of Health, Education, and Welfare. Division
of Alcohol, Drug Abuse and Mental Health. National Conference on Child Abuse. A Summary Report, 1974.
Provided is information to various groups concerned with child abuse.

1171. U. S. Office of Child Development. Report of the U. S. Department of Health, Education, and Welfare to the President and Congress of the United States on the Implementation of Public Law 93-247, The Child Abuse Prevention
and Treatment Act. Washington, D. C., August 1975 (HEW-
391). 60 p.
Provided is a report on the manner in which the provisions of The Child Abuse Prevention and Treatment Act have been carried out to date.

1172. Van Stolk, Mary. The Battered Child in Canada. See entry 806.

1173. Veillard-Cybulscy, H.; Veillard-Cybulscy, M. [The Role of the Juvenile Judge in the Protection of Children and Adolescents]. Courrier, 12:393-405, June 1962. (Fre)

1174. Volk, P. "Überleben schwerer, für die Kindestötung typischer Verletzungen" [Survival After Severe and Typically Infanticidal Injuries]. Deutsche Zeitschrift für die Gesamte Gerichtliche Medizin, 57:190-196, 1966.
Described is the legal-medical aspects of a case in which the unwed mother attempted to cover up the abuse, possibly resulting from an unsuccessful murder attempt on her newborn child. She had the baby without medical assistance and maintained that the neck and mouth injuries and scratches were due to the problems experienced in extracting the child by herself. The child survived and was given up for adoption. The prosecutor was able to show that such injuries could not have resulted from birth.

1175. Von Kerde, C. "Gerichtsmedizinische Aspekte zu Problemen der Kindesmisshandlung" [Medico-Legal Aspects of Child Abuse]. Kinderaerztliche Praxis, 42(11):513-518, November 1974.

1176. Wald, M. S. "State Intervention on Behalf of 'Neglected' Children: Standards for Removal of Children from Their Homes, Monitoring the Status of Children in Foster Care, and Termination of Parental Rights." Stanford Law Review, 28:623-706, April 1976.

1177. Waldeck, K. "Die Gerichtsarztliche Bedeutung der Kindermisshandlung" [The Significance in Forensic Medicine of Abuse of Children]. Wurzburg: Triltsch, 1938. Pp25. R. R. Willoughby (Brown).

1178. Warren, Eugene R. "Battered Child Syndrome." Journal of the Arkansas Medical Society, 62:413, March 1966.
In 1965, Arkansas enacted a statute requiring physicians to report all cases of child abuse to the appropriate police authority. The statute also provides immunity from defamation suits stemming from the report (the report is presumed to be in good faith) and abrogates the physician-patient and husband-wife immunities in any proceedings arising from the report.

1179. Weaver, Colin. "Legal Procedures in Cases of Non-Accidental Injury to Children." (Letter). British Medical Journal, 2(6028):180-181, July 1976.
To criticize the social services departments for not securing a care order from the juvenile courts in cases of non-accidental injury is not always fair. It is relatively easy to prove that a child's development is being avoidably impaired, but it is not always possible to prove that a child is in need of care or control which it is unlikely to receive unless the court makes an order.

1180. Weinberger, C. W. "The Oath Did Not Make Any Allowance for Group Practice. " (Editorial). Medical Insight, (10): 30-32, October 1973.
The federal government and particularly the Department of Health, Education, and Welfare have long been interested in child welfare and the problem of child abuse. Further DHEW efforts in the battle against child abuse are described.

1181. "Welcome to the School of Hard Knocks. " Oklahoma Observer, 7:14, February 25, 1975.
Brian G. Fraser, attorney for the National Center for the Prevention and Treatment of Child Abuse and Neglect, Denver, reviews the law pertaining to child abuse at the October annual meeting of the Oklahoma Health and Welfare Association in Oklahoma City. Agencies involved in protective services encounter the basic unresolved question: whose rights, parent's or child's. Juvenile judges represent both extremes.

1182. White, Desbert, J. , Jr. "Protecting the Abused Child in Georgia: Identifying and Reporting. " Journal of the Medical Association of Georgia, 60:86-88, March 1971.
The Georgia child abuse reporting law requires medical and social service professionals to report suspected cases; designates the county Department of Family and Children Services to provide protective services and continuing care; and outlines information to be included in both oral and written reports. The legislation aims to rehabilitate families. However, cooperation is needed to achieve effective community resources.

1183. "Who Cares for New York's Abused Children?" (Editorial). New York Medicine, 30(4):120-123, 137, April 1974.
The New York Child Protective Services Act of 1973 and the federal law which went into effect on January 31, 1974, represent enlightened legislation for the protection of the rights of children. The New York law requires reporting and the establishment of a central registry. Two projects proposed for federal funding are described.

1184. Wilcox, D. P. "Child Abuse Laws: Past, Present, and Future. " Journal of Forensic Sciences, 21(1):71-75, January 1976.
The details of a lawsuit against four California doctors who failed to report attacks on a five-month-old baby introduce this article. A brief history of child abuse, developments in child abuse detection, recent trends in child abuse laws, other legislative trends, recent federal legislation, the new model law being developed, and professional responsibility are then discussed.

1185. Wilkerson, Albert E. , editor. The Rights of Children: Emergent Concepts in Law and Society. Philadelphia: Temple University Press, 1973. 313 p.
The sections of this book are: The Child as a Person; Guarantees for the Child; Decisions About the Child; and an Epilogue on

Children's Rights.   There is one chapter under Guarantees for the
Child entitled "The Abused Child and the Law. "

1186.   Wilson, J. B. , Jr.   "The Battered Child Act--A Summary
and Analysis. "   Res Gestae, 9(6):9-10, June 1965.

1187.   Winking, Cyril H.   "Coping with Child Abuse: One State's
Experience (Illinois: Conference Paper).   Public Welfare,
26:189-192,   July 1968.
Among the significant features of the Illinois child abuse law
is the designation of a single agency to receive reports of cases and
to act on them.   Persons under 16 are designated as children to be
protected by the law and reporting is required by physicians, surgeons, dentists, and other practitioners and hospitals.   The character of the law is significantly nonpunitive and immunity is provided
for all who report.

1188.   Woolridge, E. D.   "Significant Problems of the Forensic
Odontologist in the U. S. A. "   International Journal of Forensic Dentistry, 1(2):6-12, 1973.
The author (dentist and lawyer) describes the rapid development of forensic odontology in the U. S. through the last years and
emphasizes the need for knowledge of the legal rights and limitations
in gaining, handling, and evaluating dental evidence, now and in the
future.

1189.   Wooster, K. C.   "The California Legislative Approach to
Problems of Willful Child Abuse. "   California Law Review,
54(4):1805-1831, October 1966.
The history of California laws relating to child abuse is reviewed through 1966 in terms of reporting statutes and laws pertaining to prosecution of the abuser.

1190.   Young, Leontine.   Wednesday's Children: A Study of Child
Neglect and Abuse.   See entry 233.

MANAGEMENT, PREVENTION AND TREATMENT

1191. "Abusing Parents Organize to Help Each Other. " Today's
      Child, 22:6, 1974.
      Describes the feelings of rage thousands of mothers feel to-
wards their children and discusses the merits of Parents Anonymous
groups to "turn self-hate into self-help. " Includes sources of help
and addresses for parents who are interested in forming a Parents
Anonymous group.

1192. "Action Against Child Abuse. " Canadian Welfare, 50:22-23,
      July-August 1974.
      This is overview of the action being taken against child abuse
in Canada, Britain, and the United States.

1193. Alexander, Jerry. "How Psychologists Can Help Stop Child
      Abuse. " Journal of Clinical Child Psychology, 5(1):13-14,
      May 1, 1976.
      The author, President of the Citizens Committee for Battered
Children, is a manufacturer with a lifelong concern for children.
He believes that child abuse will be stopped only through a unified
effort of citizens and professionals. In his article he enumerates
actions psychologists and others can take to aid in stopping child
abuse. (Journal Introduction.)

1194. Allison, Patricia Kay. Exploration of a Program of Preven-
      tive Intervention in the Early Parent-Infant Interaction.
      See entry 23.

1195. Alvy, Kerby T. "Preventing Child Abuse. " American Psy-
      chologist, 30(9):921-928, September 1975.
      Discussed are two major and general approaches to analyzing
child abuse: the comprehensive approach, defining child abuse as
being collective, institutional, and individual in nature; and the nar-
row approach, considering only individual abuse. Then considered
are the prevention implications of these approaches. Emphasized is
the relationship between theoretical formulation of the cause of abuse
and programs having the potential for prevention. (Journal Summary
Modified.)

1196. American Academy of Pediatrics. Committee on Infant and
      Preschool Child. "Maltreatment of Children. The Bat-
      tered Child Syndrome. " Pediatrics, 50:160-162, July 1972.
      In a policy statement, the American Academy of Pediatrics

210

Committee on Infant and Preschool Child reaffirms its policy to aid
in the prevention, identification, and management of the child abuse
problem. They predict an annual incidence of 250 cases of child
abuse per million population. In order to manage this problem better,
six new suggestions are added to their 1966 statement of recommendations.

1197. American Humane Association. Children's Division. Disci-
       pline, Your Child and You. By Robert W. Blum and Lynne
       A. Blum. Denver, Colo., 16 p. 356.
       This informative pamphlet on discipline was written by a ped-
iatrician and a psychologist. It contains helpful insights on a subject
about which most parents hold strong feelings and expectations. For
parents and for those who help, this publication offers an important
up-to-date perspective on discipline and how children grow and learn.

1198. Arizona Community Development for Abuse and Neglect. The
       Impact of Family Therapy in the On-Going Treatment of the
       Self-Admitted Child Abuser. By F. G. Bolton, Jr. Phoe-
       nix, Arizona, 1975. 15 p.
       A discussion covers various aspects of the rehabilitation of
abusive parents through family therapy. Family therapists can provide crucial intervention at crisis points by providing simple education for the family on the patient's condition, acting as a full partner
in solution of family problems, and offering new means of communication until the family is able to function fully as a stress-mediating
unit.

1199. Aubry, Ernest L. Observations on Conditions at MacLaren
       Hall Annex: A Facility for the Detention of Neglected and
       Abused Children. (Unpublished paper). Los Angeles:
       Western Center on Law and Poverty, 1972. 68 p.
       Living conditions at the MacLaren Hall Annex in Los Angeles,
a facility for detention of neglected and abused children, are described. It is concluded that the facility must no longer be used for
its present purposes, since the children housed there are subjected
to irreparable intellectual, emotional, and psychological deterioration.

1200. Avery, Jane C. "The Battered Child: A Shocking Problem."
       Mental Hygiene, 57:40-43, Spring 1973.
       Detailed is the battered child syndrome and society's role in
its prevention. The first problem is identifying the child. Then a
multi-disciplinary network of protection must be developed within the
community. The major obstacle to the program is lack of effective
coordination among elements. Avery discusses legislation, treatment, and follow-up.

1201. Baher, Edwina; Hyman, Clare; Jones, Carolyn, et al. At
       Risk: An Account of the Work of the Battered Child Re-
       search Department, NSPCC. See entry 2204.

1202. Bard, E. Ronald. "To Heal the Wounded Family." Human
       Ecology Forum, 7:6-8, Summer 1976.

1203. "Battered Babies." (Editorial). Canadian Medical Association Journal, 101(7):98, November 1, 1969.
     Rather than simply prosecuting the parents, which has no constructive effect, it is suggested that the child be maintained in the home where possible, with enlightened support from the various medical, welfare, and other people who come into contact with the parents. Legislation requiring more diligent detection and reporting on the part of Canadian physicians is suggested.

1204. "Battered Babies." (Editorial). Midwife and Health Visitor, 7:421, November 1971.
     This editorial traces since 1963 the increasing interest in the problem of child abuse in Britain. U.S. authorities in the field, Caffey and Kempe, are referred to and some of Kempe's opinion as to causes and preventive measures are given.

1205. "The Battered Baby." Clinician, 36(9):369-370, 1972.
     In order to curb the high incidence of battered babies in India, the government must take prompt action by raising the general standard of living, by imposing strict family planning, by setting up child care centers and creches for employees' children, and by social and psychological counseling of parents.

1206. "The Battered Baby Syndrome: Some Practical Aspects." Medical Journal of Australia, 2(7):231-232, 1974.
     Measures designed for controlling the abusive treatment of infants in Australia are reviewed and reference is made to the laws applicable to child abuse and the legal position of the physician. Some suggestions for community aid in alleviating tensions in the home are also included.

1207. "The Battered Family Syndrome." Emergency Medicine, 3:204-207, February 1971.
     A team of Australian pediatricians has developed an approach to parents that they feel may provide a constructive basis for treating the problem of child abuse within the family and rehabilitating, rather than breaking up, the family unit. Questions designed by Drs. Callaghan and Fotheringham to guide the physician and social worker in the often delicate interviews are provided.

1208. Bean, Shirley L. "Parents' Center Project: A Multi-Service Approach to the Prevention of Child Abuse." Child Welfare, 50:277-282, May 1971.
     Detailed is a group therapy program designed to help parents in families where patterns of child abuse are developing. The Parents' Center Project is devoted to the prevention of child abuse, and its study, through three research objectives: the development of new techniques to improve the service to young children who have been abused and to their parents, the training of personnel to pursue studies of child abuse, and the study of the origins and effects of violence as a force within the family.

1209. Belloir, A.; Jezequel, C. "Enfants victimes de sévices:

Aspects psychologiques et socio juridiques" [Child Victims
of Maltreatment: Psychological and Sociolegal Aspects].
Journal des Agreges, 7(11):373-379, 1974.
To treat and protect children suffering from the battered child
syndrome, the authors believe it is necessary to have a plan that is
well organized and one that works in cooperation with social, judicial,
psychiatric, and pediatric services in order to detect and evaluate
necessary action. Sociomedical surveillance for all children under
six years should be extended for comprehensive prevention. If temporary separation is necessary, socioeconomic action or psychological,
or both, should take place so child can return to better situation.

1210. Bellucci, Matilda T. "Group Treatment of Mothers in Child
        Protection Cases. " Child Welfare, 51:110-116, February
        1972.
A new approach to the treatment of mothers in child protection cases was attempted by the Children's Services Division of the
Hamilton County Welfare Department, Cincinnati. A co-therapy plan
through weekly group treatment for a small group of deprived women
who had neglected their large families was instituted. Whereas this
new approach has demonstrated effectiveness where little else has,
a shorter and less demanding method should be sought.

1211. Besharov, Douglas J. "Building a Community Response to
        Child Abuse and Maltreatment. " Children Today, 4:2-4,
        September 1975. Reprinted in pamphlet form by DHEW,
        Publ. No. (OHD) 76-30084.
The author contends that we must now discover how to develop
the cooperative community structures necessary to provide needed
services efficiently, effectively and compassionately in dealing with
child abuse. There has been too much fragmentation, overlapping
and uncoordination in rehabilitation services.

1212. Beswick, K. ; Lynch, M. A. ; Roberts, J. "Child Abuse and
        General Practice. " British Medical Journal, 2(6039):800-
        802, 1976.
During 1973-1976, there were 12 cases of child abuse in a
general practice of 1841 children under 10. Thirty children were
reported at risk in March of 1976. A preventive program showed
good results and no new cases.

1213. Bezzeg, Elizabeth D. ; Fratianne, Richard B. ; Karnasiewicz,
        Sally Q. ; et al. "The Role of the Child Care Worker in
        the Treatment of Severely Burned Children. " Pediatrics,
        50:617-624, October 1972.
Burns resulting from child abuse are one of the most frequent (common) situations in which burns occur. Experience with
57 children suggests that the physical and psychological rehabilitation of severely burned children is promoted in a positive and child-
oriented environment. The child care worker, functioning as an integral member of the burn team, can help establish a more peaceful
relationship between the child and his environment.

1214.   Biermann, G. "Kinder in Unserer Zeit" [Children in Our
         Time]. Medizinische Welt, 22:1411-1417, September 1971.
         Every year 90-100 children are killed by their parents in W.
Germany; 95 percent of the cases go undiscovered.   Abused children
are repeatedly sent back to parents who finally may kill them.   Better parenting education and psychotherapeutic help is needed.   Factors such as family life, play space, mass media, hospitals, and
kindergartens are discussed; also the anti-authoritarian concept.
There is further need for institutes of the sort in Mannheim and
Kölm to deal with psycho-hygienic problems.

1215.   Bishop, Frank. "The Maltreatment of Children: Some Un-
         resolved Problems. " Medical Journal of Australia, 2(7):
         245-249, August 16, 1975.
         Evidence suggests that physical results may be the least im-
portant criterion of successful management of maltreated children.
Emotional, social, intellectual and personality development results
should receive equal attention.   The maltreated child may himself
be a potential child-batterer and separation from his parents may
not alter this prognosis.   Professional ignorance, denial and collusion are all barriers to successful management, as are inadequate
treatment facilities and a cumbersome legal system whose inappropriate priorities may readily produce tragedy.   (Journal Summary.)

1216.   Bloch, Harry. "The Battered Child. " (Letter). Pediatrics,
         39(4):625, April 1967.
         The isolation of children battered by parents from children
battered by society is questioned.   Active concern for all children
abused by war, poverty, slum conditions, etc. is suggested as the
means for preventing many instances of child abuse.

1217.   Booz-Allen and Hamilton, Inc. An Assessment of the Needs
         of and Resources for Children of Alcoholic Parents. Pre-
         pared for National Institute on Alcohol Abuse and Alcohol-
         ism. (Rep. No. PB-241-119; NIAAA/NCALI-75/13.)
         xx+ 162 p. Springfield, Va. : U. S. Nat. Tech. Inform.
         Serv. , 1974.
         Characteristics, coping mechanisms and problems of children
of alcoholic parents are reviewed from the literature (45 items), reports of social agencies and institutions and personal interviews.   It
is recommended that the National Institute on Alcohol Abuse and Alcoholism assume major responsibility for the proposed national effort, enlisting the support of organizations concerned with the general welfare of children.

1218.   Borland, Marie, ed. Violence in the Family. See entry
         2360.

1219.   Brandwein, Harold. "Issue at Point: The Battered Child:
         A Definite and Significant Factor in Mental Retardation. "
         Mental Retardation, 11:50-51, October 1973.
         In the field of mental retardation, treatment is no longer the
ultimate goal--rather annihilation.   There is good reason to suspect

that child abuse may be seriously and significantly involved in contributing to the incidence of mental retardation. More research is needed relating child battering to mental retardation.

1220. Breig, Joe. "Beatniks Would Be Ashamed: Child Beating."
Ave Maria, 97:19, January 12, 1963.
Breig urges patient persuasion instead of physical abuse. The remedy is to start with toddlers who can be taught reason and love and thoughtfulness if someone will only take the time and trouble to do so.

1221. Brem, Jacob. "Child Abuse Control Centers: A Project for the Academy?" Pediatrics, 45:894-895, May 1970.
Child abuse control centers, similar to the poison control centers in existence, might be a means of dealing with the problem, Brem suggests. He advocates a team approach using the child's physician, a consultant, and social, nursing, psychiatric, and public health services. He suggests that the comprehensive Health Planning Council consider this as a project in prevention and that the American Academy of Pediatrics establish a standing committee on child abuse.

1222. Broeck, Elsa Ten. "Extended Family Center: A Home Away from Home for Abused Children and Their Parents." Children Today, 3:2-6, March 1974.
The work of the Extended Family Center in San Francisco, established with support from the Office of Child Development in 1973 as a treatment center for abused children and their parents, is described.

1223. Brown, Robert. "Training Schools for Children." Church and Society, 66:23-26, May-June 1976.
The author is concerned with the destruction that our institutions do to children in the name of law and order, and in the name of street protection. Dealing with the violent delinquent is a separate issue. What happens to many of our violent children is that parents under undue stress close out societal input in terms of what is right and wrong, and the child has no frame of reference. Recommended are very small units, probably expensive, where both a semblance of custodial control, as well as in-depth treatment programs covering all possibilities, is made available to these people.

1224. Bumbalo, Judith A.; Young, Delores E. "The Self-Help Phenomenon." American Journal of Nursing, 73:1588-1591, September 1973.
A great deal can be learned from such groups as Recovery, Inc. and Gamblers Anonymous, the authors believe.

1225. Burchill, Philip G. "The Battered Child, the Law and the Community." Quarterly, 29(3):48-51, 1972
Many child abusers lack the trust or understanding to allow others to help them. They usually marry someone who will continue the abuse, and they are likely to overpunish a child who does not

offer them fulfillment.   They are apt to expect a child to take care
of himself.   It is with these criteria in mind that support and treatment must be offered.

1226.   Burne, Brian H.   "Experts and Child Abuse. "   (Letter).
        British Medical Journal, 4(5939):290-291, November 2,
        1974.
        Concern is with the psychological, community, pediatric, and
psychiatric fields which have jointly studied the syndrome of the battered child.   Psychologists and clinical medical officers have a great
deal to offer in relation to the measurement of mental growth and
in advising parents of abused children.   Services such as these
should be made available through new community pediatric services.

1227.   Burt, M. R.   The System for Neglected and Abused Children
        in the District of Columbia: A Policy Analysis.   Bethesda,
        Md. :   Burt Associates, October 21, 1974.   55 p.
        A study focuses on means of improving the care of neglected
and abused children in the District of Columbia and on prospective
policies that may be adopted by the D. C. government.

1228.   Bysshe, Janette.   "A Battered Baby. "   Nursing Times, 72:
        986-987, June 24, 1976.
        Bysshe discusses a child's admission to the hospital, the
diagnosis, past medical history, social history, and the final decision
to remove the child from its mother who was unable to cope with
separation from her husband and unemployment.

1229.   Cantrell, Dee.   "Child Abuse. "   Ona Journal, 3:195, June
        1976.
        Problems, other than diagnosis and legal aspects, involve re-
moving abused children from untoward circumstances.   Where will
they go?   How long can they stay in foster homes?   The goal of the
Child Abuse Council in Columbus, Georgia, is public awareness of
the realities of child abuse and educating persons in child care and
parenting.

1230.   Carter, Bryan D. ; Reed, Ruth; Reh, Ceil G.   "Mental Health
        Nursing Intervention with Child Abusing and Neglecting
        Mothers. "   Journal of Psychiatric Nursing and Mental
        Health Services, 13(5):11-15, September-October 1975.
        The findings appear to suggest that such a concerted team
interventive effort based primarily upon mental health nursing services can increase the home management, child care, and mother-
child interactional skills of mothers who have been identified as having abused or neglected their children.   In order to further substan-
tiate the findings obtained in the present study, a long-term follow-up
is being conducted to assess the stability of the observed changes.
(Journal Conclusion Modified.)

1231.   Carter, Jan, ed.   The Maltreated Child.   See entry 750.

1232.   Cary, Ara C. , et al.   "Prevention and Detection of Emotional

Disturbance in Preschool Children. " American Journal of Orthopsychiatry, 37:719-724, 1967.
A ten-session program of a once-a-week nursery and mother guidance group which allows for modification of certain developmental lags and ego defects. The program is based on the premise that infancy to latency period reawakens the mother's progenital conflicts which are preconsciously or consciously communicated to the child. Therefore, the result is an increase in the child's vulnerability and the mother's uncertainty about her child care methods.

1233. Chase, Naomi Feigelson. A Child Is Being Beaten: Violence Against Children, An American Tragedy. See entry 568.

1234. Chesser, Eustace. Cruelty to Children. See entry 570.

1235. "Child Abuse: An Anonymous Answer. " Medical World News, 12(36):4, October 1971.
Describes the beginnings of Mothers Anonymous, a group with an Alcoholics Anonymous-type philosophy.

1236. "Child Abuse: Members of the Calgary Child Abuse Advisory Committee Describe a Community Approach. " Canadian Welfare, 51:15-16, May-June 1975.
Awareness of child abuse has come only recently to Canada. General community involvement in the prevention and protection of children from abuse is yet minimal. In Calgary, a small group of concerned citizens initiated a comprehensive program with virtually no budget. The results of the committee's work in various areas is presented.

1237. "Child Abuse--Nevada's Plan. " People, 2(1):4-5, 1974.
Nevada's plan for dealing with child abuse is basically a demonstration project intended to show how a program founded on strengthening parental skills can cut down on child abuse rates. The training and information activity will be carried out by six psychologists, specialists in family life. Training will also be offered to potential parents, hopefully preventing future child abuse.

1238. "Child Abuse Registry Aids in Prevention. " Pediatric News, 9(4):58, April 1975.
The maintenance of a central registry of child abuse cases in Dade County, Florida, is credited with case identification, insight into etiology, and means of prevention.

1239. [Child Abuses Demand Action]. Lakartidningen, 64:652-653, February 15, 1967.

1240. "Child Battery: Seek and Save. " Medical World News, 13 (22):21+, June 1, 1972.
A panel of recognized experts in the field of child abuse comments on a wide variety of questions dealing with this phenomenon. The use of lay therapists and crisis nurseries plays an important role in prevention. Needed also is a higher degree of suspicion on

the part of physicians, special attention to the parents with characteristics which classify them as risk, greater education, and establishment of groups such as Parents Anonymous.

1241. "Children in Danger." (Editorial). <u>Lancet</u>, 1:1090-1091,
June 1, 1974.
The author describes the work of the Department of Health
in the management of child abuse cases. Local councils and corresponding area health authorities are asked to set up joint review
committees to coordinate action and to make sure families are not
lost in follow-up when they move away.

1242. "Children in Peril." (Editorial). <u>The Nation</u>, 214:293-294,
March 6, 1972.
A 1972 ABC television documentary explodes many of the
myths surrounding child abuse. Preventive measures are known for
child abuse but funds are generally lacking to carry them out, partly
because of public hostility to social welfare programs. Typical of
this latter point is President Nixon's veto of the 1971 Child Development Act and his advocacy of employment rather than social services
for welfare recipients.

1243. <u>Children Today</u>. May-June 1975 issue on "Combatting Child
Abuse and Neglect." $1 Supt. of Documents, U.S. GPO.
Washington, D.C. 20402, Stock No. 017-090-70011-1.
This issue contains eight articles: Foster Placement of Abused
Children; Why Most Physicians Don't Get Involved in Child Abuse
Cases; an interview with Jolly K., founder of Parents Anonymous;
a crisis-intervention program; etc.

1244. Christophersen, Edward R.; Kuehn, Barbara S.; Grinstead,
Joe D.; et al. "A Family Training Program for Abuse
and Neglect Families." <u>Journal of Pediatric Psychology</u>,
1(2):90-94, Spring 1976.
Described is the Family Training Program designed to meet
the needs of abuse and neglect families. The intensive, in-home,
skill-oriented treatment program was structured to teach parents to
provide their children with a maximum amount of instruction, feedback, and consistent consequences for their behavior. In addition,
the program trained parents to strengthen appropriate behaviors and
weaken inappropriate behavior.

1245. Cobe, P. "Winning the Battle Against Child Abuse." <u>Fore-
cast for Home Economics</u>, 21:F46+, May 1976.
Basic issues are reviewed in child abuse, including: governmental action (the Child Abuse and Prevention Act of 1974), reasons
behind abuse, resource development centers, classroom programs
for families, and suggestions on how one can help (from the Future
Homemakers of America).

1246. Cohen-Matthijsen, T. "Het 'Battered Child' Syndroom" [The
Battered Child Syndrome]. <u>Nederlands Tijdschrift voor
Geneeskunde</u>, 114(4):142-149, January 24, 1970. (Dutch)

Character structure of the parents involved in the battered child syndrome and the role these highly pathogenic forms of behavior play in the care and education of children are discussed. In developing a program for the treatment of child and family, the author considers what examinations of both child and parent are necessary.

1247. Cohn, Anne Harris. Assessing the Impact of Health Programs Responding to New Problems: The Case of Child Abuse and Neglect. Dr. P.H. University of California, Berkeley, 1975. 236 p. Available from University Microfilms, Order No. 76-15,077.

The purposes of this dissertation are: to develop a set of indicators that measure the impact of services on abusers and neglectors and that can be widely applied in evaluative studies; to illustrate a method for developing and refining impact indicators for evaluative studies; and to use the identified indicators in a specific case, as part of a larger evaluation of a particular program--the Extended Family Center in San Francisco, Calif.

1248. Colman, Wendy. "Occupational Therapy and Child Abuse." American Journal of Occupational Therapy, 29(7):412-417, August 1975.

As experience with the 25 abusive families worked with over a 2-year period dictated, a particular treatment model for occupational therapy in child abuse has been developed, stressing two points: a safe group in which parents can develop socialization skills in order that contact with adults be satisfying enough to overcome the need to be isolated; and developing a means of looking at a process through a craft, or through any daily activity, so as to understand its structure and what it accomplishes. (Journal Summary Modified.)

1249. Committee on Accidents in Childhood. "The Battered Baby." British Medical Journal, 1:601-603, 1966.

1250. Court, Joan; Kerr, Anna. "The Battered Child Syndrome. A Preventable Disease?" Nursing Times, 67:695-697, June 10, 1971.

The most effective treatment for battering parents can be described as "transfusion of mother" which is best provided for by a multidisciplinary approach with one worker acting as the primary mother figure. Nurse and health visitor also play important roles in this process. The health visitor in particular should serve as a model for "mothering" skills.

1251. Crane, P. "Prevention and Cure: Hooligans." Christian Order, 5:513-514, September 1964.

1252. Criswell, Howard D., Jr. "Why Do They Beat Their Child?" Human Needs, 1(9):5-7, March 1973.

A review describes child abusers and discusses rehabilitation of abusers and possible prevention of abuse. The role of the Denver Center for the Study of Abused and Neglected Child as a training and treatment facility is provided. Also, the role of obstetricians in possibly predicting potential abusers is discussed.

1253. Cunningham, Pennie; Gebel, Marilyn; Richter, Aleda. Treatment Methods with Child Abusers: An Experience Study. Master's of Social Work Thesis. Smith College Studies in Social Work, 43(1):56-57, 1972.
    Current theoretical and practical issues in methods of treatment for the child abuser were studied. It was felt that people abuse children mainly because of their own emotional immaturity or inadequacy, and that special personality traits needed to work with such patients are not unlike those expected of an effective social worker. Abusive clients demand a more personal expenditure of energy in terms of investigative activities and bureaucratic obstacles. (Journal Summary Modified.)

1254. Dalhousie University. School of Law. Child Abuse in Nova Scotia. See entry 2217.

1255. Daniel, Glenda. "Child-Abusers: Parents Anonymous Organization." PTA Magazine, 68:32-35, September 1973.
    Daniel describes the formation of the Parents Anonymous Organization, composed of individuals who were abusing their children and who found that by meeting in small groups for discussion they could rechannel their destructive attitudes and actions. Rather than stressing guilt and rehashing mistakes, the PA program encourages parents to follow guidelines leading to increased self-understanding and self-control.

1256. Davis, Dan; Hebbert, Virginia; Hunter, Rosemary; et al. "Child Abuse and Neglect: Its Causes and Prevention." Popular Government, 41:1-4, 14, Spring 1976.
    The three basic components, as conceptualized in child abuse, are described. Programs to help families in stress should emphasize: the timeliness of help, the need to support the role of the family in the child's life, and the need for alternate ways to meet the varying needs of families in stress. Interdisciplinary programs, community education, the development of family support systems, lay therapy providing prenatal, immediate postnatal, and respite care, are some of the means of prevention suggested.

1257. Dawe, Kathleen E. "Maltreated Children at Home and Overseas." Australian Paediatric Journal, 9:177-184, August 1973.
    Overseas projects and developments in the management of maltreated children are discussed in the context of problems faced domestically. Diagnosis of "suspected maltreatment" is also discussed. Abusive patterns are considered and suggestions for treatment of the parents are presented.

1258. "Dealing with Child Abusers." Science Digest, 76:70-71, October 1974.
    Panelists in a discussion on child abuse at Purdue University

discuss types of abuse, the criminal and civil approach to offenders, and self-help groups.

1259. Debenham, A. E. "Cruelty and Neglect." In The Innocent Victims. Sydney, Australia: Edwards and Shaw, 1969. (p. 99-123)
A series of case reports of child abuse and neglect are used to show that a child is only taken away from the parents when it is clear there is no other way to have that child cared for properly and then only after every possible way has been tried to make the parent accept responsibility. When chance after chance has been given-- only then are children made wards of the state. If irresponsible parents straighten up, they may have the children returned to them. Many didn't bother--just disappeared, glad to have the children taken off their hands.

1260. De Francis, Vincent. "Parents Who Abuse Children." PTA Magazine, 58:16-18, November 1963.
The author considers the inadequacies of parents who abuse their children, what can be done with them, and how to most effectively deal with the problem of child abuse. He advocates establishment of child protective services in the community to help prevent children's exposure to injury and help families where neglect and abuse occur.

1261. De La Haye Davies, H. "Maltreated Children: Early Warning System and Follow-Up Scheme." Police Journal, 44 (3):193-196, 1971.
A report of a liaison scheme conducted by the Northampton and County Constabulary with the Consultant Paediatrician, Northampton General Hospital, and other parties involved in cases of maltreatment of children. Team now consists of four principals: consultant paediatrician, senior police surgeon, senior C. I. D. Officer, and senior inspector of NSPCC. (Journal Summary.)

1262. "Deliberate Injury of Children." British Medical Journal, 4(5884):61-62, October 13, 1973.
It is urged, in making recommendations for preventing child abuse, that rehabilitation of the family is more important than punishment and that battering parents need help not condemnation. Team work is emphasized. Also recommended are case conferences, the setting up of an area review committee and additional research into the effect of different types of management.

1263. Densen-Gerber, Judianne; Rohrs, Charles C. Drug-Addicted Parents and Child Abuse. New York: Odyssey House, 1975. 16 p.
The medical treatment available to newborn infants born to addicted mothers is seen as nothing short of scandalous and inhumane--at best fragmented and insufficient. Data indicated that in Newark, N. J. , there may be up to 40, 000 children living in unsupervised addict homes. If the mothers cannot be taught effective mothering, the children should be taken from them. It is suggested that

addiction should be taken as a prima facie basis for unfitness as a parent.

1264. _____ ; _____ . "Drug-Addicted Parents and Child Abuse. "
        Contemporary Drug Problems, 2:683-695, Winter 1973.
        Pregnant addicts who refuse help and addict parents who re-
ject intervention must be taken off the streets and placed under mandatory treatment until they either deliver drug-free children, or relinquish their claims to the children, or demonstrate an ability to
responsibly care for them.   A corollary is that adequate and meaningful facilities to provide the necessary services must be developed
for 100 percent of these families.   Addiction must be designated as
a prima facie criterion of unfitness as a parent. (Journal Summary.)

1265. De Tar, Virginia.   "Before the Juvenile Court Steps In. "
        Journal of Home Economics, 35:333-335, June 1943.
        In Maricopa County, Arizona, where many people with prob-
lems involving children looked to the juvenile court, a special project was established in October 1940 to study and assist families of
dependent, predelinquent, neglected, and abused children.   Needed
is combined intelligent efforts of all agencies offering services to
the public to uphold the health and welfare of the country during the
years of the war and the peace that follows.   The role of the home
economist is reviewed.

1266. Detert, Anne; Richardson, Barbara.   "Maltreatment of Chil-
        dren. "   (M. S. W. Thesis).   Smith College Studies in Social
        Work, 44(1):71-72, 1973.
        Causes for child abuse and implication for treatment and pre-
vention are emphasized.   Also considered are: the history, incidence,
psychiatric, social and legal aspects of child abuse.   Information was
gathered from caseworkers in protective services, treatment center
staff, juvenile probation officers, and medical personnel.

1267. Doris, John L.   "Child Abuse and Neglect: An Introduction
        to the Family Life Development Center. "   Human Ecology
        Forum, 5:4-7, Autumn 1974.
        The development of the Family Life Development Center at
Cornell University is examined from a historical perspective.   Efforts to combat child abuse and neglect in the state of New York are
traced from the landmark case of Mary Ellen Wilson in 1874.   The
Family Life Development Center is involved in community education
and legislative and planning programs.

1268. Ebeling, Nancy B. ; Hill, Deborah A. , eds.   Child Abuse:
        Intervention and Treatment.   Acton, Mass.: Publishing
        Sciences Group, 1975.   182 p.
        The authors--social workers, doctors, psychiatrists, nurses,
probation officers, project directors, parents and attorneys--provide
an enlightened look at prevention, etiology, intervention and treatment of child abuse, emotional reaction to child abuse, legal issues,
the dynamics of separation and placement, and more.   (Advertising Flyer.)

1269. Edelson, Edward. "It's the Parent Who Needs Help." Family Health, 2:15-17, July 1970.
This is an account of the work of the battered child clinic at Colorado General Hospital, Denver. It is here that Dr. C. Henry Kempe, pediatrician, works. It was he who coined the expression "battered child syndrome." Reporting his findings in 1962 to the American Academy of Pediatrics, the subject skyrocketed into the headlines.

1270. Elmer, Elizabeth. "Abused Children and Community Resources." International Journal of Offender Therapy and Comparative Criminology, 11(1):16-23, 1967.
The types of community resources offered to children and their caretakers at the time of the children's discharge from a hospital where they had been treated for multiple bone injuries were categorized and their usefulness assessed. (Author Summary Modified.)

1271. Emery, John. "Experts and Child Abuse." (Letter). British Medical Journal, 4(5935):43-44, October 5, 1974.
Factors of omission are as important as physical trauma in deaths due to child abuse. Negative abuse is much more common than that of the battered baby. Emery thinks committees, in general, require too much evidence before taking action, which could lead to unnecessary deaths. He believes another system for locating these neglected children must be developed quickly.

1272. Erwin, Donald T. "The Battered Child Syndrome." Medico-Legal Bulletin, 130:1-10, February 1964.
This paper is largely a compilation of the work of authors in this field and deals with methods to recognize and manage the "battered child" and at the same time prevent legal action against the physician for defamation, if the charges are proved groundless later.

1273. Everts-Goddard, J. E.; Doeve-Van Raalte, M. S. "Voorkomen dat het van kwaad tot erger gaat. Hulpverlening bij Kindermishandeling" [Prevent It from Going from Bad to Worse. Assistance in Cases of Child Abuse]. Sjow, 4(8): 176-179, 1976.

1274. Fitzpatrick, Mary F. "Recognition and Prevention of Child-Abuse or Non-Accidental Injury." Queen's Nursing Journal, 19(7):203-205, October 1976.
Touches upon some of the advances made in recognizing and dealing with child abuse, the social stresses of young parents, legal aspects, and the circumstances of handling cases in Hertfordshire, England.

1275. Flato, Charles. "Parents Who Beat Children." Saturday Evening Post, 235:30+, October 6, 1962.
No matter how wise the laws are, or how intelligently enforced, society will not come to grips with the tragedy of child abuse

until ordinary citizens change their attitude toward parents who mistreat their children.   Parental delinquency must not be ignored.

1276.   Fomufod, Antoine K.   "Low Birth Weight and Early Neonatal
        Separation as Factors in Child Abuse. " Journal of the
        National Medical Association, 68(2):106-109, March 1976.
        The findings in the various studies discussed in this paper
suggest that low birth weight and/or early neonatal hospitalization
are circumstances calling for careful review of the family situation
and study of parental behavior in the hope of identifying potential
child abusers.   A call is made for vigilance in detecting any warning signs so that where possible, prophylactic therapy can be instituted.   (Journal Summary Modified.)

1277.   Fontana, Vincent J.   "Child Abuse: Tomorrow's Problems
        Begin Today. " Catholic Lawyer, 22(4):297-304, Autumn
        1976.
        Fontana considers the problem of child abuse probably the
most medico-social one presently confronting this country.   He
names three fallacies that have kept us from making more rapid
progress in dealing with the problem.   Once they are destroyed, a
more thorough analysis can be made.   The teaching of parenting
skills can be the most effective means of prevention.

1278.   _____.   "Factors Needed for Prevention of Child Abuse
        and Neglect. " (Letter).   Pediatrics, 46(2):318-319, 1970.
        Fontana comments on certain defects in the present manage-
ment of child abuse cases that have contributed to the inadequate
protection of maltreated children.

1279.   _____.   "Further Reflections on Maltreatment of Children. "
        (Letter).   New York State Journal of Medicine, 68:2214-
        2215, August 15, 1968.
        Battering parents have past personal experiences of loneliness,
lack of protection, and love.   Fontana suggests that the solution to
child abuse must begin with the proper care and treatment of the
adolescent exposed to an environment lacking in parental love and
protection.   Also discussed are the many difficulties that remain in
attacking the problem of maltreatment of children.

1280.   _____.   "Letter to the Editor. " Journal of the American
        Medical Association, 223:1390-1391, March 19, 1973.
        Fontana refutes the idea that nobody can predict and thereby
prevent situations in which child abuse is likely to occur.   He further
contends that prevention of child abuse involves much more than removing the child from an abusive home.   He claims we are now
closer to finding ways of predicting and preventing abuse and neglect.

1281.   _____.   The Maltreated Child: The Maltreatment Syndrome
        in Children.   Foreword by Mother Loretto Bernard.   2d
        ed.   Springfield, Ill. : Thomas, 1971.   96 p.
        This book covers historical data; incidence; diagnosis; the
social manifestations of child abuse; preventive measures from the

standpoint of medical, social, and legal responsibility; quotes from the model child abuse law from the Penal Code of the State of California, and several case reports.

1282. _____. "The Neglect and Abuse of Children." Journal of Asthma Research, 14(1):15-17, October 1976.
People can relate to diseases in children, but not to the most common cause of their death, child abuse. Every parent should be concerned because their children will live with these mistreated children who may eventually be out on the streets battering society. Fontana urges people to face up to reality--to contribute time and energies to bring back a decent society, closely knit family units, and neighborhoods with real neighbors.

1283. _____. Somewhere a Child Is Crying: Maltreatment-- Causes and Prevention. See entry 599.

1284. _____. "We Must Stop the Vicious Cycle of Child Abuse." Parents Magazine, 50:8, December 1975.
Maltreatment of children can be stopped. Society must recognize that child abusers are not criminals but rather people badly in need of help. There are many services throughout the country to help abusing and neglectful parents understand and overcome their anger, and deal with their children lovingly and constructively. Resources for concerned parents are provided, as well as suggested books to read.

1285. _____; Robison, Esther. "A Multidisciplinary Approach to the Treatment of Child Abuse." Pediatrics, 57:760-764, 1976.
A multidisciplinary team of professionals and paraprofessionals provides an innovative therapeutic approach for the treatment of child abuse and neglect among a deprived and disadvantaged population of abusing mothers. The therapeutic approach stresses residential care for mother and child, behavior modification through corrective child care experiences, personality modifications through individual and group therapy, and environmental and social changes through staff assistance and education. (Journal Summary.)

1286. "Forensic Aspects of Pediatric Problems." Inform Newsletter, 4(3):Entire Issue, 1972.
Discussed are sudden and unexpected deaths, child abuse and battering, infanticide, accidents, suicide in adolescents, homicides in children, drug abuse and addiction. Organizations and reference sources in the field of child abuse and sudden infant death are listed.

1287. Forsyth, William B. "Committee on Infant and Preschool Child: Maltreatment of Children, the Battered Child Syndrome." Pediatrics, 50:160-162, July 1972.
The Committee on Infant and Preschool Child published in 1966 a statement concerning the status of the problem of the battered child. It now reaffirms and supports these recommendations which are listed and adds five additional elements. Priorities must be es-

tablished to allow for an expansion of the prevention, identification, and management aspects of the syndrome.

1288.　Friedman, Stanford B.; Holter, Joan C.　"Battered Babies."
　　　　New Society, 310-311, February 19, 1970.
　　　Results of two case studies, taken from hospital records at the University of Rochester Medical Center, are reviewed.　Characteristics of the abusing parents revealed many stressful situations in their lives.　Management procedure in handling such cases is suggested.

1289.　Galdston, Richard.　"Preventing the Abuse of Little Children:
　　　　The Parents' Center Project for the Study and Prevention
　　　　of Child Abuse."　American Journal of Orthopsychiatry,
　　　　45(3):372-381, April 1975.
　　　A project is described in which 73 children of 46 abusing families were enrolled in a therapeutic day care unit from four weeks to five years.　The parents attended weekly meetings of a parent group, thus preserving the integrity of the family while protecting the children from physical abuse.　The results of treatment were less clear for the parents than for the children, but it was felt that the treatment of the children over this prolonged period could not have been achieved without concurrent treatment of their parents.

1290.　Georgia University.　Regional Institute of Social Welfare Re-
　　　　search.　Child Abuse and Neglect:　Problems and Pro-
　　　　grams, by Joan C. Adams.　Athens, Georgia, 1976.　27 p.
　　　　Available from the Institute, 468 N. Milledge Ave., Heri-
　　　　tage Bldg., Athens, Ga., 30602.　$1; also from EDRS:
　　　　MF-$0.83; HC-$2.06, Plus Postage.
　　　Presented is an overview of child abuse, including definitions of child abuse and child neglect, causes and treatment processes, and legislation.　Some basic approaches to treatment, prevention, and identification are described.

1291.　Gil, David G.　"A Holistic Perspective on Child Abuse and
　　　　Its Prevention."　Journal of Sociology and Social Welfare,
　　　　2(2):110-125, Winter 1974.
　　　Child abuse is described as a complete social phenomenon. Discussed are two analytic concepts--levels of manifestation and causal dimensions--to be used for studying the nature of child abuse and for developing effective policies and programs for its prevention. The main obstacle to effective treatment of the problem is described as the fragmentary approach in which each discipline deals with it in an isolated manner rather than a societal context.　Suggestions are given for a holistic approach and for prevention.

1292.　＿＿＿＿＿.　"Preventing Violence Against Children."　Christian
　　　　Home, February 1973.

1293.　＿＿＿＿＿.　"Primary Prevention of Child Abuse: A Philosoph-
　　　　ical and Political Issue."　Journal of Pediatric Psychology,
　　　　1(2):54-57, Spring 1976; Psychiatric Opinion, 13(4):April 1976.

Gil defines child abuse as any waste of a child's developmental potential and identifies society's philosophy, its values and its concepts of humans as the deepest layer of causation of child abuse. For primary prevention of child abuse, he suggests the establishment of a truly democratic, humanistic, cooperative and egalitarian social system in place of the existing inegalitarian, selfish and competitive one. Further recommendations include the prohibition of the use of force and coercion in adult-child relations, the elimination of poverty and all sources of psychological disturbance.

1294.   _____; De Francis, Vincent. "Issues and Needs in Child Abuse and Neglect." In: Thomas, Mason P., Jr., ed. Proceedings of the Second Governor's Conference on Child Abuse and Neglect, Chapel Hill, N.C.: Univ. of North Carolina, Institute of Government, 1972.

1295.   Gilbert, M. T. "Behavioural Approach to the Treatment of Child Abuse." Nursing Times, 72:140-143, January 29, 1976.
A treatment approach to the problem of child abuse, which embodies the principles of behavior psychotherapy, was applied in the case of a 30-year-old woman and her 4-year-old daughter. The behavioral strategy aimed at eliminating the potential of physical violence to the child and at presenting a good model of how to handle the child.

1296.   Glaser, J.; Levin, S. ["Battered Child Syndrome."] Harefuah, 77(2):55-56, 1969. (Hebrew).
Appropriate authorities have taken steps to deal with the problem of the battered child syndrome in the U.S. and England where an alarming number of cases have taken place. The case of a battered child is reported because of its typical history and findings. All cases should be reported so trained personnel can handle them.

1297.   Glazier, Alice E., ed. Child Abuse: A Community Challenge. See entry 2229.

1298.   Goldberg, Gale. "Breaking the Communication Barrier: The Initial Interview with an Abusing Parent." Child Welfare, 54(4):274-282, April 1975.
The extreme difficulty of establishing effective communication in an initial interview with a parent accused of child abuse can be mitigated if the social worker employs behavior techniques that facilitate exchange of feelings and information, including positioning, reaching for feelings, waiting, "getting with" feelings, asking for information, and giving information.

1299.   Gordon, Alex. "A Child Is Being Beaten." Physician's Management, 5:22-31+, June 1965.
Once the problem of lack of awareness in child abuse cases is solved, the questions of protecting the child during medical treatment, deciding whether to send a child home, how to prevent his return when necessary, and how to improve the home situation are

still unanswered. Several recommendations from professional organizations and professionals in medical and social work fields are presented.

1300. Gottlieb, David, ed. Children's Liberation. See entry 610.

1301. Green, Arthur H. "The Child Abuse Syndrome and the Treatment of Abusing Parents. " See entry 611.

1302. Green, Frederick C. "Help in Preventing Lead Poisoning and Child Abuse. " Young Children, 31:404-415, July 1976.
    Two particular health problems relevant to infants and preschool children receive special mention--lead poisoning and child abuse and neglect. Both conditions could be identified earlier and properly cared for if comprehensive health services were available to all children.

1303. _____. "Reflections on Child Abuse and Neglect. " Clinical Proceedings, 30(2):31-34, 1974.
    A discussion of child abuse as the product of an equation containing three factors: a special kind of parent, a special kind of child, and a precipitating crisis. Suggestion is made that physicians and counselors become knowledgeable about preventive, therapeutic and rehabilitative measures as they apply to each part of the equation. A number of crisis minimizing programs are suggested to deal with the three aspects of the problem mentioned.

1304. Gregory, Robert J. "To the Rescue of Child Advocacy. " Peabody Journal of Education, 49:119-125, January 1972.
    Stemming from described social and educational concerns, the Neighborhood Learning Centers were initiated in North Carolina in 1968. A description of the project is given as an example and illustration of the problem, the tactics, and the goals. The Child Advocate Council of the NLC serves several functions.

1305. Gurry, D. L. "The Role of the Health Services in Preventions, Detection and Treatment of Child Abuse. " The Australasian Nurses Journal, 4:14+, October 1975.

1306. Hågå, P. [Child Maltreatment--'The Battered Child Syndrome']. Tidsskrift for den Norske Laegeforening, 95 (12):752-755, 779, April 30, 1975; Sykepleien, 62(12):564-568, 582-583, June 20, 1975.
    In the case of the battered child syndrome, emphasis is placed upon the possibilities of reuniting the family through therapeutic intervention. Suggestions for handling cases in Norway are provided.

1307. Harris, M. J. "Discussion on the 'Battered Child Syndrome.'" Australian Journal of Forensic Science, 3(2):77-78, 1970.
    The Denver experience with the battered child syndrome indicates that 25 percent of all accidents under two years of age are battered children; the likelihood of rebattering on returning home

after the first incident is 30 percent. The question of whether to remove the child from the home is discussed in terms of the safety of the child and the well-being of his psyche. Four steps in the diagnosis and treatment are outlined.

1308. Harris, Susan B. , ed. Child Abuse: Present and Future. See entry 616.

1309. Heins, Marilyn. "From the U.S.--a Doctor's View of Child Abuse." Canadian Welfare, 59(5):13-15, 1974.
The extent, physical and mental effects, and disposition of child abuse cases are discussed and analyzed. In addition to briefly describing the rehabilitative approach to treatment of child abusers, several preventive measures are recommended.

1310. Helfer, Ray E. The Diagnostic Process and Treatment Programs. See entry 347.

1311. _____; Kempe, C. Henry, eds. Child Abuse and Neglect: The Family and the Community. See entry 617.

1312. _____; Wheeler, J. S. "Child Abuse and the Private Pediatrician." Feelings and Their Medical Significance, 14 (3):1-4, May-June 1974.
The familiar pattern in cases of child abuse consists of a parent with the potential for abuse, a child who is or is perceived to be different, and a crisis of any dimension. The Allentown, Pennsylvania, approach is outlined, as well as a recommended program, involving three main segments: a diagnostic consultation program, an educational committee, and a therapeutic development committee. Four distinct responsibilities of the private pediatrician are outlined.

1313. "Help for Child Beaters." Newsweek, 80:66+, July 24, 1972.
Because child battering cases are increasing, what has been learned about child abuse is beginning to be applied in treating basic causes. The key to therapy is viewing parents as people who need help, rather than as criminals. Two new approaches are discussed: the use of parent aids developed at the University of Colorado Medical Center, and an organization for self-help, Mothers Anonymous.

1314. Hepworth, Philip. "Looking at Baby Battering: Its Detection and Treatment." Canadian Welfare, 49(4):12-15, 25, 1973.
Problems faced in reducing child battering in Canada and a discussion on battered babies excerpted from House of Commons Debates in Great Britain are presented. A preventative approach, utilizing specialists from different fields, including medicine, nursing, and social work, is proposed to detect situations in which child abuse might occur and develop ways to prevent its occurrence. Close follow-up of cases to prevent recurrent beatings is emphasized.

1315. Hinton, Cornelia; Sterling, Joanne W. "Volunteers Serve as an Adjunct to Treatment for Child-Abusing Families." Hospital and Community Psychiatry, 26(3):136-137, March 1975.

A child abuse volunteer corps was developed to serve as an adjunct to treatment for abusing or neglectful families and to develop a relationship of acceptance, trust, and friendship with them. Training was provided by a clinical staff team with expertise in human development, family counseling, crisis intervention and related areas.

1316.   Hobbs, Lisa. "Mothers Anonymous: A New 'Cure' for Child Battering?" Chatelaine, 45:66, 92-95, October 1972.
Mothers who have battered their own children are learning to help each other by talking out their problem in groups, with professional aid, and "blowing" to each other over the phone or on the spot whenever crisis builds to the boiling point. (Journal Summary.)

1317.   Hock, Y. O.; Hwang, W. T. "A Battered Child." Medical Journal of Malaysia, 30(1):43-47, 1975.
This is an account of a six-year-old girl whose mother sought advice from the local doctor concerning the child's placement in school and a behavior problem. The doctor found many indications of physical abuse whereupon he referred the child to a hospital for management. The manner in which the hospital handled the case is outlined.

1318.   Homemaker Service of the National Capital Area, Inc. Strengthening Family Life Through Homemaker-Home Health Aide Services: A Report of a Special Project Conducted in Washington, D. C. December 1971.
Presented are the organization, implementation, and results of a program which attempted to educate low SES families in homemaking practices, one major area of child abuse prevention. The results of the project were promising, and provide ideas as to the direction preventive measures should take.

1319.   Housden, Leslie George. The Prevention of Cruelty to Children. See entry 693.

1320.   Howells, John G. Remember Maria. See entry 1935.

1321.   _____. "Visiting Children." (Letter). British Medical Journal, 2(5488):676-677, March 12, 1966.
Separation of a child from its mother is not a mental health hazard unless it is accompanied by a deprivation of proper care. Conversely, leaving a child in a home in which the proper care is not given can be harmful. A survey of emotionally disturbed children under two years of age did not show a higher incidence of separation than a control group. These studies tend to refute the popular belief that it is better for an abused or neglected child to remain in a traumatic home than be removed.

1322.   Hudson, P. J. "How to Set Up a No-Budget Battered Child Program." Journal of the Medical Society of New Jersey, 70:441-442, June 1973.
The development of a program for the battered child in Bergen County, New Jersey, is described. Measures taken in the development are presented.

1323.   Hughes, Ronald C.   "A Clinic's Parent-Performance Training
        Program for Child Abusers. "   Hospital and Community
        Psychiatry, 25(12):779, 782, December 1974.
The development of a parent performance training program
for child abusers within a community mental health clinic is described.   Noticeable changes in parental attitudes were found during
the eighth session, and the parent performance training was considered to be a successful adjunct to therapy.

1324.   Hurley, A.   "Come and Get This Kid or I'm Going to Kill
        Him!"   California's Health, 30(1):12-14, July 1972.
A report describes the experience of Child Abuse Listening
and Mediation, Inc. (CALM), a confidential telephone listening and
referral service.   It is open 24 hours a day, 7 days a week for listening or for referral and resource services.   The nature of the
service is described as mothering, caring, and sharing.

1325.   Irwin, Theodore.   To Combat Child Abuse and Neglect.   New
        York: Public Affairs Committee, 1974.   28 p.   (Public
        Affairs Pamphlet: no. 508)
Various aspects of child abuse, such as definition, incidence,
causes, legal aspects, federal action, treatment and prevention, the
physician's role, and how concerned citizens can help are included
in this pamphlet.

1326.   Isaacs, Susanna.   "Emotional Problems in Childhood and Ado-
        lescence: Neglect, Cruelty, and Battering. "   British Med-
        ical Journal, 3:224-226, July 22, 1972.
The difficulties in dealing with emotional and physical abuse
of children by their parents is discussed, emphasizing the need for
a sympathetic, controlled and concerned curiosity in approaching the
parents in order to avoid recurring incidents.   The aim is the relief of the situation, not retribution.

1327.   _____.   "Neglect, Cruelty, and Battering. "   British Med-
        ical Journal, 3:224-226, July 22, 1972.
Leading up to the method of treating child abuse cases is information on diagnosis, the parent's personality disorder, hospital
admission, and psychiatric investigation of the family.

1328.   Jacobs, Stanley.   "Childbeaters: Monsters or Sick People?"
        Our Sunday Visitor, Inc. , 62:1+, June 24, 1973.
The author contends that punishing adults guilty of child abuse
does not seem to be an effective solution to a growing problem.
Jacobs suggests that abusive parents need professional help and religious counseling.   A profile of a child-beater is presented along
with various preventive measures.

1329.   Jacobziner, Harold.   "Rescuing the Battered Child. "   Amer-
        ican Journal of Nursing, 64:92+, June 1964.
A pediatrician tells how vast the problem of child abuse is
and what is being done by some national groups and the nation's
largest city.

1330.   James, Howard.   The Little Victims: How America Treats
        Its Children.   See entry 623.

1331.   Johnston, Carole.   "Parental Stress Service--How It All Be-
        gan. "   Journal of Clinical Child Psychology, 2(3):45, Fall
        1973.
        The origin and operation of the Parental Stress Service in
Berkeley, California is described.   The goals are: to interrupt the
intergenerational cycle of child abuse; aid caretakers at risk of los-
ing control; provide agency referral for long-term help; establish a
24-hour, seven-day a week program; and educate the public on the
problems of child abuse.

1332.   Johnston, Ernie, Jr.   "Battered Child, Troubled Parent:
        Healing the Wounds. "   Encore, 5:26-30, May 3, 1976.
        This general information article was written to sensitize the
public to the problem of child abuse, but recognizes that there are
at least two victims in every child abuse case--the abusive parent
and the abused child.   Case studies, comments by Dr. Fontana, preventive measures, indicators of child abuse and neglect, characteristics of abusive parents, and data on incidence are also included.

1333.   Justice, Blair; Duncan, D. F.   "Physical Abuse of Children
        as a Public Health Problem. "   Public Health Reviews,
        4(2):183-200, 1975.
        Reviews studies of the physical abuse of children by their
parents or other adults in an effort to present epidemiological data
which can be used in a model for public health intervention.   A model
of child abuse is presented in terms of the public health epidemio-
logist's concept of disease which involves host, environment, agent,
and vector components.   (Journal Summary Modified.)

1334.   _____ ; Justice, Rita.   The Abusing Family.   New York:
        Human Sciences Press, 1976.   288 p.
        One purpose of this book is to present a detailed description
of what can be accomplished through group therapy of parents involved
in abuse, based on the authors' work with couples since 1973.   Also
provided is a conceptual framework for therapy with abusing parents
that stems from the authors' own model concerning the causes of
abuse.   The systems nature of child abuse is emphasized so that
causes and "cures" can be properly understood and interventions
appropriately designed.   How too much change coming too fast plagues
the lives of families in which child abuse occurs is demonstrated.
Another purpose of the book is to address the question of when it is
safe for a child in custody to return home and how the effect of intervention strategies in child abuse can be measured.

1335.   _____ ; _____ .   "TA Work with Child Abuse. "   Trans-
        actional Analysis Journal, 5(1):38-41, January 1975.
        A transactional analysis approach to therapy with 10 couples
legally charged with child abuse is used.   The therapy focused on
breaking up the destructive symbiosis between the parents and between parent and child.   Eight couples had their children returned
to them on the therapist's recommendation.   (P. A.)

1336. Kempe, C. Henry. "Approaches to Preventing Child Abuse. The Health Visitor's Concept." American Journal of Diseases of Children. 130(9):941-947, September 1976.
Universal, egalitarian, and compulsory health supervision is the right of every child. It should not be left to the motivation of the parents but must be guaranteed by society. Predicting and preventing of much child abuse is practical, if standard observations are made early. The utilization of visiting nurses or, more often in most places, indigenous health visitors who are successful, supportive, mature mothers acceptable to their communities, is the most inexpensive, least threatening, and most efficient approach for giving the child the greatest possible chance to reach his potential. (Journal Conclusion Modified.)

1337. _____. "Paediatric Implications of the Battered Baby Syndrome." Archives of Disease in Childhood, 46:28-37, February 1971.
States the symptoms and characteristics of the Battered Child Syndrome and reports that frequency of occurrence may be as high as 6 in 1000. Suggests that early management of this syndrome involves an immediate separation of the child from its parents, along with treatment focused on the needs of the parents.

1338. _____. "A Practical Approach to the Protection of the Abused Child and Rehabilitation of the Abusing Parent." Pediatrics, 51(4, Part II):804-812, April 1973.
The clinical approach to child abuse starts with prediction: identifying families at high risk in prenatal clinics; observation of a mother's reaction in the first 24 hours of her child's life; and consideration of the postpartum period. Casework is insufficient to manage the problem. Foster grandparents have been useful therapeutic tools, spending many hours a week giving damaged, suspicious, unfriendly, and hurt parents their first experience in parenting.

1339. _____; Helfer, Ray E., eds. Helping the Battered Child and His Family. Philadelphia: Lippincott, 1972. 313 p.
This book concerns programs for dealing with and helping families of battered children. Included are chapters by a psychiatrist, a pediatrician, a social worker, a nurse, a psychologist, a lawyer, a policeman, and a judge, with descriptions of program such as those involving parent aides, in which these disciplines work together. Heavily relied on is the experience in Denver where a child abuse program has been put together from previously existing medical, legal, and child welfare resources. This volume offers a point of departure for initiating such programs.

1340. Kreech, Florence. "Adoption Outreach." Child Welfare, 52:669-675, December 1973.
The problem of adoption outreach to unwed mothers, to their families, and to the fathers of such children is presented in addition to adoption needs of foster and abused and neglected children.

1341. Krywulak, W.; Elias, J. C. "The Physically Abused Child." Manitoba Medical Review, 47:472-475, October 1967.

A brief review summarizes the problem of the battered child syndrome and the status of the abused child in Manitoba. How the problem has been managed is detailed.

1342. Langshaw, W. C. "The Battered Child. Paper Presented at the Tenth Plenary Session of the Australian Academy of Forensic Sciences Held in Sydney on 26th November 1970." Australian Journal of Forensic Sciences, 3(2):60-70, December 1970.
Management of child abuse is discussed from various aspects.

1343. Leavitt, Jerome Edward, comp. The Battered Child: Selected Readings. See entry 521.

1344. Lieber, Leonard L.; Baker, Jean M. "Parents Anonymous-- Self-Help Treatment for Child Abusing Parents: A Review and an Evaluation." Frontiers, 1-10, Winter 1976.
Presented are the results of a study on the impact of Parents Anonymous on the lives of its members.

1345. Light, Richard J. "Abused and Neglected Children in America." Harvard Educational Review, 43:556-598, November 1973.
Several sources of data are examined to estimate the incidence of abuse, its social and demographic features, and the nature of available child abuse reports. Three potential social policies are analyzed in detail. Each analysis has two underlying themes: even with incomplete data, it is often possible to evaluate the probable effectiveness of a social policy before it is implemented; and data initially collected in a nonexperimental setting can still be used to suggest improvement in policy.

1346. Littner, Ner. "The Challenge to Make Fuller Use of Our Knowledge About Children." Child Welfare, 53(5):287-294, 1974.
This paper considers the issues of child advocacy, of children's rights, and of prevention against the background of current knowledge about the traumatic effects of separation and placement of children.

1347. Lobsenz, Norman. "One Woman's War Against Child Abuse: SCAN Volunteers." Good Housekeeping, 181:82-83+, July 1975.
SCAN (Suspected Child Abuse and Neglect) began in a Little Rock drugstore when a woman named Sharon Pallone saw a teen-age mother slap and then try to comfort her child. In an effort to help the mother in a long-range way she got nowhere. She set out to create a service that would simultaneously protect the child and rehabilitate the parent.

1348. LoPresti, Joseph M. "The Abused 'Battered Child.'" Clinical Proceedings, 24:351-352, December 1968.
The physician-author deplores the infinitesimal progress made

in preventing child abuse. He contends that a baby has a right to be protected from bodily harm and possible death, but the battered baby continues to be much abused by legal stoicism, lethargy, inertia, and ignorance.

1349. Lovens, Herbert D.; Rako, Jules. "A Community Approach to the Prevention of Child Abuse." Child Welfare, 54:83-87, February 1975.
This article describes the development, purpose and goals of the Vulnerable Child Committee, the basis for a community program to identify vulnerable children as a way of preventing abuse and neglect and of helping the families. Through cooperative efforts, six Boston, Massachusetts, area hospitals have set up a cross-index referral system with appropriate guidelines to facilitate reporting for use in the index.

1350. Lowry, T. P.; Lowry, A. "Abortion as a Preventive for Abused Children." Psychiatric Opinion, 8(3):19-25, 1970.
Abortion has much to recommend it in the prevention of child abuse. Three different studies give estimates of parents who abuse or kill their children because they are unwanted. The utility of abortion, however, is limited by the fact that most abusing parents want children and have an excessive dependence on them to furnish the love they cannot obtain in other ways. Nevertheless, abortion is not medically hazardous and the experience of Japan seems to indicate that it is a useful social tool.

1351. Ludwig, S. State of the Art--Early Warning Signs of Child Abuse and Neglect--The Medical View. Social and Rehabilitation Service Conference on Early Warning Signals of Child Abuse, Atlanta, Georgia, November 27-29, 1973. 9 p.
The concepts involved with early warning signals of child abuse are presented from the pediatrician's point of view. Prevention is described on three levels. Primary prevention is preventing the occurrence of the illness; secondary prevention has to do with limiting illness duration (early case finding); and tertiary prevention is concerned with decreasing morbidity or long-term impairment.

1352. McDermott, J. F., Jr. "The Treatment of Child Abuse. Play Therapy with a 4-Year-Old Child." Journal of the American Academy of Child Psychiatry, 15(3):430-440, 1976.
This is an account of a 4-year-old severely regressed girl where play therapy was used in treatment.

1353. MacLeod, Celeste. "Parent to Child: Legacy of Battering." Nation, 218:719-722, June 8, 1974.
Money spent combatting child abuse may be a more effective crime prevention measure than new prisons. But whatever the effect on our national violence problem, the benefits to the children involved, and to the future generations, are incalculable. Community involvement can be the key to change. (Journal Summary.)

1354. Margolis, Clorinda G.; Edwards, Daniel W.; Shrier, Linda
P. "Brief Hotline Training: An Effort to Examine Impact
on Volunteers. " American Journal of Community Psychology, 3(1):59-67, March 1975.
In response to community needs and pressures, increasing
numbers of small crisis centers and hotline services have emerged.
This emergence of services has been possible in part because of the
mounting number of eager and interested volunteers. These services
want and need training for the volunteers. This article examines the
problem of evaluating the kind of information and the kind of training
that hotline volunteers were given in a brief training program.
(Journal Introduction.)

1355. Martin, Harold P. , ed. The Abused Child: A Multidisciplinary Approach to Developmental Issues and Treatment.
Cambridge, Mass.: Ballinger Publ. , 1976. 304 p.
All contributors to this book, with the exception of two British
authors, are affiliated with the National Center for Prevention and
Treatment of Child Abuse and Neglect in Denver. Under the guidance
of C. Henry Kempe, the Denver group have been heavily involved in
child abuse from the early 1960's. Most of this book has been taken
from programs developed at the National Center, such as a preschool
for abused children, crises nursery, and residential treatment program for abusive families. Its concern is about abused children--
the various wounds of the child--psychological, developmental, and
neurological.

1356. _____; Beezley, P. "Prevention and the Consequences of
Child Abuse. " Journal of Operational Psychiatry, 6(1):68-
77, Fall-Winter 1974.
Four variables operational in the effect of an abusive environment on children are described. It is time to concentrate not simply
on minimizing the effect of abuse to children, but rather to identify
potential victims and prevent abuse where possible.

1357. _____; _____. Symposium: Early Intervention in a
Child's Life. Prevention and the Consequences of Child
Abuse. Columbia, University of Missouri, Section of
Child Psychiatry Symposium, November 1974. 10 p.
The wide variation in specific personalities and intelligences
in children who have been abused make it impossible to accept a
simplistic cause and effect relationship in determining the consequences of abuse. However, by examining certain factors, individually, which are involved in abuse the consequences may be more
easily discerned. To effect prevention it is essential to identify and
understand precipitating factors involved in abuse cases.

1358. Mathers, James. "Experts and Child Abuse. " (Letter).
British Medical Journal, 4(5937):163, October 19, 1974.
Even though physical separation is not detrimental to an infant, emotional health and well-being should not be taken for granted
if the baby is removed from its mother. If an infant should be
placed in the hospital for medical, psychiatric, and social diagnosis

of the family whenever there is suspicion of abuse, then it is equally important that the mother should be admitted with the child. The bond between mother and infant, which is the foundation of the child's later emotional health, is probably already impaired in such cases; and separate admission of the baby can only confirm and exacerbate the impairment.

1359.   "Memorandum on Non-Accidental Injury to Children." Social
        Work Today, 5(4):110-111, 1974; first published 1974,
        April 22 by the DHSS.
        Measures to prevent, diagnose and manage cases of non-accidental injury to children need to be strengthened. There is a need
for regular joint reviews of these measures by all agencies concerned.
This circular is divided into three sections: diagnosis, care, management and rehabilitation; local organization including review committees; and prevention and training.

1360.   Miller, Mary Bailey. "Community Action and Child Abuse."
        Nursing Outlook, 17:44-46, March 1969.
        A discussion explains the formation of a community child
abuse awareness program in a North Carolina community. Public
health nurses designed the project in order to clarify child abuse
reporting procedures to the community. Attention was drawn to the
problem through radio and television exposure and personal letters
sent to community professionals.

1361.   Miller, Merle K.; Fay, Henry J. "Emergency Child Care
        Services: The Evaluation of a Project: Springfield, Massachusetts." Child Welfare, 48:496-499, October 1969.
        Presented are the summary results and an evaluation of the
first year's operation of the Springfield Emergency Child Committee.
Such a committee was formed in an effort to meet the needs of children abandoned or neglected during hours when most social welfare
agencies were not operational (holidays, nights, and weekends).

1362.   Morris, Marian G.; Gould, Robert W.; Matthews, Patricia
        J. "Toward Prevention of Child Abuse: Children's Hospital of Philadelphia." Children, 11:55-60, March 1964.
        This article details the three main groups of neglecting parents and their reactions to their abused child. It also presents the
typical reactions of the abused child to his abuse while in the hospital. Emphasis is given to implications regarding prevention and
community involvement in preventing child abuse.

1363.   Mowat, Alex P. "The Battered Baby Syndrome." District
        Nursing, 14:26-27, May 1971.
        Succinctly covered in this two-page article are the clinical
features, etiological factors, and management of child abuse.

1364.   "My Problem and How I Solved It: Battered Child." Good
        Housekeeping, 178:18+, May 1974.
        A lady suspects the child next door is being beaten. When
she takes her own son to a pediatrician, she enquires of him as to

what might be done. The physician advises her. She calls a "hot line" number and a social worker arrives shortly next door, taking the child away for a few days. Gradually, a change for the better is witnessed in the situation.

1365. "The Myth of the Battered Child Syndrome. " Current Medical Dialog, 40(4):327-334, April 1973.
To control child abuse a coherent and humane approach is needed. Required is the investment of diverse and coordinated professional energies. Acting on the really important cases requires more than isolated professional activities.

1366. NSPCC Battered Child Research Team. At Risk: An Account of the Work of the Battered Child Research Department NSPCC. See entry 1973.

1367. Nagi, Saad Z. Child Maltreatment in the United States: A Cry for Help and Organizational Response. See entry 2242.

1368. _____ . Notes on Needs Assessment for Programs on Child Abuse and Neglect. Columbus, Ohio State University, June 1975. 33 p.
Information relevant to needs assessment for improving the performance of programs on child abuse and neglect is presented. The information was derived from intensive interviews with concerned professionals in a number of communities selected on the basis of variability, and through a survey of agencies and programs related to child abuse and neglect which represent a probability sample of the U. S. population. Program needs, problems, and limitations are discussed.

1369. National Committee for Prevention of Child Abuse. Professional Papers: Child Abuse and Neglect. See entry 1063.

1370. _____ . What Every Parent Should Know, by Thomas Gordon. Chicago, 1975. 32 p.
How do you cope with a crying infant, a procrastinating toddler, an indifferent teenager? This booklet provides practical suggestions on how to cope with kids. It explains discipline concepts and techniques and gives a successful method to resolve conflicts so that the rights and needs of both the parent and the child are respected and met. Excellent material for parents, kids, teachers, and parenting courses.

1371. National Conference on Child Abuse: A Summary Report. Washington, D. C.: Children's Hospital of the District of Columbia, 1974. 51 p.
Presented are key addresses and workshop summaries of the National Conference on Child Abuse (1973). Stressed by key speakers was the need for a coordinated multidisciplinary effort at federal, state, and local levels in the areas of prevention, identification, legislation, prevention and rehabilitation, education and research. A complete list of participants with their specialities is included.

1372. National Symposium on Child Abuse, 5th, Boston, Massachusetts, 1974. See entry 1983.

1373. Nau, Elisabeth. "Kindemisshandlung" [Child Abuse]. Monatsscrift für Kinderheilkunde, 115:192-194, April 1967.
The best solution to child abuse would seem to be one which would encompass all faculties dealing with the problem. Early reporting of cases and greater punishment of the abuser is essential. Students of medicine, psychology, and law must be trained to recognize and understand child abuse, its symptoms and its results. Milieu factors, abuser's personality traits, and statistics on the deed and its consequences are discussed separately.

1374. _____. "Prophylaxe bei Kindesmisshandlung" [Prevention of Child Abuse]. Beitraege zur Gerichtlichen Medizin, 30:324-332, 1973.

1375. Nazzaro, Jean. "Child Abuse and Neglect. Exceptional Children, 40:351-354, February 1974.
The problem of child neglect and abuse is discussed in the context of action being taken by government agencies. Other topics discussed include prevention through education, the role of family stress in child abuse, the role of the federal government, intervention and rehabilitation, and guidelines to be utilized by public health clinics in identification of child abuse cases.

1376. Neimann, N. "Les sévices envers les enfants" [Child Abuse]. Semaine des Hopitaux de Paris, 44:1523-1525, May 8, 1968.
The interest of American authors has caused a revival of concern about the "battered child syndrome" in France. Since the family physician is often not in a position to make a correct diagnosis, hospitalization is recommended. If parents refuse hospitalization, the family doctor can contact the D.A.S.S. and complete examination of the case can be made. The D.A.S.S. can place the family under observation, or in more serious cases, the child may be placed with foster parents or in an institution.

1377. Nelson, Adair. "Help for Troubled Parents." Together, 17:28-30, May 1973.
The formation of Parents Anonymous, Inc., a self-help group of child abusers, is detailed. Also described are the mission, techniques, and benefits of PA in combatting physical abuse, neglect, verbal abuse, emotional abuse, emotional neglect, and sexual abuse of children.

1378. New Jersey State Division of Youth and Family Services. Bureau of Research, Planning, and Program Development. Abuse and Neglect in New Jersey. A Guide for Communities and Provider Agencies. Trenton, August 1974. 21 p.
The gap between the number of children abused or seriously neglected in New Jersey each year and the number of these children and families who receive supervision and help is documented, and a state treatment network is outlined. In the current treatment pattern in New Jersey, the most serious deficiency in the system is a lack

of programs to help develop and improve parenting behavior and skills. A model treatment network and programs are proposed, and a cost analysis is presented. Program needs are broken down by county.

1379. New York (City). Mayor's Task Force on Child Abuse and Neglect. Final Report, 1970. 99 p. Apps.
The Mayor's Task Force on Child Abuse in New York City was concerned with making specific recommendations to assist in the prevention of child abuse and to improve services. Through questionnaires from professional or agency persons who could provide relevant objective information, data were collected. Interviews with professional or agency persons most expert in the field were held. Recommendations include that a central registry be maintained on a 24-hour, 7-day-per-week basis. The availability of foster home and other custodial facilities in the community were also investigated.

1380. New York State. Legislative Assembly. Select Committee on Child Abuse. Report. See entry 788.

1381. Newberger, Eli H.; Hyde, James N. "Child Abuse: Principles and Implications of Current Pediatric Practice." Pediatric Clinics of North America, 22(3):695-715, August 1975. (Also a Paper Presented in Part at the Conference of Research in Child Abuse, Bethesda, Md., June 1974.) 47 p. Available from EDRS: MF-$0.76; HC-$1.95, Plus Postage.
This paper summarizes data and experience with child abuse pertinent to child health practice. Because of the complex origin of child abuse, and because of institutional and social changes that will have to accompany excellent practice if child abuse is to be treated and prevented, issues of program and policy development are also addressed. (Journal Summary.)

1382. _____; McAnulty, E. H. Family Intervention in the Pediatric Clinic: A Necessary Approach to the Vulnerable Child. Annual Meeting of the Ambulatory Pediatric Association, May 1974. 22 p.
A report describes development and first-year activities of a pediatric clinic designed to coordinate and provide various hospital-based and community-based treatments for physical and social problems of vulnerable children in multi-problem families. A review of 75 cases is given. Other data gathered from the 75 cases are discussed in light of recent practical and theoretical advancements in management and suggestions for improvement of the clinic are made.

1383. Nixon, H. H. "Non-Accidental Injury in Children." British Medical Journal, 4:656-660, December 15, 1973.
Discussed are types of non-accidental injuries, such as violence, aggression, and emotional deprivation. Nixon cites two studies regarding such injuries and refers to them as guides for prevention. Prevention usually depends on two prerequisites: in every locality a working system must be devised to assure that children

receive adequate protection and families receive relevant help; and all the professional workers in the locality must be prepared to use the system once their suspicions have been aroused.

1384.   "No Not Non-Accidental Injury. " (Editorial).   Lancet,
        2(7989):775-776, October 9, 1976.
        Child abuse is a scream from those failing to cope with the human predicament.   Doctors must be vigilant and sensitive of the bizarre.   The reproductive act is imperiled by many hazards, such as ignorance, inexperience, and incompetence.   Sound management practices by good pediatric units--a team of experts to deal with various aspects--are needed.   Medicine needs more than traditional techniques to deal with subtle and crude ways of doing harm.   Schools should teach children that reproduction is a long business.   Parenthood should be a choice, not a routine obligation.

1385.   "Non-Accidental Injury to Children. " British Medical Journal,
        4:96-97, October 13, 1973.
        The report entitled "Non-Accidental Injuries to Children" by Tunbridge Wells Study Group is summarized.   It is primarily concerned with techniques for ensuring maximum support for families so as to limit the harm done both physically and emotionally.

1386.   "Non-Accidental Injury to Children. " World of Irish Nursing,
        5:1, June 1976.
        Presented is a summary of the main recommendations of a committee report on non-accidental injury to children.

1387.   Oliver, J. E.   "Social Aspects of the Baby Battering Syn-
        drome in Relation to Family Planning. " (Letter).   British
        Journal of Psychiatry, 126:395-396, April 1975.
        Oliver believes that battering occurs alongside a constellation of other social inadequacies, but that there is no excuse for not being insistent in the provision of contraceptive advice which is often difficult for parents to accept.   Family planning must also be directed at the much larger numbers of less severely pathological families to raise the quality of rearing in this and the next generation.

1388.   Ounsted, Christopher; Oppenheimer, Rhoda; Lindsay, Janet.
        "Aspects of Bonding Failure: The Psychopathology and
        Psychotherapeutic Treatment of Families of Battered Chil-
        dren. " Development Medicine and Child Neurology, 16(4):
        447-456, 1974.
        Methods of treatment and prevention of child battering in two groups of families are discussed.   The first (inpatient) group consisted of families in which the child was known to have been battered. The second (outpatient) group consisted of families in which a child was at risk of being battered.   The methods of establishing relationships between the parents and children produced notable improvements in the family relationships.   (Author Abstract Modified.)

1389.   "Out of the Closet: Authorities Face Up to the Child-Abuse
        Problem. " U.S. News, 80:83-84, May 3, 1976.

Described is the extensive effort to curb an epidemic of child abuse--laws, expanded counseling, and faster, more efficient police and medical help for victims.

1390. Palmeri, Rosario. "Child Abuse and the 'Ounce of Prevention.'" Connecticut Health Bulletin, 84(11):289-293, 1970.
Physicians are often in a position to notice inconsistencies of rearing practices in parents. Careful attention should be given to mothers who feel inadequate or show outright rejection of their children. Prevention is the emphasis in pediatrics, in medicine, and in public health. That "ounce of prevention" to save a heavy load of cure can be used by concern, involvement with the parents, and education-at-large.

1391. Panel for Family Living. Nursing Assessment and Intervention with Child Abuse Families, by C. Snyder and A. L. Spietz. Tacoma, Wash., 1975. 15 p.
A pilot study of nursing assessment and intervention in child-abusing families is reported. The primary goal of the project was to assess systematically each mother-infant pair referred by the Panel for Family Living and provide feedback to the mother regarding her strengths and weaknesses. The approach is described in detail and the validity of it is supported.

1392. "Parents Anonymous and Child Abuse: Self-Help Group for Abusers." Intellect, 103:76-77, November 1974.
In a recent panel discussion on child abuse and neglect held at Purdue University, the therapeutic approach was the one all considered as appropriate in dealing with the problem. It was brought out in the discussion that parent education should be mandatory from kindergarten through high school and that learning to be a good parent does not come automatically with the birth of a child.

1393. Parry, W. H.; Seymour, M. W. "Battered-Baby Syndrome." (Letter). British Medical Journal, 3:583, September 4, 1971.
Whenever a battered child case is recognized, other children in the family should be examined for recent or past injury. The medical officer can coordinate the efforts of hospitals, general practitioners, health visitors, and directors of social services to provide necessary services to the child and the family.

1394. Paulson, Morris J. "Child Trauma Intervention: A Community Response to Family Violence." Journal of Clinical Child Psychology, 4:26-29, Fall 1975.
This paper reflects understanding and experience gained over five years with 115 mothers and fathers who have participated in the child abuse treatment program at UCLA. Paulson treats upon understanding maltreatment, concomitants of abuse in the nuclear family, and community action--a multidisciplinary, multimodality need. He recommends five proposals for implementation by the combined efforts of a professional and lay community.

1395. _____. "Multiple Intervention Programs for the Abused and Neglected Child." Journal of Pediatric Psychology, 1(2):83-87, Spring 1976.

Identified are various child oriented primary prevention programs involving hospital-based personnel, the school system, public health nurse, and social service and law enforcement agencies. Secondary intervention and rehabilitation programs include cooperative nurseries, Head Start programs, day care services, parent-education programs, nurturant mothering, family learning centers, crisis nurseries, foster centers, 24-hour hot-lines, "living in" facilities, university based child development and theater arts projects, Child Trauma Intervention Programs, and projects sponsored by professional, lay, and self-help groups.

1396. _____; Blake, Phillip R. "The Physically Abused Child: A Focus on Prevention." Child Welfare, 48(2):86-95, 1969.

Compared are the results of a study in one geographical area of Los Angeles County with results of other studies reported in the literature. Data reveal important person-social characteristics of the abusing parents, their home life, and their family structure. The need for identification of child abusers is stressed, to allow the active participation of protective services in a preventive intervention, consisting of psychotherapy, agencies' use of authority to shield the child, group encounter sessions, and protective casework.

1397. _____; Chaleff, Anne. "Parent Surrogate Roles: A Dynamic Concept in Understanding and Treating Abusive Parents." Journal of Clinical Child Psychology, 2:38-40, Fall 1973.

The authors report a study in which they conducted a rehabilitative group psychotherapy program with a sample of 61 parents of abused children. They became accepted parent-surrogates in their roles as therapists and note that "... co-therapists as parent-surrogates can be a psychological antidote to those emotionally empty...."

1398. _____; _____; Frisch, F. "Parents of the Battered Child: A Multidisciplinary Group Therapy Approach to Life-Threatening Behavior." Life-Threatening Behavior, 4(1):18-31, Spring 1974.

The demographic findings and the experience of a three-year multidisciplinary group psychotherapy program, with 31 child-abusing families are reported.

1399. Pavenstedt, E. "An Intervention Program for Infants from High Risk Homes." American Journal of Public Health, 63(5):393-395, May 1973.

An experimental day care unit for 15 children at high risk of abuse because of inadequate mothering was established and combined with a group training program for care-givers. Close supervision of trainees is emphasized.

1400. Pike, Enid L. "C. A. L. M. --A Timely Experiment in the Pre-

vention of Child Abuse. " Journal of Clinical Child Psy-
chology, 2(3):43-44, Fall 1973.
Describes the origin, goals, and functioning of C. A. L. M. --
Child Abuse Listening Mediation.

1401. Pizzo, P. D.; Cochintu, A.; Bean, S. "Child Abuse and Day
Care. " Voice for Children, 7(1):1-6, January 1974.
A review covers recognition of child abuse and neglect, etiology, levels of action that can be taken by day care programs, and
common pitfalls in attempted treatment of the problem.

1402. Polakow, Robert L.; Peabody, Dixie L. "Behavioral Treatment of Child Abuse. " International Journal of Offender
Therapy and Comparative Criminology, 19(1):100-103, 1975.
Results of a behavioral approach to the treatment of an abusing young mother and her seven-year-old son are described. Con-
tingency contracting, assertive training, and discrimination training
were the techniques employed.

1403. Polansky, N. A.; Polansky, N. F. The Current Status of Child
Abuse and Child Neglect in This Country--1968. Report
to the Joint Commission on the Mental Health of Children,
Washington, D. C., University of Georgia. Typescript.
The two-fold aim of this report was to summarize what was
currently known about child abuse and neglect and to derive recommendations for action. The focus was on the parents, the rationale
being that the phenomena of child abuse and neglect are best understood in terms of the parents, especially the mothers.

1404. Prescott, James W. "Abortion or the Unwanted Child: A
Choice for a Humanistic Society. " Humanist: 35(2):11-15,
March-April 1975; Journal of Pediatric Psychology, 1(2):
62-67, Spring 1976.
Prescott argues for abortion from a humanistic standpoint.
He asks, "Is it not more moral and humane to prevent a life than
to permit a life that may experience deprivation, suffering, and perhaps a brutal early death, which many of our child-abuse and infant-
and child-mortality statistics reflect. Is more physical existence
our highest goal and greatest moral burden. Or is the quality of
human life our highest goal and greatest moral burden?"

1405. "Preventing Maltreat of Children: I. De Francis, Vincent.
Introduction, 229-230; II. Rubin, Jean. The Need for
Intervention, 230-235; III. Fontana, Vincent J. An Insidious and Disturbing Medical Entity, 235-239; IV. Nyden,
Paul V. The Use of Authority, 239-245. Public Welfare,
24:3, July 1966.
A series of three related articles, together with a guest introduction, examine the problem of child abuse in relation to intervention procedures, protective services, community planning and education, symptoms and maltreatment syndrome, physician reporting
of cases, use of laws and welfare services and child-protective programs.

1406. "Prevention of Cruelty to Children and Animals." Charities, 9:372-373, October 18, 1902.

1407. Puerto Rico State Department of Social Service. Demonstration Unit. Progress Report--First Year, May 1, 1974-April 30, 1975. 1975. 22 p.
The progress report covers the first six months of functional operation of a child abuse or neglect demonstration project. Goals, accomplishments, and objectives are given.

1408. Rabow, L. "Kraniocerebrala skador vid barnmisshandel" [Craniocerebral Injuries in Maltreated Children]. Lakartidningen, 68(5):469-472, 1972.
Rabow presents five cases of maltreated children who received treatment in a neurosurgical clinic. An examination of the social anamnesis of these children gives rise to a discussion of the measures that have already been taken to prevent maltreatment of children and further measures which could be taken.

1409. Reavley, W.; Gilbert, M.-T. "The Behavioral Treatment Approach to Potential Child Abuse--Two Illustrative Case Reports." Social Work Today, 7(6):166-168, 1976.
Two cases of child abuse are analyzed in behavioral terms. The treatment strategies and their implementation, arising from this analysis, are reported in detail. Particular emphasis is laid upon the "educational" aspects of treatment and the active role of the patient.

1410. Reeb, K. G.; Melli, M. S.; Wald, M.; et al. "A Conference on Child Abuse." Wisconsin Medical Journal, 71:226-229, October 1972.
Deals with the problem of detecting, aiding, and prosecuting the adult who abuses the child. Recommendations include prompt reporting, remedial services, quick action by the courts, and a 24-hour receiving area for injured children.

1411. Reed, Judith. "Working with Abusive Parents: A Parent's View: Interview with Jolly K." Children Today, 4:6-9, May 1975.
This is an interview with Jolly K., founder of Parents Anonymous, Inc. of Los Angeles, California, a private organization of self-help groups. PA involves parents, professionals, and volunteers who work together to help parents control their abusive behavior toward their own children.

1412. Reinhart, John B.; Elmer, Elizabeth. "Love of Children--a Myth?" Clinical Pediatrics, 7:703-705, December 1968.
Modern society has been slow to recognize that the idealized conception of motherly love does not always exist in reality, and that many children are in need of protection from parental abuse and neglect. Help is urgently needed. Includes suggestions for services to abused and neglected children.

1413. Renvoize, Jean. Children in Danger. The Causes and Prevention of Baby Battering. See entry 645.

1414. "Report from the Prevention and Rehabilitation Work Group. "
B. Steele, Chairman. Clinical Proceedings, 30(2):42-45,
1974.
The Prevention and Rehabilitation Work Group of the National
Conference on Child Abuse recommends that therapeutic or preventive
programs for families where child abuse or neglect occurs should be
multidisciplinary with a comprehensive approach which deals with the
entire family unit. Program coordination and the delineation of responsibilities is also essential. Included are the elements of a comprehensive program.

1415. Robinson, Lawrence D. "You and Your Children: Child
Abuse. " Essence, 3:11, June 1972.
The author explains aspects of prevention for the abused and
neglected child and discusses how and why the community should become involved in reporting abuse cases and rehabilitating the abusers.

1416. Rosten, Patricia. "Spare the Rod and Save the Parent. "
McCall's, 100:35, August 1973.
Detailed is a new approach to the battered-child syndrome:
treatment for parents. At the National Center for Prevention of
Child Abuse and Neglect in Denver, Colorado, aid is provided to the
battering parent. This program was established following research
conclusions that found battering parents share certain common
traits.

1417. Rubin, Jean. "The Battered Child. " Wellesley Alumnae
Magazine, 50(3):8-9, March 1966.
The author talks about her work as a Consultant on Child
Abuse at the U. S. Children's Bureau. She reviews the work of the
Bureau as it offers consultation and technical assistance to the states.

1418. Ryan, William Burke. Infanticide: Its Law, Prevalence,
Prevention and History. See entry 1115.

1419. SCAN Service, Inc. (Suspected Child Abuse and Neglect):
A Unique Program in Arkansas. Little Rock, Arkansas:
SCAN Volunteer Service, Inc., Hendrix Hall, 4313 W.
Markham St. 5 p.
This pamphlet describes SCAN, a private agency offering a
unique program to help families with a child abuse problem make
their homes safe and happy for their children.

1420. Sampson, Paul. "Medical Progress Has Little Effect on an
Ancient Childhood Syndrome. " (Editorial). Journal of the
American Medical Association, 222(13):1605-1612, 1972.
Some aspects of the current status of the battered child syndrome were discussed at a recent panel discussion. Without preventive measures such children are in danger of brain damage or
death. Remedies within the competence of the physician are stressed.

1421. Savino, A. B.; Sanders, R. Wyman. "Working with Abusive
      Parents. Group Therapy and Home Visits." American
      Journal of Nursing, 73:482-484, March 1973.
      Presents an overview of the program of UCLA Neuro-psychia-
tric Institute in working with abusive parents, including group therapy for parents who have been charged in court with either "child
abuse" or "maintaining an unfit home." The approach emphasizes
acceptance of the parent and the inculcation of parenting skills.

1422. Scerri, V. J. P. "Battered Babies and Their Parents. The
      Welfare of the Child." Royal Society of Health Journal,
      95(3):156-158, 1975.
      The right of every child is to be protected from abuse or
harm and to have a home life. It is difficult to achieve these objectives due to complex legal processes, current practice, and confused administration. In order to protect the child, there must be
early diagnosis and prompt, clearcut decisions, along with a greater
investment in preventive services.

1423. Schmitt, Barton D.; Beezley, Patricia. "The Long-Term
      Management of the Child and Family in Child Abuse and
      Neglect." Pediatric Annals, 5(3):59-78, March 1976.
      Successful long-term management of child abuse and neglect
cases depends upon: a comprehensive diagnostic assessment of the
family; multidisciplinary team decision-making and treatment planning; availability of diversified treatment options; and periodic reassessment of treatment plans. Described are a range of treatment
modalities that should be available in a modern community.

1424. _____; Kempe, C. Henry. "The Pediatrician's Role in
      Child Abuse and Neglect." Current Problems in Pedia-
      trics, 5(5):3-47, March 1975.
      The battered child syndrome and nutritional neglect are dis-
cussed separately in detail. Pathognomonic cases of physical abuse
are considered, as are suspicious injury histories, the psycho-social
risk factors, and the typical behavior of the suspected parent in the
hospital. Guidelines for initial management are detailed, and the
use of hospital-based child protection team is discussed.

1425. Schneider, C. J. Prediction, Treatment, and Prevention of
      Child Abuse. New Orleans, La.: American Psychological
      Association Annual Meeting, September 1974. 11 p.
      A study was undertaken in Denver to test the validity of a
screening questionnaire. Of 500 mothers from varying socioeconomic
levels, 100 were defined as high abusing risk based on several criteria. The questionnaire is now ready for extensive field studies.
Treatment for the child abuse phenomenon falls into four categories
which are described. Prevention may ultimately result from widespread practices aimed at identifying potential abusers before they
abuse.

1426. Schuchter, Arnold. Child Abuse Intervention: Prescriptive
      Package. See entry 1118.

1427. Shaffer, Helen B. "Child Abuse: Search for Remedies."
    Editorial Research Reports, May 12, 1965, p. 343-359.
    A review covers the status of the problem of child abuse in
1965. Recognition of abuse has been slow because of a reluctance
to believe the phenomenon. The incidence in 1965 was thought to be
as high as 10,000 cases annually. The need for legislation requiring
reporting and new procedures for protecting injured children are
pointed out. The outlook for rehabilitating abusive parents is considered poor, and the need for further study was emphasized.

1428. Sheeran, Mary. "Symposium on the Battered Child." World
    of Irish Nursing, 5:6, July-August 1976.
    This is a report on a symposium, held by the Irish Society
for the Prevention of Cruelty to Children, on the subject of "Non-
Accidental Injury to Children--the Battered Child." After presentations by various notable persons in the field, the 68 people attending
separated into six multidisciplinary groups for deliberation. Recommendations for prevention and treatment were reported from each
group.

1429. Simpson, D. W. "Non-Accidental Injury to Preschool Chil-
    dren in New Zealand." New Zealand Medical Journal,
    81(531):12-15, January 8, 1975.
    Medical, social, legal and educational strategies for improved
prevention and treatment of physical maltreatment of young children
are outlined, using an operationally defined concept of maltreatment.
Available New Zealand data is discussed.

1429a. Sint-Van Den Heuvel, M. K. "Kindermishandeling" [Mal-
    treatment of Children] Stichting Voor Het Kind (Amsterdam)
    1971. 30 p.
    The author speaks of the little attention that child abuse has
received in The Netherlands. It has been calculated that at least
1200 are annually maltreated--the dark number being much larger.
Offenders are characterized, and the symptoms of maltreatment are
discussed. Repressive and preventive measures are outlined. It is
believed that the shared responsibility of the population is also of
importance.

1430. _____; Everts-Goddard, J. E., eds. Kindermishandeling
    [Child Abuse]. See entry 2176.

1431. Sloan, R. E.; Horrobin, R.; Wiffin, E. M. "Antenatal Bat-
    tering." (Letter). British Medical Journal, 4(5945):655,
    December 14, 1974.
    Because the antenatal period has often been neglected, it is
time to assess the risk factors for the baby. In some cases, such
assessment should be taken at the very earliest opportunity so as to
avoid calamity.

1432. _____; _____; _____. "Unborn Battered Babies."
    Social Work Today, 5(15):592, 1974.
    The authors feel that the antenatal period has been neglected

as a time to assess risk factors for the baby and that such assessment may be ideal in some cases for action to be taken at the very earliest opportunity and avoid calamity. If risk factors were considered briefly at the first antenatal appointment with the general practitioner and thought of a little more in the antenatal period, many babies could be protected from injury.

1433. Smith, Austin E. "The Beaten Child." Hygeia, 22:386-388, May 1944.
    Smith explains that abused children must be offered companionship, the value of books and pictures, the pleasures of sports, shows, and museums, and human kindness. He advocates a full community-wide effort to meet the need.

1434. Smith, Clement A. "The Battered Child." New England Journal of Medicine, 289(1):322-323, August 9, 1973.
    A discussion covers the growing recognition of the child abuse syndrome, etiology of the problem, and methods of management to prevent further battering. Although diagnosis and treatment provide protection, the major aim of health care professionals is to identify potential child abuse situations, and successfully intervene before battering.

1435. Smith, R. C. "New Ways to Help Battering Parents." Today's Health, 51:57-62+, January 1973.
    The new thinking about parents who abuse their children suggests that most of them are essentially normal, and emphasizes more sympathetic understanding and therapy that includes group sessions, self-help and parent aides. Meet some of these parents in a first-hand report from a Denver treatment center. (Journal Summary.)

1436. Smith, Selwyn M. The Battered Child Syndrome. See entry 1553.

1437/8 _____ ; Noble, Sheila. "Battered Children and Their Parents." New Society, 26:393-395, November 15, 1973.
    Case reports of two battered children in the same family point to ineffective handling of the problem. Case conferences are deemed inefficient. Proposed is a hospital-based regional team, or a new office of "children's guardian." It is believed these would improve the poor liaison now existing between various agencies involved. Other remedies rest with the courts.

1439. Solomon, Theo; Berger, Deborah; Pessirilo, Gloria. The Mayor's Task Force on Child Abuse and Neglect. See entry 1133.

1440. Sontag, A. "Preventing Child Abuse. The Use of Children's Homes to Help the Single Mother." Social Work Today, 4(20):634-735, 1973.
    Successful day care allows the mother to work and provides the opportunity for her to develop her financial independence. This

leads to greater mental stimulation, less boredom and more self-fulfillment. In turn, this would mean less aggression towards, and more toleration of the child. The author believes it is a better solution than foster care.

1441. Special Committee on Child Health of the Medical Society of New Jersey. "Medical Management of Child Abuse." Journal of the Medical Society of New Jersey, 69(6):551-553, 1972.
A guide to medical management of the battered child is presented including recognition of the battered child, focus on the abusing parent, and reporting the problem.

1442. Steele, Brandt F. Working with Abusive Parents from a Psychiatric Point of View. See entry 2181.

1443. Steinmetz, Suzanne K., comp. "Violent Parents." See entry 2417.

1444. Stephenson, P. S. Project Toddler: Interim Report. Vancouver: British Columbia University, Division of Child Psychiatry, September 1975. 112 p.
A multidimensional demonstration project dealing with very high-risk young children, their siblings, and their neglecting and abusing parents is described and evaluated. Important etiological factors in the development of child abuse are reviewed, giving special consideration to socio-cultural elements. The demonstration project was derived from these considerations and through consultations with child protective service workers, to provide early intervention to high-risk children in multiproblem families. The enrichment program focuses on cognitive and effective stimulation of the child and working to reduce any observable psychopathology.

1445. Straus, P.; Wolf, A. [A Topical Subject: The Battered Child]. Psychiatrie de L'Enfant, 12(2):577-628, 1969.
Clinical observations of cases encountered in a Parisian hospital showed that in the majority of the cases, the child must be removed from the dangerous environment, and that psychotherapy for the parents should be undertaken.

1446. Streshinsky, Shirley. "Help Me Before I Hurt My Child!" Redbook, 143:85+, June 1974.
This is an account of how CALM (Child Abuse Listening Mediation) became established. Claire Miles, a nurse, wife of a physician, and the mother of four children, saw the need to help parents who were overwhelmed by responsibilities and instigated the project.

1447. Strunk, Orlo. "Battered Children in Our Midst: A Review Article." The Journal of Pastoral Care, 25(4):252-256, December 1971.
This article reviews Dr. David Bakan's book, Slaughter of the Innocents. Strunk discovers in this book three implications for

pastoral workers: clergymen must not "look the other way" but see what is there; practical information of considerable clinical value is that abused children die more readily, are unlovable, tend to become child abusers; and a cautious hope for change even in propensities, possibly locked into man's very basic nature. Pastors will want more specific information.

1448. Sullivan, Eugene; Smith, Donald F.; Fox, Mary Alice V., et al. "Symposium: Battered Child Syndrome." Clinical Proceedings, 20:229-239, September 1964.
A discussion of the problems inherent in the handling of child abuse cases. Stresses the fact that inter-agency cooperation is needed.

1449. Sumpter, E. E. "Battered Baby Syndrome." (Letter). British Medical Journal, 1(5490):800-801, March 26, 1966.
The battered baby syndrome is distinct from and more serious than general child neglect. When it is detected, the investigation should be confined to the hospital until, at least provisional, medical and social decisions are made.

1450. Swindall, Bertha E. "Child Abuse: A Community Concern." Engage/Social Action, 2:6-11, January 1975.
The story of a nine-year-old who suffered child abuse and who was 20 years later telling it to a psychiatrist introduces this article. Ways in which the community can help from the standpoint of church seminars, sensitivity meetings in day care centers, PTA groups, and in industries where parents work are given. The role of the church is particularly emphasized.

1451. "Taking It Out on the Baby." New Zealand Medical Journal, 66:394, June 1967.
Parental assault on young children remains a major problem due to oversights and inconsistencies in detection, diagnosis, and reporting, and the lack of effective treatment of the parents. Further research and coordination of efforts are necessary for the prevention of the problem.

1452. Tangen, Ottar. "Kan barnemishandling forebygges?" [Battered Child Syndrome. Can Child Assault Be Prevented?]. Nordisk Medicine, 90(6-7):169-171, June 1975.

1453. Tapp, Jack T.; Ryken, Virginia; Kaltwasser, Carl. "Counseling the Abusing Parent by Telephone." Crisis Intervention, 5(3):27-37, 1974.
Discusses procedures and issues involved in operating a 24-hour crisis service dealing with child abuse. The focus is on ways in which phone workers can help potentially abusing parents; special problems are identified. (P. A.)

1454. Ten Broeck, Elsa. "The Extended Family Center." Children Today, 3:2-6, March-April 1974. Reprinted in pamphlet form by DHEW.

The purpose of the Extended Family Center is to develop the resources of an extended family for isolated parents who are acting out their problems through violence. Twenty-four-hour emergency services are provided. Professional therapy is required for abusive parents for four hours each week.

1455. Ten Have, Ralph. "A Preventive Approach to Problems of Child Abuse and Neglect." Michigan Medicine, 64:645-649, September 1965.
Family planning may prevent new cases of child abuse and neglect by delaying pregnancy and childbirth for couples who have shown that they are unwilling and ill-prepared psychologically for the responsibilities of parenthood.

1456. Toland, Marjorie. "Abuse of Children--Whose Responsibility." Connecticut Medicine, 28:438-442, June 1964.
Community (social) obligation as concerns the abused child, what is being done, and how, with some opinions on the future course of action.

1457. "Too Hurt to Cry! Parental Abuse of Children Is a Growing National Evil: Its Prevention and the Protection of Its Victims Are Jobs for All of Us." Social Service Outlook, 1:4-6, April 1966.
This article describes the grim reality of child mistreatment and considers its incidence, Kempe's pathfinding study, New York State's mandated reporting law, identification of the abusing parent, and community recognition of the problem.

1458. Tracy, J. J.; Ballard, C. M.; Clark, E. H. "Child Abuse Project: A Follow-Up." Social Work, 20(5):398-399, September 1975.
The first year results of a project designed to identify families affected by child abuse--to increase effective parental behavior, and to decrease abusive behavior using techniques of behavior modification--is described. A plea is made for a more precise definition of abused children and abusing parents in literature reports.

1459. Trafford, Anthony; Alison, Michael. "Battered Babies in Britain: Excerpts from Address." Canadian Welfare, 49:14-15, 25, July-August 1973.
In this excerpt from Great Britain, House of Commons Debates, two members comment on the problem of battered babies and propose various solutions, including education of parents, involvement of multi-professional teams, police, magistrates, and the public, preventive social work with families, and better local organizations for managing the problem.

1460. "Training for Child Care.: Health and Social Service Journal, 83(4333): 1019, May 5, 1973.
It should be possible to provide affected families where child abuse occurs with early assistance. Abusing parents were often denied supportive mothering themselves as babies. Approximately 10 percent of involved parents exhibit signs of serious mental illness.

1461. Trube-Becker, Elisabeth. "Körperliche Vernachlassigung des
       Kleinkindes mit Todesfolge" [Physical Negligence and Sub-
       sequent Exitus of Infants]. Medizinische Klinik, 70(10):
       417-426, March 7, 1975.
       Under the German Penal Code, persons guilty of child abuse
or malevolent negligence are punishable. Unequivocal proof of negligence, which happens relatively often, offers great difficulties in
establishing proof to medical experts. Mothers with too many children are often overcharged in comparison to their physical and mental abilities. They need urgently medical aid and care by public
welfare organizations.

1462. U. S. National Center on Child Abuse and Neglect. Child
       Abuse and Neglect. The Problem and Its Management.
       Vol. 1: An Overview of the Problem. DHEW-OHD-75-
       30073. 1976. 70 p. Available from Sup't of Documents,
       Stock No. 017-092-00018-9, $1.50; also from EDRS: MF-
       $0.83; HC-$3.50, Plus Postage.
       This booklet, first of a three-volume series, presents an
overview of the problems of child abuse and neglect. Discussions
focus on child maltreatment from various perspectives, including
characteristics of parents and children, effects of abuse and neglect,
a psychiatrist's view of the problem, and a discussion of state reporting laws.

1463. _____ . Child Abuse and Neglect. The Problem and Its
       Management. Vol. 2: The Roles and Responsibilities of
       Professionals. DHEW-OHD-75-30074. 1976. 96 p.
       Available from Sup't of Documents, Stock No. 017-092-
       00017-1, $1.90; also from EDRS: MF-$0.83; HC-$4.67,
       Plus Postage.
       This booklet, second in a three-volume series, presents dis-
cussions of the roles of some of the professionals and agencies involved in child abuse and neglect case management.

1464. _____ . Child Abuse and Neglect: The Problem and Its
       Management. Vol. 3: The Community Team: An Ap-
       proach to Case Management and Prevention. DHEW-OHD-
       75-30075. 1976. 216 p. Available from Sup't. of Docu-
       ments, Stock No. 017-092-00019-7, $2.60; also from
       EDRS: MF-$0.83; HC-$11.37, Plus Postage.
       This booklet, third in a three-volume series, presents a de-
scription of community coordination for managing and preventing child
abuse and neglect. Within the context of the "community-team approach," various resources for identification and diagnosis, treatment and education are discussed.

1465. Venkatadri, P. C. "The Battered Baby." (Editorial). Clin-
       ician, 36(9):369-370, 1972.
       Clinical manifestations of the battered baby syndrome are
provided. Recommendations include recognition of the syndrome as
a social and national problem and governmental action to raise the
standard of living, institute family planning, and set up child care

centers and parent counseling programs.   Prompt recognition of the
syndrome, on the part of physicians is urged.

1466.   Viano, E.   The Battered Child: A Review of Studies and Re-
            search in the Area of Child Abuse.   Paper presented at the
            First International Symposium on Victimology, held from
            2-6 September 1973, Jerusalem.   Institute of Criminology,
            Hebrew University of Jerusalem.   1973.
        Some of the more important studies done in the area of child
abuse are reviewed.   Findings on the parents, children, and other
relevant variables are summarized.   Highlighted are recommendations for action and policy and renewed commitment of national resources.

1467.   "Violence Against Children. "   Journal of Clinical Child Psy-
            chology, 2(3):entire issue, 1973.
        The entire issue emerged from a symposium on "Violence
Against Children" held in 1972.

1468.   Walters, David R.   Physical and Sexual Abuse of Children:
            Causes and Treatment.   See entry 2422.

1469.   Walton, Cynthia.   "Battered Baby Syndrome. "   New States-
            man, 72:348, September 9, 1966.
        What about cases of hidden cruelty to children which are
causing great concern to pediatricians and social workers?   Where
is intensive help to the family as a whole to come from?   The problem is a telling argument for the need to reorganize the welfare
services towards the positive prevention of family deterioration.
Can these claims be ignored?

1470.   Ward, S.   "Suffer the Little Children--and Their Family. "
            Medical Service Digest, 26(4):4-17, July-August 1975.
        The problem of child abuse and neglect and methods for its
identification and treatment are considered as they pertain to the
U. S. Air Force Child Advocacy Program.

1471.   Weinberger, Caspar W.   (Editorial).   "NIMH Tune-In. "   Med-
            ical Insight, 5:30-32, October 1973.
        This is a guest editorial by Secretary of Health, Education,
and Welfare Caspar W. Weinberger.   He tells of the work of the
National Institute of Mental Health, the Office of Child Development,
and the Social and Rehabilitation Service, and of various grants to
such institutions as Boston's Children's Hospital Medical Center, San
Francisco's Extended Family Center, etc.   He urges physicians to
join him in the fight against maltreatment of children.

1472.   Wichlacz, Casimer R. ; Randall, Dolores H. ; Nelson, James
            H. ; Kempe, C. Henry.   "The Characteristics and Manage-
            ment of Child Abuse in the U. S. Army--Europe. "   Clinical
            Pediatrics, 14(6):545-548, June 1975.
        A 12-month epidemiologic study of child abuse and neglect
within a population of 100,000 U.S. military personnel and family

members in a geographic area of 5, 400 square miles in Germany is reported. Living conditions may contribute to a high rate of child abuse. The evaluation, management and treatment of these cases involved the intervention of various military and German agencies and facilities. The lack of child welfare resources is a major obstacle to recognition and treatment.

1473. Wild, D. "Baby Battering and Its Prevention." Midwives Chronicle and Nursing Notes. 84(1002):242-244, July 1971.
Early diagnosis of child battering situations is formalized into a surveillance system. Included are criteria for predisposing possible child battering. Forms for reporting suspected fulfillment of criteria to the county are completed and county medical officers use the information to decide upon what action should be taken. Expediency and discretion are emphasized.

1474. Williams, Gertrude J. "Guest Editorial." Journal of Pediatric Psychology, 1(2):3-5, Spring 1976.
In this preface to a special issue on abused and neglected children, Williams challenges the beliefs that there is no place like home for abused children and that separation from abusing parents may be more harmful than the abuse. She deplores society's nonresponse to child abuse and the vacuous sentimentality upon which many crucial decisions are being made by professionals for abused children.

1475. Young, Leontine. Wednesday's Children: A Study of Child Neglect and Abuse. See entry 233.

1476. Zalba, Serapio R. "The Abused Child: I. A Survey of the Problem." Social Work, 11:3-16, 1966.
A review of child abuse covers the history, definition, etiology, and epidemiology of the problem. Efforts at formulating a precise typological system with predictive indicators of dangers to children and prognosis for treatment are discussed. The need for educating the medical profession to identify abuse at an early stage and for assigning responsibility and accountability for protective services to assure a minimum acceptable level of service is stressed.

1477. _____. "The Abused Child. II. A Typology for Classification and Treatment." Social Work, 12(1):70-79, January 1967.
Zalba presents six categories of abusing parents: psychotic; pervasively angry and abusive; depressive, passive-aggressive; cold, compulsive disciplinarian; impulsive, marital conflict; and identify-role conflict. The first three categories are termed uncontrollable with regard to abuse while the last three situations can be helped by social workers to maintain the family contact and to remove the danger to the child.

1478. Zauner, Phyllis. "Mothers Anonymous: The Last Resort." McCall's, 99:57, January 1972.
Mrs. H. J., herself a child-abuser, formed a Mothers Anony-

mous group in Redondo Beach, California, early in 1970. Three months is usually sufficient time to rehabilitate a mother, although many mothers continue to attend meetings. A professional counselor at meetings, calling one another when under stress, and swapping kids for a few days are some of the methods used.

1479. Zetterström, R. [What's Behind the Child Abuse Cases--and How to Prevent It?] Lakartidningen, 66:1182-1187, March 19, 1969.

MEDICAL ASPECTS

1480. Akbarnia, B.; Torg, J. S.; Kirkpatrick, J., et al. "Manifestations of the Battered-Child Syndrome." Journal of Bone and Joint Surgery (American Volume), 56-A(6):1159-1166, September 1974.

Out of 231 patients admitted with battered child syndrome between 1965 and 1973, the case records and X-rays of 217 were reviewed. Since one-third of the patients required orthopedic treatment, orthopedists are alerted to the prevalence of this syndrome and its medical manifestations, and to their responsibility to the injured child and its family.

1481. Allen, Hugh D.; Ten Bensel, Robert W.; Raile, Richard. "The Battered Child Syndrome. Part 1. Medical Aspects." Minnesota Medicine, 51:1793-1799, December 1968.

The co-authors discuss the incidence, characteristics, varieties, and differential diagnosis of the battered child syndrome. After an analysis of three case studies, it is concluded that the syndrome occurs not infrequently and should be suspected when evidence of trauma is disproportionate to the clinical history.

1482. Baker, D. H.; Berdon, W. E. "Special Trauma Problems in Children." Radiologic Clinics of North America, 4:289-305, August 1966.

Special pediatric trauma problems are discussed, such as the battered child syndrome, growing bone conditions, the ability of the growing skeleton to recover, semisystemic diseases, preexisting conditions, etc.

1483. Beau, A., et al. "Rupture traumatique en deux temps du canal hepatique gauche, chez une enfant victime de sevices" [Traumatic 2-Stage Rupture of the Left Hepatic Duct in a Child Victim of a Parental Beating]. Annales de Chirurgie Infantile, 12:47-52, January-February 1971.

The medical aspects and the therapeutic possibilities are given in the case of a three-year-old child beaten by her father.

1484. Benstead, J. G. "Infantile Subdural Haematoma." British Medical Journal, 3:114-115, July 10, 1971.

The concern here is with the three main distinguishable categories relating to fatal infantile subdural hematoma. The three categories are those with obviously related head injury, such as bruising or fractures or both; those with injuries elsewhere on the body, but

no significant injury to the head; those with no significant injury anywhere.

1485. Blockey, N. J. "Observations on Infantile Coxa Vara."
        Journal of Bone and Joint Surgery, 51B(1):106-111, Feb-
        ruary 1969.
        An historical account, diagnostic hypothesis, and four medical
case reports related to infantile coxa vara are presented. According
to Blockey, familiarity with the battered baby syndrome indicates
that a history of trauma is often unobtainable when skeletal changes
cannot be explained on other than a traumatic basis. Severe trauma
in normal infants or the shearing produced by normal walking in a
weakened femoral neck is sufficient to produce the changes.

1486. Bongiovi, Joseph J.; Logosso, Ronald. "Pancreatic Pseudo-
        cyst Occurring in the Battered Child Syndrome." Journal
        of Pediatric Surgery, 4:220-226, April 1969.
        A pancreatic pseudocyst occurring as a direct result of trauma
in a battered child of five years was treated successfully by external
drainage. This case represents the thirty-fifth pancreatic pseudocyst
reported in childhood and the first such case reported in association
with the battered child syndrome.

1487. Caffey, John. "On the Theory and Practice of Shaking In-
        fants. Its Potential Residual Effects of Permanent Brain
        Damage and Mental Retardation." American Journal of
        Diseases of Children, 124:161-169, August 1972.
        Caffey discusses the evidence which supports his concept that
the whiplash-shaking and jerking of infants are frequently pathogenic
and often result in grave permanent damage to infantile brains and
eyes. He also points out that potentially pathogenic whiplash-shaking
is practiced commonly in a wide variety of ways, under a wide variety of circumstances, by a wide variety of persons, for a wide
variety of reasons.

1488. _____. "Traumatic Cupping of the Metaphyses of Growing
        Bones." American Journal of Roentgenology, Radium
        Therapy and Nuclear Medicine, 108:451-460, 1970.
        Discusses examples of residual traumatic cupping. Empha-
sizes the fact that cupping is a residual lesion that develops gradually
after several months and years of bone growth.

1489. _____. "The Whiplash Shaken Infant Syndrome: Manual
        Shaking by the Extremities with Whiplash-Induced Intra-
        cranial and Intraocular Bleedings, Linked with Residual
        Permanent Brain Damage and Mental Retardation." Journal
        of Pediatrics, 54(4):396-403, October 1974.
        The theme of this report is fourfold: it presents the essential
clinical manifestations of the whiplash syndrome; it presents evidence
which indicates that many so-called battered babies are really shaken
babies; it emphasizes the high vulnerability of the infantile head,
brain, and eyes to habitual, manual, whiplash stresses of ordinary
shaking by the extremities; and it supports the hypothesis that casual,

habitual, manual whiplash shaking (WLS) of infants is a substantial primary, frequent cause of later mental retardation and permanent brain damage.

1490. Cameron, J. Malcolm. "The Battered Baby." Nursing Mirror and Midwives Journal, 134:32-38, June 9, 1972.
Cameron presents a clinical definition, the history, clinical aspects and subdivisions of child abuse. In addition, the social aspects of ill-treatment of children by parental abuse or neglect are discussed, and suggestions for treatment of the battered baby syndrome are offered.

1491. Cameron, James M. "Battered Child Syndrome." Legal Medicine Annual, 0(0):123-134, 1974.
Cameron discusses the incidence, cause, characteristic injuries, and social aspects of the battered child syndrome. He also outlines the physician's role in management of child abuse along with procedures to be followed in an examination or autopsy of an abused child.

1492. Castel, Y.; Boucly, J. Y. "Problemes poses au medein praticien par les enfants victimes de sevices" [Problems Posed to the General Practitioner by Battered Children]. Ouest Medical, 25(22):2265-2269, 1972.
Using as examples three battered babies admitted to C. H. U. pediatric department in Brest, the authors recapitulate the problems these kinds of cases cause for the general practitioner--diagnostic, sociological, and ethical. He should not be expected to act on his own.

1493. "Child with Congenital Glaucoma May Be Victim of Parental Abuse." U. S. Medicine, 11(14):6, July 15, 1975.
A news report discusses the finding of a case of congenital glaucoma in a 9-week-old infant which was a result of gross neglect. Examination revealed physical injuries as well. Treatment of the eye injuries is described. Physician's responsibilities are briefly discussed.

1494. Collins, Camilla. "On the Dangers of Shaking Young Children." Child Welfare, 53:143-146, March 1974.
A presentation by John Caffey for the 1972 AMA Convention on the effects of whiplash shaking and jolting of infants is detailed. Caffey believes that permanent brain damage and mental retardation develop in a large number of infants who have been abused. He concludes that whiplash shaking and jerking are significant causes of mental retardation, unrecognized, chronic blood clots on the brain and sometimes death. These effects warrant a nationwide education campaign to alert the public.

1495. Cozen, Lewis. "Office Treatment of Childhood Hip Conditions." Medical Times, 99:150-152, passim, November 1971.
From infancy to old age, the hip is a common site of disease. Cozen gives some tips on spotting the more common pediatric prob-

lems, including hip injury in relation to the battered baby syndrome.
Specific suggestions for treatment are also offered.

1496. Dershewitz, Robert; Vestal, Bonita; Maclaren, Noel K.; et
al. "Transient Hepatomegaly and Hypoglycemia. A Consequence of Malicious Insulin Administration." American
Journal of Diseases of Children, 130(9):998-999, September
1976.
On two occasions, a $3\frac{1}{2}$-year-old black girl had severe hypoglycemia associated with transient hepatomegaly. The plasma insulin
level during the second hypoglycemic episode was excessive and led
to a malicious insulin administration. We suggest that plasma be
obtained for insulin determination in children with hypoglycemia, and
that transient hepatomegaly may be a helpful sign in cases of insulin
overdose. (Journal Summary.)

1497. Ebeling, Nancy B.; Hill, Deborah A., eds. Child Abuse: Intervention and Treatment. See entry 1268.

1498. Eisenstein, Elliot M.; Delta, Basil; Clifford, John. "Jejunal
Hematoma: An Unusual Manifestation of the Battered-Child
Syndrome." Clinical Pediatrics, 4:436-440, August 1965.
A case is reported of intramural hematoma of the jejunum due
to trauma in a willfully abused child. Although this rare lesion is
almost always traumatic in origin, we believe that this is the first
reported instance in which the condition seems to have been associated with the battered-child syndrome. Prompt surgical intervention, plus effective social service agency follow-up, has helped secure a favorable outcome. (Journal Summary.)

1499. Elmer, Elizabeth; Gregg, Grace S. "Developmental Characteristics of Abused Children." Pediatrics, 40:596-602, October 1967.
This paper describes the developmental characteristics of a
group of abused children when they were admitted to Children's Hospital of Pittsburgh and when they were evaluated some years later.
The results of intervention are also assessed.

1500. Fontana, Vincent J. "Review" of The Battered Child, by
Ray E. Helfer and C. Henry Kempe. Crime and Delinquency, 16(1):120-122, 1970.
In this review of The Battered Child, Fontana discusses major
points emphasized by the authors and believes that the book gives information necessary to approach the problem in a very practical
manner.

1501. Franklin, Alfred W., ed. Concerning Child Abuse. See
entry 2224.

1502. Friedman, Robert M.; Helfer, Ray E.; Katz, S. N., et al.
Four Perspectives on the Status of Child Abuse and Neglect
Research. See entry 2225.

1503. Friendly, David S. "Ocular Manifestation of Physical Child Abuse." Transactions of the American Academy of Opthalmology and Otolaryngology, 75:318-332, March-April 1971.
  The purpose of this paper is to direct attention to the opthalmic aspects of the battered child syndrome, and thereby heighten general awareness, so that the possibility of child abuse will receive greater consideration than it has in the past in differential diagnosis of traumatic eye injuries.

1504. Godfrey, Joseph D. "Trauma in Children." Journal of Bone and Joint Surgery, 46:422-447, March 1964.
  In this instructional course lecture, Godfrey recalls and emphasizes the general principles for the management of various bone fractures in children through a series of X-ray photographs. Included is a short review of some of the pitfalls encountered in the diagnosis and medical management of children's fractures which indicates that many factors influence both treatment and results. Among the many types of trauma sustained by children is that inflicted by mentally deranged or depraved parents. (Journal Summary Modified.)

1505. Griffiths, D. L.; Moynihan, F. J. "Multiple Epiphysial Injuries in Babies. ('Battered Baby' Syndrome)." British Medical Journal, 5372:1558-1561, December 21, 1963.
  This article is concerned with babies who are brought into a hospital with unexplained injuries and are suspected victims of trauma, usually inflicted by parents. Case studies are reviewed with photos of such injuries as fractures or dislocations of long bones.

1506. Grislain, J. R., et al. [Child Abuse. Medical Aspects]. Annales de Pediatrie, 15:429-439, June-July 1968.

1507. Grosfeld, J. L., et al. "Surgical Aspects of Child Abuse (Trauma-X)." Pediatric Annals, 5(10):106-120, October 1976.

1508. Gunn, A. D. G. "Wounds of Violence." Nursing Times, 63(18):590-592, May 5, 1967.
  This paper is devoted largely to legal definitions of various kinds of wounds (abrasions, bruises, lacerations, incised wounds and stab wounds). The battered child syndrome is discussed peripherally; frequently the radiologist is the person who contributes most to the diagnosis of the syndrome.

1509. Guthkelch, A. N. "Infantile Subdural Haematoma and Its Relationship to Whiplash Injuries." British Medical Journal, 2:430-431, May 22, 1971.
  Guthkelch discusses aspects of subdural hematoma which is one of the commonest features of the battered child syndrome. By no means do all the patients so affected have external marks of injury on the head, however. In some cases, acceleration/deceleration

rather than direct violence is the cause of the hemorrhage, the infant having been shaken rather than struck by its parent. This hypothesis might also explain the frequency of the findings of subdural hemorrhage in battered children as compared with its incidence in head injuries of other origins.

1510. Haller, J. Alex, Jr.; Talbert, James L. "Trauma Workshop Report: Trauma in Children." Journal of Trauma, 10: 1052-1054, November 1970.
The battered child is described as the result of a unique type of home injury in children which includes the well-documented positive trauma and the less well recognized injuries of passive neglect, such as malnutrition and untreated infected lacerations.

1511. Hayden, John W. "Pathologic Fractures in Children." Wisconsin Medical Journal, 68:313-318, November 1969.
Hayden claims that in the treatment of pathologic fractures in childhood, including those stemming from the battered baby syndrome, it is imperative for the physician to make the correct diagnosis of the basic process, treat the fracture conservatively, if possible, treat the basic process, and avoid operation in specific instances.

1512. Helfer, Ray E.; Kempe, C. Henry, comp. The Battered Child. 2d ed. Chicago: University of Chicago, 1974. 262 p.
The co-editors have assembled a comprehensive volume, dealing with the historical, medical, psychiatric, social, and legal aspects of child abuse. Individual chapters deal with the responsibility and role of the physician, radiologic aspects of the battered child syndrome, the pathology of child abuse, parents who abuse children, and the roles of the social worker and law enforcement agency. Better interdisciplinary cooperation and coordination are urged in dealing with the problem. Appendices list a summary of neglect and traumatic cases, and child abuse legislation in 1973.

1513. Helpern, Milton. "Medical Examiners and Infant Deaths." (Letter). New England Journal of Medicine, 287:1050-1052, November 16, 1972.
Helpern, Chief Medical Examiner, defends his Office in the investigation of a sudden infant death against the accusations of Judith Choate and Dr. A. B. Bergman both of the National Foundation for Sudden Infant Death (NFSID). Mrs. Choate, president of the organization, was dissatisfied with the investigation of the death of her son on March 16, 1965, and Dr. Bergman of another infant death investigation.

1514. Holder, V. "The Battered Child at School." Health and Social Service Journal, 86(4472):71-72, January 10, 1976.
School problems experienced by physically and emotionally abused children are reviewed. Nearly 10 percent of the total child abuse cases in England each year result in some level of brain damage. Aside from physical impairment, learning problems can stem from anxiety so severe that the child's eyes cannot focus.

1515. Howells, J. G. "Ill-Health and Child Abuse." (Letter).
    Lancet, 2(7932):454, September 6, 1975.
    The episodes of ill-health associated with child battering may
be secondary to a more basic cause. It must be identified and resolved.

1516. Joos, Thad H. "Child Abuse: A Different Point of View."
    Pediatrics, 45(3):511, March 1970.
    In the Allergy Clinic, Joos encounters many children suffer-
ing from a different form of child abuse. Severe allergic rhinitis
or asthma often result from constantly present allergens which are
never removed from the house, even after explanations of cause and
effect repeated by the physician. Abnormalities caused by this atopic
disease include ear infection, hearing loss, malocclusion of the
teeth, school absenteeism, tension fatigue syndrome, and fixed chest
deformities secondary to long-term asthma.

1517. Kempe, C. Henry. "Uncommon Manifestations of the Battered
    Child Syndrome." American Journal of Diseases of Chil-
    dren, 129(11):1265, November 1975.
    Kempe refers to the typical, and most common radiological
features of the battered child syndrome classically described by Caffey and Silverman. Besides Caffey's more recent description of the
whiplash-shaken infant syndrome, Kempe lists eleven other clinical
findings requiring immediate and accurate diagnosis to prevent further
damage to child and to allow for effective intervention.

1518. Kerr, W. C. "Lithium Salts in the Management of a Child
    Batterer." Medical Journal of Australia, 2(11):414-415,
    September 11, 1976.
    This is an account of the use of lithium salts in the manage-
ment of a child batterer whose case history is provided. After the
establishment of a treatment regime of lithium in a therapeutic dos-
age the patient's mood improved, her irritability disappeared and
she was no longer subject to explosive rages.

1519. Köttgen U. "Kindesmisshandlung" [Child Abuse ("Battered
    Child Syndrome")]. Medizinische Klinik, 61:2025-2028,
    December 23, 1966.
    The "battered child syndrome," described and discussed in
the USA for years, was scarcely noted by Germany before 1966.
Typical cases involved a combination of subdural hematomas with
multiple, traumatic damage to the skeletal structure. Permanent
damage or death is not infrequent. Symptoms and causes of German
child abuse are discussed.

1520. Leavitt, Jerome Edward, comp. The Battered Child: Se-
    lected Readings. See entry 521.

1521. Levine, Milton I. "A Pediatrician's View." Pediatric An-
    nals, 5(3):6-9, March 1976.
    Levine discusses the many aspects of detecting and treating
cases of child abuse and neglect as seen by a pediatrician. He then

introduces the guest editor of this special issue of Pediatric Annals and comments briefly on each article.

1522. Lindenberg, Richard; Freytag, Ella. "Morphology of Brain Lesions from Blunt Trauma in Early Infancy." Archives of Pathology, 87:298-305, 1969.
Cerebral lesions from blunt trauma in young infants represent a characteristic entity, whether they result from accident or maltreatment. The lesions take the form of tears rather than contusions because of the soft consistency of the not yet myelinated brain, the skull's pliancy, the smoothness of the intracranial fossae, and the shallowness of the subarachnoid space.

1523. Lonsdale, Derrick; Evarts, Charles M. "Guide to the Battered Child Syndrome." Hospital Medicine, 8:8-12+, March 1972.
In this illustrated article, the authors present various aspects of the battered child syndrome, including incidence, forms of abuse, diagnosis, psychological features, and medicolegal features.

1524. MacCarthy, D. "The Physical Effect of Maternal Rejection on a Child Living at Home." Update, 7(11):1399-1406, 1973.
Dwarfism is one of the physical effects produced in a child suffering long lasting emotional deprivation. Dejection, apathy, and signs of rough treatment are the general aspects in the clinical picture.

1525. MacKeith, Ronald. "Speculations on Non-Accidental Injury as a Cause of Chronic Brain Disorder." Developmental Medicine and Child Neurology, 16:216-218, April 1974.
Statistics are presented regarding the death of battered children in relation to brain damage by wilful violence. MacKeith then compares the United Kingdom and the United States regarding battered children. He also points out other injuries which may affect a battered child from non-accidental injury, such as cerebral palsy.

1526. Mant, A. Keith. "The Battered Baby Syndrome." Medico-Legal Bulletin, 188:1-8, December 1968.
This paper deals primarily with the medicolegal investigation of fatal cases of child abuse; the difficulties which must be overcome; and some of the tactics employed by the defense.

1527. Martin, H. P.; Beezley, P.; Conway, E. F.; Kempe, C. H. "The Development of Abused Children." Advances in Pediatrics, 21:25-73, 1974.
The coauthors contend that the abused child is at high risk for damage to his nervous system and maldevelopment of ego functions. In addition, the report deals with physical and intellectual findings of a group of 58 previously abused children.

1528. Meacham, William F. "The Neurosurgical Aspects of the Battered Child." Southern Medical Bulletin, 58(3):33-36, 1970.

The different types of head trauma due to child maltreatment
are described and suggested treatment is given.

1529.   "Medical Progress Has Little Effect on an Ancient Childhood
        Syndrome." Journal of the American Medical Association,
        222(13):1605-1612, 1972.
        This is a panel discussion by physicians and law enforcement
officials on child abuse.

1530.   Miller, Donald S.   "Fractures Among Children." Minnesota
        Medicine, 42:1209-1213, September 1959; 1414-1418, 1423-
        1425, October 1959.
        Part I.   Parental Assault as Causative Agent: General cases
of fractures in children with parent assault as probable causative
agent.   Mentions incidence of abuse and urges physicians to consider
parental assault as a possible cause of fracture in many cases.
Part II.   Some Practical Principles of Treatment of Common Fractures: Describes types of fractures and appropriate treatment.

1531.   Money, John; Needleman, Andrea.   "Child Abuse in the Syn-
        drome of Reversible Hyposomatotripic Dwarfism-Psycho-
        social Dwarfism." Journal of Pediatric Psychology, 1(2):
        20-23, Spring 1976.
        Abuse dwarfism is also known as reversible hyposomatotropin-
ism.   Secretion of pituitary growth hormone (somatotropin) is deficient but can be reversed.   The formula for reversal is simply to
change the domicile from an abusing to a non-abusing one.   The authors also describe various behavior pathologies related to abuse
dwarfism, ranging from unusual eating and drinking patterns to col-
lusional family psychopathology.

1532.   Moyes, Peter D.   "Subdural Effusions in Infants." Canadian
        Medical Association Journal, 231-234, February 1, 1969.
        Over a 10-year period, 60 children were treated for subdural
hematoma.   Birth trauma and post-meningitic effusion accounted for
most of the cases, with child abuse representing four cases.   Symptoms are given.   Diagnoses were confirmed by radiological evidence
of skull expansion or fracture and subdural taps showing fresh blood
or an elevated protein content.   Method of treatment is described.
The severity of the initial injury, and the promptness of treatment
affected the outcome.

1533.   National Symposium on Child Abuse, Rochester, N. Y., 1971.
        See entry 786.

1534.   National Symposium on Child Abuse, 4th, Charleston, S. C.,
        1973.   See entry 1982.

1535.   Nelson, Gerald D.; Paletta, F. X.   "Burns in Children."
        Surgery, Gynecology and Obstetrics, 128:518-522, March
        1969.
        A group of 460 children sustaining second and third degree
burns were treated using occlusive dressing technique without topical

agents. Although only one case of deliberate abuse was identified, more were suspected. The overall mortality rate (14 of 460) was 45 percent of the standard predicted mortality rate, a result superior to that obtained by silver-nitrate-Sulfamylon (mafenide) treatment. Topical application of silver nitrate is not as important as frequent changes of dressings and early skin grafting.

1536. Noack, R.; Welcker, U. "Zwei aussergenwohnliche schadel-verletzungen bei sauglingen" [Two Unusual Skull Injuries in Infants]. Zentralblatt für Chirurgie, 94(17):582-585, 1969.
    Two cases of intracranial injuries are described. The injuries were from foreign bodies in infancy--the result, probably, of criminal intent.

1537. Orton, C. I. "Loss of Columella and Septum from an Unusual Form of Child Abuse. Case Report." Plastic and Reconstructive Surgery, 56(3):345-346, September 1975.
    This is a report of a case where a mother obsessively scoured the nasal secretions from the noses of her two children with a bobby pin. The injuries resulted in intermittent bleeding. The columellar loss in one child and its reconstruction is described.

1538. Owens, Mark P.; Wolfman, Earl F., Jr.; Chung, George K. "The Management of Liver Trauma." Archives of Surgery, 103:211-215, August 1971.
    A series of 150 consecutive cases of liver trauma reveals a mortality of 8.3 percent for penetrating trauma and 47.7 percent for blunt trauma. A progressive increase in mortality was noted for increasing numbers of associated organ injuries. Three of the cases resulted from child battering; one child died. Treatment, complications, and results are detailed.

1539. Pena, Sergio D. J.; Medovy, Harry. "Child Abuse and Traumatic Pseudocyst of the Pancreas." Journal of Pediatrics, 83:1026-1028, December 1973.
    Pseudocyst of the pancreas in children is often caused by child battering. This is particularly true in preschool children.

1540. Pfundt, Theodore R. "The Problem of the Battered Child." Postgraduate Medicine, 35:426-431, April 1964.
    A description of pathological findings of children who died from parental abuse. Stresses the varieties of assault on the children and describing these as "incredible." Emphasizes the physician's critical role in detection and assuring later protection for the child. Includes case examples and illustrations.

1541. Quigley, Thomas B.; Banks, Henry H.; Leach, Robert E., et al. "Advances in the Management of Fractures and Dislocations in the Past Decade." Orthopedic Clinics of North America, 3:793-825, November 1972.
    In discussing orthopedic surgical management of fractures and dislocations, the authors report on 50 cases of child abuse at the Children's Hospital of Pittsburgh, Pa. X-ray evidence of recent and

old injury to the skeleton was found in all; this included fractures of the skull, ribs, clavicle and long bones. These children also are presented often with dehydration, macrocephaly, superficial bruising, hemorrhages, and pallor.

1542. Rees, B. "The Immunological Identification of Foetal Haemoglobin in Bloodstains in Infanticide and Associated Crimes." Medicine, Science and the Law, 14(3):163-167, 1974.
The means of differentiating cord blood stains from those of adult blood are described.

1543. Reuter, G. [Surgical Aspects of the Problem of Child Abuse with Special Reference to Injuries of the Internal Organs]. Paediatrie und Grenzgebiete, 15(5):253-263, 1976.

1544. Roaf, Robert. "Trauma in Childhood." British Medical Journal, 5449:1541-1543, June 12, 1965; Nursing Mirror and Midwives Journal, 123:x+, May 5, 1967.
Article deals with the various traumas in childhood which are mainly caused by combustion engines and battering parents. The focus is on certain types of traumas, how they were inflicted, their symptoms, and their treatment. Mechanical injuries in battered babies are seen as common fractures, nerve-tendon and blood vessel injuries, and as burns.

1545. Roberts, Albert, F., ed. Childhood Deprivation. See entry 649.

1546. Robertson, I.; Hodge, P. R. "Histopathology of Healing Abrasions." Forensic Science, 1:17-25, April 1972.
In the practice of forensic pathology it is occasionally important to estimate the interval of time between the infliction of an injury, and death. This problem, among others, has been encountered in fatal cases of the "battered-baby syndrome," in particular. The histological examination of abrasions is of value in determining their age and the age of associated underlying subcutaneous bruises, provided multiple sections are examined and special stains (commonly used in routine histological laboratories) are employed. (Journal Summary Modified.)

1547. Rosen, S. R.; Hirschenfang, S.; Benton, J. G. "Aftermath of Severe Multiple Deprivation in a Young Child: Clinical Implications." Perceptual and Motor Skills, 24:219-226, 1967.
A 3-year-old boy abandoned by his mother showed broad developmental retardation on being hospitalized for dehydration and severe malnutrition. A medical history of the case is given.

1548. Salmon, M. A. "The Spectrum of Abuse in the Battered-Child Syndrome." Injury: British Journal of Accident Surgery, 2:211-217, January 1971.
Offers six case histories to illustrate the range of injuries encompassed by the general definition of the Battered Child Syndrome.

States the need to have a clear picture of the spectrum of abuse from which to work.

1549. Sarsfield, J. K. "The Neurological Sequelae of Non-Accidental Injury. " Developmental Medicine and Child Neurology, 16(6):826-827, December 1974.
Sarsfield discusses the brain damage which may occur in non-accidental injuries of children. He gives various statistics and examples of the many injuries which may affect the battered baby. Also presented are some studies in regard to brain-damaged children and effects these injuries have caused.

1550. Schacter, M. "De l'enfant maltraité au 'syndrome de l'enfant battu. ' A propos de la soi-disant 'actualite' d'un vieux probleme" [From the Mistreated Child to the 'Battered Child Syndrome. ' About the So-Called 'Actuality' of an Old Problem]. Praxis, 64(39):1248-1253, September 30, 1975.
A critical review of the medical literature from 1930 to the end of 1973 discusses the finding from the standpoint of the severity of the problem, incidence, injuries, diagnosis, and causes. Finally, the author states that the concept of the battered child of the American authors brings no new facts. (English Abstract Modified.)

1551. Schechner, S. A. , et al. "Case Reports. Gastric Peforation and Child Abuse. " Journal of Trauma, 14:723-725, August 1974.
Gastrointestinal tract injuries caused by child abuse has been widely discussed but the stomach, as a site for traumatic perforation, has been mentioned infrequently. Reported are two cases of gastric rupture carrying suspicion of abuse.

1552. Shulman, Kenneth. "Late Complications of Head Injuries in Children. " Clinical Neurosurgery, 19:371-380, 1972.
This paper reviews the operative and nonoperative late complications of head injuries in children, one of which is repeated trauma by a sibling, parent, or other adult--the battered child syndrome. A hopeful attitude is justified because of the favorable long-term prognosis in the pediatric age group. (Journal Summary Modified.)

1553. Smith, Selwyn M. The Battered Child Syndrome. London, Boston: Butterworths, 1975. 292 p.
A practical and clinical study of the various aspects of child abuse. Smith states that the aim of this book has been to improve the lack of systematic knowledge by bringing together the published professional opinions on the characteristics of the parents and children involved so that systematic testing of hypotheses can be carried out. Part I covers the Background to the Problem: A Review of the Medical, Social and Legal Literature; Part II presents 134 Battered Children and Their Parents: A Controlled Study; Part III covers the Psychiatric, Psychological, and Social Characteristics of the Parents; and Part IV is the Interpretation of the Findings. Four appendices and a glossary.

1554. Steigrad, J. "The Battered Child Syndrome. Paper Presented at the Tenth Plenary Session of the Australian Academy of Forensic Sciences Held in Sydney on 26th November 1970. " Australian Journal of Forensic Science, 3(2):57-59, 1970.

Steigrad presents a short resume of the medical features of the battered child syndrome and indicates the suspected incidence of this syndrome. The syndrome exists as a clinical entity and is recognizable in spite of the difficulty of obtaining a history or obtaining proof that there has been wilful maltreatment.

1555. Stettnisch, K. D.; Wagner, P.; Richter, H. "Candidameningitis nach Misshandlung" [Candida Meningitis in Battered Children]. Zeitschrift für Aerztliche Fortbildung, 70(1): 29-32, 1976.

The medical aspects of a case of Candida meningitis in a battered baby is reported in detail. Symptoms and treatment are fully given.

1556. Stricker, M. "Les Mutilations de la Columelle" [Trauma of the Columella]. Revue de Stomatologie et de Chirurgie Maxillo-Faciale, 73:485-494, September 1972.

Columellar mutilation results from the exeresis of a cutaneous epithelioma, but even more often from a traumatism in view of the fact that so-called agenesis of the columella is, in reality a progressive reduction due to repeated traumatism suffered by children who have been ill-treated. Ways of repairing the columella, which is a differentiated structure and very tricky to handle, are given. (Journal Summary Modified.)

1557. Stroud, C. E. "Three Dysfunctional Environmental Influences in Development: Malnutrition, Non-Accidental Injury and Child Minding. Introduction. " Postgraduate Medical Journal, 51Suppl 2: Suppl 15:17-18, 1975.

If attempting to help each child achieve its genetic potential is accepted as a pediatrician's lot in child health, a grave responsibility is taken. Genetically determined differences in intellectual potential cannot be altered, but environment, which has a greater effect, can be altered in such a way as to make it easier for children to achieve their true potential.

1558. Suson, Eduardo M.; Klotz, Donald, Jr.; Kottmeier, Peter K. "Liver Trauma in Children. " Journal of Pediatric Surgery, 10(3):411-417, June 1975.

Awareness of the possibility of liver injury in children with blunt abdominal trauma, prompt operative intervention with adequate vascular control prior to the attempted repair of liver of associated major vessel injuries should significantly increase the salvage of these pediatric trauma victims. (Journal Summary Modified.)

1559. Talukder, M. Q.; Dawson, K. P. "Nutritional Marasmus in an Affluent Society. " Practitioner, 212(1269):359-362, March 1974.

1560. Till, Kenneth. "Subdural Haematoma and Effusion in Infancy."
British Medical Journal, 3:804, September 28, 1968.
Till begins with a defense of earlier investigations regarding
subdural hematoma and effusion in infancy. He then discusses the
home life situations of infants investigated who have sustained subdural hematoma. Statistics regarding unstable homes, foster homes,
and broken homes of these infants are presented. Investigations and
follow-ups are suggested to protect these children from further injury.

1561. Tomasi, Lawrence G.; Rosman, N. T. "Purtscher Retinopathy in the Battered Child Syndrome." American Journal
of Diseases of Children, 129(11):1335-1337, November 1975.
Purtscher retinopathy is described with symptoms found in
adults and in infants. Two battered infants had like symptoms.
Purtscher retinopathy should be added to the list of physical signs
suggesting child abuse. (Journal Summary Modified.)

1562. Watt, J. M. "Ill-Thrift." New Zealand Medical Journal,
75(480):285-287, May 1972.
Failure-to-thrive resulting from emotional deprivation is an
important pediatric problem which may be present as an emergency.
Fully detailed are the medical aspects of this syndrome. The often
rapid dramatic change in the infant upon hospital admission frequently
makes the diagnosis. This syndrome should be attacked as vigorously
as the battered child syndrome.

MULTIPLE ASPECTS

1563. American Humane Association. Children's Division. Child
     Abuse: A Preview of a Nationwide Survey, by Vincent De
     Francis. Denver, Colo., 1963. 20 p. $.40. (Presented
     to the annual forum of the National Conference on Social
     Welfare, held in Cleveland, May 1963.)
     Preliminary study of incidence, characteristics, community
attitudes and patterns of dealing with the battered child problem.

1564. "Assaulted Children." Lancet, 1:543-544, March 7, 1964.
     This article deals generally with child abuse--the welcome
recent publicity in the U.S. which will alert doctors to this condition,
the history of medical findings beginning with Caffey in 1946, diagnosis and management, and legal aspects.

1565. Bahr, Robert. "The Murder They Get Away With." Today's
     Family Digest, 23:65-69, October 1967.
     By referring to a typical case of child abuse, Bahr discusses
the incidence of the battered child syndrome. He emphasizes the
ineffectiveness of reporting laws, the difficulty in getting physicians
to report suspected cases, and the significance of community protective services.

1566. Bain, Katherine. "The Physically Abused Child." Pediatrics,
     31:895-897, June 1963.
     In this commentary, the Deputy Chief of HEW's Children's
Bureau describes the growing incidence of child abuse, the reasons
for physician failure to act in behalf of the abused child, and the
nature and effects of child abuse.

1567. _____; Milowe, Irvin D.; Wenger, Donald S., et al.
     "Child Abuse and Injury." Military Medicine, 130(8):747-
     762, August 1965.
     This article is based on the 1964 Forensic Sciences Sympos-
ium presented at the Armed Forces Institute of Pathology. Five
medical and legal authorities discuss various perspectives of child
abuse with special reference to the military population. Emphasis
is given to identification of child abuse cases, the reluctance of social workers and psychiatrists to believe that many of the families
involved cannot be improved, problems of removing the abused child
from the family, and legal aspects of physician reporting procedures.

1568. "Battered Babies." Royal Society of Health Journal, 90:282-
     283, passim, September-October 1970.

A review covers briefly the history, incidence, etiology, clinical picture, and management of the battered child syndrome.

1569. "The Battered-Child Syndrome. " (Editorial). Journal of the American Medical Association, 181(1):42, July 7, 1962.
This editorial presents a general overview of the incidence, symptoms, diagnosis, and disposition of child abuse cases, including the role of the physician and mandatory reporting laws.

1570. Brown, George; Wolf, Jeanne; Ure, Barbara, et al. "Child Abuse and Neglect in Alaska. " Alaska Medicine, 16(5): 108-111, 1974.
Child abuse and neglect in Alaska are discussed as broad, multifactorial problems. Reporting began in 1971, and sample cases of a severe nature are cited. Symptoms and signs of abuse are listed. National medical, political, community, and volunteer attention is focused on the problem.

1571. Brown, Rowine H. "The Battered Child Syndrome. " Journal of Forensic Sciences, 21(1):65-70, 1976.
Brown presents the many views of the battered child syndrome: legal, statistics, types of injuries, offenders, causes, and diagnosis. In spite of numerous problems, attempts are being made to solve the problem of the battered child and to save his life. Nine ways in which action is, or should be, taken are given.

1572. Carter, E. J. "The Battered Baby Syndrome. " Police College Magazine, 13(1):39-46, 1974.
After a review of the literature, the general aspects of the problem are discussed.

1573. "Child Abuse and Neglect. " Journal of the Indiana State Medical Association, 69(8):580-581, August 1976.

1574. "Child Abuse: Perspective, Politics, and Programs. " Journal of Clinical Child Psychology, 5(1):16-32, 1976.
The following articles are included on this theme: "The eighth amendment ... 'cruel and unusual', " Adah Maurer (p. 16); "Severe parental punishment and delinquency: a development theory, " R. S. Welsh (pp. 17-21); "Children's rights: countering the opposition, " R. H. Starr, Jr. , C. J. Zook and P. Hauser (pp. 21-23); "The professional's role and perspective on child abuse, " L. M. Riscalla (pp. 24-26); "If you don't stop hitting your sister, I'm going to beat your brains in, " S. Bordin-Sandler (pp. 27-30); "A behavior modification program to remediate child abuse, " R. E. Jensen (pp. 30-32).

1575. "Child Abuse Reported Increasing. " IEA Reporter, 29(3):6, November 1974.
Reviewed are the opinions of pediatrician James E. Mahan concerning the problem of child abuse--characteristics of parents, the reporting aspects of the law, visible signs and symptoms of the syndrome, and means of management.

1576. Crockett, Art. "The Battered-Child Syndrome." Ave Maria, 108:8-12, August 24, 1968.
In this general article, the author presents some statistics on the incidence of child-battering, examines causative factors, comments on legislative counter measures, and offers several preventive measures. Crockett contends that the ultimate solution to this problem rests with the parent.

1577. Delaney, D. W. "The Physically Abused Child." World Medical Journal, 13:145-147, September-October 1966.
The author draws attention to the problem of child abuse.

1578. Dziedzic-Witkowska, T., et al. [Battered Child Syndrome]. Polski Tygodnik Lekarski, 31(6):239-240, February 9, 1976. (Polish)

1579. Ealing Battered Baby Conference, 1973. The Ealing Battered Baby Conference: Proceedings of a One-Day Conference Organized by the Health Department of the London Borough of Ealing, November 1973. London: B. Edsall and Co. Ltd., 1974. 34 p. il.

1580. Falk, W.; Maresch, W. "Klinisch-pädiatrische und forensische Aspekte der Kindesmisshandlungen" [Clinical Pediatric and Forensic Aspects of Child Abuse]. Monatsschrift für Kinderheilkunde, 115:196-197, April 1967.
This article reports a pediatrician's conference in Graz on the many aspects of child abuse. The crime of child abuse is committed most often by parents, but also by others in authority, and results often in physical and psychological damage. The pediatrician is often the first to suspect and establish the child abuse case. German-speaking pediatrics lag behind the U.S. in dealing with child abuse. Eighteen cases, discovered through the university children's clinic in Graz, are described at this conference.

1581. Fleming, G. M. "Cruelty to Children." British Medical Journal, 2:421-422, May 13, 1967.
Fleming explains what "cruelty to children" entails, the extent of the problem, the nature of the injuries which might be involved, whether it was an accident or intentional, the nature of the parents, and the action which should be taken in such cases. He also discusses the doctor's viewpoints and feelings when exposed to such cases.

1582. Fontana, Vincent J. "To Prevent the Abuse of the Future." Trial Magazine, 10:14-16+, May-June 1974.
Fontana discusses child abuse as a medical-social disease that has assumed epidemic proportions and encompasses a child rearing pattern which is becoming more entrenched in our population. He describes the incidence, detection, diagnosis, causes, management, and legal aspects of the problem.

1583. Fraser, Brian G. "Tragedy of Child Abuse: Momma Used to Whip Her." Compact, 8:10-12, March 1974.

Beginning with a case study in which a child dies as a result of a brutal whipping, Fraser continues with a discussion on how our society has finally recognized the extent of child abuse. Also pointed out are various legislative laws regarding the reporting of child abuse and which states actually have any laws regarding any aspect of child abuse.

1584. Fruchtl, Gertrude, Sr. "The Case of the Battered Baby." Liquorian, 58:17-22, January 1970.
    The author describes the nature, incidence, and causes of the battered baby syndrome. She also comments on the various child abuse laws in an attempt to heighten the awareness and interest of parents and the public.

1585. _____; Brodeur, A. "The Battered Child." Catholic World, 209:156-159, July 1969.
    The coauthors discuss the nature, incidence, diagnosis, social and moral, and legal aspects of the battered child. Effective treatment begins with the establishment of parental responsibility, according to the authors.

1586. George, James E. "Spare the Rod: A Survey of the Battered-Child Syndrome." Forensic Science, 2:129-167, May 1973.
    The author surveys the battered-child syndrome from its historial origins to the present. He discusses the psychosocial aspects, including incidence, the nature of the beater, the beaten, and circumstances surrounding the episode of battering. Discussion of the medical aspects covers case studies, radiological dermatologic and pathologic findings and other clues. The author also deals with the legal milieu. (Journal Summary Modified.)

1587. Grumet, Barbara R. "The Plaintive Plaintiffs: Victims of the Battered Child Syndrome." In: Sanford N. Katz, ed., The Youngest Minority: Lawyers in Defense of Children (p. 151-172). Chicago: American Bar Association, Section of Family Law, 1974. 350 p.
    Causes of child abuse, incidence, diagnosis, and legal aspects are discussed.

1588. "Ill-Treated Children: From the Royal College of General Practitioners." Journal of the Royal College of General Practitioners, 26(172):804-815, November 1976.
    In numbered order, this article covers child abuse from the standpoint of definitions, history, prevalence, causes, pathology, natural history, characteristics of the families, and clinical features in general practice. It then takes up the role of the general practitioner, the organization of care, and concludes that in the years ahead care of the ill-treated child will continue to be one of the most difficult and complex clinical problems in family practice.

1589. Joyner, Edmund N., III. "Symposium on Child Abuse." Pediatrics, 51(4, Part 2):771-812, April 1973.

A report of the Symposium of Child Abuse sponsored by the Medical Society of the County of New York on June 15, 1971, includes papers discussing present knowledge concerning etiology, diagnosis, and treatment of the abused child; the legal as well as the medical and social methods of handling the problems; and current and possible future approaches to the handling of the child and family involved. Transcripts of two panel discussions are also included.

1590. Kosciolek, Edward J. "Who Is the Battered Child?" Minnesota Welfare, 17-26+, Summer-Fall 1966.
Incidence of child abuse is reported from Hennepin County, Minnesota, along with an analysis of 30 cases. Parent characteristics, response to counseling, and police involvement are touched upon. The law of Minnesota is discussed.

1591. Lockett, Patricia W. "Dealing with Abuse." Tennessee Public Welfare Record, 55-57+, June 1971.
Highlights of talks given at a symposium held in Denver on the battered child are reported.

1592. Manzke, H. "Battered Child Syndrome." Padiatrische Praxis, 11(3):361-368, 1972.
Various aspects of this problem are described.

1593. Mattingly, R. "Children at Risk. ..." Health and Social Service Journal, 85:1008, May 3, 1975.
The recent burgeoning interest in child abuse experienced in England is examined and some of the important determining characteristics of a potentially abusive situation are discussed. The threshold of suspicion of doctors, social workers, and health visitors depends both on a knowledge of the circumstances commonly associated with abused children and on public awareness.

1594. Mitchell, Ross G. "The Incidence and Nature of Child Abuse." Developmental Medicine and Child Neurology, 17(5):641-644, October 1975.
This presentation offers a general well-rounded view of child abuse, its incidence, causes and resolution. Mitchell discusses who is more likely to abuse a child, why it will happen, and how it might be prevented. It is suggested that child abuse should be seen primarily as a problem of a disturbed family relationship and psychologically stressed parents who need help and treatment, rather than the vengeance of an outraged society.

1595. Mulligan, Elizabeth. "Broken Children." St. Anthony Messenger, 82:14-18, October 1974.
This article is introduced by a case of child abuse. Then generally discussed is diagnosis, etiological factors, legal and reporting aspects, the physician's role, and prevention and treatment.

1596. Mutch, David. "Rescuing Abused & Neglected Children." Christian Science Monitor, October 21, 22, 23, 24, 25, 1974.

A series of articles in the Christian Science Monitor examined the plight of abused and neglected children in the U. S. Information is given about incidence, emphasis of rescue agencies, where child abuse occurs, etc. As if in unwitting revenge, a good percentage of these children turn against society in later years.

1597.   National Conference on Child Abuse and Neglect. Proceedings of the First..., (Atlanta, Ga.), January 4-7, 1976. 123 p. (DHEW) Pubn. No. (OHD) 77-30094 pa--National Center on Child Abuse and Neglect, Children's Bureau, Washington, D. C. 20201.
Sponsored by the Regional Institute of Social Welfare Research, Athens, Georgia.

1598.   Neimann, N.; Rabouille, D. "Les Enfants victimes de sévices" [The Battered Child]. Revue du Praticien, 19(27):3879-3888, 1969.
Given is a survey on the many aspects of the battered child problem in France. Prevention is stressed which it is believed lies in medico-social factors.

1599.   Non-Accidental Injury to Children: Proceedings of a Conference Held at [and organized by] the Department of Health and Social Security on 19 June 1974. London: H. M. S. O., 1975. 74 p.

1600.   Ocampo, T. P. "The Battered Child Syndrome." Journal of the South Carolina Medical Association, 70(11):356-358, November 1974.
The child abuse syndrome is discussed, with focus on the following aspects: historical, statistical, legal, diagnostic, psychodynamic, and therapeutic. It is recommended that, since the problem is both medical and social, a team approach involving physicians and paramedical personnel, social workers, lawyers, and the whole community be used.

1601.   Parry, Wilfrid H.; Seymour, Margaret W.; Smith, Selwyn M. "Child Abuse Syndrome." British Medical Journal, 3:113-114, July 8, 1972.
Written as two letters to refute a letter printed earlier by a third party, this article discusses how battered children are found in all social classes and usually in the younger ages. Both letters expressed consternation with the lack of concern displayed by professionals. Statistics are given concerning child abuse. Hospitals are urged to become more involved.

1602.   "Reflections on Child Abuse and Neglect." (Editorial). Clinical Proceedings, 30(2):31-58, February 1974.
The proceedings of the June 1973 National Conference on Child Abuse are presented. The conference, sponsored by the Children's Hospital National Medical Center and the National Institute of Mental Health in June 1973, under the chairmanship of C. Henry Kempe, focused on five major topics: identification, legislation, prevention

and rehabilitation, education, and research. The concerns of each group are outlined. A summary of Senator Mondale's Keynote Address is included.

1603. Riley, Harris D., Jr.; Woodworth, Karen L. "Battered Children and Their Families: How We Can Help Them." American Baby, 37:44-45+, September 1975.
A case of child abuse introduces this article which continues with the causes of child abuse, diagnosis and management, the law, how physicians can help, and a look at the future in dealing with the problem.

1604. Rubin, Jean. "The Need for Intervention." Public Welfare, 24(3):230-235, July 1966.
A review covers briefly the incidence of child abuse, characteristics of the abused child and abusing parent, and various facets of dealing with the problem.

1605. Schavil, I., et al. "The Battered Child Syndrome." Harefuah, 78:248-249, March 1, 1970.

1606. Scoville, A. B. "The Battered-Child Syndrome." (Editorial). Journal of the Tennessee Medical Association, 64(4):346-347, April 1971.
A brief review covers the battered child syndrome: mandatory laws, from whence comes battering parents, reasons for battering, etc. The importance of reporting is stressed.

1607. Segerburg, Osborn, Jr. "Our Biggest Child Killer; Reprint from Girl Talk." Today's Family Digest, 27:55-59, October 1971.
Segersburg reviews child abuse from the standpoint of incidence, particular cases of abuse, legislative action of the states, professional responsibility, causes, and treatment.

1608. Simpson, Keith. "The Battered Baby Problem." South African Medical Journal, 42:661-663, July 6, 1968; Royal Society of Health Journal, 87:168-170, May-June 1967.
A discussion covers definition, injuries, incidence, legal problems, and prevention of the battered child syndrome. Awareness on the part of health personnel is important for early recognition. Included are six characteristic features of this syndrome. A table compares 29 original explanations for traumatic injury with the truth. Five case histories are presented.

1609. "Suffer the Little Children." Emergency Medicine, 7(9):140-178, September 1975.
In this lengthy article, child abusers are examined in terms of their characteristics and motivations. The abused children are described in terms of their frequently presenting symptoms of abuse. The physician's role in detection, diagnosis, and management is also presented along with a detailed analysis of the legal responsibility of the attending doctor.

1610. "Symposium: Child Abuse: The Problem of Definition.
       T. J. Clements; Child Abuse: An Overview. R. H. Hays;
       The Neglect and Abuse of Children: The Physician's Per-
       spective. R. W. Ten Bensel; Child Abuse: The Legal
       Framework in Nebraska. Dealing with Child Abuse in a
       Unified Family Court. Mandatory Reporting of Child Abuse
       in Nebraska. " Creighton Law Review, 8:729-802, June
       1975.

1611. Symposium on Child Abuse, New York University Medical
       Center, June 15, 1971. Edited by Aaron R. Rausen.
       (Evanston, Ill.: American Academy of Pediatrics, 1973).
       Sponsored by the Medical Society of the County of New
       York. Pediatrics, 51(4)Pt. 2:771-812, April 1973.
       Outstanding authorities in the field of child abuse, such as
Helfer, Fontana, and Kempe, present papers at this Symposium on
the following subjects: history and demography, etiology, diagnosis,
the law, child protective organizations, the role of the physician,
and the rehabilitation of the abused parent.

1612. Thomas, Mason P., Jr. "Child Abuse Cases: A Complex
       Problem. " Popular Government, 32:17-18+, October 1965;
       North Carolina Public Welfare News, 1-2+, September
       1965.
       The complexity of the child abuse problem is explored by the
author who emphasizes difficulties in diagnosis, determining true incidence, understanding causes of parental child abuse, protection of
children from such abuse, and legal approaches to reduction of the
problem.

1613. Van Dyke, V. Understanding Child Abuse. Springfield,
       Illinois State Department of Children and Family Services,
       1974. 6p.
       While the true incidence of child abuse is unknown, it has
been estimated at between 250 and 300 cases per million population
per year in New York City and in Denver. Abuse of a child results
from the interaction of several factors which are named. The 1973
amendment to the Illinois child abuse act expanded the list of those
required to report. It also stipulated that investigation by the Department of Children and Family Services was to be initiated within
24 hours of the receipt of the report and provided for establishment
of a central registry. Provisions for treatment are given.

1614. Watt, J. M. "The Battered Baby. " The New Zealand Nurs-
       ing Journal, 58:14, June 1965.
       This article covers incidence in the U. S., Britain, and New
Zealand, as well as diagnosis and the action that should be taken to
treat and prevent further abuse.

1615. Weber, A. [Child Abuse]. Praxis, 57:188-190, February
       13, 1968.
       Weber discusses many facets of child abuse: frequency, age,
clinical picture and diagnosis, psychiatric and legal aspects, and personality of the abused.

PROFESSIONAL RESPONSIBILITY
(PHYSICIANS, NURSES, ETC.)

1616. "The Abused. " Pictorial. Emergency Medicine, 7:152-154+,
September 1975.
So long as no social or government agency is charged with
actively overseeing the welfare of preschool children, the physician
is the only outsider in a position to spot child abuse--and the single
person legally mandated to mount rescue operations. Physical clues
to look for, diagnostic steps, and situations in which the physician
should be suspicious are outlined. Hospitalization is recommended
even if the injury is not serious enough to warrant it in order to
give time for an investigation.

1616a. Akbarnia, Behrooz A. ; Akbarnia, Nasrin O. "The Role of
Orthopedist in Child Abuse and Neglect. " Orthopedic
Clinics of North America, 7(3):733-742, July 1976.
The diagnosis of child abuse is contingent upon having a high
index of suspicion. Orthopedic surgeons and other surgical specialists should be more involved in a team approach for prevention, detection and management in cases of child abuse in the hope of breaking the cycle of this mutilating and often fatal tragedy. (Journal
Summary.)

1617. Alberts, M. E. "Child Abuse. " Journal of the Iowa Medical
Society, 62:242, May 1972.
Alberts presents a brief history of child abuse, outlines a
statement from the American Academy of Pediatrics Committee on
Infant and Pre-School Child relating to maltreatment of children, and
urges physicians to be aware of child abuse and to alert responsible
agencies to bring about a cessation of prevalent maltreatment of children.

1618. Anderson, J. P. ; Fraser, F. Murray; Burns, Kevin. "Attitudes of Nova Scotia Physicians to Child Abuse. " Nova
Scotia Medical Bulletin, 52:185-189, October 1973.
This paper attempts to summarize some of the knowledge and
attitudes of 144 Nova Scotian physicians with regard to child abuse
and related subjects.

1619. Arnoldi, A. [Child Abuse: Preventive, Diagnostic and Referral Tasks of the Nurse in Social Health Care]. Tijdschrift voor Ziekenverpleging, 27(21):478-481, May 21,
1974. (Dutch)

1620. Baker, Helen. "A Question of Witness." Nursing Times,
        67:691-694, June 10, 1971.
        A questionnaire administered to 18 nursing officers and 26
home visitors and augmented by personal interviews evaluated nurses'
attitudes toward testifying when cases of child abuse reached the
courts.

1621. Bakwin, Harry. "Report of the Meeting of the American Hu-
        mane Society." Newsletter of the American Academy of
        Pediatrics, 13(8):5, September-October 1962.
        Bakwin reports on a special meeting of the American Humane
Society which concerned the abused child. Discussion was limited
to the physically abused child and studies by the Massachusetts Society for Prevention of Cruelty to Children. Emphasized at the
meeting was the need to alert physicians to the frequency and seriousness of the problem, and the need to report cases to legal authorities.

1622. Barnard, Martha U.; Wolf, Lorraine. "Psychosocial Failure
        to Thrive. Nursing Assessment and Intervention." Nurs-
        ing Clinics of North America, 8:557-565, September 1973.
        Failure to thrive (psychosomatic) is a reversible syndrome
with early detection and intervention. The authors have demonstrated
that the nurse clinician or practitioner, through the process of systematic assessment and problem identification, is in a critical position to initiate and support early intervention. As pointed out, the
nurse assists the family (or family surrogate) in reaching mutually
agreed on goals for the maximum health and well-being of the infant.
(Journal Summary.)

1623. Barnett, Bernard. "Violent Parents." (Letter). Lancet,
        2:1208-1209, November 27, 1971.
        The role of the general practitioner in cases of child mis-
treatment has not been adequately defined. In a recent case, which
is described, the family physician was not involved in early medical-
social service contacts and effective case conferences were not conducted.

1624. Barowsky, Ellis I. "The Abuse and Neglect of Handicapped
        Children by Professionals and Parents." Journal of Pedia-
        tric Psychology, 1(2):44-46, Spring 1976.
        Revealed are various forms of abuse and neglect of disabled
children, including delays in pursuing professional assistance, mis-
interpretation of progress reports, failure to accept the child's disability, refusal to make referrals, over-prescription of psychomi-
metics and behavior modification techniques, use of technical skills
by untrained personnel, utilization of experimental treatment programs, placement of all handicapped children in non-handicapped educational facilities, and parental failure to comply with necessary
medical intervention. Although the parent must share the common
culpability, the greater responsibility rests with the professional.

1625. Barta, Rudolph A., Jr.; Smith, Nathan J. "Willful Trauma to Young Children: A Challenge to the Physician." Clinical Pediatrics, 2:545-554, October 1963.

The battered child syndrome is increasing in incidence as a problem in pediatric practice. The attending physician must make every attempt to remove the child from his troubled environment into a safer atmosphere, and to insist on a complete investigation of the home situation by a social agency or legal body. Problems arising in management are also discussed. (Journal Summary Modified.)

1626. Bassett, L. B. "How to Help Abused Children--and Their Parents." RN, 37:44-46+, October 1974.

A review of the nurse's role in child abuse case finding and treatment covers descriptions of typical behavior patterns in abusive parents and of injury and behavior patterns in the child, reporting requirements, and common factors in abuse-prone parents.

1627. "Battered Baby Syndrome." (Letter). Medical Journal of Australia, 2:1073, December 8, 1973.

Two letters to the editor deal with a survey of hospitalized children who had sustained trauma in Brisbane, and legal liability for reporting suspected cases of child abuse in Australia, respectively.

1628. "The Battered Child Syndrome." (Editorial). Journal of the Louisiana State Medical Society, 115:322-324, September 1963.

The problem of child abuse and the many situations associated with it should be presented to the medical profession. The most important requirement for the recognition of this syndrome would be the knowledge that such things exist, and a high index of suspicion on the part of the physician. His duty to the child involves a heavy responsibility, but by discharging this responsibility, the physician may be giving the child his own chance to live.

1629. "Battered-Child Syndrome: Child Beating." Time, 80:60, July 20, 1962.

This article reviews an earlier one appearing in JAMA. The physician's responsibility is stressed. He must overcome reluctance to accept the implications of bony lesions, and he must assume responsibility for the safety to the child.

1630. Becker, Walter. "Kindesmisshandlung und ärztliche Schweigepflicht [Child Abuse and Professional Secrecy]. Medizinische Klinik, 66:209-212, February 5, 1971.

This article concerns itself with many problematic aspects of handling child abuse cases with special reference to the need to reaffirm the doctor's oath of silence while at the same time guaranteeing the protection of the child's right to freedom from abuse.

1631. Birenbaum, Arnold. "The Pediatric Nurse Practitioner and Preventive Community Mental Health." Journal of Psychiatric Nursing and Mental Health, 12(5):14-19, September-October 1974.

This paper attempts to report five ways in which Pediatric Nurse Practitioners act as community mental health workers. Child abuse and neglect is included as one of the problems they will encounter.

1632. Brenneman, George. "Battered Child Syndrome." Alaska
        Medicine, 10:175-178, December 1968.
    Presented is a general review of the problem of battered children. According to Brenneman, the purpose of this article will be served if the medical profession in Alaska is made more aware of the battered child syndrome and of its role in the management of the problem.

1633. Browne, Kenneth M. "Wilful Abuse of Children." Nebraska
        Medical Journal, 50:598-599, December 1965.
    In outlining the physician's role in the management of willful abuse of children, Browne presents three points: suspect that a willful injury was inflicted when the extent of injury is not compatible with the history obtained; search carefully for evidence of previous abuse; and report promptly all suspected cases to law enforcement officers.

1634. Bussey, Kenneth L.; Rapp, George F. "The Battered Child
        Syndrome." Journal of the Indiana State Medical Associa-
        tion, 67(6):383-385, 1974.
    It is felt that physicians should develop an awareness of the battered child syndrome. This is particularly true when the clinical and X-ray findings are different from what could be expected from the history. The incidence of the condition in Marion County, Indiana, its clinical manifestations, radiologic features, differential diagnosis and the law in regard to the abused child are presented.

1635. Cameron, J. Malcolm. "The Battered Baby Syndrome."
        Practitioner, 209:302-310, September 1972.
    The phenomenon of child abuse is discussed from the point of view of the doctor who treats the child. It is difficult for doctors to identify cases of child abuse since they must generally accept the parent's story of how the injury occurred. Physiological signs which should arouse the doctor's awareness of the possibility of abuse are described.

1636. _____; Johnson, H. R. M.; Camps, F. E. "The Battered
        Child Syndrome." Medicine, Science and the Law, 6:2-21,
        January 1966.
    The purpose of this paper is to substantiate the frequent occurrence of inflicted injury on children and to recognize the immediate and very imperative need for protection of such helpless children. Regardless of the doctor's personal reluctance to become involved in such cases, complete investigation, including a full radiographic study, is necessary for the child's protection, together with steps to prevent repetition of the ill-treatment through normal medical channels, social services, and, in extreme cases, by legal sanctions. (Journal Summary Modified.)

1637. Chadwick, David L. "Child Abuse. " Journal of the American Medical Association, 235(18):2017-2018, May 3, 1976.
Chadwick sums up his article by saying that doctors can do much about child abuse. Their services are essential to recognition of cases and most important in reporting, helping the child, the family, and the community. If his efforts are to be effective, the physician must take the trouble to become informed about the problem.

1638. Chamberlain, Nancy. "The Nurse and the Abusive Parent. " Nursing, 4:72-73+, October 1974.
Two case reports demonstrate how mothers will give false excuses for injuries to battered children. Characteristics of parents who abuse, detecting child abusers, working with the parents, and reporting child abuse make up the substance of this article.

1639. Chang, Abert; Oglesby, Allan; Wallace, Helen; et al. "Child Abuse and Neglect: Physicians' Knowledge, Attitudes, and Experiences. " American Journal of Public Health, 66(12): 1199-1201, December 1976.
Reported are the results of a 1974 nationwide study of physicians' knowledge, attitudes, and practice on child abuse and neglect. Responses of pediatricians, radiologists, and "other" physicians to nine specific questions are compared and analyzed, revealing a gap between stated attitudes and practice in regard to reporting cases.

1640. "Child Abuse. " Bulletin of the Cleveland Dental Society, 25:18-19, October 1969.
Discussed is the child abuse law which hinges on the judgment of physicians and other professionals. They are reminded that it will only be as good as their willingness to use it. Highlights of the Ohio Child Abuse Law are presented.

1641. "Child-Abuse Laws in the 50 States. " RN, 31:67-68, December 1968.
In 20 states (which are listed), the registered nurse is included in the child abuse law as being required to report suspected cases. The alert nurse can give potential child-abusing mothers support and guidance during pregnancy and the neonatal period.

1642. "Child Abuse Reporting Laws. " Journal of the American Dental Association, 75:1070, November 1967.
Dentists are required in 22 states, plus the District of Columbia, to report cases in which they suspect child abuse. They should be alert to the possibility of a child's injuries being due to abuse, and it is their duty to report those instances.

1643. Clark, Ann L.; Affonso, Dyanne D. "Mother-Child Relationships. " MCM, The American Journal of Maternal Child Nursing, 1:95-99, March-April 1976.
All nurses in the field of maternal child health are involved in some phase of the development and maintenance of a healthy relationship between a child and his primary caretaker. Considering

the roles of both mother and infant in the early interaction between them and their ultimate bonding to each other, these authors outline the nurse's role in easing them into a positive relationship.

1644. Coles, Robert. "Terror-Struck Children." New Republic, 150:11-13, May 30, 1964.
A psychiatrist discusses the importance of recognition, both public and legal, of child abuse. He emphasizes the need for physicians, and other professionals, to report child abuse cases and for the establishment of institutional means for receiving reports, dealing with them, investigating situations and providing help. He calls for immediate action.

1645. Cordell, Chris. "The Abused Child." Imprint, 21:34+, April 1974.
The nurse-author presents a brief overview of child abuse and emphasizes the role of nurses in breaking the cycle of abuse to children. Specific topics treated are signs and symptoms of abusive parents and abused children, recognition of accidents, detection of child abusers, and role functions of emotional support, guidance, teaching, advising, and referral.

1646. Court, Joan. "The Battered Child Syndrome. 1. The Need for a Multidisciplinary Approach." Nursing Times, 67: 659-661, June 3, 1971.
Describes symptoms of a battered baby, and cites importance of physician's role in detection and treatment. Resistance to intervention must be overcome.

1647. Court, J. "Kindermishandeling. Wat Kunne Wij Doen?" [Maltreatment of Children. What Can We Do?]. Tijdschrift voor Maatschappijvraagstukken en Welzijnswerk, 26(10):255-259, 260-265, 1972.
The physician can do two things in child abuse cases: notify the court of law, and appeal to workers in other disciplines. The author argues in favor of the latter course. This, however, is not a guarantee of a solution to problems in which professional discretion also plays an important role. (Journal Summary Modified.)

1648. Courter, Eileen M. "Physicians Must Cooperate in Child Abuse Cases." Michigan Medicine, 72:361-362, May 1973.
According to the Children's Protective Services Section of the Michigan Department of Social Services, the number of reported child abuse and neglect cases in Michigan is growing, and the help of physicians and other medical personnel is needed to tackle the problem. Michigan's child abuse law is examined with reference to the responsibility of the physician involved in such cases.

1649. Cremers, H. T. [Battery and Rape: Medico-Ethical Problems in the Examination and Reporting to the Police Court]. Nederlands Tijdschrift voor Geneeskunde, 119(32):1259-1262, August 9, 1975. (Dutch)

1650. Curphey, Theodore J.; Kade, Harold; Noguchi, Thomas;
      et al. "The Battered Child Syndrome. Responsibilities
      of the Pathologist. " California Medicine, 102:102-104,
      February 1965.
      The coauthors contend that the contribution of the pathologist
to the problem of the abused child hinges on his awareness of the
problem and the consequent procedural pattern he follows in the autopsy study, complemented by information resulting from the medical
and police investigation of the case. Four cases illustrate the function of the pathologist in dealing with the battered child syndrome.

1651. Davies, J. M. "Detection and Prevention. " Nursing Mirror
      and Midwives Journal, 140:56-57, June 12, 1975.
      The role of the health visitor in the detection and prevention
of child abuse is outlined. "Parentcraft" classes for expectant
mothers and fathers and playgrounds and nurseries are preventive
measures. Management of cases is to be found in full examination
of the child, notification of social services, case conferences, obtaining cooperation of the parents, and good record keeping.

1652. Dennis, James L. "Child Abuse and the Physician's Respon-
      sibility. " Postgraduate Medicine, 35:446, April 1964.
      Dennis emphasizes the role of the physician in the ultimate
prevention of child abuse, primarily in the detection of victims,
management of the clinical situation, and reporting of suspected
cases.

1653. "Dentists Required to Report Cases of Abused and Maltreated
      Children. " New York State Dental Journal, 39:629, De-
      cember 1973.
      A description of reporting procedures for dentists who sus-
pect child abuse. States that dentists are required by law to report.

1654. Disbrow, Mildred A. "Parents Who Abuse Their Children. "
      Washington State Journal of Nursing, 44:5-9, Summer 1972.
      Disbrow discusses why so few child abuse cases are reported,
the factors that hamper adequate reporting, and the characteristics
of child abusers. She asserts that child abuse is self-perpetuating
and that nurses can be helpful in case finding and by working with
new parents.

1655. "The Doctor. " Emergency Medicine, 7:168-173, September
      1975.
      Outlined are the procedures a doctor should follow in cases
of suspected child abuse.

1656. Dominguez Martinez, J. M.; Romero Palanco, J. L. "Com-
      entarios Sobre el Sindrome de Malos Tratos Infantiles"
      [Comments on the Child Abuse Syndrome]. Revista Es-
      pañola de Pediatria, 31(185):755-774, 1975.
      The purpose of this paper is to bring to the attention of doc-
tors in general, and pediatricians, in particular, their obligation to

inform the authorities of any case they may observe in which there is sound evidence of child abuse.

1657. Drogendijk, A. C. "Het mishandelde kind" [The Battered Child]. Nederlands Tijdschrift voor Geneeskunde, 114(23): 949-954, 1970.
The advantages and disadvantages of the legal obligation of physicians to report child abuse cases are spelled out. The law takes no cognizance of psychic maltreatment. A central registry is discussed.

1658. Eisen, Peter. "The Maltreatment Syndrome in Children." Medical Journal of Australia, 1(9):466-467, 1967.
Professional apathy to the problem of child abuse must be replaced by professional responsibility. The medical profession can help stimulate new legislation on neglect and abuse. Full physical and psychological care for the child is the best preventive medicine.

1659. Elmore, Joyce; Alexander, Betty; Lyman, Laura; et al. "The Nurse's Role in the Care of the Battered Child: Panel Discussion." Clinical Proceedings, 24:364-374, December 1968.
This article details a panel discussion of the nurse's role in the care of the battered child in three settings: the emergency room; the clinical nursing unit; and the community.

1660. "The Enigma of Child Abuse." Journal of Practical Nursing, 26:29-31, July 1976.
The reluctance of third parties to become involved in suspected cases of child abuse is the theme of this article, directed at licensed practical nurses. Problems of reporting, preventing, and treating are also discussed.

1661. "Experts and Child Abuse." (Editorial). British Medical Journal, 3(5932):641-642, September 14, 1974.
This editorial refers to the abuse death of Maria Colwell and discusses the lessons which have been learned from this wasteful death. The author cites one change--the courts and social services no longer attach as much significance to the bloodtie. Other changes are probable now that attention has been drawn to professional fallibility.

1662. Fairchild, Don. "Child Abuse: What a Nurse Can and Should Do." Texas Nursing, 50:10, August 1976.
Nurses are in a strategic position to identify and report child abuse and also to observe the effects of emotional abuse or neglect. A review of who abuses children, how to recognize abusers, the role of the DPW, the law, and prevention is given.

1663. Fontana, Vincent J. "Battered Children." (Letter). New England Journal of Medicine, 289:1044, November 8, 1973.
Child maltreatment is not a rare disease, or found only in the ghetto, or committed by the mentally ill (only 10 percent). It

is more than a symptom of the times; it is inextricably linked with
unbearable stress, living conditions, and other social ills. If physicians cannot feel for the children, they should at least feel for
themselves and the kind of future they are shaping for themselves
and their children.

1664. _____ . "An Insidious and Disturbing Medical Entity."
Public Welfare, 24(3):235-239, July 1966.
The range of child abuse is broad and extends from deprivation to serious physical damage and even death. Obtaining accurate
information is often difficult since the abused child is usually less
than three years old, and the parent is likely to be reticent or dis-
honest. The lack of attention to this syndrome in medical education
is lamented. Physicians are apparently still reluctant to report
cases.

1665. _____ . "Recognition of Maltreatment and Prevention of
the Battered Child Syndrome." Pediatrics, 38:1078, December 1966.
Prevention and decreased incidence of the battered child de-
pend on educating physicians and pediatricians to recognize the broader
and more insidious symptoms of the abused child and to assume the
responsibilities of reporting cases of abuse, protecting the child,
and alleviating factors responsible for parental abuse.

1666. Fotheringham, B. J. "Non-Accidental Injuries to Children."
The Australasian Nurses Journal, 3:13+, September 1974.

1667. Fricker, A. "Child Abuse." The Australasian Nurses Journal, 3:27, April 1975.

1668. Friedman, Allison L.; Juntti, M. Jeanette; Scoblic, Mary A.
"Nursing Responsibility in Child Abuse." Nursing Forum,
15(1):95-112, 1976.
The major intent of this presentation was to demonstrate:
nursing responsibility according to legal mandate, using the example
of legislation signed into Michigan Public Law in September 1975;
components of child abuse and neglect services including identification, reporting, diagnosing, and treatment; and to identify for other
health professionals providing services to families and children, the
nurse's role in dealing with the child abuse and neglect phenomenon.
(Journal Summary.)

1669. "From the States. Legislation & Litigation." Journal of the
American Dental Association, 75:1081-1082, November 1967.
Special attention is called to child abuse legislation for it is
not uniform in including dentists among those persons under a duty
to report suspicious injuries to local officials. Every dentist should
be familiar with the law of his own state.

1670. Fulk, Delores Leusby. "The Battered Child." Nursing
Forum, 3(2):10-26, 1964.
The nurse has a special set of obligations in matters of the

abused child--to recognize potential cases, reporting, encouraging psychiatric therapy for those who need it, and following up every situation. The discourse continues with information on underlying causes, clinical manifestations and diagnosis, treatment, protection and legislation, guidelines for hospitals, the need for public education, and the nurse's role.

1671. Fuller, M. G. "Child Abuse: The Physician's Responsibility." Journal of Legal Medicine, 3(5):24-29, May 1975.
The major role of the physician in identifying and reporting cases of child abuse is discussed. The present level of nonreporting is due in part to the physician's lack of knowledge regarding the immunity provisions of the reporting statutes which virtually exclude physicians from any legal liability in reporting child abuse, even if their diagnosis is judged incorrect. The reporting laws also provide a waiver of the physician-patient privilege.

1672. Furst, William D. "The Medical Profession and Child Abuse in Texas." Texas Medicine, 71(7):87-89, July 1975.
Furst encourages the physician to join with other professionals in his community in stimulating the collaborative local action necessary to meet the increased reporting of child abuse in Texas. Advice on the diagnosis, treatment and management of child abuse is also presented.

1673. _____. "A Pediatric Generalist's Experiences with Child Abuse and Neglect in a Small, Isolated Community." Pediatric Annals, 5(3):79-87, March 1976.
Using four case studies to illustrate his experiences with the problems of child abuse and neglect, Furst describes his involvement in community activities dealing with public education, professional awareness, legal aspects, and in-service training of school personnel.

1674. George, James E. "Law and the Emergency Nurse: Battered-Child Syndrome and the ED Nurse." Journal of Emergency Nursing, 1:11, May-June 1975.
The responsibilities of the ED nurse from the standpoint of detection, diagnosis, and reporting are outlined.

1675. Gnehm, H. E. "Le Syndrome de l'enfant battu" [Battered Child Syndrome]. Helvetica Paediatrica Acta, 31:Suppl 31:1-27, 1973.
The physician is often loathe to disbelieve parents when confronted with a case of child abuse. He should be more aware of the high incidence of the battered child syndrome. His duty is to have the child admitted to a hospital in order to protect him and have the diagnosis confirmed.

1676. Golub, Sharon. "The Battered Child: What the Nurse Can Do." RN, 31:42+, December 1968.
A discussion of the nurse's role in dealing with child abuse and neglect; characteristics of parents which are helpful in diagnos-

ing the problem, and characteristics of children who have been abused or neglected.

1677. Gordon, Bianca. "Battering: Unfortunate Backlash." (Letter). British Medical Journal, 2:443, May 25, 1974.
There is an urgent need to recognize the danger of hasty and insensitive steps being taken against innocent parents by social workers who act on uncorroborated assumptions of child abuse. The author discusses how workers in this field should be trained so as not to cause trouble or problems within families, or between the family and social case workers.

1678. Gower, M. D. "Non-Accidental Injury and the Health Visitor." Nursing Times, 72(40):1563-1564, October 7, 1976.
Non-accidental injury to children is discussed only from the point of view of the domiciliary midwife and the health visitor. Proper procedure when battering has been observed is detailed. Prevention is also discussed. Mrs. Gower is divisional nursing officer (community), Essex AHA, Southend-on-Sea.

1679. Green, F. C. "Child Abuse and Neglect. A Priority Problem for the Private Physician." Pediatric Clinics of North America, 22(2):329-339, May 1975.
Any physician should clearly understand the complex problem of child abuse and neglect.

1680. Green, Karl M. "The Abused Child." Maryland State Medical Journal, 15:47-49, March 1966.
Green presents the nature, incidence, clinical symptoms, and management of the battered child syndrome. He concludes that physicians can contribute much not only to the medical aspects, but to the legal and social aspects of this problem also.

1681. Gregg, Grace S. "Infant Trauma." American Family Physician, 3:101-105, May 1971.
After initiating emergency treatment, the physician should analyze the environmental factors which led to the infant's injury. Trauma in infancy suggests a lowering of child-care practices, although there are "passive" or "act-of-God" accidents. Abused babies rarely present with the classic battered child syndrome. The physician must sift out abuse cases from the many infant injuries he sees. Constructive intervention, designed to support the family and protect the child, is the best approach. (Journal Summary.)

1682. _____. "Physician, Child-Abuse Reporting Laws, and Injured Child. Psychosocial Anatomy of Childhood Trauma." Clinical Pediatrics, 7:720-725, December 1968.
Abuse may occur at any age. It is the young non-verbal child, unable to escape and totally dependent on his caretakers, who is in the greatest danger of future injury. A comprehensive approach and a plan of action for the physician to follow when faced with the problem of an injured child is presented. Suggestions for arriving at a reasonably certain diagnosis and recommendations for correcting the background disturbances are also discussed. (Journal Summary.)

1683. Hall, Marian. "The Right to Live." Nursing Outlook, 15: 63-65, August 1967.
    The battered child syndrome is discussed from the nursing point of view. Nurses, particularly those in public health and pediatrics, have an important role in detection. Those nurses in planned parenthood are in a good position to identify emotionally immature mothers.

1684. Halpern, S. R. "The Battered Child (Continued)." (Letter). Pediatrics, 40(1):143,144, July 1967.
    The role of pediatricians in the prevention of child abuse and neglect is discussed in the context of professional ethics. The pediatrician is obliged to actively pursue improved prophylaxes for child abuse.

1685. Hansen, Christian M., Jr. "Physician Responsibility in Child Abuse." (Editorial). Journal of the Medical Society of New Jersey, 72(7):559, July 1975.
    Hansen addresses the problem of why physicians are failing to recognize or report instances of child abuse and neglect. He then recommends that treatment resources be made available to communities throughout New Jersey.

1686. Hansen, Marie M. "Accident or Child Abuse? Challenge to Emergency Nurses." Journal of Emergency Nursing, 2: 13-20, January-February 1976.
    The role of the emergency department nurse, who is in a unique position to initiate therapy with the abusing family, is outlined. The two abilities focused on are: accurate assessment of injuries and appropriate reporting.

1687. Hartley, Albert I. "Identifying the Physically Abused Child." Texas Medicine, 65:50-55, March 1969.
    This article offers guidelines which may help the physician decide what cause of action will be of maximum value to the child's welfare, and fulfill his own legal, ethical, and moral as well as medical responsibilities in identifying the possibly physically abused child.

1688. Hays, Richard. "Child Abuse and Our Responsibility." Nebraska Nurse, 3:24, May 1970.
    Hays insists that the health-related professions must assume the responsibility of bringing to the attention of child protective agencies those children suspected of being neglected or abused, although such reporting may jeopardize parent-professional relationships.

1689. Hazlewood, Arthur I. "Child Abuse: The Dentist's Role." New York State Dental Journal, 36:289-291, May 1970.
    Because parental maltreatment is a major killer of American children today, the Maltreatment Syndrome is a major pediatric problem. Consequently, dentists are charged with the legal responsibility of reporting both proven and suspected cases of child abuse. The moral obligation has always existed.

1690. "The Health Professions and Child Abuse and Neglect. A
Guide to Fulfilling the Legal Responsibilities of the Medical Profession in Cases of Suspected Child Abuse or Neglect." Journal of the Medical Society of New Jersey, 72
(7):605-609, July 1975.
The legal responsibilities of the medical profession of suspected child abuse or neglect in the state of New Jersey are reviewed.
In addition to mandatory reporting, the physician should maintain protective custody of the child in severe cases. Two New Jersey statutes which directly address the role and responsibilities of the physician are discussed. The social services that are available to the
family after the abuse is officially reported are summarized.

1691. Helfer, Ray E. "Why Most Physicians Don't Get Involved in
Child Abuse Cases and What to Do About It." Children
Today, 4(3):28-32, May-June 1975.
Helfer cites eight reasons why doctors don't become involved
in child abuse cases. Some recommendations are also discussed to
help alleviate the difficult problem of reporting child abuse faced by
physicians.

1692. _____; Pollock, Carl B. "The Battered Child Syndrome."
Advances in Pediatrics, 15:9-27, 1968.
The authors present data on the incidence of child abuse and
examine the legal and moral obligations of the physician. Recommendations are offered in dealing with the medical, radiologic, and
psychiatric problems of the abused child, abusing parents, and community agencies in order to develop a multifaceted approach to reducing the incidence.

1693. Helpern, Milton. "Fatalities from Child Abuse and Neglect:
The Responsibility of the Medical Examiner and Coroner."
Pediatric Annals, 5(3):42-57, March 1976.
Citing the disadvantages of a coroner system or one in which
postmortem studies are provided on a fee-for-service basis, Helpern
proposes the medical examiner's system of detecting violent death
from child abuse or neglect. He also describes the many problems
in determining the antemortem and postmortem trauma, and criticizes the often casual preparation of autopsy reports.

1694. Henson, Donna D. "Cries of Children." Journal of Practical
Nursing, 25:26-27+, December 1975.
A case study of a maltreated child serves to alert student
and licensed practical nurses to the nature and extent of child abuse.
Nursing personnel are urged to provide emotional support for the
child as well as psychological understanding in dealing with the abusive parent.

1695. Herber, F. [On the Securing of Evidence by the Physician].
Zeitschift für Aerztliche Fortbildung, 343-345, March 15,
1969.

1696. Hiller, Renate B. "The Battered Child--A Health Visitor's

Point of View. " <u>Nursing Times</u>, 65:1265-1266, October 2, 1969.

Early identification of abnormal marital and family relationships and a child's failure to thrive are one of the health visitor's main tasks and objectives. Some examples usually regarded as difficult family situations that could easily lead to injury of the child are given. The health visitor is often the only person who continues to visit and provide parents with opportunities to talk about the stresses and strains of raising a family. Teamwork and cooperation with other professionals ensures a more effective service to the families.

1697. Hopkins, Joan. "The Nurse and the Abused Child. " <u>The</u> <u>Nursing Clinics of North America</u>, 5(4):589-598, December 1970.

A tremendous responsibility lies with the nursing profession in case finding, prevention, and treatment of the abused child. Nurses are taught to observe symptoms, and they have pediatric training that is invaluable in teaching parents child rearing practices. The ability to recognize the problem and the needs of the parents is important in developing a meaningful relationship with these families.

1698. Hurd, Jeanne Marie L. "Assessing Maternal Attachments: First Step Toward the Prevention of Child Abuse. " <u>Jogn</u> <u>Nursing</u>, 4:25-30, July-August 1975.

Effective treatment of child abuse must be initiated long before abuse begins by identifying the potential child abuser. The obstetric nurse can initiate this process in the first crucial postpartum days by assessing maternal attachment. She can then become instrumental in the development and implementation of an effective system of referral and follow-up. (Journal Introduction Modified.)

1699. Hyman, C. A. "Accidents in the Home to Children Under Two Years. " <u>Health Visitor</u>, 47:139-141, May 1974.

1700. Isaacs, Susanna. "The Battered Baby. " (Letter). <u>British</u> <u>Medical Journal</u>, 2(5497):1233, May 14, 1966.

Psychiatrists play an important role in protecting children whose parents cannot help damaging them physically or emotionally. The psychiatrist may alleviate family psychopathology by helping parents control their aggression, helping children avoid aggression-provoking situations, or otherwise aiding parents in meeting their responsibilities.

1701. Isaacson, E. K. "The Emotionally Battered Child. " (Letter). <u>Pediatrics</u>, 38(3):523, September 1966.

Pediatricians are not sufficiently involved in recognizing and advising emotionally deprived children. They should be alert to unhealthy behavior by either the parent or the child which might indicate stress or neglect at home. A few minutes of every examination should be used routinely to inquire into the family situation. Time should be taken to probe and advise.

1702. Jackson, R. H. "Trauma in Childhood." (Letter). British
     Medical Journal, 2(5456):299-300, July 31, 1965.
     Discussions of trauma in childhood should not be restricted
by the over-specialization of medicine. A doctor's specialization
in orthopedics may lead him to over-emphasize fractures while neglecting head injuries, burns, poisoning, and epidemiology. Centers
should be established where orthopedic surgeons, pediatricians, neurosurgeons, and plastic surgeons could study the problem as a whole.

1703. Jensen, A. D.; Smith, R. E.; Olson, M. I. "Ocular Clues
     to Child Abuse." Journal of Pediatric Ophthalmology,
     8(4):270-272, 1971.
     Forty-eight child abuse patients seen at Johns Hopkins Hos-
pital showed that 40 percent had ocular findings. As ophthalmologists
are the first medical personnel to observe such patients, they should
be aware that physical child abuse is manifested in diverse fashion.
They should be on the alert and should report the problem if morbidity and mortality is to be reduced.

1704. Johnson, Mildred. "Symposium: The Nursing Responsibili-
     ties in the Care of the Battered Child." Clinical Proceed-
     ings, 24:352-353, December 1968.
     A symposium was presented to enable the members of the
nursing profession to understand the physical and psychological needs
of the abused child and to inform them of the legal and social agencies they will encounter in dealing with child abuse.

1705. Johnson, N. Child Abuse in North Dakota. Grand Forks,
     North Dakota University, Bureau of Governmental Affairs,
     February 1974. 12 p.
     A survey of 620 physicians in North Dakota on child abuse
resulted in 234 responses. In general, the responses revealed a
low rate of abuse reporting, a lack of familiarity with the state's
child abuse laws, and the desire to be better informed of the legal
aspects of child abuse. On the basis of the survey responses, six
recommendations are advanced.

1706. Johnson, T. D.; Holder, Angela R. "Child Abuse and the
     Physician." Journal of the American Medical Association,
     222(4):517-518, October 23, 1972.
     In this statement prepared for the AMA Office of the General
Counsel, the authors describe aspects of physical cruelty and denial
of medical attention to children. Physicians are encouraged to accept their responsibility and intervene in suspected child abuse cases.

1707. Josten, Lavohn. "The Treatment of an Abused Family."
     Maternal-Child Nursing Journal, 4:23-34, Spring 1975.
     Nursing intervention by public health nurses in the area of
child abuse is illustrated in an individual case report stemming from
the initial public health nurse contact over a period of one year and
subsequent six-month contact after the family had a third child.

1708. Kalisch, Beatrice J. "Child Abuse: What Is It? What Can

Be Done About It?" Nursing Care, 7:22-25, June 1974.
Kalisch depicts the tragedy of child abuse via several vignettes
and then defines child abuse, identifies characteristics of abusing
parents, and the abused child, and discusses several techniques to
alleviate abuse of children.

1709. _____. "Nursing Actions in Behalf of the Battered Child."
Nursing Forum, 12:365-377, 1973.
Opportunities for action by the nursing profession in cases of
child abuse fall into four areas: case finding, relationship with the
parent, fostering community assistance programs, and public education. These areas are described.

1710. Kempe, C. Henry; Silver, Henry K. The Problem of Parental
Criminal Neglect and Severe Physical Abuse of Children.
Transactions of American Pediatric Society, 69th Annual
Meeting, Buck Hill Falls, Pennsylvania, May 6-8, 1959;
American Journal of Diseases of Children, 98(4):528,
October 1959.
Cases reviewed illustrate that the pediatrician must have an
awareness of criminal neglect and physical abuse of children when
the first instance of abuse in a family occurs so that he may be prepared to make a specific diagnosis and recommendations that will
lead to the institution of protective measures for the remaining children. The frequent failures of physicians, social services, and the
law, in coping with these problems require a frank reappraisal of
this difficult problem.

1711. Kohlhaas, Max von. "Schweigepflicht bei Kindesmisshandlungen" [Duty to Secrecy in Cases of Child Abuse]. Munchener Medizinische Wochenschrift, 108:1941-1944, September 30, 1966.
The physician's duty to secrecy on one hand and toleration of
most severe maltreatment of children on the other is a problem.
The physician is not an assistant to the police nor can he silently
tolerate injustice in more severe cases. If requested by police to
examine a child, he may perform this examination on the basis of
paragraph 81 c STPO even though the parents are opposed to the
examination. (English Abstract Modified.)

1712. Kornfeld, Betty. "Children Too Have Rights." AARN News
Letter, 31(2):6, February 1975.
After reviewing the Child Abuse Project which became a reality in August 1974 (a part of The Family Resource Centre at The
Alberta Children's Hospital), the author speaks of the role and functions of the nurse as regards this problem. She offers guidelines
for detection and management and suggests various ways nurses can
help.

1713. Laskin, Daniel M. "The Battered-Child Syndrome." (Editorial). Journal of Oral Surgery, 31:903, December 1973.
The role of the oral surgeon in combating the battered child
syndrome is outlined. Greater attention to this condition in the den-

tal teaching institutions is suggested. Dentists should acquaint themselves with the laws regarding reporting in their own states. They should also be thoroughly aware of the signs and symptoms of the syndrome.

1714. Laupus, W. E. "Child Abuse and the Physician." Virginia Medical Monthly, 93(1):1-2, January 1966.
Hospitalization of an abused child should be followed by an oral report to the police or appropriate children's protective service. It is suggested that legislation should go beyond reporting and provide for protective services and investigation of the reported incident.

1715. Layton, J. J. "The Watchdog of Medicine." Community Health, 4(2):58-63, September-October 1972.
In a general discussion of the role of the forensic pathologist and the problems he faces, the battered child syndrome is briefly discussed.

1716. Learoyd, Sandra; Williamson, Ann. "The Battered Child Syndrome--Nursing Care." Nursing Mirror and Midwives Journal, 140(22):54-55, June 12, 1975.
The authors discuss the difficulties of nursing abused children with both senior and student nurses. Superficially, the patient study outlined is satisfactory, but, if one investigates further, many nurses are dissatisfied with their efforts. Although there are individual differences, a pattern of their feelings and suggestions for improved practice is emerging.

1717. Lesermann, Sidney. "There's a Murderer in My Waiting Room." Medical Economics, 41:62-71, August 24, 1964.
This is a true and shocking story of child-abuse and the legal helplessness of the doctor who was confronted by it. The author uses a pen name, but the essential facts are matters of record. Only names and places have been disguised. (Journal Summary.)

1718. "Lesson Not Yet Learned." (Editorial). British Medical Journal, 1(5956):477-478, March 1, 1975.
The concern here is with the case of a three-year-old boy who was battered by his foster parents. The child did not die but will never recover from his injuries. It is pointed out that alert physicians and social workers should be aware of such occurrences and attempt to remove children from such situations.

1719. Lewis, H. N. "Adoption." British Medical Journal, 2(5461):577-580, September 4, 1965.
A physician examining an adopted child should be alert for the physical and emotional signs of rejection by the adopting family. These may take any form from minor psychosomatic symptoms, such as enuresis to the well-known battered child syndrome. The rights of the physician and the children's officer in Great Britain as provided under the Adoption Act of 1958 are stated.

1720. "MD Has Role in Child Abuse Cases." (Editorial). Pennsylvania Medicine, 73(9):102, September 1970.

A Pennsylvania Department of Public Welfare survey revealed that 586 cases of child abuse and 27 fatalities took place in Pennsylvania in 1969. The survey illustrates the need for the family physician to take a more active role in detection and diagnosis and in cooperating with welfare authorities.

1721. "MD Responsibility for the Protection of the Battered Child."
New York Medicine, 26(2):59+78, 1970.

The responsibility of the physician in cases of child abuse is outlined. He must become familiar with this widespread disease and its manifestations.

1722. MacCarthy, Dermod. "Physical Effects and Symptoms of the
Cycle of Rejection." Proceedings of the Royal Society of
Medicine, 67(10):1057-1061, October 1974.

The pediatrician's role in the cycle of deprivation is to alert all those who have the primary care of sick or healthy children to the possible implications of poor nutrition, short stature and cold extremities in the under-fives, and of failure to thrive, failure to grow and coldness of the hands and feet of babies. Rejection may do permanent damage to physical and mental health and the child must be safeguarded. (Journal Conclusion Modified.)

1723. McCauley, Mary Ann. "RNs Often Involved. Reporting Child
Abuse Is Everyone's Responsibility." American Nurse,
7(10):6, October 31, 1975.

Nurses are often the child's first contact and, therefore, should be aware of possible signs of mistreatment. The implications which a model law has for nurses and the nursing profession are outlined.

1724. McKenzie, Michael W.; Stewart, Ronald B.; Roth, Sally S.
"Child Abuse--What the Pharmacist Should Know." Journal
of the American Pharmaceutical Association, 15(4):213-217,
April 1975.

Some valuable services to the family of a battered child that can be performed by pharmacists are offered. It is emphasized that pharmacists should report cases even when there is only a suspicion of child abuse. Eight signs or symptoms to look for in the parent and child are listed.

1725. "Maltreatment: Don't Look the Other Way." Emergency
Medicine, 4:180-183, January 1972.

Physicians are asked to be more cooperative in reporting suspected cases of child abuse which are less evident than the more obvious forms of maltreatment. Attending physicians must learn to diagnose the disease in its subtler forms.

1726. Martin, Harold P., ed. The Abused Child: A Multidisciplinary Approach to Developmental Issues and Treatment.
See entry 1355.

1727. Maxwell, I. D. "Assault and Battery of Children and Others. "
Nova Scotia Medical Bulletin, 45:105-107, April 1966.
A discussion emphasizes the Canadian physician's medical
responsibility to report suspected cases of child abuse; clarifies reporting and legal procedures; and suggests methods for notifying the
proper authorities. Although reporting is not mandatory, hospital
personnel are urged to notify the regional police office when battering is suspected.

1728. "Medical Management of Child Abuse. " Journal of the Medical Society of New Jersey, 69:551-553, June 1972.
Stresses importance of alerting the physician to his moral,
professional, and legal responsibilities in the area of child abuse.
The general problem of the battered child is reviewed and suggestions are offered about management.

1729. Mindlin, Rowland L. "Child Abuse and Neglect: The Role of
the Pediatrician and the Academy. " Pediatrics, 54(4):393-
395, October 1974.
The author discusses a report on visits to health-based child
abuse and neglect treatment programs conducted by a Task Force in
cooperation with the Academy's Committee on Infant and Preschool
Child to point out needs in recognition, treatment, and prevention of
child abuse. The role of individual pediatricians is to increase
awareness of the problem of child abuse and to join with concerned
persons in the community to deal with it. One step in that direction
is a self-instructional course in the recognition, management and
community aspects of child abuse and neglect sponsored by the Committee.

1730. Montgomerie, D. E. "Child Abuse in New Zealand. "
(Letter). New Zealand Medical Journal, 81(537):361, 1975.
Physicians are more aware than anyone else of the incidence
and prevalence of child abuse in New Zealand, but for a variety of
reasons they are reluctant to become actively involved. They should
maintain unofficial records of child abuse to satisfy their own uncertainty regarding the extent of the problem; awareness of these figures
may precipitate their active involvement in prevention programs.

1731. Morris, Vivian G.; Taneja-Jaisinghani, Vijay. "Call for Action on the Child Abuse Problem. " Journal of Home Economics, 68:17-20, May 1976.
Home economists are urged to learn rapidly to recognize
existing, changing, and newly evolving problems facing individuals
and families and to formulate and implement policies and programs
for remedying and eradicating the problem of child abuse.

1732. Morse, Thomas S. "Child Abuse, a Neglected Form of
Trauma. " Journal of Trauma, 15(7):620-621, July 1975.
Surgeons have neglected the problem of child abuse because
they are unfamiliar with the steps required to protect the child and
help the parents. They fear time-consuming entanglement or liabil-

ity. Once the surgeon overcomes his natural reluctance, he finds his part in the process to be surprisingly easy. The hallmarks of abuse are described.

1733. Moysen, F., et al. [Ignored Fractures and Mistreated Children]. Bruxelles-Medical, 46:857-871, September 18, 1966. (French)

1734. Mueller, G. "Zur Problematik der Kindesmisshandlung aus padiatrischer sicht" [Problems of Child Abuse from the Pediatric Point of View]. Kinderaerztliche Praxis, 44(3): 124-130, 1976.
Child abuse is defined and indicators and social causes of abuse are spelled out. The pediatrician's duty is described.

1735. Mundie, Gene; Fontana, Vincent J. "Child Abuse Our Responsibility." Pictorial. Journal of Practical Nursing, 24:14-17, December 1974.
Outlined are the responsibilities of a LP/VN (Licensed Practical/Vocational Nurse). Provided are incidence statistics in New York and nationwide, etiology, prevention, treatment, and a table showing factors when child abuse and neglect are present.

1736. _____; _____. "The Maltreated Child and the E. D. Nurse." Point of View, 11:12-14, October 1974.
The role of the E. D. nurse is described from the standpoint of diagnosis; the reporting process; communication with others, such as the social worker; and prevention.

1737. Neill, Kathleen; Kauffman, Carole. "Mother-Child Relationships. Care of the Hospitalized Abused Child and His Family: Nursing Implications." Part 5. The American Journal of Maternal Child Nursing, 1:117-123, March-April 1976.
Before nurses can effectively work with the abused child and his family, they must become knowledgeable about the state of the art of assisting the child and the abusive parent. Based on this need for information the nurse's role and responsibility in caring for these troubled families is explored.

1738. "New Law on Child Abuse and Neglect." Virginia Medical Monthly, 102(7):568, July 1975.
This brief article acquaints Virginia physicians with the provisions of a comprehensive new law dealing with child abuse and neglect which became effective on June 1, 1975.

1739. "Non-Accidental Injury to Children." (Editorial). The Medical Journal of Australia, 1(26):986, June 26, 1976.
In light of a report prepared by a Community Welfare Advisory Committee (Enquiry into Non-Accidental Physical Injury to Children in South Australia), indicating that only 22 percent of 615 doctors replied to the prospective survey questionnaire, it is suggested that attitudes of doctors will need to be carefully reexamined.

The report has numerous recommendations, many of which have direct implications for doctors. The child abuse law is discussed.

1740. Norman, Mari. "A Lifeline for Battering Parents." Nursing
      Times, 70(39):1506-1507, September 26, 1974.
      The role of the health visitor in reducing cases of child abuse
is discussed. The health visitor visits all families approximately 11
days after the birth of a new baby and continues to visit according
to her assessment of need until the child starts school. Because
she spends much time working with "normal" well-functioning families, she has the ability to recognize very early signs of possible
child abuse.

1741. Oppe, T. E. "The First 28 Days." Part 3. "The Vulner-
      able Baby." Midwives Chronicle, 87:310-312, September
      1974.

1742. O'Toole, Thomas J. "The Speech Clinician and Child Abuse."
      Language, Speech & Hearing Services in Schools, 5(2):
      103-106, April 1974.
      Suggests the possibility of alleviating the problem of child
abuse through a speech clinician experienced in working with children.
The range of contact is wide enough to provide opportunities for detecting and reporting child abuse and for helping the abused child
and his parents. (P. A.)

1743. Patterson, Peter H. ; Char, Donald. "Child Abuse in Hawaii. "
      Hawaii Medical Journal, 25:395-397, May-June 1966.
      More than half of 715 physicians belonging to the Hawaii Med-
ical Association replied to a questionnaire on detection and reporting
of child abuse. Sixty-one cases of abuse were detected by the respondents; about half the cases reported. Reporting and handling of
cases and suggestions and recommendations for education and study
in this area are discussed.

1744. Paul, J. "Die Misshandlung von hirngeschädigten Kindern"
      [The Abuse of Brain Damaged Children]. Monatsschrift
      für Kinderheilkunde, 115:202-206, April 1967.
      Under a period of permanent stress, parents of brain-damaged
children may develop child abuse tendencies, however latent in the
beginning. It is the duty of the doctor to recognize the sociopatho-
logical conditions of the abuse situation and get help for the parents.
The doctor can do this with good conscience as long as no other
institution has been given the right or assumed it.

1745. Pickett, L. K. "Role of the Surgeon in the Detection of
      Child Abuse." Connecticut Medicine, 36:513-514, Septem-
      ber 1972.
      Current and previous experience with child abuse mandates
that the surgeon has a vital role in its detection. Surgeons who
treat injured children are obligated by law to report any child suspected of being abused and must recognize that child abuse is prevalent among all socioeconomic classes. The program established at
the Yale-New Haven Hospital is described.

1746. Piekut-Warszawska, E. [Children in the Oświecim Camp
       (memoirs of a nurse)]. Przeglad Lekarski, 23:204-205,
       1967. (Polish)

1747. Pieterse, J. J. "De vertrouwensarts inzake kindermishandel-
       ing" [The Confidential Physician in Child Maltreatment].
       Maandblad voor de Geestelijke Volksgezondheid, 29(3):129-
       134, 1974.
       In January of 1972 four major cities in the Netherlands ap-
pointed a confidential physician to deal with child maltreatment. His
duties are described. It is expected more will be appointed.

1748. Pietroni, R. G. "The Battered Baby and the GP." Midwife
       Health Visitor and Community Nurse, 12:145-147, August 1976.

1749. "Please, Nurse! Help Prevent Child Abuse." Nursing Up-
       date, 4:1+, April 1973.
       Based upon a round-table discussion of the abused and poten-
tially abused child, this article discusses the abusing parent or adult,
forms of maltreatment and punishment, the key signs of early and
later abuse, and the role of nurses in preventing further abuse. The
emphasis in prevention is shifting toward identifying and helping those
persons who have the potential to abuse children and toward spotting
signs of abuse early enough to prevent severe abuse.

1750. Polier, Justine Wise. "Professional Abuse of Children: Re-
       sponsibility for the Delivery of Services." American Jour-
       nal of Orthopsychiatry, 45(3):357-362, April 1975.
       Determination of which children will receive or will be ex-
cluded from services, as well as the nature and extent of those services, is largely in the province of medical, welfare, teaching, and
legal professionals. Often discretion in such matters is all but unchecked, and leads to withholding of services which is seen as a kind
of child abuse.

1751. Prilook, Marion E. , ed. "The Repeatedly Ill Child: How
       Physicians Can Help Prevent Child Abuse." Part 7.
       Patient Care, 7:131-134+, February 15, 1973.
       This final article, developed from the Patient's Care round-
table of seven parts, deals with problems of a large group of children who are repeatedly ill in only a figurative sense. They are
the abused and potentially abused children. Included are ways to recognize any abused, neglected, or battered child; recommendations for action when one is spotted, and constructive guidelines to help those parents who as yet have only the potential to mistreat their children.

1752. Rectanus, Daniel R. "The Battered Child Syndrome." Med-
       ical Insight, 1:48+, November 1969.
       Medico-legal responsibilities are reviewed in the light of child
abuse laws. It is important that the physician understand the differences between criminal action and dependency proceedings. Incidence, psychological and sociological findings in parents, the neces-

sity of the physician's persistence in his efforts to learn of the
events leading to injury, and the physical examination are discussed.

1753. Redfern, Dorothy L. "Children in the Community. A Com-
        munity in Search of a Better Way: The Multidisciplinary
        Approach to the Problems of Child Abuse and Neglect ...
        Guilford County, North Carolina. " ANA Clinical Sessions,
        126-133, 1974.
        Some of the responsibilities nurses working in community
agencies have for abused and neglected children have been presented.
The author has focused on the problems related to identification and
reporting. There is much yet to be learned about treatment strategies that are effective. The question is not whether nurses should
be involved but what direction this involvement should take. (Journal Summary Modified.)

1754. "Reporting Child Abuse. " Pediatric Currents, 16(10):37-40,
        November-December 1967.
        A sampling of the literature dealing with child abuse in 1967
revealed that while all 50 states had passed reporting laws, many
physicians were still unaware of the specific provision of the law
in their state, and they were equally unfamiliar with the proportions
of the problem.

1755. "The Reporting of Child Abuse. " Bulletin of the Menninger
        Clinic, 28:271-272, September 1964.
        This article comments on several aspects of the Kansas State
Attorney General's opinions on the reporting of child abuse by Kansas
physicians. Following the official opinions, the Kansas Medical Society recommended to the state legislature that physicians, nurses,
and hospitals be required to report instances of suspected child abuse.

1756. "Reporting on Abused Child: One Physician's Experience. "
        Roche Image of Medicine and Research, 14:24-27, May 1972.

1757. Rijkmans, J. M. "Kindermishandeling" [Child Abuse Postbus
        145, Groningen]. Delikt en Delinkwent, 4(10):510-516, 1974.
        This article pertains to the confidential physician.

1758. Riley, Harris D. "The Battered Child Syndrome: General
        and Medical Aspects. " Southern Medical Journal, 58(3):
        9-13, 1970.
        The physician's roles and responsibilities to the abused child, the
abusing family, and the court are summarized. A hospital examination
checklist for medical detection of possible child abuse, including guidelines for history, observations, and physical examination, is presented.

1759. Riscalla, Louis Mead. The Professional's Role and Perspec-
        tives on Child Abuse. (Paper presented at the Annual
        Meeting of the American Psychological Association, 83rd,
        Chicago, Ill. August 30-September 3, 1975.) 13 p. Avail-
        able from EDRS: MF-$0. 83; HC-$1. 67, Plus Postage.
        This paper explores some of the ways in which professionals

inadvertently or deliberately abuse children and perpetuate child abuse. Pressures from school personnel, teachers, parents, or psychologists; various forms of discipline; labeling of children in special education; court handling of abused children; and children's rights are touched upon.

1760. Ryan, James H. "The Battered Child Deserves a Better Deal." Prism, 1(5):39-43, 1973.
The problem of child abuse is examined with particular reference to the role of the physician. He must have an unrelenting dedication to the effective treatment of the battering personality. Under the oath to support life, the physician must take the first step by reporting abuse.

1761. Sanders, R. Wyman. "Resistance to Dealing with Parents of Battered Children." Pediatrics, 50:853-857, December 1972.
Resistance to dealing with parents of battered children appears to be a transcultural phenomenon as well as an individual issue involving the caretakers who work with each battered child and his family. The author reviews some of the pertinent literature on the topic and gives some specific case examples to support this hypothesis. Finally, some suggestions are made of ways to deal more effectively with these families. (Author's Abstract.)

1762. Sarsfield, James K. "Battering: Dangers of a Backlash." (Letter). British Medical Journal, 2:57-58, April 6, 1974.
Sarsfield points out the possible harmful effects of precipitant action in the investigation of suspected cases of baby-battering. He feels that a close liaison between all interested parties and the practice of restraint are absolute when guarding against false accusations of child abuse. Such accusations could lead to destroyed confidence in doctors as well as the medical profession.

1763. Schmidt, Rebecca. "What Home Economists Should Know About Child Abuse." Journal of Home Economics, 68:13-16, May 1976.
Home economists have had little or no formal training in dealing with the problem of child abuse, but they have a role--reporting cases, offering help and guidance, relying on their expertise in child development, family relations, and parenting skills. This article shares with the home economist the requirements of prevention and treatment programs and pleads for her commitment to their initiation.

1764. Schmitt, Barton D.; Kempe, C. Henry. The Pediatrician's Role in Child Abuse and Neglect. Chicago: Year Book Medical Publishers, 1975. 47 p. illus. (Current Problems in Pediatrics, v. 5, no. 5)

1765. Schrotel, S. R. "Responsibilities of Physicians in Suspected Cases of Child Brutality." Cincinnati Journal of Medicine, 42:408, October 1961.

Editorial urging physicians to report cases of suspected abuse to aid police in taking action.

1766. Schuurmans-Stekhoven, W. [Child Abuse and Professional Secret]. Nederlands Tijdschrift voor Geneeskunde, 114: 170-171, January 24, 1970. (Dutch)

1767. Scott, P. D. "Victims of Violence." Nursing Times, 70(27): 1036-1037, July 4, 1974.
This article is written to provide underlying causes of crimes of violence which may help the nurse in her care of victims. During the convalescent period some prophylactic action may be taken. This is particularly clear in the case of babies brought into the hospital with unexplained injuries. After an act of violence, it is not only the victim who should take stock, nor the offender, but society and its social services as well.

1768. Sgroi, Suzanne M. "The Abused Child--Physicians' Obligations." (Editorial). Connecticut Medicine, 39(7):418, July 1975.
The Connecticut child abuse law is reviewed in light of the physician's responsibility. Information on the Child Abuse Care-Line and the Central Child Abuse Registry which physician's may use is reviewed. He is urged to be on the alert to all forms of physical and sexual abuse.

1769. Shade, Dolores A. "Limits to Service in Child Abuse." American Journal of Nursing, 69:1710-1712, August 1969.
Shade contends that prevention and recognition of high-risk families is the area in which nurses can contribute most in solving the problem of child abuse. Once the nurse is certain of the diagnosis of child abuse, she must recognize her limitations, such as the lack of preparation to be therapist for abusive parents and their pathologic social situation.

1770. Shaheen, Eleanor; Husain, S. A.; Hays, Janice. "Child Abuse--A Medical Emergency." Missouri Medicine, 72(9): 532-535, September 1975.
Child abuse is examined from the standpoint of its historical background, definition, incidence, characteristics of the abused and abusers, diagnosis, and legal and reporting aspects. The physician has three main responsibilities--detection, reporting, and participation in the family treatment process.

1771. Shaw, Anthony. "How to Help the Battered Child." RISS, 6(12):71-104, December 1963.
A discussion of doctor-parent relationships and legal problems involved in attempting to secure protection of abused children.

1772. Shydro, Joanne. "Child Abuse." Nursing '72, 2:37-41, December 1972.
A nurse, who learned that in order to help the battered child she must first help the parents, relates her first case of the battered child. She explains procedure in working with parents.

1773. Silber, David L.; Bell, William E. "The Neurologist and the Physically Abused Child." Neurology, 21:991-999, October 1971.

Because of his special interest in the diagnosis and management of cerebral trauma, the neurologist is included among those responsible for identification and protection of physically abused children. Head trauma holds a prominent position in this unpleasant chapter of human-induced disease which may take one of many forms. The primary responsibility of the neurologist is recognizing the possibility and reporting such cases to the appropriate involved agencies. The importance of roentgenographic assessment as an identifying tool is stressed in children with head trauma. (Journal Summary Modified.)

1774. Silver, Larry B. "Child Abuse Syndrome: A Review." Medical Times, 96:803-820, August 1968.

A review of the literature from all disciplines in the hope that such a summary will assist the practicing physician to become more alert to the child abuse syndrome and to his role in working with the community.

1775. _____; Barton, William; Dublin, Christina. "Child Abuse Laws--Are They Enough?" Journal of the American Association, 199:65-68, January 9, 1967. tables.

The physicians in the Washington, D. C. metropolitan area were questioned to assess their knowledge of the battered child syndrome, their awareness of the community procedures available, their attitude toward reporting such cases under the protection of the new child abuse laws. Results suggest that methods of communication between medical and community organizations and the physician have not been completely effective in familiarizing the physician with the battered child syndrome or with the community procedures to be used for reporting. Several considerations appear to inhibit the physician from reporting suspected cases of child abuse. (Journal Abstract.)

1776. _____; Dublin, Christina C.; Lourie, Reginald S. "Child Abuse Syndrome: The 'Gray Areas' in Establishing a Diagnosis." Pediatrics, 44:594-600, October 1969.

This is an exploration of situations in which the physician found it difficult to establish or rule out the diagnosis of child abuse. In such cases, the major issues were the physician's subjective personal feelings, his misunderstanding of the child abuse laws, and his role and responsibilities. The five main reasons for non-reporting are indicated.

1777. Sint-Van Den Heuvel, M. K.; Doek, J. E. "Kindermishandeling. De functie van de vertrouwensarte" [Maltreatment of Children. The Function of the Confidential Physician]. Algemeen Politieblad, 121(9):211-214, 1972.

In the Netherlands, the increasing interest in the problem of maltreatment of children has led to the formation of the Interdepartmental Commission on Maltreatment of Children. Functions and duties of confidential physicians and of this society are briefly outlined.

1778. Storlie. "What About John-John?" (Nursing Care Studies). Catholic Nurse, 17:44+, September 1968.

1779. "A Symposium on Battered Children. " Nursing Mirror and Midwives Journal, 140(22):47-58, June 12, 1975.
Four separate articles, each with one or multiple authors, present an analysis of the medical, nursing, community, and legal aspects of child abuse. The major purpose of the symposium was to enable the nurse to give more effective, lasting help to children who have suffered non-accidental injury to those at risk, and--equally important--to their parents.

1780. "Symposium on Child Abuse. " Clinical Proceedings, 24:351-393, 1968.
This article focuses on the role of the nurse in the care and prevention of the battered and neglected child. Includes summaries of various presentations.

1781. Tagg, Peggy I. "Nursing Intervention for the Abused Child and His Family. " Pediatric Nursing, 2(5):36-39, September-October 1976.
The author feels that the nurse, more than any other health professional, must be aware of her increased accountability for the identification of the abused or neglected child and his family. The purpose of this article is to familiarize nurses with the Child Abuse Syndrome and to recommend appropriate nursing intervention.

1782. Ten Bensel, Robert W. ; King, Kurt J. "Neglect and Abuse of Children: Historical Aspects, Identification, and Management. " Journal of Dentistry for Children, 42(5):348-358, September-October 1975.
The dentist's role primarily involves awareness of the problem of maltreatment, a method of approach to identify and report suspected cases, the documentation of the injuries or neglect which have been observed, and follow-up of any orofacial injuries. Further studies in the dental field are needed to delineate the types and incidences of orofacial injuries and their relationship to child abuse. Dentists and all professionals must work together, if adequate services are to be provided to protect children and rehabilitate families. (Journal Summary Modified.)

1783. _____ ; Raile, Richard B. "The Battered Child Syndrome. " Minnesota Medicine, 46:977-982, October 1963.
A review of the literature and a report of two cases of the "battered child syndrome" has been presented to assist the physician in his management of these cases under two new Minnesota State laws. (Journal Summary.)

1784. Tessier, Barbara. "My Unforgettable Nursing Experience: A Child Abused. " The Journal of Practical Nursing, 16:18, March 1966.
This is a personal account of a nurse's reaction to a three-

year-old patient, a victim of child abuse, who is admitted to a hospital. Tessier traces the child's gradual deterioration and miraculous recovery.

1785. Teuscher, G. W. "The Battered Child: A Social Enigma."
      (Editorial). Journal of Dentistry for Children, 41(5):335-
      336, September-October 1974.
      Teuscher appeals to the profession of dentistry to aid in the
fight to solve the battered child problem.

1786. Trouern-Trend, John B. G.; Leonard, Martha. "Prevention
      of Child Abuse: Current Progress in Connecticut. I. The
      Problem." Connecticut Medicine, 36:135-137, March 1972.
      From October 1, 1967, to August 31, 1968, Connecticut re-
corded a child abuse incidence of 11.5 per 100,000 children per year.
The actual rate is probably higher than this figure, since many physicians remain either unaware of the problem or are unwilling to report. Tips are given to the physician as to when he should suspect
child abuse. He should report the incident; he is granted legal immunity.

1787. Trube-Becker, Elisabeth. "Ärztliche Schweigepflicht und
      Kindesmisshandlung" [The Physician's Professional Discre-
      tion and Child Abuse]. Medizinische Klinik, 62:1398-1400,
      September 8, 1967.
      In child abuse cases, the intimate nature of the family, and
especially the physician's professional discretion or oath of silence,
is discussed. The doctor must decide which action will most benefit the child: working with the parents or reporting the case to the
police. As the German law now stands, the doctor is given the
choice of what action to take. This should remain so, because a
law forcing reporting of the case would result in the destruction of
the basis of trust between doctor and patient.

1788. _____. "Schweigenpflicht und Zeugnisverweigerungsrecht
      des Ärztes bei Delikten Gegen das King" [The Doctor's
      Pledge of Secrecy and His Right as a Witness to Refuse to
      Answer in Crimes Against Children]. Munchener Medizin-
      ische Wochenschrift, 114:389-392, March 3, 1972.
      The physician has the possibility of gaining insight into cul-
pable behavior towards a child and into the condition of the child.
The conflict of two legal principles deserving protection (that of the
physician's professional secrecy and the right to inviolability of life
and limb) cannot be solved otherwise than by infringing one of these
legal principles. The physician must decide on his own responsibility.
He should not rigidly insist on his pledge of secrecy; he must cure
and help.

1789. Turner, Eric. "Battered Baby Syndrome." British Medical
      Journal, 5378:308, February 1, 1964.
      Turner points out that many of the head injuries in infants and
small children are caused by parental abuse. However, he feels it
is not the place of the doctor to play judge or lawyer and condemn

the parent. Rather, the role of the physician is to prevent disease and treat injuries.

1790. Van Rees, R. "Hulpverlening en Kindermishandeling" [Aid and Maltreatment of Children]. Tijdschrift voor Maatschappijvraagstukken en Welzijnswerk, 29(15):293-295, 1975.
The attitude and personality of the persons who give aid in child maltreatment are analyzed on the basis of some features of the aid given. Trust is a primary requirement; giving aid is discussed as a growth process; the relationship between those who give and those who receive aid is discussed as well as the commitment and emotions of the persons who give aid and the aid-giving system as a process of renovation. (Journal Summary Modified.)

1791. Van Stolk, Mary. The Battered Child in Canada. See entry 806.

1792. "Vertrouwensartsen Kindermishandeling. Jaarvelslag 1973" [Confidential Physicians on Maltreatment of Children]. Medisch Contact, 29(48):1564-1565, 1974.

1793. "Vertrouwensartsen kindermishandeling voorzien in een behoefte" [Confidential Physicians for Child Abuse Cases Meet a Need]. Medisch Contact, 28(33):960, 1973.
The interdepartmental (Ministry of Public Health and Environmental Hygiene and the Ministry of Justice) committee on Child Abuse (The Netherlands) presented their annual report on 1972 concerning the experiment with confidential physicians for child abuse cases. This experiment got under way in January 1972. The number of children who in 1972 could be (further) assisted due to the mediation of the confidential physician is regarded by the committee as sufficient justification for this system.

1794. Wolff, Howard. "Are Doctors Too Soft on Child Beaters?" (Editorial). Medical Economics, 43(21):84-87, October 3, 1966.
Private physicians fear that their relationship with the accused family will be permanently impaired, or that misdiagnosis will lead to embarrassment while other physicians remain ignorant of the symptoms of child abuse. Possible solutions include teaching physicians to recognize the telltale signs of child abuse and emphasizing to them that the spirit of the law is to report suspicions and protect health and welfare, not to establish guilt or to punish.

1795. Woods, Walter. "From the President. Expanding Our Responsibility." Journal of Dentistry for Children, 42(2):86, March-April 1975.
Woods believes dentists must involve themselves in the problems of child abuse and neglect. He asks, "As respected professional people, how much more must we probe, question, suggest, and do?" In his opinion, dentists need only to expand their already-highly developed powers of observation and work organization to place their profession in proper relation to the total well-being of society, individually, and collectively.

1796. Woodward, J. W. "Battering: Unfortunate Backlash."
       (Letter). British Medical Journal, 1:452, March 9, 1974.
       Woodward cites the case of suspected child abuse which was
not confirmed upon investigation. The mother involved was approached by a legal authority regarding the child. After the incident was cleared up as a mistake, the harm had been done. The
mother now feels she cannot punish her child for wrongdoing for fear
of being reported once again. The author feels that without adequate
means of communication between members of the health team, parents who wish to chastise their children had better do so in private
or some ill-meaning informer may report them.

1797. Woodworth, R. M. "The Physician and the Battered Child
       Syndrome in the United States and in Oklahoma." Journal
       of the Oklahoma State Medical Association, 67(11):463-475,
       November 1974.
       The problem of child abuse, especially as it concerns the
physician, is overviewed. How the problem of child abuse is handled
at both the state and county level in Oklahoma is described.

1798. Woolley, Paul V., Jr. "The Pediatrician and the Young Child
       Subjected to Repeated Physical Abuse." Journal of Pedia-
       trics, 62:628-629, April 1963.
       Woolley praises the literary contributions of social workers
and lawyers in the matter of physical child abuse. He encourages
every pediatrician, and other workers in the field of child health,
to read "A Project to Rescue Children from Inflicted Injury" by
Helen E. Boardman. Each physician should familiarize himself with
the clinical and roentgenologic appearances of infants subjected to repeated trauma. A broader attack on this problem than is possible
by the individual physician is suggested.

1799. Young, Harold A. "The Battered Child." Journal of the
       Iowa Medical Society, 64(10):438-439, October 1974.
       The medical practitioner's treatment of the abused child is
considered. It goes beyond the body-mending process and involves
measures to curb likelihood of recurrence. It is urged that physicians report all suspected cases of the battered child syndrome.
(Journal Summary Modified.)

1800. Young, Marjorie. "Comparison of Physician Responses to
       Child Abuse, Tulsa County, Oklahoma: 1969 and 1974."
       Journal of the Oklahoma State Medical Association, 69(4):
       125-127, April 1976.
       According to the variables measured in the 1969 and 1974
surveys, the majority of physicians favored active intervention to
protect a child being abused and viewed supervision and treatment of
the child abuser as preferable to punishment. There were no significant differences between physician attitudes and behavior concerning child abuse in 1969 and those in 1974. Rather, the findings are
almost identical and, for the variables considered, can be viewed as
showing a fixed, stable perspective. The so-called "new look" at
child abuse is not statistically demonstrated in this study. (Journal
Summary.)

1801. Zadik, Donna. "Social and Medical Aspects of the Battered Child with Vision Impairment." New Outlook for the Blind, 67:241-250, June 1973.

The possibility that many children may be visually handicapped or blind due to child abuse is discussed. Workers in agencies and school programs serving visually handicapped children should be alert to medical conditions and eye disorders related to child abuse, the general characteristics of battering parents or caretakers, and legal procedures designed to protect the abused child. (Author Abstract Modified.)

1802. Ziering, William; Vawter, Gordon F. "The Battered Baby Syndrome." Journal of Pediatrics, 65:321-322, August 1964.

Two letters to the editor from Fresno County General Hospital pediatricians on the battered baby syndrome stress the role of the pediatrician in these cases. It is imperative that physicians no longer consider the matter a "social problem." The need for a central registry to index instances of suspicious cases and more X-ray examination is voiced.

PROTECTIVE COOPERATION AND SERVICES

1803. Alabama State Department of Pensions and Security. Bureau of Family and Children's Services. Protective Services Manual for Administration of Services for Children and Their Families. Chapter V. Montgomery, Ala., June 7, 1974. 15 p.

A chapter on protective services to be incorporated in a state children and family services administrative manual discusses the statutory provision for protective services under the Alabama Department of Pensions and Security and outlines characteristics of and criteria for protective services and procedures for providing such services. Legal forms for court petition and summons, foster care agreement, and child abuse reports are included.

1804. Alexander, Jerry. "Protecting the Children of Life-Threatening Parents." Journal of Clinical Child Psychology, 3(2): 53-54, 1974. (Summer)

As president of the Citizen's Committee for Battered Children, Alexander describes the strategy and tactics of his organization's efforts to stop life-threatening behavior against children. Additionally, he suggests how professionals can help reduce this modern form of barbarism.

1805. American Academy of Pediatrics. Committee on Infant and Pre-School Child. Maltreatment of Children: The Physically Abused Child. 6 p. (Reprinted from Pediatrics, 37(2):377-382, February 1966.)

This committee report focuses on the nature and function of community child protective services, reporting laws, the role of the physician and of the community in child abuse cases, and the importance of a central register. The article concludes with principles to be followed in legislation pertaining to child abuse.

1806. American Humane Association. Children's Division. Child Protective Services--A National Survey. Denver, Colo., 1967. 316 p. OP

This exhaustive study presents the major findings of a survey which reached into every state, county and community of the country. The data is reported in clear and concise form on a state-by-state basis. Most significant is the analysis and discussion from a national perspective of the different laws, policies and practices found to exist in the 50 states and the territories.

1807. _____ . _____ . Child Protective Services and the Law,
by Thomas T. Becker. Denver, Colo., 1968. 24 p.
$.35.
Exploration of the impact of Supreme Court decisions on neglect proceedings. How may due process be assured? Will court
hearings be adversary trials? Who represents the child? How may
conflicts of interest be resolved?

1808. _____ . _____ . Child Protective Services Standards.
Denver, Colo. $.20.
This brief brochure presents in capsule form a statement of
CPS development and philosophy, the eight steps in the CPS process,
and 12 operational standards for today's CPS agencies based upon the
long experience of American Humane and its member agencies.

1809. _____ . _____ . Children Who Were Helped--Through
Child Protective Services, by Vincent De Francis. 14 p.
$.25.
Non-technical community interpretation of the purpose and
method of Child Protection through the use of "case stories."

1810. _____ . _____ . Community Cooperation for Better
Child Protection, by Vincent De Francis. Denver, Colo.,
1959. 20 p. $.25. (This paper was read at the 86th
Annual Forum of the National Conference on Social Welfare
held in San Francisco May 24-29, 1959.)
Discussion of the cooperative roles of the court, police,
school, church and voluntary agencies and how they may contribute
best to the protection of children.

1811. _____ . _____ . The Court and Protective Services--
Their Respective Roles, by Vincent De Francis. Denver,
Colo. 19 p. $.45.
A discussion of the purpose and functions of the two agencies--
a recognition of their separate and mutual responsibilities and how
they may achieve optimum cooperation on behalf of neglected children.

1812. _____ . _____ . Due Process in Child Protective Pro-
ceedings--Intervention on Behalf of Neglected Children, by
Thomas T. Becker. Denver, Colo., 1971. 24 p. $.50.
Discusses the implications of the mandate for due process as
it applies to the neglect proceeding in juvenile court; defines the elements of due process, and interprets the precarious balance required
to protect conflicting rights.

1813. _____ . _____ . Emotional Neglect of Children, by
Robert M. Mulford. Denver, Colo. 11 p.
A penetrating analysis of the challenge to child protection
posed by this difficult area of child neglect.

1814. _____ . _____ . Family Life Education and Protective
Services, by Norman W. Paget and G. Lewis Penner. Denver, Colo. 24 p. $.35.

Explores the techniques for involving protective service clients in a program of family life education; discussion of course content; evaluation of participation as means for strengthening casework relationships and parental capacity for child care.

1815. _____. _____. In the Interest of Children: A Century of Progress, by Katherine Brownell Oettinger, Arthur Morton, and Robert M. Mulford. Denver, Colo. 28 p. $.35.
Review and assessment of problems and progress in child protection in the United States and England during the 20th century. Discussion of needs, approaches, trends, and future goals.

1816. _____. _____. Innovative Approaches in Child Protective Services, by Duane W. Christy, and Norman W. Paget. Denver, Colo., 1969. 24 p. $.50.
This pamphlet discusses some new and imaginative approaches contributing to better protection of neglected and abused children.

1817. _____. _____. An Intensive Casework Project in Child Protective Services, by Julia Ann Bishop, Barbara W. Burton, and William A. Bourke. Denver, Colo. 34 p. $.45.
Three papers report significant findings on the constructive use of time limits; planned periodic inventories of progress toward change and goals; authority in casework.

1818. _____. _____. Let's Get Technical, the "Why and What" of Child Protective Services. Denver, Colo. 10 p. $.25.
Explores special skills and their application through the use of a case history.

1819. _____. _____. Protecting the Battered Child, by Edgar J. Merrill, Irving Kaufman, Philip R. Dodge, et al. Denver, Colo. 30 p. $.70.
Report of a statewide study and analysis of child abuse cases; discussion of implications as viewed by experts in psychiatry, medicine, law and social work.

1820. _____. _____. Protective-Preventive Services: Are They Synonymous? by Robert M. Mulford and Hans W. Hoel. Denver, Colo. 24 p. $.35.
Are the preventive services provided in many social work settings identical in scope and function with Child Protective Services? Two papers explore and define areas of similarity and difference.

1821. _____. _____. Protective Services and Community Expectations, by Vincent De Francis. Denver, Colo. 17 p. $.25.
A discussion of community responsibility for providing protective services--the legal frame of reference for physical and emotional neglect--the problems involved in obtaining a legal finding of emotional neglect.

1822. _____ . _____ . Protective Services and Emotional Neglect, by Max Wald. Denver, Colo. 20 p. $.50.
A discussion of emotional neglect; description of skills and
attitudes necessary to change destructive parental behavior; illustrations of techniques through case history.

1823. _____ . _____ . The Protective Services Center, by
G. Lewis Penner and Henry H. Welch. Denver, Colo.,
1967. 20 p. $.35.
Discussion of the conceptualization and development of a multi-
service facility designed to provide a comprehensive program for
families in need of protective services. The first year's experience
of a research and demonstration project.

1824. _____ . _____ . Public Welfare Responsibility for Child
Protective Services, by Jane Lacour, Harriet C. Erickson,
Guy R. Justis. Denver, Colo., 1965. 22 p. $.35.
Problems in engaging community support for child protective
services and in developing countywide and statewide programs are
discussed. Advice is provided to child protective service adherents
on how to mobilize community support and move reluctant legislators.
The problems encountered in setting up a protective services program in Los Angeles County and in the State of Colorado are reviewed.

1825. _____ . _____ . Round-the-Clock Coverage in Child
Protective Services, by Lena Cooke, Ping Kyau Minn, and
Dorothy Washburn. Denver, Colo. 20 p. $.30.
Discussion of responsibility and patterns for meeting after-
hour emergencies of child neglect and abuse.

1826. _____ . _____ . Speaking Out for Child Protection, by
Vincent De Francis. Denver, Colo., 1973. 28 p. $.50.
Highlights of testimony before U.S. Senate Subcommittee on
Children and Youth. Strongly points to urgency of implementation
of Child Protective Services. Gives perspective on progress in this
specialized field.

1827. _____ . _____ . Special Skills in Child Protective Services, by Vincent De Francis. 16 p. $.25.
Explores special skills and their application through the use
of a case history.

1828. _____ . _____ . The Status of Child Protection--A National Dilemma, by Vincent De Francis and Boyd Oviatt.
Denver, Colo., 1971. 29 p. $.50.
Discussion of the general failure to mount Child Protective
Services programs of sufficient magnitude and competency to effectively treat the needs of neglected, abused children; questions are
raised and directions for needed changes proposed.

1829. Arnold, Mildred. "Training Trainers to Reach Abusive and
Neglectful Parents." Social and Rehabilitation Record, 3(2):
9-11, June 1976.

In the fall of 1973, the Public Services Administration developed a prospectus for a national training program for protective services and services in related fields to abused and neglected children and their families. This training program is described.

1830. Arthur, L. J. H.; Moncrieff, M. W.; Milburn, W.; et al. "Non-Accidental Injury in Children: What We Do in Derby." British Medical Journal, 1(6022):1363-1366, 1976.
Described is how social workers, doctors, and policemen have managed child abuse in Derby since 1971.

1831. Awana, R. An Interdisciplinary Approach to Protecting Children. Honolulu, Hawaii State Department of Social Services and Housing. Children's Protective Services Center, 1972. 10 p.
An interdisciplinary team for child protection services in Hawaii is discussed. The team consists of the public welfare social work supervisor, and the hospital's pediatrician, psychiatrist, and psychologist. In some cases a legal counsel participates. The social worker's most complex cases were presented to the team.

1832. Baher, Edwina; Hyman, Clare; Jones, Carolyn, et al. At Risk: An Account of the Battered Child Research Department, NSPCC. See entry 2204.

1833. Baio, P. "Personal View: Caseworker or Policeman? NSPCC Social Worker's Dilemma." Social Work Today, 6(7):197-198, 1975.
The NSPCC must make up its mind as to whether it is a social work agency or a law enforcement agency. Otherwise, the workers in the NSPCC cannot understand their role with clarity or certainty. Nor will other social work organizations be able to respond effectively until this decision is made. The argument is explored.

1834. Bard, Morton; Zacker, J. "The Prevention of Family Violence: Dilemmas of Community Intervention." Journal of Marriage and the Family, 33(4):677-682, November 1971.
The authors deal with the problem of intervention by the community which takes from the families the right to privacy and individual civil rights. The principles which govern community intervention may require highly sophisticated adaptations in the shadowy interface between the social sciences and the law.

1835. Barnett, Bernard. "Battered Babies." (Letter). British Medical Journal, 4(5680):432, November 15, 1969.
For long-term treatment and active social intervention, greater communication between physicians and social workers is necessary. The urgency of the need and the small possibility of misuse outweigh the possible ethical problem involved in giving confidential information to a member of another profession.

1836. _____. "Battered Babies." Lancet, 2:567-568, September 12, 1970.

Hospitals are not the best institutions for preventing child abuse. Instead, effective family services incorporating the family physician must be established to identify high-risk families and offer family support.

1837. Bath Department of Social Services. Joint Consultative Committee for Concealed Parental Violence. Battered Babies. England, March 1974. 7 p.
A brief report describes the role of a consultative committee concerned with child abuse in Bath, England, and enumerates diagnostic factors associated with the battered baby syndrome.

1838. "The Battered." (Editorial). Lancet, 1(7918):1228-1229, May 31, 1975.
The need for effective evaluation of services provided to abused or neglected children and their families is discussed. The present preoccupation with abuse and neglect in Britain has overly entangled pediatricians at the risk of neglecting other needy families and ill children. The British Department of Health and Social Security must audit the national situation keeping in mind the problems of other disadvantaged and abused children and assess its priorities in the use of staff and resources.

1839. Bell, Cynthia J. "Medical Consultants: Appropriate Selection and Utilization in Child Welfare." Child Welfare, 55(7):445-458, July-August 1976.
This paper describes the organization and functioning of a medical consultation program serving an agency as it deals with child abuse cases. Specialized medical consultant roles are discussed in the following functions: health care educator, psychiatric adviser, pediatric adviser, and medico-legal adviser. This approach is applicable to public and private agencies that are family oriented and serve children in their own homes or in alternate care.

1840. Bertram, M. Beck. "Protective Casework: Revitalized." Child Welfare, 34:1-20, 1955.
A historical tracing of protective service intervention, originating as a coercive socializing force which was considered disreputable by other social workers, becoming more acceptable with the notions of "aggressive casework," ego strengths even in disturbed individuals, and family as a Gestalt. Finally tied together with a discussion of the acknowledgment and use of authority by protective caseworkers.

1841. Billingsley, Andrew. "Agency Structure and the Commitment to Service." Public Welfare, 24:246-251, 1966.
The comparison of problems and functions of child protection services as they are rendered under different agencies.

1842. _____. The Role of the Social Worker in a Child Protective Agency: A Comparative Analysis. Ph.D. Brandeis University, Waltham, Mass., 1964. Available from University Microfilms, Order No. 64-12,850.
This study describes patterns of role performance, orienta-

tions, and satisfaction among social workers in two voluntary, non-sectarian social casework agencies in Massachusetts: a child protective agency (CPA) and a family counseling agency (FCA). The sample of 110 includes all full-time caseworkers and supervisors in both agencies. Data was collected by questionnaire and self-administered activity time sheets.

1843. Bishop, Julia A. "Helping Neglectful Parents." Annals of the American Academy of Political and Social Science, 355:82-89, September 1964.
Bishop claims that since 1870, the greatest change in child protective services has been in the emphasis on help to parents to provide needed care as opposed to punishment of parents and removal of children. Protective service is a direct joint effort of community and social agency involving identification of abusing parents, provision of authoritative intervention, and availability of services and resources which support parental functioning.

1844. Blue, M. T. "The Battered Child Syndrome from a Social Work Viewpoint." Canadian Journal of Public Health, 56: 197-198, May 1965.
This article represents the comments made by the author in a panel discussion on child abuse held at a meeting of the Canadian Public Health Association. Blue concludes that welfare agencies and professional social workers must cooperate in every way to protect a "battered child" from abusive, neglectful parents.

1845. Borland, Marie, ed. Violence in the Family. See entry 2360.

1846. Bosanquet, Nicholas. "Who Is Really to Blame?" Nursing Times, 72(4):126-127, January 29, 1976.
This is an exploratory account of the report of the review body into the death of a boy, Steven Meurs in King's Lynn, who was killed by his mother. Was the mother, who was looking after six children, her own two and four others, totally to blame? The review body report seems to underestimate the amount of support that mothers like Sandra Meurs need if they are going to be able to cope.

1847. Bradford, Kirk Anshelm. Critical Factors That Affect the Judgments of Protective Services Workers in Child Abuse Situations. D. S. W. Catholic University of America, Washington, D. C., May 1976. 516 p. Available from University Microfilms, Order No. 76-20,989.
The purpose of this study was to identify critical factors that affect the decision-making processes of protective services social workers as they consider whether or not to place a child after an incident of child abuse.

1848. Breslow, Lester. "Proposals for Achieving More Adequate Health Care for Children and Youth." American Journal of Public Health, 60:Suppl:106-122, April 1970.
Discussed are several influences on child health: malnutri-

tion, deficiencies in dental care, speech defects, and child battering. Breslow reviews recent health program developments and the role of Medicaid. In proposing a national program for child health, the author studies resources and financing of a program, and principles and services to be incorporated therein.

1849. Brieland, D. "Emergency Protective Service in Illinois." Child Welfare, 44:281-283, May 1965.
The emergency after-hours protective service for neglected or abused children in Illinois is outlined. The central ingredient in the program is an answering service in the state capital to receive calls from throughout the state which are then referred to the local or regional branch or office for investigation of the situation.

1850. _____. "Protective Services and Child Abuse: Implications for Public Child Welfare." Social Service Review, 40(4):369-377, 1966.
Passage of new child abuse laws in 49 states and the high volume of reports that have resulted make serious new demands on public welfare agencies. Providing both emergency and regular coverage requires caseworkers to serve children in their own homes, homemaker service, and shelter facilities for temporary care. Special staff development efforts are also essential. The new laws and their administration have several special problems which are named.

1851. Brumbaugh, Oliver L. "Discussion." Child Welfare, 36:13-15, February 1957.
Treatment used by CPS workers includes giving parents a choice to involve themselves in intervention as soon as possible, respecting their privacy by informing them of intent to investigate, and regarding parents' problems with warmth and understanding.

1852. Burt, Marvin R. "Final Results of the Nashville Comprehensive Emergency Services Project." Child Welfare, 55(9): 661-664, 1976.
This demonstration program was originally described in Child Welfare's March 1974 issue. This summary of its results in coordinating the wide variety of services provided for neglected and abused children in a metropolitan area indicates that objectives were met, at a substantial reduction in costs. (Journal Introduction.)

1853. _____; Balyeat, Ralph. "New System for Improving the Care of Neglected and Abused Children." Child Welfare, 53:167-179, March 1974.
A new system for improving the care of neglected and abused children is discussed. Previously the program in metropolitan Nashville and Davidson County was highly fragmented with no one agency designated for program coordination. It is concluded that the new system is achieving the stated objectives.

1854. Calgary Child Abuse Advisory Committee. "Child Abuse." Canadian Welfare, 15-16, 1975.
A community approach to the problem of child abuse and neg-

lect was developed by the Calgary Child Abuse Advisory Committee.
The following areas were identified for program development: prevention, self-help, treatment, resources, detection and statistics,
local statistical information, and funding. The efforts of the Committee are detailed.

1855. California. Legislature. Assembly. Interim Committee on
      Social Welfare. Protective Services for Children: Report.
      Sacramento, Assembly of the State of California, 1967.
      40 p. illus. (Assembly Interim Committee Report 1965-
      1967, v. 19, no. 15)

1856. Cameron, J. "The Battered Child Syndrome." Medicine,
      Science, and the Law, 6:2-21, 1966.
      Substantiates the frequent occurrence of inflicted injury on
children and recognizes the immediate and imperative need for protection of such children.

1857. Cameron, James S. "Role of the Child Protective Organiza-
      tion." Pediatrics, 51(4):793-795, April 1973.
      In the Symposium on Child Abuse held in 1971, the role of the
child protective organization within the New York State Public Social
Services Department was discussed as it relates to treating cases of
child abuse and neglect. Also discussed are reporting laws, protective custody, and the overall aim of protective services.

1858. Carey, William L., et al. The Complaint Process in Pro-
      tective Services for Children. Salem, Oregon, Governor's
      Commission on Youth, 1971. 60 p.
      "A group project submitted in partial fulfillment of the re-
quirements for the degree of Master of Social Work, Portland State
University, 1969."

1859. Carstens, C. C. "Prevention of Cruelty to Children." Pro-
      ceedings of the Academy of Political Science, 2:613-619,
      July 1912.
      The broadening significance of the word "cruelty" is examined
in light of the organization work of the New York Society for the
Prevention of Cruelty to Children when it was first organized in 1874
and was principally concerned with the enforcement of law and the
punishment of the offender.

1860. Carter, Jan, ed. The Maltreated Child. See entry 750.

1861. Caulfield, Ernest. The Infant Welfare Movement in the
      Eighteenth Century. New York: Paul B. Hoeber, 1931.
      This is an historical account of the Infant Welfare Movement
in England, and more particularly London. Here is the picture of
the conditions of the poor where neglect, cruelty, and infanticide
were abundant. Here is found the first real changes. The book is
concerned with men who occupy important positions in pediatric history.

1862. Chase, Naomi Feigelson. A Child Is Being Beaten: Violence Against Children, an American Tragedy. See entry 568.

1863. "Child Abuse and Neglect. " International Juvenile Officers' Association Newsletter, 3(4):17-18, July-August-September 1974.
The 1973 Child Abuse Prevention and Treatment Act has granted much needed federal money ($10 million the first year to be administered by the DHEW) for an attack on the problem. Juvenile officers, public health nurses, and social service organizations can effectively join together to combat the problem.

1864. Child Welfare League of America. Child Welfare League of America Standards for Child Protective Service. New York, 1973. 85 p.
Presented are standards developed by the Child Welfare League of America for protective services on behalf of neglected, abused or exploited children.

1865. Class, Norris. "Some Comments on the Child Welfare League of America Standards for Child Protective Services. " Child Welfare, 139-140, March 1963.
Administrative policies need to be standarized for CPS workers and the role of law enforcement should be explained and defined.

1866. Coigney, Virginia. Children Are People Too: How We Fail Our Children and How We Can Love Them. See entry 575.

1867. Committee on Infant and Preschool Child, American Academy of Pediatrics. "Maltreatment of Children: The Battered Child Syndrome. " Pediatrics, 50:160-162, July 1972.
The Council on Child Health, composed of a committee of physicians, in its policy statement reaffirms and supports earlier recommendations and calls for the expansion of the prevention, identification, and management aspects of the battered child syndrome via predictive questionnaires, crisis management programs, establishment of diagnostics and/or treatment centers, increased responsibility by physicians and hospitals, and utilization of day care centers.

1868. Connecticut Child Welfare Association. The Care Line. (Report). Hartford, Conn. , 1974. 41 p.
The Care Line was established in October 1973 by the Connecticut Child Welfare Association, Inc. , as a statewide 24-hour-a-day, 7-day-a-week information and referral service for callers concerned about child mistreatment. Full details concerning the first year of operation are given.

1869. Costin, Lela B. Child Welfare: Policies and Practice. New York: McGraw-Hill Book Co. , 1972. 423 p. illus.
The reader is referred particularly to Chapter 9 of this book, "Protecting Children from Neglect and Abuse, " which covers the his-

torical development; the nature, aims and special attributes; and the focus and aspects of protective services in regard to child abuse and neglect.

1870. Court, Donald; Lister, James; Franklin, Alfred W.   "Experts and Child Abuse. " (Letter). British Medical Journal, 3(5934):801-802, September 28, 1974.
    The authors attempt to clear the air regarding each profession's function in child abuse cases. Each profession would be better off if none tried to interfere with the job of another profession. Communication is the key to progress in a particular case, not interference.

1871. Crane, John A.   "A Framework for Studies of Separation in Child Welfare. " The Social Service Review, 44(3), September 1970.
    The author presents a critique of clinical research in the separation in child welfare. He then presents a number of models which would control some of the biases inherent in clinical studies. Crane contends that while clinical research with small and possibly unrepresentative samples is a "source of fruitful speculation" there are few "hard findings. "

1872. Cromwell, J.; Perkins, E.   "The Battered Child-Dilemmas in Management. " Medical Social Work, 22:160-168, 1969.
    A summary of papers on child abuse, dealing with the dilemmas and function and administrative set-up of agencies, dilemmas within the law, dependence of agencies upon others for referrals, and lack of experience of workers.

1873. Cushing, Grafton D.   "Work of Societies for the Prevention of Cruelty to Children Essential in the Prevention of Crime. " Conference of Charities and Correction, National. Proceedings, 1906:106-111.
    Cushing discusses the two theories which describe the proper sphere of Prevention of Cruelty to Children Societies, namely: they may be thoroughly organized investigating and prosecuting agencies; or they may stand ready also to take part in any movement which will directly or indirectly improve the conditions under which children live. The author prefers the latter option in promoting the growth and progress of communities.

1874. D'Agostino, Paul A.   "Dysfunctioning Families and Child Abuse: The Need for an Interagency Effort. " Public Welfare, 30(4):14-17, 1972.
    The united effort of the Welfare Department and two private organizations in the establishment of a therapeutic infant child care center, the formation of an interagency, interdisciplinary group for the prevention of child abuse, and two steps the Boston community has taken in its management of child abuse, are described.

1875. Dalecká, M., et al. [Social and Legal Aspects of the Protection of the Child in the Family]. Ceskoslovenska Pediatrie, 26:251-255, May 1971.

1876. Dalhousie University. School of Law. Child Abuse in Nova
      Scotia. See entry 2217.

1877. Danckwerth, E. T. "Techniques of Child Abuse Investiga-
      tions." Police Chief, 43(3):62-64, 1976.
      The role of the police officer in child abuse cases is outlined.

1878. Davies, Joann. "When the Agency Must Intervene." Public
      Welfare, 102-105, April 1965.
      The main emphasis is that the social worker must assume
an authoritative role and at the same time be sensitive, objective,
and compassionate.

1879. Davoren, Elizabeth. "Foster Placement of Abused Children."
      Children Today, 4(3):41, May-June, 1975.
      Although foster homes usually provide a better home environ-
ment for an abused child, they also have their disadvantages. Specific disadvantages include the child's reaction to being taken out of
his natural home environment and placed into a new home, the child's
treatment when returning home and not receiving the attention given
by foster parents, and the curiosity of foster parents which precipi-
tates their asking questions which may bring back frightening memor-
ies.

1880. _____. "Working with Abusive Parents. A Social Work-
      er's View." Children Today, 4(3):2, 38-43, May-June 1975.
      Working with abusive parents is a proven way of protecting
children, while, at the same time, encouraging recognition of the
child abuse problem. The author discusses the etiology of child
abuse, how to report abusing parents, treatment services which are
provided, what type of person best works with abusive parents, and
the various supportive services offered to abusive parents.

1881. Day Care Council of New York, Inc. Children at Risk: The
      Growing Problem of Child Abuse. New York, January
      1972. 28 p. Available from the Council, 114 E. 32nd
      St., New York, N.Y., 10010. $1.75; also from EDRS:
      MF-$0.65; HC-$3.29, Plus Postage.
      This booklet describes what people can do about child abuse,
including the doctor, the hospital, those legally responsible to report
suspected abuse, and the social agency. Day care programs can
recognize and report suspicious incidents, prevent abuse, help rehabilitate families and educate the public. The report concludes that
a solution of this problem requires the full range of social, medical,
psychiatric, legal and educational resources.

1882. De Francis, Vincent. "Child Protective Services--1967."
      Juvenile Court Judges Journal, 19:24-30, Spring 1968.
      This article summarizes a 1967 nationwide survey to assess
the status and availability of a specialized and preventive child welfare program. While the findings are encouraging, there is a long
way to go before child protection becomes a reality in all geographic
areas of every state.

1883. _____. "Preventing Maltreatment of Children." Public
        Welfare, 24:229-230, 1968.
        Brief outline of problems of child protection.

1884. De Lesseps, Suzanne. "Child Abuse." Editorial Research
        Reports, 1(4):67-83, January 30, 1976.
        De Lesseps describes the severity of child abuse and neglect,
the common characteristics of abusive parents, the reluctance to
report cases, and the rising interest in incidents of wife battering.
In an analysis of child protection in tradition and law, the author
comments on the ancient view of children as chattel of parents, the
landmark case of Mary Ellen, the Kempe Report, the Child Abuse
Prevention and Treatment Act of 1974, and Congressional hearings
on psychiatric centers. In her concluding remarks, she investigates
various actions to protect children from abuse.

1885. Delsordo, James D. "Protective Casework for Abused Chil-
        dren." Children, 10:213-218, November 1963.
        The author cites many cases of abused children where there
is a need for the children to be removed from the home until rehabilitation has been established for the parents. Different types of
parental abuse are identified. Protection of the child from such
abuse should be a primary concern of caseworkers.

1886. Denver Department of Welfare. Division of Services for Fam-
        ilies, Children, and Youth. The Battered Child: A Study
        of Children with Inflicted Injuries, by Betty Johnson and
        Harold Morse. Denver, Colo., 1968. 22 p.
        The Division of Services for Families, Children, and Youth
of the Denver Department of Welfare conducted a study of battered
children to review the consistency of its approach, to determine the
effectiveness of the various methods, and to assess its long-term
results. The findings are reported.

1887. _____. _____. Child Abuse, 1972. Denver, Colo.,
        1973. 36 p.
        The 1972 operations of the Child Protection Program are de-
scribed. The program's work on behalf of 143 children reported to
the local battered child registry is statistically analyzed and compared with 1971 figures. Variables are discussed. Services provided and the outcome for 72 children during the first six months are
reviewed for each child. An effort was made to determine the where-
abouts of the children reported in 1971 and 1972. Recidivism was
thought to be at 15 percent and 17 families contained more than one
abused child. It is estimated that 2400-2600 children come to the
attention of the program each year.

1888. Denzin, Norman K., ed. Children and Their Caretakers.
        New Brunswick, N.J.: Transaction Books, 1973. 333 p.
        A series of articles which focus on the institutions that so-
ciety creates to provide for child protection or growth is presented.
The articles draw attention to the oppressive nature of child welfare
policies and to the ways in which the intended and unintended conse-

quences of these policies inhibit both effective protection and meaningful growth. Day-care centers, legal response to the battered child,
and summer military camps are examined.

1889. Diggle, Geoffrey; Jackson, Graham. "Child Injury Intensive
Monitoring System." British Medical Journal, 3:334-336,
August 11, 1973.
The authors have been developing a child intensive monitoring
system since 1970 and present here a general outline. The system
has been developed mainly to record physically abused or injured
children because of their easier definition, but it is sufficiently flex-
ible to cover the neglected or deprived child.

1890. Duke, R. F. N. "Battered Babies." (Letter). British Medical Journal, 2(5964):194, April 26, 1975.
Duke deals with self-appointed committees which are set up
to investigate parents who may be harming their children. He does
not approve of this procedure or the way such committees conduct
their investigations. Labeling them as "sneaky" and a little bit too
powerful for everyone's good, Duke wonders why such committees
have not been set up to investigate wife-batterings, drunken drivers,
or powerful people with psychotic disorders.

1891. East Sussex, Eng. County Council. Children at Risk: A
Study by the East Sussex County Council into the Problems
Revealed by the Report of the Inquiry into the Case of
Maria Colwell. Lewes: East Sussex County Council,
1975. 133 p.

1892. Ebeling, Nancy B.; Hill, Deborah A., eds. Child Abuse:
Intervention and Treatment. See entry 1268.

1893. Education Commission of the States. State Services in Child
Development: Regional Conference Highlights, Spring 1975.
Report No. 75. Early Childhood Report No. 14. Denver,
Colo., November 1975. 45 p. Available from the Com-
mission, 300 Lincoln Tower, 1860 Lincoln Street, Denver,
Colo., 80203. Paper, $1; also from EDRS: MF-$0.83;
HC-$2.06, Plus Postage.
This report includes highlights of three regional ECS Early
Childhood Project conferences which dealt with needs assessment
and planning, child abuse, and day care services. Speakers during
the second conference day focused on child abuse: the need for and
form of a model child abuse reporting law and various methods of
detecting and dealing with child abuse problems. The present and
future roles of federal and state governments were reviewed and
analyzed with reference to these conferences topics.

1894. Elmer, Elizabeth. "Abused Young Children Seen in Hospitals." Social Work, 5:98-102, October 1960.
Elmer believes that the repugnance of society for the subject
of abused children is the chief reason that so little systemic study
has been devoted to them and their families. She reviews the grad-

ual medical recognition of the problem, and discusses the attitudes of doctors and social workers who are subject to the same kinds of feelings that can be observed in other segments of society. She stresses the challenge to the social work profession.

1895. [Ever More Children Are Removed from Their Parents].
Sygeplejersken, 74(28):3, July 17, 1974.

1896. Everett, M. G.; Lewis, I. C.; Mair, C. H.; et al. "The Battered Baby Syndrome: The Tasmanian Approach. " Medical Journal of Australia, 2:735-737, October 13, 1973.
Tasmania appears to experience as many cases of child abuse as anywhere else. The laws of the state protect those who report. The procedures of the multidisciplinary approach are outlined.

1897. Fairburn, Anthony. "Small Children at Risk. " Lancet, 1:199-200, January 27, 1973.
Description of child abuse monitoring system in a population of 90, 000.

1898. _____; Jones, Susan. "Beta 5 and Battering. " New Society, 33:249-250, July 31, 1975.
This article has its setting in Bath, England. It stresses the consultative committee's monitoring role in early identification of Beta Group Children (at severe risk) and Q Group Children (at low risk), and continuing surveillance with a background of staff support and training, backing up statutory departments when difficult decisions are made. It does not offer an answer to the problems of the traceless, migratory family, and must wait for effective record-linkage systems.

1899. Fairchild, Henry P. "Preventing Cruelty to Children. " American Journal of Sociology, 18:556-573, January 1913.
Fairchild recounts his experience working for the Massachusetts Society for the Prevention of Cruelty to Children. He states that the existence of the Society acts as a powerful check on the actions of some parents and accomplishes many positive results.

1900. Fenby, T. Pitts. "The Work of the National Society for the Prevention of Cruelty to Children (NSPCC). " International Journal of Offender Therapy and Comparative Criminology, 16(3):201-205, 1972.
The NSPCC believes that the only way to break the vicious circle of depression, repeating a pattern of living going back for generations, is to get to know the parents and to work with the children while they are still young. Concern for the child is shown through the parents--they are encouraged to understand their children's needs and to care for them.

1901. The First American International Humane Conference Conducted Under the Auspices of The American Humane Association in Conjunction with Its Thirty-Fourth Annual Meeting Held in the City of Washington, D. C. , October

10-15, 1910; also First International Humane Exposition.
Report of the Proceedings. Albany, N. Y. : American
Humane Association, 1910. 228 p.
The thirteen sessions of the First American International Humane Conference are recorded. Speakers from several countries
spoke of the various aspects of cruelty to children and animals, e. g. ,
one speaker gave a graphic historical account of the binding of the
feet of female infants in China and how this practice was eventually
eradicated. Testimonials are given as to how members became interested in some particular phase of the prevention of cruelty and the
progress made by humane societies. Resolutions by each section of
the Conference are included along with reports, membership lists,
statistics, registrants, directories of societies outside and inside the
U. S. , etc.

1902. Flammang, C. J. The Police and the Underprotected Child.
Springfield, Ill. : Charles C. Thomas, 1970. 310 p.
The problem of child protection is examined, particularly as
it pertains to the law enforcement officer. Necessary techniques
and information are included to assist working police officers in such
cases. Practical police methods are described in the areas of investigation, collection, and preservation of physical evidence; interviewing, and interrogation. A realistic analysis of interagency relationships is provided for the police administrator, with suggestions
to improve needed liaison with other groups having a role in the protection of children. The roles and procedures of other disciplines
that are involved in child abuse and neglect are considered.

1903. Follis, P. "Recognizing Non-Accidental Injury in Children. "
Nursing Times, 71(51):2034-2035, December 18, 1975.
A successful program, with a multidisciplinary approach, for
the identification of non-accidental injuries to children at the Royal
Infirmary, Preston, Lancashire, England, is described.

1904. Fontana, Vincent J. "Child Abuse: A Tragic Problem. "
Parents' Magazine & Better Homemaking, 48:20, March
1973.
A brief overview of the child abuse problem is discussed.
Dr. Fontana suggests organizations who may serve in child abuse
cases, emphasizing parents' personal involvement as a vital role
in halting the problem.

1905. . "The Neglect and Abuse of Children. " New York
State Journal of Medicine, 64:215-220, January 15, 1964.
Fontana discusses the diagnostic clinical criteria and social
manifestations of and preventive measures for child abuse. The
responsibilities of the community, the physician, and legal authorities are presented, and the author makes a plea for their proper
integration and cooperation.

1906. Foresman, Louise. "Homemaker Service in Neglect and
Abuse. Strengthening Family Life. " Part 1. Children,
12:23-26, January-February 1965.

Highlighted is the importance of the caseworker-homemaker teams with regard to families having problems at home. Foresman identifies the contributions to be made by the homemaker and how these contributions affect a home situation both physically and mentally.

1907. Francis, H. W. S. "Child Health--Points of Concern." Public Health, 81:246-249, July 1967.

Effective child health care requires coordination between the different branches of medicine and social welfare work impinging on the child. For example, child guidance workers should recognize the instances in which emotional disturbances are rooted in physical causes. All practitioners and family physicians should be alert to the role poverty plays and the indications of child neglect.

1908. Franklin, Alfred W., ed. Concerning Child Abuse. See entry 2224.

1909. Fraser, Brian G. "Towards a More Practical Central Registry (Child Abuse Cases)." Denver Law Journal, 51(4): 509-528, 1974.

The concept and need for central registries for the recording of suspected child abuse reports, problems arising from the existence of such registries, and potential solutions for these problems are discussed. Thirty-three states maintain a registry, but the nature of the material filed and other aspects of operation differ widely from state to state.

1910. Friedman, Robert M.; Helfer, Ray E.; Katz, S. N.; et al. Four Perspectives on the Status of Child Abuse and Neglect Research. See entry 2225.

1911. Gardner, John W. "Abused Child." McCall's, 94:96-97+, September 1967.

Gardner offers these questions: How can we organize community resources to make them accessible to battered children? What measures should be taken to protect abused children? How can we learn more about involved families? He discusses examples of programs already begun in some areas to prevent child abuse and suggests actions the individual may undertake.

1912. Geiser, Robert L. The Illusion of Caring: Children in Foster Care. Boston: Beacon Press, 1973. 184 p. illus.

Presentation of case examples of plight of children who were removed from their parents and placed in foster homes. States incalculable psychiatric damage is inflicted upon these children since rehabilitation services are not provided for either parents or children as they sit in limbo for major part of childhood. Attributes later serious adult disturbance to experience in foster home.

1913. Glazier, Alice E., ed. Child Abuse: A Community Challenge. See entry 2229.

1914. Goldacre, Patricia. "Registering Doubt." Times (London) Educational Supplement, 3135:20-21, July 4, 1975.
Examined are the complex problems that may arise for parents when all injuries of children, accidental and non-accidental, are registered for the rest of their lives. A register raises grave questions of confidentiality for the medical profession and it may discourage parents from coming forward of their own free will. The register is seen by many as being punitive.

1915. Great Britain. Committee of Inquiry into the Care and Supervision Provided in Relation to Maria Colwell. Report of the Committee of Inquiry into the Care and Supervision Provided in Relation to Maria Colwell. London: H.M.S.O., 1974. 120 p. (At head of title: Department of Health and Social Security.)

1916. Grechishnikova, L. V. [June 1--An International Day for Protection of Children]. Pediatriia, 40:3-8, June 1961. (Russian)

1917. Gretton, John. "When No One Is Minding the Children." Times (London) Educational Supplement, 3056:4, December 21, 1973.
Flaws are examined in the social services system that allows battered babies--and ill treatment of older children--to go unnoticed until it is too late. This is done in the wake of the Maria Colwell inquiry.

1918. Hammell, Charlotte L. "Preserving Family Life for Children." Child Welfare, 48(10):591-594, December 1969.
One of the major goals of child welfare is the prevention of abuse and neglect of children. If family life is to be preserved, basic to it is the recognition of parents' needs and vast programs to insure adequate standards of living for the disadvantaged segment of the population that produces so many neglected and dependent children.

1919. Harrison, Stanley L. "Child Abuse Control Centers: A Project for the Academy?" Pediatrics, 45:895, May 1970.
The author acknowledges Dr. Brem's letter concerning the establishment of child abuse centers similar to poison control centers and the creation of a standing committee on child abuse within the academy. He states that he will forward these recommendations to the appropriate chairman for consideration.

1920. Hartman, Louise G.; Fisher, Alfra Dean. "Using the Group Method in Protective Services." Tennessee Public Welfare Record, 59-60, June 1969.
The advantages of the group process over casework in working with mothers who neglect or abuse their children are explored.

1921. Hawaii State Department of Social Services. Division of Pub-

328 / Child Abuse

lic Welfare. Protective Services for Children. Operational Plan. Oahu Branch. Honolulu, May 1, 1970. 8 p.
The Oahu Branch Child Protective Services Unit of Hawaii was established in 1969 to receive and investigate complaints of child abuse and neglect. This operational plan for the Unit describes the functions and relationships of the Unit to the Child Protective Services Center at Kaukeolani Children's Hospital and to other units of the Oahu branch, the persons served, and the methods of implementation.

1922. Helfer, Ray E. "Plan for Protection: The Child-Abuse Center. " Child Welfare, 49:486-494, November 1970.
Outlined is a family-centered approach to a therapeutic program for child abuse. It proposes the establishment of a center for the study and care of abused children in the hopes of reaching these goals: to develop a family-centered therapeutic approach, make the method efficient and practical, develop an on-going training program for utilization in day-to-day care, and phase all of the service load into a special child abuse section.

1923. _____; Kempe, C. Henry, eds. Child Abuse and Neglect: The Family and the Community. See entry 617.

1924. Herman, Bernice J. "Cucumber from Roberta; Work of the Child and Family Advocates of Evanston. " MH, 60:19-21, Summer 1976.
The story of Roberta exemplifies the work of the Mental Health Association of Evanston, Illinois, begun on a HEW grant to the Child and Family Advocates of Evanston to facilitate coordination and development of services for child-abusing parents and their children and to prevent potential abusers. The organization cares about the quality of family life, striving to help families under stress.

1925. Herre, E. A. A. "Aggressive Casework in a Protective Services Unit. " Social Casework, 46:358-362, 1965.
Describes the organization and functions of a protective services agency in some detail. Lists the financial and psychological benefits to society of children who are left in their homes as opposed to foster placements.

1926. _____. "A Community Mobilizes to Protect Its Children. " Public Welfare, 23(2):93-98, 1965.
Full responsibility for cases of neglect and abuse of children was given to the County Department of Public Welfare after a pilot project was completed in Milwaukee in 1959. The Protective Service Unit, established by federal funds, provides emergency service and long-term treatment, co-ordinates community resources and action, and acts as consultant to other divisions of the department. An aggressive reaching-out approach is encouraged.

1927. Herrmann, Kenneth J. , Jr. I Hope My Daddy Dies, Mister. Philadelphia: Dorrance, 1975. 111 p.
This is a day-to-day account, Monday through Friday, of the

life of a social worker as he deals with an overwhelming caseload of severe cases of child abuse and neglect. An epilogue provides the final outcome of his efforts with the various families discussed.

1928. Hessel, Samuel J.; Rowe, Daniel S. "Rights of Parents and Children." (Letters). New England Journal of Medicine, 283:156-157, July 16, 1970.

Hessel questions the use of child abuse registers. He believes any physician who sees D. A. R. T. in large block letters on a record will approach the patient and family with a different psychological, if not medical, point of view. Such a designation can be a lifelong stigma to an entire family. Rowe answers Hessel by naming safeguards in the use of the registry. If attention is directed toward protection of the child, not toward prosecution of the parents, the possibility of harm to innocent persons is lessened.

1929. Hoffman, Mary. "From Baby Farms to Yo-Yo Children." Times (London) Educational Supplement, 3135:21, July 4, 1975.

Yo-Yo children are seen as marital footballs. The changing role of the NSPCC is examined. Part of its energies have been diverted to research and setting up therapeutic playgrounds, but the true role is seen as providing inspection to protect children. It also runs special courses for educational welfare officers and teachers. Although some think the services of NSPCC overlap social services, the author feels there will always be a role for it to play.

1930. Holland, Mary. "Children at Risk." New Statesman, 86:721-722, November 16, 1973.

Holland discusses the difficulty in arousing sufficient interest and action in England concerning children at risk. She praises the NSPCC for setting up in 1969 a Battered Child Research Unit to register cases of child abuse. The NSPCC has pleaded that a willingness to undertake long-term casework should be matched by a readiness to bring cases before the juvenile court.

1931. Holmes, Sally A.; Barnhart, Carol; Cantoni, Lucile; et al. "Working with the Parent in Child-Abuse Cases." Social Casework, 56(1):3-12, January 1975.

Characteristics of abusive parents and clues to look for in a family are given. Working with the parent involves developing a treatment relationship, understanding rage, parenting and educating the parent, expanding life's satisfactions, helping parents modify behavior, breaking the barrier of isolation, helping parents allow for setbacks in treatment, and recognizing the need for placement. The relationship between agencies is discussed.

1932. "Homemaker Service in Neglect and Abuse." Children, 12:23-29, January-February 1965.

I. Strengthening Family Life, by Louise Foresman. II. A Tool for Case Evaluation, by Elizabeth A. Stringer. See also entry 2028.

1933. Hornbein, Ruth. Social Worker's Orientations to the Use of

Authority in Initiating and Maintaining a Social Casework Relationship with Parents Who Abuse and Parents Who Neglect Their Children. D. S. W. University of Denver, 1972. 184 p. Available from University Microfilms, Order No. UM 72-32, 079.

A study of the orientations of social workers in child protection services to the use of authority in initiating and maintaining a casework relationship with abusive and neglectful parents included compilation and analysis of data from a complex questionnaire. A group of social workers and a group of judges in Denver replied to questions concerning use of authority developed from 55 case studies of child abuse. Topics extensively discussed include concepts of authority, use of authority in social casework, and specific criteria for development of the study.

1934. Horner, Gerald. "Support Your Social Workers (The Problem of "Battered Children" in Britain). " Municipal and Public Services Journal, 82:862+, July 19, 1974.

1935. Howells, John G. Remember Maria. Toronto: Butterworths, 1974. 115 p.

After having been in the care of foster parents for six years, a child is returned to her mother and stepfather who battered her to death. Brief vignettes of many other instances of child abuse that have resulted from administrative, legal, and bureaucratic insensitivities are given. The assumption that natural parents should have the authority in managing their children is challenged. Several misconceptions are examined--the so-called link between natural parent and child, the role of the father, and the relationship between separation and deprivation. Evaluation, diagnosis, and treatment of the entire family is advocated when the issue of child abuse is involved.

1936. _____. "Whose Responsibility?--Parent, Foster Parent, or Local Authority? (a) Separation or Death. " Royal Society of Health Journal, 95(5):257-261, October 1975.

Three misconceptions are briefly considered: the "special feeling or mystical bond" between parent and child is always present; in all circumstances the mother-child bond is so unique that it cannot be replaced by any other; the above misconceptions held in conjunction lead to the idea that the child's natural family is better for him than any other family. The responsibility to act on new concepts lies with the social worker, the helping professions, the government, and the public. See also entry 2006.

1937. Hudson, Bob. "Whose Responsibility? 'Battered' Children. " Municipal and Public Services Journal, 83:999-1001, August 8, 1975.

1938. Hughes, A. F. "The Battered Baby Syndrome--A Multidisciplinary Problem. " Case Conference, 14(8):304-308, 1967.

Hughes lists six symptoms and characteristics of child abuse cases. Once identified, the Battered Baby Syndrome ceases to be the sole concern of doctors and becomes the equal responsibility of social workers operating within the existing legal framework. The syndrome must be dealt with by many different professionals and disciplines.

1939. Ireland, William H. "A Registry on Child Abuse." Children, 13:113-115, May 1966.
    This article deals with processes of registering cases of child abuse in order to design effective methods of control. It explains why a registry is important and how it is utilized.

1940. James, Howard. The Little Victims: How America Treats Its Children. See entry 623.

1941. Jenkins, E. Fellows. "New York Society for the Prevention of Cruelty to Children." Annals of the American Academy of Political and Social Science, 31:492-494, March 1908.
    The role and functions of the New York Society for the Prevention of Cruelty to Children are described by the organization's secretary-superintendent.

1942. Johnson, Betty; Morse, Harold A. "Injured Children and Their Parents." Children, 15:147+, July-August 1968.
    Since 1951, the Division of Services for Children and Youth of the Denver Department of Welfare has participated in a Protective Service Program in cooperation with the Denver Juvenile Court, the Denver Police Department, and the Denver General Hospital. The purpose of the program is to help, not punish, parents who neglect or injure their children.

1943. Johnson, Clara L. Child Abuse: Public Welfare Agency-Juvenile Court Relationships. See entry 1001.

1944. _____. Child Abuse: State Legislation and Programs in the Southeast. See entry 1002.

1945. _____. Two Community Protective Service Systems: Comparative Evaluation of Systems Operations. Athens, Georgia University, Regional Institute of Social Welfare Research. March 1976. 54 p. Available from the Regional Institute, 468 N. Milledge Avenue, Heritage Building, Athens, Georgia 30601. $5; also from EDRS: MF-$0.83; HC-$3.50, Plus Postage.
    Presented are the findings of a study conducted to evaluate two community protective service systems in terms of the mechanisms for identifying and handling child abuse and neglect cases and the effectiveness of intervention. The two sites were Nashville, Tennessee, (an emergency reporting system and a 24-hour protective service program) and Savannah, Georgia, (a more traditional protective service system with no internal provision for 24-hour intake.) In a final chapter the similarities and differences between the two systems are discussed, and recommendations are presented.

1946. Juvenile Protective Association. The Bowen Center Project.

A Report of a Demonstration in Child Protective Services.
1965-1971. Chicago, Ill. , 1975. 168 p.
This extensive and highly documented report covers the organization and operation of the Bowen Center Project in Chicago from
1965 to 1971, a program for delivering coordinated social, educational, and health services to families of neglected and mistreated
children, with the ultimate goals of helping the children and restab-
ilizing the families. Specific results obtained with each of the families are summarized, and some general conclusions regarding the
parents and the children are drawn.

1947. Kaufman, Irving. "The Contribution of Protective Services. "
        Child Welfare, 8-15, February 1957.
        A protective supervisory person, although frequently resented
at the outset by neglecting or abusing parents, is many times received with gratitude and relief later on. Some special techniques
for dealing with parents are discussed.

1948. Kempe, C. Henry; Helfer, Ray E. , eds. Helping the Bat-
        tered Child and His Family. See entry 1339.

1949. Kent County Department of Social Welfare. Child Protective
        Services. The Abused Child in This Community. Grand
        Rapids, Michigan, October 25, 1965.

1950. Klibanoff, Elton B. "Child Advocacy in Action. " Childhood
        Education, 52:70-72, November-December 1975.
        Efforts to improve coordination among various agencies in-
volved in child protective services are examined, with emphasis on
the Massachusetts Office for Children. Two components are cited
as necessary for coordination. The Office is not a direct service
provider but is a community-based agency with mandated functions
at state and local levels.

1951. Knapp, Vrinda Sharma. The Role of the Juvenile Police in
        the Protection of Neglected and Abused Children. San
        Francisco: R and E Research Associates, 1975. 117 p.
        (Originally presented as the author's thesis, University of
        Southern California, D. S. W. 1961.)
        This is a study of the role of juvenile police in the protection
of children who are the victims of adult neglect and abuse in one
geographic area of a metropolitan city. Its focus is on the activities
of the juvenile police from the time a complaint of child neglect or
abuse is brought to their attention until their responsibility ends.

1952. Kristal, Helen F. ; Tucker, Ford. "Managing Child Abuse
        Cases. " Social Work, 20(5):392-395, September 1975.
        Casework can often be used to good advantage in managing
child abuse cases. The procedure described in this article is coordinated by a social worker who works closely with the physician
and helps train new professional staff members from various disciplines. (Journal Introduction.)

1953. Lahiff, Maureen. "Talking Point: Softly, Softly." Nursing Times, 72(50):1950-1951, December 16, 1976.
  Lahiff questions the involvement of the police in case conferences on child abuse, contending that such action could create more problems than it solves. She believes that the police has the potential of decreasing the effectiveness of the health visitor's role.

1954. Landriau, M. "Studies in Child Abuse." Social Service Quarterly, 50(1):175-178, 1976.
  The author looks at ways in which the NSPCC in the United Kingdom has attempted to assist families involved in non-accidental injury to their children. It began its pioneering research in 1968. Its aims were to find ways of effectively intervening in family situations where children under the age of four suffered, or were at risk of suffering, and to create an informed body of knowledge about the syndrome. The research carried out by NSPCC into one aspect of child abuse has been utilized here to illustrate some methods by which a more effective programme of preventing non-accidental injury to children might be achieved.

1955. Laudinet, J. [The Protection of Childhood]. Techniques Hospitalieres Medico-Sociales et Sanitaires, 15:45-47, November 1959. (French)

1956. Learning Institute of North Carolina. Social Services and the Family, edited by Jamice Ryan. 1975. 63 p. Available from the Learning Institute, 800 Silver Avenue, Greensboro, North Carolina 27403. Paper, $1.25; also from EDRS: MF-$0.76; HC-$3.32, Plus Postage.
  Short articles and materials focus on various aspects of intervention, child abuse, neglect and advocacy, family problems, services, and parent education. A general review of the last ten years of early intervention programs is included. A schedule for training a social services/parent involvement staff, guidelines for developing helping relationships, and reading lists pertaining to emotional deprivation in early life and professional support to the family is also included.

1957. Leavitt, Jerome Edward, comp. The Battered Child: Selected Readings. See entry 521.

1958. Lewis, Harold; Jahn, Julius A.; Bishop, Julia Ann. Designing More Effective Protective Services--Intervening in the Recurrence Cycle of Neglect and Abuse of Children. Philadelphia, University of Pennsylvania School of Social Work, Research Center, June 1967.

1959. Lister, John. "By the London Post. The Price of Oil--Death of a Baby--No Sex, Please--We're British." New England Journal of Medicine, 294(13):710-712, March 25, 1976.
  Oil rigs, tugs, and giant tankers are now a familiar sight off the East Coast of Scotland, and with the influx of workers, many

social and medical ills have arisen, including the increasing frequence
of violence of all kinds and in particular the battering of children and
women. The death by starvation of a 16-month-old baby boy brought
general criticism of the competence of social workers and a demand
for more resources devoted to social services.

1960. McCrea, Roswell Cheney. The Humane Movement: A De-
       scriptive Survey Prepared on the Henry Bergh Foundation
       for the Promotion of Humane Education in Columbia Uni-
       versity. New York: Columbia University Press, 1910;
       College Park, Md.: McGrath Publ. Co., 1969.
       Chapter V. The prevention of cruelty to children, p. 135-
146. Table II. Summary of state laws for the protection of children, p. 389-431.

1961. McFerran, Jane. "Parents' Groups in Protective Services."
       Children, 5:223-228, November-December 1958.
       Self-help groups were formed in Louisville, Kentucky, to help
abusing parents face their problem and try to correct it. Discussions and simple meetings were held and proved to be valuable in
assisting most parents to make sincere efforts to apply at home
some of the ideas developed in the meetings. Group feelings and
group effort are positive attributes in helping abusing parents.

1962. McKinney, Geraldine. "Child Abuse and Neglect: A Search
       for Answers." Social and Rehabilitation Record, 2(3):13-
       14, April 1975.
       Ten states and 30 local departments of social services were
surveyed on an interview basis by the Social and Rehabilitation Service to assist states in improving their services to abused and neglected children and their families. The problem areas which showed
up were: inadequate reporting requirements, inadequate legal requirements and processes, and not enough trained people.

1963. McNairy, Darst M.; Sharpless, Martha; Doyle, Cynthia; et al.
       "A Community Approach to Child Abuse and Neglect."
       Popular Government, 41:10-14, Spring 1976.
       CAPS (Child Abuse Prevention Services), a multifaceted ap-
proach to helping abusive parents and their children that involves
doctors, social workers, public health and mental health staffers,
lawyers, and the courts, is described.

1964. "Maria Colwell." Queen's Nursing Journal, 17:155, October
       1974.
       This is a formal response by Barbara Castle, Secretary of
State for Social Services, to a Committee report on the Maria Colwell case in Great Britain. The Secretary emphasizes the need to
strengthen measures to prevent, diagnose, and manage cases of non-
accidental injury to children, and promises to introduce a children's
bill into Parliament pertaining to adoption, guardianship, fostering,
and other aspects of children in care.

1965. "Maria Colwell and After." (Editorial). British Medical
       Journal, 1:300, February 23, 1974.

This is an editorial comment on the child abuse death of Maria Colwell. It discusses where the blame should be placed regarding her death and how incidents like this one can be prevented. Additional problems are explored, including: finding abusive families, identifying high-risk families, and who should decide when and where an abused child is supposed to go, and with whom the authority is placed.

1966. Marin County Interagency Committee on Child Abuse. <u>Child Abuse Report.</u> San Rafael, Calif. , Marin County Probation Department, March 1972. 59 p.
The problem of child abuse as it related to the community services of Marin County, California, is surveyed, and recommendations are offered concerning ways to deal with the problem.

1967. Marsh, Benjamin T. "Some Functions of a Society to Protect Children from Cruelty. " <u>Annals of the American Academy of Political and Social Science,</u> 27:458-461, March 1906.
The secretary of the Pennsylvania Society to Protect Children from Cruelty discusses various functions of the Society, including: having charge of Juvenile Court; making sure children are given suitable physical, mental, and moral care; prevention activities which emphasize parent responsibility; investigation of conditions affecting childlife; rehabilitation of family life, and the prevention of crime.

1968. Melville, Joy. "A Mothers' Meeting: N. S. P. C. C. Pilot Scheme in South Central London. " <u>New Society,</u> 141, April 17, 1975.
This is an account of a meeting, sponsored by social workers, of abusing mothers who were suffering from depression, isolation, and the inability to make relationships.

1969. Michael, Marianne K. "Social Report: Child Abuse. " <u>Iowa Journal of Social Work,</u> 5(1):22-26, 1972.
Action taken regarding the treatment of 49 cases of child abuse reported by the University of Iowa Hospitals over the period of 1965-1971 is reported, with stress on the role of the new Iowa code for child abuse which went into effect in 1965. Information was collected from records, interviews, and survey of social service resources regarding the family situation of each child and the kinds of services available, such as foster care, etc. Actions of the court were also determined. There is still much to do on the part of state social service agencies.

1970. Minn, Ping Kyau. "Operation Help: An Approach to Child Protection. " In: <u>Social Work Practice,</u> 1964. p. 172-180. New York: Columbia University Press, 1964.
Described is the 24-hour service in cases of child abuse and neglect in the Hawaiian Department of Social Services.

1971. Mitchell, Betsy. "Working with Abusive Parents. A Caseworker's View. " <u>American Journal of Nursing,</u> 73:480-483, March 1973.

In a review of her experience with abusive parents, a case-worker in the Child Protective Service Unit of the Bureau of Child Welfare in a large eastern city reveals that helping parents is the key to improving the abused child's situation.

1972. Moorehead, Carolina. "7-Man Team Helps Parents of Bat-tered Babies." Times (London) Educational Supplement, 2897:12, November 27, 1970.
The methods employed in prevention and treatment by the Battered Child's Research Department of NSPCC, which was estab-lished in 1970, are described. Joan Court, experienced psychiatric social worker, is head of the Battered Child Unit. Five social workers, a psychiatrist and psychologist man the unit. Miss Court would like to see children at school receive preparation for the eventual tensions of having a baby.

1973. NSPCC Battered Child Research Team. At Risk: An Account of the Work of the Battered Child Research Department NSPCC. London, England: Routledge & Kegan Paul, 1976. 246 p.
Treatment of child abuse in 25 families through a total fam-ily, multiple-modality approach is described. (P. A.)

1974. Nagi, Saad Z. Child Maltreatment in the United States: A Cry for Help and Organizational Response. See entry 2242.

1975. _____. The Structure and Performance of Programs on Child Abuse and Neglect. Interim Report. Child Abuse and Neglect Programs--A National Overview. Columbus, Ohio State University. Department of Sociology and Public Policy, March 1975. 16 p.
A total of 1, 969 interviews were conducted among judges, physicians, law enforcement officers, caseworkers, and others in agencies related to child abuse and neglect in a nationwide survey in 1972-1973. Extrapolating from the Florida data, it is estimated that there were 925, 000 reportable cases nationally in that year, of which approximately 600, 000 were reported. Substantiated abuse or neglect might be expected in 555, 000 cases. The source of highest reporting, information on placement of abused and neglected children, level of participation of coordinating groups, etc. , are given. Coun-seling was the most lacking in all agencies.

1976. National Committee for Prevention of Child Abuse. Profes-sional Papers: Child Abuse and Neglect. See entry 1063.

1977. National Society for the Prevention of Cruelty to Children (England). Battered Child Research Department. The "Battered Baby" Syndrome. An Analysis of Reports Sub-mitted by Medical Officers of Health and Children's Offi-cers. London, May 1972. 10 p.
Clinical and social management of the individual family and administrative aspects of the problem of child abuse in England are discussed based on progress reports submitted by Medical Officers

of Health and Children's Officers during the period 1970-1971. Primary and secondary prevention are discussed, and four alternative rehabilitation plans are outlined. The structure and function of review committees and case committees are examined. Also considered are education and training, child abuse registers, and role of the police.

1978. _____ . _____ . A Study of Suspected Child Abuse, by R. L. Castle and A. M. Kerr. London, September 1972. 19 p.
The incidence of cases of suspected child abuse referred to England's National Society for the Prevention of Cruelty to Children (NSPCC) in 1970 was determined, and the findings were compared to an early retrospective study conducted by the NSPCC. Further, the work of NSPCC social workers in this field was analyzed. More parents were referring themselves, while general practitioners continued to report at a low rate. The NSPCC also became more popular as a treatment agency. More central registries are recommended.

1979. _____ . National Advisory Centre on the Battered Child. Battered Children: Myth and Realty--Some Problems of Providing Service, by R. L. Castle. London, May 1973. 4 p.
Some of the myths and realities of the battered child syndrome are examined, including some of the problems relevant to diagnosis, management, and treatment in England at the present time.

1980. National Symposium on Child Abuse, Rochester, N. Y. , 1971 See entry 786.

1981. National Symposium on Child Abuse, 2d, Denver, 1972. A Collection of Papers Presented at a National Meeting in Denver, Colorado, October 11, 1972, to Explore on an Interdisciplinary Basis the Problems of Child Abuse and Sexual Exploitation of Children. Denver, American Humane Assn. , Children's Division, 1973. 60 p. (96th Annual Meeting of AHA)
This symposium was co-sponsored by the National Council of Juvenile Court Judges and by several agencies in the Greater Denver Metropolitan Area. National experts discuss multidisciplinary approaches for protecting victims of neglect and abuse. Roles and responsibilities of professionals involved in the process are interpreted and related to cooperative and coordinated services.

1982. National Symposium on Child Abuse, 4th, Charleston, S. C. , 1973. A Collection of Papers Presented at a National Meeting in Charleston, South Carolina, October 23, 1973, to Explore on an Interdisciplinary Basis the Problems of Child Abuse and Neglect. Denver, American Humane Assn. , Children's Division, 1975. 92 p. $1.20. (97th Annual Meeting of the AHA and co-sponsored by the American Legion, National Commission on Children and Youth, the American Public Welfare Association, and many other organizations.)

Selected papers delivered at a national symposium brought together panels of experts in areas of identification and protection of
neglected, maltreated and sexually abused children. Papers deal
with multidisciplinary approaches, medical problems and legal aspects
in terms of invoking the authority of the courts.

1983. National Symposium on Child Abuse, 5th, Boston, 1974. Collection of Papers Presented at a National Meeting in Boston, Massachusetts, October 15-16, 1974, to Examine Contemporary Issues and Therapeutic Approaches to the Problems of Child Abuse and Neglect. Denver, Colo. , American Humane Association, Children's Division, 1976. 151 p.
$2.
An intensive examination of contemporary issues and therapeutic approaches to the problems of child abuse and neglect. Selected papers relate to reporting and registries, appropriate use of
the courts, therapeutic group service modules, and realities and
frustrations in child protection.

1984. New York State Assembly. Select Committee on Child Abuse.
A Guide to New York's Child Protection System. Albany,
July 1974. 38 p.
New York State's statutory creation of a child protective system was the result of the premise that child protective workers offer a distinct advantage over law enforcement officers in child protective investigations because of their particular abilities. The law
creates a system with five fundamental components. Specific definitions and procedures of these five system components are described
and responsibilities of all persons involved are detailed. A directory
of New York child protective agencies is included.

1985. New York State Department of Social Services. Child Protective Services in New York State, 1976 Annual Report.
Albany: The Department. 43 p. 19 Tables.
This report provides a description of the advances made in
New York State during 1976 on behalf of abused and maltreated children. In addition to a complete statistical compendium, the report
provides information on the continuing development of the State Central Register automated system.

1986. Northern Virginia Mental Health Association. Is Anybody
Listening? Creative Approaches in the Delivery of Child
Protective Services. A Public Forum. Arlington, 1974.
98 p.
The proceedings of a public forum on Creative Approaches in
the Delivery of Child Protective Services held in Reston, Va. , from
September 30 to October 1, 1974, are presented. The problem, the
magnitude, services presently available, and the future directions for
services are discussed.

1987. Nyden, Paul V. "The Use of Authority. " Public Welfare,
24(3):239-245, 1966.

A comprehensive, cogent treatment of the issues involved in child protection. Outlines agency responsibility.

1988. Oettinger, Katherine B. "Protecting Children from Abuse." Parents' Magazine & Better Homemaking, 39:12, November 1964.
A brief overview of the child abuse problem is presented, and the problem is described socially and legally. Oettinger asks that readers support child abuse reporting and be alert to the growing need for more adequate protective services.

1989. "One Problem, Two Answers." Economist, 255:31, May 3, 1975.
Two cases of child murder--Maria Colwell and Lisa Godfrey-- are reviewed from the standpoint of social services. In Maria's case, there was little liaison between a considerable number of agencies involved. In Lisa's case, not enough agencies were involved. Conflicting views seen in the Seebohm and Godfrey reports are examined. There no longer can be any excuse for all concerned--voluntary and statutory authorities and the police--to fail to work together, the article contends.

1990. Orriss, Harry D. "Lessons from a Tragedy." Nursing Times, 70:140-141, January 31, 1974.
The case of Maria Colwell, who was beaten to death by her stepfather, William Kepple, January 6, 1973, is reviewed. The case was the result of a breakdown in communication, and a failure to do what integrated social services departments were primarily set up to do--coordinate. It is for the inquiry to decide whether departmental organization, division of responsibilities, methods and procedures contributed to the failure evident in Maria's case.

1991. Osborn, Maria L. "Inadequate Mothers." (Letter). Lancet, 2(7892):1322, November 30, 1974.
Osborn believes a shorter, simpler and surer procedure than providing "constant manipulation at every juncture" to inadequate mothers is to separate the infant from an inadequate mother and provide him with love and care from a substitute parent. A baby cannot wait for love, and the mother is relieved of the burden of unwanted mothering.

1992. Page, Geraldine. "Detection of Child Abuse." Nursing Mirror and Midwives Journal, 141:53-54, September 18, 1975.
Through a family consisting of two children where child abuse is suspected, a field worker traces her association with the mother, children, and a registered child-minder. The author feels it is very difficult to know when to act in an unpredictable situation, but contends that every neighbor, relative, doctor, teacher, nurse, and social worker has a responsibility to the abused child. Attempting to scapegoat the community-care system when something goes wrong merely emphasizes the double standards of society as a whole.

1993. Patti, Rino John. Child Protection in California, 1850-1966.

An Analysis of Public Policy. D. S. W. University of
Southern California, Los Angeles, June 1967. 412 p.
Available from University Microfilms, Order No. 67-17, 692.
The purpose of this study was to trace the development and
implementation of public policy in California pertaining to the pro-
tection of neglected children from 1850 to 1966.

1994. Paul, S. D. "Recognition of the Entity 'The Battered Child
Syndrome' in India. " Indian Journal of Pediatrics, 39:58-
62, February 1972.
A review of the battered child syndrome emphasizes the need
for child protection in India. In view of the problems in managing
child abuse cases, recommended legislation includes physicians' responsibility to report, a child welfare agency to provide continuing
care, and juvenile court involvement to protect the child.

1995. Piersma, Harry L. "Administrative Problems in Child Abuse
Services. " Journal of Pediatric Psychology, 1(2):41-44,
Spring 1976.
In describing the administrative structure of existing child
abuse services at Fort Bragg, N. C. , Piersma identifies several
common administrative problems related to professional coordination,
lines of authority and responsibility, abundance of red tape, and attitudes of dissension and frustration. Suggestions are given for rec-
tifying administrative problems that have interfered with the development of effective treatment programs.

1996. Pizzey, Erin. Scream Quietly or the Neighbours Will Hear.
Edited by Alison Forbes. Harmondsworth; Baltimore [etc.]:
Penguin, 1974. 143 p. (A Penguin Special)
This book is an account of the work of Chiswick Women's
Aid in England, a house established to help battered women and their
children in a practical way--offering asylum when there is no other
place to go. Pizzey takes to task the social services, police, social
security, hospitals, doctors, and marriage counselors who fail to
help in practical ways. She praises the work of the Probation Service and health visitors. If children are not to grow up to be batterers, supportive help must be available. Up to now wives with
children had no means of extricating themselves from an impossible
situation.

1997. Powis, D. "Violence to Children. " Police Review, 82(4270):
1473-1475, 1974.
The patrol officer is told what to look for and what to do when
there is a reasonable suspicion that child abuse is occurring.

1998. "Prevention of Cruelty to Children. " Annals of the American
Academy of Political and Social Science, 26:774-777, No-
vember 1905.
This article details the origin and functions of the New York
Society for the Prevention of Cruelty to Children. According to the
society's secretary, the organization should not be considered a mere

alms-giving unit, but rather as an agent of the law in the enforcement of the criminal law.

1999. "The Problem of Battered Children. " (Editorial) Nursing
Mirror and Midwives Journal, 138:39, May 3, 1974.
This editorial describes the short-term and long-term management of child abuse cases developed in response to the Maria Colwell
incident in Great Britain.

2000. "Protecting Children from Abuse and Neglect: Phase II. "
Currents in Public Health, 7(10):1-4, November-December
1967.
The goal of protective services is outlined. When the parents
cannot fulfill even minimal responsibilities of parenthood, then society
must be willing to terminate the parental rights. Describes how prevention can be accomplished.

2001. "Protective Services for Children. " In: Encyclopedia of
Social Work, p. 1007-1013. New York: National Association of Social Workers, 1971.
History is given of the child protective movement in the U. S. ,
beginning in the 1870s when the Society for the Prevention of Cruelty
to Animals intervened in a situation of extreme abuse in the case of
a nine-year-old named, Mary Ellen. Protective standards and services, preventive services; methods (direct casework); background of
child abuse legislation, trends and needs in protective services, and
the increases in research are touched upon.

2002. Protective Services in Public Welfare--Davidson County,
Tennessee. Children's Bureau Project Number D-283.
Presents complete results of a project done under the direc-
tion of the Tennessee Department of Public Welfare, Davidson County,
Tennessee, designed to develop a Child Protection Agency for that area.

2003. Puerto Rico State Department of Social Services. Evaluation
Plan for the Child Abuse and Neglect Demonstration Unit,
Bayamon, Puerto Rico, by N. Moreno. Research and Evaluation Division, 1973-1974. 20 p.
An evaluation plan for the Child Abuse and Neglect Demonstration Unit at Bayamon, Puerto Rico, is outlined. Its general
goals are given.

2004. _____. Overview of the Child Abuse and Neglect Demonstration Unit. Bayamon, February 28, 1975. 25 p.
The Child Abuse and Neglect Demonstration Unit in Bayamon,
Puerto Rico, that handles cases coming to the attention of the local
social service offices of the nine towns that constitute this region,
is described.

2005. Raiford, William H. "Helping the Hopeless. How Physically
and Psychologically Battered Children Were Helped Toward
Better Lives. " Social and Rehabilitation Record, 3(5):28-32,
September 1976.

When the Juvenile Protective Association of Chicago launched a project to demonstrate that families living below the lowest rung of society's ladder can be rescued, they were appalled at what they found upon visiting homes in impoverished areas. In a follow-up study four years after the project ended in 1971, 13 families that could be contacted were found to have maintained family relations on a higher level without regression. The project is described.

2006. Reeves, Christine. "Whose Responsibility?--Parent, Foster Parent, or Local Authority? (b) Whose Responsibility?" Royal Society of Health Journal, 95(5):261-263, October 1975.

Little priority is given to education and preparation for parenthood. Society's lack results in families being continually added to social agency's caseloads. Child in Care (foster care service) is examined. Foster parents shape children into the kind of future society that lies ahead. They should be allowed to play a greater part in the decisions and planning. The establishment of the National Foster Care Association is a step in the right direction. See also entry 1936.

2007. Reid, B. "Social Agencies and the Police in the London Borough of Southwark." Police Journal, 49(3):210-215, 1976.

2008. Reid, Joseph H.; Phillips, Maxine. "Child Welfare Since 1912." Children Today, 1:13-18, March-April 1972.

Described in this article are the growth, history, and services of the Children's Bureau. Specific functions rendered are identified as adoption, foster care, one-parent families, and child abuse.

2009. Rein, Martin. Child Protective Services in Massachusetts. Waltham, Mass.: Florence Heller Graduate School for Advanced Studies in Social Welfare, Brandeis University, November 1963. 171 p.

2010. Reinitz, Freda G. "Special Registration Project on the Abused Child." Child Welfare, 44:103-105, February 1965.

Explained is the procedure, entitled Red X, which alerts participating agencies of the fact that evidence of neglect or abuse was of such order as to require referral for protective care for those designated cases. It is the hope of this program, begun in Philadelphia in February 1964, that case finding and handling will improve and become more effective.

2011. "Remember Maria." (Editorial). Midwife, Health Visitor and Community Nurse, 11(7):205, July 1975.

2012. Renvoize, Jean. Children in Danger. The Causes and Prevention of Baby Battering. See entry 645.

2013. Richette, Lisa Aversa. The Throwaway Children. See entry 1104.

2014. Roberts, Robert Winston. A Comparative Study of Social
Caseworkers' Judgments of Child Abuse Cases. Doctoral
Dissertation. New York, Columbia University, School of
Social Work. 1970. 275 p. Available from University
Microfilms, Order No. 71-6247.
A comparative study analyzes 194 social caseworkers' diag-
nostic, prognostic, and placement judgments of child abuse cases.
The caseworkers were selected from Chicago and California protec-
tive services, family services, child welfare, and public assistance
agencies.

2015. Rochel, M., et al. "Effektivität der Mabbnahmen bei Kinder-
smisshandlungen" [Protective Measure Against Child Abuse
and Child Neglect]. Beitraege zur Gerichtlichen Medizin,
31:110-114, 1973.

2016. Sandusky, Annie Lee. "Services to Neglected Children. "
Children, 7:23-28, January-February 1960.
Various community services are identified which provide help
to abused children and families with problems resulting in child neglect and abuse. Services include child welfare workers, welfare departments, justice courts, lawmakers, the police, and the community as a whole. Also discussed are why these services are needed
and why they work toward curbing child neglect and abuse.

2017. "Saving Battered Children. " Time, 85:43, January 8, 1965.
Incidence of child abuse is reviewed and the model state law
drawn up by U. S. Children's Bureau is discussed. Is law enough?
There must be social services available in an effort to prevent further abuses, safeguard and enhance the welfare of such children and
preserve family life wherever possible. Do they have the manpower
to implement all the reports made mandatory by law?

2018. Sayre, James W.; Foley, Frank W.; Zingarella, Leonor S.,
et al. "Community Committee on Child Abuse. " New
York State Journal of Medicine, 73:2071-2075, August 1973.
The development, membership and accomplishments of the
Committee on Child Abuse of Monroe County, New York are reported.
People representing medical, social, and legal aspects of child abuse
met to discuss mutual concerns. Interagency problems and misunder-
standings are identified and discussed, and ways of improving care
are suggested. (Author Abstract Modified.)

2019. Schmidt, Dolores M. "The Challenge of Helping the 'Untreat-
ables. ' " Public Welfare, 98-102, April 1965.
The father of a family on public assistance is suspected of
abusing the children. Described is how the situation was handled
by social services.

2020. Schmidt, F. [Studies on the Registration and Care of Socially
Endangered Groups of Persons in a District]. Zeitschrift
für die Gesamte Hygiene und Ihre Grenzgebiete, 19:378-384,
May 1973.

2021. Sherman, E. A.; Phillips, M. H.; Haring, B. L.; et al. *Service to Children in Their Own Homes: Its Nature and Outcome.* New York: Child Welfare League of America, Inc., 1973. 156 p.

The nature and outcome of service to abused and neglected children in their own homes provided over the period 1970-1971 were examined. Intake and Decision Schedules were filled out on a total of 553 children in 246 cases in which the decision was to serve children at home by plan or in lieu of placement. Cases were drawn from one voluntary and three public agencies.

2022. Shultz, William John. *Humane Movement in the United States, 1910-1922.* (Columbia University Studies in History, Economics and Public Law, v. 113, no. 1; whole no. 252) New York: Longmans, Green & Co., n. d.

2023. Silver, Larry B.; Dublin, C. C.; Lourie, R. S. "Agency Action and Interaction in Cases of Child Abuse." *Social Casework*, 52(3):164-171, March 1971.

A retrospective review of hospital and community agency records was made in order to study the roles played by individual agencies in cases of child abuse, and the effectiveness of agency intervention in preventing further abuse. The study supports the concept that child abuse is reflective of family pathology.

2024. Smith, Selwyn M. "Child Injury Intensive Monitoring System." *British Medical Journal*, 3:593-594, September 15, 1973.

Smith discusses the value of having a computer-based system working at all levels of authority regarding the scale and nature of the battered baby. He points out that although it is already being used at the authoritative level, it might work better if it was used in hospitals rather than social service departments. He also thinks the system should incorporate accurate records of abuse from all doctors.

2025. Sokoloff, Burton. "The Battered Child." (Letter). *Western Journal of Medicine*, 121(6):509, December 1974.

This letter refers to an excellent article by Richard J. Kohlman concerning "Malpractice Liability for Failing to Report Child Abuse" which, however, failed to include the failure of police authorities to continue to follow through in the cases that physicians do report. Sokoloff tells of his own experience with the police.

2026. Streshinsky, M.; Billingsley, A.; Gurgin, V. "A Study of Social Work Practice in Protective Services: It's Not What You Know, It's Where You Work." *Child Welfare*, 45:444-450, 471, October 1966.

From a study of the responses of a large sample of workers to questions relating to hypothetical, but realistic, case situations involving physical neglect and physical abuse of children, some conclusions were drawn regarding where in the welfare department protective services would most appropriately be lodged. Nine communities were studied.

2027. Streshinsky, Naomi, et al. "Social Work Practice in Protective Services. " Child Welfare, 444-450+, October 1966.
The organization of the welfare department and community support of its function are the important determinants in adequate service to all clients and particularly for the maltreated child.

2028. Stringer, Elizabeth A. "Homemaker Service in Neglect and Abuse. Part 2. A Tool for Case Evaluation. " Children, 12:26-29, January-February 1965.
Stringer discusses selected cases of child abuse and neglect and explains why there is a need for a Homemaker Service. This service provides an individual to assist a social caseworker in the evaluation of family strengths and weaknesses. The homemaker will provide facts based on direct observation and can be invaluable in helping a responsible agency take appropriate action for the protection of the child.

2029. Suarez, Mary L.; Ricketson, Mary A. "Facilitating Casework with Protective Service Clients Through Use of Volunteers. " Child Welfare, 53:313-322, May 1974.
An experiment in the use of volunteers in direct protective service has proved of benefit to clients, social workers, and the agency. The informal, trusting relationship of volunteer and client met the client's personal needs, freed the caseworker for concentration on other areas, and promoted community understanding of the agency. (Journal Summary.)

2030. Surdock, P. W., Jr. A Community's Team Approach to Abuse and Neglect. Helena, Montana State Department of Social and Rehabilitation Services, Social Services Bureau, October 2, 1974. 8 p.
Montana has established eight community consultation teams to deal with child abuse and neglect. Each team consists (with some variation) of a pediatrician, county welfare social worker, county attorney, public health nurse, psychiatrist, and the representative of a local hospital, all of whom work as part-time volunteers, and a full-time professional team coordinator. Gradually, the team members have developed a sense of unity and institutional integrity, while retaining the uniqueness of each member's individual role.

2031. Swanson, Lynn D. "Role of the Police in the Protection of Children from Neglect and Abuse. " Federal Probation, 25:43-48, March 1961.
Reviews police procedures: investigation, referrals, custody, shelter, care, community planning for protection of children.

2032. Swedish Association of Psychologists. "Forbundet om Barnmisshandel. " (Society for the Prevention of Cruelty to Children), Psykolognytt, 15(6):14-16, 1969.
Procedures of the Social Administration in handling cases of child mistreatment are reviewed and criticized. Recommendations include a central committee, the type of professionals who should staff it, and other preventive measures to be pursued in the schools and other community centers.

2033. Syre, J.; Foley, F.; Zingarella, L., et al. "Community
        Committee on Child Abuse." New York State Journal of
        Medicine, 73:2071-2075, 1973.
    A four-page descriptive article on the development and work-
ings of a community child abuse committee.

2034. Tennessee State Department of Public Welfare. Study on
        Child Abuse and Child Neglect in Tennessee. Memphis,
        March 1975. 72 p.
    The services needed by and available to neglected, dependent,
and abused children and their families in Tennessee were studied by
conducting a survey of each county. Data were gathered on every
child in each active Protective Service family-child case, on each
child in a random sample of active, non-protective service family-
child cases, and on the view of knowledgeable professionals outside
the Tennessee Department of Public Welfare. Recommendations are
provided in the following areas: statewide planning and policy-making,
programming for service delivery, staffing and staff development, and
ongoing research.

2035. Texas State Department of Community Affairs. Office of
        Early Childhood Development. The Darker Side of Child-
        hood: 46 Things You Need to Know About Texas Children,
        by Barbara Langham. Austin, Texas, November 1974.
        96 p. Available from EDRS: MF-$0.76; HC-$4.43, Plus
        Postage.
    This illustrated book lists 46 facts relating to child care,
families, nutrition, health, and public services. It was prepared to
call attention to the needs of young children in Texas. The information was collected from such sources as the U.S. Census Bureau and
the State Department of Health's Bureau of Vital Statistics, as well
as from the Texas Nutrition Survey of 1968-69 and the Texas Household Survey of Families with Children Under Six.

2036. "Theory and Practice." Nursing Times, 71(18):678, May 1,
        1975.
    Failure to intervene effectively in child abuse cases due to
the lack of communication between the different caring agencies is
discussed, citing a case mishandled by the London Borough of Lam-
beth. While communication was a major problem in this case, in-
experience, excessive caseloads, ineffectual statutory powers, and
the delegation of critical interagency negotiations to one harassed
social worker played important accessory roles.

2037. Thomas, Mason P., Jr. Protective Services in North Caro-
        lina. 1976. 44 p. Institute of Government, University
        of North Carolina, Box 990, Chapel Hill, N.C. 27514.
    Protective services for abused or neglected children and dis-
abled adults.

2038. Tocchio, Octavio J. "Procedural Problems Inhibiting Effec-
        tive County and Community-Wide Resolution of Battered

Child Problems (Fresno, California). " Chart. <u>Police</u>,
14:16-21, May-June 1970.

Tocchio examines the legal and functional procedures being
utilized in Fresno County, California, for the effective control and
resolution of the battered child syndrome. He identifies several
problem areas, including the probation department, juvenile court,
police agencies, hospitals, and welfare departments and agencies.

2039. Underhill, Evi. "The Strange Silence of Teachers, Doctors,
and Social Workers in the Face of Cruelty to Children. "
<u>International Child Welfare Review</u>, 21:16-21, 1974.

The author, a former magistrate, refers to the child abuse
case of Maria Colwell and asks who is responsible--the social workers? local courts? the doctors? the teachers? She believes it
is a matter of urgency that new laws for the protection of children
be passed and that abortion laws be strengthened and made more
liberal. Social workers should absorb, contribute, and push forth
knowledge about human behavior and motivation to avoid such cases.

2040. U. S. Law Enforcement Assistance Administration. National
Institute of Law Enforcement and Criminal Justice. Office
of Technical Transfer. <u>Child Abuse Intervention:</u> Prescriptive Package. Schuchter, Arnold. December 1976.
157 p. charts. paper. $3.50. Supt. Docs.

2041. U. S. Office of Child Development. <u>Comprehensive Emergency
Services: A System Designed to Care for Children in
Crisis.</u> Department of Health, Education and Welfare,
Washington, D. C. , 1976. 35 p.

This is a report of a project in metropolitan Nashville which
uses a network of community services in child abuse and neglect
cases.

2042. Varon, Edith. <u>The Client of a Protective Agency in the Con-
text of the Community: A Field Study of the Massachusetts
Society for the Prevention of Cruelty to Children.</u> Ph. D.
Brandeis University, Waltham, Massachusetts, 1961. 312 p.
Available from University Microfilms, Order No. 62-1215.

This study was concerned with the responses of clients to an
agency, one of whose functions was social control. It assumed that
the response was influenced by community attitudes and sought to
learn the relation among the responses of agency clients, non-clients,
workers, and some other agents of social control in the community.

2043. _____ . "Communication: Client, Community, and Agency. "
<u>Social Work</u>, 51-57, April 1964.

This is a study of the work of the Massachusetts Society for
the Prevention of Cruelty to Children--assessing the degree and
quality of communication between a protective agency and its clients.

2044. Vaughan, Mark. "Hungry Children Scavenge in Portsmouth
Dust Bins. " <u>Times (London) Educational Supplement,</u>
2911:3, March 5, 1971.

Primary school children in Portsmouth who scavenge dust bins for food and who are inadequately clothed for the elements are a matter of concern to teachers who try to help them personally by small gifts. It is felt that much more liaison between schools and welfare departments is needed.

2045. Wagner, Mary; Wagner, Marsden. Child Advocacy in Den-
        mark: 70 Years of Experience with This "New" Idea.
        Copenhagen, Denmark: Copenhagen University, Institute
        of Social Medicine. Available from EDRS: MF-$0.75;
        HC-$1.50, Plus Postage.
    Denmark's child advocacy system is made up of local "kom-
mune" (county) Child and Youth Welfare Committees which watch
over the well-being of children. Each child and youth committee
serves as an effective advocate for the children of its community
in three areas: promotion, protection, and prevention. Further
details of the system are provided.

2046. Wayne, Julianne; Ebeling, Nancy B.; Avery, Nancy C. "Dif-
        ferential Groupwork in a Protective Agency." Child Wel-
        fare, 55:581-591, October 1976.
    This paper describes the evolution of a successful groupwork
program in an agency that once provided treatment through the casework method alone. (Journal Introduction.)

2047. Werble, Beatrice; Henry, Charlotte S.; Millar, Margaret W.
        "Motivation for Using Casework Services." Social Case-
        work, 39:124-138, February-March 1958.
    The authors describe a number of techniques and strategies
they have developed to overcome problems in casework treatment of
"hard to reach" families who are neglecting or abusing their children
or whose children have other problems.

2048. West, Joy. "Inadequate Mothers." (Letter) Lancet, 2(7894):
        1451, December 14, 1974.
    West deplores separation of the child from its inadequate
mother; for one thing it presupposes an inexhaustible supply of long-
term foster parents. Months of skilled nursing supervision may be
needed to bring about appreciable improvement in mother/child relationship. Despite slow gains, this method is preferable to an inevitable succession of short-term placements in care, perpetuating the
cycle of deprivation.

2049. Whitehorn, Katherine. "C&A." Spectator, 206:775-776, May
        26, 1961.
    Reports the publication of the history of the NSPCC in the
same month as the history of RSPCA. Reviewed are the attitudes
toward animals and children over the years and attempts to alleviate
these circumstances.

2050. Yelaja, Shankar A. "The Concept of Authority and Its Use
        in Child Protective Service." Child Welfare, 44:514-522,
        1965.

Discusses the fact that authority can be viewed as a power of communication and that legitimatized authority can facilitate effective therapeutic relationships with abusive/neglectful parents.

2051. Young, Leontine. Wednesday's Children: A Study of Child Neglect and Abuse. See entry 233.

2052. Yudkin, S. "Battered Baby Syndrome." (Letter). British Medical Journal, 2(5493):980-981, April 16, 1966.
When a battered child is detected, there is no justification for confining the investigation to within the hospital; other agencies are likely to have important information. The duty of the physician on detecting a battered child (in Great Britain) is to report it to the children's department of the local authority, not to the police.

PSYCHOLOGICAL ASPECTS

2053. Adams, Earl H. "Psychiatry and Protective Work. " Mental
        Hygiene, 22:625-633, October 1938.
        Adams discusses his experience serving as psychiatric con-
sultant to the Brooklyn Society for the Prevention of Cruelty to Children.   He believes that the attitude of the psychiatrist is all-impor-
tant.   He stresses the use of the psychiatric approach in dealing
with problems of cruelty to children.

2054. Allison, Patricia Kay. Exploration of a Program of Preven-
        tive Intervention in the Early Parent-Infant Interaction.
        See entry 23.

2055. American Humane Association. Children's Division. Treat-
        ing Parental Pathology, by Elizabeth Philbrick. Denver,
        Colo. 18 p. $.45.
        A superb exposition of how authority in casework is employed
in the process of treating the pathology of neglecting parents.

2056. Anthony, E. James. "It Hurts Me More Than It Hurts You
        --An Approach to Discipline as a Two-Way Process. "
        Reiss-Davis Clinic Bulletin, 7-22, Spring 1965.
        This article concerns itself with pathological expressions of
parental discipline and their negative effects on the children.

2057. Appelbaum, Alan S. "The Psychologist as a Client-Centered
        Case Consultant in Protective Service. " Journal of Ped-
        iatric Psychology, 1(2):87-90, Spring 1976.
        Contending that there is a tremendous need for well-controlled
psychological investigations of the child abuse phenomenon, the author identifies the potential roles of the psychologist as assessment
of the total family situation and the emotional and cognitive development of the abused child, psychological evaluations of parents, recommendations of meaningful interventions, and preparation of court
testimony when required.

2058. Arnold, M. "Children in Limbo. " Public Welfare, 25(3):
        221-228, July 1967.
        The child in limbo is defined as one in whom psychological
growth and development are stagnant.   Types of children in limbo
are identified.   Retrieving these children from their status could be
facilitated by increased federal funds, changes in state laws, permanent foster family care, and courageous innovation in child welfare.

2059. Asch, Stuart S. "Crib Deaths: Their Possible Relationship to Post-Partum Depression and Infanticide." Journal of the Mount Sinai Hospital, 35:214-220, 1968.
The phenomenon of sudden unexplained death in infants or "crib deaths" is described. The dynamics and phenomenology of postpartum depression is also described; and the relationship of suicide to homicide is emphasized. The hypothesis is presented that a large proportion of the annual 20,000 to 30,000 "crib deaths" in the United States are covert infanticides, manifestations of a postpartum depression in the mother. As a result of confusion in identities between mother and fetus/baby, in the pregnant or postpartum woman, infanticide may occur in place of suicide. (Journal Summary.)

2060. _____; Rubin, Lowell J. "Postpartum Reactions: Some Unrecognized Variations." American Journal of Psychiatry, 131:870-874, August 1974.
Four postpartum syndromes that are not often recognized, including infanticide and child battering, are described based on case report material. These reactions derive from experiences involving the mother's mental representations and are not confined to the biological mother. The phenomenon of successive generations of postpartum reactions in women is described and explained as being grandmother oriented. Awareness of this sequence should aid in the anticipation of postpartum psychopathology.

2061. Babow, Irving; Babow, Robin. "The World of the Abused Child: A Phenomenological Report." Life-Threatening Behavior, 4(1):32-42, Spring 1974.
A verbatim interview of a 21-year-old suicidal woman, who had a long history of abuse by her mother, is presented. Some theoretical issues concerning the scientific and clinical usefulness of phenomenological reports in the understanding of child abuse, and other aberrant behavior are briefly discussed.

2062. Becker, Walter. "Die Kindesmisshandlung--ein familien-pathologisches Syndrom" [The Battered Child--A Pathological Family Syndrome]. Zentralblatt für Jugendrecht und Jugendwohlfahrt, 62(2):66-72, 1975.
Child battering usually takes place in a sick family. Also, the socially-accepted method of physical punishment is at fault. However, psychological punishment can be even more harmful. Maltreatment of children indicates a need in the general and vocational schools to train senior classes in family life and parental duties.

2063. _____. "Zum Problem der Kindesmisshandlungen" [On the Problem of Child Abuse]. Therapie der Gegenwart, 107:135-136 passim, February 1968.
Maltreatment of children, often mentally as well as physically damaging to the child, is often a reflection of some kind of hostility between the husband and wife. The wife, being governed by subjective attitudes deals out the punishment.

2064. Bennie, E. H.; Sclare, A. B. "The Battered Child Syndrome." American Journal of Psychiatry, 125(7):975-979, 1969.
  The assailant as the patient is reviewed in ten cases of the battered child syndrome. Aggression can be acted out upon a child in persons with poor emotional control.

2065. Bloch, D. "Some Dynamics of Suffering: Effect of the Wish for Infanticide in a Case of Schizophrenia." Psychoanalytic Review, 53(4):532-554, Winter 1966-1967.
  Parental hatred of a child and the concealed wish to destroy him results in intolerable suffering in the child. The child bends all efforts toward creating the illusion of being loved. He is torn between attempting to win their love by becoming more worthy and his own murderous feelings toward his parents. He is condemned to a life of perpetual suffering.

2066. Block, Myna. "Child Abuse: What Can We Do to Stop It?" Forecast for Home Economics, 19:F24-26+, March 1974.
  Block discusses who abuses children and the common psychological/sociological/cultural traits of abusive parents, why there is an "upswing," what is being done, and ideas for help.

2067. Blumberg, Marvin L. "Psychopathology of the Abusing Parent." American Journal of Psychotherapy, 28:21-29, January 1974.
  A psychopathological study of the abusing parent is presented. The current epidemic of child abuse is discussed. Successful treatment includes psychotherapy for parents and temporary removal of the children from the homes. Personality characteristics of the abusing parent are given.

2068. Brett, Dawn Irene. The Battered and Abused Child Syndrome. D. S. W. University of California, Berkeley, 1966. 157 p. Available from University Microfilms, Order No. 67-08510.
  This study explores physical abuse of children aged five years and under as a symptom of dysfunctional family behavior. Brett concludes that the control and management of abusive behavior rests upon access to the most inarticulate and helpless age group in the population, the preschool child.

2069. Broadbent, P. "Mrs. Jones: 22 Years: Gravida 2: Potential Batterer." Health Visitor, 45:321, October 1972.

2070. Brown, John A.; Daniels, Robert. "Some Observations on Abusive Parents." Child Welfare, 47(2):89-94, February 1968.
  The authors deal with the abusive parent within a psychodynamic framework, presenting three case histories based on personal observation which illustrate some of the dynamics that seem to contribute to the aggressive act. Abusive parents are seen as emotionally empty and intellectually limited.

2071. Brozovsky, Morris; Falit, Harvey. "Neonaticide. Clinical and Psychodynamic Considerations." Journal of the American Academy of Child Psychiatry, 10:673-683, October 1971.

The killing of a newborn by its mother at birth presents a specific clinical entity, to be distinguished from the murder of an older infant by his mother. Through a consideration of two cases studied by the authors, and of cases reported in the literature, the clinical characteristics associated with neonaticide are discussed, and psychodynamic formulations are offered.

2072. Buist, Neil R. M. "Deliberate Injury of Children." (Letter). British Medical Journal, 4:739, December 22, 1973.

The author points out that in addition to physical abuse, psychological abuse is a major component of child abuse cases. While it is easier to find and care for physically abused children it is far more difficult to pinpoint psychological abuse, such as emotional deprivation. Buist appeals to everyone to become aware of this problem and to explore aspects of psychological abuse so better medical, social, and legal systems may be developed.

2073. _____. "Violent Parents." Lancet, 1:36, January 1, 1972.

Psychological abuse may in the long run cause more damage to children than the more dramatic but relatively short-lived effects of physical abuse. It is difficult to detect, and it is difficult to draw the line between sadistically motivated punishment and punishment motivated by legitimate authoritarian attitudes.

2074. Button, Jesse H.; Reivich, Ronald S. "Obsessions of Infanticide. A Review of 42 Cases." Archives of General Psychiatry, 27:235-240, August 1972.

Obsessions of infanticide were a central psychopathologic feature in 42 of 1,317 consecutive patients' evaluations at a university medical center. Among these 42 patients, diagnoses were made of 17 as schizophrenic, 11 as depressive, and 7 as obsessive-compulsive. Supportive psychotherapy as well as chemotherapy or convulsant therapy produced relatively prompt remission of symptoms. (Journal Summary Modified.)

2075. Caldwell, Bettye. "The Effect of Psychosocial Deprivation on Human Development in Infancy." Merrill Palmer Quarterly, 260-277, 1970.

After Spitz pointed out maternal deprivation, more knowledge in the field was desired. However, researching this age group was difficult because of changing mores which presented a great variable.

2076. Calef, Victor. "The Hostility of Parents to Children: Some Notes on Infertility, Child Abuse, and Abortion." International Journal of Psychoanalytic Psychotherapy, 1:76-96, February 1972.

This article is based primarily on material from four female patients. Child abuse, infertility, and abortion are considered as manifestations of hostility on the part of parents (mothers) toward their children, and all share certain psychological meanings and mechanisms. In most instances, the destructive overt behavior is carried out without conscious guilt, though secondary guilt is evident. The behavior itself is usually denied and rationalized. The crime against the child is often carried out to expunge or hide a more serious, unconscious crime. (Journal Summary Modified.)

2077. Chandra, R. K. "The Battered Child." Indian Journal of Pediatrics, 35:365, July 1968.
    Psychological considerations are as important in dealing with child abuse as physical trauma. If the physician responds to a case of abuse in a harsh punitive fashion, lasting harm may be done to the child. The child and the parents need sympathy and possibly, psychotherapy.

2078. Chazaud, J., et al. [Mental Disorders in a Child with Silverman's Syndrome]. Revue de Neuropsychiatrie Infantile et d'Hygiene Mentale de l'Enfance, 20:411-415, May 1972. (French)

2079. Child Guidance and Mental Health Clinics of Delaware County. Behavior Profile of Abused Children, by R. M. Fitti and A. Gitt. Media, Pa., April 1975. 11 p.
    Records of 28 children, aged 2-6, who had undergone psychotherapy at the Child Guidance and Mental Health Clinics of Delaware County, Pennsylvania were reviewed to construct a behavior profile of abused children.

2080. Child Welfare League of America. The Neglected Battered-Child Syndrome: Role Reversal in Parents, by Helen E. Boardman, Giulio J. Barbero, Marian G. Morris, et al. New York, 1963. 49 p.
    This pamphlet is presented in three parts: Who Insures the Child's Right to Health?; Malidentification of Mother-Baby-Father Relationships Expressed in Infant Failure to Thrive; and Role Reversal: A Concept Dealing with Neglected-Battered-Child Syndrome.

2081. Corbett, James T. "A Psychiatrist Reviews the Battered Child Syndrome and Mandatory Reporting Legislation." Northwest Medicine, 63:920-922, December 1964.
    In this critical review of professional and lay interest in child abuse and mandatory reporting legislation, Corbett suggests that the battered child syndrome should be considered as a psychiatric problem in the parent as well as a medical problem in the child. The parent should be seen as the prime target for psychiatric assistance. Referral of these matters to the police tends to further the misconception that the psychiatrically ill are primarily criminal in intent.

2082. Croughs, W., et al. [Psychogenic Growth Disorder and Battered Child Syndrome in Three Children]. Nederlands Tijdschrift voor Geneeskunde, 114:672-678, April 18, 1970. (Dutch)

2083. Currie, J. R. "A Psychiatric Assessment of the Battered
Child Syndrome. " South African Medical Journal, 44:635-
639, May 30, 1970.
A general survey of the literature is presented and a psychodynamic formulation of the battered child syndrome is offered. The
management of two cases is described and a suggested programme
for the treatment of further cases is discussed. (Journal Summary
Modified.)

2084. Curtis, George C. "Violence Breeds Violence--Perhaps?"
American Journal of Psychiatry, 120:386-387, October 1963.
One consequence of child abuse which must be considered is
the probable tendency of abused children to become tomorrow's perpetrators of crimes of violence. Theoretically, the child should have
an unusual degree of hostility; and empirically, studies cited have
led to the observation that child abuse and later expressions of violence may be interrelated.

2085. David, C. A. "The Use of the Confrontation Technique in the
Battered Child Syndrome. " American Journal of Psychotherapy, 28(4):543-552, October 1974.
This paper focuses on the treatment of the battering parent
by confrontation technique--a special technique in psychotherapy. A
case history of such a parent is detailed. The underlying psychodynamics are postulated and the verbal and nonverbal goals clarified.
Based on these an appropriate "confrontation statement" is used in on-
going psychotherapy.

2086. David, Lester. "Shocking Price of Parental Anger. " Good
Housekeeping, 158:86-87+, March 1964; also Reader's Digest, 85:181-182+, September 1964.
Some parents are able to retain a sense of proportion and
keep their actions within reasonable bounds. Those who cannot are
emotionally ill, immature, and unhinged. Often their illness is not
evident to society or to themselves. Some of the causes of child
abuse, symptoms to look for, diagnosis, and the law are covered.

2087. DeCourcy, Peter. A Silent Tragedy: Child Abuse in the
Community. See entry 58.

2088. "Der Kinder Cruelty. (Cruel Child-Rearing Practices Produced Nazi Leaders). " Human Behavior, 4:71, March
1975.
Two psychiatrists wandering through playgrounds in Germany
were struck by the violence both in the play of the children and in
the handling of the children by their parents. Deciding to undertake
a systematic comparison of aggressive behavior on the playgrounds
of different nations, German children were rated significantly more
aggressive toward one another than were Italians or Danes. A poll
in West Germany indicated that 60 percent of parents believe in
"beating, " not slapping or spanking their children. The study describes an apparent relationship between the aggression an individual
endures and that which he will mete out.

2089. Eickhoff, L. F. "Inadequate Mothers." (Letter). Lancet,
2(7889):1152-1153, November 9, 1974.
In women not predisposed to mothering at menarche, first
parturition fails to initiate full maternal powers resulting in inadequate mothering and emotional damage to the child. Such mothers
tend to be unresponsive to their infants, who in turn languish from
lack of attention, slipping into bizarre patterns of behavior and emotional dullness. Intervention to rectify inadequate mothering and its
associated damage will be more rewarding than efforts to eliminate
battered child syndrome.

2090. Feshbach, Norma D. "The Effects of Violence in Childhood."
Journal of Clinical Psychology, 2(3):28-31, Fall 1973.
A number of observations on the use of violence by parents
in childrearing are put forth by Feshbach. Laboratory studies are
cited which support the article's thesis that punishment is not conducive to learning. Moreover, physical punishment by the adult is
likely to lead to personality problems for the parent as well as the
child.

2091. Flynn, William R. "Frontier Justice: A Contribution to the
Theory of Child Battery." American Journal of Psychiatry,
127:375-379, September 1970.
Child abuse, the author believes, is often dependent upon
structural and dynamic elements within the adult. He reports two
cases of mothers who beat one of their children and concludes that
defective defense structures of the ego are frequently responsible
for child abuse. Abusing parents, he finds, tend to project their
anger onto their children, while denying and repressing it in themselves. (Journal Summary.)

2092. Fontana, Vincent J. "Children in Peril." Keynote, 3(3):12-
14, 1975.
Fontana contends that the criminal is the child who survives
his maltreatment physically, but who suffers at the hands of unre-
strained, aggressive, and psychotic adults affected by divorce, alcoholism, drug addiction, mental retardation, recurring mental illness, unemployment, and financial stress.

2093. Forrest, Tess. "The Family Dynamics of Maternal Violence."
Journal of the American Academy of Psychoanalysis, 2(3):
215-230, 1974.
The mother's ability to show tenderness to a child's needs
for care and love is a prime example of the most human expression
of rationality. When maternal deprivation intercedes, it is an assault on the integrity of the child, exemplifying irrational and dis-
integrative processes in the mother. Therapeutic efforts to revital-
ize an abusing mother and to sensitize marital partners, may help
break the cycle that visits the ills of one generation to the next.

2094. Fraiberg, Selma; Adelson, Edna; Shapiro, Vivian. "Ghosts
in the Nursery. A Psychoanalytic Approach to the Problems of Impaired Infant-Mother Relationships." Journal

of the American Academy of Child Psychiatry, 14(3):387-
421, Summer 1975.
Described are the psychoanalysis and treatment of two mothers
who allowed ghosts out of their past to enter the nursery and prevent
the bonding process between them and their infants.

2095. Fray, Pierre. "Crimes et délits par réactivité primitive"
[Crimes and Offenses by Primitive Reactivity]. Annales
Médico-Psychologiques, 1:701-708, May 1970. (P. A.)

2096. Freedman, David A. "The Battering Parent and His Child:
A Study in Early Object Relations." International Review
of Psycho-Analysis, 2(2):189-198, 1975.
Suggests the use of data about battered children to draw inferences between presumed developmental causal experiences and observed end results. The syndrome is a transmissible entity with
origins in the events of the first few postpartal months, and has
been shown to recur in a single family in as many as four successive generations. (P. A.)

2097. Friedrich, William N.; Boriskin, Jerry A. "The Role of the
Child in Child Abuse: A Review of the Literature." American Journal of Orthopsychiatry, 46(4):580-590, October
1976.
Abuse is the product of a complex set of interactions: a special child is not the sole contributor to abuse; neither is abuse exclusively the function of a parent defect.

2098. Galdston, Richard. "Dysfunctions of Parenting: The Battered
Child, the Neglected Child, the Exploited Child." In:
Modern Perspectives of International Child Psychiatry,
by John G. Howell (ed.) Edinburgh, Scotland: Oliver and
Boyd, October 1968.
Defines problems of battered, neglected or exploited child in
terms of parental dysfunction; development of child sacrificed for
maintenance of parent's psychological homeostasis.

2099. _____. "Violence Begins at Home: The Parents' Center
Project for the Study and Prevention of Child Abuse."
Journal of the American Academy of Child Psychiatry,
10:336-350, April 1971.
Experience of the Parents' Center Project for the Study and
Prevention of Child Abuse in Boston indicates that it is in the mastery of the potential for violent behavior that parents who abuse their
children have failed; they have an inability to abstract, symbolize,
or displace anger. The failure to master violence within the home
in turn serves as a basis for increased social violence.

2100. Gibbens, T. C. N. "Female Offenders." British Journal of
Hospital Medicine, 6(3):279-286, September 1971.
Female offenders tend to be more seriously disturbed mentally than male offenders and can be characterized, in terms of behavior, by the type of crime they have committed. Medical prob-

lems usually play a large part in the offenses of women. Those who
murder or abuse their children are often severely depressed or suffering from mental and physical exhaustion.

2101. Glaser, Helen H. , et al. "Physical and Psychological Development of Children with Early Failure to Thrive. "
Journal of Pediatrics, 73(5):690-698, November 1968.
Failure to thrive may be connected with emotional neglect,
however one-third of the families had no detectable evidence of physical, emotional, or psychological abnormalities. Many of the symptoms and problems of non-thriving children are included.

2102. Gluckman, L. K. "Cruelty to Children. " New Zealand Medical Journal, 67:155-159, January 1968.
The origins of cruelty to children and various subtle forms
of cruelty are discussed from the viewpoint of clinical psychiatry.
A differential diagnosis of those who maltreat children is attempted.
The maltreated child cannot be considered in isolation but often must
be considered in relation to the family group.

2103. Gosselin, J. Y.; Bury, J. A. "Approche Psychopathologique
d'un cas d'infanticide" [Psychological Approaches of a
Case of Infanticide]. Canadian Psychiatric Association
Journal, 14:473-480, October 1969.
This paper relates the case of a twenty-year-old woman who
was hospitalized after an acute psychotic reaction suddenly appeared
in the immediate postpartum period of her first pregnancy. Her baby
daughter died when nine days old; asphyxiation by talcum powder
sprinkled by the mother during a short period of confusion or dis-
sociative reactions. Discussed is a specific type of infanticide: the
"acutely psychotic filicide" committed under the influence of delir-
ium. (English Summary Modified.)

2104. Grabowska, H. [Character Disorders in a Physically Mistreated Child]. Psychiatria Polska, 2:463-465, July-September 1968. (Polish)

2105. Green, Arthur H. Child Abusing Fathers. Brooklyn, N. Y. :
Downstate Medical Center, Division of Child and Adolescent
Psychiatry, 1976. 28 p.
Typical personality traits, psychodynamics, and environmental
influences operating in child-abusing fathers are described. Similarities and contracts between child-abusing fathers and mothers are
discussed in the context of their divergent roles in the family. Based
on the data presented, a rationale for psychiatric intervention and
treatment of child-abusing fathers is suggested.

2106. _____. A Psychodynamic Approach to the Study and Treatment of Child Abusing Parents. Brooklyn, N. Y. : Downstate Medical Center, Division of Child and Adolescent
Psychiatry. (Paper presented at the American Medical
Association Annual Meeting, New York, June 26, 1973.
22 p.)

The characteristics of and potential treatments for child-abusing parents are considered psychodynamically. Abusive parents submit their children to traumatic experiences similar to those they endured during childhood. Three factors in family interaction significantly associated with child abuse are given. Case reports are cited to illustrate each factor. Obstacles to the successful treatment of such parents are explored and treatment objectives for parents are proposed.

2107. _____; Gaines, R. W.; Sandgrund, A. Psychological Sequelae of Child Abuse and Neglect. Brooklyn, N.Y.: Downstate Medical Center, Division of Child and Adolescent Psychiatry. (Paper presented at the American Psychiatric Association 127th Annual Meeting, Detroit, Mich., May 6-10, 1974. 17 p.)
The impact of chronic physical abuse and neglect on the ego functions and behavior of school-aged, inner-city children was explored. On the basis of psychiatric interviews and psychological tests, 60 abused children, 30 neglected children, and 30 normal controls were compared with respect to intellectual and ego function impairment as measured by 13 scales.

2108. Harlow, H. F. "Harlow Duplicates Battered Child Syndrome in Monkey Experiments." Psychiatric News, 11(2):16-17, 1976.
This article reviews the author's acceptance speech of the Kittay International Award for his work with primates on the "mother-infant attachment bond."

2109. Harrington, J. A. "Violence: A Clinical Viewpoint." British Medical Journal, 1:228-231, January 22, 1972.
In distinguishing between aggression and violence, Harrington discusses various theories regarding violent and aggressive behavior, including psychological, psychodynamic, personality, and biological theories, imitation, group factors, neurophysiology of violence, and alcohol and drugs. He also discusses violence to children and babies, and violence in hospitals. He believes the professional medical personnel should be constantly aware of violent and aggressive behavior and should try to prevent it.

2110. Havens, Lester L. "Youth, Violence, and the Nature of Family Life." Psychiatric Annals, 2:18-29, February 1972.
This article examines what provokes child-beating from a psychological viewpoint.

2111. Haward. "Some Psychological Aspects of Pregnancy." Midwives Chronicle, 82:199, June 1969.

2112. Helfer, Ray E.; Kempe, C. Henry, comp. The Battered Child. See entry 1512.

2113. Hyman, C. A. "A Psychological Study of Child Battering." Health Visitor, 48(8):294-296, August 1975.

2114. Johansson, A. [The Emotionally Abandoned Children]. Tidskrift for Sveriges Sjukskoterskor, 41(15):8-10, August 29, 1974.

2115. Katz, J. "The Battered Child Syndrome--Psychiatric Aspects. " (Paper Presented at the Tenth Plenary Session of the Australian Academy of Forensic Sciences Held in Sydney on 26th November 1970.) Australian Journal of Forensic Science, 3(2):71-76, 1970.
This syndrome must be seen as a multi-dimensional phenomenon with a complex set of causal factors from the psychiatric viewpoint. Although the basic cause of the abuse lies in the parental make-up, certain babies are more likely to stimulate attack. The approach to the parent must be remedial, rather than punitive.

2116. Katz, Morton Lawrence. A Comparison of Ego Functioning in Filicidal and Physically Child-Abusing Mothers. Ph. D. California School of Professional Psychology, Los Angeles, California. 1975. 105 p. Available from University Microfilms, Order No. 76-10,422.
The focus of the present investigation was to compare the ego functioning in filicidal and physically child-abusing mothers. It was hypothesized that the filicidal mother's behavior is governed by a rigid and constricted ego while the physically child-abusing mother's behavior is governed by an ego which is impulsive and has a low frustration tolerance.

2117. Kirkpatrick, Francine Karen. Patterns of Role Dominance-Submission and Conflict in Parents of Abused Children. Ph. D. California School of Professional Psychology, Los Angeles, California. 1975. 167 p. Available from University Microfilms, Order No. 76-10,423.
The significance of this study is the empirical demonstration of what has been clinically observed and suggested in the literature regarding the relationship between the child abuser and his or her spouse. The commonality of patterns of dominance and submission in the majority of parents of abused children, despite other differences, gives strong suggestion that the dynamics behind collusion between the couple in child abuse include this dominant-submissive relationship pattern.

2118. Klaus, Marshall H.; Kennell, John H. "Mothers Separated from Their Newborn Infants. " Pediatric Clinics of North America, 17:1015-1037, November 1970.
Observations in human mothers suggest that affectional bonds are forming before delivery, but that they may be easily altered in the first days of life. A preliminary inspection of fragments of available data suggests that maternal behavior may be altered in some women by a period of separation, just as infant behavior is affected by isolation from the mother. (Journal Summary Modified.)

2119. Kline, Donald; Christiansen, James. Educational and Psychological Problems of Abused Children. Final Report. See entry 2310.

2120. Kreindler, Simon. "Psychiatric Treatment for the Abusing Parent and the Abused Child. Some Problems and Possible Solutions." Canadian Psychiatric Association Journal, 21(5):275-280, August 1976.
Psychological characteristics of abusing parents are discussed. In the classical sense, they are not "good patients" because they may refuse to be involved in treatment. Abused children may manifest any type of psychopathology. Some of the major problems encountered in providing treatment for abusing parents and their children are given.

2121. Künzel, E. [Juvenile Delinquency and Neglect. Their Origin and Treatment from the Viewpoint of Depth Psychology]. Praxis der Kinderpsychologie und Kinderpsychiatrie, 1-136, 1965. (German)

2122. Lansky, Shirley B.; Erickson, Harold M., Jr. "Prevention of Child Murder. A Case Report." Journal of the American Academy of Child Psychiatry, 13(4):691-698, Autumn 1974.
Presented here is a case involving family dynamics illustrative of the "Medea complex" in which the wish to kill the husband's favorite child was manifested in the hospital, a hitherto unreported phenomenon. The successful treatment of the family is examined to demonstrate how a severely disturbed family can be salvaged and developed into a nurturing, supportive unit.

2123. Laury, Gabriel V. "The Battered-Child Syndrome: Parental Motivation, Clinical Aspects." Bulletin of the New York Academy of Medicine, 46:676-685, September 1970.
There are many motivations for child battering. Parents give many explanations, but the underlying motivations are multiple and often unknown to the parent. Usually, they reflect deeper seated hostility in the parent.

2124. _____; Meerloo, Joost A. M. "Mental Cruelty and Child Abuse." Psychiatric Quarterly Supplement, 41(2):203-254, 1967.
Mental cruelty as a form of child abuse is discussed. Presents examples of forms of child abuse, such as parental deprivation, excessive overconcern, and perfectionalism beyond the capabilities of the child. Suggests treatment to stop cycle of child abuse.

2125. _____; _____. "Subtle Types of Mental Cruelty to Children." Child and Family, 6:28-34, 1967.
Information on the extent of mental cruelty to which parents subject their children is provided. The authors explain how children, subjected to mental cruelty, often become emotionally crippled, and consequently, turn against their own children. Prevention for this type of child is suggested as the key course of action, with treatment and mental health education for the whole family.

2126. Leavitt, Jerome Edward, comp. The Battered Child: Selected Readings. See entry 521.

2127. Lebensohn, Z. M. "Legal Abortion as a Positive Mental
       Health Measure in Family Planning. " Comprehensive Psy-
       chiatry, 14(2):95-98, March-April 1973.
       The birth of an unwanted child has been shown to result in
abuse, neglect, or abandonment of the child, behavioral and psychiatric problems, and economic hardship. Because no contraceptive is
foolproof and because dangerous illegal abortions will flourish in the
absence of a legal alternative, abortion should be legalized for family planning purposes.

2128. Lukianowicz, Narcyz. "Parental Maltreatment of Children. "
       British Journal of Social Psychiatry, 3(3):189-195, 1969.
       By a simple classification of various forms of maltreatment
of children, the dynamics of the phenomenon are presented. As
clinical examples, four cases are summarized to illustrate four different types of maltreatment. Milder forms of cruelty pose inherent
difficulties in recognition.

2129. Lynch, Margaret A.; Lindsay, Janet; Ounsted, C. "Tran-
       quilizers Causing Aggression. " (Letter). British Medical
       Journal, 1(5952):266, February 1, 1975.
       The authors discuss how the use of drugs sometimes leads
mothers to abuse their children. Benzodiazepines and antidepres-
sants make them aggressive and hostile. Then they take out their
hostilities on their children. They are then usually treated for isolated anxiety or for depression. The authors advise that prescribing
of drugs should be done with extreme caution and knowledge.

2130. Majláth, György. "A sértett gyermekkoruak szavahihetőségé-
       ről és a megítélés általános lehetőségeiről az igazsagugyi
       pszichólogiai szakértol tevékenységben a megrontás és vér-
       fertőzes bűntettében" [On the Veracity of Injured Juveniles
       and on the General Possibilities of Drawing up an Adequate
       Psychological Expertise in Cases of Deprivation and Incest].
       Pszichológiai Tanulmányok, 11:623-640, 1968. (Hungarian)

2131. Malone, C. "Safety First: Comments on the Influence of
       External Danger in the Lives of Children of Disorganized
       Families. " American Journal of Orthopsychiatry, 39:3-12,
       1966.
       Descriptive findings on the psychological characteristic and
developmental problems of a group of 21 preschool children who were
raised in homes where external danger from parents abuse was present.

2132. Martin, Harold P. , ed. The Abused Child: A Multidisciplin-
       ary Approach to Developmental Issues and Treatment. See
       entry 1355.

2133. _____; Rodeheffer, Martha A. "The Psychological Impact
       of Abuse on Children. " Journal of Pediatric Psychology,
       1(2):12-16, Spring 1976.
       The authors state that the abused child has psychological

wounds as incapacitating and chronic as his physical wounds. They indicate that some of the unusual behaviors of the abused child are important adaptations with survival value within the abusive environment. However, those very adaptations play an active role in the etiology of developmental delays so frequently observed in abused children.

2134. Maurer, Adah. "Corporal Punishment." American Psychologist, 29(8):614-626, August 1974.
Two sets of literature are examined: the laboratory literature as analyzed by Johnston and the field study literature. It is shown that the laboratory literature has under-emphasized the reality of educational and child-rearing customs, while the field study literature has underestimated the scientific aspects of the data. Recent studies indicate a near perfect correlation between the amount and severity of physical punishment endured by a child and severity of antisocial aggressiveness that he displays during adolescence.

2135. Medveckỷ, J.; Kafka, J. [Psychiatric Aspects of Neonaticide Committed by Mothers]. Ceskoslovenská Psychiatrie, 68: 16-22, February 1972.

2136. Meerlo, J. A. [Mental Cruelty]. Nederlands Tijdschrift voor Geneeskunde, 113:2238-2239, December 13, 1969. (Dutch)

2137. Milowe, Irvin D.; Lourie, Reginald S. "The Child's Role in the Battered Child Syndrome." Journal of Pediatrics, 65(6):1079-1081, December 1964.
A discussion of the contributions which some children seem to make in the etiology of child battering in the context of a classification of abusive parents into four categories.

2138. _____; _____. "Some Provocative and Controversial Mental Health Problems Posed by the Battered Child Syndrome." In: Proceedings of the Third Annual Conference: Mental Career Development Program, May 26-28, 1964. p. 70-76. Washington, D. C., National Institute of Mental Health, Publ. No. 1245, 1964.

2139. Mohr, J. W.; McKnight, C. K. "Violence as a Function of Age and Relationship with Special Reference to Matricide." Canadian Psychiatric Association Journal, 16(1):29-53, 1971.
The author discusses the risk that children may be killed by parents suffering from a severe depressive illness. This risk becomes grave when the patient is actively suicidal. A case is presented in detail.

2140. Money, J., et al. "Folie à deux in the Parents of Psychosocial Dwarfs: Two Cases." Bulletin of the American Academy of Psychiatry and the Law, 4(4):351-362, 1976.

2141. Moore, Jean G. "Yo-Yo Children: Victims of Matrimonial Violence." Child Welfare, 54:557-566, September 1975.

An analysis of matrimonial psychopathology reveals that children are often used as pawns and scapegoats in husband-wife violence. This study was conducted by a British agency which is working out treatment approaches to this facet of the child neglect and child abuse spectrum.

2142. _____. "The Yo-Yo Syndrome: A Matter for Interdisciplinary Concern. " Medicine, Science, and the Law, 15(4): 234-236, 1975.
The effects of violent domestic situations on children are examined. This effect is divided into four categories: turned against self; school problems; scapegoating, and pawns. Children most favored by one parent are rejected by the other. As pawns, they are perceived as irrelevant to the central conflict and are used as weapons in the marital war.

2143. Morris, Marian G. "Psychological Miscarriage: An End to Mother Love. " Transaction, 8-13, January-February 1966.
This article examines the dynamics of maternal rejection.

2144. _____. Gould, Robert W. "Neglected Children. Role Reversal: A Necessary Concept in Dealing with the 'Battered Child Syndrome'" American Journal of Orthopsychiatry, 33(2): 298-299, March 1963. (Reprinted in The Neglected Battered Child Syndrome. New York: Child Welfare League of America, July 1963. 49 p.)
The parent sees the child as having adult powers for deliberately displeasing or judging, similar in attitude to their own parents who could not be satisfied and who did not satisfy. Brutality seems their prerogative, as it was that of their parents, whom they hated. The child becomes an easy target in acting out their sufferings from other life situations. Understanding this role reversal concept is necessary to assess parents' attitudes and to help them.

2145. Nau, Elisabeth. "Das Delikt der Kindesmisshandlung in forensisch-psychiatrischer Sicht" [The Crime of Child Abuse from a Forensic-Psychiatric Viewpoint]. Munchener Medizinische Wochenschrift, 106:972-974, May 22, 1964.
In child ill treatment, the particular situation, the close culprit-victim relationship, the peculiar personality of the culprit, and the low tendency of the neighborhood to inform the police render the discovery of the crime difficult. The calamitous effect of repeated emotional and physical injuries was demonstrated in a high percentage of future criminals. (English Summary Modified.)

2146. New York State Assembly. Selected Committee on Child Abuse. Report on the Feasibility of Studying the Relationship Between Child Abuse and Later Socially Deviant Behavior. See entry 2245.

2147. Ney, P. G. "Four Types of Hyperkinesis. " Canadian Psychiatric Association Journal, 19(6):543-550, December 1974.

2148. Nichamin, Samuel J. "Battered Child Syndrome and Brain Dysfunction. " (Letter). Journal of the American Medical Association, 223:1390, March 19, 1973.
Nichamin believes that in certain instances the abused child, in some fashion, exerts a provocative effect on an unstable, emotionally labile parent, precipitating a violent assault of variable degree by the latter. He recommends the detection and medical treatment of young adults with brain dysfunction, learning disabilities, and emotional problems as a way of lessening the incidence of battered infants and children.

2149. Ostow, M. "Parents' Hostility to Their Children. " Israel Annals of Psychiatry and Related Disciplines, 8:3-21, April 1970.

2150. Ounsted, C.; Oppenheimer, R.; Lindsay, J. "Aspects of Bonding Failure. The Psychopathology and Psychotherapeutic Treatment of Families of Battered Children. " Developmental Medicine and Child Neurology, 16:447-456, 1974.
Relates lack of affectional relationship of parent to infant with severe battering of child. Describes in-patient and out-patient therapy. Describes state of a "frozen watchfulness" seen in abused children. Links behavior sequences with psycho-dynamic relationships.

2151. Paulson, Morris J.; Afifi, Abdelmonen A.; Chaleff, Anne, et al. "An MMPI Scale for Identifying 'At Risk' Abusive Parents. " Journal of Clinical Child Psychology, 4(1): 22-24, 1975.
The present study represents the use of an accredited psychometric instrument for the psychological assessment of a specific population of subjects whose reason for referral is maltreatment and abuse of children. The success of this scale in identification, prediction, and treatment of abusive parents will contribute greatly to the ultimate goals of prevention of physical and psychological abuse of children. (Journal Conclusion.)

2152. _____; Blake, Phillip R. "The Abused, Battered and Maltreated Child: A Review. " Trauma, 9:1-3, December 1967.

2153. Pereira, Francisco. [Applications of Psychology of Learning to the Rehabilitation of the "gamin. "] Revista Latinoamericana de Psicologica, 7(3):391-399, 1975.
The principles of the psychology of learning can be applied to the problem of the "gamin, " the abandoned child of the Colombian Cities. Several points in which psychology can contribute to understanding and solving this important social problem are described. English Summary. (P. A.)

2154. Peterson, Karen L. "Contributions to an Abused Child's Un-

lovability: Failure in the Developmental Tasks and in the Mastery of Trauma. " M. S. W. Thesis. Smith College Studies in Social Work, 44(1):24-25, 1973.
The trauma of child abuse and subsequent placement was examined in relation to normal developmental tasks of childhood and early adolescence. A theoretical view of the abused child's attempt to master and to integrate psychosexual, psychosocial, affective and cognitive developmental tasks is presented, and the child's vulnerability to psychological injury and his innate resiliency to psychological injury are demonstrated.

2155. _____. "There's a Link Between Animal Abuse and Child Abuse. " PTA Magazine, 68:14-16, June 1974.
A free-lance writer quotes Phyllis Wright, internationally known animal welfare expert, who contends that she's 100 percent sure there's a connection between children who abuse animals and adults who abuse children. The author explores the theory through conversations with other animal welfare experts, police officials, authorities on the battered child syndrome, a contention of Margaret Mead, and beliefs of other authorities. Children who take out their frustrations on pets are many times abused themselves and if not checked and helped become our future criminals.

2156. Póltawska, W. , et al. [Results of the Psychiatric Studies of Persons Born or Imprisoned in Childhood in Nazi Concentration Camps]. Przeglad Lekarski, 22:21-36, 1966. (Polish)

2157. Rheingold, Joseph C. The Fear of Being a Woman: A Theory of Maternal Destructiveness. New York: Grune and Stratton, 1964. 756 p.
Part I of this book traces the destructive effects of certain maternal attitudes and childrearing practices.

2158. Richette, Lisa Aversa. The Throwaway Children. See entry 1104.

2159. Rigler, David; Rigler, Marilyn. Persistent Effects of Early Experience. Los Angeles, California, Los Angeles Children's Hospital, Psychiatric Division, 1975. 14 p. (Presented at the Society for Research and Child Development, Denver, Colorado, April 1975.)

2160. Rindfleisch, Nolan. A Study of the Influence of Background and Organizational Factors in Direct Care Workers' Attitudes Toward Use of Physical Force on Children. Ph. D. Case Western Reserve University, Cleveland, Ohio, June 1976.
In this ex post facto field study child abuse was viewed in terms of Goode's multidimensional model. Role-playing techniques were used to examine voluntary harm-doing behavior. The dependent variable was level of justified force. Findings indicated that the model can be used to investigate the dynamics of the child-abuse

problem that an unidimensional approach ignores. Sanctioned use of physical force was substantially mediated by the organizational context and then expressed in individual attitudes toward the use of force.

2161. Riscalla, Louise Mead. The Professional's Role and Perspectives on Child Abuse. See entry 1759.

2162. Roberts, Albert F., ed. Childhood Deprivation. See entry 649.

2163. Rodenburg, Martin. "Child Murder by a Depressed Mother: A Case Report." Canadian Psychiatric Association Journal, 16:49-53, 1971.
Describes the risk factor of child murder involved when a parent is depressed or psychotic. Presents a case history of child murder, with a psychological interpretation of the incident.

2164. _____. "Child Murder by Depressed Parents." Canadian Psychiatric Association Journal, 16(1):41-48, February 1971.
Reviews the dynamics of child murder by depressed parents, and presents several factors of murders performed by parents in a depressed state. Parental factors can be recognized and specified and this may help in child abuse prevention.

2165. Rogers, Sinclair. Isolation in Early Childhood. (Paper presented to the Select Committee on Violence in the Family, The House of Commons, May 1976.) 14 p. Available from EDRS: MF-$0.83; HC-$1.67, Plus Postage.
Presented is information on isolated children. A study being undertaken to examine the role of isolation in reported cases of child abuse and neglect is described. Emphasized are the effects of extreme isolation on language and psychological development.

2166. Rolston, Richard Hummel. The Effect of Prior Physical Abuse on the Expression of Overt and Fantasy Aggressive Behavior in Children. See entry 189.

2167. Rosenberg, Judith Elise; Cook, JoAnn Hohman. "Differences in Parenting and Subsequent Character Structure Development in Child Abuse and Child Neglect." Journal of Pediatric Psychology, 1(2):72-75, Spring 1976.
Using a theoretical model which sees child abuse and neglect as polarized experiences of parenting paralleling polarized experiences of being, the co-authors examine three developmental areas of parenting: initial bonding; development of trust; and development of self-worth. In contrasting these experiences with an ideal model, these are implications for specific and differentiated psychotherapeutic treatment.

2168. Rosenblatt, S.; Schaeffer, D.; Rosenthal, J. S. "Effects of Diphenylhydantoin on Child Abusing Parents: A Preliminary

Report. " Current Therapeutical Research, Clinical and Experimental, 19(3):332-336, 1976.
This article reports on the use of Diphenylhydantoin (DPH) in treating anxiety, depression, and somatic symptoms of child abusing parents. It was found to have a significant short term effect. So far as attitudes toward children, aggressiveness, impulsiveness, or hostility is concerned, no effects were noted.

2169. Schreiber, Flora Rheta. Sybil. See entry 195.

2170. Schwartz, Emanuel K. "Child Murder Today (Playwrights and Psychologists View Filicide in Life, Drama). The Human Context, 4(2):360-361, 1972.
The denial by parents of their hostile feelings towards their own children was a dominant theme of a weekend seminar on filicide attended by playwrights and psychologists. All of the playwrights had written at least one play on the subject. Doubts were expressed regarding public acceptance of and producer interest in such plays. The planners of the seminar feel that playwrights can make a major contribution to help save children by heightening awareness of filicide and other forms of child abuse and neglect.

2171. Schwartz, L. "Psychiatric Case Report of Nutritional Battering with Implications for Community Agencies. " Community Mental Health Journal, 3:163-169, 1967.
A psychiatric case report of a child starved by parents. Presents implications for community involvement.

2172. Shengold, Leonard. "The Effects of Over-Stimulation: Rat People. " International Journal of Psycho-Analysis, 48:403-415, 1967.
A "rat person" syndrome has been observed in adults who were the victims of childhood beatings or sexual attack, particularly prolonged incestuous relationships. This syndrome is described in detail. Parallels may be drawn between the patient and the protagonists of Sophocles' Oedipus Rex and Orwell's 1984. Several case histories are available for illustration of the syndrome.

2173. Shenken, L. "Proceedings: A Child Is Being Beaten. " Australian and New Zealand Journal of Psychiatry, 7:243-248, December 1973.
It was Freud's conclusion that the beating fantasy was a regression to the preoedipal, anal sadistic phase of libido development during which the patients were fixated. Verification of this assumption would seem to be provided through the present case material. Psychoanalytic psychotherapy in the treatment of personality disorder is stressed.

2174. Silver, Henry K. ; Finkelstein, Marcia. "Deprivation Dwarfism. " The Journal of Pediatrics, 70(3, 1):317-324, March 1967.
Deprivation dwarfism is a physical and psychological syndrome characterized by extreme short stature, voracious appetite, and

marked delay in skeletal maturation. The condition develops in children who have suffered from emotional and psychological deprivation.
Emotional disorders in the parents of grossly disturbed family relationships are generally present.

2175. Silver, Larry B. "The Psychological Aspects of the Battered
        Child and His Parents." Clinical Proceedings, 24:355-364,
        December 1968.
        Several criteria may be used in the hospital to distinguish
parents and children involved in child abuse from those involved in
accidental injury. The reactions of the non-abusive parent and the
abusive parent are given, as well as the reactions of the nonabused
and the abused child. Several other general observations are made.

2176. Sint-Van Den Heuvel, M. K.; Everts-Goddard, J. E., eds.
        Kindermishandeling [Child Abuse]. Van Loghum Slaterus,
        1974.
        This book comprises several papers on maltreatment of chil-
dren and discusses medico-psychiatric and legal aspects as well as
various types of aid in this respect. Suggestions are made on possible ways to prevent maltreatment of children and to deal with its
various consequences. The chapters concern: interdisciplinary cooperation; medico-psychiatric and legal aspects in The Netherlands;
the problem of child abuse in relation to upbringing and education in
general; mental cruelty; various types of aid in The Netherlands and
abroad.

2177. Sloboda, Sharon B. "The Children of Alcoholics: A Neglected
        Problem." Hospital and Community Psychiatry, 25(9):605-
        606, 1974.
        Sloboda says that most experts in the field of alcoholism agree
that treating the alcoholic without including the family is ludicrous.
Yet far too often children are left out of family therapy sessions.
She reviews some of the psychological and sociological implications
for the child.

2178. Smith, Selwyn M. The Battered Child Syndrome. See entry
        1553.

2179. Spinetta, John J.; Rigler, David. "The Child-Abusing Par-
        ent: A Psychological Review." Psychological Bulletin,
        77:296-304, April 1972.
        Presents an overview of recent literature on the parents of
battered children. A critique is made of a recent demographic survey in light of the data.

2180. Steele, Brandt F. "Working with Abusive Parents. A Psy-
        chiatrist's View." Children Today, 4(3):3-5, 44, May-June
        1975.
        Abusing parents are analyzed through a psychiatrist's eyes.
It is found they have about the normal incidence of neuroses, psychoses, and character disorders which exist, but there is a small
group of abusive parents (less than 10 percent) who suffer from

serious psychiatric disorders. These parents should be screened
out at regular treatment centers and treated as in-patients or out-
patients. Understanding is most important and should be displayed
by therapists when working with abusive parents.

2181. _____. Working with Abusive Parents from a Psychiatric
      Point of View. Washington, D. C. , U. S. DHEW: National
      Center on Child Abuse and Neglect. Report No. DHEW-
      OHD-76-30070, 1975. 25 p. Price: $.45.
   Child abuse and neglect is seen as an abnormal parenting behavior which has resulted from neglect or abuse of the abusive parents during their early lives. This is one of six booklets published
by the National Center, three of which are concerned with the role
of professionals and the community team approach and three of which
deal with diagnosis, working with abusive parents, and setting up a
central registry.

2182. Steinmetz, Suzanne K. , comp. "Violent Parents. " See entry
      2417.

2183. Stoerger, R. "Die kindesmisshandlung in forensich psychia-
      trischer sicht" [Maltreatment of Children from the Forensic
      Psychiatric Viewpoint]. Medizinische Welt, 38:2083-2088,
      September 20, 1969.
   The psychiatric type of those responsible for the maltreatment of children and their possible motives are discussed in detail.
Forensic methods of examination are touched upon. Preventive possibilities are listed.

2184. Stone, F. H. "Psychological Aspects of Early Mother-Infant
      Relationships. " British Medical Journal, 4:224-226, Oc-
      tober 23, 1971.
   Stone focuses upon the relationship of the mother and the infant and how they react to each other. He discusses the various
psychological needs of the mother, the infant, and the needs of the
two together. He points out that child battering may stem from the
unwanted child, the fatherless child, or the child whose mother is
"fed up" with the pains of caring for a child.

2185. Straus, M. "Some Antecedents of Physical Punishment: A
      Linkage Theory Interpretation. " Journal of Marriage and
      the Family, 33:658-663, 1971.
   Presentation of a linkage theory which holds that physical
punishment by parents is influenced by parents' conception of the
roles the child is to play as an adult.

2186. Straus, P.; Kreisler, L. "Le Jeune Enfant brutalise" [Bru-
      tally Treated Young Children]. Gazette Medicale de
      France, 79(14):2313-2326, 1972.
   Diagnosis of maltreatment is not always evident even though
symptoms may be numerous. Rarely mental cases, many child
abusers belong to the category of social cases. They are also
found in other classes of society--cultural and wealthy. Some grave

event in early childhood is behind the diversity of circumstances but
all have in common aggressiveness with perversion of the feelings
that the normal adult person has towards the young child.

2187. Stuchlik, S. "K Problematice Patologie Osobnosti Agresív-
ních Rodičů" [Pathologic Personality of Aggressive Par-
ents]. Ceskoslovenska Pediatrie, 26:247-251, May 1971.
(Czech)

2188. Tascari, A. "The Abused Child." Journal of the Iowa Medical Society, 62:229-232, 1972.
A brief description of the type of parent who is likely to be
an abuser and the characteristics of the typically abused child. Outlines the common types of injuries and reporting procedures for
physicians.

2189. Tizard, Jack. "Three Dysfunctional Environmental Influences
in Development: Malnutrition, Non-Accidental Injury and
Child-Minding." Postgraduate Medical Journal, 51 Suppl
2: Suppl 15:19-27, 1975.
Along with malnutrition and dysfunctional child-minding practices, various aspects of non-accidental injury to children are discussed with regard to the normal development of children. Tizard
emphasizes the need for a psychiatric explanation of non-accidental
injury for clinical purposes, treatment and prevention of battered
children.

2190. Togut, Myra R.; Allen, John E.; Lelchuck, Louis. "A Psychological Exploration of the Nonorganic Failure-to-Thrive
Syndrome." Developmental Medicine and Child Neurology,
11:601-607, October 1969.
An exploratory study of psycho-social factors in non-organic
failure-to-thrive infants is presented, focusing on familial relationships and other pertinent environmental factors implicated in this
disorder. It is apparent that a comprehensive medical work-up is
mandatory for every patient in whom this diagnosis is entertained.
The diagnosis of nonorganic Failure-to-Thrive Syndrome appears to
require the identification of three primary elements. These are
given. (Journal Summary Modified.)

2191. Tooley, Kay. "The Choice of a Surviving Sibling as 'Scapegoat' in Some Cases of Maternal Bereavement: A Case
Report." Journal of Child Psychology and Psychiatry,
16:331-339, October 1975.
This paper presents a description of a pathological variation
of the mourning process in mothers who have suffered a narcissis-
tically damaging psychologic or actual loss of a child. The parent-
child estrangement continues for years after the trauma with an ex-
tremity and severity that often necessitates court intervention. Counseling by available professionals at the time of bereavement would
be both economical and effective in forestalling this variety of pathological family scapegoating. (Journal Summary Modified.)

2192. Treffers, Ph. D. A.; DeLeeuw, R.; Smit Beek, E. "Premature Birth from the Point of View of Child Psychiatry." Nederlands Tijdschrift voor Geneeskunde, 120(32):1371-1379, 1976.

On the basis of the family's reaction to the birth of a premature or dysmature child, an attempt is made to explain the child psychiatric problems.

2193. Wasserman, Sidney. "The Abused Parent of the Abused Child." Children, 14:175-179, September 1967.

Wasserman describes what goes on inside the "battering parent" and why he abuses his child. Rejection from parents, uninhibited rage, and the inability to have a close relationship are cited as possible causes leading to the "battering parent." Also discussed are some treatment processes for the parent, such as group therapy, individual therapy, and community therapy.

2194. Waterman, J. "Role Reversal: A Necessary Concept in Dealing with a Battered Child Syndrome." American Journal of Orthopsychiatry, 3:298-300, 1963.

A psychodynamic explanation of "role reversal" in battering parents.

2195. Welsh, Ralph S. "Violence, Permissiveness and the Overpunished Child." Journal of Pediatric Psychology, 1(2): 68-71, Spring 1976.

Based upon 1800 delinquent evaluations, Welsh concludes that severe parental punishment is not only a significant precursor of delinquent behavior but appears to be the only variable to be consistently found in the background of each recidivist male delinquent studied. In effect, the juvenile delinquent appears to be on a continuum, beginning at the level of the battered child and extending upward to the level of the overpunished child.

2196. "Who Batters Children?" Human Behavior, 4:51, January 1975.

Psychologist John A. Haberland of California's Orange County Medical Center devised the "Child Abuse Rating Scale" to ferret out actual and would-be battering parents. The test was tried out on 30 parents and proved to be an accurate predictor of child abuse. Provided are examples.

2197. Wille, Reinhard, et al. "Kindesmisshandlungen. Psychosoziale Konstellationen und Katamnesen" [Child Abuse. Psychosocial Situations and Case Histories]. Munchener Medizinische Wochenschrift, 109:989-997, May 5, 1967.

Maltreatment of children frequently is an expression of a structural defect within the family. Its psycho-dynamics are specific. Certain psychosocial situations may be recognized only with the aid of social agencies. Every physician should consider the etiology of certain child injuries from the point of view of suspicion of maltreatment. Placing the endangered child in a home must be considered in the case of disharmonic "ambivalent" maltreaters, who are discontented with themselves. (English Abstract Modified.)

2198. Williams, Arthur H. "The Mind of a Child Murderer."
    Mental Health, 26:6-8, 1967.
    A great deal of emotion, prejudice, and rage faces the man who kills a child. Dr. Arthur Hyatt Williams, consultant psychiatrist at the Tavistock Clinic and Oakwood Hospital, is a psychotherapist at Wormwood Scrubs prison. Here, he analyzes the public reaction and the motives of the offender. (Journal Summary.)

2199. Woolcott, N. "The 'Stranger' Mother." Australasian Nurses Journal, 3(10):39, passim, May 1974.

2200. Worling, R. "Maternal Deprivation--A Re-Examination."
    Canada's Mental Health, 14:3-11, 1966.
    Discusses childhood psychiatric illness as related to maternal deprivation. Concludes that lack of love and attention in early years is related to psychiatric disturbance.

2201. Wright, Logan. "Psychologic Aspects of the Battered Child Syndrome." Southern Medical Bulletin, 58(3):14-18, 1970.
    Discusses the psychological aspects of child abuse, including the personalities of the children and parents based on a 10-year follow-up study of abused children. Over extended periods of observation the parents were a paradox in that while significantly disturbed and capable of abusing their children they were also adept at convincing others that they were not disturbed and not capable of abusive behavior. Group therapy, home visitation, birth control, and medical consultation are presented as remedial courses of action.

RESEARCH

2201a. "Aid to Abused and Neglected Children: A Los Angeles Project to Assess Service." Intellect, 102:415, April 1974.
    A project to assess the effectiveness of a community program for physically abused and neglected children and their parents will be undertaken in Los Angeles. The project will be funded over a five-year period by NIMH and Mental Health Administration. The program will assess the impact of making available to the children and their parents extensive medical, legal, and social assistance.

2202. Allison, Patricia Kay. Exploration of a Program of Preventive Intervention in the Early Parent-Infant Interaction. D. S. W. See entry 23.

2203. Auerbach, Mary C., et al. The Abused Child in Washington, D. C., June 1, 1963-November 30, 1964. Master's Thesis, Howard University School of Social Work, June 1965.

2204. Baher, Edwina; Hyman, Clare; Jones, Carolyn, et al. At Risk: An Account of the Work of the Battered Child Research Department, NSPCC. London: Routledge & Kegan Paul, 1976. 246 p. (Routledge Direct Editions)
    The authors of this volume, all members of the NSPCC, Battered Child Research Department, have, in a comprehensive way, presented results of their treatment of abusive parents. The philosophy of a total family approach uses a variety of treatment modalities and very much includes the needs of the child. The findings have broad implications for general adoption of these methods by local child protection authorities as well as by private agencies in the field of family care. (From Preface by C. Henry Kempe.)

2205. Berg, Pamela Ione. Parental Expectations and Attitudes in Child-Abusing Families. Ph. D. See entry 33.

2206. Billingsley, Andrew. The Role of the Social Worker in a Child Protective Agency: A Comparative Analysis. See entry 1842.

2207. Bradford, Kirk A. Critical Factors that Affect the Judgments of Protective Services Workers in Child Abuse Situations. See entry 1847.

2208. Branigan, Eileen, et al. An Exploratory Study of the Neglected-Battered Child Syndrome. See entry 560.

2209. Brett, Dawn Irene. The Battered and Abused Child Syndrome.
       See entry 2068.

2210. Brown, Marsena; Pappas, Margaret McCullough. Eight Chil-
       dren with Suspected Inflicted Injury: A Follow-Up Pilot
       Study. See entry 38.

2211. Burns, Alice; Feldman, Myra; Kaufman, Anita, et al. Child
       Abuse and Neglect in Suffolk County. Setauket, N. Y.:
       Edmond Publishing Co., 1973. 39 p. (Paper)
       This report was designed to evaluate reporting of child abuse
and neglect in Suffolk County. Reporting methods and procedures of
hospitals, the health department, and the Department of Social Services having the most contact with children were studied. All evidence indicated the problem is large enough to warrant an evaluation
of the current methods used in casefinding, identification, reporting,
prevention and education.

2212. "Child Abuse Study." The Atlantic Advocate, 63:50, August
       1973.
       A two-year study of child abuse in Nova Scotia, carried out
by students from Dalhousie University's law and medical schools and
the Maritime School of Social Work, has resulted in the release of
a comprehensive report outlining causes and possible cures for the
problem. Major recommendations are included.

2213. Clark, Karen Noelle. Knowledge of Child Development and
       Behavior Interaction Patterns of Mothers Who Abuse Their
       Children. See entry 573.

2214. Cohen, M. I. Neglect and Abuse of Children in the Middle
       Class. See entry 574.

2215. Cohn, Anne Harris. Assessing the Impact of Health Pro-
       grams Responding to New Problems: The Case of Child
       Abuse and Neglect. See entry 1247.

2216. Cunningham, Pennie; Gebel, Marilyn; Richter, Aleda. Treat-
       ment Methods with Child Abusers: An Experience Study.
       See entry 1253.

2217. Dalhousie University. School of Law. Child Abuse in Nova
       Scotia. A Research Project About Battered and Maternally
       Deprived Children. Halifax, Nova Scotia, 1973. 292 p.
       The causes and treatment of cases involving battered and
emotionally deprived children in Nova Scotia were investigated, and
an interdisciplinary approach to the research of problems in child
abuse was developed. Attitude survey data are presented on a wide
range of topics, including beliefs regarding the extent and seriousness of child abuse, case dispositions, etiological factors in child
abuse, the use of violence in child rearing, and child abuse legislation. Recommendations are offered regarding a central registry,
a child's advocate, the rights of children, elimination of corporal

punishment in the schools, the family court, legal counsel, preventive services, need for more social workers, and other areas pertaining to the identification, prevention and treatment of child abuse.

2218. Davoren, Elizabeth. The Battered Child in California: A
Survey. San Francisco Consortium, California, March
1973. 17 p.
Information gathered from a questionnaire sent to all California county welfare and probation departments and hospitals reporting more than 1,000 births per year and from telephone interviews of key people interested in child abuse indicated that many people were unaware of the problem and those who were aware were reluctant to confront cases for various given reasons. What needs to be done is given and current programs and projects in California are listed and briefly described.

2219. Dawe, Kathleen E. "Child Abuse in Nova Scotia." Australian Paediatric Journal, 9:294-296. December 1973.

2220. Detert, Anne; Richardson, Barbara. "Maltreatment of Children." See entry 1266.

2221. Draft Report of Phase I of the Family Development Study.
See entry 61.

2222. Fergusson, David M.; Fleming, Joan; O'Neill, David P.
Child Abuse in New Zealand. See entry 594.

2223. Fitch, Michael J.; Cadol, Robert V.; Goldson, Edward; et al.
"Cognitive Development of Abused and Failure-to-Thrive
Children." Journal of Pediatric Psychology, 1(2):32-37,
Spring 1976.
Reported is a research project in the city and county of Denver, the four-year longitudinal study of the cognitive development of children hospitalized for nonorganic Failure-to-Thrive or Non-Accidental Trauma. Fitch and associates conclude that: children who fail to thrive were hospitalized at a younger age than those who were non-accidentally traumatized; abused children appear to be at greater risk for scoring lower in more areas of cognitive development than are those who have not been abused; and children who fail to thrive may be at greater risk for scoring lower on measures of cognitive development than those who experience non-accidental trauma.

2224. Franklin, Alfred White, ed. Concerning Child Abuse: Papers
Presented by the Tunbridge Wells Study Group (Tunbridge
Wells, Eng., May 15-18, 1973) on Non-Accidental Injury
to Children. Edinburgh, Scotland: Churchill Livingstone
(distr. in U.S. by Longman, New York). 1975. 189 p.
This volume is a written record of the papers presented by the Tunbridge Wells Study Group on non-accidental injury to children. After a brief outline of the nature of the task by the editor, the subject is considered in five sections: the medical aspects, the social service element, the police point of view, the legal aspects, and the need for education.

2225. Friedman, Robert M.; Helfer, Ray E.; Katz, S. N.; et al.
Four Perspectives on the Status of Child Abuse and Neglect Research. Prepared for: National Center on Child
Abuse and Neglect (DHEW), Washington, D. C. Available
from the National Technical Information Service, 278 p.
(NTIS PB-250852-AS), March 1976.
The current status of child abuse and neglect research is reviewed from the four traditional perspectives of mental health, medicine, law, and social work.

2226. Gibson, Geoffrey. "Emergency Medical Services: The Research Gaps." Health Services Research, 9(1):6-21,
Spring 1974.
There is need to take stock of research gaps in developing
better emergency medical services (EMS) and to determine how well
current research activities meet these needs.

2227. Gil, David G., et al. Nationwide Epidemiologic Study of
Child Abuse. Progress Report. Waltham, Mass.: Brandeis University, Florence Heller Graduate School for Advanced Studies in Social Welfare, 1967. 23 p. Available
from EDRS: MF-$.25; HC-$1.
The progress report on the Nationwide Epidemiologic Study
of Child Abuse reviewed the study foci of the survey, the scope of
participation, the basis and comprehensive levels of the data collection, and participation of two non-public agencies for estimates and
comparison. Processing, analysis, reporting, and interpretation
will be concluded by June 30, 1969, and will include a clinical interview substudy in two sampling units. Additional stages in the proposal will also be investigated.

2228. Giovannoni, Jeanne M. Research in Child Abuse: A Way of
Seeing Is a Way of Not Seeing. Paper presented at National Symposium on Child Abuse, Chicago 1974.
General discussion of state of child abuse research in comparison to that of juvenile delinquency and mental illness research.

2229. Glazier, Alice E., ed. Child Abuse: A Community Challenge.
East Aurora, N. Y.: Henry Stewart, 1971. 169 p.
"A report on a four-year demonstration-research program
conducted from November 1, 1966, to October 31, 1970, by the
Children's Aid and Society for the Prevention of Cruelty to Children
of Erie County, in cooperation with the Children's Hospital of Buffalo, and financed by the James H. Cummings Foundation."

2230. Greeland, Cyril. Child Abuse in Ontario. Toronto, Ministry
of Community and Social Services, 1973. 70 p. (Ontario,
Ministry of Community and Social Services Research and
Planning Branch. Research Report 3)

2231. Harris, Susan B., ed. Child Abuse: Present and Future.
See entry 616.

2232. Holland, Cathleen Grant. An Examination of Social Isolation

and Availability to Treatment in the Phenomenon of Child
Abuse. See entry 104.

2233. Hornbein, Ruth. Social Worker's Orientations to the Use of
Authority in Initiating and Maintaining a Social Casework
Relationship with Parents Who Abuse and Parents Who Neg-
lect Their Children. See entry 1933.

2234. Johnson, Clara L. Child Abuse in the Southeast: Analysis
of 1172 Reported Cases. See entry 117.

2235. Kamerman, Sheila B. "Eight Countries: Cross-National
Perspectives on Child Abuse and Neglect." Children Today, 4(3):34-37, May-June 1975.
In a study of eight countries' views on child abuse and neglect,
it was found that researchers in all the countries agreed that there
were no firm data on incidence. The major debate related to whether
or not child abuse represented a phenomenon distinct from maltreatment of children generally and whether it warranted special policies
and programs. The perception of the problem differed in the various countries which made the study difficult to evaluate.

2236. Katz, Morton Lawrence. A Comparison of Ego Functioning
in Filicidal and Physically Child-Abusing Mothers. See
entry 2116.

2237. Kenel, Mary Elizabeth. A Study of the Cognitive Dimension
of Impulsivity-Reflectivity and Aggression in Female Child
Abusers. See entry 123.

2238. Kirkpatrick, Francine Karen. Patterns of Role Dominance-
Submission and Conflict in Parents of Abused Children.
See entry 2117.

2239. Kline, Donald; Christiansen, James. Educational and Psychological Problems of Abused Children. Final Report. See
entry 2310.

2240. Knapp, Vrinda Sharma. The Role of the Juvenile Police in
the Protection of Neglected and Abused Children. See
entry 1951.

2241. Nagi, Saad Z. "Child Abuse and Neglect Programs: A National Overview." Children Today, 4(3):13-17, May-June
1975.
Nagi discusses a study which was planned to gain a general
overview of programs in the U.S. concerning child abuse and neglect, to identify gaps in the design and problems, in the performance
of these programs, and to identify needs and directions for new program development. The study plan was developed around two aspects: intensive interviews with judges, doctors, caseworkers, policemen and others to gain an understanding of the issues in child
abuse and neglect; and surveys of agencies and programs involved
in abuse and neglect of children.

2242. _____. Child Maltreatment in the United States: A Cry
for Help and Organizational Response. Columbus: Ohio
State University, 1976. 231 p.
Reported are the research results from a national child maltreatment study planned around three aspects--intensive interviews
with individuals in the field, a survey of organizations and programs
related to child abuse and neglect, and the formulation of recommendations for policy and program planning. Some of the areas covered
are the rights of children, status of knowledge and technology, in-
compatibilities between punitive and therapeutic approaches, the magnitude of the problem and epidemological patterns, findings on the
structure and performance of programs, etc.

2243. _____. Child Maltreatment in the United States: A Cry
for Help and Organization Response. Appendix. Columbus: Ohio State University, 1976. 295 p.
The appendix to the report on a national child maltreatment
study includes sample forms used in interviewing individuals in child
protective services, public health departments, school systems, hospitals, hospital social service departments, courts, and police and
sheriff's departments. Included in each survey form are sections
with questions in flow chart format pertaining to organization, case
identification, case management, interagency teams and liaisons,
opinions, and observations made by the interviewer.

2244. National Conference on Child Abuse: A Summary Report.
See entry 1371.

2245. New York State Assembly. Select Committee on Child Abuse.
Report on the Feasibility of Studying the Relationship Between Child Abuse and Later Socially Deviant Behavior.
New York, August 1973. 43 p.
The feasibility of studying the interrelationship between child
abuse and neglect and later socially deviant behavior is examined.
The early 1950's were selected tentatively as the years from which
the identifying data on children officially suspected to be abused or
neglected could be drawn. Eight counties selected for the study were
found suitable, and no difficulty was anticipated in obtaining all the
records necessary.

2246. O'Hearn, Thomas P., Jr. A Comparison of Fathers in Abusive Situations with Fathers in Non-Abusive Situations.
See entry 166.

2247. Patti, Rino J. Child Protection in California, 1850-1966.
An Analysis of Public Policy. See entry 1993.

2248. Perrin, Helen Joyce. Child Abuse in Naval Regional Medical
Centers: San Diego and Long Beach, California. Long
Beach: Academic Press, 1976. 44 ℓ. (Originally pre-
sented as the author's thesis, University of California,
Los Angeles.)

2249. Reich, John W. "Experimental Assessment of a Treatment

Project." Journal of Pediatric Psychology, 1(2):94-97, Spring 1976.

Described is a research study assessing the impact of a treatment project aimed at aiding child-abusing parents. Involved is the application of Kempe's concept of the "Parent Aide," essentially a lay therapist who establishes and maintains close, long-term friendship contacts with the parents. Analyzed data appear to indicate significant positive change occurring in the parents.

2250. Reidy, Thomas Joseph, Jr. The Social, Emotional and Cognitive Functioning of Physically Abused and Neglected Children. See entry 184.

2251. "Report from the Research Work Group." Eli H. Newberger, Chairman. Clinical Proceedings, 30(2):49-50, 1974.

In the report from the Research Work Group of the National Conference on Child Abuse, an attempt to set priorities for continued study of the problem of child abuse in order to reduce existing fragmentation of effort is examined. The focus of research efforts on the courts, the police, the professions, and the study of the family, the parents, and children is suggested. Five requirements for further research programs are discussed.

2252. Rindfleisch, Nolan. A Study of the Influence of Background and Organizational Factors in Direct Care Workers' Attitudes Toward Use of Physical Force on Children. See entry 2160.

2253. Roberts, Robert Winston. A Comparative Study of Social Caseworkers' Judgments of Child Abuse Cases. See entry 2014.

2254. Rolston, Richard H. The Effect of Prior Physical Abuse on the Expression of Overt and Fantasy Aggressive Behavior in Children. See entry 189.

2255. Schlesinger, Benjamin. "Child Abuse." Chatelaine, 43:16, March 1970.

Schlesinger reviews the results of a continuing study conducted by Brandeis University.

2256. Seaberg, James R. Physical Child Abuse: An Expanded Analysis. See entry 2409.

2257. Segal, Rose S. A Comparison of Some Characteristics of Abusing and Neglecting, Non-Abusing Parents. See entry 201.

2258. Smith, Selwyn M. "The Battered Child Syndrome--Some Research Aspects." Bulletin of the American Academy of Psychiatry and the Law, 4(3):225-243, 1976.

2259. Starr, R. H., Jr.; Ceresnie, Steven; Rossi, JoAnn. "What

Child Abuse Researchers Don't Tell About Child Abuse Research. " Journal of Pediatric Psychology, 1(2):50-53, Spring 1976.
In describing a research design to examine both psychological and social factors as possible determinants of child abuse, the co-authors encountered four classes of issues in their research: problems with sample selection and criteria, measurement problems, ethical issues, and the role of the researcher studying social problems. The researchers conclude that the difficulties involved in both research and treatment make it vital that social agency and research personnel cooperate and understand the roles each plays.

2260. "The State of Child Abuse Research. " Child Protection Report, 2:3-6, January 1976.

2261. Stultz, Sylvia L. Childrearing Attitudes of Abusive Mothers: A Controlled Study. See entry 662.

2262. Theisen, William Maurice. Implementing a Child Abuse Law: An Inquiry into the Formulation and Execution of Social Policy. See entry 1144.

2263. Tocchio, Octavio J. Legislation and Law Enforcement in California for the Protection of the Physically Battered Child. See entry 1147.

2264. U. S. Office of Child Development. Child Abuse and Neglect: A Report on the Status of the Research, by Maure Hurt, Jr. 1975. 63 p. DHEW Pubn. no. OHD 74-20. pa $1. 25, Sup't. docs. Also available from EDRS: MF-$0. 76; HC-$3. 32, Plus Postage.
This state-of-the-art report provides preliminary information on the status of child abuse and neglect research projects currently in progress or recently completed. Each chapter discusses a particular research problem area and outlines the relevant demonstration projects. Three useful appendices are included: the text of the Child Abuse Prevention and Treatment Act, abstracts of current Federal research and demonstration projects on child abuse and neglect, and an annotated bibliography of research.

2265. Varon, Edith. The Client of a Protective Agency in the Context of the Community: A Field Study of the Massachusetts Society for the Prevention of Cruelty to Children. See entry 2042.

2266. Webb, K. W. ; Burt, M. R. ; Friedman, F. G. A. ; et al. Report and Plan for Recommended Approaches and Methods for Determination of National Incidence of Child Abuse and Neglect. Vol. I. Bethesda, Md. : Burt Associates, Inc. , 1975. 164 p. Available from National Technical Information Service. NTIS PB-250 853-AS.
A report describes the development of a methodological approach for determining the incidence of child abuse and neglect during

an initial 12-month period as baseline and detecting trends during succeeding years of implementation. Thirteen possible approaches for estimating incidence are identified, discussed, and evaluated according to specific criteria.

2267. _____; _____; _____; et al. Report and Plan on Recommended Approaches and Methods for Determination of National Incidence of Child Abuse and Neglect. Vol. II. Bethesda, Md.: Burt Associates, Inc., 1975. 224 p. Available from National Technical Information Service. NTIS PB-250 854-AS.

A methodological approach for estimating child abuse and neglect incidence in the U.S. utilizes separate citizen surveys of abuse and neglect. In-person interviews by social workers using structured questionnaires are suggested for determining the incidence of child neglect. Questionnaire development, evaluation of the neglect survey data, and sampling plans for the neglect methodology are examined in detail. Telephone nomination interviews and in-person randomized response questioning are recommended for estimating the incidence of child abuse. Special problems associated with sampling institutional, American Indian, military, and migrant populations are considered, and a questionnaire adaptable for institutional surveys is suggested.

2268. Young, M. Some Selected Dimensions of Alienation in Abusive and Non-Abusive Families: A Comparative Study. See entry 2426.

SCHOOL'S ROLE

2269. "APHA Conference Report, 1968. School Health. " <u>Public</u>
<u>Health Reports</u>, 84:215-220, March 1969.

2270. "Abused Child. " <u>Today's Education</u>, 63:40-43, January 1974.
Child abuse may have reached epidemic proportions. Since
many abused children are over age five, and of school age, the
school can take a role in preventing abuse. It has been suggested
that schools institute child abuse reporting procedures, that they
abolish corporal punishment, and that they institute education-for-
parenthood programs.

2271. American Humane Association. Children's Division. <u>Guide-</u>
<u>lines for Schools to Help Protect Neglected and Abused</u>
<u>Children</u>. Denver, Colo. , 1971. 6 p. $2.50 per 100.
School personnel have a unique amount of contact with and
opportunity to observe children. They can be of major assistance
in early case finding and reporting instances of abuse. The child's
behavior may point to neglect or abuse; appearance may be another
signal; and the attitude of the parents may be grounds for suspicion.
All of these signals are explained in detail.

2272. Amiel, Shirley. "Child Abuse in Schools. " <u>Northwest Med-</u>
<u>icine</u>, 71:808, November 1972.
Amiel condemns the public school system for its deliberate
sadistic mistreatment of, and discrimination against, children. She
claims that 4.5 million students are exposed annually to seriously
maladjusted teachers, and then describes several examples of generalized discrimination and abuse of children as it occurs in schools.

2273. Badner, George. "Child Abuse Cases Increase: Pennsylvania. " <u>Pennsylvania School Journal</u>, 124:20-22, October
1975.
If the child abuse legislation being considered by the state
General Assembly is signed into law, teachers and top school officials will be required to detect and report child abuse cases from
among their students. They will need to know the causes, sources,
and treatment, and now is the time to start learning.

2274. Batinich, Mancina E. "How School Can Aid the Abused Child:
Principal's Role Central in Protecting Children. " <u>Chicago</u>
<u>School Journal</u>, 46:57-62, November 1964.
Described are several steps which a school principal should

take in any or all cases of child abuse: record keeping, arranging psychological testing, possible consultation with a social caseworker, filing of appropriate reports, contacting agencies, and participation in court hearings. Batinich also encourages school personnel to become aware of the problem and to participate in child abuse countermeasures.

2275. Bechtold, Mary L. "Silent Partner to a Parent's Brutality."
School and Community, 52:33, November 1965.
Describes case of abuse and school's handling of it. Calls for uniform procedure for reporting and protecting child.

2276. _____. "That Battered Child Could Be Dead Tomorrow."
Instructor, 77:20, April 1968.
As an elementary counselor, Bechtold details personal involvement in handling a child abuse case. She offers guidelines for teachers if they suspect children are being physically abused.

2277. Björck, S. [The School Nurse Is Important in Discovering
Child Abuse]. Tidskrift for Sveriges Sjukskoterskor, 41
(15):4, August 29, 1974.

2278. Broadhurst, Diane D. "Policy Making: First Step for
Schools in the Fight Against Child Abuse and Neglect."
Elementary School Guidance and Counseling, 10:222-226,
March 1976.
The model program at Montgomery County Public Schools (Maryland), called Project PROTECTION, is one of three funded by the U.S. Office of Education under Title III of the Elementary and Secondary Act to train educators to recognize and properly refer children who may be abused or neglected. Initiated in 1974, it involves four phases: staff development, direct service to county nonpublic schools, curriculum development, and policy revision. The latter is the most important and is described.

2279. _____. "Project Protection: A School Program to Detect
and Prevent Child Abuse and Neglect." Children Today,
4:22-25, May 1975.
The development of a protection service for abused children in Montgomery County, Maryland, school's project is described. Protection is concerned with policy revisions, staff development, and curriculum development. These phases involve defining an abused child, developing a staff of adequately trained professionals, formulating reporting procedures, and preventing the problem through education for responsible parenthood.

2280. _____. "School Program to Combat Child Abuse: Montgomery County, Md." Education Digest, 41:20-23, October
1975.
Broadhurst outlines the Montgomery County, Md. Public School's Project PROTECTION to train teachers to recognize and properly refer children suspected of being abused or neglected. Aspects of curriculum development which focus on prevention are also included.

2281. _____ ; Howard, Maxwell C. "More About Project Pro-
        tection. " Childhood Education, 52:67-69, November-Decem-
        ber 1975.
    Montgomery County, Maryland, one of the largest school dis-
tricts in the nation, has made significant progress in developing a
school-based program to detect and prevent child abuse and neglect.
Its program--Project PROTECTION--can now serve as a model for
other school systems.   The four phases of the Project are discussed.

2282. Carroll-Gardner, Judi.   "Child Neglect and Abuse. "   North
        Carolina Education, 6:20-21, January 1976.
    The tenets of the North Carolina child abuse law, which calls
for reporting to the Director of Social Services, is reviewed, as
well as the goal of Protective Services.

2283. Caskey, Owen L.; Richardson, Ivanna.   "Understanding and
        Helping Child-Abusing Parents. " Elementary School Guid-
        ance and Counseling, 9:196-208, March 1975.
    The problem of child abuse is discussed concentrating on fac-
tors relevant to treatment of the abusing adult.   Ways that school
counselors, social workers, and psychologists could assist abusive
parents in a school-centered approach to treatment are described.

2284. "Child Abuse and Neglect Statute Has Important Implications. "
        School Board Notes, 3:9, April 1, 1975.
    It is important that school personnel be familiar with the pro-
visions of P. L. 1974 c. 119, the New Jersey Child Abuse and Neglect
Statute, which became effective January 8, 1975.   A review of the
provisions is given.   An informational packet is available from:
Division of Youth and Family Services, One S. Montgomery Street,
Trenton, N. J. 08625.

2285. "Child Abuse Is Growing Problem. "   Educator's Advocate,
        6(7):8, March 19, 1976.
    With greater teacher awareness of the child abuse problem
and sensitivity to the early clues, social service agencies could be
alerted much sooner and preventive measures begun before irreparable physical or psychological damage is done.   Local association
policy should state clearly steps for teachers and other school personnel to take.

2286. "Child Abuse Law Stressed. "   Alabama School Journal, 91
        (20):3, October 15, 1974.
    Discussed is a new pamphlet on the State's child abuse law which
the State Department of Education is distributing to local school super-
intendents who will be able to make copies available to teachers.

2287. "Child Abuse Reporting Statute. "   Maine School Management
        Association Bulletin, 1-5, November 1975.
    The school's role is addressed in light of the Maine child
abuse reporting statute.

2288. "Child Abuse: The Importance of Early Detection. "   Ohio
        Schools, 53:26+, October 24, 1975.

Early determination of suspected child abuse on the part of educators can be the factor that helps prevent major emotional or physical damage to the child. The responsibilities of the teacher, the Ohio reporting law, visible signs to look for, and organizations to contact for help, are provided.

2289. "Child Abuse: What Teachers Can Do to Combat It." Ed News, 30:7, December 4, 1975.

2290. Covington, Cleta. "Battered Child (New North Carolina Law Makes Reporting of Abuses to Children Easier)." North Carolina Education, 33:23+, September 1966.
Teachers are acquainted with various aspects of child abuse and those procedures to be followed in the case of a suspected battered child.

2291. _____. "Battered Child (Teachers' Responsibility in Preventing Child Abuse)." North Carolina Teachers Record, 36:25-28, October 1966.

2292. Duncan, Carole. "They Beat Children, Don't They?" Journal of Clinical Child Psychology, 2(3):13-14, Fall 1973.
This article pertains to corporal punishment in the public schools of Dallas and other institutions.

2293. "Educators, Local Associations Can Help Stop Rise of Child Abuse Incidents." Nevada Education, 10:5, January 1976.

2294. Ferro, Frank. "Protecting Children: The National Center on Child Abuse and Neglect." Childhood Education, 52: 63-66, November-December 1975.
The work of the National Center on Child Abuse and Neglect is described. One of the funded resource-projects is the Education Commission of the States whose major concern is the role of educational systems in child abuse and neglect. Teachers and other educational personnel have major contributions to make as our society attempts to cope with the pervasive and nationwide problems involved in protecting children. Hopeful signs are the growing efforts to incorporate information about child abuse into the curriculum of teacher-training programs.

2295. Forrer, Stephen E. "Battered Children and Counselor Responsibility." The School Counselor, 22:161-165, January 1975.
Discusses three general areas in which counselors can work to combat child abuse. A model of the function and community relationship of the child abuse council is illustrated. The development of a preventive approach through training and education is essential. (P. A.)

2296. Fraser, Brian G. "Child Abuse and What the Schools Can Do About It." Illinois School Board Journal, 43:31-34, January-February 1975.

Fraser introduces this article with a case of child abuse that resulted in death. Some common questions and answers that teachers might ask about the Illinois law and reporting are provided. The teachers and the schools have a large role to play in the arena of child abuse and neglect. Their resources must be utilized to fill gaps that agencies cannot investigate and offer services to.

2297. Freeman, C. B. "The Children's Petition of 1669 and Its Sequel." British Journal of Educational Studies, 14:216-223, May 1966.

Corporal punishment and its abuse in British schools are detailed. The author states that children should not be beaten in school but punished according to the offense. Teachers should never severely punish their students, for it is not in their jurisdiction to do so.

2298. Gil, David G. "What Schools Can Do About Child Abuse." American Education, 5:2-4, April 1969; also in Social Service Outlook, 8-12, February 1970.

Gil advocates recognition of child abuse cases in the schools since most children subjected to abuse are of school age and come into contact with schools almost daily. Baltimore public schools illustrate the role of the institution in facilitating reporting and assuring medical and social services for abused children and their families. The author discusses aims for preventing or reducing the incidence of abuse by attacking causes of the problem.

2299. Gray, Anne. "Child Abuse. Some Signs for Teachers." Ed News, 30:3, March 4, 1976.

The author provides 16 indicators of child abuse/neglect for teachers. She also urges teachers to listen quietly for hints which a child might drop. A pick-up clue assures the student you are interested and DO CARE! This is the second of a series of five articles written by the same author.

2300. _____. "Parental Abuse Most Often Caused by Stress Problems." Ed News, 30:9, March 11, 1976.

Anne Gray enumerates the stressful problems for parents and guardians of children. No socioeconomic level of society is more prone to become the abuser. Those on the lower socioeconomic level are more readily exposed. Gray names four indicators for teachers to be aware of in the parent/guardian. This is the third article in a (short) series of five articles by the same author.

2301. Hagebak, Robert. Disciplinary Practices in Dallas Contrasted with School Systems with Rules Against Violence Against Children. September 8, 1972. 11 p. (Paper presented at the Annual Convention of the American Psychological Association, 80th, Honolulu, Hawaii). Available from ERIC: MF-$0.65; HC-$3.29; Journal of Clinical Child Psychology, 2(3):14-16, Fall 1973.

Corporal punishment and its implications are discussed in this speech in Dallas, where corporal punishment is officially sanctioned as a method of school discipline; and in many other parts of the country, the prevailing opinion is that corporal punishment is necessary, effective and harmless. Teachers using corporal punishment should examine their motives and consider what sort of model they should be providing students.

2302. Henke, Lorraine J. "A Health Educator's Role in the Problem of Child Abuse." Health Education, 6(3):15-18, May-June 1975.
Henke names three areas in which the educator can help solve the problem of child abuse. To identify the abused child, she quotes the characteristics of a child in need of protection, as published by the American Humane Association. To serve as a resource person, she suggests the teacher requires additional knowledge and a dedication to involvement. Also, there should be a variety of courses geared toward teaching the students how to be effective parents.

2303. Herbert, D. L. "The Family Educational Rights and Privacy Act of 1974 vs. Child Abuse Reporting Laws: The Teacher's Dilemma." Juvenile Justice, 26(3):15-19, August 1975.
The impact of the federal Family Educational Rights and Privacy Act of 1974 on state and local child abuse reporting laws, and the dilemma of educators in such cases, are discussed. Such laws are particularly relevant to teachers who see the majority of children for approximately 75 percent of the year.

2304. Hyman, Irwin; Schreiber, Karen. "Selected Concepts and Practices of Child Advocacy in School Psychology." Psychology in the Schools, 12:50-58, January 1975.
The rationale for the position that the school psychologist is and must be a child advocate is stated, and concepts concerning the ways in which the school psychologist can work as a child advocate are presented.

2305. Kempe, C. Henry; Helfer, Ray E., eds. Helping the Battered Child and His Family. See entry 1339.

2306. Kibby, Robert. "The Abused Child." California School Boards, 34:23-26, May 1975.
The principal of Moreno Elementary School reports that confrontation with abusive parents did not improve the home situation of the most urgent cases and parents often became hostile to the school. He presents a case that the school attempted to handle and a case in which the school collaborated with the social agency and their method of intervention. The school's experience with the child protective services made it aware of its ignorance in matters relating to child abuse. Kibby feels that the school has only begun to successfully cope with the broad aspects of the problem.

2307. _____; Sanders, Lola; Creaghan, Sidney, et al. "The Abused Child--The Need for Collaboration." Thrust for Educational Leadership, 4:11-13, May 1975.

"Relevant" teaching is teaching the "whole child. " Teachers
must be learners before each student--only through awareness of
their personal prejudices can they relinquish them.   Teaching, however, is never "relevant" to the experiences of the battered child.
Turning to child protective services and to workshops on the battered child, the Kernville Union School District teachers learned
much about child abuse and how to handle such cases when they occurred in their school.

2308.   Kliman, A.   "Children in Crisis. " Journal of the New York
        State School Nurse-Teachers Association, 7:21-33, Winter
        1976.

2309.   Kline, Donald F.   Child Abuse and Neglect: A Primer for
        School Personnel.   56 p. $4.   Available from: The
        Council for Exceptional Children, Publications Sales, 1920
        Association Drive, Reston, Virginia 22091.
           This pamphlet provides helpful information for the educator
and gives guidelines for writing education policy.   A sample reporting form is included.   (Advertisement.)

2310.   _____ ; Christiansen, James.   Educational and Psychological
        Problems of Abused Children.   Final Report.   Logan, Utah
        State University, Department of Special Education, 1975.
        174 p.
           The frequency of educational and psychological problems was
examined in 138 school-aged abused children.   Related literature was
reviewed to present the history, magnitude, and demographic aspects
of child abuse and to analyze current knowledge in terms of the ade-
quacy of research methodology and design.   Data for the study were
drawn from juvenile court records and the following variables were
investigated: frequency of special education placement; frequency of
speech therapy and psychological counseling; frequency of institutional
placement; type and frequency of traits and behaviors which may be
indicative of psychological problems, and academic achievement levels.   The findings are reported.

2311.   Leavitt, Jerome Edward, comp.   The Battered Child: Se-
        lected Readings.   See entry 521.

2312.   "Let's Protect Our Children. "   (from child abuse).   Action
        Line, 10:2, December 1, 1976.
           Members of the teaching profession, by the very nature of
their profession, have an advantage in detecting possible cases of
child abuse and taking positive steps to prevent it.   The provisions
of the Maryland law are detailed, and teachers are urged to report
to the local department of Social Services or an appropriate law enforcement agency.

2313.   Leuchter, H. J.   "Are Schools to Be or Not to Be Community
        Health Centers?" (Letter).   American Journal of Psychi-
        atry, 125(4):575-576, October 1968.
        Schools must serve as community mental health centers to

intervene against the emotional distress of children whose family
life is unhealthy. Psychiatrists must aid in devising programs for
teachers and others in direct contact with abused, neglected, and
disturbed children and must educate the public on the essentials of
health and family life and the need to support programs for their
advancement.

2314. Lynch, Annette. "Child Abuse in the School-Age Population:
       Philadelphia." The Journal of School Health, 45:141-148,
       March 1975.
       Recognition of child abuse as a phenomenon of the older child
--the school child--has been slow. It is conjectured that less than
5 percent of the nation's schools have viable procedures. The setting for this report is late 1970--a large metropolitan district. Facts
in regard to child abuse are noted and three methods used to better
understand the condition and the response of school staff are outlined. Recommendations to overcome deficiences are offered.

2315. McRorie, Dennis G. C. "Child Abuse and School Personnel."
       Wyoming Education News, 41(2):34-35, October 1974.

2316. Martin, David L. "The Growing Horror of Child Abuse and
       the Undeniable Role of the Schools in Putting an End to It."
       American School Board Journal, 160:51-55, November 1973.
       Discussed is how the school can help in abuse prevention and
reasons why it should become involved. School officials should establish specific policies and procedures for child abuse reporting.
School board members should encourage proper reporting by sensi-
tizing school employees to the existence of the problem and methods
of reporting it.

2317. Maurer, Adah. "Spare the Child!" Journal of Clinical Child
       Psychology, 2(3):4-6, Fall 1973.
       Using three types of teachers, as portrayed by Charles Dick-
ens, Maurer describes the flogger; the gentle, put-upon patsy; and
the guru who teaches with quiet strength. She believes that children
brutalized in schools will live to drive cars upon our highways to
add to the disgraceful toll of the slaughtered. As they rejected the
school system run by one set adults, they are likely to reject the
highway system run by another set of adults. She calls upon the
psychologist and the educator to break this cycle of violence. Her
article is signed "Peace Without Paddles!"

2318. Montgomery County Public Schools. A Policy Statement on
       Child Abuse and Child Neglect. Rev. Rockville, Mary-
       land, August 26, 1974. 4 p.
       A policy statement on child abuse and child neglect developed
by the Montgomery County, Maryland, Public Schools is presented;
guidelines for staff members in reporting suspected child abuse or
child neglect cases are outlined. The content of written reports to
file in such cases is summarized, and a sample child abuse and
neglect reporting form is provided.

2319. Montgomery County Public Schools. Proceedings. Project Protection Child Abuse and Neglect Conference and Workshops. Rockville, Md., September 1974. 57 p.
The proceedings of a conference and workshops held to sensitize Montgomery County, Maryland, school personnel to the problems of child abuse and neglect and to make them aware of their own responsibilities in this area are reported. The conference and workshops were conducted under the auspices of Project PROTECTION, a federally-funded county program to deal with the educational problems associated with child abuse and neglect.

2320. Morgan, Sharon R. "The Battered Child in the Classroom." Journal of Pediatric Psychology, 1(2):47-49, Spring 1976.
Morgan presents the need for school programming in mental health and then enumerates specific characteristics resulting from abusive treatment that are especially pertinent for classroom teachers. Despite the prevalent use of corporal punishment and its exacerbation of abuse, the author identifies the school as one of the major resources in the community wherein normal development is possible.

2321. Murdock, C. George. "The Abused Child and the School System." American Journal of Public Health and the Nation's Health, 60:105-109, January 1970.
A program was started in Syracuse, N.Y., on the premise that the school system would be valuable in detecting cases of abused children. Presented are the program and the results of the program for the first four years of operation.

2322. Nicholas, Wanda. "Check New Child Abuse Law." Teacher's Voice, 53(9):1, January 26, 1976.
The implications of Michigan's new child abuse law is reviewed for teachers. They should read the complete law and help make the implementation of the law fulfill its intent. Copies of the law can be obtained through your legislator by asking for Act 238, Public Acts of 1975, as approved by the Governor on September 2, 1975.

2323. Nordstrom, Jerry L. "Child Abuse: A School District's Response to Its Responsiblity." Child Welfare, 53:257-260, April 1974.
The public school system could play a pivotal role in the detection and prevention of child abuse and neglect, but few systems have recognized and acted effectively to discharge this responsibility. This paper describes the organized efforts of one school district to play a role as the advocate of children's rights, and the results of the program. (Journal Summary.)

2324. "Nurses Declare Policy Statement on Child Abuse." IEA Reporter, 29:8, November 1974.

2325. "Protecting Children: Freeing Them from Mental and Phys-

ical Abuse: Symposium. " Childhood Education, 52:58-75, November 1975.
"What teachers need to know about child abuse and neglect" is a collection of articles which deal with the problem of child abuse. Included are practical suggestions for ways in which teachers and school systems can become more effective in detecting and reporting mistreatment of children, efforts of the federal government to provide multidisciplinary supports for human-services agencies, and suggestions to help people who want to help combat child abuse.

2326. Regalis, M. T. "Child Abuse--Care Enough to Act!" Journal of the New York State School Nurse-Teachers Association, 7:15-19, March 1976.

2327. "Report Child Abuse. " NJEA Review, 49:30, March 1976.
Teachers are urged to report suspected cases of child abuse. A checklist of the visible signs to look for, as well as the provisions of the New Jersey law are provided. Steps to take in reporting are given.

2328. "Report Child Abuse. " Ohio Schools, 54:21-24, September 24, 1976.
Child abuse or neglect is defined. Visible signs teachers should watch for, traits of abusers, guidelines for reporting abuse, the provisions of the Ohio law, and some do's and don'ts for teachers are provided.

2329. "Reporting of Child Abuse by School Personnel. " (Editorial). Public Health Reports, 84(1):219-220, January 1969.
Syracuse (N. Y.) school personnel are required to report instances of suspected child abuse to the department of social welfare. During the years 1964-1968 the schools have been the largest single source of reports (18-24 per year). Despite the successes of the program, many school personnel are still reluctant to report due to unfounded fears.

2330. Reskow, Judith. "Child Abuse: What the Educator Should Know. " NJEA Review, 47:14-15, November 1973.
The school's role in playing a very important part in detection of child abuse is stressed. Ways in which to help, symptoms and signs for the teacher to look for, and some common personality traits exhibited by abusive parents are provided. It is important for teachers to know the law and how it affects them in regard to this problem.

2331. Richards, Laurel A. "Can the Schools Help Prevent Child Abuse?" Illinois Teacher for Contemporary Roles, 17:43-45, September-October 1973.
Richards states that the schools seem ill-prepared to deal with problems of child battering, basically because teachers are not trained to recognize the signs of abuse. The author discusses battering parents and avenues of help for those parents.

2332. Riscalla, Louis Mead. The Professional's Role and Perspectives on Child Abuse. See entry 1759.

2333. Rochester, Dean E. , et al. "What Can the Schools Do About Child Abuse?" Today's Education, 57:59-60, September 1968.
Limited though it was, we feel that we may draw a few broad conclusions from [our survey]. One thing is clear: Elementary school teachers, principals, and counselors have a vital role to play in breaking up the battered child syndrome. When they act, they can help in child abuse situations; they can even at times eliminate them. (Journal Summary.)

2334. Sanders, Lola; Kibby, Robert W. ; Creagham, Sidney, et al. "Child Abuse: Detection and Prevention." Young Children, 30:332-338, July 1975.
This article is an account of how Moreno School in Sunnymead, California, eventually began to deal with child abuse. The steps being taken are outlined.

2335. Schmitt, Barton D. "What Teachers Need to Know About Child Abuse and Neglect. " Childhood Education, 52:58-62, November 1975. Education Digest, 41:19-21, March 1976.
Presented is information to aid teachers in detecting and reporting child abuse and neglect. Discussed are injurious conditions to look for which include physical abuse, nutritional deprivation, drug abuse, medical care neglect, sexual abuse, emotional abuse, severe hygiene neglect, and educational neglect. In diagnosing the situation, several approaches (such as talking to the child in a private setting) are described; and once diagnosis is certain, it is recommended that the case be reported to a child protective agency. (Journal Summary.)

2336. "School Nurses' Responsibilities Viewed. " California State Nurses' Association Bulletin, 63:7, June 1967.
This special announcement alerts school nurses in the state of California that they should report suspected cases of child abuse to designated officials within the school system rather than report directly to law enforcement officials.

2337. Shanas, Bert. "Child Abuse: A Killer Teachers Can Help Control. " Phi Delta Kappan, 56(7):479-482, March 1975.
Large numbers of teachers, unfortunately, are still failing to meet the responsibility of reporting child abuse cases. Reviewed are some of the reasons why. Whether or not the principal and school system are willing to help, it is the teacher's responsibility to report. The list of possible child abuse and neglect tipoffs, published by the American Humane Association, is provided, along with a list of places for teachers to write for further information.

2338. Spindel, Jerome N. "Child Abuse: Can You Spot It?" Massachusetts Teacher, 54:16-17, November 1974.

The purpose of this article is to help teachers spot and carry through on suspected cases of child abuse. Provided are the tenets of the Massachusetts reporting law, what to watch for in abuse cases, and phone numbers and locations of the offices of the Department of Public Welfare and of the CPS offices.

2339. "Teachers Can Help Stop Child Abuse." GEA Update, 8(19): 4, May 14, 1976.
   With greater teacher awareness of child abuse and sensitivity to the early clues, social service agencies could be alerted much sooner and preventive measures begun before irreparable physical or psychological damage is done. Six steps the local association can take to help stop the epidemic are given.

2340. "Teacher's Role in Reporting Child Abuse." Illinois Education News, 3:8-9, 1974.
   Discussion of teacher's responsibility in recognizing and reporting child abuse cases to the Illinois Department of CPS (Department of Children and Family Services).

2341. Ten Bensel, Robert W.; Berdie, Jane. "Neglect and Abuse of Children and Youth: The Scope of the Problem and the School's Role." Journal of School Health, 46:453-461, October 1976.
   This article focuses primarily on the school's role and responsibilities in cases of child abuse and neglect. Suggested guidelines cover the need for comprehensive policy and training on a district-wide basis, ways to work with families and other agencies, and the special role of the schools, i. e., recognizing, identifying, and reporting abuse and providing a physically and emotionally secure environment for pupils.

2342. Thomas, M. Angele, ed. Children Alone: What Can Be Done About Abuse and Neglect. The Council for Exceptional Children, 1976. 128 p. Available from The Council, $7.50.
   Information on what schools can and should be doing in the treatment of abused and neglected children is provided in this book.

2343. Thomson, Ellen M. "Child Abuse Is No Myth." Interview edited by Leanna Landsmann. Instructor, 83:84-85, January 1974.
   This is an interview with Ellen M. Thomson who is a social worker at the Child Care Center of Child and Family Services in Buffalo, N. Y., and who co-authored Child Abuse, A Community Challenge. She focuses on why parents abuse their children and what can be done to help them stop. Teachers should be willing to become involved by keeping records of visible signs when a child is suspected of being abused and by reporting to the proper authorities.

2344. Understanding Child Maltreatment: Help and Hope. A Course of Study. Pilot Edition. Rockville, Md.: Montgomery

County Public Schools, 1976.   568 p.   (Sponsoring Agency: Bureau of Elementary and Secondary Education, DHEW/OE, Washington, D.C.)

Intended for use in inservice teacher and professional education, as well as with secondary level students, the curriculum guide is designed as part of Project PROTECTION to promote understanding of the individual and societal problems of child maltreatment in terms of prevention.   The document contains six units.   The Montgomery County (Maryland) school system's current policy statement and reporting procedures for child abuse and neglect are also provided, as well as an annotated bibliography of selected literature for use at the professional level.

2345.   Wall, Charles M.   "Child Abuse: A Societal Problem with Educational Implications."   Peabody Journal of Education, 52:222-225, April 1975.

No single agency can deal with the problem of child abuse; the complexity of the problem renders necessary implementation of a multidisciplinary and multiagency approach.   The school's role as a part of this approach becomes greater as it incorporates even younger children into its program.   Through identification, prevention, and treatment, the school can aid society in preventing child abuse.   (Journal Summary Modified.)

2346.   "What Teachers Can Do When Kids Come to School Battered, Bruised."   UEA Action, 8:5, December 1976.

The Utah child abuse law is interpreted in light of the teacher's responsibility.   A list of symptoms to alert teachers to child abuse or neglect is provided.

2347.   Zurcher, J. C.   Identifying the Battered or Molested Child. A Handbook for School Staff Members.   Palo Alto Unified School District, Palo Alto, Calif., 1972.   8 p.

School personnel are in the front line in the defense of children who are unable to protect themselves against maltreatment by adults.   Factors to help them identify abused children are outlined, as well as the steps to be taken if a teacher has reason to believe that the child is being maltreated in any way.

SOCIOLOGICAL ASPECTS

2348. Adams, Wayne V. "The Physically Abused Child: A Re-
           view." Journal of Pediatric Psychology, 1(2):7-11, Spring
           1976.
           After tracing the historical developments leading to a recog-
nition of child abuse as a real socio-medical problem, Adams discusses the incidence, etiology, and treatment approaches related to
child abuse.

2349. Allen, Hugh D.; Kosciolek, Edward; Ten Bensel, Robert W.,
           et al. "The Battered Child Syndrome. II. Social and
           Psychiatric Aspects." Minnesota Medicine, 52:155-156,
           January 1969.
           The co-authors present a profile of child abusers in terms
of socioeconomic background, education, age, sex, degree of estrangement from the community, prevalence of mental disturbance,
personality characteristics, impulsiveness, aggressiveness, childhood experiences, incidence of pre-marital unwanted pregnancy, marital instability, sexual promiscuity, criminal offenses, and alcoholic
tendencies.

2350. Alvy, Kerby T. "On Child Abuse: Values and Analytic Ap-
           proaches." Journal of Clinical Child Psychology, 4(1):36-
           37, Spring 1975.
           Argues that the traditional definition of child abuse must be
expanded from abuse perpetrated by an individual to abuse encouraged
and fostered by cultural attitudes and institutions (e.g., rearing beliefs and school policies that suggest the need of physical force to
control behavior). (P.A.)

2351. American Humane Association. Children's Division. Neg-
           lecting Parents: A Study of Psychosocial Characteristics,
           by Morton I. Cohen, Robert M. Mulford, and Elizabeth
           Philbrick. Denver, Colo. 28 p.
           Interpretation of the findings in a research project to identify
the psychosocial characteristics of neglecting parents in almost 1,000
families.

2352. Ariés, Philippe. Centuries of Childhood: A Social History
           of Family Life. See entry 683.

2353. Bakan, David. "Slaughter of the Innocents." Journal of Clin-
           ical Child Psychology, 2(3):10-12, Fall 1973.

396

This article is a series of excerpts from the author's book of the same title. The hypothesis is presented that child abuse is related to the biological population-resource balance. This hypothetical result is tempered by the possibility that by knowing what is "natural" man may be able to make modifications in accordance with his own value system. Bakan suggests cultural rectification through elimination of force or violence to gain obedience or social compliance and the realization that the welfare of society is dependent on its children.

2354. _____. Slaughter of the Innocents: A Study of the Battered Child Phenomenon. San Francisco: Jossey-Bass, 1971. (The Jossey-Bass Behaviorial Science Series.) 128 p.

This book covers the subject of child abuse and infanticide from several interesting points of view. The problem is defined in detail and the psychodynamics of the principles and of society are discussed. The history of child abuse and infanticide are considered from antiquity through the present. The account of the modern awareness in the last 30 years is detailed and complete. A revealing insight into the nature of the disorder as presented to children forms the core of the third chapter which deals with songs, nursery rhymes, and fairy tales in which the theme recurs again and again. Infanticide in the context of the larger problem of balance of resources and population is considered. If the Universal Declaration of Human Rights of the United Nations were adopted universally in man's consciousness, law, and custom, substantial progress would have been made.

2355. Bandura, Albert. "Institutionally Sanctioned Violence. " Journal of Clinical Child Psychology, 2(3):23-24, Fall 1973.

Society sanctions various forms of violence, the author points out, and has developed a number of self-absolving practices through which moral people can be led to behave aggressively and violently without self-condemnation. A number of practices are described and examples given together with solutions which society may well implement.

2356. Bilainkin, George. "Children in Peril. " Contemporary Review, 201:67-71, February 1962.

In the United Kingdom, an estimated 300 children will be assaulted, thrashed, starved, maimed, and subjected to many more cruel and inhumane acts of violence each year for the next 50 years. The author discusses how society fails to protect its children from this abuse and how many individuals have more or less pushed this problem to the back of their minds. Bilainkin briefly looks at some possible answers for the prevention of child abuse.

2357. Bird, Harmony. "Battered Babies: A Social and Medical Problem. " Nursing Times, 69:1552-1554, November 22, 1973; Zeitschrift für Krankenpflege, 67(12):455-457, December 1974.

A report of two young children physically beaten by their

father since birth is given. The information indicates the frequent
occurrence of abuse by one parent without the knowledge of the other.
The role of the nursing staff and social worker in helping parents
who are torn between loyalty to their spouses and love for their
children is stressed.

2358. Blumberg, Myrna. "When Parents Hit Out." Twentieth Cen-
        tury, 173:39-44, Winter 1964-1965.
        Blumberg reports on recent research into the neglected topic
of parental violence towards children. Discussed are both "smack-
ing" as punishment or normally accepted violence, and the uncontrollable assaults which rank as cruelty when they are detected and
brought into the open. (Journal Summary Modified.)

2359. Blumenthal, Monica D. "Justifying Violence: Attitudes of
        American Men." Aggression, Violence and Childhood,
        Fifth Annual Seminar, Children's Medical Center, Tulsa,
        Oklahoma, October 1972.
        A discussion of forces influencing attitudes toward violence
and conclusions drawn from studies of attitudes toward violence.

2360. Borland, Marie, ed. Violence in the Family. Manchester,
        England: Manchester University Press; Atlantic Highlands,
        N.J.: Humanities Press, 1976. 148 p.
        A series of articles written by eight different authors on an
overview of physical violence in the family: sociological aspects,
medical diagnosis of children, management of the problem, the legal
framework, battered wives, police involvement, and interagency collaboration.

2361. Calkins, C. F., et al. "Children's Rights: An Introductory
        Sociological Overview." Peabody Journal of Education,
        50:89-109, January 1973.
        The authors formulate a sociological definition of children's
rights through delineating prerequisite conditions (to rights) and explore how these conditions are fulfilled under varying patterns of
social organization.

2362. Chase, Naomi Feigelson. A Child Is Being Beaten: Violence
        Against Children, An American Tragedy. See entry 568.

2363. Child Study Center. Parental Alienation: Ominous Precursor
        of Child Abuse, by M. Young. Oklahoma City, Okla., No-
        vember 1975. 15 p.
        Alienation was compared between a group of families who were
recognized as abusive and families who had no history of abuse.
Abusive families were found to be significantly more socially isolated
than controls.

2364. Court, Joan; Robinson, W. "The Battered Child Syndrome."
        Midwives Chronicle and Nursing Notes, 83(990):212-216,
        July 1970.
        Psychosocial characteristics of parents in child abuse situa-

tions include loneliness, isolation, fear of social relationships, lack of roots in the community, and suffering from parental rejection. Midwives are frequently in a position to note these characteristics and to help abusive mothers.

2365. Dunovský, J., et al. [Complexity of Social Background in the Case of a Battered Child]. Ceskoslovenske Zdravot-nictvi, 21:341-344, August 1973. (Czech)

2366. Eisenberg, Leon. "The Sins of the Fathers: Urban Decay and Social Pathology." American Journal of Orthopsy-chiatry, 32:5-17, 1962.
The characteristics of parents, treatment, and problems of foster children for whom special consultation is requested, are discussed.

2367. Erlanger, Howard S. "Social Class and Corporal Punishment in Childrearing: A Reassessment." American Sociological Review, 39:68-85, February 1974.
The relationship of social class to the type of punishment used on children is discussed, and data on this subject available in the literature, are analyzed. This analysis suggests that, although various studies have found a statistically significant relationship, the relationship is rather weak.

2368. Fleck, Stephen. "Child Abuse." Connecticut Medicine, 36:337, June 1972.
Fleck suggests that the incidence of child abuse represents only the top of an iceberg of a vast reservoir of unwanted children in society. The existence of child abuse and unwanted children reveals two American myths commonly indulged: we are a child-centered society and we are future oriented. The author punctures both myths successfully.

2369. Fontana, Vincent J. "Child Abuse and Neglect--A Social Disease." Journal of the New York State School Nurse-Teachers Association, 5:18-21, June 1974.
One of the nation's leading authorities on child abuse discusses the problem as a social disease of epidemic and endemic proportions. Fontana claims that if child abuse is allowed to continue at its present pace, this disease will threaten the future of society and the entire fabric of civilization.

2370. _____ . The Maltreated Child: The Maltreatment Syndrome in Children. See entry 1281.

2371. _____ . Somewhere a Child Is Crying, Maltreatment--Causes and Prevention. See entry 599.

2372. Fried, Jeanine. "Values, Norms and Child Abuse." New Mexico School Review, 51(4):49, Spring 1976.
This article is introduced by statements representing value positions concerning parent-child relations held by many persons.

A community standard of parenting expects that the parenting role
will result in children who at maturity will be able to function effectively in society. A standard of physical care is also set by society
but norms for the emotional and social quality of a child's life are
not universally agreed upon, however.

2373. Garbarino, James. "Preliminary Study of Some Ecological
Correlates of Child Abuse; The Impact of Socio-Economic
Stress on Mothers." Child Development, 47:178-185,
March 1976.
In this research project, the ecological correlates of child
abuse and maltreatment are explored. Data suggest that the degree
to which mothers in a particular New York State county are subjected
to socioeconomic stress without adequate support systems accounts
for a substantial proportion of the variance in rates of child abuse
and maltreatment. Economic conditions more generally affecting the
family accounted for a much smaller proportion.

2374. Garcia Vila, A.; Moya Benavent, M.; Borrajo Guadarrama,
E. "Síndrome del Niño Maltratado" [Battered Baby Syn-
drome]. Medicina Española, 70(413):81-86, 1973.
Examined are four cases of the battered baby syndrome representative of environmental characteristics of the children, i.e., sociocultural and psychological.

2375. Gelles, Richard J. "Child Abuse as Psychopathology: A
Sociological Critique and Reformulation." American Journal of Orthopsychiatry, 43(4):611-621, July 1973.
Much current research on child abuse employs a psychopathological model which explains child abuse as a function of a psychological pathology, or a sickness. It is hypothesized that major deficiences of this model are inconsistency and narrowness. It is suggested that a more dimensional approach to child abuse is possible
by focusing on the sociological and contextual variables' association
with abuse. (Author Abstract.)

2376. _____. "A Psychosocial Approach to Child Abuse." Nursing Digest, 2:52-59, April 1974.
The dominant theme is that the parent who abuses a child
suffers from a psychological sickness. A critical look is taken at
this theory and a number of deficiences are found with the model.
The purpose of this paper is to provide a more dimensional analysis
of the generative sources of child abuse. Data is re-examined in
terms of three aspects of child abuse: social characteristics of
abusing parents, social characteristics of the victims, and the situational properties of the act.

2377. _____. "The Social Construction of Child Abuse." American Journal of Orthopsychiatry, 45(3):363-371, April 1975.
Research on child abuse has traditionally focused on incidence,
causes, and prevention and treatment. One facet overlooked is that
abuse is social deviance, and is the product of social labeling. Em-
ploying the perspective of labeling theory, this paper proposes that

causes of abuse are products of social definitions applied by gate-
keepers charged with identifying children injured by their caretakers.
Gaps in our knowledge of child abuse are pointed out, and suggestions for empirical research are offered. (Journal Summary.)

2378. _____. The Violent Home: A Study of Physical Aggres-
sion Between Husbands and Wives. Beverly Hills, Calif:
Sage Publications, 1972. 230 p. (Sage Library of Social
Research, v. 13)
Conjugal violence is the dominant focus of this research.
However, attitudes toward corporal punishment of children are included. Empirical data on violence between family members definitely tend to indicate that violent individuals grew up in violent families and were frequently victims of familial violence as children.
In the author's research, it was found that many of the respondents
who had committed violence towards spouses had been exposed to
conjugal violence as children and had been frequent victims of parental violence.

2379. Gil, David G. "Abusing Parents: Cultural and Class Factors." In: Social Life Series of the Richmond School of
Social Work. Virginia Commonwealth University, 1970.

2380. _____. "Physical Abuse of Children." Pediatrics, 45:
510-511, March 1970.
Gil supports his epidemiological study with these points.
Findings from reports obtained from every state government in the
U.S. on every legally reported case (1967-1968) suggest that the root
cause of child abuse is part of our culture. Whereas battered children have received more attention by news media, the massive abuse
which society inflicts on millions of children who grow up in poverty
and deprivation is far more of a serious problem. He feels he has
used a more balanced approach by studying child abuse from a social rather than a clinical perspective.

2381. _____. "A Sociocultural Perspective on Physical Child
Abuse." Child Welfare, 50(7):389-395, July 1971. Also
available in pamphlet form.
A broad study--on a nationwide scale--of physical child abuse,
conducted by Brandeis University, stressed the sociological and cultural aspects of this phenomenon. The findings suggest a series of
measures as a basis for prevention through education, legislation,
elimination of poverty, and social services. (Pamphlet Introduction.)

2382. _____. "Unraveling Child Abuse." American Journal of
Orthopsychiatry, 45(3):346-356, 1975.
An attempt is made to clarify the dynamics of child abuse
within egalitarian value premises, as inflicted gaps in children's
circumstances that prevent the actualization of their inherent potential. The three related levels of manifestation are: interpersonal
level in the home; institutional level through policies and practices
of child care settings; societal level through social policies that determine lives of all children. These dimensions exert their influ-

ence through multiple interactions with each other. (Author Summary Modified.)

2383. _____. "Violence Against Children." Journal of Marriage and the Family, 33:637-648, November 1971.
This paper develops a definition and conceptual model of violence against children on the basis of a series of nationwide epidemiologic studies, public opinion, and press surveys. Culturally sanctioned use of physical force in child rearing, poverty and discrimination, deviance in bio-psycho-social functioning, and chance events are identified as causal dimensions of physical child abuse. The scope of the phenomenon and selected findings from the surveys are discussed and social policies aimed at primary, secondary, and tertiary prevention are suggested. Attention is drawn to massive societal abuse of children, which is a related but much more serious social problem. (Journal Summary.)

2384. _____. Violence Against Children--Physical Child Abuse in the United States. See entry 767.

2385. _____; Noble, John H. Public Knowledge, Attitudes and Opinions About Physical Child Abuse in the United States. Waltham, Mass.: Brandeis University, Florence Heller Graduate School for Advanced Studies in Social Welfare, 1967. 48 p. Available from EDRS: MF-$0.25; HC-$2.
The knowledge, attitudes, and opinions of the general public on child abuse and related issues were investigated with a standard, multi-stage area probability sample of non-institutional United States residents 21 or older (1520 respondents).

2386. _____; _____. "Public Knowledge, Attitudes and Opinions About Physical Child Abuse in the U.S." Child Welfare, 48(7):395-401,426, 1969.
Findings from Gil's 1965 survey of the general public to determine their knowledge of child abuse are reported. Recommends use of more advertising by public agencies to increase public recogniton of the problem.

2387. Giovannoni, Jeanne M. "Parental Mistreatment: Perpetrators and Victims." Journal of Marriage and the Family, 33: 649-657, November 1971.
Parental mistreatment of children is seen as a manifestation of noxious societal forces infringing on families. Data from a series of comparative studies of families who mistreated their children and those who had not is analyzed according to this proposition.

2388. Gottlieb, David, ed. Children's Liberation. See entry 610.

2389. Heinild, S. "Børnemishandling--et samfundsproblem" [Child Assault--A Society Problem]. Nordisk Medicin, 90(6-7): 172-173, June 1975.

2390. Helfer, Ray E.; Kempe, C. Henry, comp. The Battered Child. See entry 1512.

2391. James, Howard. The Little Victims: How America Treats Its Children. See entry 623.

2392. Keller, Oliver J. "Hypothesis for Violent Crime." American Journal of Correction, 37:7, March 1975.
Keller suggests the existence of a correlation between the increasing amount of brutal crime against the individual and the large number of unwanted and rejected children in our country. Since child abuse is not fully reported we cannot envision the true extent of it. However, the author does see a relationship between the abused child and the later resultant sociopathic criminal.

2393. Kobayashi, Noboru. "Child Abuse: From the Standpoint of Social Pediatrics." Popular Medicine, 52:12-17, 1974.
Literature on child abuse is reviewed. The gradual development of human rights for children is described. Socioeconomic characteristics of child abusing parents are considered.

2394. Leavitt, Jerome Edward, comp. The Battered Child: Selected Readings. See entry 521.

2395. Lenard, H. G. "Diskussionsbemerkung zur Arbeit H.-Ch. Steinhausen: Sozialmedizinische Aspekte der körperlichen Kindesmisshandlung (diese Z. 120,314-318 (1972))" [Discussion Comment on the Article of H.-Ch. Steinhausen: Sociomedical Aspects of Physical Child Abuse (This J. 120, 314-318 (1972)]. Monatsschrift für Kinderheilkunde, 121: 84-85, February 1973.
Lenard questions the emphasis of Steinhausen's article (entry 2415) on the low socioeconomic and intelligence levels of child abusers. He believes the central problem to be psycho-pathological, and that an unjustified over-emphasis on socioeconomic factors could lead to a significant number of battered children not being diagnosed because the parents don't "look like that." He cites several American studies that find child abusers are not limited to any one socioeconomic group. See also entry 2414.

2396. Lindenthal, Jacob Jay; Bennett, Arletha; Johnson, Sylvia. "Public Knowledge of Child Abuse: Newark, N.J." Child Welfare, 54:521-523, July 1975.
A report of a survey of 75 Newark adults reveals to what degree the survey population knew about child abuse. Five facets of public knowledge and attitudes about child abuse were measured. It was concluded that an increasingly educated public would be increasingly oriented toward treatment of offenders rather than arrest.

2397. Machanik, Gerald. "Parents Are Not Always a Child's Best Friend." S. A. Nursing Journal, 36:10-12, March 1969.
Mistreatment of children is looked upon as a social disease-- people can't control themselves when they hear a child cry, parents are starved for love themselves and expect too much maturity from child, there is a revulsion against the obligations of parenthood, and the maternal instinct seems extinct. The rearing of children is badly in need of change.

2398. Maurer, Adah. "Institutional Assault on Children." Clinical
    Psychologist, 29(2):23-25, Winter 1976.
    Contends that American society in general, and institutions in
particular, sanction and encourage assaultive behavior toward children because of traditional acceptance of corporal punishment and
"discipline." Psychologists are guilty of assault on children through
their use of aversive conditioning procedure to suppress unwanted
behavior. (P. A.)

2399. Mawby, R. I. "Child-Minding and Social Change." Social
    Service Quarterly, 48(2):208-211, 1974.
    Baby-farmers are the subject of this article. It is shown
that the problems of child-minding today can be better understood
through an analysis of the kinds of guardians who operated in the
19th century. As social, demographic and legal conditions changed,
so did child-minding in British society.

2400. Moore, P. "A Look at the Disintegrating World of Child-
    hood." (Editorial). Psychology Today, 9(1):32,34,36,
    June 1975.
    A disintegration of the family structure in our society is
viewed as a major factor in the failure of children to develop fully.
Divorce rates, working mothers, and single-parent families sharpen
the intensity of the problem. Infant mortality is another example of
the problem, and abuse, and even murder, of children is on the rise.

2401. National Committee for Prevention of Child Abuse. Profes-
    sional Papers: Child Abuse and Neglect. See entry 1063.

2402. Newberger, Eli H. "Book Review: Violence Against Children,
    by David Gil." Pediatrics, 48:688-690, 1971.
    A critique of Gil's (1970) monograph. Highly critical of Gil's
treatment of child abuse, specifically citing the format and methodology employed by Gil from which he drew macrospective conclusions
on the cause, nature, and incidence of child abuse.

2403. _____; Reed, R. B.; Daniel, J. H., et al. Toward an
    Etiologic Classification of Pediatric Social Illness. See
    entry 163.

2404. Oppe, T. E. "Battered Babies." Health Trends, 4(4):74-76,
    1972.
    The battered child syndrome has much in common with other
social and medical pathologies associated with parental failure. Under three years of age and suffering repeated non-accidental injuries
through episodic violence is the typical battered child. There are
differences from a social, psychiatric, and legal standpoint between
the battered child syndrome, child murder and continuous physical
persecution of children practiced by sadistic adults.

2405. "Panel Workshop: Violence, Crime, Sexual Abuse and Addic-
    tion (Will, Brigham, Ottenberg, Aytch, Booher, Cox, Cus-
    key, Del Rio, Densen-Gerber, Francis, Henderson, Mc-

Laughlin, Peters, Roether, Sobel, Stokes, Velimesis, Wright)." Contemporary Drug Problems, 5:385-440, Fall 1976.
The discussion in this panel workshop centered around chronic problems of society which perpetuate and multiply violence, crime, sexual abuse and incest, the powerlessness of children, domestic violence, the subservient role of women in society, and conditions in prison which reinforce violent behavior of prisoners. (Journal Summary Modified.)

2406. Roberts, Albert F., ed. Childhood Deprivation. See entry 649.

2407. Sage, Wayne, "Violence in the Children's Room." Human Behavior, 4(7):41-47, July 1975.
This is a lengthy article, exploring mainly the causes of child abuse. Most experts agree that the problem is deeply rooted on both the personal and social levels. It is a social tragedy that no one can ignore.

2408. Schmideberg, Melitta. "The Child Murderer." In: Crime in America: Controversial Issues in Twentieth Century Criminology, p. 202-210, by Herbert Aaron Bloch, ed. New York, Philosophical Library, 1961.

2409. Seaberg, James Rexford. Physical Child Abuse: An Expanded Analysis. Ph.D. The University of Wisconsin (Madison), 1974. 195 p. Available from University Microfilms, Order No. 74-26512.
Dr. David G. Gil conducted in 1967 and 1968 the first national study of physical child abuse. Seaberg's research was an attempt to expand Gil's analysis, using his data, to test structural causal models of injury severity in physical child-abuse behavior.

2410. Smith, Selwyn M. The Battered Child Syndrome. See entry 1553.

2411. _____. "Parents of Battered Babies." (Letter). British Medical Journal, 2:443, May 25, 1974.
The focus here is the assumption that anomalies of family status have a bearing on the circumstances leading to baby battering. Smith points out that because of the striking similarities between baby battering and other forms of deviant behavior, doctors must be authoritative, intrusive, and insistent if they are to help prevent rebattering. Prevention of battering must lie in the effective education of the next generation and, if possible, legal changes in child care.

2412. Soman, Shirley Camper. Let's Stop Destroying Our Children. New York: Hawthorn Books, 1974. 274 p.
A broad survey of societal neglect of children includes several case histories to support the hypothesis that child abuse is caused by community neglect of family problems. Isolation, loneliness, and inability to communicate are conditions leading to child abuse. A

more humane approach by institutions and professionals concerned
with child abuse is strongly recommended.   Victimization of children
by toys, bicycles, recreational programs, vehicles, furniture, appli-
ances, poisonous substances, poor living conditions, lack of material
necessities, and dangerous occupational situations are also discussed.

2413.   Steele, Brandt F.   "Child Abuse: Its Impact on Society."
        Journal of the Indiana State Medical Association, 68(3):191-
        194, March 1975.
        Social issues, in the past 20 years, have become the emphasis
in child care rather than the treatment of diseases.   Special education programs are needed for those children who are abused or neglected.   The circumstances under which they exist may cause them
to become juvenile delinquents and continue the chain of abuse and
neglect.

2414.   Steinhausen, H.-Ch.   "Schlusswort zur Diskussionsbemerkung
        von H.-G. Lenard zur Arbeit H.-Ch. Steinhausen: Sozial-
        medizinische Aspekte der körperlichen Kindesmisshandlung.
        I.   diese Z.   120, 314-318 (1972)" [Conclusion to the Dis-
        cussion Comment of H.-G. Lenard on the Article Aspects
        of Physical Child Abuse I.   This J. 120, 314-318 (1972)].
        Monatsschrift für Kinderheilkunde, 121:86-87, February
        1973.
        Steinhausen answers Lenard's criticism (entry 2395) of his
study on the socio-medical aspects of physical child abuse.   While
Lenard uses research from other countries to refute him, he, Steinhausen was concerned with only that data from the Federal Republic.
He denies that he has presented the problem of child abuse as one
that is primarily socioeconomic.   Rather, he has tried to interpret
the data on the psychological aspects in a socio-genetic context.   He
points to the physical-authoritarian parental basis of the lower classes
as contributing to child abuse as contrasted with the love-oriented educational techniques of the middle and upper classes.   He suggests
that abuse in these classes may be more often in the form of with-
drawal of love, rather than physical abuse.   Finally, he accuses
Lenard of one-sided quotes, quotes out of context and inaccurate
quotes.

2415.   _____.   "Sozialmedizinische Aspekte de körperlichen Kin-
        desmisshandlung" [Social Medicine Aspects of Physical
        Child Abuse].   Monatsschrift für Kinderheilkunde, 120:314-
        318, August 1972.
        This paper presents epidemiological data as well as charac-
teristic features of delinquent parents, battered children, and motivations for maltreatment.   An attempt is made to interpret the individual features of the delinquency in the light of their psycho-social
determinants.   (English Abstract.)

2416.   Steinmetz, Suzanne.   "Occupation and Physical Punishment:
        A Response to Straus."   Journal of Marriage and the Fam-
        ily, 33:664-666, 1971.
        An exploratory study suggesting that the type of work done,

not the traditional social class identification is related to the type
of control devices workers use with their children.

2417. _____, comp. "Violent Parents." In: <u>Violence in the
Family</u> (p. 141-229). New York: Dodd, Mead, 1974.
Part Three of this book is devoted to the background of physical punishment of children, the history of child abuse and infanticide,
sociological and psychological aspects, and helping parents and protecting children. Other parts of the book include an overview of the
subject on violence in the family, violence between spouses and kin,
and the influence of familial violence on societal violence.

2418. Stephenson, P. S. <u>Project Toddler: Interim Report.</u> See
entry 1444.

2419. Straus, Murray A. "Cultural and Social Organizational Influences on Violence Between Family Members." (Paper read
at the Mental Hygiene Institute Conference on "Sex, Marriage and the Family," November 30, 1972, Montreal,
Canada.)
Studies show that abusing parents have learned an abusive role
model from their parents which is brought into effect when a stress
condition occurs. The larger the number of children in a family,
the more often physical punishment is used.

2420. "Unsuspected Trauma." (Editorial). <u>Journal of the American
Medical Association,</u> 176(11):942-943, June 17, 1961.
The social and legal aspects of unsuspected trauma have many
ramifications. Incidence of injury to infants in family life varies in
inverse proportion to the intelligence of the parents, and particularly
increases with any addiction to drugs, including alcohol. Social services and legal authorities are expressing an increased interest whenever the need is apparent for the infant's protection.

2421. Van Stolk, Mary. <u>The Battered Child in Canada.</u> See entry
806.

2422. Walters, David R. <u>Physical and Sexual Abuse of Children:
Causes and Treatment.</u> Bloomington, Ind.: Indiana University Press, 1975. 192 p.
The central thesis is that abuse is rooted in our cultural heritage of denigrating children and institutionalizing violence and that
abusive parents are not usually mentally ill but are simply repeating
patterns in which they were reared. The author attempts to inform
the reader about the overall problem of child abuse in America and
to provide some understanding of adults who are labeled "abusive."
He presents the human aspects of child abuse and how it can be
treated by professionals, rather than a litany of horrors done to
children.

2423. Wertham, Frederic. "Battered Children and Baffled Adults."
<u>Bulletin of the New York Academy of Medicine,</u> 48(7):887-
898, August 1972.

The close interrelation of psychological and social factors in the battered child syndrome is discussed. The idea that human violence is an eternal, inborn instinct amounts to a biological justification for violence, and this attitude carries over to the battered child syndrome. Alcoholism, presence of a defective child in the home, and mental illness in parents are other contributory factors.

2424. Yelaja, Shankar A. "The Abused Child ... A Reminder of Despair." Canadian Welfare, 49(2):8-11, 1973.

Child abuse and neglect is explored as part of the family situation. Three types of parents are involved: those who are willfully or deliberately neglectful; parents who are ignorant of child care; and those who are poor in every sense of the word--in money, in health, in housing, in employment and in social circumstances. Often the child is neglected by the family and by the institutions of society and the social structure itself. It is suggested that child welfare services be alerted to include services to the whole family in order to prevent sociopathologies that affect children in need. (Journal Summary.)

2425. Young, Leontine. Wednesday's Children: A Study of Child Neglect and Abuse. See entry 233.

2426. Young, M. Some Selected Dimensions of Alienation in Abusive and Non-Abusive Families: A Comparative Study. Master's Thesis. Norman: University of Oklahoma, 1975. 99 p.

The relationship of alienation to child abuse is explored. Two dimensions of the sociological concept of alienation are relevant to abusive parents: social isolation and powerlessness. Hypotheses are tested regarding the differences between abusive and non-abusive parents in their social relationships and integration into the community; and regarding the social learning of the parental role and its effect in the functioning of parents. Public health nurses completed psychological and demographic surveys on abusive and non-abusive families they had encountered to provide data to assess the various hypotheses. Eight hypotheses received at least partial confirmation. The implications of the findings are discussed, and recommendations are offered.

UNCLASSIFIED FOREIGN LANGUAGE PUBLICATIONS

2427. [Anyone Who in Error Hurts His Child, Hurts Himself When He Is a Parent]. Tidskrift for Sveriges Sjukskorterskor, 38:18-19, October 20, 1971. (Swedish)

2428. "Barnmisshandel i Sverige--en Skakande Utställning" [Child Abuse in Sweden--A Distressing Exhibit]. Tidskrift for Sveriges Sjukskorterskor, 38:16-17, October 20, 1971. (Swedish)

2429. Bergstrand, C. G., et al. [Cases of Child Abuse in Malmö 1967-1974]. Lakartidningen, 73(33):2671-2677, August 11, 1976. (Eng. Abstr.)

2430. Beskow, B. [Abandoned Children]. Svenska Lakartidningen, 57:344-351, June 29, 1960. (Swedish)

2431. Betancourt, G. L. "Familias con Niños Presuntamente Maltratodos." Boletin de la Asociacion Medica de Puerto Rico, 63:216-218, September 1971. (Spanish)

2432. Bleistein, R. "Kinderfeindliche Gesellschaft?" Stimmen der Zeit, 194:1-2, January 1976.

2433. Brězina, A., et al. [Experiences in Ostrava with Child Abuse. Comments on the Article of Dunovsky J. Karabelova H: "Complications in the Social Background in a Case of Child Abuse," Ceskoslovenske Zdravotnictvi, 21, 1973, p. 344]. Ceskoslovenske Zdravotnictvi, 21:439, October 1973. (Czech)

2434. Cabanis, D. "Ein Ungewönhnliches Aggressionsdelikt" [Unusual Act of Aggression]. Beitraege zur Gerichtlichen Medizin, 27:176-181, 1970. (German)

2435. [Child Abuse]. Nederlands Tijdschrift voor Geneeskunde, 108:2418-2419, December 12, 1964. (Dutch)

2436. Christiansen, W. F. [Child Abuse. Case Material from General Practice]. Ugeskrift for Laeger, 130:1215-1219, July 18, 1968. (Danish)

2437. Coyle, J. T. "Alkali Retinopathy." (Letter). Archives d'Ophtalmologie, 94(9):1629, September 1976.

2438. De La Torre, J. A. [Aggression in the Pediatric Age. I. Syndrome of the Battered and Underdeveloped Child]. Gaceta Medica de Mexico, 109(4):215-222, April 1975. (Spanish)

2439. _____. [Battering the New Born Infant]. (Editorial). Boletin Medico del Hospital Infantil de Mexico, 32(3):363-364, May-June 1975. (Spanish)

2440. Drogendijk, A. C., Sr. "Wat Zijn Dat Toch Voor Ouders die hun Kind Mishandelen." Tijdschrift voor Ziekenverpleging, 24:858-861, September 14, 1971. (Dutch)

2441. Frick, A. [Mistreated Small Children]. Svenska Lakartidningen, 61:3004-3012, October 7, 1964.

2442. Gjerdrum, K. [The "Battered Child Syndrome"]. Tidsskrift for den Norske Laegeforening, 84:1609-1612, December 1, 1964. (Norwegian)

2443. Gostomzyk, J. G. [Child Abuse]. ZFA: Zeitschrift für Allgemeinmedizin, 52(20):1048-1055, July 20, 1976.

2444. Harlay, A. [The Abused Child]. L'Infirmière Francais, (180):5-9, December 1976.

2445. Harlem, O. K. [Child Abuse]. Tidsskrift for den Norske Laegeforening, 84:1635-1636, December 1, 1964. (Norwegian)

2446. Hedeby, Berit. Barnmisshandeln i Sverige. Göteborg: Zinderman, 1975. 170 p.

2447. Hiramatsu, Y., et al.[So-Called Battered-Child Syndrome]. Rinsho Hoshasen, 16:843-846, October 1971. (Japan)

2448. Hoagoa, P. [Child Abuse--The Battered Child Syndrome]. Sykepleien, 62(12):564-568, 582-583, June 20, 1975.

2449. Ignatov, Aleksei Nikolaevich. Ugolovnyĭzakon okhraniaet prava nesovershennoletnikh. Moskva, Iuridicheskala literatura, 1971.

2450. Jaeger, W. "Descemetruptur bei van der Hoeve-Lobstein-Syndrom mit Ausbildung einer Keratoschisis." Bericht; Deutsche Ophthalmologische Gesellschaft, 70:639-646, 1970. (German)

2451. Johansson, E. E.; Lukács, J. "Barnens rätt i Samhället-Nágot att Kämpa for. Tidsskrift for Sveriges Sjukskoterskor, 38:47-50, November 3, 1971. (Swedish)

2452. Joyal-Poupart, R. "Le Silence qui fait de nous des bourreaux." Le Revue Juridique Thémis, 9:115-120, 1974.

2453. "Kindermishandeling." Nederlands Tijdschrift voor Geneeskunde, 114:971-972, June 6, 1970.

2454. Kluska, V., et al. [Battered Child Syndrome]. Casopis Lekaru Ceskych, 111:153-157, February 18, 1972.

2455. Kokavec, M., Dobrotka, G. "Kotázke Motivácie Zlého Zaobchádzania s Defmi." Ceskoslovenska Patologie, 7:55-58, November 1971.

2456. Kugelmann, J. "Uber Symmetrische Spontanfrakturen Unbekannter Genese beim Säugling." Annales de Pediatrie, 178: 177-181, 1952.

2457. Kuipers, F., et al. [Child Abuse (Battered Child Syndrome)]. Nederlands Tijdschrift voor Geneeskunde, 108:2399-2406, December 12, 1964. (Dutch)

2458. _____. "De Taak Van de Verpleegster bij Mishandelde Kinderen." Tijdschr Ziekenverpl, 22:836-838, September 15, 1969. (Dutch)

2459. Lievre, J. A.; Camus, J. P.; Guillien, P.; Duclos, H. "Osteoarticular Manifestations of Congenital Generalized Analgesia." Revue du Rhumatisme et des Maladies Osteoarticulaires, 35:583-589, November 1968.

2460. Marie, J.; Apostolides, P.; Salet, J.; Eliachar, E.; Lyon, G. "Hématome sous-dural du nourrisson associé a des fractures des membres." Annales de Pediatrie, 30:1757-1763, 1954.

2461. Marquezy, R-Z.; Bach, Ch.; Blondeau, M. "Hématome sousdural et fractures multiples des os longs chez un nourrisson de 9 mois." Archives Francaises de Pediatrie, 9:526-531, 1952.

2462. Marten, J. [Problem of Child Abuse]. Ceskoslovenska Pediatrie, 30(9):429-431, September 1975. (Eng. Abstr.)

2463. Marti, J.; Kaufmann, H. J. "Multiple Traumatische Knochenläsionen beim Säugling." Deutsche Medizinische Wochenschrift, 84:984-988,991,992, 1959.

2464. Medynśka, L. "Battered Child Syndrome." Pediatria Polska, 49:767-772, June 1974. (Polish)

2465. Meneghello, J.; Hasbun, J. "Hematoma Subdural y fractura de los huesos largos." Revista Chilena de Pediatria, 22: 80-83, 1951.

2466. Muller, G. [Child Abuse from the Pediatric Viewpoint]. Kinderaerztliche Praxis, 44(3):124-130, March 1976.

2467. Olsson, U. "Undervisning om Barnmisshandel för vårdper-
       sonal. " Tidskrift for Sveriges Sjukskoterskor, 38:16-18,
       October 6, 1971. (Swedish)

2468. Pérez, C. , et al. [Battered Child Syndrome. Traumatologi-
       cal Aspects]. Revista Chilena de Pediatria, 46(4):363-365,
       July-August 1975. (Spanish)

2469. Pieterse, J. J. [The Battered Child]. Nederlands Tijdschrift
       voor Geneeskunde, 114:1000-1002, June 13, 1970. (Dutch)

2470. Racine, A. [Introductory Discussion of Child Abuse]. Les
       Enfants Victimes de Mauvais Traitements, 28:5-16, 1971.

2471. Rebattu, J. P. , et al. [Silverman's Syndrome]. Journal
       Francais d'Oto-Rhino-Laryngologie, et Chirurgie
       Maxillo-Faciale, 25(4):345, 347, April 1976

2472. Renard, G. , et al. [Is the Silverman Syndrome a Battered
       Child Syndrome?] Bulletin des Societes d'Ophtalmologie
       de France, 75(9-10):827-829, September-October 1976.

2473. Ringel, J. [Cruelty to Child in the Family]. Ceskoslovenska
       Pediatrie, 26:243-246, May 1971.

2474. Selander, P. [Child Abuse]. Lakartidningen, 72(1-2):42-43,
       January 8, 1975. (Swedish)

2475. Soto Viera, M. E. "Comentarios en Torno a una Tesis Sobre
       Atropello y Maltrato Infantil. " [Comments on a Thesis of
       Child Abuse]. Boletin de la Asociacion Medica de Puerto
       Rico, 63:219-222, September 1971. (Spanish)

2476. Sweden. Socialstyrelsen. Barn som far illa; en undersökning
       om barnmisshandel och skadlig uppväxtmiljö(av) Socialstyrel-
       sen i samarbete med Allmänna barnhuset. (Stockholm,
       Distributor: Nya Lagerblads trychkert, Karishamn, 1975).
       86 p.

2477. Tangen, Ottar. Barnesmishandling i Norgo: the maltreat-
       ment syndrome in children, child neglect and/or abuse,
       the battered child phenomenon. Oslo: Holstad, 1975.
       123 p. ill. Norwegian or English; English summary.

2478. Trube-Becker, E. "Tötungsdelikte Durch die Mutter. " Beit-
       raege zur Gerichtlichen, 27:166-175, 1970. (German)

2479. Ullrich, Wolfgang. Die Kindesmisshandlung in strafrechtlicher,
       kriminologischer und gerichtsmedizinischer Sicht. (Neu-
       wied a. Rh.) Luchterhand (1964) 139 p. (Strafrecht, Stra-
       fverfahren, Kriminologie, Bd. 8)

2480. Vesterdal, Jørgen. The Battered Child Syndrome. Abstracts:

The Battered Child. (Lindau, Nestlé Scientific Services, 1972). 76 p. port. (Annales Nestlé. [English ed.] no. 27)

2481. Weigel, W., et al. [Child Abuse and Neglect]. (author's transl.). Roentgenblaetter, 28(10):463-470, October 1975. (Eng. Abstract) (German)

2482. Witaszek-Napierala, A. [Germanization of Polish Children]. Przeglad Lekarski, 25:109-110, 1969. (Polish)

2483. Witkowski, J. [Further Information on the "Polen-Jugendver-wahrlager" in Lódz]. Przeglad Lekarski, 25:97-108, 1969. (Polish)

2484. Wyss, Rudolf. Unzucht mit Kindern; Untersuchungen zur Frage der sogenannten Pädophilie. Berlin; New York: Springer, 1967. 72 p. (Monographien aus dem Gesamt-gebiete der Neurologie und Psychiatrie, Heft 121)

DIRECTORY OF INFORMATION SOURCES

AIMS Instructional Media Services, Inc.
626 Justin Avenue
Glendale, Calif.   91201
(213) 240-9300

American Academy of Pediatrics
1801 Hinman Avenue
Evanston, Ill.   60204
(312) 869-4255

American Humane Association
5351 S. Roslyn Street
Englewood, Colo.   80110

Brigham Young University
Media Marketing W-STAD
Provo, Utah   84602
(801) 374-1211, X 4071

CEC Information Services and
   Publications
The Council for Exceptional
   Children
1920 Association Drive
Reston, Va.   22091

CRM McGraw-Hill Films
Del Mar, Calif.   92014
(714) 481-8184

Child Abuse Listening Mediation
   (CALM)
P. O. Box 718
Santa Barbara, Calif.   93102
(805) 963-1115

Child Protection Report
1301 20th Street, N. W.
Washington, D. C.   20036

Child Welfare League of America
67 Irving Place
New York, N. Y.   10003

Children Before Dogs (CBD)
15 W. 81st Street
New York, New York   10024
(212) 873-5507

Children's Memorial Hospital
Division of Child Psychiatry
Attn: Jean Stiman
2300 Children's Plaza
Chicago, Ill.   60614
(312) 649-4589

Children's Rights, Inc.
3443 17th Street, N. W.
Washington, D. C.   20010
(202) 462-7573

Day Care Council of New York,
   Inc.
114 E. 32nd Street
New York, N. Y.   10010

Education Commission of the
   States
300 Lincoln Tower
1860 Lincoln Street
Denver, Colo.   80295

End Violence Against the Next
   Generation (EVAN-G)
977 Keeler Avenue
Berkeley, Calif.   94708
(415) 527-0454

ERIC Document Reproduction
   Services (EDRS)
P. O. Box 190
Arlington, Va.   22210

414

Films, Inc.
1144 Wilmette Avenue
Wilmette, Ill.   60091
(312) 256-6600

Fort Wayne Public Library
Attn: Steven Fortriede
900 Webster Street
Fort Wayne, Ind.   46802

High Court of Southern Califor-
    nia
Attn: Mr. James Martin
100 Border Avenue
Solana Beach, Calif.   92075
(714) 755-5158

Indiana University
Audio-Visual Center
Bloomington, Ind.   47401
(812) 337-8087

Medcom, Inc.
1633 Broadway
New York, N.Y.   10019

Michigan State University
Department of Human Develop-
    ment
College of Human Medicine
East Lansing, Mich.   48823

Mike Williams Associates
329 A 17th Street
Manhattan Beach, Calif.   90266

Motorola Telegrams, Inc.
7919 Cliffbrook Drive, Suite 243
Dallas, Texas 75240
(214) 661-8464 (call Collect)

Motorola Teleprograms, Inc.
4825 N. Scott Street, Suite 23
Schiller Park, Ill.   60176
(312) 671-0141 (call Collect)

National Center for Child Abuse
    and Neglect
1205 Oneida
Denver, Colo.   80220

National Center on Child Abuse
    and Neglect

Office of Child Development
Children's Bureau
330 Independence Avenue, S.W.
Washington, D.C.   20201
(202) 755-7762

National Committee for Preven-
    tion of Child Abuse
Suite 510
111 E. Wacker Drive
Chicago, Ill.   60601

Parental Stress Center
918 S. Negley Avenue
Pittsburgh, Pa.   15232
(412) 661-2674

Parents Anonymous
2810 Artesia Boulevard
Redondo Beach, Calif.   90278
(213) 371-3501

Parents' Magazine Films, Inc.
52 Vanderbilt Avenue
New York, N.Y.   10017
(212) 685-4400

Paulist Productions
P.O. Box 1057
Pacific Palisades, Calif.   90272
(213) 454-0688

Regional Institute of Social Wel-
    fare Research
468 N. Milledge Avenue
Heritage Building
Athens, Ga.   30602

SCAN Volunteer Service, Inc.
    (Suspected Child Abuse and
    Neglect)
Hendrix Hall
4314 W. Markham Street
Little Rock, Arkansas   72205
(501) 371-2773

Trikon Productions
P.O. Box 21
La Jolla, Calif.   92038
(714) 459-5233

University Microfilms Interna-
    tional

300 North Zeeb Road
Ann Arbor, Mich.   48106
(1-800-521-3042) (Toll Free)

Xerox Films
Xerox Educational Publications
245 Long Hill Road
Middletown, Conn.   06457
(203) 347-7251

AARN News Letter
ANA Clinical Sessions
Acta Paedopsychiatrica
Acta Psychiatrica Scandinavica
Action Line
Addictive Diseases
Adolescence
Advances in Pediatrics
Alabama School Journal
Alaska Medicine
Alcohol Health and Research
World
Algemeen Politieblad
America
American Academy of Child
Psychiatry Journal
American Baby
American Bar Association Journal
American Criminal Law Review
American Education
American Family Physician
American Journal of Community
Psychology
American Journal of Correction
American Journal of Diseases
of Children
The American Journal of Maternal Child Nursing
American Journal of Mental Deficiency
American Journal of Nursing
American Journal of Occupational Therapy
American Journal of Ophthalmology
American Journal of Orthopedics
American Journal of Orthopsychiatry
American Journal of Psychiatry
American Journal of Psycho-
therapy
American Journal of Public
Health and the Nation's
Health
American Journal of Roentgenology, Radium Therapy and
Nuclear Medicine
American Journal of Sociology
American Medical News
American Nurse
American Psychologist
American School Board Journal
American Sociological Review
Annales de Chirurgie Infantile
Annales de Dermatologie et
Syphiligraphie
Annales de Pediatrie
Annales de Radiologie
Annales d'Oculistique
Annales Médico-Psychologiques
Annales of the American Academy of Political and Social
Science
Annual Progress in Child Psychiatry and Child Development
Applied Radiology and Nuclear
Medicine
Archiv für Kriminologie
Archives d'Ophtalmologie
Archives Françaises de Pediatrie
Archives of Dermatology
Archives of Disease in Childhood
Archives of General Psychiatry
Archives of Ophthalmology
Archives of Pathology
Archives of Surgery
The Atlantic Advocate
The Australasian Nurses Journal

Australian and New Zealand Journal of Psychiatry
Australian Journal of Forensic Science
Australian Paediatric Journal
Ave Maria

Beitraege zur Gerichtlichen Medizin
Bericht; Deutsche Ophthalmologische Gesellschaft
Biomedical Communications
Boletín de la Asociacion Medica de Puerto Rico
Boletín Medico del Hospital Infantil de Mexico
British Journal of Criminology
British Journal of Delinquency
British Journal of Educational Studies
British Journal of Hospital Medicine
British Journal of Medical Psychology
British Journal of Ophthalmology
British Journal of Oral Surgery
British Journal of Preventive & Social Medicine
British Journal of Psychiatry
British Journal of Radiology
British Journal of Social Psychiatry
British Medical Journal
Bruxelles-Medical
Buffalo Law Review
Bulletin de la Societe Française de Dermatologie et de Syphiligraphie
Bulletin des Societes d'Ophtalmologie de France
Bulletin of the American Academy of Psychiatry and the Law
Bulletin of the Calcutta School of Tropical Medicine
Bulletin of the Cleveland Dental Society
Bulletin of the Menninger Clinic
Bulletin of the New York Academy of Medicine
Bulletin of the Tulane Medical Faculty

CMD (Current Medical Dialog)
Les Cahiers de Droit
California Law Review
California Medicine
California School Boards
California State Bar Journal (title varies)
California State Nurses' Association Bulletin
California Western Law Review
California's Health
Canada's Mental Health
Canadian Hospital
Canadian Journal of Public Health
Canadian Medical Association Journal
The Canadian Nurse
Canadian Psychiatric Association Journal
Canadian Welfare
Case and Comment
Case Conference
Casopis Lekaru Ceskych
Catholic Lawyer
Catholic Library World
Catholic Nurse
Catholic World
Ceskoslovenska Patologie
Ceskoslovenska Pediatrie
Ceskoslovenska Psychiatrie
Ceskoslovenske Zdravotnictvi
Charities
Chatelaine
Chicago-Kent Law Review
Chicago Schools Journal
Child and Family
Child Development
Child Protection Report
Child Welfare
Childhood Education
Children
Children Today
Chirurgische Praxis
Christian Century
Christian Home
Christian Order
Christian Science Monitor
Christianity Today
Church and Society
Cincinnati Journal of Medicine
Cleveland-Marshall Law Review

Clinical Neurosurgery
Clinical Pediatrics
Clinical Proceedings of Children's Hospital of the District of Columbia
Clinical Psychologist
Clinician
Columbia Journal of Law and Social Problems
Columbia Law Review
Commonweal
Community Health
Community Mental Health Journal
Compact
Comprehensive Psychiatry
Connecticut Bar Journal
Connecticut Health Bulletin
Connecticut Law Review
Connecticut Medicine
Consultant
Contemporary Drug Problems
Contemporary Review
Cornell Law Review
Courrier
Creighton Law Review
Crime and Delinquency
Criminologie
Crisis Intervention
Cumberland Law Review
The Cumberland-Samford Law Review
Current Problems in Pediatrics
Current Therapeutical Research, Clinical and Experimental
Currents in Public Health

Day Care and Early Education
Delaware Medical Journal
Delikt en Delinkwent
Denver Law Journal
DePaul Law Review
Deutsche Gesundheitswesen
Deutsche Medizinische Wochenschrift
Deutsche Zeitschrift für die Gesamte Gerichtliche Medizin
Developmental Medicine and Child Neurology
Dickinson Law Review
Dimensions in Health Service
Diseases in the Nervous System
Dissertation Abstracts International
District Nursing
Duquesne Law Review

East African Medical Journal
Economist
Editorial Research Reports
Education Digest
Education News
Educator's Advocate
Elementary School Guidance and Counseling
Emergency Medicine
Emory Law Journal
Encore American & Worldwide News
Les Enfants Victimes de Mauvais Traitements
Engage/Social Action
Essence
Exceptional Children

FBI Law Enforcement Bulletin
Family Coordinator
Family Health
Family Law Quarterly
Federal Probation
Feelings and Their Medical Significance
Fordham Law Review
Forecast for Home Economics
Forensic Science
Fortschritte auf dem Gebiete der Roentgenstrahlen und der Nuklearmedizin
Fortune
Frontiers

GEA Update
GP
Gaceta Medica de Mexico
Gazette Medicale de France
George Washington Law Review
Georgetown Law Journal
Good Housekeeping
Guy's Hospital Reports

Harefuah
Harvard Educational Review
Hastings Law Journal

Hawaii Medical Journal
Health and Social Service Journal
Health Education
Health Services Research
Health Trends
Health Visitor
Helvetica Paediatrica Acta
History of Childhood Quarterly
Hospital and Community Psychiatry
Hospital Medicine
Hospital Physician
Hospital Practice
Hospital Topics
Hospitals
Howard Journal of Penology and Crime Prevention
Howard Law Journal
Human Behavior
The Human Context
Human Ecology Forum
Human Needs
Humanist

IEA Reporter
Illinois Education News
Illinois Medical Journal
Illinois School Board Journal
Illinois Teacher for Contemporary Roles (title varies)
Imprint
Indian Journal of Pediatrics
Indian Pediatrics
Infirmière Canadienne
L'Infirmière Français
Inform Newsletter
Injury: British Journal of Ancient Surgery
Instructor
Intellect, the Magazine of Educational and Social Affairs
International Child Welfare Review
International Journal of Forensic Dentistry
International Journal of Law and Science
International Journal of Offender Therapy and Comparative Criminology
International Journal of Psycho-Analysis
International Journal of Psychoanalytic Psychotherapy
International Juvenile Officers' Association Newsletter
International Review of Psycho-Analysis
International Surgery
Iowa Journal of Social Work
Irish Medical Journal
Israel Annals of Psychiatry and Related Disciplines

JOGN Nursing
Journal des Agreges
Journal Francais d'Oto-Rhino-Laryngologie et Chirurgie Maxillo-Faciale
Journal of Asthma Research
Journal of Autism and Childhood Schizophrenia
Journal of Bone and Joint Surgery
Journal of Child Psychology and Psychiatry and Allied Disciplines
Journal of Clinical Child Psychology
Journal of Clinical Psychology
Journal of Consulting and Clinical Psychology
Journal of Dentistry for Children
Journal of Emergency Nursing
Journal of Family Law
Journal of Forensic Sciences
Journal of Home Economics
Journal of Laryngology and Otology
Journal of Legal Medicine
Journal of Marriage and the Family
Journal of Neurosurgery
Journal of Operational Psychiatry
Journal of Oral Surgery
The Journal of Pastoral Care
Journal of Pediatric Ophthalmology
Journal of Pediatric Psychology
Journal of Pediatric Surgery

Journal of Pediatrics

The Journal of Practical Nursing

Journal of Psychiatric Nursing and Mental Health Services

The Journal of School Health

Journal of Sociology and Social Health

Journal of Sociology and Social Welfare

Journal of the American Academy of Child Psychiatry

Journal of the American Academy of Psychoanalysis

Journal of the American Dental Association

Journal of the American Medical Association

Journal of the American Pharmaceutical Association

Journal of the Arkansas Medical Society

Journal of the Canadian Association of Radiologists

Journal of the Canadian Dental Association

Journal of the College of Radiologists of Australia

Journal of the Florida Medical Association

Journal of the Forensic Science Society

Journal of the Indiana State Medical Association

Journal of the International Association of Pupil Personnel Workers

Journal of the International College of Surgeons

Journal of the Iowa Medical Society

Journal of the Kansas Medical Society

Journal of the Kentucky Medical Association

Journal of the Louisiana State Medical Society

Journal of the Maine Medical Association

Journal of the Medical Association of Georgia

Journal of the Medical Association of the State of Alabama

Journal of the Medical Society of New Jersey

Journal of the Mississippi State Medical Association

Journal of the Mount Sinai Hospital

Journal of the National Association

Journal of the National Medical Association

Journal of the New York State School Nurse-Teachers Association

Journal of the Oklahoma State Medical Association

Journal of the Royal College of General Practitioners

Journal of the Royal Naval Medical Service

Journal of the South Carolina Medical Association

Journal of the State Bar of California

Journal of the Tennessee Medical Association

Journal of Trauma

Journal of Youth & Adolescence

Juvenile Court Judges Journal

Juvenile Justice

Keynote

Kinderaerztliche Praxis

Kriminalistik

Lakartidningen

Lancet

Land & Water Law Review

Language, Speech & Hearing Services in Schools

Law and the Social Order

The Law Society's Gazette

Legal Medicine Annual

Library Counselor

Life

Life-Threatening Behavior

Liguorian

Loyola Law Review

Lyon Medical

MCN: The American Journal

of Maternal Child Nursing
MH (Mental Hygiene)
Maandblad voor de Geestelijke Volksgezondheid
McCall's
Maine School Management Association Bulletin
Manitoba Medical Review
Maryland State Medical Journal
Massachusetts Physician
Massachusetts Teacher
Maternal-Child Nursing Journal
Medecine Legale et Dommage Corporel
Medical Annals of the District of Columbia
Medical Economics
Medical Insight
Medical Journal of Australia
Medical Journal of Malaysia
Medical Science
Medical Service Digest
Medical Social Law
Medical Social Work
Medical Times
Medical Trial Technique Quarterly
Medical World News
Medicina Española
Medicine, Science and the Law
Medico-Legal Bulletin
Medico-Legal Journal
Medisch Contact
Medizinische Klinik
Medizinische Welt
Memphis State University Law Review
Mental Health
Mental Health Program Reports
Mental Hygiene
Mental Retardation
Merrill Palmer Quarterly
Michigan Law Review
Michigan Medicine
Midwife and Health Visitor
Midwife Health Visitor & Community Nurse
Midwives Chronicle
Military Medicine
Minerva Pediatrica
Minnesota Law Review
Minnesota Medicine
Minnesota Welfare

Mississippi Law Journal
Missouri Medicine
Monatsschrift für Kinderheilkunde
Monatsschrift für Unfallheilkunde
More
Munchener Medizinische Wochenschrift
Municipal and Public Services Journal

NJEA Review
Nation
Nebraska Medical Journal
Nebraska Nurse
Nebraska State Medical Journal
Nederlands Tijdschrift voor Geneeskunde
Nederlands Tijdschrift voor Kriminologie
Neue Praxis
Neurology
Neuropsihijatrija
Nevada Education
New England Journal of Medicine
New Mexico School Review
New Outlook for the Blind
New Physician
New Republic
New Society
New Statesman and Nation-Week-End Review
New York Medicine
New York State Dental Journal
New York State Journal of Medicine
New York University of Law Review
New Yorker
The New Zealand Medical Journal
New Zealand Nursing Journal
New Zealand Psychologist
Newsletter of the American Academy of Pediatrics
Newsweek
Nordisk Kriminalteknisk Tidsskrift
Nordisk Medicin
North Carolina Education
North Carolina Law Review
North Carolina Medical Journal

North Carolina Public Welfare News
North Carolina Teachers Record
North Dakota Law Review
Northwest Medicine
Northwestern University Law Review
Nova Scotia Medical Bulletin
Nursing
Nursing Care
The Nursing Clinics of North America
Nursing Digest
Nursing Forum
Nursing Journal of India
Nursing Mirror and Midwives Journal
Nursing Outlook
Nursing Research
Nursing Times
Nursing Update

Ohio Schools
Ohio State Law Journal
Ohio State Medical Journal
Oklahoma Law Review
Oklahoma Observer
Ona Journal
Oregon Law Review
Orthopedic Clinics of North America
Orvosi Hetilap
Ouest Medical
Our Sunday Visitor, Inc.

The PTA Magazine
Padiatrische Praxis
Paediatrie und Grenzgebiete
Parents' Magazine & Better Homemaking
Patient Care
Peabody Journal of Education
Pediatria Polska
Pediatric Annals
Pediatric Clinics of North America
Pediatric Currents
Pediatric News
Pediatric Nursing
Pediatrics
Pediatrics Digest

Pediatrie
Pediatriia
Pennsylvania Medical Journal
Pennsylvania Medicine
Pennsylvania School Journal
People
Pepperdine Law Review
Perceptual & Motor Skills
The Pharos of Alpha Omega Alpha
Phi Delta Kappan
Physician's Management
Plastic and Reconstructive Surgery
Point of View
Police
Police Chief
Police College Magazine
Police Journal
Police Review
Police Surgeon
Polizeiblatt
Polski Tygodnik Lekarski
Popular Government
Popular Medicine
Postgraduate Medical Journal
Postgraduate Medicine
Practitioner
Prakticky Lekar
Praxis
Praxis der Kinderpsychologie und Kinderpsychiatrie
Presse Medicale
Prism
Pro Juventute
Probation Journal
Problemy Alkoholizmu
Proceedings of the Academy of Political Science
Proceedings of the Royal Society of Medicine
Proces
The Progressive
Prosecutor
Przeglad Lekarski
Psychiatria Clinica
Psychiatria Polska
Psychiatric Annals
Psychiatric News
Psychiatric Opinion
Psychiatric Quarterly Supplement
Psychiatrie de l'Enfant

Psychiatry
Psychoanalytic Quarterly
Psychoanalytic Review
Psychological Bulletin
Psychology in the Schools
Psychology Today
Psychoneuroendocrinology
Psykológnytt
Pszichológiai Tanulmányok
Public Health
Public Health Reports
Public Health Reviews
Public Law
Public Welfare

Quarterly
Queen's Nursing Journal

R. N.
Radiography
Radiologe
Radiologia Diagnostica
Radiologic Clinics of North
    America
Radiology
Reader's Digest
Recht der Jugend und des
    Bildungswesens
Record of the Association of
    the Bar of the City of New
    York
Redbook
Reiss-Davis Clinic Bulletin
Res Gestae
Resident and Staff Physician
Revista Chilena de Pediatria
Revista Española de Pediatria
Revista Latinoamericana de
    Psicologica
Revue de Droit Pénal et de
    Criminologie
La Revue de l'Alcoolisme
Revue de Neuropsychiatrie In-
    fantile et d'Hygiene Mentale
    de l'Enfance
Revue de Stomatologie et de
    Chirurgie Maxillo-Faciale
Revue du Praticien
Revue du Rhumatisme et des
    Maladies Osteoarticulaires
Revue Internationale de l'Enfant

Le Revue Juridique Thémis
Rhode Island Medical Journal
Rinsho Hoshasen
Riss
Rivista Sperimentale di Frenia-
    tria e Medicine Legale Delle
    Alienazioni Mentali
Roche Image of Medicine and
    Research
Rocky Mountain Medical Jour-
    nal
Roentgenblaetter
Royal Society of Health Journal

S. A. Nursing Journal
Saint Anthony Messenger
San Diego Law Review
Saturday Evening Post
School and Community
School Board Notes
The School Counselor
School Library Journal
Schweizerische Medizinische
    Wochenschrift
Science Digest
Semaine des Hopitaux de Paris
Seton Hall Law Review
Sjow
Smith College Studies in Social
    Work
Social and Rehabilitation Record
Social Casework
Social Service Outlook
Social Service Quarterly
Social Service Review
Social Welfare Court Digest
Social Work
Social Work Today
South African Medical Journal
Southern Medical Journal
Special Children
Spectator
Stanford Law Review
Stanford Medical Bulletin
State Government
Stimmen der Zeit
Suggested State Legislation
Surgery, Gynecology and Ob-
    stetrics
Surgical Clinics of North Amer-
    ica
Surgical Neurology

Svenska Lakartidningen
Sygeplejersken
Sykepleien

Teacher's Voice
Techniques Hospitalieres Medico-
Sociales et Sanitaires
Tennessee Public Welfare Rec-
ord
Texas Medicine
Texas Nursing
Texas State Journal of Medicine
Therapie der Gegenwart
Thrust for Educational Leader-
ship
Tidskrift for Sveriges Sjuks-
koterskor
Tidsskrift for den Norske Laege-
forening
Tijdschrift voor Maatschappi-
jvraagstukken en Welzijn-
swerk
Tijdschrift voor Ziekenverpleg-
ing
Time
Times (London) Educational
Supplement
Today's Child
Today's Education
Today's Family Digest
Today's Health
Together
Transaction
Transactional Analysis Journal
Transactions of the American
Academy of Ophthalmology
and Otolaryngology
Transactions of the Ophthalmol-
ogical Societies of the United
Kingdom
Trauma
Trial
Trial and Tort Trends
Trial Law Quarterly
Tunisie Medicale
Twentieth Century

U E A Action (Utah Education
Association Action)
U. S. Catholic
U. S. Medicine

U. S. News
Ugeskrift for Laeger
University of Baltimore Law
Review
University of Detroit Law Jour-
nal
University of Florida Law Re-
view
University of Kansas Law Re-
view
University of Maryland Law
Forum
University of Miami Law Re-
view
University of Michigan Journal
of Law Reform
University of Missouri Law
Review
University of Pittsburgh Law
Review
University of Western Australia
Law Review
Update
Utah Public Welfare Review

Valparaiso University Law Re-
view
VEB Gustav Fischer Verlag
Vie Medicale au Canada Fran-
cais
Villanova Law Review
Virginia Health Bulletin
Virginia Medical Monthly
Voice for Children

Washburn Law Journal
Washington and Lee Law Review
Washington Law Review
Washington State Journal of
Nursing
Wellesley Alumnae Magazine
West Virginia Law Review
Western Journal of Medicine
Western Reserve Law Review
What's New (Abbott Laborator-
ies)
Wiener Medizinische Wochens-
chrift
Willamette Law Journal
William & Mary Law Review
Wisconsin Medical Journal

Woman's World
Women Lawyers Journal
World Medical Journal
World of Irish Nursing
Wyoming Education News

Young Children

ZFA: Zeitschrift für Allgemeinmedizin
Zeitschrift für Aerztliche Fortbildung

Zeitschrift für Allgemeinmed-
izin; der Landarzt
Zeitschrift für die Gesamte
Hygiene und Ihre Grenzgebiete
Zeitschrift für Kinderchirurgie
und Grenzgebiete
Zeitschrift für Krankenpflege
Zeitschrift für Morphologie und
Anthropologie
Zeitschrift für Rechtsmedizin
Zentralblatt für Chirurgie
Zentralblatt für Jugendrecht
und Jugendwohlfahrt

AUTHOR INDEX

Adams, Earl H. 2053
Adams, Joan C. 1290
Adams, P. C. 236
Adams, Wayne V. 2348
Adelman, Lynn 1087
Adelson, Edna 2094
Adelson, Lester 19, 20, 21, 22
Adler, M. 811
Affonso, Dyanne D. 1643
Afifi, Abdelmonen A. 177, 178, 2151
Ahmed, S. 89
AIMS Instructional Media Services, Inc. 500, 502
Akbarnia, Behrooz A. 1480, 1616A
Akbarnia, Nasrin O. 1616A
Alabama State Department of Pensions and Security 1803
Alberts, M. E. 1617
Alexander, Betty 1659
Alexander, Jerry 1193, 1804
Alimohammadi, A. 24
Alison, Michael 1459
Allen, Ann Frances 547
Allen, Hugh D. 818, 819, 1481, 2349
Allen, John E. 2190
Allen, M. 820
Allison, Patricia K. 23
Altman, Donald H. 237
Alvy, Kerby T. 1195, 2350
Ambuel, J. Phillip 235
Ameli, N. O. 24
American Academy of Pediatrics 671, 1196, 1805, 1867
American Broadcasting Co. 505
American Humane Association 468, 469, 470, 496, 497, 744, 821, 822, 1197, 1563, 1806, 1807, 1808, 1809, 1810, 1811,
1812, 1813, 1814, 1815, 1816, 1817, 1818, 1819, 1820, 1821, 1822, 1823, 1824, 1825, 1826, 1827, 1828, 2055, 2271, 2351
Amiel, Shirley 2272
Anchorage Child Abuse Board, Inc. 25
Anderson, Doris 823
Anderson, J. P. 1618
Anderson, J. R. 745
Anderson, Lee R. 250
Anderson, William R. 239
Andreini, M. 25
Andrews, C. 824
Andrews, John P. 240
Andrews, Roberta G. 43
Angel, K. 958
Annecillo, Charles 152, 154
Anthony, E. James 2056
Antoni, P. 241
Apostolides, P. 2460
Appelbaum, Alan S. 2057
Arcadio, F. 242
Areen, J. 826
Ariés, Philippe 683
Arizona Community Development for Abuse and Neglect 1198
Arkansas. Legislative Council 827
Arnold, George L. 828
Arnold, Mildred 1829, 2058
Arnoldi, A. 1619
Aron, J. J. 243
Arthur, L. J. H. 1830
Asch, Stuart S. 2059, 2060
Askwith, Gordon K. 829
Aubry, Ernest L. 1199
Auerbach, Mary C. 2203
Auvert, B. 244
Avery, Jane C. 1200

427

Stein, A. M. 64
Steinberg, Derek 726
Steinberg, Rose 134
Steinfels, Peter 215
Steinhausen, H.-Ch. 2414,
2415
Steinmetz, Suzanne K. 2416,
2417
Stender, W. 216
Stephenson, P. Susan 217,
1444
Sterling, Joanne W. 1315
Stern, Leo 126, 660
Stern, U. 1137
Stettnisch, K. D. 1555
Stevenson, W. 435
Stewart, Ronald B. 1724
Stoenner, Herb 496
Stoerger, R. 2183
Stoetzer, J. B. 1138
Stone, F. H. 2184
Stone, N. H. 436
Stone, Richard K. 437
Storey, Bruce 438
Storlie, 1778
Stover, William H., Jr. 661
Strand, R. D. 236
Straus, M. 2185
Straus, Murray A. 2419
Straus, P. 132, 227, 439,
440, 1445, 2186
Strauss, P. 1139
Streshinsky, M. 2026
Streshinsky, Naomi 2027
Streshinsky, Shirley 1446
Stricker, M. 1556
Stringer, Elizabeth A. 1932,
2028
Stroud, C. E. 1557
Strunk, Orlo 1447
Stuchlik, S. 2187
Stultz, Sylvia L. 662
Sturdock, P. W., Jr. 218
Suarez, Mary L. 2029
Subramanyam, M. V. G. 246
Sullivan, Eugene 1448
Sullivan, Michael F. 1140
Sumpter, E. E. 1449
Surdock, P. W., Jr. 2030
Suson, Eduardo M. 1558
Sussman, Alan 753, 1141,
1142
Sussman, Sidney J. 219, 441

Swanson, D. 663
Swanson, Lynn D. 2031
Sweden. Socialstyrelsen. 220,
2476
Swedish Association of Psy-
chologists 2032
Swindall, Bertha E. 1450
Swischuk, Leonard E. 128,
442, 443, 444
Symons, John 183
Symposium on Child Abuse,
New York University Medi-
cal Center, June 15, 1971
1611
Syre, J. 2033

Tagg, Peggy I. 1781
Taipale, V. 221
Talbert, James L. 446, 1510
Talukder, M. Q. 1559
Taneja-Jaisinghani, Vijay 1731
Tangen, Ottar 1452, 2477
Tapp, Jack T. 1453
Tascari, A. 2188
Tate, R. J. 447
Taylor, Audrey 169, 171
Taylor, David 448
Taylor, M. R. H. 737
Teague, Russell E. 1143
Ten Bensel, Robert W. 540,
739, 819, 1481, 1610, 1782,
1783, 2341, 2349
Ten Broeck, Elsa 137, 1454;
see also Broeck, Elsa Ten
Teng, Ching Tseng 449, 450
Ten Have, Ralph 1455
Tennessee State Department of
Public Welfare 2034
Terr, Lenore C. 222, 223
Tessier, Barbara 1784
Teuscher, G. W. 1785
Texas State Department of
Community Affairs 2035
Theisen, William Maurice
1144
Théodorides, M. 288
Theron, H.-P. 244
Thomas, G. 451
Thomas, M. Angele 2342
Thomas, Mason P., Jr. 1145,
1146, 1612, 2037
Thomason, Mary L. 178